FOUNDATIONS FOR INQUIRY

FOUNDATIONS FOR INQUIRY

Choices and Trade-Offs in the Organizational Sciences

Craig C. Lundberg
and Cheri A. Young

STANFORD BUSINESS BOOKS
An imprint of Stanford University Press
Stanford, California 2005

Stanford University Press
Stanford, California

Printed in the United States of America on acid-free, archival-quality paper

Library of Congress Cataloging-in-Publication Data
Lundberg, Craig C.
  Foundations for inquiry : choices and trade-offs in the organizational sciences /
Craig C. Lundberg and Cheri A. Young.
    p.   cm.
  Includes bibiliographical references and index.
  ISBN 0-8047-4153-0 (cloth : alk. paper)
  1. Organization—Research—Methodology. 2. Social sciences—Research—
Methodology. 3. Decision making. I. Young, Cheri Ann. II. Title.

HD30.4.L86 2005
302.3′5′072—dc22

2005003048

Typeset by G & S Book Services in 9.7/11.5 Sabon
Original Printing 2005

Last figure below indicates year of this printing:
14   13   12   11   10   09   08   07   06   05

Contents

Preface

C. West Churchman (1971, vii) notes that "a preface should explain and thank; it has two audiences, those who might be interested in reading the book and those who have made the reading possible." Our preface provides an explanation; our acknowledgment provides the "thank you."

Readers of novels for enjoyment often select a new book simply because it is written by a favorite author or because there are clues that it is a type of novel they prefer—romance, historical, mystery—or that it is about a setting, era, occupation, or activity they prefer to read about. Having begun the novel, they judge its escape and/or entertainment value early on and either read on or abandon it. Potential readers of nonfiction or academic-looking books, however, often want to know "up front" what the books are about and why they are worth reading. Readers seem to get answers to these questions in a couple of ways. Sometimes they browse and skim, quickly reading brief samples of text, checking to see who is cited, studying one or a few figures or tables, or looking at the table of contents or other cues to organization. Sometimes they read the preface or the introduction to see what the author says about the focus and worthiness of the book. Because you are reading our preface, let us try to anticipate your questions, hoping, unabashedly, to tempt you to pursue this book more thoroughly.

What Is This Book About?

The key words of our title help to define what this book is about—foundations, inquiry, and organizational sciences. "Inquiry" is used throughout in its most generic sense: an activity that produces knowledge; "foundations" implies the philosophic or intellectual support base on which inquiry rests; and "organizational sciences" (nowadays often called "organization studies") draws together the many applied social and behavioral fields that are concerned with describing, understanding, and modifying the structures and dynamics of those purposive social-technical systems called "organizations."

We portray inquiry as a distinctive, human process (activities for posing questions and finding, making sense of, and sharing meaningful answers) that occurs within contexts of foundational ideas as well as social relations and that, hence, also has a political/ethical dimension. Our thesis, reflected in the book's subtitle, is that there are alternatives in every aspect of inquiry (for instance, alternative foundational ideas, alternative activities at each stage of the research process, alternative ways of assembling resultant knowledge as models and theories), that choices are made among the alternatives, and that trade-offs always occur as a result of these choices. This thesis implies that it is personally and socially valuable for inquirers to be aware of these choices and trade-offs. Thus, this book is not simply a manual of research techniques and/or technical resources, nor does it knowingly promote one mode of inquiry over another.

Why Bother to Pursue This Book?

This book is both a primer and a resource. It is a primer for readers who are curious about and unacquainted with serious inquiry, and who wish to begin to understand what it involves. By "serious inquiry" we mean doing research to find answers to questions not previously asked (not simply searching for answers already available). As a primer, this book will enable readers not only to become informed about inquiry in general but also to gain a somewhat nuanced understanding of the foundations on which research projects are erected, the theoretical reservoirs of research findings, the cycle of activities that constitute the research process, and much more. Readers will be able to make more informed judgments about their research-related training, better assess the research work they run across, and think more clearly about their own research endeavors. We believe that being a sophisticated creator and consumer of scientific knowledge means more than simply possessing a kit bag of research techniques, which are inevitably narrow and biased. We also believe that a heightened awareness of the many choices and trade-offs involved in serious inquiry will not only promote an enhanced appreciation of it but also enable the reader to become both a more discriminating consumer of research-based knowledge and a more adept contributor to such knowledge. We further hope that this book will demystify scientific inquiry, encourage its readers to expand their repertoire of research-related practices, think more clearly about their own projects, and make more informed decisions about their research training. For experienced scholars this book may provide a "refresher course," encourage ongoing discourse about inquiry, and perhaps stimulate further development.

In addition to being a primer, this book is intended as a resource in two different ways: it provides a general framework that shows the "big picture" of inquiry and how each piece of the inquiry mosaic relates to the whole, and it contains ideas and materials that are sometimes hard to come by because they are scattered across a variety of literatures and many, many decades. By collecting them together, this book makes them more readily available.

Who Are the Intended Audiences of This Book?

We hope that anyone interested in social and behavioral research—especially those associated with the management and organizational sciences—might benefit from this book. The simply curious should find that they will better understand what is involved in scientific inquiry and the preparation for it. For those relatively new to organizational studies and serious scholarship, this book's "big picture" and its emphasis on the many choices and trade-offs involved should prepare them to effectively assess the work they come across and selectively pursue their own further development. For those who believe their previous research training was overly technique-oriented, design or methodologically narrow, or simply now dated, this book may provide a modest, even gentle, corrective. For those who are serious about inquiry, we hope our book will lead to the many specialist literatures available and assist readers in seeing them for what they are and are not.

How Should You Read This Book?

For those readers relatively new to research, we suggest reading the book systematically, cover to cover, in the order presented. This will take time, for the book is long, but take your time; *really* take your time. Read a part and digest it, referring often to Figure 2-3 in Chapter 2 to remind yourself where you are.

For those readers with previous research training and/or experience, we suggest first carefully reading the introduction and Chapter 2, which map the book's subject matter, then browsing in Chapter 1, and then giving attention to those materials you feel curious or less informed about.

All readers will probably benefit from having conversations with others, perhaps stimulated by what has been read here. Clarity often comes from articulating what we think as well as comparing it with what others think.

Acknowledgments

This book had its origins in, and is partially based on, materials from a seminar about inquiry given at Cornell University over the course of several years. The seminar profited from the participation of intelligent and hard-working graduate students who, as they wrestled with the ideas of the seminar, taught us as they learned.

We are especially thankful to the many thoughtful and articulate scholars whose work we have included in the readings and drawn on in our discussions. In a very real sense, this book is theirs.

Our appreciation also extends to many, many others, near and far. We both had generous, wise, and demanding mentors at Cornell, challenging colleagues at several other institutions, and supportive friends and family. We have borrowed ideas shamelessly from others as they touched our scholarly lives. We hope that they will notice their influence.

While our intellectual indebtedness to others is both widespread and enormous, several people deserve special mention. As models for us of what persistent, careful, bold thinking can accomplish, we acknowledge the influence of John Hennessey Jr., James G. March, Karl Weick, and William Foote Whyte. This book exists in part because of the direct and daily support of our living-working partners, Jenna Lundberg and David Corsun. They not only enrich our lives but also provide the time, space, and sustenance that writing requires. Assistance was also provided by Rachel Shinnar, whose friendly smile and quick study of the *Chicago Manual of Style* made our lives so much easier. A special "thank you" goes to Sheri Gilbert, our independent copyright permissions hero, who did the seemingly impossible task of tracking down and documenting the numerous permissions necessary for this book. And there is Bill Hicks, our first editor at Stanford

University Press. Without Bill's initial enthusiasm and ongoing caring attention, this book would still be just a vague wish.

Additionally, we wish to acknowledge the financial support provided by a Stimulation, Implementation, Transition, and Enhancement grant offered through the Office of Research at University of Nevada, Las Vegas. This grant demonstrates what a modest investment can do in terms of yielding meaningful and creative results.

Finally, we wish to acknowledge one another. We have brought our gender, generational, and experience differences to several collaborative projects over the years. Long good friends and respected associates, we have strengthened, deepened, and tested our relationship through the labor of love that is this book.

Craig C. Lundberg
Ithaca, New York

Cheri A. Young
Las Vegas, Nevada

FOUNDATIONS FOR INQUIRY

Introduction: Themes and Exemplars

A person who can identify the inevitable tradeoffs in inquiry and relax gracefully having done so is a seasoned inquirer.

—*Karl E. Weick*

The general argument behind this book is that inquiry in the organizational sciences is usefully understood through the following five intertwined contentions:

1. There are alternatives for every activity, every practice, every aspect of inquiry; choices have to be made among alternatives; and there are trade-offs for each choice made (i.e., there is no one best way to do inquiry).
2. Inquiry is manifestly a patterned process of learning what the world (or parts of it) is really like and/or how it really works (i.e., inquiry is not something one is born knowing how to do; it can be learned).
3. The inquiry process, comprised of a series of choices and trade-offs, is based upon and reflects a foundation of alternative assumptions about the nature of reality and humanity and how these can be known (i.e., different assumptive sets will influence choices among inquiry alternatives).
4. Inquiry is conducted by people for people and hence is always both social and political (i.e., inquiry is a relationship- and value-infused human endeavor).
5. The learning outcomes of the inquiry process are contained or reside in conceptual frameworks of varying degrees of confirmation and clarity (i.e., shared frames of reference, models, theories) as well as in the enhanced competencies of inquirers.

As reasonable as these contentions may seem, each has been contested not only historically but also even today. Just a few decades ago, the majority of scientists believed that inquiry should be value-free, that science was simply just the accumulation of more and better facts, that there was just one scientific method, and that reality was "out there" to be straight-forwardly observed, measured, and counted. For nearly three decades the social and behavioral sciences have experienced a resurgence of interest in the philosophic basis of science, paradigmatic impact, theoretic develop-ment, alternative inquiry strategies and research designs, the adequacy of data gathering methods, the utility of alternative analytic methods, and much else. The organizational sciences have been the subject as well as the arena in which much of this interest and its resulting ferment have oc-curred. To be sure, however, most intellectual differences of opinion were and sometimes still are handled with diversionary strategies, such as silence (a competing perspective is simply not expressed), marginalization (com-peting views are relegated to parenthetical asides or footnotes), and un-derstatement (within a wide review of perspectives, only those that are pre-ferred are focused on).

The Orthodox Ideal of Inquiry

At present, a large and multifaceted literature addresses the adequacy of the earlier ideal of sciencing in the social and behavioral disciplines and their applied offspring. What was this espoused, conventional ideal of inquiry that once dominated organizational research? It seems to go, even if over-simplified, as follows: (1) fieldwork or previous experience is used to identify and get a feel for some phenomena; (2) survey work is then used to discover distributions of the phenomena and associations among entities or within processes; (3) with this "understanding" and the models induced, more rig-orous work, such as experimentation, is used to test hypotheses and clarify relationships; and (4) with the accumulation of confirmed findings, theory is progressively verified or modified. Modal analysis (i.e., typicality) is the name of the game; nomothetic (i.e., universal seeking), the name of the approach.

If we further ask, "What was the ideal research design?" the response has to be a rigorous experiment (e.g., D. T. Campbell and Stanley 1966). The researcher is presumed to know what is significant at the outset. He or she controls for all other variables, measures the relevant variables carefully, is concerned with validity and reliability, and reports the research fully so that replication is possible. If we ask why an experiment was considered the ideal design, the response has to be because an experiment is consistent with both a positivistic paradigm and is unidirectional and causal (i.e., there is a one-way flow of influence, over time, from "cause" to "effect," in which the determination of all the conditions of a cause enables identification of the effect; thus, if all of an effect is registered, then the cause can be in-ferred). Specific casual findings permit the eventual induction of more gen-eral, logically related premises, axioms, or laws. A set of related premises, axioms, or laws thus constitutes the heart of a theory from which subordinate propositions and statements may be logically deduced. We further note that this type of sciencing seeks to develop descriptive theories about facts external to the researcher, and this requires the tightest possible unilateral control by the researcher over the research setting. Following the advice of the English philosopher Locke, there are simple facts to be observed; hence, reality is objectified. The observer is differentiated from the objects observed, and there is a simple, positivistic causation behind the research strategy and methods. This empirical, logically positivistic "orthodoxy" was—and is still—held up by many as the ideal for both the social and organizational sciences (Daft and Lewin 1990). Mitroff and Pondy (1978) summarize the ideal nicely: "We are conditioned by our scientific training to associate progress with greater rigor, greater precision, disintegrative analysis, more empirical documentation of a phenomenon, and the progressive exorcism of value-laden questions in favor of a purer pursuit of 'truth' that is a closer and closer fitting of our theories to the one objective reality we presume exists" (p. 145).

Reactions: Critical, Defensive, and Constructive

As the well-trod ideal of logical empiricism became more and more widely articulated, advocated, and accepted, new theory and research was judged for its connection and relevance to earlier scholarship rather than for its importance to practice (Wing 1994). This inevitably also generated a series of reactions.

One reaction was straightforwardly critical. Critics of the prevailing ideal orthodoxy have pointed with disapproval to just about every facet of it:[1]

- from its pseudo-objectivity (e.g., Pondy and Boje 1975);
- to its limited epistemology (e.g., Evered and Louis 1979);
- to its restricted methodological examples (e.g., Churchman 1972);
- to its overemphasis on modal analysis (e.g., Pondy and Olson 1977);
- to its domination by goal-oriented exemplars (e.g., Georgiou 1973);
- to researcher effects, even in rigorously controlled studies (e.g., Rosenthal 1966);
- to the assumption that respondents share a universe of discourse with investigators, allowing conceptual ratings on scales (e.g., Benson 1977a);
- to the overuse of causalistic explicative explanations and the ignoring of teleological ones (e.g., Evered 1976);

1. The following listing is replete with scientific jargon. All of it will become understandable by the end of the book. The point here is simply to demonstrate that there has been a lot of criticism.

- to the dysfunctionality of its dominant paradigm (e.g., Lundberg 1981);
- to the essentially authoritarian nature of research that is unilaterally researcher controlled (e.g., Galtung 1977);
- to the implicit sociolinguistic perspective that means results cannot in any simple way criticize that perspective (e.g., Habermas 1971);
- to its biases such as the overestimation of the utility of simple bivariate relationships;
- to the intentional overdetermination of causes; and
- to the overgeneralization that comes from contextual insensitivity.

Many of these criticisms share the underlying belief that rigor is somehow synonymous with quantitativeness, that precision comes from numbers and their manipulation, rather than from the strength of inference made possible by a given research study (Staw 1985). The ultimate criticism may be that of Torbert (1977), who notes that researchers seldom seem to develop the quality of attention necessary to test whether their purposes, strategies, and actual behaviors are congruent with one another, because the practice of organizational science tends to focus on only one of these aspects at a time.

The preceding list permits us to make the following general points. First, these "early" criticisms continue to be echoed and sometimes even amplified right up to the present (e.g., Marsden 1993). Second, each of these criticisms tends to focus on one or only a few facets of prevailing science. We should note that inquirers in different countries probably have different conceptions of what constitutes normal everyday science and mainstream organizational research. Our characterization is from a North American perspective. In Europe, in contrast, the logical positivist tradition has been substantially eroded in some fields. There, normal science often includes a preference for qualitative methods, and radical, critical, and postmodern approaches have established a much firmer foothold than in North America.

Two types of reactions have appeared in the organizational sciences in defense of its normal science ideal. On the one hand, there are those who argue that the empirical, logically positivistic, natural sciences model for research (e.g., Popper 1964) on which the organizational science ideal is based, while imperfect and needing thoughtful application, remains the primary means for understanding all phenomenon (e.g., Behling 1980). Variants of this stance include the argument that the central role of research is to choose among the proliferating set of theories (e.g., Laudan 1977), thereby assuming that the study of organizations and behavior of and within them is amenable to relatively few universal laws and that clutter is bad (Hauge 1994), and the argument for a consensus in a scientific discipline's general orientation and all that follows (e.g., Pfeffer 1993). On the other hand, there are those whose defense of the empirical, logico-positivistic ideal is to more finely tune criticized facets, for example, by adding variables to regression equations, inductively searching for common gestalts, limiting the number of units of analyses, using more disciplined case analyses or more longitudinal designs, and so on.

Reacting to the critics and the defenders of the organizational science ideal are many whose intent appears to be constructive. They offer arguments that attempt to dissolve disputes about the ideal by showing

1. that dichotomies, such as those between quantitative and qualitative methods (Martin 1990; Morgan and Smircich 1980), micro and macro levels of analysis (Rousseau 1985), and various research purposes, such as description and prediction (Blalock 1982), are oversimplified;
2. that combining multiple approaches—for example, paradigms (Gioia and Pitre 1990), methods (Jick 1979), and research strategies (McGrath 1982)—is useful;
3. that integration between positivist and interpretive approaches is possible, even desirable (Lee 1991); and
4. that the tensions engendered by debates are, in fact, functional at this time (Fabian 2000).

Toward Undermining Debate

The numerous debates continuing to riddle discussions about inquiry in the organizational sciences range, as we have seen, from basic assumptions to methods. To be sure, many of these debates do not appear to be inconsequential. What they have in common, of course, is their either/or quality. In the epigraph offered at the outset, however, Weick notes the "inevitable tradeoffs in inquiry," implying the potential value of all positions. To take Weick seriously suggests that these debates can be undermined. To begin to undermine the debates within organizational science inquiry, let us note several fundamental points that are widely accepted by scholars but often conveniently overlooked by the advocate of one or another debate position.

Theorists and researchers, as well as members of organizations, have cognitive limitations. Singularly and in sets, researchers do not have the value-free cognitive complexity to comprehend the "true" dynamics and patterns of all relevant aspects of any unit of analysis in a single epiphanic moment, much less to communicate it in a disciplined manner. One consequence of this "bounded rationality" is that they are prone to identify with subgoals of large, complex undertakings, to narrow their attention, and to satisfice with regard to their search, choice, and justification behavior. Thus, advocacy will be based on partial rather than comprehensive understandings (Hauge 1994; Simon 1991).

Organizational scientists, like those they study, have allegiances to their community, personal values and self-interests, needs for recognition, status and security, identities to foster, propensities for risk taking and risk aversion, and many other qualities of being human. In addition, in conducting their research, they study some stakeholders rather than every constituent group, and their findings will tend to benefit some stakeholders but not others. Scientists are human beings too; neutrality and objectivity are always just beyond reach. Thus advocacy is always, at least partially, political (Townley 1993).

Organizational theorizing and inquiry rests on some belief of "essential human nature." To some scientists, human beings are acted on by circumstances. Other scientists believe people shape and control their destinies. To still other scientists, human behavior is seen as both autonomous and determined. While no consensus exists concerning which of these "taken-for-granteds" is true, each is complemented by a method of science and colors other beliefs behind inquiry debates. Thus, advocacy is always grounded on a debatable foundation (Galtung 1977).

All organizational science phenomena of interest can be studied in terms of a unit of analysis at several levels, and each unit of analysis can be studied in an array of contexts, that is, from complicated individual decision makers to international arenas. Choices among units of analysis and contexts do not reflect any widely accepted scientific criteria (Korukonda 1989). Phenomena are therefore defined arbitrarily. Thus advocacy tends to be between theoretical schools that talk past each other about the phenomena of interest, their context, and the dynamics of those phenomena (Aldrich and Whetten 1981).

The phenomena of the organizational sciences are always in flux. All units of analysis are moving into states or conditions that have never occurred before in history and, as knowledge about these phenomena is developed and disseminated, it more or less alters the circumstances in which it was discovered. Hence, any espousal that takes an inflexible stand about an inherently unstable phenomena has to be suspect (Cziko 1989).

We must remember that the phenomena of the organizational sciences are richly complex and that any simple, dogmatic advocacy about how to understand such phenomena is likely to be specious at best. Once we abandon our allegiance to one or the other side of the debates about inquiry, we inevitably face many choices about how to create scientific meanings and do scientific work.

Equivoque, Alternatives, and Trade-offs

We have argued several points so far. We have contended that the present, normal-science ideal of the organizational sciences has been, and still is, capable of being criticized. In addition, the debates about inquiry we have noted are really about particular facets of the process and may be undermined when examined in terms of fundamentals about inquirers and phenomena. Another claim of ours is that inquiry is usefully understood as a process where the choices made about each component may be influenced by the choices made about other components.

The choices inherent in inquiry are essentially equivocal ones. "Equivoques are indeterminate, inscrutable, ambivalent, questionable, and they permit multiple meanings" (Weick 1979, 174). In Koestler's (1978) memorable phrasing, an equivoque is a term with at least two meanings, two disparate strings of thought tied together by an acoustic knot. Every facet of all the components of inquiry has more than one possible meaning. The richness and multiplicity of meanings that can be superimposed on any phenomena through inquiry are what organizational scientists must thoughtfully manage. The inquirer's major task is to be aware of and select among the alternatives inherent in every aspect of the inquiry process, knowing and appreciating the trade-offs among the choices of alternatives adopted or rejected, and how these choices and subsequent trade-offs will affect most of the other choices to be made.

In every aspect of inquiry, real alternatives lie in wait. Most involve trade-offs, and some may even be dilemmas involving choices between two equal, and sometimes unpleasant, alternatives. Does this mean we should resign ourselves to a cognitive free-for-all and accept the bitter division that competition among rival beliefs and methods foster, or should we heed the siren calls for the one best way of theorizing and doing research? Believing organizational reality is both complex and changeful and that imposing a multiplicity of meanings on it increases our understanding of these phenomena, we suggest that variety of all aspects of inquiry is natural, endemic, and potentially constructive. While sympathetic to the confusion a seemingly endless proliferation of methodological strategies, designs, and techniques may cause, we believe that thinking a small number of them will capture organizational reality is unrealistic. While likewise sympathetic to the overwhelming proliferation of models and theories that exist, we contend it is unrealistic to think a small number of models and theories will suffice in making sense of organizational reality. And while sympathetic to the perennial debates over inquiry's assumptions, values, and beliefs, we yet again believe it may be unrealistic to think one set is sufficient for making meaning of organizational reality. Perhaps the time has come to eschew mainstream inquiry for multistream inquiry; celebrate the abundance of methods, theories, and meanings; appreciate the equivoque in organizational phenomena as well as in the activities of inquiry; and approach organizational sciencing more thoughtfully than it has been approached before.

Toward Making Sense of Choices

Accepting and welcoming paradigmatic, theoretic, and methodological variety requires much of us. Accepting that differences of attention to, and understanding of, phenomena are natural and necessary requires more than simply being tolerant of or simply respecting the work of others who work differently than we do. We will have to actively dispel our ignorance of other beliefs and approaches. We will have to actively explore across philosophies, paradigms, theories, and methods to discover their applicable domains. We will have to compare across these domains to keep communication progressing and to see that the complexity of our inquiry processes keeps up with the complexity of the phenomena of interest. It is, after all, the richness and multiplicity of meanings that can be superimposed on organizational phenomena that organizational scientists must contribute to.

In the chapters that follow,[2] we provide a framework and materials designed to enhance appreciation and understanding of the processes and components of inquiry. The two chapters of Part 1, in combination, outline a way of making sense of inquiry as a very human, very social, learning process that encompasses the activities of doing research within philosophic and theoretic frames. Parts 2 and 3 then elaborate these nested frames. The five chapters of Part 2 expand on the philosophic context of inquiry, and the three chapters of Part 3 elaborate the theoretical reservoir of knowledge at the center of inquiry. A common theme in our discussion of these two frames is the multiplicity of possible alternative philosophic configurations that shape the many alternative forms of theory, and how both frames combine to shape and guide research. Part 4, through its five chapters, describes the sequence of activities that constitute the research process, where again there are trade-offs among the many alternatives at each activity stage. In the final part of this book, Part 5, we return full circle to inquiry as human and social, and hence learningful for those persons engaged in knowledge-production projects and research careers as well as for the human communities that search for and utilize research findings.

To study the complexity of organizational phenomena, with its many units of analysis and dynamic contexts, requires the deep understanding of many approaches and perspectives. Appreciating the equivoque of inquiry will allow us, individually and collectively, to, in Weick's words, "relax gracefully" and get on with the important and always fascinating work of the organizational sciences.

2. Editors' note: The chapters that follow include selections from the works of others, some of which were originally published many years ago. Readers will no doubt notice that in these older works, individuals are referred to as males, a common practice back then. We ask our readers, when appropriate, to mentally insert "he or she" when an individual is referred to only as "he."

Part 1

Getting Acquainted with Inquiry

In Part 1, we introduce serious inquiry and sketch its scope and themes through two chapters. Each chapter offers a different response to the general question, What is involved in inquiry?

The response provided in Chapter 1, "Embracing Inquiry as Learning," suggests that serious inquiry may be conceived as several kinds of learning, from the personal learning of inquirers to the focused learning that accrues from research projects to the cumulative learning for society from advancing scientific knowledge. Inquiry as learning emphasizes inquiry as an inherently human and social process.

The response provided in Chapter 2, "Mapping the Domain of Inquiry," suggests that serious inquiry may also be viewed as three sets of linked components, the first set involving the philosophic context of inquiry; the second, models and theories, the repositories of knowledge. These two sets of linked components frame and shape scholarship generally, as well as the sequence of activities that constitute the third component, the process of scientific research.

The two responses to the question of what inquiry involves both contribute to a view of inquiry as a generalized, cyclical, social-technical learning process, a view elaborated in the remainder of this book. The two chapters that follow should do much to demystify inquiry as well as prepare the reader to appreciate some of its subtleties and complexities.

1   Embracing Inquiry as Learning

Writing, for me, has always been an adventure of discovery.
—*Richard J. Bernstein*

Science affects the way we think together.
—*Lewis Thomas*

I think that Aristotle was profoundly right in holding that ethics is concerned with how to live and with human happiness, and also profoundly
right in holding that this sort of *knowledge* ("practical knowledge")
is different from theoretical knowledge. A view of knowledge that
acknowledges that the sphere of knowledge is wider than the sphere
of "science" seems to me to be a cultural necessity if we are to arrive
at a sane and human view of ourselves *or* of science.
—*Hilary Putnam*

In the four selections that make up this chapter we will be able to see and
appreciate two major points. First, inquiry is a very human and social endeavor, and, second, inquiry is, in its essence, a process through which both
persons and communities learn.

The first selection, notes from a lecture by an eminent chemist to a class
of undergraduate science majors, provides a window into the reality of serious inquiry—what is actually involved when scientists go about their
craft. This insider's account does much to dispel popular notions of serious
inquiry as simply the application of a set of techniques or a recipe to follow
or as merely a set of high-minded values or what a heroic genius does. Inquiry is shown to be something very personal, emotional, social, political,
usually constrained, often risky, sometimes creative, and entailing a lot of
careful, not always glamorous work. Greenwood and Levin's guest lecturer
also nicely reminds us that inquiry is a process of many steps or stages.

The next two selections are by a distinguished scientist, in fact, a Nobel
laureate! Richard Feynman worked in the physical sciences and is widely

recognized as a creative, productive, influential scientist. First, Feynman writes about his beginnings as a lifelong inquirer. As a boy, in conversations with his father, he developed habits of curiosity, questioning, and of always looking closely. Then, in the second selection, taken from a talk to high school science teachers, Feynman helps us step back and see the long-term consequences of inquiry, to appreciate what the accumulation of learning does for the human community, and how scientific knowledge evolves and improves through doubt and questioning.

The last selection, written for this volume, reminds us that inquiry is fundamentally a cyclic learning process that produces individual and collective knowledge at several levels of sophistication.

The Guest Lecturer
Davydd J. Greenwood and Morten Levine

The episode that we recount happened to Greenwood 15 years ago. He has retold the story often enough that, in the way of narratives, his recollection of it is as much tied up with the retellings as with the original episode. He did not document the episode with anything other than lecture notes because only on reflection over the years did the larger meanings become clearer. Still, Greenwood feels that he is being true to the episode that he participated in.

At the time this occurred, Greenwood was the chair of the Biology and Society major at Cornell University. A program for students in their first 4 university years in the U.S. higher education system, this multidisciplinary, multicollege major was designed to link the basic biological and physical sciences with the social sciences and humanities. It provided opportunities for students with a strong interest in the basic sciences to explore the social sciences and the humanities systematically. Greenwood was responsible for the core, upper-level course that included an overview of the relationship between biology and society, as well as discussions of science and scientific method.

Having taught this course several times, Greenwood discovered that good, advanced undergraduates with strong backgrounds in mathematics, physics, chemistry, and biology had very little in the way of concrete, behavioral understanding of the scientific method. They were sophisticated enough at using the appropriate language to describe the rules of the scientific method, but they did not understand the scientific method as a form of behavior. Instead, they used their notions about the scientific method mainly as a way of talking about scientific values.

On reflection, Greenwood realized that it was not really surprising be-

Source: *Introduction to action research: Social research for social change* by Davydd J. Greenwood and Morten Levine, 57–64. Copyright © 1998 by Sage Publications, Inc. Reprinted by permission of Sage Publications, Inc.

cause, by their third year at the university, most students had done only rote science work in the introductory courses they had taken. They had very little experience of science as a form of discovery and interpretation in a laboratory setting.

Although this situation was understandable, Greenwood found it unacceptable for the Biology and Society major. Many of the majors were preparing for careers in medicine or in other branches of health care where their understanding of the scientific method as a form of behavior would have direct consequences for thousands of patients. He cast around to find some way to deal with the problem. He knew that, despite his good relations with the students, as a cultural anthropologist, his views about the scientific method would have little credibility to them. He thus decided to invite a Nobel Prize winning chemist from Cornell to come to the class and lecture on the scientific method. He made this choice partially because he knew the scientist and partly because this professor was known to be an extraordinary good and committed teacher of science.

The lecture given by the chemist lasted the standard 50 minutes, and the students were on the edge of their seats throughout. The prestige of this individual, combined with his congenial and down-to-earth manner, made the lesson effective for most present. It was clear at the outset that the students expected a very abstract and theoretical lecture from this eminent scientific intellectual. They apparently equated great science with great abstractions, very general laws, and big theories. What they got was something different. The chemist chose to describe his activities as a scientist and to bring the students into his world through a behavioral perspective, particularly through the perspective of the principal investigator in charge of a scientific research project.

He began by pointing out to the students that the first issue in any scientific inquiry is to generate a problem to study. He explained that this is not a simple process. It was evident from the students' reaction that they had not been asked previously to think about how scientists come up with questions to ask. Probably this was because students are generally given a set of pre-digested questions to address in their class work. The chemist pointed out that there are many problems in the world and many more suggested in the scientific literature. Some of these are interesting to the researchers in question; some are not. What is interesting, he argued, is partly a matter of personal preferences and histories. Also, some problems require equipment and funding that are not available; others touch on elements of previous experience that make them attractive or unattractive. Occasionally, an anomaly picked up through observation generates a questioning process and a review of the literature that eventually causes a group of people to decide it has a problem worth studying.

It was already clear at this point that the students were hearing ideas new to them. Most had not considered the matrix of ideas, experiences, organizational structures, and histories that provide the context in which scientists ask questions. Yet the chemist's statements accord well with studies carried out in the philosophy of science (Kuhn 1962) and the social studies of science (Barnes 1977; Barnes and Shapin 1979; Latour and Woolgar 1979; Rabinow 1996; Zabusky 1995). There are few convincing accounts of the scientific problem generation process. The exception is a study by Paul Rabinow (1996) that addresses this issue to good effect for one discovery in recombinant DNA work. This subject is now a central concern of the field of science and technology studies.

Problem selection tends to be bracketed under the headings of "individual creativity," "genius," and so on, converting science into a story of individual heroes that, we note, is a story with a hierarchical and authoritarian moral to it. The lecture pointed out that this process turns on the creativity of an individual or team in thinking up and defining problems well enough so they can be studied. The individual and team operate in a social context locally, through the scientific literature, and through their ongoing contacts around the world that place problems in a complex social, intellectual, and spatial web.

The chemist then asked the class how anyone could know that a selected problem is worth studying. Again the students were puzzled. He pointed out that there are many rational tests of the consequences arising from particular subjects, but none guarantees that the problem itself is worth the effort. Whether or not a researcher or a team becomes committed to the study of a problem is a matter of individual preference, intuition, insight, and the availability of the required resources, including money. It often is also the result of a chain of previous work in which this particular activity forms a link.

Having defined a problem and decided it is important enough to pursue, the next issue for researchers is to figure out how to study it. The group must ask itself what would be potentially relevant data for the study of the selected problem. The professor problematized this deliberately by showing that it is often not obvious what relevant data might be for a particular problem. In his view, much valuable effort often goes into trying to decide what data could bear some reasonable relationship to the problem and other researchers would find convincing.

Again the students were surprised. The ambiguity of what constitutes data, the amount of social processing that goes on in a scientific research team, and the dependence of local researchers on their wider networks and on the limitations of local equipment and funding were all dimensions of science that their introductory science courses had not revealed to them. They had been given a view of scientific method primarily as an individual encounter with a world of facts and individualistic formulations of hypotheses, research strategies, experiments, and reports. That is, they had been given the heroic view of science, and they were listening to a scientific hero who was giving them an antiheroic narrative of science, yet one that was filled with a profound respect for the activity of scientists.

They seemed particularly bewildered by the notion that the data also are determined, to an extent, by the kind of equipment available at the research site. What is at hand plays some role in what data are thought to be relevant and the way data might be collected. Greenwood could see the students were uncomfortable with this, as if it was a form of cheating because of the idealization of scientific processes they were familiar with.

The chemist also emphasized the large number of decisions about how to document the information being collected and organizing the activity among a team of researchers to make it efficient and reasonable. The notions that a Nobel Prize chemist would have to be a team leader, an accomplished grant writer, and a social actor skilled in organizing and motivating groups were surprising to the class. That compromises would be made to design an activity that would not cause the research group to run out of resources before the data collection was completed was also new. Of course, this is not the students' fault, because few had ever faced the need to write grants, collect resources, and conduct experiments within a budget.

Having emphasized the intellectual and social embeddedness of all the elements in the scientific process, the chemist then argued that it is difficult to decide when data collection is complete. He pointed out that deciding how much data are enough often is a pragmatic matter, not always justifiable in abstract terms. It may be a decision based on fatigue; the exhaustion of financial, physical, or temporal resources; or the sense that there are enough data to say something others will believe about the problem in question. The students realized that this was a much more indeterminate view of the closure of the data collection phase of a scientific process than they had expected.

At this point, the chemist moved on to the second phase of hypothesis or question formulation. He pointed out that, although the activity is initially guided by a sense of a particular problem and possibly by a hypothesis, once a body of data has been collected and is examined, the issue becomes how to account for the array, or the distribution, or the structure of the sort of data at hand. In the physical and natural sciences, this part of the process often is a group activity. A variety of hypotheses is often formulated by a brainstorming activity through interaction influenced by a reading of the literature, flurries of e-mail, interpersonal and interunit relationships, and other interactions.

The chemist then asked the class members how they would know when they had formulated enough hypotheses. The students were mystified because hypothesis formulation as a form of behavior is apparently not often discussed in science courses. His sober answer was that hypothesis formulation is over when you cannot think of any more hypotheses or when you are too tired to go on. The students initially thought he was joking, but it became clear that he was not. He wanted the students to understand that science is not an activity that takes place in some idealized metaphysical space with perfect information, infinite resources to spend, and perfectly rational human beings in attendance. Science is a form of human activity that combines a set of pragmatic compromises between all the elements present at any given moment.

Beyond the pragmatics of the situation, the chemist also wanted to make a deeper point. We believe he was arguing that there is no rational way to know when one has formed enough alternative kinds of explanations for the array of data in question. The world is more complex than our apprehension of it can be, and thus we will always be approaching this complexity through a series of imperfect compromises. Being trained in a particular institution with a particular group of scientists is likely to have a powerful effect on judgements about how many hypotheses are sufficient. The appetites for complexity and other characteristics of these groups will, probably, socialize a young scientist to a particular standard. However this occurs, the chemist was pointing out that one can never know that all the relevant, possible ways of accounting for the data have been formulated. Science, as powerful as it is, is not a means for transcending the human condition.

Having completely perplexed his audience, the chemist then moved on to the next step: the process of testing questions or hypotheses against the data. Doing prestructured experiments with finite solutions in laboratory exercises did not prepare the students very well for what he said. In the students' experience, all the puzzles had specific answers, and they would receive grades for solving the puzzles with a specific set of resources and in a limited amount of time. They know the answers were there, and they simply had to uncover them. These scientific training practices did not prepare them for the chemist's much less determinate view.

He pointed out that translating hypotheses into testable propositions and matching data to hypotheses are complex, ambiguous, and creative activities. Chains of assumptions and definitions are required to link data and hypotheses, and these chains have to be built so they are capable of convincing others that the reasoning and research process gone through is sensible and, therefore, that the results are acceptable. Doing this in laboratory situations is often a group process with rapid brainstorming and much trial and error, eminently social activities.[1]

Once the group has inventoried all the questions or hypotheses it can think of against the data collected and organized, the lecturer said that the

1. One relevant dimension of science as a form of action that was not touched on in the lecture is the sheer amount of trial-and-error experimentation and troubleshooting that goes on in any scientific work. Most experienced scientists know that science is composed of a few insights and discoveries and a vast amount of routine, tiresome, and often frustrating laboratory work. Troubleshooting, false positives, false negatives, and confusion are all part of the daily routine of scientific work.

best possible outcome is that the group has not invalidated all the explanations that it initially developed. The hope is that it would have at least one left. Quite often, this does not happen, and the group must return to the process of hypothesis formulation because none of the hypotheses is left standing. Alternatively, the data may not provide the basis for choosing among alternative explanations, and the experiment has to be redesigned.

At this point, the students were relieved because this began to sound like the sort of science that they could identify with. At the end of the process, the group has a validated explanation. But the chemist was not through. He explained that, having not invalidated all the hypotheses did not mean that the remaining hypotheses had been proved true. He insisted that one could only say that the group had not invalidated all the hypotheses that it had been able to think of.

In making this argument, he was not being perverse. Having pointed out that the initial process of hypothesis formulation is indeterminate, in the sense that there always exists the possibility of hypotheses that the group did not think of and that financial and human resources are finite, he was being consistent. If a single hypothesis were left after the testing procedures were complete, one could only say that, of the hypotheses thought of, at least one had not yet been invalidated. It might be invalidated in the future, but other better hypotheses might be formulated to account for the data in the future. Thus, the remaining explanation could not be said to be correct. It is simply the only one left of those thought of.

The 50 minutes were over. Greenwood's class seemed stunned, though appreciative. Rather than making the usual quick and noisy exodus, they wandered out of the room silently.

The chemist had given a master class, but more important, he had conveyed a view of science as a form of human action involving complexity, ambiguity, creativity, group dynamics, and many pragmatic concessions to the limitations imposed by the time and resources available. Rather than diminishing or demystifying science, this view helps us understand that science is a way of behaving, a way of acting in relation to the nonhuman and human worlds that has resulted in remarkable improvements in our understanding of how those worlds work and our ability to change the state of those worlds. Good scientific practice centers on constant cycles of thought and action.

Something the chemist did not mention at any point was prediction. Although it was clear that a good explanation could be used to generate a prior idea of the way the data should be arrayed if the explanation were to hold, he did not stress prediction itself as a core element in science. Rather, he emphasized explanation. Yet, commonsense views of science almost always equate science with prediction. We believe the chemist was right to deemphasize prediction as a fundamental criterion for science.

Scientists seek to explain arrays of data. Predicting the expected array of data under given conditions is a powerful way of testing explanations, but the goal is having an explanation that makes sense. Prediction is a tool to be used in this effort, and its use varies a great deal with the conditions. Under some conditions, prediction, in the ordinary sense, is out of the question, as in the historical studies of evolution.[2] Under other conditions, predictions take the form of statistical generalizations about huge populations and cannot accurately capture what is happening in particular segments of those populations. In other situations, predictive activity takes the form of intervening in the phenomenon under study to change its state in a desired direction. This is precisely what the experimental method in science does and what [action research] aims to achieve in the social world.

The chemist's view matches closely with our experiences of scientists and engineers at work. It puts them, as human actors, at the center of the combined social-research activity that is science. He made it clear that scientists and engineers are not the enactors of some abstract, perfect, determinate system. The chemist conveyed to the students that scientific method is a form of social behavior, a form that is not foolproof, but one that used human capabilities to pose questions and attempts to examine those questions through rational but fully social inquiry. He stressed the need to recognize the significant gaps and imperfections in any process of this sort, and he affirmed that human judgement, creativity, and social interaction are an intrinsic part of the process.

Repeatedly, he emphasized that science is a collective activity carried out by members of research teams within a larger scientific community. The larger community provides the literature on which the research is built to some degree, as well as the resources used to carry out the research. The research team and the laboratory form a complex, dynamic social system of people acting on phenomena and sharing their thoughts within the pragmatic limitations set by the availability of key resources and the dynamics of human relationships involved.

2. Occasionally the term *retrodiction* is used to refer to an attempt to build a prediction about past processes out of a theoretical formulation and then compare the predicted result with what happened historically. This seems to us simply another meaning of prediction, albeit a useful one.

The Making of a Scientist
Richard P. Feynman

I have a friend who's an artist, and he sometimes takes a view which I don't agree with. He'll hold up a flower and say, "Look how beautiful it

Source: *Surely you're joking, Mr. Feynman! Adventures of a curious character* by Richard P. Feynman as told to Ralph Leighton, 11–19. Copyright © 1985 by Richard P. Feynman and Ralph Leighton. Used by permission of W. W. Norton & Company, Inc., and The Random House Group Limited.

is," and I'll agree. But then he'll say, "I, as an artist, can see how beautiful a flower is. But you, as a scientist, take it all apart and it becomes dull." I think he's kind of nutty.

First of all, the beauty that he sees is available to other people—and to me, too, I believe. Although I might not be quite as refined aesthetically as he is, I can appreciate the beauty of a flower. But at the same time, I see much more in the flower than he sees. I can imagine the cells inside, which also have a beauty. There's beauty not just at the dimension of one centimeter; there's also beauty at a smaller dimension.

There are the complicated actions of the cells, and other processes. The fact that the colors in the flower have evolved in order to attract insects to pollinate it is interesting; that means insects can see the colors. That adds a question: does this aesthetic sense we have also exist in lower forms of life? There are all kinds of interesting questions that come from a knowledge of science, which only adds to the excitement and mystery and awe of a flower. It only adds. I don't understand how it subtracts.

I've always been very one-sided about science, and when I was younger, I concentrated almost all my effort on it. In those days I didn't have time, and I didn't have much patience, to learn what's called the humanities. Even though there were humanities courses in the university that you had to take in order to graduate, I tried my best to avoid them. It's only afterwards, when I've gotten older and more relaxed, that I've spread out a little bit. I've learned to draw and I read a little bit, but I'm really still a very one-sided person and I don't know a great deal. I have a limited intelligence and I use it in a particular direction.

Before I was born, my father told my mother, "If it's a boy, he's going to be a scientist." [3] When I was just a little kid, very small in a highchair, my father brought home a lot of little bathroom tiles—seconds—of different colors. We played with them, my father setting them up vertically on my highchair like dominoes, and I would push one end so they would all go down.

Then after a while, I'd help set them up. Pretty soon, we're setting them up in a more complicated way: two white tiles and a blue tile, two white tiles and a blue tile, and so on. When my mother saw that she said, "Leave the poor child alone. If he wants to put a blue tile, let him put a blue tile."

But my father said, "No, I want to show him what patterns are like and how interesting they are. It's a kind of elementary mathematics." So he started very early to tell me about the world and how interesting it is.

We had the *Encyclopaedia Britannica* at home. When I was a small boy he used to sit me on his lap and read to me from the *Britannica*. We would be reading, say, about dinosaurs. It would be talking about the *Tyrannosaurus*

---

3. Richard's younger sister, Joan, has a Ph.D. in physics, in spite of this preconception that only boys are destined to be scientists.

rex, and it would say something like, "This dinosaur is twenty-five feet high and its head is six feet across."

My father would stop reading and say, "Now, let's see what that means. That would mean that if he stood in our front yard, he would be tall enough to put his head through our window up here." (We were on the second floor.) "But his head would be too wide to fit in the window." Everything he read to me he would translate as best he could into some reality.

It was very exciting and very, very interesting to think there were animals of such magnitude—and that they all died out, and that nobody knew why. I wasn't frightened that there would be one coming in my window as a consequence of this. But I learned from my father to translate: everything I read I try to figure out what it really means, what it's really saying.

We used to go to the Catskill Mountains, a place where people from New York City would go in the summer. The fathers would all return to New York to work during the week, and come back only for the weekend. On weekends, my father would take me for walks in the woods and he'd tell me about interesting things that were going on in the woods. When the other mothers saw this, they thought it was wonderful and that the other fathers should take their sons for walks. They tried to work on them but they didn't get anywhere at first. They wanted my father to take all the kids, but he didn't want to because he had a special relationship with me. So it ended up that the other fathers had to take their children for walks the next weekend.

The next Monday, when the fathers were all back to work, we kids were playing in a field. One kid says to me, "See that bird? What kind of bird is that?"

I said, "I haven't the slightest idea what kind of bird it is."

He says, "It's a brown-throated thrush. Your father doesn't teach you anything!"

But it was the opposite. He had already taught me: "See that bird?" he says. "It's a Spencer's warbler." (I knew he didn't know the real name.) "Well, in Italian, it's a *Chutto Lapittida*. In Portuguese, it's a *Bom da Peida*. In Chinese, it's a *Chung-long-tah*, and in Japanese, it's a *Katano Tekeda*. You can know the name of that bird in all the languages of the world, but when you're finished, you'll know absolutely nothing whatever about the bird. You'll only know about humans in different places, and what they call the bird. So let's look at the bird and see what it's *doing*—that's what counts." (I learned very early the difference between knowing the name of something and knowing something.)

He said, "For example, look: the bird pecks at its feathers all the time. See it walking around, pecking at its feathers?"

"Yeah."

He says, "Why do you think birds peck at their feathers?"

I said, "Well, maybe they mess up their feathers when they fly, so they're pecking them in order to straighten them out."

"All right," he says. "If that were the case, then they would peck a lot just after they've been flying. Then, after they've been on the ground a while, they wouldn't peck so much any more—you know what I mean?"

"Yeah."

He says, "Let's look and see if they peck more just after they land."

It wasn't hard to tell: there was not much difference between the birds that had been walking around a bit and those that had just landed. So I said, "I give up. Why does a bird peck at its feathers?"

"Because there are lice bothering it," he says. "The lice eat flakes of protein that come off its feathers."

He continued, "Each louse has some waxy stuff on its legs, and little mites eat that. The mites don't digest it perfectly, so they emit from their rear ends a sugar-like material, in which bacteria grow."

Finally he says, "So you see, everywhere there's a source of food, there's *some* form of life that finds it."

Now, I knew that it may not have been exactly a louse, that it might not be exactly true that the louse's legs have mites. That story was probably incorrect in *detail*, but what he was telling me was right in *principle*.

Another time, when I was older, he picked a leaf off of a tree. This leaf had a flaw, a thing we never look at much. The leaf was sort of deteriorated; it had a little brown line in the shape of a C, starting somewhere in the middle of the leaf and going out in a curl to the edge.

"Look at this brown line," he says. "It's narrow at the beginning and it's wider as it goes to the edge. What this is, is a fly—a blue fly with yellow eyes and green wings has come laid an egg on this leaf. Then, when the egg hatches into a maggot (a caterpillar-like thing), it spends its whole life eating this leaf—that's where it gets its food. As it eats along, it leaves behind this brown trail of eaten leaf. As the maggot grows, the trail grows wider until he's grown to full size at the end of the leaf, where he turns into a fly—a blue fly with yellow eyes and green wings—who flies away and lays an egg on another leaf."

Again, I know that the details weren't precisely correct—it could have even been a beetle—but the idea that he was trying to explain to me was the amusing part of life: the whole thing is just reproduction. No matter how complicated the business is, the main point is to do it again!

Not having experience with many fathers, I didn't realize how remarkable he was. How did he learn the deep principles of science and the love of it, what's behind it, and why it's worth doing? I never really asked him, because I just assumed that those were things that fathers knew.

My father taught me to notice things. One day, I was playing with an "express wagon," a little wagon with a railing around it. It had a ball in it, and when I pulled the wagon, I noticed something about the way the ball moved. I went to my father and said, "Say, Pop, I noticed something: When I pull the wagon, the ball rolls to the back of the wagon. And when I'm pulling it along and I suddenly stop, the ball rolls to the front of the wagon. Why is that?"

"That, nobody knows," he said. "The general principle is that things which are moving tend to keep on moving, and things which are standing still tend to stand still, unless you push them hard. This tendency is called 'inertia,' but nobody knows why it's true." Now, that's a deep understanding. He didn't just give me the name.

He went on to say, "If you look from the side, you'll see that it's the back of the wagon that you're pulling against the ball, and the ball stands still. As a matter of fact, from the friction it starts to move forward a little bit in relation to the ground. It doesn't move back."

I ran back to the little wagon and set the ball up again and pulled the wagon. Looking sideways, I saw that indeed he was right. Relative to the sidewalk, it moved forward a little bit.

That's the way I was educated by my father, with those kinds of examples and discussions: no pressure—just lovely, interesting discussions. It has motivated me for the rest of my life, and makes me interested in *all* the sciences. (It just happens I do physics better.)

I've been caught, so to speak—like someone who was given something wonderful when he was a child, and he's always looking for it again. I'm always looking, like a child, for the wonders I know I'm going to find—maybe not every time, but every once in a while.

Around that time my cousin, who was three years older, was in high school. He was having considerable difficulty with his algebra, so a tutor would come. I was allowed to sit in a corner while the tutor would try to teach my cousin algebra. I'd hear him talking about x.

I said to my cousin, "What are you trying to do?"

"I'm trying to find out what x is, like $2x + 7 = 15$."

I say, "You mean 4."

"Yeah, but you did it by arithmetic. You have to do it by algebra."

I learned algebra, fortunately, not by going to school, but by finding my aunt's old schoolbook in the attic, and understanding that the whole idea was to find out what x is—it doesn't make any difference how you do it. For me, there was no such thing as doing it "by arithmetic," or doing it "by algebra." "Doing it by algebra" was a set of rules which, if you followed them blindly, could produce the answer: "subtract 7 from both sides; if you have a multiplier, divide both sides by the multiplier," and so on—a series of steps by which you could get the answer if you didn't understand what you were trying to do. The rules had been invented so that the children who have to study algebra can all pass it. And that's why my cousin was never able to do algebra.

There was a series of math books in our local library which started out with *Arithmetic for the Practical Man*. Then came *Algebra for the Practical*

Man, and then *Trigonometry for the Practical Man*. (I learned trigonometry from that, but I soon forgot it again, because I didn't understand it very well.) When I was about thirteen, the library was going to get *Calculus for the Practical Man*. By this time I knew, from reading the encyclopedia, that calculus was an important and interesting subject, and I ought to learn it.

When I finally saw the calculus book at the library, I was very excited. I went to the librarian to check it out, but she looked at me and said, "You're just a child. What are you taking this book out for?"

It was one of the few times in my life I was uncomfortable and I lied. I said it was for my father.

I took the book home and I began to learn calculus from it. I thought it was relatively simple and straightforward. My father started to read it, but he found it confusing and he couldn't understand it. So I tried to explain calculus to him. I didn't know he was so limited, and it bothered me a little bit. It was the first time I realized that I had learned more in some sense than he.

One of the things that my father taught me besides physics—whether it's correct or not—was a disrespect for certain kinds of things. For example, when I was a little boy, and he would sit me on his knee, he'd show me rotogravures in the *New York Times*—that's printed pictures which had just come out in newspapers.

One time we were looking at a picture of the pope and everybody bowing in front of him. My father said, "Now, look at those humans. Here's one human standing here, and all these others are bowing in front of him. Now, what's the difference? This one is the pope"—he hated the pope anyway. He said, "This difference is the hat he's wearing." (If it was a general, it was the epaulets. It was always the costume, the uniform, the position.) "But," he said, "this man has the same problems as everybody else: he eats dinner; he goes to the bathroom. He's a human being." (By the way, my father was in the uniform business, so he knew what the difference is in a man with the uniform off and the uniform on—it was the same man for him.)

He was happy with me, I believe. Once, though, when I came back from MIT (I'd been there a few years), he said to me, "Now that you've become educated about these things, there's one question I've always had that I've never understood very well."

I asked him what it was.

He said, "I understand that when an atom makes a transition from one state to another, it emits a particle of light called a photon."

"That's right," I said.

He says, "Is the photon in the atom ahead of time?"

"No, there's no photon beforehand."

"Well," he says, "where does it come from, then? How does it come out?"

I tried to explain it to him—that photon numbers aren't conserved; they're just created by the motion of the electron—but I couldn't explain it very well. I said, "It's like the sound that I'm making now: it wasn't in me before." (It's not like my little boy, who suddenly announced one day, when he was very young, that he could no longer say a certain word—the word turned out to be "cat"—because his "word bag" had run out of the word. There's no word bag that makes you use up words as they come out; in the same sense, there's no "photon bag" in an atom.)

He was not satisfied with me in that respect. I was never able to explain any of the things that he didn't understand. So he was unsuccessful: he sent me to all these universities in order to find out those things, and he never did find out.

Although my mother didn't know anything about science, she had a great influence on me as well. In particular, she had a wonderful sense of humor, and I learned from her that the highest forms of understanding we can achieve are laughter and human compassion.

What Is Science
Richard P. Feynman

What science is, I think, may be something like this: There was on this planet an evolution of life to the stage that there were evolved animals, which are intelligent. I don't mean just human beings, but animals which play and which can learn something from experience (like cats). But at this stage each animal would have to learn from its own experience. They gradually develop, until some animal could learn from experience more rapidly and could even learn from another's experience by watching, or one could show the other, or he saw what the other one did. So there came a possibility that all might learn it, but the transmission was inefficient and they would die, and maybe the one who learned it died, too, before he could pass it on to others.

The question is, is it possible to learn more rapidly what somebody learned from some accident than the rate at which the thing is being forgotten, either because of bad memory or because of the death of the learner or inventors?

So there came a time, perhaps, when for some species the rate at which learning was increased reached such a pitch that suddenly a completely new thing happened; things could be learned by one animal, passed on to another, and another, fast enough that it was not lost to the race. Thus became possible an accumulation of knowledge of the race.

This has been called time-binding. I don't know who first called it this. At any rate, we have here some samples of those animals, sitting here trying to bind one experience to another, each one trying to learn from the other.

This phenomenon of having a memory for the race, of having an accumulated knowledge passable from one generation to another, was new in the world. But it had a disease in it. It was possible to pass on mistaken ideas. It was possible to pass on ideas which were not profitable for the race. The race has ideas, but they are not necessarily profitable.

So there came a time in which the ideas, although accumulated very slowly, were all accumulations not only of practical and useful things, but great accumulations of all types of prejudices, and strange and odd beliefs.

Then a way of avoiding the disease was discovered. This is to doubt that what is being passed from the past is in fact true, and to try to find out *ab initio*, again from experience, what the situation is, rather than trusting the experience of the past in the form in which it is passed down. And that is what science is: the result of the discovery that is it worthwhile rechecking by new direct experience, and not necessarily trusting the race experience from the past. I see it that way. That is my best definition.

I would like to remind you all of things that you know very well in order to give you a little enthusiasm. . . . I think it is necessary to inspire again and again, and to remember the value of science for children, for grown-ups, and everybody else, in several ways; not only so that we will become better citizens, more able to control nature and so on. There are other things.

There is the value of the worldview created by science. There is the beauty and the wonder of the world that is discovered through the results of these new experiences. That is to say, the wonders of the content which I just reminded you of; that things move because the sun is shining, which is a deep idea, very strange and wonderful. (Yet, not everything moves because the sun is shining. The earth rotates independent of the sun shining, and the nuclear reactions recently produced energy on the earth, a new source. Probably volcanoes are generally [powered by] a source different from the shining sun.)

The world looks so different after learning science. For example, the trees are made of air, primarily. When they are burned, they go back to air, and in the flaming heat is released the flaming heat of the sun which was bound in to convert the air into trees, and in ash is the small remnant of the part which did not come from air, that came from the solid earth, instead.

These are beautiful things, and the content of science is wonderfully full of them. They are very inspiring, and they can be used to inspire others.

Another of the qualities of science is that it teaches the value of rational thought, as well as the importance of freedom of thought; the positive results that come from doubting that the lessons are all true. You must here distinguish—especially in teaching—the science from the forms of procedures that are sometimes used in developing science. It is easy to say, "We write, experiment, and observe, and do this or that." You can copy that form exactly. But great religions are dissipated by following form without remembering the direct content of the teaching of the great leaders. In the same way it is possible to follow form and call it science but it is pseudoscience. In this way we all suffer from the kind of tyranny we have today in the many institutions that have come under the influence of pseudoscientific advisers.

We have many studies in teaching, for example, in which people make observations and they make lists and they do statistics, but they do not thereby become established science, established knowledge. They are merely an imitative form of science—like the South Sea Islanders making airfields, radio towers out of wood, expecting a great airplane to arrive. They even build wooden airplanes of the same shape as they see in the foreigners' airfields around them, but strangely, they don't fly. The result of this pseudoscientific imitation is to produce experts, which many of you are—experts. You teachers who are really teaching children at the bottom of the heap, maybe you can doubt the experts once in a while. Learn from science that you *must* doubt the experts. As a matter of fact, I can also define science another way: Science is the belief in the ignorance of experts.

When someone says science teaches such and such, he is using the word incorrectly. Science doesn't teach it; experience teaches it. If they say to you science has shown such and such, you might ask, "How does science show it—how did the scientists find out—how, what, where?" Not science has shown, but this experiment, this effect, has shown. And you have as much right as anyone else, upon hearing about the experiments (but we must listen to *all* the evidence), to judge whether a reusable conclusion has been arrived at. . . .

I think we live in an unscientific age in which almost all the buffeting of communications and television words, books, and so on are unscientific. That doesn't mean they are bad, but they are unscientific. As a result, there is a considerable amount of intellectual tyranny in the name of science.

Finally, a man cannot live beyond the grave. Each generation that discovers something from its experience must pass that on, but it must pass that on with a delicate balance of respect and disrespect, so that the race (now that it is aware of the disease to which it is liable) does not inflict its errors too rigidly on its youth, but it does pass on the accumulated wisdom, plus the wisdom that it may not be wisdom.

It is necessary to teach both to accept and to reject the past with a kind of balance that takes considerable skill. Science alone of all the subjects contains within itself the lesson of the danger of belief in the infallibility of the greatest teachers of the preceding generation.

Kim Encounters Atlas
Craig C. Lundberg and Cheri A. Young

This note assumes that most of us, most of the time, wish to have knowledge that is clear, communicable, and trustworthy—that is, knowledge that accurately describes the world we encounter and usefully explains how it works. The knowledge we do possess, however, ranges greatly, from relatively naive to relatively sophisticated. Despite this variation, our knowledge can be enhanced, and enhanced knowledge occurs when how we learn becomes progressively more conscious, clearer, and more factually based. In what follows, we outline how people, individually and collectively, can become more sophisticated in their learning and knowing.

Our discussion of sophistication enhancement will unfold in three parts. The first part describes a true incident in which a young child, Kim, provides an archetypal example of how learning occurs. In the second part, we use Kim's experience to conceptualize learning as a cyclical process. Last, we show how to develop ever more sophisticated learning and knowing through a progressively focused, fact-centered, shared, repetitive, cycling of learning.

The Atlas Encounter

On a warm, sunny afternoon in New York City, Kim, a five-year-old girl, and her father explored Central Park for a couple of hours. At about four o'clock, they began to slowly walk hand-in-hand in the crowd southward down Fifth Avenue, on the west side of the street, toward a scheduled meeting with a friend. As they strolled along, Kim's father pointed out what he thought were interesting things to his daughter. Soon they came to Rockefeller Center and immediately noticed a large setback in the building. Conspicuous in the setback was a large, muscular statue of Atlas (by sculptor Lee Lawrice) on a tall pedestal, holding a large sphere on his shoulders. Altogether the statue was large and imposing, particularly when seen from the viewpoint of a five-year-old child. Upon seeing the Atlas statue, Kim asked, "Who is that Daddy?" Her father responded by naming Atlas and providing the popular condensed version of the Atlas myth. "A long time ago, Kim, people believed that Atlas held up the world."[4] Dropping her father's hand, Kim wrinkled her forehead and looked the statue up and down. After a moment's pause, she turned to her father and inquired, "But Daddy, what was *he* standing on?" At that her father threw back his head and laughed. He replied to his inquisitive daughter, "Kim, when people finally

Source: Written by the authors for this book.

4. This is, of course, inaccurate, for in Greek mythology Atlas held heaven and earth apart.

got around to asking your question they gave up on the Atlas story and be-gan to search for other explanations of how the world seems to stay up."

Right now you might be thinking, "What a precocious child!" But lest the moral of the story be lost, let us pause to briefly reflect on Kim's en-counter with Atlas. Before she sees the statue Kim knows that people stand on and move upon the earth, and, in fact, when she initially sees the Atlas statue, she and her father are standing on the sidewalk. When Kim hears the popular account of the myth that omits what is under Atlas's feet, she ap-parently senses a disparity, becomes curious, and asks her last question. Her father's response probably reinforced Kim's knowledge that people have to stand on something.

On Learning

The incident of Kim's encounter with Atlas, while a small and simple one, seems indicative of how all of us create and refine our knowledge. All of us, like Kim, always have something in mind in the form of knowledge. This knowledge (a set of beliefs) is more or less accurate and describes what things are and how things work. As we go through life, what we have in mind allows us to notice things and once in a while we also notice that what we have in mind is not what we perceive, that is, there is an unexpected dis-crepancy (an anomaly). If we are bothered by a discrepancy, we sometimes get curious. We wonder how what we have noticed, different from what we expected based on our beliefs, can be so. This questioning sometimes leads us to seek additional information or other beliefs or to clarify facts or ideas previously acquired (to inquire). Either way, we thereafter tend to under-stand things differently—that is, the something in mind we began with has been modified (we have learned). Figure 1-1 graphically portrays the belief modifying–learning cycle just sketched.

We can now see, in general, how beliefs are modified, and, might easily concur that Kim probably learned something that summer afternoon in New York. The learning cycle outlined also seems to describe how human communities learn, because members of human communities of all sorts do tend to share many beliefs—from uncritically held, not very factual ones (e.g., fictions, fantasies, myths) to well tested, fact-based ones (e.g., sci-entific knowledge)—which prompt the noticing, comparison of belief to ob-served reality, and inquiry process that improves shared beliefs.

Let us pause here and comment more fully on beliefs as the residuals of learning. Beliefs may, and do, vary in two ways. They can vary in how well they are substantiated factually—from one or a few imagined "facts" to a great many carefully described facts gathered by independent observers. Be-liefs can also vary in terms of their generality or scope—from encompassing or including a few to a great many specific facts. The more a belief is narrow

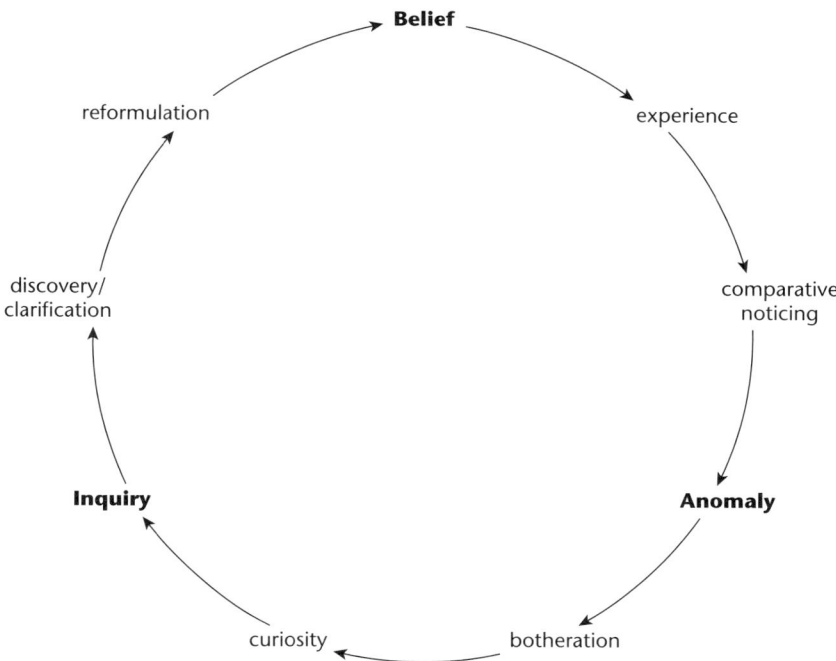

FIGURE **1-1**   The cycle of belief modification

in scope and well substantiated by observable facts, the less likely the belief will be brought into question by noticed anomalies. Regardless of their factual foundation or their scope, beliefs are stated in just two basic forms. One form is about association—something is believed to coexist with something else at a point in time. Beliefs of association are also probability statements— that is, when we observe the presence of one thing we believe that at some level of chance that we will observe another thing. The other form of belief is about causation (also a probability)—that is, when we observe one thing (a cause) at one time we believe there is some chance that at a later time we will observe something else (the effect). We prefer beliefs that are fact-based and clear about the probability of either the association or causality of two or more facts because they are the most accurate about the world we live in.

Enhancing Sophistication

Being more sophisticated in our knowledge means having and using beliefs that accurately reflect reality—that is, beliefs that refer to valid facts and have a high probability in their relationship. Learning, we have argued, is modifying beliefs through a cycle of noticing anomalies and doing inquiry. Beliefs enable us to perceive both those facts that confirm a belief and those that do not.

To be naive is to hold beliefs that frequently lead to unexpected observations. The better our beliefs reflect reality, the less often they lead to the unexpected—and we say that our knowledge is more sophisticated. How does sophistication enhancement occur? The general answer is that sophistication accrues when the belief modification cycle is repeated, when each repetition is more carefully, more consciously performed and beliefs become increasingly reality based.

Let us illustrate how increasingly sophisticated inquiry occurs, and thus how knowledge becomes increasingly more sophisticated, by describing the successive learning of Kim, now a young adult, who holds some beliefs about a phenomenon, say education for senior citizens. At the outset, Kim is very naive. Her beliefs about educating senior citizens are just unconscious assumptions. With ongoing experiences and interactions with other people, Kim's assumptions turn into the sorts of things people say to one another to capture their experiences in language—commonsense sayings and simplistic generalizations. Typically, however, these are both pretty general (for instance, "you can't teach an old dog new tricks") and often contradictory (for instance, "you're never too old to learn"). When Kim acknowledges such contradictions, she sometimes seeks new experiences that aid in discovering which, if either, commonsense saying makes the most sense to her. To do this, for example, Kim may volunteer at a nursing home to gain more experience.

As Kim acquires an ever wider base of experience, and thus, more and better facts, she finds that her beliefs apply in some situations and not others and they tend to be less general. These more refined, context-specific beliefs are usually referred to as "rules of thumb," which are essentially simple assertions that something is so under such and such conditions. For example, senior citizens in a supportive, caring environment where life-long learning is valued will be open to learning opportunities. These sorts of belief tend to be believable to Kim because they are based on her personally relevant, situational experience. Sooner or later, however, when Kim applies a rule of thumb, there are unanticipated consequences—the rule somehow does not seem to work or the situation does not seem right. When this happens, Kim may look for different things in different situations to explain the unanticipated. Such searching is usually not very careful and typically ceases with the first "next best" explanation that makes sense in terms of the facts available and/or the opinions of authorities or experts listened to. For instance, Kim may speak with the nursing home director, who tells her that it is the healthier elder person who has a college degree that is more likely to sign up for a workshop. Such clarifications of the contexts and contingent conditions where rule-of-thumb assertions seem to be true tends to give Kim the basis for increasingly error-free, more effective behavior.

Many, if not most, people content themselves with the level of sophistication that experience-based knowledge provides. Sometimes, however, people want to know even more accurately about something of importance to their work or life and push themselves to utter or write their beliefs more rigorously. These may be either (a) descriptive of reality (e.g., "under conditions [a, b, c . . .], then [proposition]," where the proposition is an associative or causative statement that relates two or more ideas) or (b) prescriptive rules (e.g., "under conditions [a, b, c . . .], then do [behavior m, n, o . . .] to achieve outcome [x, y, z . . .]"). For example, Kim's descriptive belief may be that when the nursing home environment supports life-long learning, educational opportunities are available, and the senior citizen has had positive experiences involving education, then he or she will enroll in a continuing education course offered at the home. Such rigorous statements not only structure her beliefs more clearly and are clearly communicated, but they also sensitize her to look at the relevant facts more carefully. Kim may notice unpredicted things, and sometimes these will prompt the sort of careful, systematic research for information needed to improve or correct the statement. As findings of systematic research cumulate, she may attempt to summarize them in models focused around the idea of senior education. A model typically combines a number of ideas and how the ideas relate to one another. Such models, just like rigorous statements they are composed of, aid one's understanding of the phenomena and guide the model's testing. One's colleagues may join in this testing and a whole program of research may ensue.

With time, as interrelated sets of rigorous statements and models get progressively clarified and confirmed, they coalesce into theoretical configurations termed schools of thought. Inquiry at this stage of sophistication is largely devoted to the verification and refinement of extant theory. Sooner or later competing theoretical perspectives sometimes develop—that is, two or more major theories come into existence, all of which ostensibly explain the same phenomena. When alternative theoretical explanations exist, allegiances occur and intertheoretical debates tend to reign. This state of affairs, when publicly acknowledged, sometimes prompts research designed to show which competing theory explains best (technically this is called "strong inference"). The winner among such theoretical competitions—as well as the research assumptions, designs and methods it embraces—becomes the exemplar for a field and defines "normal" scientific knowledge within it. Such theories continue to dominate research endeavors until the time comes when a new, clear anomaly is noticed and acknowledged—that is, until the theory cannot fully explain the phenomena of interest. This, of course, is quite rare, and when it happens the scientific discipline's accepted

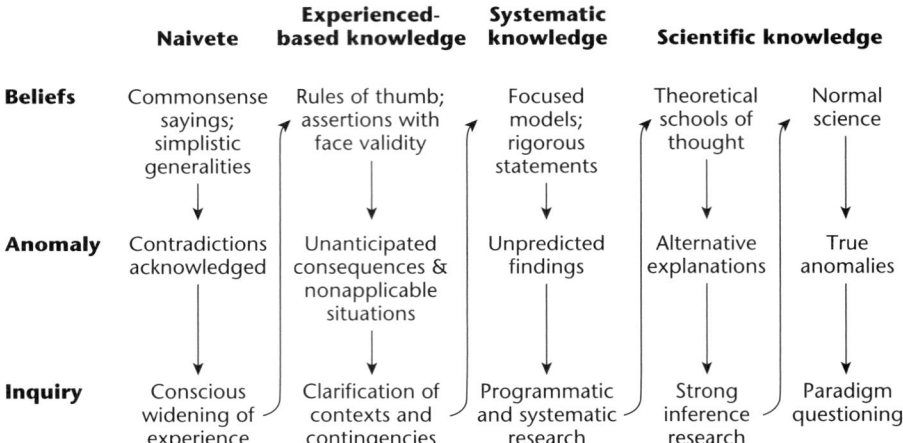

	Naivete	Experienced-based knowledge	Systematic knowledge	Scientific knowledge	
Beliefs	Commonsense sayings; simplistic generalities	Rules of thumb; assertions with face validity	Focused models; rigorous statements	Theoretical schools of thought	Normal science
Anomaly	Contradictions acknowledged	Unanticipated consequences & nonapplicable situations	Unpredicted findings	Alternative explanations	True anomalies
Inquiry	Conscious widening of experience	Clarification of contexts and contingencies	Programmatic and systematic research	Strong inference research	Paradigm questioning

FIGURE **1-2**   Knowledge enhancement

way of seeing and understanding (the prevailing paradigm) is brought into question and new forms of theorizing begin.

The progressive series of belief modification cycles we have described, from naivete through increasing sophistication on to science is shown graphically in Figure 1-2. We see that sophistication enhancement comes when each successive cycle uses more clearly stated beliefs (ideas and their relationships) that permit the noticing of anomalies and prompt more careful and focused inquiry.

Concluding Commentary

The cycle of belief modification and its repetitive, progressive application to develop ever more sophisticated knowledge that we have described appear to be pretty straightforward processes. The more sophisticated our beliefs, the more clearly we can communicate, the better our understanding, and the more effective our behavior should be. Why then does there seem to be so much relatively unsophisticated thinking? In part, the answer to this question is simply that not many people understand how more sophisticated knowledge creation occurs. Another part of the answer, however, is that many of us prefer our current beliefs, are unpracticed in comparative noticing, do not allow ourselves to be bothered by the discrepancies we perceive, do not state our beliefs very clearly, keep a lid on our curiosity, and so on. Still another part of the answer is that many of us learn early and strongly not to question the beliefs we acquire or not to subject them to the concrete

facts of our experience or other observed reality. And, of course, fact finding, comparison of facts to beliefs, and belief reformulation may not only be
unfamiliar; they are also demanding tasks requiring persistence and energy.
It may be more comfortable to accept the answers (beliefs) of others than to
do the hard work of constructing and improving our understandings of how
the world is and how it works.

Summary

In the selections in this chapter, inquiry is seen to be a distinctly human
and social endeavor. Questions occur and get answered, over and over, by
people, usually with others. Regardless of age, gender, personality, focal interests, or circumstances, the process of inquiry allows for the possibility
that currently available facts may change beliefs that were based on previously accepted "facts." The cyclic nature of serious (i.e., sophisticated) inquiry ensures that erroneous beliefs will be modified when research data fail
to support them—and in this process, people and their human communities learn from the ever more sophisticated knowledge produced.

While the overview of inquiry seems straightforward enough—be curious or bothered by something noticed, think up or listen to others for some
new understanding of it, and gather some information that might help determine whether the new understanding seems reasonable or not—our
chapter selections suggest that inquiry actually requires much of us. What
seems so obvious to someone naive—that is, what knowledge is not being
confirmed by our observation? What is a new and useful question to ask?
What information might shed some light on a new question? How can we
gather enough of the right kind of information? When should we change
our minds? Such questions turn out to be much more subtle, complicated,
and contentious when carefully thought about. To create knowledge that is
relatively lasting, that achieves relatively widespread agreement, and that
seems to justify changes in our actions, activities, and life circumstances,
obviously requires quite sophisticated inquirers.

2   Mapping the Domain of Inquiry

> To talk about sensemaking is to talk about reality as an ongoing accomplishment that takes form when people make retrospective sense of the situations in which they find themselves and their creations. There is a strong reflexive quality to [these] processes. People make sense of things by seeing a world on which they already imposed what they believe. People discover their own inventions, which is why sensemaking understood as invention, and interpretation understood as discovery, can be complementary ideas.
>
> —*Karl Weick*

Up to this point, we have stated more than once that serious inquiry, while simple and straightforward in outline, is in actuality quite complex. The purpose of this chapter is to map the domain of inquiry by identifying its components and how they relate to one another. There are three primary components to inquiry. A configuration of philosophic assumptions (what we refer to as the philosophic context) shapes the conceptual forms in which knowledge resides (models and theories). This conceptual frame of models and theories influences the research activities of knowledge creation (the research process). These three components—the research process, models and theories, and philosophic assumptions—are what we are calling the *domain of inquiry.*

The chapter will unfold in four parts. In the first part, we will define "inquiry" as making meanings and show how meaning-making is in fact a special case of the human learning process known as sensemaking. In the second part, we look at the research process through the lens of sensemaking, noting that the research process consists of a generally ordered sequence of activities that begins with questions and ends with what new knowledge can contribute. In the third and fourth parts of this chapter, we describe the two other components of the domain of inquiry in which the research process is embedded: models and theories, and the philosophic context. Models and theories may serve as the reservoirs of knowledge from which questions arise, from which questions are framed, and into which answers are deposited. The set of philosophic assumptions that constitute the philosophic context of inquiry shapes both conceptual frameworks (models and theories) and the research process.

Inquiry as Making Meanings

For serious inquirers, the meanings of interest are, generally speaking, of just three kinds: (1) what the world is like (actually, how some part or aspect of the world may be more accurately *described*); (2) how it works (how some natural process or human practice more accurately *happens*); and (3) how the first two kinds of meanings are discovered, progressively clarified, and verified. Meaning-making, or what is termed *sensemaking*, literally means the making of sense. For inquiry this involves making sense of the world (what it is like, how it works, etc.) or, in other words, figuring out what things mean. Sensemaking "involves taking whatever is clearer, whether it be a belief or an action, and linking it with that which is less clear" (Weick 1995a, 135). Interestingly, the essence of sensemaking has just three elements: a frame, a cue, and a connection. A frame allows one to notice, extract, and make sense of cues.

> Frames and cues can be thought of as vocabularies in which words that are more abstract (frames) include and point to other less abstract words (cues) that become sensible in the context created by the more inclusive words. . . . A cue in a frame is what makes sense, not the cue alone or the frame alone (Weick 1995a, 110).

Meaning thus occurs when a more inclusive idea or set of ideas (i.e., conceptual models and theories) and the facts they represent allow us to notice some particular new facts as well as notice whether these particular facts are consistent with the earlier set. The frames that are ideas and sets of ideas are, of course, learned before the present moment of experiencing a cued particular fact. Frames can be personalized but for the most part tend to be past moments of socialization (i.e., learned with and from as well as shared with other people). For individuals and human communities of various sizes, "sensemaking edits continuity into discreet categories, observations into interpretations, experience into bounded events, and perceptions into pre-existing plans and frameworks" (Weick 1995a, 108). For example, imagine a student, asked to code some interview data, who does not know what the research is about or the theory being tested.

When people make sense they also make meaning. When cues are unclear or nonsensical they are anomalies (see Fig. 1-1), and sometimes anomalies prompt the process of making more or better sense—the process of doing research.

TABLE 2-1
The research process

Stage	Activities
Project conception and initiation	Selection of phenomena/topic/issue/problem Specify focal concerns/guiding questions Clarify project sponsorship and stakeholders
Project design	Project significance justified, ideological allegiance acknowledged Project related to existing knowledge Clarify the nature of reality assumed Select and justify project strategy and research design Key ideas defined conceptually and operationally Formulate specific questions/hypotheses
Data surfacing	Designate appropriate context Specify sampling Select data gathering methods Gather data
Data processing/management	Specify form of data Design data reduction Determine data storage and retrieval
Data examination	Specify what meaning consists of Do analysis Do interpretation Compile and display findings
Dissemination of the research	Determine appropriate actions Select appropriate timing, voice, style, medium Share/utilize findings
Termination of research project	Project assessment Identification of further research

The Research Process

The process of producing meaningful answers to puzzling, bothersome questions is the research part of inquiry. While descriptions of how to conduct research vary considerably in the number of activity stages or steps involved, their general sequencing remains similar. Our synthesis of the research literature reveals a sequence of seven stages of major activities, each of which usually embraces several more specific activities. Table 2-1 summarizes this elaborated seven-stage research process.

Research projects begin by being conceived and initiated. Whether because of intentional searching within a known conceptual frame or simply inadvertent noticing within an unconsciously held frame, some topic, issue, problem area or phenomena of interest is selected; focal concerns or general guiding questions are specified; and possible project sponsorship and project stakeholders clarified. The second major activity is the design of the research. Research design involves justifying the project's significance in practical and theoretical terms and acknowledging consciously or unconsciously the project's or the researcher's ideological allegiance. In addition, how the study is related to, based on, and/or an extension of existing knowledge is shown. Furthermore, beliefs about the fundamental nature of the phenomena should be clarified, although they are typically assumed. A strategy of subsequent activities is designed, key ideas are defined conceptually and how they are known in data, and the study's questions are more precisely formulated. As a third stage, relevant data are acquired after a suitable context is designated, the parameters of the sampling specified, and data collection methods selected (in accord with standards of reliability and validity). Once the designated type and amount of relevant data are collected, the fourth major activity is the processing of the data (i.e., sorting and ordering it in forms appropriate for storage, retrieval, and manipulation). The fifth major activity is to examine the data: analyzing and interpreting the data to provide responses to the study's questions in the form of research findings—new knowledge—and to compile and display these new understandings and explanations. With the study's findings explained, their dissemination becomes the sixth major activity. Some action is outlined, either to enact some intervention or to talk and/or write so as to influence action somewhere sometime—and with choices of voice, style, and medium of influence selected, the study's findings are actively disseminated. The seventh and final major activity in the research process is the termination of the project (and ideally, assessing it).

While the sequence of activities outlining the research process is arguably what experienced researchers do, not all steps are always performed or performed consciously. Some activities are given attention because the researchers anticipate the "reconstructed logic" (Kaplan 1964) of research reports. Some activities are simply presumed because the researcher is working within the modality currently in ascendance within a school of thought. Some activities are ignored or glossed because of naivete or personal proclivities of the researcher or because of resource constraints. For these and other reasons, researchers quite often do not appreciate the many distinct activities, their alternatives, or the multitude of real choices that exist in designing and executing research endeavors. Nevertheless, no major activities can be ignored without serious negative consequences to the research project (Daft 1984). Because activities may overlap (the initiation of one may occur before an earlier activity is completed) and/or be interdependent, some early activity choices may determine the nature of later ones (e.g., Selltiz, Wrightsman, and Cook 1976).

In addition to the seven major activity stages, the research process embraces some twenty-five subactivities. Each subactivity holds alternatives of a substantive nature requiring one or more choices. Research is always therefore replete with decisions. Our point is obvious but is usefully stated: the whats, wheres, hows, and whos of research are very many indeed. Beginning with the first activity of noticing something of interest to study, the decision tree of subsequent choices can be remarkably complex.

Framing Research: Models and Theories

The research process does not exist in a vacuum. It will reflect, to a considerable degree, the nature and extent of the more or less elaborated, more or less factually based, more or less organized body of existing knowledge (found in models and/or theories) that is relevant to a research project's focus. This conceptual foundation of models and/or theories provides the proximate frame for all systematic and scientific research projects.

The frame provided by conceptual models and theories serves research in two basic ways. On the one hand, research findings (i.e., new knowledge) may be incorporated into existing models and theories—filling gaps in them and refining and elaborating them. New findings become meaningful only in terms of existing conceptual frames. On the other hand, these frames provided by extant knowledge are what permit us to notice anomalous cues (e.g., some previously unnoticed facts, some facts that are not readily explained) and see them as raising meaningful questions. How models and theories frame and receive research is graphically depicted in Figure 2-1.

Interestingly, models and theories vary in several ways: the number of kinds of facts they embrace (scope), the degree of their explicitness (formality), the extent of their factual confirmation (validity), the structure of the knowledge contained (form), etc. These features of conceptual frameworks

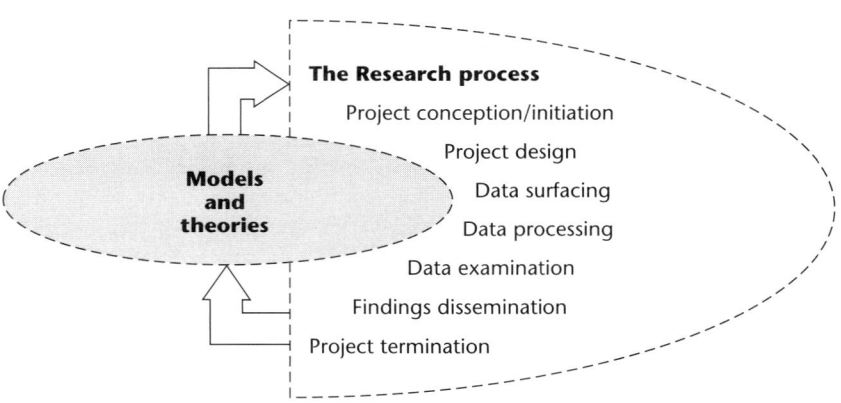

FIGURE **2-1**   The conceptual frame of research

combine to give many alternative types. The variety of models and theories subtly shape research through the emphasis that a conceptual frame provides on what can be noticed and questioned, and, what form of findings permit their inclusion into extant theoretical work. Research without theory is meaningless; theory without research stagnates.

Framing Knowledge: Philosophic Context

If conceptual frameworks in the form of models and theories frame and thereby shape the research process, what influences the scope and form of these models and theories, and, by extension, the research process? Conceptual frameworks (models and theories) and research activities are both nested within and shaped by the more distal frame that is constituted by the several types of fundamental assumptions and beliefs that form the philosophic context of inquiry. We are in agreement with Bentz and Shapiro (1998) who state:

> We are old-fashioned in believing that the scientist or working researcher is always a kind of philosopher, at least an applied philosopher. We are even pre-modern in the sense that before the nineteenth century the sciences did not exist as separate disciplines and were considered part of philosophy. We believe that it is impossible to fully understand the nature of research or to make the best choices about it without some attention to its philosophical context, its assumptions, its a priori constructions of reality, its knowledge values. No matter how technical and mechanical research may be, at least at some points in the process, it always is also a form of philosophical inquiry. That is, it always involves philosophical assumptions about the nature of knowledge and of the world and about what the point of knowledge and research are in the first place. Consciously or unconsciously, research is always contributing to the advancement of some philosophical "project"—and to a personal and social one as well. (31)

What sorts of assumptions lie behind how we theorize and do research? Assumptions, by definition, are both ubiquitous and out of consciousness. Nevertheless they can be categorized, at least generally, and their types within categories specified, again at least generally. Five categories of core philosophic assumptions about inquiry can be designated: assumptions about the nature of reality (*ontology*), assumptions about how reality is known (*epistemology*), assumptions and metaphors about human nature (*images of human nature*), assumptions about sets of emotionally charged values and beliefs that bind some people together and help them make sense of their worlds (*ideology*), and assumptions held by researchers working within a theoretical community about how they should work to advance

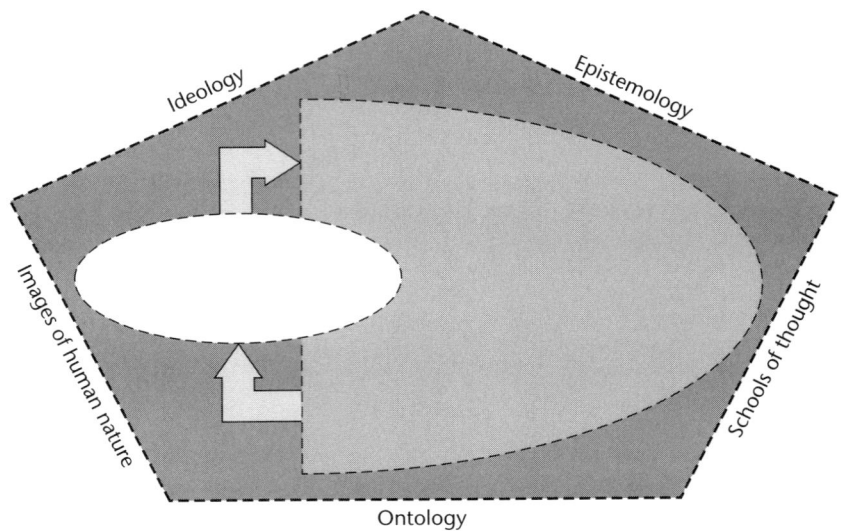

FIGURE **2-2**   The philosophic context of inquiry

their field of knowledge and enhance their reputations (*schools of thought*). There are alternatives within each of these five assumptive categories. "Paradigm" is the name given to a configuration of such assumptions. Because these philosophic assumptions frame and thus shape models and theories (which in turn frame the research process), we label this paradigmatic set of philosophic assumptions the *philosophic context of inquiry* (see Fig. 2-2). The *domain of inquiry*, which consists of the philosophic context of inquiry, models and theories, and the research process is shown in Figure 2-3. Each part of the domain of inquiry will be discussed in detail in future chapters.

Summary

Inquiry allows us to make meaning by using frames, such as models and theories, that allow us to notice some particular facts (cues) and make sense of them. When the cues are unclear or nonsensical, anomalies prompt the process of doing research. The research process, however, is framed by relevant models and theories. The models and theories themselves may stimulate the search for new knowledge (making sense of anomalies) and, at the same time, may include the outcome of the research process. Knowledge may be created when models and theories are refined, changed, updated, and/or discarded because of findings from the research process.

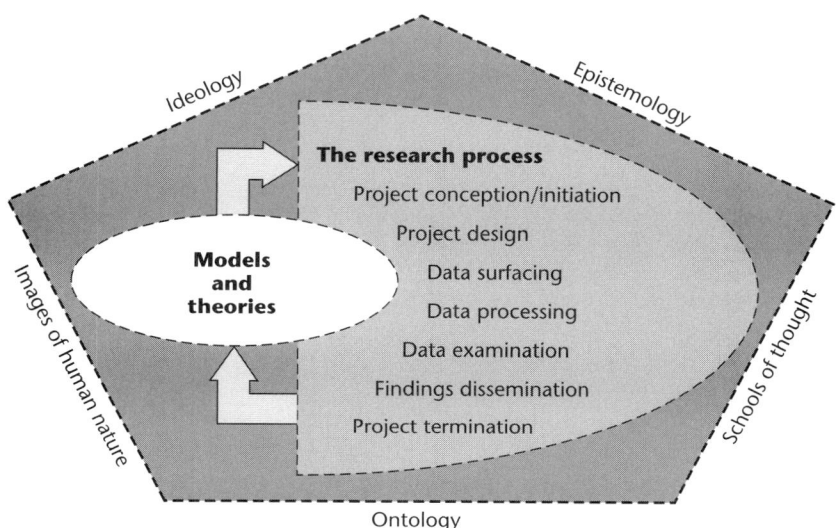

FIGURE **2-3**   The domain of inquiry

While models and theories frame the research process, the philosophic context of inquiry frames models and theories, and, hence, the research process. The philosophic context of inquiry consists of five categories of core assumptions, including ontology (the nature of reality), epistemology (how reality is known), human nature (images of humans), ideologies (values and beliefs that bind some people together and help them make sense of their worlds), and schools of thought (assumptions held by researchers regarding how to work to advance their field of knowledge and reputation). Although the research process may appear mechanical and technical, it always involves philosophical assumptions that frame or influence the type of questions asked, the type of data sought, and the type of knowledge created.

The domain of inquiry has now been mapped as three related component areas: an area of practices (described as a general sequence of activities that constitute the *process of research*), an area of consciously shared, developing repositories of knowledge (described as *models and theories* that act as conceptual frameworks of various degrees of systematization, formalization, and confirmation), and an area of *philosophic context* (described as a paradigmatic frame composed of five types of basic philosophic assumptions). It is useful to remember that the domain of inquiry is known and is used by people, singularly and collectively, and thus is subject to both human attention and learning—thus contributing to our personal understanding and appreciation of inquiry as well as contributing to the development of inquiry itself.

Part 2

The Philosophical Context of Inquiry

Serious inquiry, like all human endeavors, is based upon a foundation of core assumptions. These deep-seated assumptions are culturelike in that they are usually out of our awareness, shared to some degree with others, and relatively stable, although, because they are learned, they can be chosen and modified when brought to consciousness. This assumptive set forms the philosophic context of inquiry and as such frames and shapes both conceptualization and research. The chapters of Part 2 that follow each specify and describe the five assumptive components of inquiry's philosophic context.

In Chapter 3 paradigms are described, their filtering and shaping functions noted, social science and organizational science paradigm types given, and a few contemporary issues briefly discussed. In addition, we suggest the trade-offs and consequences for alternative paradigmatic frames. The remaining chapters of this part—Chapters 4 through 7—each focus on one or more of the five philosophic assumptions—about human nature, ontology and epistemology, ideologies and values, and the theoretical schools of thought that organize scientific fields and disciplines. Consistent with the major theme of this book, we endeavor to present the range of alternatives of each of the five philosophic assumptions.

Be forewarned: the chapters of Part 2 will require considerable concentration simply because they discuss things usually not discussed. We encourage readers to be patient with themselves as they encounter ideas that may be unfamiliar and/or difficult to grasp at first. While we will endeavor to summarize key points, some of the material in Part 2 just takes time to comprehend. The philosophic context of inquiry deserves your full attention—it is vital for everyone who wishes to understand, appreciate, and do organizational science research. And it is not just the province of philosophers!

The Frame of Paradigm

The most difficult thing in science, as in other fields, is to shake off accepted views.
> —*George Sarton*

A wise man proportions his belief to the evidence.
> —*David Hume*

In place of fundamental truths I put fundamental probabilities— provisionally assumed *guides* by which one lives.
> —*Friedrich Nietzsche*

It requires a very unusual mind to undertake the analysis of the obvious.
> —*A. N. Whitehead*

This chapter is concerned with philosophical frames of inquiry, or paradigms, their assumptions, and the implications of those assumptions for a variety of conceptual and research issues, not with the relative popularity or utility of any particular paradigm. Paradigms are the critical precondition for serious inquiry. Given its centrality, importance, and shaping power, as well as its elusiveness, we will begin by showing why the idea of paradigms emerged, what it means, and how it works.

Origins, Definition, and Function

About a century ago, science and philosophy were seen as being in a state of chaos; heterogeneity and fragmentation characterized most disciplines. It was believed that a common scientific language was needed, from which, eventually, a unified science would emerge. Most laypeople believed then, as they do now, that science advances in a cumulative manner, with each discovery building inexorably on all those that precede it—accelerated from time to time by heroic individual discoveries. Scientific progress thus supposedly moved toward a fixed goal set by nature.

In 1962, Thomas Kuhn, in *The Structure of Scientific Revolutions*, argued that organized communities of specialists, not individual minds, were the central actors in scientific development, and that these communities made progress in two distinctive modes. In "normal science" researchers did narrow, technical theoretical work guided by a "paradigm," a view of their field that served as a set of predictions for what investigators would find. When these researchers observed, instead, a lot of things that did not fit their expectations ("anomalies"), the community then entered a period of "revolutionary science." This period prompted the community to debate the utility of alternative paradigms and eventually select one that enabled better explanations of a greater range of relevant phenomena and promised thereby to better guide the next phase of normal science. Kuhn's model of scientific changes is shown in Figure 3-1.

Science does not proceed, according to Kuhn, by facts revealing themselves to clever thinkers or by scientists attempting to falsify their own

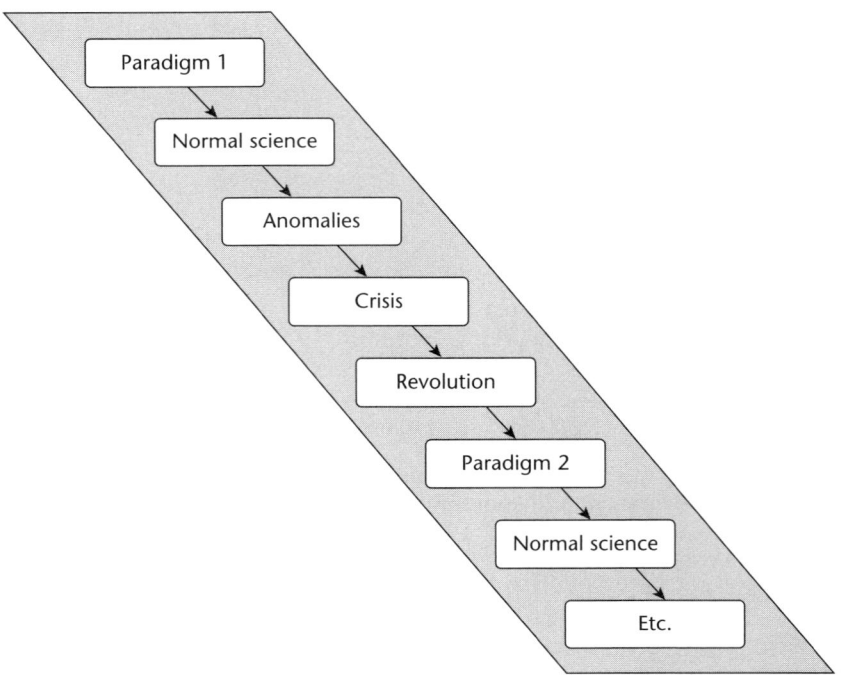

FIGURE **3-1**   How science changes, according to Kuhn

hypotheses in every experiment. Rather, progress moves from existing knowledge toward more fully confirmed answers to new questions scientists put to nature. Since the questions themselves sometimes change, the progress of science is discontinuous. Kuhn emphasizes the power of preconceived assumptions to guide the conceptualizations of scientists. He insists that without the focusing effect of these conceptualizations, scientists would not be able to actually investigate phenomena, the explanation of which was essential to the creation of new knowledge. While scientists always have something in mind, they are open-minded in the sense of always questioning inherited ideas.

> Established ways of seeing the world are replaced, throughout history, by tremendous upheavals in thought. Those changes are so expansive that the old ways of thinking are totally incompatible with the new. To embrace the new is to undertake a conversion experience. By no means are all scientists in the field willing to contemplate this move from a comfortable stability. The new view of the world—an Einsteinian one rather than a Newtonian one, for example—creates a new structure, a new set of community agendas, a revolutionary new set of social arrangements, a new paradigm which revolutionizes our understanding. (Burrell 1996, 646–647)

The backbone term in Kuhn's book is "paradigm." The idea of a paradigm itself, however, is somewhat elusive. According to Masterman (1970), Kuhn uses the term in at least twenty-one different ways. Understanding of the idea may be facilitated by first referring to a definition of paradigm used by Friedrichs (1970): "A fundamental image a discipline has of its subject matter" (55). How this occurs is suggested by Guba and Lincoln (1994), who state that a "paradigm may be viewed as a set of *basic beliefs* (or metaphysics) that deals with ultimates or first principles. It represents a *worldview* that defines, for its holder, the nature of the 'world,' the individuals' place in it, and the range of possible relationships to that world and its parts, as, for example, cosmologies and theologies do" (107).

R. H. Brown (1978) sharpens and extends the meaning of paradigm when he states, "By paradigm we refer to those sets of assumptions, usually implicit, about what sorts of things make up the world, how they act, how they hang together, and how they become known" (373). And Ritzer (1980) sweeps most other definitions into this comprehensive one: "A paradigm is a fundamental image of the subject matter within a science. It serves to define what should be studied, what questions should be asked, and what rules should be followed in interpreting the answers obtained. The paradigm is the broadest unit of consensus within a science and serves to differentiate one scientific community (*or sub-community*) from another. It subsumes, defines, and interrelates the exemplars, theories, and methods and tools that exist within it" (189).

TABLE 3-1
Types of paradigmatic assumptions

Assumption	Question
Human nature	What is the relationship between human beings and their environments?
Ontological	What is the nature of reality?
Epistemological	What is the relationship of the researcher to that which is being researched?
Ideological	Whose interests are being supported?
School of thought	What conceptual work and its investigators deserve allegiance?

The preceding definitions permit the appreciation of the three meanings of paradigms identified by Morgan (1979a).

First, there is the concept of paradigm in a metatheoretical or philosophical sense, where the term is used to capture a complete view of reality, or "way of seeing." Second, there is the concept of paradigm relating to the social organization of science in terms of schools of thought built around a set of scientific habits connected with particular kinds of scientific achievements. Third, there is the concept of paradigm relating to the concrete use of specific kinds of tools and texts for the process of scientific puzzle solving. (137)

Ritzer's definition of paradigm exemplifies Morgan's first meaning and generally guides our discussion herein. Thus, inquiry paradigms define for inquirers what it is they do and what falls within and without the limits of legitimate inquiry. The kinds of assumptions that compose inquiry paradigms are known to us through a set of questions, which are interconnected in such a way that the answer given to any one question, taken in any order, constrains how the others may be answered. Table 3-1 displays the five types of key assumptions defining a paradigm and their associated focal questions.

These five types of assumptions are basic and fundamental in the sense that they must be accepted simply on faith—there is no way to establish the ultimate truthfulness of their answers. And, we emphasize, the sets of answers given to the defining questions are, in all cases, human constructions; that is, they are all inventions of the human mind and are subject to human error and further learning. Normal science does, we recall, occasionally lead to paradigm change.

The first two selections in this chapter provide examples of paradigm types and typologies. While both are well known, let us emphasize that they are illustrative, not definitive—both inform us of major paradigms in use today and how they may be differentiated. In the first selection, Burrell and Morgan derive four major paradigms using two dimensions: one that asserts that social theory is primarily concerned with reality as either subjective or

objective; the other asserts that social change is either primarily the consequence of stabilizing societal regulation or a natural process of continuous
change. They instructively show how the major known social theories fit into
their four paradigms. Ritzer, in the second selection, offers an alternative to
Burrell and Morgan. He outlines three major social paradigms and notes the
theories and preferred methodologies of each. Ritzer's paradigm types are
used by Pondy and Boje in the next selection to group most of the well-
known theories in organization studies. The existence of several paradigms
means, on the one hand, that little paradigm consensus currently exists and
that at present "normal science" in the organizational sciences is pluralistic, and, on the other hand, that paradigm development may be needed.
Lincoln, in the final selection, succinctly outlines seven discernable ways that
paradigms are currently being modified—reminding us that paradigms are
never really static.

Two Dimensions, Four Paradigms
Gibson Burrell and Gareth Morgan

. . . We have focused upon some of the key assumptions which charac-
terise different approaches to social theory. We have argued that it is possible to analyse these approaches in terms of two key dimensions of analysis, each of which subsumes a series of related themes. It has been suggested
that assumptions about the nature of science can be thought of in terms of
what we call the subjective-objective dimension, and assumptions about the
nature of society in terms of a regulation-radical change dimension. [Now]
we wish to discuss the relationships between the two dimensions and to develop a coherent scheme for the analysis of social theory.

We have already noted how sociological debate since the late 1960s has
tended to ignore the distinctions between the two dimensions—in particular, how there has been a tendency to focus upon issues concerned with
the subjective-objective dimension and to ignore those concerned with the
regulation-radical change dimension. Interestingly enough, this focus of attention has characterised sociological thought associated with both regulation and radical change. The subjective-objective debate has been conducted independently within both sociological camps.

Within the sociology of regulation it has assumed the form of a debate
between interpretive sociology and functionalism. In the wake of P. L. Berger
and Luckmann's treatise on the sociology of knowledge (1966), Garfinkel's
work on ethnomethodology (1967) and a general resurgence of interest in

Source: "Two dimensions: Four paradigms," in *Sociological paradigms and organizational analysis* by Gibson Burrell and Gareth Morgan, 21–25, 35. Copyright © 1979 by
Gibson Burrell and Gareth Morgan. Used by permission of Gibson Burrell.

phenomenology, the questionable status of the ontological and epistemolog-ical assumptions of the functionalist perspective have become increasingly exposed. The debate has often led to a polarisation between the two schools of thought.

Similarly, within the context of the sociology of radical change there has been a division between theorists subscribing to "subjective" and "objec-tive" views of society. The debate in many respects takes its lead from the publication in France in 1966 and Britain in 1969 of Louis Althusser's work *For Marx*. This presented the notion of an "epistemological break" in Marx's work and emphasised the polarisation of Marxist theorists into two camps: those emphasising the "subjective" aspects of Marxism (Lukács and the Frankfurt School, for example) and those advocating more "objective" approaches, such as that associated with Althusserian structuralism.

Within the context of the sociologies both of regulation and radical change, therefore, the middle to late 1960s witnessed a distinct switch in the focus of attention. The debate *between* these two sociologies which had char-acterised the early 1960s disappeared and was replaced by an introverted dialogue *within* the context of each of the separate schools of thought. In-stead of "speaking" to each other they turned inwards and addressed their remarks to themselves. The concern to sort out their position with regard to what we call the subjective-objective dimension, a complicated process in view of all the interrelated strands, led to a neglect of the regulation-radical change dimension.

As a consequence of these developments, recent debate has often been confused. Sociological thought has tended to be characterised by a narrow sectarianism, from which an overall perspective and grasp of basic issues are conspicuously absent. The time is ripe for consideration of the way ahead, and we submit that the two key dimensions of analysis which we have identified define critical parameters within which this can take place. We present them as two independent dimensions which resurrect the sociologi-cal issues of the early 1960s and place them alongside those of the late 1960s and early 1970s. Taken together, they define four distinct sociological para-digms which can be utilised for the analysis of a wide range of social theories. The relationship between these paradigms, which we label "radical human-ist," "radical structuralist," "interpretive" and "functionalist," is illustrated in Figure 3-2.

It will be clear from the diagram that each of the paradigms shares a com-mon set of features with its neighbours on the horizontal and vertical axes in terms of one of the two dimensions but is differentiated on the other dimen-sion. For this reason they should be viewed as contiguous but separate—contiguous because of the shared characteristics, but separate because of the differentiation is, as we shall demonstrate later, of sufficient importance to warrant treatment of the paradigms as four distinct entities. The four

The sociology of radical change

Radical humanist	Radical structuralist
Interpretive	Functionalist

Subjective — Objective

The sociology of regulation

FIGURE **3-2**   Four paradigms for the analysis of social theory

SOURCE: "Two dimensions: Four paradigms," *Sociological paradigms and organizational analysis* by Gibson Burrell and Gareth Morgan, 22, fig. 3. Copyright © 1979 by Gibson Burrell and Gareth Morgan. Used by permission of the author.

paradigms define fundamentally different perspectives for the analysis of social phenomena. They approach this endeavor from contrasting standpoints and generate quite different concepts and analytical tools.

The Nature and Uses of the Four Paradigms

Before going on to discuss the substantive nature of each of the paradigms, it will be as well to pay some attention to the way in which we intend the notion of "paradigm" to be used.[1] We regard our four paradigms

1. For a full discussion of the role of paradigms in scientific development, see Kuhn (1970). In his analysis, paradigms are defined as "universally recognised scientific achievements that for a time provide model problems and solutions to a community of practitioners" (p. viii). Paradigms are regarded as governing the progress of what is called "normal science," in which "the scientist's work is devoted to the articulation and wider application of the accepted paradigm, which is not itself questioned or criticised. Scientific problems are regarded as puzzles, as problems which are known to have a solution within the framework of assumptions implicitly or explicitly embodied in the paradigm. If a puzzle is not solved,

as being defined by very basic meta-theoretical assumptions which under-write the frame of reference, mode of theorising and *modus operandi* of the social theorists who operate within them. It is a term which is intended to emphasise the commonality of perspective which binds the work of a group of theorists together in such a way that they can be usefully regarded as approaching social theory within the bounds of the same problematic.

This definition does not imply complete unity of thought. It allows for the fact that within the context of any given paradigm there will be much debate between theorists who adopt different standpoints. The paradigm does, however, have an underlying unity in terms of its basic and often "taken for granted" assumptions, which separate a group of theorists in a very fundamental way from theorists located in other paradigms. The "unity" of the paradigm thus derives from reference to alternative views of reality which lie outside its boundaries and which may not necessarily even be recognised as existing.

In identifying four paradigms in social theory we are in essence suggesting that it is meaningful to examine work in the subject area in terms of four sets of basic assumptions. Each set identifies a quite separate social-scientific reality. To be located in a particular paradigm is to view the world in a particular way. The four paradigms thus define four views of the social world based upon different meta-theoretical assumptions with regard to the nature of science and of society.

It is our contention that all social theorists can be located within the context of these four paradigms according to the metatheoretical assumptions reflected in their work. The four paradigms taken together provide a map for negotiating the subject area, which offers a convenient means of identifying the basic similarities and differences between the work of various theorists and, in particular, the underlying frame of reference which they adopt. It also provides a convenient way of locating one's own personal frame of reference with regard to social theory, and thus a means of understanding why certain theories and perspectives may have more personal appeal than others. Like any other map, it provides a tool for establishing where you are,

---

the fault lies in the scientist, and not in the paradigm" (Keat and Urry 1975, 55). "Normal science" contrasts with relatively brief periods of "revolutionary science," in which "the scientist is confronted by increasingly perplexing anomalies, which call into question the paradigm itself. Scientific revolution occurs when a new paradigm emerges, and becomes accepted by the scientific community" (ibid., 55).

We are using the term "paradigm" in a broader sense than that intended by Kuhn. Within the context of the present work, we are arguing that social theory can be conveniently understood in terms of the co-existence of four distinct and rival paradigms defined by very basic meta-theoretical assumptions in relation to the nature of science and society. "Paradigms," "problematics," "alternative realities," "frames of reference," "forms of life" and "universe of discourse" are all related conceptualisations although of course they are *not* synonymous.

where you have been and where it is possible to go in the future. It provides a tool for mapping intellectual journeys in social theory—one's own and those of the theorists who have contributed to the subject area.

In this work we intend to make much use of the map-like qualities of the four paradigms. Each defines a range of intellectual territory. Given the overall meta-theoretical assumptions which distinguish one paradigm from another, there is room for much variation within them. Within the context of the "functionalist" paradigm, for example, certain theorists adopt more extreme positions in terms of one or both of the two dimensions than others. Such differences often account for the internal debate which goes on between theorists engaged in the activities of "normal science" within the context of the same paradigm[2]. . . .

Our research suggests that whilst the activity within the context of each paradigm is often considerable, inter-paradigmatic "journeys" are much rarer. This is in keeping with Kuhn's (1970) notion of "revolutionary science." For a theorist to switch paradigms calls for a change in meta-theoretical assumptions, something which, although manifestly possible, is not often achieved in practice. As Keat and Urry put it, "For individual scientists, the change of allegiance from one paradigm to another is often a "conversion experience," akin to *Gestalt*-switches or changes of religious faith" (1975, 55). When a theorist does shift his position in this way, it stands out very clearly as a major break with his intellectual tradition and is heralded as being so in the literature, in that the theorist is usually welcomed by those whom he has joined and often disowned by his former "paradigm colleagues." Thus we witness what is known as the "epistemological break" between the work of the young Marx and the mature Marx—what we would identify as a shift from the radical humanist paradigm to the radical structuralist paradigm. At the level of organisational analysis, a distinct paradigm shift can be detected in the work of Silverman—a shift from the functionalist paradigm to the interpretive paradigm. . . .

. . . In British and American sociology the radical structuralist view has received relatively little attention outside the realm of conflict theory. This paradigm, located as it is within a realist view of the social world, has many significant implications for the study of organisations, but they have only been developed in the barest forms. . . .

2. Some *inter*-paradigm debate is also possible. Giddens maintains "that all paradigms . . . are mediated by others" and that within "normal science" scientists are aware of *other* paradigms. He posits that: "The process of learning a paradigm . . . is also the process of learning what that paradigm is not" (1976, 142–44).

Interestingly, he confines his discussion to the mediation of one paradigm by another one. We believe that a model of four conflicting paradigms within sociology is more accurate and that academics' knowledge of "scientists" within the other three paradigms is likely to be very sketchy in some cases. Relations between paradigms are perhaps better described in terms of "disinterested hostility" rather than "debate."

Paradigmatic Communities
George Ritzer

The Social Facts Paradigm

Exemplar

The exemplar for the social factist is the work of Émile Durkheim, in particular, *The Rules of Sociological Method* (1964) and *Suicide* (1951).

Image of the Subject Matter

In *The Rules of Sociological Method* Durkheim argued that the basic subject matter of sociology is the social fact. He demonstrated that contention empirically in *Suicide*. As Blau (1960) has pointed out, there are two types of social facts—social structures and social institutions. Sociologists who define either, or both, of these types as the basic subject matter of sociology are social factists. They accept, following Durkheim, that these social facts should be treated as "real" things. Some even go further arguing that they *are* real things (Warriner 1956). A social fact can be a "real" structure (such as a group or a bureaucracy) or a "real" institution (such as a family or religion). The social factist focuses on the nature of these structures and institutions and their interrelationships. He is usually not content to remain at this level and frequently encroaches on the subject matter of the other two paradigms. He also endeavors to explain social definitions and behavior. Conversely, those who accept the other two paradigms are far from reluctant, as we will see, to try to explain social structures and social institutions. In fact, *the adherents of each paradigm attempt to deny the validity of the other paradigms.* The social factist sees behavior and social definitions more or less determined by social structures and institutions.

Theories

The social facts paradigm encompasses a number of theoretical perspectives. Structural-functional theory tends to see social facts as rather neatly interrelated. Conflict theory tends to emphasize disorder among social facts, or the fact that order is maintained by coercive forces within society. Structural-functional and conflict theory are the two dominant theories within the social facts paradigm. Systems theory is another, but much of systems theory can be included under the heading of modern structural-functionalism. It is important to emphasize the point that structural-functionalism and conflict theory are theories, not paradigms as both Friedrichs and Effrat would have us believe. They both can be included under the heading of the social facts paradigm since they both accept the centrality of the study of social facts. I believe this approach is far more parsimonious and realistic than the ones presented by Friedrichs or Effrat.

Methods

The preferred method of the social factist engaged in empirical research is the questionnaire and/or interview. This preference is an anomaly since questionnaires and interviews are designed to gather information from individuals. How can one study social facts by asking individuals questions? I will argue later that one cannot really study social facts in this way. Instead, the comparative and historical method should be used by those who seek to study social facts.

The Social Definition Paradigm

Exemplar

To the social definitionist, the unifying exemplar is Max Weber's (Gerth and Mills 1958) work on social action.

Image of the Subject Matter

Weber's work led to an interest in the way individuals define their social situations and the effect of this definition on ensuring action. This is the basic subject matter of the social definition paradigm. The subject matter is not social facts, but the way in which people define those social facts. The basic premise here is W. I. Thomas' dictum: if people define things as real, they will be real in their consequences. The crucial object of study is intrasubjectivity and intersubjectivity and the action that results. This also entails a rejection of the behaviorist position. Behavior is not seen as a simple stimulus-response phenomenon, but rather as a result of an evaluative process undertaken by the individual. The acceptance of the social definition paradigm entails a simultaneous rejection of the validity of the other two sociological paradigms.

Theories

There are three major theories that can be subsumed under the social definitionist paradigm. The first is action theory, stemming directly from Weber and later in the work of Parsons (1937) and MacIver (1942). The second theory is symbolic interactionism, which also owes a debt to Weber, but developed primarily at the University of Chicago in the 1920s and 1930s in the work of Mead (1956), Cooley (1902), W. I. Thomas (1951), and later, Blumer (1969) and others. Finally, there is phenomenological sociology. This theoretical orientation was also influenced by Weber, as well as Schutz (1971), Husserl (1965), and Garfinkel (1967).

Methods

The social definitionist tends to use some form of observation if he is oriented toward research. Although other methods are used by some in this paradigm and others shun empirical methodology altogether, observation is the preferred method of the social definitionist. As with the questionnaire/interview methods of the social factist, I will later question whether the observation method really allows the social definitionist to study the subject matter of concern to him—intrasubjectivity and intersubjectivity and the resulting action.

The Social Behavior Paradigm

Exemplar

The major exemplar for the sociologist who accepts the social behavior paradigm[3] is the work of the psychologist, B. F. Skinner (1971).

Images of the Subject Matter

The behaviorist downgrades the importance of social definitions and social facts. To the behaviorist, these are metaphysical concepts which get in the way of the real subject matter of sociology—human behavior. The behaviorist seeks to understand, predict, and even determine the behavior of man. Of particular interest are the rewards that elicit desirable behaviors and the punishments that inhibit undesirable behavior.

Theories

There are two theoretical approaches in sociology that can be included under the heading of social behaviorism. The first is behavioral sociology,

3. The meaning of the phrase social behavior should not be confused with Mead's use of the same phrase. Mead used the phrase to differentiate his brand of social definitionism from behaviorism, while I use it for the sociological variant of behaviorism. I am indebted to Marston McCluggage for this point.

which is very close to pure psychological behaviorism applied to social questions. The work of Burgess and Bushell (1969) is of this genre. The second is exchange theory, which is most often associated with George Homans (1961). Homans integrates pure behaviorism with some elements native to sociology.

Methods

Owing heavy debt to psychology, it is not surprising to find that the behaviorist tends to use experimental methods when conducting research. This may take the form of laboratory experiments or experiments conducted in real-life situations. I will argue that the method of the behaviorist comes closest to tapping the subject matter of concern to his paradigm.

Applications to Organization Theory
Louis R. Pondy and David M. Boje

Ritzer's scheme is helpful in reorganizing our conception of the field of organization theory (or complex organizations, or organizational behavior, depending on the reader's labeling preferences). Organization theory has been and is dominated by social facts and social behavior paradigms. Social definitionism is relatively undeveloped within organization theory. And relatively few attempts have been made to build bridges between the paradigms as a first step toward mounting a multi-paradigm attack on organizational analysis. Two frontier problems of a programmatic sort facing our field are (a) to develop the social definition paradigm of organizations to a level of parity with the other two paradigms, and (b) to begin a process of what Maruyama (1974) has called "transpection," or communication among paradigms.

Work legitimately classified within the *social facts paradigm* would include that on structural differentiation, contingency theory, organization role sets, interorganizational relations, socio-technical systems, power structures, and organization design. At the risk of offending people by omission or improper classification (or even the effrontery of classification itself!), the set of social factists would include Perrow, Richard Hall, Etzioni, post-exchange-theory Blau, Evan, Pugh and the Aston School, Lawrence and Lorsch, Woodward, Aiken and Hage, and more recently Schönherr, Pfeffer, Freeman, Meyer, Aldrich and Duncan, to cite only a few names that pop into mind. Much of the late Jim Thompson's work (e.g., 1967) also belongs within the

Source: "Bringing mind back in: Paradigm development as a frontier problem in organization theory" by Louis R. Pondy and David M. Boje. Paper presented at the annual meeting of the American Sociological Association (San Francisco, CA, 1976). Reprinted with permission of David M. Boje.

social facts paradigm, although his use of such subjective concepts as "preferences" and "beliefs about causality" and his emphasis on the administrative process suggests an active, creative model of man that bridged over to social definitionism.[4] As Ritzer suggests, interviews and questionnaires (and the reliance on archival data) are the empirical mainstays of the social factists.

The *social behavior paradigm* tends to outcrop more among industrial and organizational psychologists than sociologists. Means for controlling reinforcement contingencies, according to this paradigm, include management or leadership style, job design, group pressures, incentive systems, and organizational climate, and much of the organizational research spawned by the social behavior paradigm has been aimed at studying how manipulations of these characteristics of the individual's environment affect his productivity, satisfaction and turnover in work settings. Skinner's (1971) operant conditioning lies at the root of most of this work, although related versions of it (that picture man as a more complex, but still essentially passive, interface between stimuli and responses) are in use—e.g., expectancy and equity theories. The number of prominent organizational theorists that can be fairly classed as social behaviorists is very large, but a sampling might include Vroom, Lawler, Porter, Likert, Fiedler, Hulin, Hackman, to name only an illustrative few.

As exemplars of the *social definition paradigm* within organization theory, a classic and two contemporaries are singled out. The classic exemplar is March and Simon's *Organizations* (1958) and the contemporaries are Weick's work (1969, 1974a) on the processes of organizing, and Silverman's (1971) treatment based in action theory.

It is an irony that *Organizations* is most frequently cited for its eloquent summary (in Chapters 3 and 4) of research findings generated by the behaviorist, and to a lesser extent the factist, paradigm. But usually overlooked is their more significant contribution of reformulating those research findings within a definitionist paradigm. For example, high productivity and low turnover are conceptualized to be the result of each individual's creative act of choice. And choice is conceived of as taking place within each individual's own framework or definition of the situation. Thus, individuals must actively search for information; they do not wait passively for an environmental experimenter to provide it in the form of some controlled situations. They picture organizations as collections of interacting performance programs whose structure must be inferred by observing the natural course of decision processes.

4. It is [Pondy's and Boje's] opinion that Thompson's work has been seriously misunderstood as advocating a broad technological and environmental determinism. It is clear from reading the second half of *Organizations in Action* that Thompson viewed skilled human administrators as necessary to bring about a "co-alignment" of structure, environment, and technology.

It is a further irony that, for the most part, March and Simon discouraged the observational strategy of data collection by phrasing empirical propositions in such a way ("if x increases, y will increase") as to encourage questionnaire measurement of "variables" and their subsequent correlational analysis. However, in other work (Cyert and March 1963; Newell and Simon 1972) it is clear that they intended descriptions of behavior to be in terms of contingent processes rather than in terms of "variables," and that those processes or behavior-producing rules were to be inferred from detailed *in situ* observation of people making choices and from asking them, simply, what they were doing.

Both substantively and methodologically, the frontier discovered ("invented" would be more an appropriate term, given the definitionist paradigm!) by March and Simon remains unsettled except for a few isolated pioneers. One of them is Weick.

Several characteristics type Weick as a social definitionist. Methodologically, he favors passive observation of everyday life rather than obtrusive measurement of large organizations too complex and "opaque" to be understood (1974a). This methodological stance is consistent with his belief that the object of observation ought to be the on-going processes rather than static structural characteristics of organizations. Thus, his interest in "organizing." Two key processes are: (1) retrospective, subjective sense making, and (2) evolutionary processes of development *from* the existing state (but *not toward* a desired end state). The emphasis on subjective meaning is clearly a part of a definitionist position. And retrospective understanding of lived (Weick's term is "enacted") experience is central to the phenomenology of Alfred Schutz (1967). Evolutionary processes less obviously belong to the definitionist paradigm. In fact, the view that variations are reinforced by the existing system is closer to behaviorist theories, if not to behaviorist methods and world views.[5] (But the point here is not to stereotype Weick as exclusively a definitionist, but only to point out the ways in which he has contributed to a definitionist approach to organizations.)

Paradigm Concerns and Development

John Stuart Mill is said to have been the first to urge social scientists to emulate their older, "harder" cousins, promising that following this advice would lead to rapid maturation of these fields. To a surprising degree, social scientists took this counsel to heart, and quantification reigned, as did an objective view of reality and its congruent sister assumptions. In recent

5. However, one basis on which variations are selected and retained is whether they "make sense" within the system's frame of reference. And this provides one way of linking Weick's notions of evolutionary development and retrospective sense-making.

decades, however, strong counter-pressures have emerged and alternative responses to all key assumptions have been explored and alternative paradigms proposed and utilized. Considerable debate has ensued, although the metaphor of "paradigm wars" described by Gage (1989) is undoubtedly overdrawn.

At the present time little consensus on paradigm development exists. On the one hand are pleas for paradigm consensus (e.g., Pfeffer 1993) and the more efficient communication and coordinated and collaborative researcher action, ease and certainty of research evaluation, etc. that would follow. On the other hand are those who bemoan a positivistic hegemony (e.g., Marsden 1993) and condemn the tyranny of the "Pfefferdigm" (Elsbach 1994), arguing that constraining paradigmatic variety is dysfunctional given the present level of paradigm development especially in the organizational sciences. Between these extremes are some who believe that the issue for organizational sciences is whether the field can strike an appropriate balance between theoretical tyranny and an anything-goes attitude (perhaps characteristic of the present state). Hidden behind these paradigm debates are beliefs about whether theory is advanced with a unified paradigm, a selected few paradigms, or many paradigms with no one paradigm dominant (Fabian 2000). Although it is generally believed that the organizational sciences are multiparadigmatic, beliefs differ regarding how to progress. Beliefs differ regarding whether to simply strive for communicating better across paradigms (e.g., Maruyama 1974), create a metaparadigm amalgam (e.g., Gioia and Pitre 1990), or await a paradigm revolution.

Paradigm Shifts
Yvonna S. Lincoln

In analyzing the paradigm shifts in all of these disciplines, Schwartz and Ogilvy (1979) make clear that the paradigms are . . . characterizing whole world views. In their analysis they have abstracted seven major characteristics of the new paradigm. These seven are important because they fly in the face of the dominant scientific paradigm. . . .

The first shift is from a simple and probabilistic world toward a view of reality that is *complex and diverse*. We have treated our world as a series of elements and processes that could be reduced to laws about their relationships and elements. We have behaved as if the world were simply additive; that is, complex elements were simply aggregations of much simpler entities. We are now beginning to understand that systems are not merely the sum of more simple units; they are separate entities that possess idiosyncratic, dynamic, and unique properties all their own.

The second shift is from a hierarchically ordered world to a world ordered by *heterarchy*. Our belief that the old order was hierarchical, indeed pyramidal, and based on a "pecking order" of natural and social laws is rapidly giving way to a belief that there is not one set or order, but several or a plurality. The key words here are interactive influence, mutual constraints, simultaneous interests. Which order is dominant at any given time depends on a number of shifting and interactive factors.

The third shift is from the image of a mechanistic and machine-like universe toward one that is *holographic*. The push-pull, single-action conception of the world is clearly more complex than levers and inclined planes could indicate. Moving toward the metaphor of the hologram, we begin to recognize a world—one that we already know is complex and heterarchic—that is the creation of constant differentiation and interaction. As Schwartz and Ogilvy (1979, 14) point out, "everything is interconnected like a vast network of interference patterns," each part containing information about the whole.

The holograph is important as a metaphor because of a unique property it possesses. If a normal recording or film has some part erased or clipped out, that portion of the file is gone forever. Not so with the holograph. In holography, even when large sections of the recorded laser interference patterns are lost, the remaining pieces contain complete information about the whole and can be used to reproduce the original image in its entirety and in three dimensions. The power of this metaphor is that every piece contains complete information about the whole. This is a particularly powerful concept when considering, for instance, genetic materials, in which a single cell is said to contain information about the entire organism, or in organizations, in which information about some subunit might provide information regarding the whole operation.

The fourth shift in world view is from the image of a determinate universe to that of an *indeterminate* one. The world as we know it, particularly the social world, is simply not predictable or controllable, even in the most sophisticated mathematical models. Witness the mess in attempting to predict economic behavior or money markets. The implication of such a shift is that future states of complex systems are not determinate or predictable. The future is ambiguous, and the condition or nature of things only in part knowable as a result of our choices.

The fifth shift is from an assumption of direct causality to the assumption of *mutual causality*. Most causal models proceeding from positivistic philosophies postulate some variety of an "if-then" notion of causal relationships. That is, the relationship between an action and an outcome is linear. Mutual causality implies that there is a symbiosis and a nonlinearity in systems such that A and B cannot be separated into simple cause and effect relationships. They grow, evolve, or otherwise change "in such a way as to make the distinction between cause and effect meaningless" (Schwartz and Ogilvy 1979, 14).

The sixth shift in paradigms is reflected in the move away from the metaphor of assembly—that is, of construction of complex systems from a series of more simple units—toward the metaphor of *morphogenesis*. Morphogenesis describes the creation of a new form. The best example of morphogenesis in the physical sciences is the process of creation of planetary systems and stars from galactic garbage—elements that are in part identifiable, but whose identity give no clue as to what the new configuration will be like. They act mutually and symbiotically to constrain the makeup of the new form, but they do not allow us to predict what the new form will be. In order for morphogenesis to occur, we need most of the previous six elements: diversity, complexity, indeterminacy, openness, and nonlinear causality.

Finally, the seventh shift is from one of pure objectivity—the posture that has been thought to characterize the scientist or researcher—to a posture that is *perspectival*. We finally have understood that it is impossible to be neutral—or objective—about our investigations, our experiments, our methods, or our rational processes. Objectivity as a pursuit in empirical investigations turns out to be a chimera, a Holy Grail, an illusion, and a snare. Subjectivity, however, is not the appropriate or only alternative. The concept of perspective may be more useful, as it implies multiple views of the same phenomenon, multiple foci that may be brought to bear, and multiple realities that are constructed of the same phenomenon. Schwartz and Ogilvy (1979) link the term perspective with engagement: "To know something requires engagement with it so that it is seen in the context of our concerns, and multiple perspectives so that we are not blinded by our own biases. This acknowledgement of the inescapability of perspective is very different from the attempt to gain objectivity by abstracting from all perspectives" (16).

Summary

Paradigm, which we now may more fully appreciate, is the frame that bundles our assumptions and thus guides scientific sensemaking. At a point in time, the "normal" paradigm ascendant in a field or discipline draws attention to some properties of some phenomena. As our selections have shown, the phenomena of interest are assumed to be either objectively real and thus discoverable or more-or-less human-defined and thus partly invented. Further, the dominant paradigm tends to focus our attention on elements or on processes, either of which is assumed to be relatively simple and determinate or relatively complex and indeterminate. Paradigms vary therefore along a continuum, defining the phenomena of interest as inherently stable to changeful, and we need the ideas of paradigm and usually the long view provided by history to discern paradigmatic changes and alternatives. Nevertheless, choice amongst paradigm alternatives exists for inquirers, and this choice has major consequences for theorizing and for research practices—whether our choice of paradigm is conscious or not.

Despite Kuhn's seminal work in opening up serious inquiry to the framing power of paradigm for "normal science," he left us with little more than a general understanding of how new frameworks were opened by inconsistencies and inadequacies of normal science to handle all data within its logic. As Kuhn left it, we are inevitably if haltingly moving toward a more "mature" paradigm that will (eventually) be able to guide all the research of a group of related disciplines. As new answers to core assumptive questions continue to be explored, however, paradigm variety increases, consolidations occur, and debates wax and wane. Paradigms point a discipline, a society, or an age toward those data and those practices that tend to reproduce the human interests at hand. In the case of the organization sciences these interests have historically been prediction and control, but more and more they are concerned with variety, plurality, discontinuity, and change. As always new paradigms call forth the theories and data that are used to validate the paradigms.

In this chapter, we have seen that there are alternative paradigms to choose among, each which frames an assumed perspective on any particular phenomena of interest. In the next four chapters, we turn to the major assumptive components of any paradigm.

4   Images of Human Nature

OUR AGE
Some of the descriptive labels: Age of *Uncertainty*; Age of *Science*; Age of *Nihilism*; Age of *Massacres*; Age of *Masses*; Age of *Globalism*; Age of *Dictatorships*; Age of *Design*; Age of *Defeat*; Age of *Communication*; Age of *Common Man*; Age of *Cinema and Democracy*; Age of the *Child*; Age of *Anxiety*; Age of *Anger*; Age of *Absurd Expectations*
   —*Jacques Barzun*

As we have seen in the previous chapter, Kuhn has provided us with the term "paradigm" to refer to the total pattern of perceiving, conceptualizing, validating, and valuing associated with investigating some general phenomena. Paradigms shape and guide serious inquiry in that they provide a frame for making sense out of observations. The frame of paradigm is composed of a set of core assumptions (see Table 3-1). One core assumption of the frame of paradigm, the prevailing image of human nature, is the focus of this chapter.

All bodies of knowledge and all human communities in which research takes place have one, or at most a few, images of human nature that influence what is studied. The several parental disciplines and the many fields that constitute the organization sciences are influenced in this way (i.e., their contents are affected by their prevailing image of humans). These images also influence the interpretation of observed phenomena. A serious inquirer almost inevitably refers back to the implicit model of explanation contained within the more basic images of humans to decide on an acceptable interpretation of his or her data and findings.

About Images

Our concern with human images is no doubt part and parcel with our species' self-consciousness—and the perennial focal question of identity. The question of who we are, as individuals and as a people, is perpetually with us. We want to know, somehow, what human nature would be like without the effects of cultural socialization. The very nature of inquiry in the social and organizational sciences suggests one answer. As Robert Young (1973, 235) notes, "We seek a basis in science for our goals and the order-ing of society." Researchers become "secular priests" in their efforts to help our disciplines "order our conduct, our work and the world that we live in." Much of serious inquiry seems to suggest we are looking for lasting funda-mentals for the essences in and of most phenomena. This search makes us susceptible to the assumption that pervades natural science: that explana-tions follow from identifying the essences—with humans as both the ob-jects and instruments of inquiry.

Images of human nature function metaphorically—they imply a way of thinking and a way of seeing that pervades how we understand not only ourselves but our world generally. Images of human nature, like metaphors, provide insight and understanding through an implicit or explicit assertion that A *is* (or is like) B—for instance, a scholar's mind is like a trap, suggest-ing it holds fast to its facts. Images of humans frame our understanding of people in a distinctive yet partial way—some essences are highlighted, others shadowed. And images, more subtly, condition how we understand all patterned social phenomena. Of course, these insights are more one-sided than anyone's reality. Thus, in drawing attention to a scholar's mind as capable of firmly grasping facts, the image glosses the fact that the same scholar may well also be chauvinistic, saintly, boring, or highly social. Qual-ities ascribed to individuals all too often characterize our knowledge about the world and how it works and the way we study it.

The impact of assumptive images of humans has prompted many schol-ars to state them explicitly, thereby attempting to raise the consciousness of investigators generally. In the selections that follow, we share several lists. The first is one developed by the Stanford Research Institute some time ago that traces major images of humans throughout recorded history and the di-mensions along which they differ. The second is a list of modern era social science images. And last is a discussion by Ali Mir of major human images recognizable in organizational studies. These examples, we caution, are nei-ther definitive nor exhaustive. Among them you may discover one or more that captures your own assumptions about the essence of human nature.

Images Throughout History
Stanford Research Institute

By identifying a number of underlying issues and dimensions along which the various images that have dominated human history have differed [see Table 4-1], we not only can better portray the dominant image of hu-

Source: "Changing images of man" by Stanford Research Institute, in *Policy Research Report 4* (Menlo Park, CA, 1974), 22a–22d, 45–48. Commissioned by the Charles F.

mankind in our society, but we can contrast that image with the images of other cultures. This may prove of vital importance in the coming "spaceship earth" era, for not only will various dissimilar cultures have to coexist more interactively, but there is an increased possibility for a creative synthesis of differences—to the extent that these differences are highlighted in an appropriate context.

Free Will

Does the human have free will, or are his actions (including his choices) determined by various internal or external forces? Many, if not most, of the ancient images saw man as determined by magical, divine, or naturalistic forces, a theme that has returned via biological and behavioral science. Most modern images of man, however, see him as free, restrained only by the natural laws of the universe and those arbitrary laws he has constructed for his own convenience.

Good versus Evil

Is human nature essentially good or evil? Or is the human neither, being shaped for good or ill by his choices or by his environment? Although many cultures have not dealt with this issue, it was made explicit in the Near East and has significantly affected the development of Western culture, having become an essential part of the Judeo-Islamic-Christian tradition. Most Western images of humankind can therefore be clearly evaluated with respect to this question.

Man and Nature

Is the human a competitor in a ruthless natural world, or is he an agent in a harmoniously balanced natural world? Or is he separate from and superior to nature, which he is to dominate for his own ends? Most cultures have assumed that the human being was intrinsically part of nature. The Semitic tradition was thus unique in setting him apart from nature. It was this tradition that has exerted the strongest influence on Western images of humankind and, indeed, may have been a necessary condition for the development of applied science as we know it today.

Kettering Foundation; coauthored by Joseph Campbell, Duane Elgin, Willis Harman, Arthur Hastings, O. W. Markley, Floyd Matson, Brendan O'Regan, and Leslie Schneider. Reprinted by permission of SRI International (formerly Stanford Research Institute).

Mind versus Matter

Are we essentially mind, consciousness, spirit? Or are we composed of physical matter alone, a construction in whom life and thought is but a characteristic of the state of organization of the material? Most cultures have seen the human as essentially spiritual; only with the rise of objective science has the materialistic emphasis developed.

Mortal versus Immortal

Some images have death as the end of individual existence and experience. Others hold that the person has a soul or spirit which continues to exist consciously after physical death, either by reincarnation into another body or by moving onto some other non-material plane of existence. Virtually all mythic images of man see him as somehow surviving physical death.

Divinity of Human Beings

Are the divine and the human essentially distinct, or is God the human's experience at a more profound level of the universal reality? This is the issue which most clearly separates the images of the mystical core of most "high" religions from the images popularized in their traditional teachings.

Individual versus Society

Is the individual important for his own sake, or is he important primarily as a member of the group? Similarly, is he valued for his intrinsic uniqueness, or for his extrinsic qualities and skills? The images of man in most ancient and modern cultures have emphasized him as a member of a society and have valued him for his extrinsic qualities. Only in the history of Greek and European culture have individualism and individuality come to be valued. And only in the French and American Revolutions did individual identity come to be idealized as the source of the equal worth of persons.

Progress

Is there a positive future toward which man and society are moving? Or is the notion of progress absent, replaced by an image of the essential unchangeability of the world? Although the idea of linear progress appears to have originated with Zoroaster and from thence to have influenced Western thought generally, the notion of the continuing rise and fall on a human and cosmic scale predominates in other cultures, finding its most notable expression in the Vedas of India.

TABLE 4-1

Images throughout history

Source period	Approximate date	Dominant image	Culture in which image is at present active	Significance for postindustrial era
Middle Paleolithic	250,000–40,000 B.C.	The hunter, focus of the male-dominated culture field of the "Great Hunt"	Few cultures in its pure form; most in its militaristic equivalent	Jeopardizes cross-cultural peace; likely necessary for police operations, however
Upper Paleolithic	30,000–15,000 B.C.	Spiritual affinity between beasts and humans, of which totemism is an expression	Various American Indian cultures with traditions intact	Has relevance for a renewed sense of partnership with other life forms on the planet
Neolithic	After 9000 B.C.	The planter, the child of the Goddess; woman the giver of life	Hindu and certain other cultures	Has possible relevance for balancing male-emphasis of Western culture
Sumerian	3500 B.C.	The human civilized through submission to seasonal variations and ruling elites	Most cultures	Has relevance as historical analogy: humans systematically explore their "inner" world
Semite	2350 B.C.	The human as a mere creature fashioned of clay to serve the gods—or some god—as a slave, but superior to and having dominion over nature; notion of "chosen people"	Orthodox Jewish, Christian, and Islamic faiths	Stands in its present form as an obstacle to emergence of new ecological understandings
Zoroastrian	1200 B.C.	The human as possessor of free will, having to choose between good and evil; mythology of individual salvation	All Western cultures in a secular form	Presents a basic polarity needing to be dialectically transcended/synthesized

Age of the Polis	500 B.C.	India: people are deluded by *maya*; the Buddha representing the absolute fulfillment of the Indian ideal of humans as *yogi* released from the wheel of karma, death and rebirth; intrinsic divinity of humans realizable through own efforts	Hindu/Buddhist	Could contribute to a new "self-realization ethic" for any culture if incorporated into a larger synthesis
		China: Confucius and the "superior man" as politically and socially concerned *sage*	Oriental cultures	Could contribute to a new "ecological ethic" for any culture if incorporated into a larger synthesis
		Levant: A *slave*, submissive to God in the image of a despot	Some forms of Islam, Christianity	Possible to see ecological requirements in this light
		Greece: Aeschylus and the human as *tragic hero*	Most Western cultures to some degree	Could provide a guiding image for personal/societal transformation in time of crisis
		Greece: Mystery religions—people become so attached to the material things of this world that they have lost touch with their own true nature, which is not of these things, but of spirit; they are the very being and model of that Spirit of which each is but a particle	All cultures, but never very visible	Could contribute to ecological understanding, de-emphasizing material overconsumption
		Greece: Humans' appreciation of science and objective knowledge as aesthetic rather than utilitarian activity; naturalistic emphasis in science, art, and philosophy	None in which dominant	Has relevance to counterbalancing the "technological ethic."

(continued)

TABLE 4-1
(continued)

Source period	Approximate date	Dominant image	Culture in which image is at present active	Significance for postindustrial era
Early Christian and Muslim	A.D. 100 and A.D. 622	Two contrary images: (1) God's servant, obey or be damned, following the Semite and Zoroastrian traditions; (2) humans "saved" by self-knowledge; Gnostic, similar to the image of the Greek mystery religions	(1) Traditional Judeo/Christian/Muslim cultures; (2) most cultures as an underground view	(1) A dominant image that needs to be incorporated into a larger synthesis; (2) could contribute to a new "self-realization ethic" for any culture if incorporated into a larger synthesis
Industrial Revolution/Enlightenment	A.D. 1500	"Economic man": individualistic, materialistic, rationalistic; objective knowledge, utilitarian/economic values coming into dominance	Most modern industrial nations	Probably inappropriate for transition to postindustrial era
Modern social science	A.D. 1900	Human as "beast": instinctual drives predominant, a "creature of evolution" whose survival depends on competitive adaptation and/or suppression of base instincts	Most modern industrial nations	An image needing to be incorporated into a larger synthesis

Modern behavioral science	A.D. 1913	Human as "mechanism"; to be understood in ways found successful by nineteenth-century physics	Primarily United States	Promoted as providing the most appropriate basis for humankind's next era, perhaps now itself needing to be incorporated into larger synthesis
Modern transdisciplinary science	A.D. 1954	Human as a "goal-directed adaptive learning system"	Image has not yet reached "takeoff point"	Provides a possible conceptual basis for integrating most other images of humans in an evolutionary frame of reference
	Various times and places from ca. 1500 B.C. to the present	Humans as "Spirit"; the "philosophia perennis" view of humans and the universe as essentially consciousness in manifest form	Most cultures, in various degrees of purity	Could contribute to needed synthesis of "opposing" images because it sees apparent opposites as differing aspects of the same underlying reality

SOURCE: Adapted from Stanford Research Institute, *Policy Research Report 4* (Menlo Park, CA, 1974), 22a–22d, table 2A, with permission of SRI International (formerly Stanford Research Institute).

Morality, Ethics, and Regulation

On what kind of ethical principles should human behavior be based? Naked power? Divine revelation? Traditional myths? Democratic agreements? Although the ethical aspects of various images of humankind have been based on all of these, there does seem to be an evolutionary ordering that takes place both in individuals and across cultures at differing stages of development.

Social Science Images

As we have just seen, images of human nature have a long history. Related to the social sciences, the idea of what is human nature, and its concomitant image, begins at least with Plato and extends into the modern era. The diversity of beliefs among scholars over time is considerable, and their positions about the essential nature of man has fueled much controversy.

Plato expressed a dual view of humanity, separating the soul, as a non-material entity, from the body. Soon, however, Aristotle defined mankind as a social animal, complemented by the Cartesian contention that human nature is manifested in rational thought—exemplified by Plato's intellectual heir Descartes' well-known statement, "cogito ergo sum" ("I think, therefore I am").

While these early philosophers attempted to grapple with an idealized human essence, the emerging field of psychological inquiry focused much more on the impulses that drove human nature toward its innate form. The psychological conception of human nature is exemplified by three positions along a continuum of assumptions about humans. Freud's psychodynamic theory (Rickman 1957) views humans as being driven by innate sexual and aggressive energy—which, for society's sake, needed to be kept in check. Later, B. F. Skinner's (1953) behaviorist approach placed human nature in a socio-physical context where the consequences of human nature determined its essence. Still later, phenomenologists, such as Carl Rogers (1961) and Abraham Maslow (1954), believed that humans were driven by innate motives toward personal growth and self-actualization.

Economics produced its own continuum, beginning with "laissez faire" humans, who Adam Smith (1937) postulated would, under the absence of supervision, seek to maximize their gains. The rather skeptical early theories of opportunism (e.g., Knight 1965) promoted an image of individuals who indulged in opportunistic behavior as a perversion of human nature. And, finally, there was the image of humankind promulgated by the influential theories of Marx. This image emphasized human nature as a response to the oppressive economic and class conditions on human consciousness.

TABLE 4-2
Major conceptions of human nature in the social sciences

Thinkers	Key idea of human nature
Plato	Human nature embodied in a soul, distinct from the body
Aristotle	People are social animals
Christianity	Human nature as an imperfect image of God
Descartes	Humanity as rational and deductive
Locke	Human nature as pursuit of happiness and freedom
Hobbes	Humanity as brutal, selfish, and aggressive
Freud	Human nature as determined by innate sexual, aggressive drives
Skinner	Human nature as a function of social contact
Rogers	Human nature as driven toward self-actualization
Marx	Human nature as productive, at odds with economic system
Sartre	No human nature, human reality is to choose oneself
Chomsky	Deterministic human nature as manifested in language recognition
Foucault	Human nature as a creation of the power/knowledge discourse

Formulations of a generalized human nature have been challenged from time to time. The strongest challenge in recent decades has come from existentialists who have contended that every person is a singular and individualized combination of traits, abilities, and characteristics that do not lend themselves to generalization. Sartre, for example, asserted that there is no such thing as human nature and that humans can aspire to be unique and authentic by using their capabilities to shape themselves into any image of their own choosing—human reality is to choose oneself.

In recent times human nature has been fiercely debated among structuralist and poststructuralist philosophers, perhaps exemplified by the contrasting viewpoints of Noam Chomsky and Michel Foucault. Chomsky (1987) uses data from linguistic research to suggest that there is a biophysical-mental structure that is manifested in individual ability to deduce language, which he claims points to the existence of an innate and predetermined human nature without which true scientific comprehension would be impossible. Foucault (1980) is less concerned with the question, "Does human nature exist?" Rather, he asks, "How has the idea of human nature existed in society?" Poststructuralists such as Foucault are more concerned with the variety of roles in which human nature has been exhibited and the futility of using any kind of image of mankind as a benchmark for humanity.

Clearly the discussion on human nature in the social sciences is contentious, given the political ramifications assumed and articulated by various theorists. Different disciplines have defined human nature within the boundaries of their own historical and experiential realities (see Table 4-2).

It is also important to emphasize how images of humankind reflect assumptions that serious inquirers have about the nature of reality. Morgan

TABLE 4-3
Assumptions about ontology and human nature

OBJECTIVE APPROACHES ←   CORE ONTOLOGICAL ASSUMPTIONS   → SUBJECTIVE APPROACHES

Reality as a concrete structure	Reality as a concrete process	Reality as a contextual field of information	Reality as symbolic discourse	Reality as a social construction	Reality as a projection of human imagination
The social world is a hard, concrete, real thing "out there," which affects everyone in one way or another. It can be thought of as a structure composed of a network of determinate relationships between constituent parts. Reality is to be found in the concrete behavior and relationships between these parts. It is an objective phenomenon that lends itself to accurate observation	The social world is an evolving process, concrete in nature, but everchanging in detailed form. Everything interacts with everything else, and it is extremely difficult to find determinate causal relationships between constituent processes. At best, the world expresses itself in terms of general and contingent relationships between its more stable and clearcut elements. The situation is fluid and	The social world is a field of everchanging form and activity based on the transmission of information. The form of activity that prevails at any one time reflects a pattern of "difference" sustained by a particular kind of information exchange. Some forms of activity are more stable than others, reflecting an evolved pattern of learning based on principles of negative feedback.	The social world is a pattern of symbolic relationships and meanings sustained through a process of human action and interaction. Although a certain degree of continuity is preserved through the operation of rulelike activities that define a particular social milieu, the pattern is always open to reaffirmation or change through the interpretations and actions of individual members.	The social world is a continuous process, created afresh in each encounter of everyday life as individuals impose themselves on their world to establish a realm of meaningful definition. They do so through the medium of language, labels, actions, and routines, which constitute symbolic modes of being in the world. Social reality is embedded in the nature and use of these modes	The social world and what passes as "reality" is a projection of individual consciousness; it is an act of creative imagination and of dubious intersubjective status. This extreme position, commonly known as solipsism, asserts that there may be nothing outside one's mind is one's world. Certain transcendental approaches to phenomenology assert a reality in

and measurement. Any aspect of the world that does not manifest itself in some form of observable activity or behavior must be regarded as being of questionable status. Reality by definition is that which is external and real. The social world is as concrete and real as the natural world.

creates opportunities for those with appropriate ability to mold and exploit relationships in accordance with their interests. The world is in part what one makes of it: a struggle between various influences, each attempting to move toward achievement of desired ends.

The nature of relationships within the field is probabilistic; a change in the appropriate pattern and balance within any sphere will reverberate throughout the whole, initiating patterns of adjustment and readjustment capable of changing the whole in fundamental ways. Relationships are relative rather than fixed.

The fundamental character of the social world is embedded in the network of subjective meanings that sustain the rule-like actions that lend it enduring form. Reality rests not in the rule or in rule-following, but in the system of meaningful action that renders itself to an external observer as rulelike.

symbolic action. The realm of social affairs thus has no concrete status of any kind; it is a symbolic construction. Symbolic modes of being in the world, such as through the use of language, may result in the development of shared, but multiple realities, the status of which is fleeting, confined only to those moments in which they are actively constructed and sustained.

consciousness, the manifestation of a phenomenal world, but not necessarily accessible to understanding in the course of everyday affairs. Reality in this sense is masked by those human processes that judge and interpret the phenomenon in consciousness prior to a full understanding of the structure of meaning it expresses. Thus the nature of the phenomenal world may be accessible to the human being only through consciously phenomenological modes of thought.

(continued)

TABLE 4-3
(continued)

OBJECTIVE APPROACHES ← ASSUMPTIONS ABOUT HUMAN NATURE → SUBJECTIVE APPROACHES

Humans as responding mechanisms	Humans as adaptive agents	Humans as information processors	Humans as social actors	Humans create their realities	Humans as transcendental beings
Human beings are a product of the external forces in the environment to which they are exposed. Stimuli in their environment condition them to behave and respond to events in predictable and determinate ways. A network of causal relationships links all important aspects of behavior to context. Though human perception may influence this process to some degree, people always	Human beings exist in an interactive relationship with their world. They influence and are influenced by their context or environment. The process of exchange that operates here is essentially a competitive one, the individual seeking to interpret and exploit the environment to satisfy important needs, and hence survive. Relationships between individuals and environment express a	Human beings are engaged in a continual process of interaction and exchange with their context— receiving, interpreting, and acting on the information received, and in so doing creating a new pattern of information that effects changes in the field as a whole. Relationships between individual and context are constantly modified as a result of this exchange; the individual is but an element	Human beings are social actors interpreting their milieu and orienting their actions in ways that are meaningful to them. In this process they utilize language, labels, routines for impression management, and other modes of culturally specific action. In so doing they contribute to the enactment of a reality; human beings live in a world of symbolic significance, interpreting and en-	Human beings create their realities in the most fundamental ways, in an attempt to make their world intelligible to themselves and to others. They are not simply actors interpreting their situations in meaningful ways, for there are no situations other than those which individuals bring into being through their own creative activity. Individuals may work together to create a	Humans are viewed as intentional beings, directing their psychic energy and experience in ways that constitute the world in a meaningful, intentional form. There are realms of being and realms of reality, constituted through founding acts, stemming from a form of transcendental consciousness. Human beings shape the world within the realm of their

Behaviorism / Social learning theory	Open systems theory	Cybernetics	Social action theory	Ethnomethodology	Phenomenology
respond to situations in a lawful (i.e., rule-governed) manner.	pattern of activity necessary for survival and well-being of the individual.	of a changing whole. The crucial relationship between individual and context is reflected in the pattern of learning and mutual adjustment that has evolved. Where this is well developed, the field of relationships is harmonious; where adjustment is low, the field is unstable and subject to unpredictable and discontinuous patterns of change.	acting a meaningful relationship with that world. Humans are actors with the capacity to interpret, modify, and sometimes create the scripts that they play upon life's stage.	shared reality, but that reality is still a subjective construction capable of disappearing the moment its members cease to sustain it as such. Reality appears as real to individuals because of human acts of conscious or unwitting collusion.	own immediate experience.

SOME EXAMPLES OF RESEARCH

OBJECTIVE APPROACHES ← ──────────────────────────────── → SUBJECTIVE APPROACHES

SOURCE: "The case for qualitative research" by Gareth Morgan and Linda Smircich, *Academy of Management Review* 5 (1980): 494–495, table 2. Copyright © 1980 by Academy of Management. Reproduced with permission of the Academy of Management via Copyright Clearance Center.

and Smircich (1980, 494–495) have provided a rough typology for thinking about what various social scientists believe about human beings and how they see their world (see Table 4-3). Each view is manifested in important kinds of social thought and theory, and each continues to underlie continuing research.

Human Nature and Organization Theory
Ali H. Mir

Most theories in organizational scholarship are predicated upon some concept of human nature (Ryan 1974). The process of organizational sense-making and reality-enactment (Weick 1979) also involves the modeling of the "nature" of organizational constituents into a demystified and malleable variable. A survey of influential organizational literature appears to reveal a multiplicity of assumptions about human nature, from pithy categories like "economic man" (F. W. Taylor 1911) and "administrative man" (March and Simon 1958) to complex networks of bounded rationality, opportunism, organic rationality, obedience and self-seeking interest (Williamson 1985). . . .

Our point of departure is the theory of scientific management which is based upon Frederick Taylor's time-motion studies, the division of labor into units that were detailed and planned according to scientifically set standards, and the deployment of such a standard through the reorganization of both human and mechanical processes of production. In this train of thought, human beings were characterized in the manner of machines—under this system, they were predictable, controllable, and replaceable (J. L. Gibson 1966). The active measurement of performance under specified standards prevented "loafing" or "soldiering," and the designed incentive system attempted to promote additional diligence. The resulting shift in control from workers to managers was primarily justified by the Taylorian view of human nature—workers were naturally lazy, [and] managerial authority and appeals to personal ambition were needed to offset this tendency.

The school of thought which has come to be known as Classical Organization Theory (COT) reiterates the need for managerial control. In a very illustrative comment Urwick (1967, 12) claims that "it is only necessary to make one reasonable simple assumption about human behavior: that human beings cannot be expected to cooperate efficiently for any common purpose unless both they and those who guide the system know what they as, individuals, are expected to do and when." Clearly, the source of this knowledge is the monopoly of a select group of owners/managers. COT's focus on

Source: "Intertwined paradigms, intertwined histories" by Ali H. Mir. Paper presented at the annual meeting of the Eastern Academy of Management (Crystal Springs, VA, 1996). Reprinted with permission by Ali H. Mir.

stability and reliability, its strong concern for constancy and certitude and its conceptualization of human beings have been critiqued extensively (March and Simon 1958; W. Whyte 1955), the most telling being the observation that the implicit assumptions of human beings in COT characterize a human being as one who is "lazy, short-sighted, liable to make mistakes, has poor judgment, and may even be a little dishonest" (Haire 1962, 86).

It would be simplistic and problematic to attribute the discourse of scientific management and COT to the authorship of the individual theorists alone. The themes that were articulated in these theories were part of a larger set of discursive and non-discursive (materialist) practices that were taking shape in the context of rapid industrialization and the metamorphosis of organizational forms towards large conglomerations. However, the setback suffered by the Taylorist dream of efficient, machine-like factories during the depression and the consequent challenges to managerial authority demanded new champions to the cause of managerial control. It found them in the forerunners of many current organizational theorists—Elton Mayo and Chester Barnard. Responding to sentiments that the concentration of resources in the hands of a small number of corporations and corporation heads was creating economic empires, the control of which had been "delivered into the hands of a new form of absolutism" (Berle and Means 1932, 124), Mayo (1933) and Barnard (1938) argued that managerial authority served the function of holding society together. They claimed that individuals were driven by emotions, that they were inclined to indulge in socially destructive acts and that they were unfit for cooperation unless they were appropriately guided. The depression was a convincing proof of that unfitness. What was needed to combat these emotions as well as the threat of future social chaos was more managerial authority and control, not less. The implications of this argument are again clear. Managerial authority and control dictated by the assumptions and the demands of the managerial class were deemed necessary to ensure that the workers became part of the Barnardian view of organizations as cooperative systems. In the absences of this control, claimed Barnard and Mayo, the system would fall apart (P. Miller and O'Leary 1989).

The fall out of the depression led to a significant turn in some arenas of managerial discourse which drew upon the shift in the economic paradigm of the nation state. The economy underwent a transformation from a philosophy of laissez-faire to one of the Keynesian welfare model—a transformation aimed at producing a "partnership" between the employee and the employer. The principles of mass-production—mass-consumption and its resulting material conditions produced a new set of managerial practices and discourses that were aimed at balancing the authoritarian structure of the organization against the welfare oriented goals of society. It was in this fertile ground that the Human Relations school flourished. This school of thought contended that the managerial practices under scientific management alienated the workers and promoted acts of resistance. In an attempt to inculcate a sense of unity between labor and capital, the Human Relations school sought to involve the workers in an orchestrated partnership with the managers, thereby attempting to align goals across hierarchies. Although the movement seemed to support and foster social grouping and workplace harmony, the underlying assumptions of the continued need for managerial control were not much different from those of the theorists who preceded this program. As Sullivan (1986, 540) puts it, it was "a manager's task to manipulate behavior by either (a) identifying a specific worker's needs and then offering need-satisfying incentives in return for work, or (b) manipulating tasks and environments to influence the creation of needs, and then to offer need-satisfying incentives."

While much of management theory that has emerged subsequently has shown a strong urge to create a balance between the two discourses of scientific management and human relations (Mathew 1993), the notion of control and regulation has seldom been abandoned. Nor has the image of the self-centered and potentially destructive human beings. The neo-Weberian model (Perrow 1981a) of March and Simon (1958) builds on the Barnardian notion of the organization as a vehicle for cohesive activity. Simon (1957) argues that people are rational only within the bounds of their habits and thus sets the stage for the claim that organizations need to control the premises of decision making of its individual members. The neo-Weberian organization is therefore derived keeping in mind "the limits of human intelligence capacities" (March and Simon 1958, 169) and the need to "neutralize or eliminate the dysfunctional characteristics of sub-group organization" (p. 78). In order to prevent individuals from going their "own selfish way" (Perrow 1981a, 129), scholars of this persuasion urge organizations (managers) to control the cognitive premises of individual decision making by controlling information flow, programming tasks and procedures, and managing organizational vocabularies in an attempt to restrict the range of stimuli—and thus temptation—available to organizational members. Drucker's (1954) concept of Management-by-Objectives insists on the creation of "objectives that could be fully measured," the objectives to be supposedly decided in consultation with the employee, a concept that is fairly well-aligned with Barnard's "benign authority."

Chandler's (1977) analysis of the visible hand takes the notion of top down managerial practices at the operational levels of the firm and succeeds in taking it to another realm of the organization—the strategic. In an argument where his Taylorian legacy becomes self-evident through the emphasis on top-down system design, control, and output-measurement, Chandler (1977, 412) argues that the visible hand of management works to help perfect "new complex machines and the modern form of factory organization" as well as "the new techniques of cost accounting." Chandler's visible hand locates its subjects in asymmetric relations of power, and reinforces the systems of discipline through the exercise of managerially controlled mechanisms of surveillance.

While the Chandlerian perspective of human nature is indicated through the repeated theme of control, it finds its full articulation in Williamson's treatment of the theory of transaction cost economics which rests on the premise that opportunistic individuals, while pursuing their self-interest and maximizing their "personal felicific calculus" (Donaldson 1990, 371), would shirk from working, be deceitful, use guile, and behave in ways that would constitute a moral hazard.

Management discourse since the end of the Second World War has revolved around the axis of control in a constant engagement of two seemingly contradictory sets of practices—the exercise of top-down management and the procedure of involvement and participation. But the image of the protagonists of this complex dance that emerges is that of the organizational human who is guileful, self-centered, driven by personal ambition, untrustworthy, apathetic, and opportunistic. The justification of the forms of managerial practice rests on the formulation of this image. The image verifies the need for control and discipline. . . .

Our concepts of human nature are, to a considerable extent, mediations of our social, economic, and ideological preconceptions. A transcending view of human nature must look at its reifications, its fetishisms, and its role in the alienation of human beings in work organizations. One of the important tasks we need to undertake towards this end is to unmask the political character of the "natural" in human nature.

It is within this epistemological context that we must place our discussion of the concept of human nature in organization theory. As practice, organizations constitute the primary mechanism through which economic production is activated. As discourse, organization theories constitute the mechanism through which the practices are legitimized and rendered acceptable (Alvesson 1990). As Chio (1992, 4) puts it, "in a society where the 'technical' relations of production are well entrenched (structurally, legally, etc.), hegemonic control is increasingly based on a 'war' over meanings and representations of reality." Our claim is that one of these ideological representations has been the construction of human nature in organizational theorizing.

Summary

Shared images of human nature, based upon assumptions about human nature, have existed throughout human history and no doubt have affected its course. Images are thus quite naturally an important component of the frame of paradigm, influencing serious inquiry in two ways. On the one hand, what is assumed to be essential about human nature will guide our substantive choices about what we wish to observe, understand, and explain, especially in those sciences—social and organizational—that attend to humans individually and collectively. As our selections have shown, the range of images is very great indeed—from fate-controlled pawns to puppeteers manipulating the world, from species-wide innate traits to culturally unique. On the other hand, shared images of human nature also will shape how we go about research—that is, the assumed nature of inquirers will be reflected in inquiry practices. Again, the range of possibilities is a wide one—from passive observers to active interveners, from self-serving individuals to embedded members of society.

Because ever more maturing scientific disciplines are devoted to the study of human beings, accumulating fact-based knowledge can and sometimes does impact the assumptive base of the discipline. The psychological essentialist emphasis in human nature, for example, is waning; replacing it is an emphasis on how philosophical and social factors, by affecting assumptions about human nature, influence what human nature is taken to be (e.g., Clegg, Hardy, and Nord 1996). Recent images derive increasingly from developments in more rapidly developing disciplines, such as biology, man-machine systems, and ecology. Still there are major blind spots— for instance, images are, in a phrase of Fineman (1993), "emotionally anorexic"; and some tenaciously held images do seem naive—for instance, "Economics can be distinguished from other social sciences by the belief that most (all?) behavior can be explained by assuming that agents have stable, well-defined preferences and make rational choices consistent with those preferences in markets that (eventually) clear" (Dawes and Thaler 1988, 187).

The range of alternative images assumed about humans is very great indeed. Their power to shape behavior is well known, hence their importance as a foundational assumption in all inquiry paradigms.

5   Choices about Reality and Knowing

If your mind isn't clouded by unnecessary things, this is the best season of your life.
    —Wei-Men

Rational, adj. Devoid of all delusions save those of observation, experience, and reflection.
    —Ambrose Bierce (The Devil's Dictionary)

It is possible to be a master of false philosophy—easier, in fact, than to be a master in the truth—because a false philosophy can be made as simple and consistent as one pleases.
    —George Santayana

In the *Wizard of Oz*, Dorothy learned that the only person who could help her (and her little dog, Toto, of course) return to Kansas was a wizard in the Emerald City. After several adventures, Dorothy, Toto, and her new friends (the Scarecrow, the Tin Man, and the Lion), followed the yellow brick road to seek an audience with the Wizard. Entry to the city, however, depended on our troop's donning spectacles—selected from a proffered tray. All the spectacles were green, and on entering the city, everything appeared green, emerald green! The multicolored reality observed with the naked eye had been transformed into a monochrome world when viewed through the spectacle lenses. This anecdote reminds us that nature is perceived, and perception is a function of what the perceiver assumes reality to be and how reality is known.

Our assumptions about reality and how it can be known—basic philosophical categories formally labeled ontology and epistemology, respectively—are key assumptions of the foundational frame of inquiry that we have called the philosophic context. Actually, this pair of assumptions "colors" how we perceive and understand everything, from molecules to the cosmos, from self to society, and, significantly, the conceptual edifices with which we perceive and understand all else. It follows that these assumptions shape our understandings of theory and research.

When many of us initially hear that reality need not just be "out there," observed identically by everyone, it may seem incredible, even though most of us have experienced culture shock of one kind or another. People, it seems, living in what we assumed to be the same reality somehow experience it differently. It's as if they were each wearing spectacles with different colored lenses! Assumptions about the nature of reality and how it is known are at the heart of all cultures, including the cultures of inquirers.

If the things we study are unchanging and we are pretty sure that our observation of the them will not change them, then "good" research would be characterized by careful sampling, precise measurement, sophisticated design, and rigorous analysis in the testing of hypotheses derived from tentative general laws—and it would produce "objective" knowledge. This approach serves the natural sciences (e.g., physics, chemistry, biology) so well that Popper (1964) labels the social science approximation of it the "natural science model." If, however, the entities and relationships of research interest are changeable because they are human and social, or because they are touched by us, and observing them may change them because the observer, with or without instrumentation, is human and social too, then there may not be just one best way to do "good" research, and the knowledge derived may take different forms. And so it is that the social-behavioral sciences (embracing organizational science, of course) can—and do—conduct inquiry with a variety of ontological and epistemological (and other) assumptions. As key components of paradigms, such assumptions strongly influence the form of theory as well as theory-improvement practices—especially our choice of methods. Methods draw attention to and reinforce theories and, by extension, paradigmatic assumptions, as Weick (1987a) reminds us.

> The commonly used data collection procedures smooth over the irregularities, imperfections, and discontinuities that occur in daily organization life (Kimberly 1980; Leach 1967), and so we researchers persist in using a term that exaggerates order. Researchers who study large organizations try to capture their size and apparent complexity by using surveys, averages, and synoptic measures in an attempt to say something about everything they observe. The costs of these strategic decisions are becoming clearer in the deepening irrelevance of organizational researchers for organizational participants (Perrow 1981b; Thoenig 1982). (p. 10).

In organizational science, with its growing literature that explores epistemologically significant themes,

> there typically remains an expressed or implied tendency to treat knowledge as being essentially of one kind. That is, the epistemology assumed in the literature tends to privilege the individual over the group, and the

explicit over the tacit (as if, for example, explicit and tacit knowledge were two variations of one kind of knowledge, not separate, distinct forms of knowledge). . . . We view these [explicit/tacit and individual/group] forms of knowledge as constituting . . . *the epistemology of possession,* since these forms of "what is known" are typically treated as something people possess. To say, for example, "Robert knows auto mechanics" points to Robert *possessing* knowledge of auto mechanics (S. D. N. Cook and Brown 1999, 382).

Cook and Brown could have opened our eyes much further, for they only "privilege" (their term) disinterested scientists of the epistemological position of early systemic modernism (R. Cooper and Burrell 1988), with its belief in the essential capacity of humanity to perfect itself through the power of rational thought. There are other voices. There are the late modern voices of postpositivism, the postmodern voices of critical modernism/critical theory, and constructivism (both going beyond Cartesian epistemologies and critically questioning, and often outright rejecting, the ethnocentric rationalism championed by modernism). The ontological and epistemological alternatives of these major paradigmatic positions are sketched in Table 5-1.

A perusal of this book might lead to the hunch that modernism is more fully represented than is postmodernism. This is no doubt so. In the social and behavioral sciences for some time, and in organizational science more recently, postmodernism has been articulated in several guises. Let us briefly describe a couple ontological-epistemological nexuses found in postmodernism by way of indicating how different they are from modernism.

Common to postmodernism is the idea of difference. The world of humankind is simultaneously driven toward consensus and determinacy—organizations, for example, are arenas of both bondage and emancipation. Parts of all social units, through mastery and domination, maintain a state of continuous difference and provocation but rarely attempt annihilation (Lyotard 1984). Postmodernists believe, however, that taken-for-granted institutions and ways of thinking and acting commonly privilege some groups and social classes over others, giving rise to social injustice. Historically, both research and practitioner literatures have mostly provided a voice for only a predominantly male, white elite. Giving voice to those who fall outside this epistemologically narrow cadre is the emancipatory value of postmodernism.

Feminism, for example, corrects theory that renders gender and gendered identities invisible (Calas and Smircich 1996). Feminism has been instrumental in reframing theory encumbered by formulations that unconsciously ignored race, social class, ethnicity, and other disadvantaged groups (Olesen 1994). Critical theory offers another postmodern perspective, viewing organizations as largely political sites. It seeks to revise structures and

TABLE 5-1
Alternative paradigmatic beliefs

	MODERNISM		POSTMODERNISM	
	Positivism	Postpositivism	Critical theory	Constructivism
Ontology	"Real" out-there reality	Reality imperfectly and probabilistically apprehensible	Historical realism—socially, politically, economically, ethnically and gender valued	Local and specific constructed realities
Epistemology	True findings	Probably true findings	Value-mediated findings	Subjectivist, created findings
Voice	Disinterested scientists	Disinterested scientists	Advocate/activist, transformative intellectual	Passionate facilitator of multivoice reconstructions
Nature of knowledge	Verified hypotheses	Nonfalsified hypotheses	Historical structural insights	Individual reconstructions sometimes coalescing

SOURCE: Adapted from Denzin and Lincoln (1994), pp. 109–112.

processes of power and domination hidden in the legitimate and taken-for-granted aspects of the social world (Deetz 1992; Forester 1983).

In this chapter's initial selection, Ralph Stablein provides a useful review of the various philosophical positions taken by researchers, highlighting the range of and relationship between their ontological and epistemological stances. With the understanding of these two philosophical frame components that Stablein offers, we can more readily appreciate the next two selections.

Roger Evered and Meryl Reis Louis, group epistemologies into two contrasting sets based on the degree of experiential involvement of the researcher: one detached and analytic in its stance toward data (i.e., inquiry from the outside); the other highly involved and more phenomenological (i.e., inquiry from the inside). In the third selection, Gareth Morgan and Linda Smircich describe the spread of both ontological and epistemological assumptions along a subjective-objective continuum and how they often pair up, as well as suggesting the metaphors and research methods associated with each.

The fourth and fifth selections amplify the ends of the Morgan and Smircich continuum. Allen Lee describes the objective end by carefully characterizing the fundamentals of traditional positivism. W. Graham Astley describes the not-quite-pure subjectivism termed "social constructivism" and argues that our dependence on language in research means that organizational science phenomena are naturally socially constructed.

The True and the Known
Ralph E. Stablein

The purpose of this paper is to provide a framework for the discussion of research issues in the organisational sciences. Discussion of these issues has frequently been characterized by controversy and even acrimony. While controversy is an important element in the advancement of any discipline, the heat surrounding the discussion of research issues tends to produce more smoke than light. . . . The strategy of [this] paper is to identify and explore the structure of debate in organisational studies. . . .

Any given debate is usually a complex web of many issues. The basic categories of philosophy provide a starting point for untangling the web. Conceptual clarity requires that we recognize that the discussion of research issues involves one or more of the following hierarchical levels: the ontological, the epistemological, and the methodological. The true, the known, and the correct. . . .

Source: "Structure of debate in organisational studies" by Ralph E. Stablein. Working paper, University of Otago (Dunedin, New Zealand, 1988). Reprinted with permission of Ralph E. Stablein.

The broadest level of disagreement in discussions of research issues reflects differences in the ontological positions of the disputants. Ontology refers to the study of the nature and relations of being. Its concern is with ultimate reality, truth with a capital T. Burrell and Morgan (1979) have discussed the variety of ontological positions that various organisational scholars may hold. Morgan and Smircich (1980) have summarized the variability in ontologies on a continuum emphasizing the degree of human subjectivity involved in defining reality. At the objective extreme, a concrete reality exists independent of human involvement. At the subjective extreme, there is no reality independent of the individual person, i.e., each of us creates a reality as the projection of our human imagination. In between are a variety of positions which allow for greater or lesser amounts of human involvement and intersubjectivity in the constitution of reality. It is important to note that an ontology deals with the actual state of reality not human understanding of whatever the true reality may be.

This distinction brings us to the level of epistemology. Epistemology is the study of the methods and grounds of knowledge especially with reference to its limits and validity. The concern is knowledge rather than truth. Knowledge, what a human community has learned, may or may not correspond to true reality.

Burrell, Morgan, and Smircich (Burrell and Morgan 1979; Morgan and Smircich 1980; Morgan 1983a) have suggested that an organisational scholar's epistemological position is very closely related to his or her ontological position. In fact, they describe a one-to-one correspondence along the same subjective-objective continuum used to describe ontologies. At the objective extreme is positivism. At the subjective extreme is solipsism. Their task of defining broad sociological paradigms (Burrell and Morgan 1979)[1] may not have required developing the difference between ontology and epistemology but it is a critical distinction for describing the structure of debate in organisational science.

While a particular ontology may be comfortably linked with epistemologies of a similarly subjective/objective nature, this need not necessarily be the case. For example, an organisational scholar at the extreme objective end of the ontology distribution may accept that our knowledge of the very concrete real world is funneled through imperfect human perceptual, cognitive, and communication apparatus (e.g., Piaget 1971). The acceptance of these limitations could lead our ontological realist to a position that is quite subjective on the epistemological continuum, e.g., a view emphasizing the ability of a community of scholars to achieve common understandings of the concrete reality. A more subjectively oriented scholar on the ontological level could share the same epistemological position while continuing to

1. Editors' note: See Burrell and Morgan in Chapter 3.

deny the existence of an underlying concrete reality. Both may share the same knowledge of reality while holding very different views regarding the ultimate Truth about reality.

This is much more than a logical possibility. It describes the contemporary situation in the history, sociology and philosophy of science. There is a near consensus on epistemology despite a wide divergence of ontological positions, ranging from idealism to realism. There is a convergence on a view of knowledge as the inherently fallible, social product of an interacting community of scholars. Many roads lead to this central conclusion. Perhaps more than any other, Kuhn's (1970) book, *The Structure of Scientific Revolutions* has popularized this notion in his description of normal and extraordinary science. Pragmatists (Mulaik 1984), Popperians (Lakatos and Musgrave 1970), phenomenologists (Latour and Woolgar 1979), realists (T. D. Cook and Campbell 1979) and critical theorists (Gouldner 1979; Bernstein 1976) would all subscribe to this general position. . . .

There are three points that are important for the structure of debate in the organisational studies. First, that epistemological agreement does not require ontological agreement. Second, that there are many epistemological communities and thus many bodies of knowledge which may, or may not, overlap. Third, that within any given community, the validity criteria for knowledge are relatively well known and accepted. . . .

Ontological debates are about the true nature of reality, generally regarding its objectivity. As the debaters are part of the reality that is in dispute, there is no logical resolution to these debates. Any arguments or evidence offered depends on premises that are exactly what is at issue in an ontological dispute. These exchanges quickly reach the impasses of mutually exclusive assertions. Ultimately, ontological disputes are the subject matter of philosophical speculation and religious, or secular, belief.

Epistemological debates are about knowledge and knowledge generating processes. These debates are, in theory (i.e., logically) resolvable as the subject of the debate is external to, and subordinate to, the debaters. However the consensus arising out of an examination of the empirical, as well as the logical, yields the conclusion that these debates can be settled only tentatively. The basis of settlement is both rational argumentation and empirical evidence. Thus, for example, the contributors to the Lakatos and Musgrave (1970) reader tussle over the degree of discontinuity in scientific revolutions, the importance of tenacity, etc. by appeal to rational argument and evidence from the history of science. Others have argued for the relevance of empirical evidence from the sociological and political spheres (Latour and Woolgar 1979; Callon, Law, and Rip 1986).

Implications for Organisational Studies

. . . As mentioned above, Burrell and Morgan (1979) have reviewed the variety of ontological positions adopted in organisation studies. An example of a debate containing ontological elements would be Locke's attack on the proponents of behaviour modification in organisations (Locke 1977) and subsequent response to it (Gray 1979; Locke 1979; Parmerlee and Schwenk 1979). One of the key issues in this exchange was the real nature of human nature.

As might be expected from our consideration of the rules of ontological debate, this issue was not resolved on the journal pages, though it is clear that in the mind (Locke 1979) or the private events (Parmerlee and Schwenk 1979) of the authors it was resolved satisfactorily. Parmerlee and Schwenk (1979) suggest that the debate might clarify differences and lead to integration of the two paradigms. For the ontological aspects of the debate integration is simply not a possible outcome.

Because of the basic irreconcilability of ontological positions and inability to resolve differences at the ontological level, I suggest that we be wary of such debates. They consume energy, time, journal pages, etc. when organisation studies suffers from constraints on these resources.

Organisation studies is about knowledge, not faith. Thus the epistemological level is of central importance. In organisation studies we can identify two major issues which divide the field into epistemological camps. The first has to do with the level of analysis and the attitude toward reductionism. This has a lot to do with the historical and contemporary ties of the study of organisations to psychology and sociology. The psychologists require that all phenomenon be explained in terms of individual persons. The sociologists insist on the importance of explanation at the level of organisations and other social units. Often this difference is framed as an ontological one. However, I suggest that the issue is: "Does explanation using the concept of organisations help understanding?" not, "Do organisations really exist?" The true existence of organisations is irrelevant to the utility of the concept in helping people know more about social life.

The utility of the concept is determined by the agreement of a group of people. If the concept only helps some of the people, a subdiscipline evolves. Depending on the degree of inconsistency in positions and the number of differences, communication between groups will range from impossible to free-flowing. Judging by our journals, we have managed to maintain communication between the psychologists and sociologists interested in organisations.

A second clear break between epistemological communities in organisation studies is that between the majority of positivist-like scholars and a minority of phenomenologically oriented scholars. Morey and Luthans (1984) characterize this polarization as an etic (objectivist, nomothetic, quantitative, outsider) perspective versus an emic (subjective, ideographic, qualitative, insider) perspective. They argue for rapprochement between the two camps. However, this break appears to be deeper and more difficult to bridge than the psychological/sociological rift. . . .

In addition to these major differences in epistemology, there are more specific differences that arise, as well. What appear as minor differences in position to nonmembers of an epistemological community may impair agreement on the validity criteria within the community. For example, there are significant differences within what we have called the emic perspective. Taken together, epistemological differences result in a splintering of scholars interested in organisational phenomena into many subcommunities. For the most part, these communities are not isolated from each other and continue to attempt to develop a common definition of, and criteria for, contributions to knowledge in organisational studies.

Two Contrasting Modes of Inquiry
Roger D. Evered and Meryl Reis Louis

. . . Our aim here is to explicate some critical assumptions underlying the diverse approaches to organizational inquiry and to help bring order to what sometimes resembles a developing chaos in the organizational sciences.

Toward that end, we will identify and contrast two predominant approaches to current organizational inquiry. . . .

We have called the two *inquiry from the outside* and *inquiry from the inside*, highlighting what we consider an essential point of contrast. Most organizational research is oriented by one or the other of these two paradigms. Although it may be feasible and at times preferable for researchers to blend or cycle between the two, most organizational researchers seem to have implicitly adopted some particular inquiry-guiding paradigm. We hope our comments will help raise the level of awareness concerning heretofore tacit commitments to particular modes of inquiry. To help explicate the differences, we will present . . . essentially polar extremes. We recognize, however, that there may be a spectrum of approaches in which elements of both are combined.

Our fundamental purpose . . . is to increase the general level of understanding and appreciation of epistemological issues in organizational inquiry. Such an appreciation has a number of potential benefits. Articulation

Source: "Alternative perspectives in the organizational sciences" by Roger D. Evered and Meryl Reis Louis, *Academy of Management Review* 6 (1981): 385–391. Copyright © 1981 by Academy of Management. Reproduced with permission of the Academy of Management via Copyright Clearance Center.

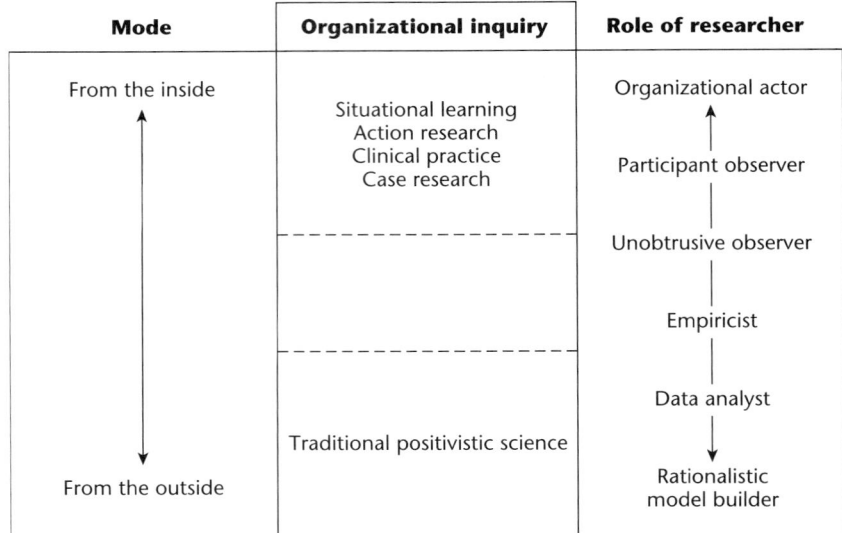

Mode	Organizational inquiry	Role of researcher
From the inside ↑	Situational learning Action research Clinical practice Case research	Organizational actor ↑ Participant observer Unobtrusive observer Empiricist Data analyst
↓ From the outside	Traditional positivistic science	Rationalistic model builder

FIGURE **5-1**   Alternative modes of inquiry

SOURCE: "Alternative perspectives in the organizational sciences" by Roger D. Evered and Meryl Reis Louis, *Academy of Management Review* 6 (1981): 388, fig. 1. Copyright © 1981 by Academy of Management. Reproduced with permission of the Academy of Management via Copyright Clearance Center.

of the epistemological differences should foster greater awareness of the appropriateness of different kinds of knowledge for different purposes; it may thereby help legitimate the adoption of alternative and more appropriate knowledge-yielding paradigms in organizational inquiry. It should also help reduce fruitless conflicts within the field, by justifying and providing a basis for tolerance of diversity and multiplicity in research design. Greater epistemological appreciation seems to be an essential prerequisite to developing an appropriate inquiry approach whereby researchers would explicitly select a mode of inquiry to fit the nature of the problematic phenomenon under study, the state of knowledge, and their own skills, style, and purpose. Moreover, appreciation of epistemological issues has implications for the evaluation of research products. It leads to a belief that the quality of a piece of research is more critically indicated by the appropriateness of the paradigm selected than by the mere technical correctness of the methods used. . . .

The distinctions we are making between coping and inquiry in relation to insider versus outsider are presented in Figure [5-1]. At the right side of the figure a spectrum of possible researcher roles is presented. We surmise that the critical aspect of this continuum is the degree of immersion of the researcher in the organization—that is, the extent of experiential involvement in and existential commitment to the organization. Operationally, it may translate into the extent of physical involvement in the setting. . . .

Two Modes of Inquiry

Inquiry from the inside and inquiry from the outside can both serve research purposes, but in different ways and with different effects. When would either be used? We address this question by contrasting the two modes on a number of analytic dimensions, summarized in Figure [5-2].

We begin by comparing the *researcher's role and relationship to the setting* under the two modes of inquiry, and by identifying the epistemological and *validity assumptions* underlying the choice of role and relationship. Knowledge and understanding of an organizational situation can be acquired in two ways: (1) by studying, *from the outside*, data generated by the organization (and other organizations deemed to be similar in certain respects), and

Dimension of difference	Mode of inquiry	
	From the outside	From the inside
Researcher's relationship to setting	Detachment, neutrality ←——→ "Being there," immersion	
Validation basis	Measurement and logic ←——→ Experiential	
Researcher's role	Onlooker ←——→ Actor	
Source of categories	A priori ←——→ Interactively emergent	
Aim of inquiry	Universality and ←——→ Situational relevance generalizability	
Type of knowledge acquired	Universal, nomothetic: ←——→ Particular, idiographic: theoria praxis	
Nature of data and meaning	Factual, context free ←——→ Interpreted, contextually embedded	

FIGURE **5-2** Differences between the two modes of inquiry

(2) by becoming a part of the organization and studying it *from the inside*. We can come to "know" the Ford Motor Company or Texas Instruments by examining annual reports, employment statistics, union announcements, questionnaire results, or observational records; or, alternatively, by functioning within these organizations for a period of time (or talking with those who do).

Inquiry from the outside is characterized by the researcher's detachment from the organizational setting under study. The detachment derives, in part, from the assumption that the thing under study is separate from, unrelated to, independent of, and unaffected by the researcher. Astronomy provides an ideal illustration. The objects of interest are measured with instruments, the data are analyzed to determine if logical patterns seem to exist, and rational theories are constructed to integrate, explain, and perhaps predict a multitude of facts. Knowledge is validated by methodical procedure and logic. Underlying the detachment of the researcher inquiring from the outside are critical epistemological assumptions: the researcher is guided by belief in an *external* reality constituted of *facts* that are *structured* in a law-like manner. This is what Habermas (1971), after Husserl, has referred to as the "objectivist illusion."

In contrast, inquiry from the inside carries with it the assumption that the researcher can best come to know the reality of an organization by *being there*: by becoming immersed in the stream of events and activities, by becoming part of the phenomena of study. "Being there" is essentially what (Heidegger 1962) means by his term *Dasein*. Knowledge is validated experientially. Underlying the immersion of a researcher inquiring from the inside is a very different set of epistemological assumptions from those of inquiry from the outside. Fundamental to it is the belief that knowledge comes from human *experience*, which is inherently continuous and *nonlogical*, and which may be *symbolically representable*. It is close to what Polanyi (1958) has termed "personal knowledge." The danger here is normally considered to be that the findings could be distorted and contaminated by the values and purposes of the researcher. This bias has been referred to by Russell (1945) as the "fallacy of subjectivism."

The researcher's role in inquiry from the outside can best be characterized as that of an onlooker. The researcher may use a telescope, microscope, or any other instrument; the essential feature is looking in from the outside at a selected piece of the world. At the extreme is the pure rationalist, sometimes referred to as a speculator, who needs to collect no data from the world to carry out the task of theorizing.

In inquiry from the inside, the researcher becomes an actor in real situations. The researcher must attend to the total situation and integrate information from all directions simultaneously. The relevant world is the field surrounding the individual actor/researcher.

Another difference between the two modes of inquiry is the *source of the analytical categories* around which data are organized. In a typical piece of outside research, the investigator pre-selects a set of categories that will guide the inquiry. Hypotheses are phrased in terms of these categories, and only those data pertaining to them are collected. The life in the organizational microcosm under study is viewed through the lens of a limited number of categories, such as centralization and formalization, or commitment and job involvement. At the extreme, this may lead to a form of perceptual "screening," so that the researcher sees only what is being sought.

The a priori categories may have been derived from personal idiosyncrasy, from theoretical formulation, or may have emerged in previous from-the-inside research. In the case of inside research, there are no intentionally prescribed categories to constrain the researcher. Instead, important features emerge through the individual's experience in and of the situation, as figure against ground in a perceptual field. Features are noticed and identified through an interpretive, iterative process whereby data and categories emerge simultaneously with successive experience. The process represents an experiential exploration and is particularly suited to early inquiry into a new research territory. Inquiry from the inside is useful for generating tentative categories grounded in the concrete circumstance of a particular situation. Such emergent categories may subsequently be used as the a priori categories guiding the more deductive, hypothesis-testing inquiry from the outside.

A further difference is the *aim of inquiry*. The aim of inquiry from the outside is to generalize from the particular to construct a set of theoretical statements that are universally applicable. The aim is to develop understanding of classes of organizational phenomena, rather than to focus on particular instances in particular settings. Inquiry from the inside, in contrast, is directed toward the historically unique situation, what Lewin (1951) called that "full reality of the whole, here-and-now individual situation." The situationally relevant products of inside research serve both practical and theoretical purposes. They can provide guides for action in the immediate situation and inputs in developing hypotheses to guide inquiry from the outside.

The different modes of inquiry are also associated with different *types of knowledge*. The aim of situational relevancy pursued in inside research is served by knowledge of the particular organization under study. This knowledge of the particular is a necessary, but not sufficient, condition for praxis. By *praxis*, we mean a knowledge of how to act appropriately in a variety of particular situations. The aim of generalizability sought by outside research is served by the development of universal knowledge, or theoria (Heidegger 1962). Habermas (1971) informs us that the original Greek meaning of *theoria* was "looking on," in the sense of witnessing a particular public celebration. Later, it came to mean "looking on" in the sense of examining the external order of the natural world and reproducing its presumed logical form. Over time, the meaning shifted focus from the particular to the universal. Praxis, on the other hand, focuses on the particular; it is knowledge that is infused with human organization and human interest, as represented in the situation under study. In the extreme, theoria implies a dissociation of universal knowledge from human interest (Habermas 1971). And, at the other extreme, praxis implies a preoccupation with the idiosyncratic.

While both modes of inquiry are concerned with understanding everyday happenings in organizations, they differ sharply in what they consider to be *data* and the level at which they consider issues of *meaning*. In inquiry from the inside, the aim of understanding particular situations necessitates that researchers make direct experiential contact with the organization under study. Understanding the events, activities, and utterances in a specific situation requires a rich appreciation of the overall organizational context. Context refers to the complex fabric of local culture, people, resources, purposes, earlier events, and future expectations that constitute the time-and-space background of the immediate and particular situation. Facts have no meaning in isolation from the setting. Meaning is developed from the point of view of the organizational participant. Inside research yields knowledge that is keyed to the organization member's definition of the situation, what Rogers (1951) has termed the "phenomenal field" of the person. Researchers involve themselves directly in the setting under study in order to appreciate organizational phenomena in light of the context in which they occur and from the participants' points of view.

In inquiry from the outside, the aim of developing universal principles of organizational life necessitates stripping away the idiosyncrasies of the particular organization(s) studied to reveal what is generally applicable to all organizations. The separation of the universal from the particular is accomplished through several processes. With the aid of sampling, aggregation, and other analytic techniques, the uniqueness of individual organizations is randomized, controlled for, and otherwise "washed," revealing the kernel of presumed common truths. The validity of such efforts rests on the comparability of measurements across observations, settings, and times, as well as the completeness with which the observational procedures and situations are documented. Hence, the concern with instrumentation, specification, and precision.

Outside research is designed to be detached from, and independent of, a specific situation under study in a particular organization. The researcher determines the frequencies of, and associations among, events with respect to a set of hypothesized categories and relationships. Meaning is assigned to events on the basis of a priori analytic categories and explicit researcher-free procedures. Interpretations of the researcher are viewed as inherently confounding. The spectrum of organizational life is filtered through the researcher's preset categories; elements related to the categories are selected, coded as data, and simultaneously given meaning by the categories. As a result, data are considered factual when they have the same meaning across situations and settings. That is, they are context-free.

Related Dichotomies

Before we discuss the uses of these two contrasting paradigms of inquiry, it may be instructive to comment on the inside/outside distinction in relation to other dichotomies presented in the literature. A surprising consequence of discussing this inside/outside dichotomy with colleagues has been the wide array of parallels that it has evoked.

Included among these were Geertz's (1973) distinction between *thick* and *thin* description; E. T. Hall's (1976) *high context* and *low context*; Chomsky's (1965) *deep* and *surface* structure; Pike's (1967) *emic* and *etic*; Kaplan's (1964) *logic-in-use* and *reconstructed logic*; and the distinctions between *acquaintance with* and *knowledge about* as variously construed by [William] James ([1890] 1918), Dewey (1933), Schutz (1962, 1967), and Merton (1972). That there is a fundamental difference between the two modes of inquiry is further suggested by the fact that in many languages there are different verbs to distinguish among different ways of knowing. For instance, French has *savoir* and *connaitre*; German has *wissen* and *kennen*; and Latin has *scire* and *noscere*.

The distinction we have made has commonly (and regrettably) evoked the distinction between *ideographic* research (individual case, situational facts, and particular patterns) and *nomothetic* (general laws, universal variables, large number of subjects), originally made by Windelband and introduced later into the social sciences by Allport (1937). Overall, the ideographic/nomothetic dichotomy has been dysfunctional for the development of the social sciences, because it carries the presumption that only nomothetic research can yield general laws. Even in the early 1930s, both Lewin and Goldstein demonstrated convincingly that nomothetic laws were at best approximations, since they can never characterize any particular event or situation. However, events occurring in the unique or particular situation *are* lawfully connected, and systematic clinical research can extricate these laws by the study of successive cases (K. Goldstein 1938; Lewin 1931).

Most commonly and naturally, the similarity between from-the-outside inquiry and *positivism* has been noted. There are many varieties of positivism (Susman and Evered 1978); we acknowledge a close correspondence between the kind known as logical empiricism and our description of inquiry from the outside. In one respect, our contribution here is to systematically articulate the positivistic mode of inquiry both by direct description and by contrast with a recognizable alternative.

TABLE 5-2

Network of basic assumptions characterizing the subjective-objective debate with social science*

SUBJECTIVIST APPROACHES TO SOCIAL SCIENCE ←——————————————————————→ OBJECTIVIST APPROACHES TO SOCIAL SCIENCE

Core ontological assumptions	Reality as a projection of human imagination	Reality as a social construction	Reality as a realm of symbolic discourse	Reality as a contextual field of information	Reality as a concrete process	Reality as a concrete structure
Assumptions about human nature	Man as pure spirit, consciousness, being	Man as a social constructor, the symbol creator	Man as an actor, the symbol user	Man as an information processor	Man as an adaptor	Man as a responder
Basic epistemological stance	To obtain phenomenological insight, revelation	To understand how social reality is created	To understand patterns of symbolic discourse	To map contexts	To study systems process, change	To construct a positivist science
Some favored metaphors	Transcendental	Language game, accomplishment, text	Theater, culture	Cybernetic	Organism	Machine
Research methods	Exploration of pure subjectivity	Hermeneutics	Symbolic analysis	Contextual analysis of Gestalten	Historical analysis	Lab experiments, surveys

SOURCE: "The case for qualitative research" by Gareth Morgan and Linda Smircich, *Academy of Management Review* 5 (1980): 492, table 1. Copyright © 1980 by Academy of Management. Reproduced with permission of the Academy of Management via Copyright Clearance Center.

*EDITORS' NOTE: Descriptions of the ontological and human nature assumptions may be found in Chapter 4, Table 4-3.

The Range of Core Assumptions
Gareth Morgan and Linda Smircich

Our basic thesis is that the case for any research method, whether qualitative or quantitative (in any case, a somewhat crude and oversimplified dichotimization) cannot be considered or presented in the abstract, because the choice and adequacy of a method embodies a variety of assumptions regarding the nature of knowledge and the methods through which that knowledge can be obtained, as well as a set of root assumptions about the nature of the phenomena to be investigated. Our aim is to examine the issues relating to methodology within this wider and deeper context, and in so doing develop a framework within which debates about rival methods in social science might be fruitfully and constructively considered.

We take our lead in this endeavor from the scheme of analysis offered by Burrell and Morgan (1979), which suggests that all approaches to social science are based on interrelated sets of assumptions regarding ontology, human nature, and epistemology. Table [5-2] provides a general overview of the relationships between ontology, human nature, epistemology, and methodology in contemporary social science. In order to simplify presentation, and make this article of manageable length, we shall restrict our attention to what Burrell and Morgan have described as the Interpretive and Functionalist paradigms. The social thought embraced by these two paradigms raises a number of important research issues, but they are wedded to ideological perspectives that overplay the tendency to spontaneous order and regulation in social affairs, while ignoring modes of domination, conflict, and radical change. This is a serious omission. A full discussion and critique of contemporary research practice should also consider perspectives characteristic of the Radical Humanist and Radical Structuralist paradigms, within which the qualitative/quantitative research issue would be regarded as an ideological debate of minor significance. With this qualification in mind, we shall now seek to show how assumptions about ontology and human nature, which provide the grounds of social theorizing, are captured metaphorically in ways that define different methodological positions. . . .

. . . In essence, [the assumptions] are intended to provide a rough typology for thinking about the various views that different social scientists hold about human beings and their world. All the views have a distinguished history, are the products of long discussion and debate by their advocates, and their basic ideas are manifested in powerful kinds of social thought. Each has evolved in awareness of the existence of the other points of view, and indeed has to some extent developed in reaction to competing perspectives. . . . Most have left their mark on contemporary organization theory, although the influence of approaches represented by positions on the right-hand side of the continuum have been dominant. . . .

Problems of Epistemology

The different assumptions regarding ontology and human nature pose interesting problems of epistemology. The different world views they reflect imply different grounds for knowledge about the social world. As we pass from assumption to assumption along the subjective-objective continuum, the nature of what constitutes adequate knowledge changes. To take the extremes of the continuum by way of illustration, an objectivist view of the social world as a concrete structure encourages an epistemological stance that emphasizes the importance of studying the nature of relationships among the elements constituting that structure. Knowledge of the social world from this point of view implies a need to understand and map out the social structure, and gives rise to the epistemology of positivism, with an emphasis on the empirical analysis of concrete relationships in an external social world. It encourages a concern for an "objective" form of knowledge that specifies the precise nature of laws, regularities, and relationships among phenomena measured in terms of social "facts" (Pugh and Hickson 1976a, 1976b; Skinner 1953, 1957).

At the other end of the continuum, the highly subjectivist view of reality as a projection of individual imagination would dispute the positivist grounds of knowledge in favor of an epistemology that emphasizes the importance of understanding the processes through which human beings concretize their relationship to their world. This phenomenologically oriented perspective challenges the idea that there can be any form of "objective" knowledge that can be specified and transmitted in a tangible form, because the knowledge thus created is often no more than an expression of the manner in which the scientist as a human being has arbitrarily imposed a personal frame of reference on the world, which is mistakenly perceived as lying in an external and separate realm (Husserl 1962). The grounds for knowledge in each of these perspectives are different because the fundamental conceptions of social reality to which the proponents of each position subscribe are poles apart.

Science as Metaphor

We thus encounter a fundamental issue that has attracted the attention of social philosophers for many centuries. It is the issue of whether or not human beings can ever achieve any form of knowledge that is independent of their own subjective construction, since they are the agents through which knowledge is perceived or experienced. A strong case can be made for the view that science of all kinds, whether nominalist or realist in its basic orientation, is primarily metaphorical (R. H. Brown 1977; Morgan 1980; Schön 1963). It is through the use of metaphor that scientists seek to create knowledge about the world. The metaphors that theorists choose as a basis for detailed theorizing usually derive from very fundamental, and often implicit, core assumptions about ontology and human nature. In selecting different metaphors for elaborating their theories, they implicitly commit themselves to an epistemological position emphasizing particular kinds and forms of knowledge. Debates about epistemology hinge largely on the advocacy of different kinds of metaphoric insight as a means of capturing the nature of the social world. It is worth examining this point in detail.

Reality as a Concrete Process

As we proceed from right to left along the subjective-objective continuum illustrated . . . epistemology of extreme positivism, derived from a mechanical conception of the universe as a closed structure, gives way to an epistemology emphasizing the need to understand process and change. It is a change in epistemology that reflects a move away from a conception of the world as a machine, or closed system, to a conception of the world as an organism, an open system. The metaphor of organism has exerted a dominant influence on the development of open systems theory within social science, providing a mode of conceptualization appropriate to theorizing about the social world as if it were a concrete process evolving through time. This epistemological position stresses the importance of monitoring process, the manner in which a phenomenon changes over time in relation to its context (e.g., Burns and Stalker 1961; Emery and Trist 1965). The metaphors of machine and organism call for different modes of research as a means of generating knowledge; they define different epistemologies, since the knowledge required to examine a view of the world as a closed mechanical structure is inadequate for examining the world as an organismic system.

Reality as a Contextual Field of Information

Similarly, the epistemological framework for examining the world as an organismic system proves inadequate for studying the world if it is regarded, in accordance with the next ontological position along the continuum, as a process of information. This ontological position calls for epistemologies based on cybernetic metaphors, which emphasize the importance of understanding contexts in a holistic fashion (Morgan 1979b). The metaphor of organism encourages the theorist to draw boundaries around the subject of study, elevating it in importance against the wider background. Thus the organization theorist often is concerned with the somewhat arbitrary relationship between organization and environment, structuring the research process and knowledge thus generated around this conceptualization. A more context-oriented epistemology, such as that provided by the cybernetic metaphor, would consciously seek to avoid this abstraction of "figure" from "ground," and search for what Bateson has described as "systemic wisdom." As he points out, it is possible to attempt to explain the evolution of the horse (figure) in terms of a one-sided adaptation to the nature of grassy plains (ground); however, this is to miss the point that the grassy plains have evolved along with the horse and may equally well be seen as an adaptation to the horse, as the other way around (1972, 155). The same is true with "organization" and "environment."

The point is that it is *contexts* which evolve, and that an adequate understanding of the *process* entails grasping the ecological nature of the context as a whole. Epistemologies based on the organismic metaphor are inadequate for this end, and need to be replaced by epistemologies concerned with the mapping of contexts (Gadalla and Cooper 1978) and facilitating understanding of the patterns of systemic relationships inherent in the ecological nature of those contexts. Thus, as far as research in organization theory is concerned, the contextual approach would stress a need to understand how organizations and environment evolve together, rather than presuming that the adaptation of organization to environment is one way, as the organismic metaphor tends to presume. The contextual approach is not concerned with the notion of causality, which underlies positivist epistemology, because it becomes impossible to find a point at which causal forces begin. The nature of interaction and feedback between elements within a contextual field is such that there are always causes, which cause causes to cause causes (Wilden 1972, 39). The beginning of systemic wisdom lies in an awareness that relationships change in concert and cannot be reduced to a set of determinate laws and propositions, as positivist epistemology would have it. A view of social reality as a contextual field carries with it distinctive requirements as to what constitutes an adequate epistemology.

Reality as a Realm of Symbolic Discourse

The next position along our continuum, which characterizes the social world as a realm of symbolic discourse, implies yet another set of epistemological requirements. Emphasis is now placed on understanding the nature and patterning of the symbols through which individuals negotiate their social reality. It is an epistemological position that rejects the idea that the social world can be represented in terms of deterministic relationships, in favor of a view that knowledge, understanding, and explanations of social affairs must take account of how social order is fashioned by human beings in ways that are meaningful to them. This epistemological position, which often draws on the metaphors of theatre (Goffman 1959; Silverman 1970) or culture (Pondy and Mitroff 1979; B. A. Turner 1971), emphasizes how social situations should be researched in a manner that reveals their inner nature. Thus, within the context of organizations there may be a concern for understanding the roles that language, symbols, and myths play in the shaping of any given reality, and a concern for generating ethnographic accounts of specific situations that yield insight with regard to the way reality works. The epistemology involved here does not hold that the findings thus obtained would be universally generalizable, but it does regard them as providing nonetheless insightful and significant knowledge about the nature of the social world. Such knowledge is inevitably seen as being relative and specific to the immediate context and situation from which it is generated, building what Glaser and Strauss call "substantive theory" (1967).

Reality as a Social Construction

The epistemology that views reality as a social construction focuses on analyzing the specific processes through which reality is created. Here, reality resides in the process through which it is created, and possible knowledge is confined to an understanding of that process. Thus emphasis tends to be on the metaphors of text (Ricoeur 1971), accomplishment (e.g., Garfinkel 1967), and language game (e.g., Winch 1958) as means of generating insight regarding the methods through which individuals make sense of their situation, thus creating and sustaining a semblance of reality. Garfinkel's term *ethnomethodology* aptly characterizes an important aspect of this approach to social inquiry, since the whole aim of inquiry is to understand the *methods* relevant to the production of common-sense knowledge in different *(ethno)* areas of everyday life. The task of epistemology here is to demonstrate the methods used in everyday life to create subjectively an agreed or negotiated social order. As Douglas (1970, 18) has indicated, the theoretical orientation that underlies ethnomethodology and other similar approaches to the study of society does not permit the generation of a form of knowledge that meets the demands of positivist epistemology; the ontological position implied here gives rise to an existential mode of social analysis the adequacy of which must be judged on quite different epistemological grounds.

Another Look at Extreme Subjectivism

The most subjectivist position on the continuum presented in our tables also carries with it its own particular grounds for knowledge. As has already

been indicated in our general discussion of the nature of subjectivist epistemology, knowledge here rests within subjective experience. The appreciation
of world phenomena is seen as being dependent on the ability to understand
the way in which human beings shape the world from inside themselves.
Epistemologies consistent with this position draw on a number of different
sources. Some draw on the phenomenological tradition deriving from Husserl (1962, 1965) and emphasize the importance of obtaining understanding
in terms of the nature of a transcendental form of consciousness. Others emphasize the importance of studying experiential learning phenomenologically (e.g., Torbert 1972, 1976). Yet others draw on non-Western modes of
philosophy (e.g., Herriegel 1953). In each case, the grounds for knowledge
demand that human beings transcend conventional scientific modes of understanding and begin to appreciate the world in revelatory, but as yet largely
uncharted, ways.

It is convenient that we should end our discussion of possible epistemologies with a view rooted in such extreme subjectivism, because it stands
in such stark contrast to positivism that many will regard it as antithetical
to science. Far from pursuing the ideal of generating "objective" forms of
knowledge, in terms of determinate relationships between facts, it denies
that such knowledge is possible. Yet we have arrived at that position by
merely following the epistemological implications of a gradual change in ontological assumptions. In so doing, we have sought to demonstrate how the
whole of scientific activity is based on assumptions. Positivism follows from
one particular set of ontological assumptions, as naturally as antipositivist
epistemologies follow from others.

Traditional Positivism
Allen S. Lee

The positivist approach to organizational research puts into practice a
view of science that has its origins in a school of thought within the philosophy of science known as "logical positivism" or "logical empiricism." A
major tenet of logical positivism is its "thesis of the unity of science"
(Hempel 1969; Kolakowski 1968, 178), which maintains that the methods of natural science constitute the only legitimate methods for use in social science. This approach has been explicitly recognized, and advocated,
as the "natural-science model" of social-science research, and has found

Source: "Integrating positivist and interpretative approaches to organizational research" by Allen S. Lee, *Organization Science* 2 (November 1991): 343–347. Published by
the Institute for Operations Research and the Management Sciences (INFORMS), 901
Elkridge Landing Road, Suite 400, Linthicum, Maryland 21090-2909 USA. Reprinted by
permission.

widespread application in social science in general, and in organizational research in particular (see Schutz 1973, 48; Behling 1980, 483; Schön, Drake, and Miller 1984, 9; Burrell and Morgan 1979, 4; Daft 1983, 539; Lee 1989a, b).

Only by applying the methods of natural science, according to the positivist school of thought, will social science (including organizational research) ever be able to match the achievements of natural science in explanation, prediction, and control. The difficulties of capturing social reality in formal propositions, quantifying it, and subjecting it to experimental controls, are said to be the reasons that organizational research, like the rest of social science, has not yet reached the same level of scientific maturity that characterizes natural science. At the same time, this also means that organizational researchers must try harder to make the study of organizations fit the natural-science model, since (according to the positivist approach) this is the only way in which organizational research can become truly scientific.

In a nutshell, the positivist approach involves the manipulation of theoretical propositions using *the rules of formal logic* and *the rules of hypothetico-deductive logic*, so that the theoretical propositions satisfy *the four requirements* of falsifiability, logical consistency, relative explanatory power, and survival. Immediately following are the details to this outline.

The Rules of Formal Logic

In the positivist approach, a scientific explanation is expressed in formal propositions, so that the rules of formal logic may be applied. This is important because the rules of formal logic provide a powerful means by which to relate propositions to one another, and to deduce new ones. The axiomatic systems of mathematics, like Euclid's system of geometry, provide the ideal for how this system of logic is supposed to work (Feigl 1970; Hanson 1969; Nagel and Newman 1960). For this reason, it is preferred, and sometimes even required, that scientific explanations be stated mathematically, since this would allow the scientist to use a well-established subset of the rules of formal logic—a subset widely known as the rules of algebra.

Whether or not mathematical, the rules of formal logic have two important consequences for the development of a scientific explanation. First, the process of logical deduction is able to extract consequences that are contained only implicitly in the explanation's opening premises, thereby leading to unanticipated discoveries (S. F. Barker 1969, 238, citing Hempel). Second, any proposition that cannot be shown to be logically connected to, or logically deducible from, the remaining propositions would be "exposed" as groundless (Hanson 1969, 61). In this way, the scientist can use the rules of formal logic to eliminate propositions that originate from the scientist's own "subjective" opinions, values, and biases. In the positivist approach, the origin of all deduced propositions must be found in the explanation's own "objective" foundational premises.

The Rules of "Hypothetico-Deductive Logic"

The rules of formal logic in general, and the rules of mathematics in particular, pertain to the task of how to relate propositions to one another. As such, these rules meet the needs of the formal logician or pure mathematician, who restricts his or her attention to the world of ideal relations—the strictly artificial world of formal propositions and the relationships between them. The scientist, however, works not only in the artificial world of propositions—propositions that are of his or her own invention—but also in the "real world" that he or she is observing. The scientist, therefore, faces not only the task of how to relate these propositions to one another (so that they are *logical*), but also the additional task of how to relate these propositions to the empirical reality of interest (so that the propositions are *true*). Therefore, in addition to the rules of formal logic (which include the rules of mathematics), the scientist needs a distinct set of procedural rules with which to relate his or her propositions to the empirical reality being investigated.

A major obstacle confronting such a procedure is that scientific propositions are resistant to testing by direct observation. The reason is that scientific propositions typically posit the existence of entities, phenomena, or relationships that are not directly observable, for whatever reason. The researcher can only *theorize* that they exist, like protons, electrons, and photons in physics, black holes in astronomy, evolution in biology, elasticities in economics, social structures in sociology, and so forth. None of these things can be seen directly. By what procedure, then, may the scientist relate his or her propositions to empirical referents that are not directly observable? Researchers who take the positivist approach address this concern by using what is called "hypothetico-deductive logic." The main idea behind hypothetico-deductive logic is that theorized entities have consequences that are observable, even if the entities themselves are not.

Hypothetico-deductive logic is a particular way of applying the logic of the syllogism. The standard syllogism (see Figure [5-3]) involves applying a major premise, such as "All men are mortal," to a minor premise, such as "Socrates is a man," in order to reach a conclusion, which, in this case, would be "Socrates is mortal." In syllogistic reasoning, the conclusion can be true only if the major premise is true and, conversely, the major premise can be true only if the conclusion is true. In other words, each serves as an indicator of the truth or falsity of the other.

In hypothetico-deductive logic (see Figure [5-3]), the major premise is a general theory, the minor premise is a set of facts (the "initial conditions")

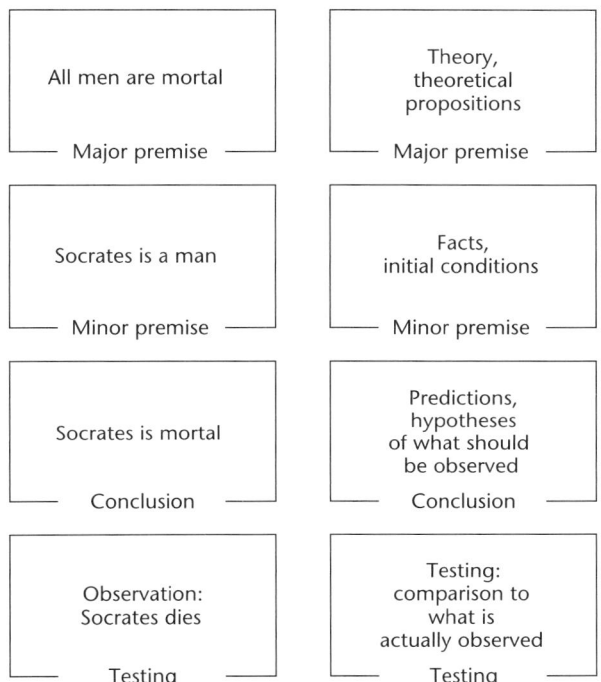

FIGURE **5-3** Hypothetico-deductive logic

SOURCE: "Integrating positivist and interpretative approaches to organizational research" by Allen S. Lee, *Organization Science* 2 (November 1991): 345, fig. 1, the Institute for Operations Research and the Management Sciences (INFORMS), 901 Elkridge Landing Road, Suite 400, Linthicum, Maryland 21090-2909 USA. Reprinted by permission.

describing a situation, and the conclusion is what the theory predicts or hypothesizes to be observed in that specific situation. This means that, even if a theory is not directly verifiable because it refers to unobservable entities, it can still be tested indirectly, through the observable consequences (equivalently called "predictions" or "hypotheses") that are logically deducible from it. For example, the theory that "All men are mortal" can be tested through its prediction that "Socrates is mortal" by observing whether or not Socrates dies. This also means that no theory can be conclusively verified as true, since a new situation and a new prediction ("Plato is mortal") would re-open the possibility for its being disproven. A theory that is said to be "confirmed" or "corroborated" is one that has survived such a test, but remains open to being disproven in future tests (see Copi 1986 and Popper 1968).

Of course, the testing of hypotheses and predictions calls for rigorous controls. This means that when the scientist tests what the theory predicts to happen, against what he or she actually observes to happen, the scientist must be able to attribute the phenomenon or relationship being observed to the factor of interest being tested, where the potentially confounding effects of the remaining factors are somehow removed or "controlled for." The controls of laboratory experiments and the controls of inferential statistics exist for this purpose.

Four Requirements for the Theoretical Propositions to Satisfy

When the rules of formal logic and the rules of hypothetico-deductive logic are used to manage theoretical propositions, there are *four "checks" or requirements* that the propositions must satisfy, so that the researcher knows that he or she is managing the propositions properly (Popper 1968, 32–33).

The first requirement is *falsifiability*. The presence of inaccuracies in the empirical content of theoretical propositions can be detected only through contradictory observations—observations that disconfirm a prediction and thereby falsify the theory from which the prediction follows. In this regard, Popper (1968, 37) takes the position that the Marxist theory of history, "in spite of the serious efforts of some of its founders and followers," eventually adopted the practice of making predictions so vague that the predictions could hardly be disconfirmed. The lack of falsifiability in the Marxist theory of history therefore had the effect of concealing any inaccuracies in it; "by this strategem they destroyed [their theory's] much advertised claim to scientific status." The now common characterization of scientific theories as falsifiable, refutable, testable, and disconfirmable is an indication of the widespread extent to which the rules of hypothetico-deductive logic have been put into practice.

The significance of the requirement of falsifiability is magnified in the situation where the scientist must evaluate competing theories. In general, it is possible for the same observation to be consistent with several theories simultaneously. This means that the accumulation of more and more observations consistent with a particular theory does not prove that it is the true one, or, if considered alone, that it is true at all. The key, therefore, is not to accumulate observations that are consistent with a theory, but to seek observations that disconfirm or falsify a theory; the result would be a reduction in the number of theories considered viable, with the surviving one(s) thus earning the status of "confirmed" or "corroborated." Unlike the Marxist theory of history, at least in the way that Popper characterizes it (above), such theories must be formulated in a way that allows their disconfirmation or falsification.

The second requirement is *logical consistency*. One test for logical consistency, already mentioned, is that all of a theory's propositions must be shown to be related to one another by the rules of formal logic, or be logically deducible from the same set of premises. Another test—one that the hypothetico-deductive framework emphasizes—is that the different predictions which follow from a theory must be compatible with one another. In other words, a theory that allows predictions of contrary or mutually exclusive events is said to lack logical consistency.

For instance, consider a set of theoretical propositions that explain race-based and gender-based employment discrimination in terms of the dynamics of psychological and group processes. Suppose further that the theoretical propositions, when applied to the facts and figures describing a certain organization, lead to the following three predictions about the actual salaries in the organization (where all factors but race and gender are held constant): on average, the white women earn more than the black men, the black men earn more than the black women, and the black women earn more than the white women. Clearly, the situations posed by any two of the predictions logically preclude the situation posed by the third. The methodological result, in which all three predictions are deducible from the same theory, would be a sign that the theoretical propositions, from which the predictions follow, lack consistency and must be "tightened up" before they are ready for empirical testing.

The third requirement is *relative explanatory power*. A given theory must be able to explain, or predict, the subject matter as well as any competing theory. As an example, consider two theories that purport to explain the same phenomenon. Each theory undergoes testing in the same five laboratory experiments, where each experiment poses a different set of empirical conditions. The predictions of the first theory are confirmed in all five laboratory experiments. The predictions of the second theory, however, are confirmed in only three of the experiments; in the remaining two experiments, the results are unfavorable or inconclusive. The second theory, in not predicting as well as the first theory, is rejected for its relative deficiency in explanatory power.

The fourth and last requirement is *survival*. While falsifiable, a theory must survive the actual attempts aimed at its disconfirmation through controlled empirical testing. Passing an empirical test, however, can never verify conclusively that the theory of interest is true. "It should be noted that a positive decision can only temporarily support the theory, for subsequent negative decisions may always overthrow it" (Popper 1968, 33). The rules of hypothetico-deductive logic therefore necessitate the on-going testing of previously confirmed theories. . . .

Socially Constructed, Administrative Science Is
W. Graham Astley

. . . This view of knowledge as a product of social negotiation within a scientific community highlights the importance of theoretical language as the vital medium through which the community's negotiations are effected. Once we relinquish the view that theoretical constructs are direct representations of external reality, language itself becomes the essential subject matter of scientific deliberation. Language is not simply a vehicle for transmitting information. Rather, it is the very embodiment of truth; our knowledge structures are linguistic conventions (Gergen 1982, 101). Scientific fields are word systems created and maintained through a process of negotiation between adherents to alternative theoretical languages.

Objective reality may have little relevance in determining the composition of these word systems. The relationship of a particular theoretical interpretation to a particular empirical phenomenon is often largely negotiable. The best example of this is dialectical analysis: the simultaneous superimposition of two or more competing analytical interpretations on the same empirical phenomenon. For instance, several divergent explanations can be offered to explain the phenomenon of internalization—the inclusion of activities that were formerly part of an organization's environment within the boundaries of the enterprise (Astley and Van de Ven 1983). Internalization has been variously explained as an absorption of critical contingencies that might potentially impede the efficient functioning of the organization's technical core (J. D. Thompson 1967, 39), an adjustment of portfolios designed to exploit product-market opportunities (Leontiades 1980), a reestablishment of the economy's efficient allocation of resources under conditions of market failure (Williamson 1975), and an attempt to eliminate fair market exchange and bring the economy under the political control of an elite of giant corporations (Edwards 1979).

It is quite possible that any one instance of internalization may simultaneously exhibit all of the empirical elements needed to lend support to each of these respective theories, in which case each theory would capture a different aspect of the phenomenon. This, however, is not the point. Rather, the key issue is that different observers tend to apply favored theoretical perspectives in a more or less exclusive manner. Some authors, for example, interpret virtually all occurrences of internalization as instances of market failure, while others interpret virtually all such occurrences as instances of

Source: "Administrative science as socially constructed truth" by W. Graham Astley, published in *Administrative Science Quarterly* 30 (September 1985): 499–503, 509–510. Copyright © 1985 Johnson Graduate School of Management, Cornell University. Reprinted with permission.

elite control (Van de Ven and Joyce 1981, ch. 8). The adherents of different positions typically do not concede that their perspective reveals only part of the whole story or that a theoretical synthesis would be desirable. Such adherence to distinctive, biased, essentially partial views of reality is, furthermore, rewarded within the discipline. Persistence in advocating the merits of a particular research paradigm creates visibility and is a common hallmark of academic success.

In many instances, moreover, objective reality cannot be the final arbiter in deciding which theoretical perspective is most valid. The notion of "loose coupling" (Weick 1976) provides a good illustration. What appears as loose coupling from one point of view might equally well be viewed as tight coupling from another point of view. If we focus attention on the leeway that organizational subunits have to pursue their own subgoals and on the degrees of autonomy they possess vis-à-vis the remainder of the organization, we will likely conclude that organizations are loosely coupled systems. But such leeway and autonomy can never be total if the organization is to retain its corporate identity. Furthermore, different subunits possess different mounts of autonomy. Consequently, some degree of interdependence and constraint impinges on all subunits, and the activities of some subunits are more closely governed by functional interdependencies and operating ties with the rest of the organization than are other subunits. Thus, it makes as much sense to emphasize degrees of tight coupling as it does to emphasize degrees of loose coupling. Organizations are always both loosely coupled and tightly coupled, depending on the analytical lens we adopt. As Lincoln (1985, 35) observed, there can be no objective choice between alternative perspectives: the validity of the perspective employed depends on the context of inquiry and on the research concerns that guide investigation. The variety of ways to reconstitute our knowledge of organizational reality is, in this sense, bounded only by theoretical ingenuity in inventing new linguistic constructions.

Linguistic Ambiguity

Not only is language, rather than objective fact, the chief product of research, but ambiguous, empirically imprecise language, dominates theorizing. The maintenance of linguistic ambiguity enhances a theory's conceptual appeal by widening its potential applicability. The very generality of ambiguous constructs assures their widespread importance in the discipline, since a great number and variety of more specific propositions can be included within their overarching frame of reference. The most general and abstract theories, the ones farthest removed from empirical reality, exert a disproportionate influence on the field by virtue of their sheer ubiquity as umbrella concepts to which a multiplicity of more explicit hypotheses can be attached.

The abstract, empirically nonrefutable hypotheses of general systems theory, for example, had substantial influence on administrative science because they provided a way to organize a large body of what might otherwise seem to be unrelated findings (Peery 1972). Resource dependence theory fulfills a similar role: its popularity as a general orienting framework of analysis is enhanced because virtually any organizational activity can be defined as a resource (Pfeffer and Salancik 1978, 259). Again, much of the appeal of transaction-costs theory rests on its claim to produce a "genuine synthesis between economics and organization theory" (Williamson and Ouchi 1981), a claim that can only be upheld because of the very broad connotation of the theory's central concept (Perrow 1981c, 375; K. S. Cook and Emerson 1984, 23; Leblebici 1985, 100).

The scientific appeal of abstract analytical frameworks lies in the symbolic, sense-making functions they fulfill (Frost and Morgan 1983). Analytical frameworks offer a satisfying sense of understanding; they "explain" why things are related in a certain manner. Linguistic ambiguity, moreover, is what allows such analytical frameworks to function symbolically, as reference points to which multiple, diverse, sometimes even contradictory meanings can be attached. By fixating cognition on common points of reference, ambiguous constructs bridge subgroup differences in perception and world view and facilitate communication. Ambiguous language allows researchers to "talk past one another" (Frost and Morgan 1983, 220) and yet talk to each other. Abstract concepts give meaning and structure to the researcher's psychological reality; they are robust mechanisms for generating scientific communion.

Linguistic ambiguity, furthermore, enhances the pragmatic value of administrative theory, while empirical precision only diminishes a theory's applicability. Generality and abstraction do not reduce the usefulness of theoretical constructs; the maintenance of ambiguity is crucial to their practical functioning. By avoiding specification of particular courses of action relevant for particular circumstances, theories can provide justification for a wide variety of different actions to take place. Managers intent on applying such theories do not mechanically translate theoretical prescriptions into behavior; instead, they rationalize their activities by pointing to events that seem credibly related to the theories' abstract terms. In doing so, managers must rely on their inside knowledge of the organizational setting and use ingenuity in accounting for practical actions by an appeal to general ideas. Theory, in this event, functions not as a technical guide to action, but as a device for enabling the manager to activate knowledge already possessed.

The theoretical frameworks offered by consulting firms specializing in specific consulting "packages" illustrate this point. Such firms have more or less standard sets of analytical tools which, through an artful redefinition of clients' problems, they can apply in one combination or another to every client in their portfolio. "Strategic planning" consultants provide one currently popular example of how this works. These consultants incorporate everything a firm does under its "corporate strategy." This notion is so vague it defies most efforts to define it; it can mean as little or as much as consultants or managers want it to mean. Owen (1982, 10) attributed the success of the Boston Consulting Group's market growth/market share matrix to exactly this kind of flexibility: "[The matrix] can be used to illustrate why a client company ought to fire a group of managers, or attempt an unfriendly merger, or unload an ailing division. It is, in short, the philosopher's stone of the consulting business." While this kind of consulting offers little in the way of specific techniques with direct application, it does legitimate managerial action through oblique symbolic references to the mystique of "strategic" necessity.

The Role of Imagery

The abstraction of theoretical language from empirical reality is nowhere better demonstrated than in the use of compelling visual imagery that requires an audience to join an author in a kind of make-believe. Theorists often self-consciously move beyond the data as they generate fictional constructs, products of imagination for which no empirical counterpart exists. In this regard, Kaplan (1964, 297) noted that "theoretical" means not only "abstract," in that theories select from the materials of experience, but also "conceptual," in that theories construct from the selected materials something that has no basis in experience at all. While theories must have empirical referents, they are also constituted by purely ideational ingredients. "A theory must somehow fit God's world, but in an important sense it creates a world of its own" (Kaplan 1964, 309).

The widespread use of ideal types, such as Burns and Stalker's (1961) "mechanistic" and "organic" organizations and Mintzberg's (1979a) "structural configurations," provides a good example. Such constructs are not merely compilations of empirical phenomena in taxonomical categories; they are intentional fictionalizations of the reality under examination. Typologically formed theory is, thus, empirically unverifiable, by its very nature (Hendricks and Peters 1973, 38). Ideal types function not just as a summary and classification of observable phenomena but also as an embodiment of the theorist's sense of logical aesthetics. In the process of constructing an ideal type the scientist deliberately departs from reality by accentuating certain of the type's attributes:

> An ideal type is formed by the one-sided accentuation of one or more points of view and by the synthesis of a great many diffuse, discrete, more or less present and occasionally absent concrete individual phenomena, which are arranged according to those one-sided emphasized viewpoints into a unified analytical construct. In its conceptual purity, this mental construct cannot be found anywhere in reality (Weber 1963, 398).

An equally important use of fictional imagery lies in the use of metaphorical constructs. Morgan (1980) argued that the successful use of metaphor always involves a degree of creative invention because it is based on partial truth only; a selective comparison between the subjects involved in the metaphorical process emphasizes features of similarity between them while it suppresses features of dissimilarity between them. "Effective metaphor is a form of creative expression which relies upon constructive falsehood as a means of liberating the imagination" (Morgan 1980, 612). Pinder and Bourgeois (1982), consequently, argued that the use of metaphors is not honest science and is misleading as a guide to objective truth. Despite lack of objectivity, however, a large amount of intellectual activity within administrative science is devoted to the trading of metaphors, representing organizations, for example, in the compelling imagery of "machines" (Ward 1964), "garbage cans" (M. D. Cohen, March, and Olsen 1972), "iron cages" (Weber 1946), "theaters" (Mangham and Overington 1983), "psychic prisons" (Morgan, Frost, and Pondy 1983), and so on.

Crystallizing theory in attractive images is an important part of scientific writing. Imagery, not the bare reporting of facts, captures the scientific imagination. As Daft (1983) noted, our research products must have "symmetry" and "beauty"; they must "hang together" in meaningful units having a "poetic" quality. Theories gain favor because of their conceptual appeal, their logical structure, or their psychological plausibility. Internal coherence, parsimony, formal elegance, and so on prevail over empirical accuracy in determining a theory's impact. Published theoretical works generally attract greater attention than purely empirical studies because of their ability to excite these essentially aesthetic sensibilities. . . .

Conclusion

The body of knowledge constituting administrative science is not an objective representation of administrative practice; it does not, through literal correspondence, simply reflect events and activities in the managerial world. Instead of discovering enduring facts of organizational life and reporting them through neutral description, we actively create truth by assigning meaning to the phenomena we observe and experience. This is not to deny the existence of an objective reality independent of minds, as critics of the social constructionist view sometimes imply (e.g., Armstrong 1980); the point is only that our *knowledge* of objective reality is subjectively constructed. Just as organizational participants subjectively interpret events in order to experience everyday life as meaningful, so administrative scientists superimpose analytical frameworks on empirical observations to render knowledge meaningful.

Summary

While Dorothy and her friends had no choice about the color of their spectacle lenses, serious inquirers have many choices regarding assumptions about reality and how it might be known. There is the choice of whether reality is assumed (because we will never *really* know) to be simply out there or a projected fantasy or something in between. Will we elect to know it from the insider's or the outsider's perspective? Surprising for some, we can also choose to believe our findings are true, probable, value-mediated, or completely subjective. Further, we can choose our voice as inquirers—if we understand that our work always represents some value and interest set. These and other choices, bundled into paradigms, outlined in this, the previous, and the following two chapters, will be made, we hope, with awareness of their consequences for theorizing and research.

6   The Impact of Ideology and Values

We are none of us tolerant in what concerns us deeply and entirely.
    —*Samuel Taylor Coleridge*

Science is not a disinterested examination of the structures of reality.
Objective truths about the world can be captured only in the thicket
of cultural belief, refined experience and honed intuition.
    —*Robert J. Richards*

The fourth core assumptive component of the frame we have termed
the philosophical context of inquiry is ideology—a set of beliefs and values
underlying and unifying group action. Through two entwined questions,
two philosophical assumptions come into play: Whose interests are being
furthered and how? What values are being enacted? Answers to these questions shape inquiry. Like the other philosophical assumptions of this foundational frame, ideology tends to be out of awareness and underdiscussed
even as it impacts the research process and research products.

The *beliefs* that compose an ideology specify the causal relations between courses of action and outcomes. *Values* refer to preferences for certain courses of action and outcomes (Beyer 1981). Ideologies, thus, may be
defined as relatively coherent sets of beliefs and values that bind some
people together and are used to explain their world in terms of preferred
cause-and-effect relations. Strongly held beliefs and values will, as consistency theory (Heider 1958; Zajonc 1960) predicts, tend to be in harmony
or balance because they are emotionally charged as well as shared. Ideologies thus explain the hows and whys of events and may specify that
some courses of action are not only more likely but more desirable than
others. Ideologies become like uniforms: one wears the same ideas as
one's comrades; the emphasis is to be one with others (Feuer 1975). The
social functions of ideologies are several. They provide solidarity by binding like-minded individuals together. They enable a group to rationalize its
vested interests and its understandings of the world (Apter 1964; P. L. Berger 1963). Ideologies function therefore to create a semblance of order and

come to be viewed as natural, nondebatable behavioral guides. They serve therefore as cognitive-emotional filters that direct and focus attention.

Ideology has, historically, been used in two quite different ways—one scientific, the other critical. The former use maintains that sets of beliefs and values can be used analytically to characterize and explain the sociopolitical behavior of intellectual groupings. The later use of the term ideology maintains that because all ideas originate in interest groups, neutral truth cannot exist. This point of view explains that social classes and political groups thus can only claim uncertainties (not the "search and doubt" that characterizes serious inquiry). Normative associations and organizations and those occupations that constitute a way of life tend to be ideologically homogeneous and to attract and retain members on the basis of distinctive ideologies. Ideologies, in the scientific sense, may be distinguished at several levels—from the ethos of science as a whole to the norms of a particular research group. At all of these levels, ideologies impact research by defining phenomena deemed worthy of study, by specifying how good answers may be obtained, how to interrupt the meanings of particular findings, and so on. Inquiry, ideology reminds us, is never really neutral or value-free—although, surprisingly, this is a relatively modern notion.

Seven selections about ideology and values follow. In the first, using ideology as sociopolitical critique, Mats Alvesson and Stanley Deetz summarize ideological critiques in organization studies. Switching to the scientific meaning of ideology, culture scholars Harrison Trice and Janice Beyer, in the second selection, explain the origins and roles of ideology; and Ralph Stablein, in the third selection, outlines four major ideological groups in organization studies and shows how these ideological groupings relate to ontology and epistemology.

Values are the focus of the remaining selections. First, a sociologist of science, Harriett Zuckerman, usefully reminds us of the value-infused norms that supposedly apply across all of science. Next, Ernest Nagel details persuasively the reasons that social science cannot be fully value-neutral. Howard Becker reminds us that research is always from someone's point of view, and thus we end up taking sides in our research. Finally, in the last selection, Abraham Kaplan clearly and patiently explains just how values color facts, meanings, problem selection, and much else in inquiry.

Ideology Critique
Mats Alvesson and Stanley Deetz

The earliest ideological critiques of the workplace were offered by Marx. In his analysis of work processes he focused primarily on practices of economic exploitation through direct coercion and structural differences in work relations between owners of capital and the owners of their own labor. However, Marx also describes the manner in which the exploitative relation is disguised and made to appear legitimate. This is the origin of ideology critique. Economic conditions and class structure still were central to the analysis whether this misrecognition of interests was a result of the domination of the ruling class's ideas (Marx 1844) or of the dull compulsions of economics relations (Marx 1867).

The themes of domination and exploitation by owners and later by managers have been central to ideology critique of the workplace in this century by Marxist inspired organization theorists (for example, Braverman 1974; Clegg and Dunkerley 1980; Edwards 1979; Salaman 1981). Attention by analysts from the left focused on ideology since workers often seemed to fail to recognize this exploitation and their class-based revolutionary potential in the industrial countries. Gradually these later analyses became less concerned with coercion and class and economic explanations as their focus changed to why coercion was so rarely necessary and to systemic processes that produced active consent. Issues of "workers' self-understanding of experience" become more central (for example, Gramsci 1971; Burawoy 1979; Willmott 1990). To an increasing degree, ideology critiques do not only or even strongly address class issues, but broaden the picture and study how cultural-ideological control operates in relationship to all employees, including levels of management (Hodge, Kress, and Jones 1979; Czarniawska-Joerges 1988; Deetz and Mumby 1990; Kunda 1992). Ideology produced in the workplace would stand alongside that present in the media and the growth of the consumer culture and welfare state as accounting for workers' failure to act on their own interests. Ideology would also account for professionals' and managers' failure to achieve autonomy in relationship to needs and wants and the conformist pressure to standardize paths for satisfying these (conspicuous consumption, careerism, and self-commodification: see Heckscher 1995). This would fill out the tradition of ideology critique.

A considerable amount of critical work has addressed management and organization theory as expressions, as well as producers, of ideologies which

Source: "Critical theory and postmodernism approaches to organizational studies" by Mats Alvesson and Stanley A. Deetz, in *Handbook of organization studies*, eds. Stewart R. Clegg, Cynthia Hardy, and Walter R. Nord, 199–202. Copyright © 1996 by Mats Alvesson and Stanley Deetz. Reprinted by permission of Sage Publications Ltd.

legitimize and strengthen specific societal and organizational social relations and objectives (Burrell and Morgan 1979; Alvesson 1987; Alvesson and Willmott 1996; Steffy and Grimes 1992). Academics, particularly those in management studies, are often viewed as ideologists. They serve dominant groups through socialization in business schools, support managers with ideas and vocabularies for cultural-ideological control at the workplace level, and provide the aura of science to support the introduction and use of managerial domination techniques.

Four themes recur in the numerous and varied writings about organizations working from the perspective of ideology critique: (1) the naturalization of social order, or the way a socially/historically constructed world would be treated as necessary, natural, rational and self-evident; (2) the universalization of managerial interests and suppression of conflicting interests; (3) the domination of instrumental, and eclipse of competitive, reasoning processes; and (4) hegemony, the way consent becomes orchestrated.

Naturalization

In naturalization a social formation is abstracted from the historical conflictual site of its origin and treated as a concrete, relatively fixed, entity. As such the reification becomes the reality rather than life processes. Through obscuring the construction process, institutional arrangements are no longer seen as choices but as natural and self-evident. The illusion that organizations and their processes are "natural" objects and functional responses to "needs" protects them from examination as produced under specific historical conditions (which are potentially passing) and out of specific power relations. In organization studies, organismic and mechanistic metaphors dominate, thereby leading research away from considering the legitimacy of control and political relations in organizations (Morgan 1986). Examining the naturalization of the present and the reifications of social processes helps display the structural interrelation of institutional forces, the processes by which they are sustained and changed, and the processes by which their arbitrary nature is concealed and hence closed to discussion. Ideology critique reclaims organizations as social-historical constructions and investigates how they are formed, sustained, and transformed by processes both internal and external to them (see Lukács 1971; Benson 1977b; Giddens 1979; Frost 1980, 1987; J. B. Thompson 1984; Deetz 1985, 1994). The self-evident nature of an organizational society, the basic distinctions and division of labor between management and workers, men and women, and so forth are called into question by ideology critique which demonstrates the arbitrary nature of these phenomena and the power relations that result and sustain these forms for the sake of discovering the remaining places of possible choice.

Universalization of Managerial Interests

Lukács (1971) among many others (see Giddens 1979) has shown that particular sectional interests are often universalized and treated as if they were everyone's interests. In contemporary corporate practices, managerial groups are privileged in decision-making and research. Management is ascribed a superior position in terms of defining the interests and interest realizations of the corporation and thereby of wide segments of the population. The interests of the corporation are frequently equated with specific managerial self-interests. For example, worker, supplier, or host community interests can be interpreted in terms of their effect on corporate—i.e., universalized managerial—interests. As such they are exercised only occasionally and usually reactively and are often represented as simply economic commodities or "costs"—for example, the price the "corporation" must pay for labor, supplies, or environmental clean-up (Deetz 1995). Central to the universalization of managerial interest is the reduction of the multiple claims of ownership to financial ownership. The investments made by other stakeholders are minimized while capital investment is made central. Management by virtue of its fiduciary responsibility (limited to monetary investors) speaks for (and is often conceptually equated with) the corporation (Storey 1983). In such a move, since the *general* well-being of each group is conceptually and materially tied to the *financial* well-being of the corporation as understood by management, self-interest by nonmanagerial stakeholders is often ironically reinterpreted as accomplished by minimizing the accomplishments of their own self-interests. In ideological critique managerial advantages can be seen as produced historically and actively reproduced through ideological practices in society and in corporations themselves (see P. Tompkins and Cheney 1985; Knights and Willmott 1985; Lazega 1992; Deetz 1992). Critical studies explore how interest articulation is distorted through the dominating role of money as simple and powerful medium (Offe and Wiesenthal 1980) and confront productivity and consumption with suppressed values such as autonomy, creativity and pleasure as objectives for the organization of work (Burrell and Morgan 1979; Willmott and Knights 1982; Alvesson 1987).

The Primacy of Instrumental Reasoning

Habermas (1971, 1975, 1984, 1987) has traced the social/historical emergence of technical rationality over competing forms of reason. Habermas described *technical reasoning* as instrumental, tending to be governed by the theoretical and hypothetical, and focusing on control through the development of means-ends chains. The natural opposite to this Habermas conceptualizes as a *practical interest*. Practical reasoning focuses on the process of understanding and mutual determination of the ends to be sought rather than control and development of means of goal accomplishment (Apel 1979). As Habermas described the practical interest: "a constitutive interest in the preservation and expansion of the intersubjectivity of possible action-oriented mutual understandings. The understanding of meaning is directed in its very structure toward the attainment of possible consensus among actors in the framework of a self-understanding derived from tradition" (1971, 310). In a balanced system these two forms of reasoning become natural complements. But, in the contemporary social situation, the form and content of modern social science and the social constitution of expertise align with organizational structures to produce the domination of technical reasoning (see Stablein and Nord 1985; Alvesson 1987; Alvesson and Willmott 1992, 1996; Mumby 1988; Fischer 1990). To the extent that technical reasoning dominates, it lays claim to the entire concept of rationality and alternative forms of reason appear irrational. To a large extent studies of the "human" side of organizations (climate, job enrichment, quality of work life, worker participation programs, and culture) have each been transformed from alternative ends into new means to be brought under technical control for extending the dominant group interests of the corporation (Alvesson 1987). Sievers, for example, suggests that "motivation only became an issue—for management and organization theorists as well as for the organization of work itself—when meaning either disappeared or was lost from work; that the loss of meaning is immediately connected with the way work has been, and still is organized in the majority of our Western enterprises" (1986, 338). The productive tension between technical control and humanistic aspects becomes submerged to the efficient accomplishment of often unknown but surely "rational" and "legitimate" corporate goals.

Hegemony

Although Gramsci's (1971) analysis and development of the concept of "hegemony" aimed at a general theory of society and social change with the workplace as one component, his conceptions have been widely used as a foundation for an examination of the workplace itself (for example, Burawoy 1979; Clegg 1989). Gramsci conceives of hegemony as a complex web of conceptual and material arrangements producing the very fabric of everyday life. Hegemony in the workplace is supported by economic arrangements enforced by contracts and reward systems, cultural arrangements enforced by advocacy of specific values and visions, and command arrangements enforced by rules and politics. These are situated within the larger society with its supporting economic arrangements, civil society (including education/intellectuals/media), and governmental laws.

The conception of hegemony suggests the presence of multiple dominant groups with different interests and the presence of power and activity even in dominated groups. The integration of these arrangements, however, favors dominant groups and the activity of both dominant and dominated groups is best characterized as a type of produced "consent." The hegemonic system works through pervading common sense and becoming part of the ordinary way of seeing the world, understanding one's self, and experiencing needs (see Angus 1992). Such a situation always makes possible a gap between that inscribed by the dominant order and that which a dominated group would have preferred. As Lukes argues, "Man's wants themselves may be a product of a system which works against their interests, and in such cases, relates the latter to what they would want to and prefer, were they able to make the choice" (1974, 34). A number of studies have investigated a variety of "consent" processes (for example, Burawoy 1979; Kunda 1992; Vallas 1993). Several studies have shown how employees "strategize their own subordination," achieving marginal gains for themselves through subordination but also perpetuating dominant systems which preclude their autonomy and ability to act on their own wider interests (see Burawoy 1985; Deetz 1995, 1998; Willmott 1993).

Organization studies in the 1980s and 1990s have exhibited a rather wide body of critical theory addressing corporate culture or proceeding from cultural perspectives on organizations, where culture and cultural engineering are defined as pointing towards hegemony (for example, Alvesson 1993; Alvesson and Willmott 1996; Deetz 1985; Jermier 1985; Knights and Willmott 1987; Mumby 1988; Rosen 1985). Willmott, for example, has explored how "corporate culture programmes are designed to deny or frustrate the development of conditions in which critical reflection is fostered. They commend the homogenization of norms and values within organizations . . . Cultural diversity is dissolved in the acid bath of the core corporate values" (1993, 534). In practice, as Willmott and other critical theorists point out, management control strategies are seldom fully successful. Resistance and some level of cultural diversity normally prevail. The role of critical theory, but even more so postmodernism, can be seen as trying to preserve and reinforce this diversity.

A Critique of Ideology Critique

Each of these four concerns raised in various ideological critiques has value. Yet, limitations of ideology critique have been demonstrated by many. Three criticisms appear most common. First, ideology critique often appears *ad hoc* and reactive. Most studies explain after the fact why something didn't happen rather than making predictive and testable statements about the future. Second, it appears elitist. Concepts like false needs and false consciousness which were central to early studies presume a basic weakness in insight and reasoning processes in the very same people it hopes to empower. The irony of an advocate of greater equality pronouncing what others should want or how they should perceive the world "better" is not lost on either dominant or dominated groups. And, third, the accounts from early studies of ideology critique appear far too simplistic. According to Abercrombie, Hill, and Turner's (1980) critique of the "dominant ideology thesis," the conception of the dominant group remains singular and intentional, as if an identifiable group worked out a system whereby domination through control of ideas could occur and its interest could be secured.

A more sophisticated critique, coming from postmodernism, points out that the idea of the centered agent-subject is as central to ideology critique as it is to dominant groups and the systems that advantage them. The hope for a rational and reflective agent who is capable of acting autonomously and coherently may in itself be a worthy target of ideology critique. The modern corporation's legitimacy is based on both the assumption of the existence of such an individual and its ability to foster that individual's development. Ideology critique does not, on the whole, question this basic notion of the individual, even though authors are quick to point to the discrepancy between actual production of people and a potential development.

Clearly the power of ideology critique can be maintained without falling to these criticisms and many critical theorists have accomplished this as they have pulled the concept of ideology away from traditional Marxism. They have responded to the critics by (a) advocating research that empirically investigates expressions of dominating systems of thought in particular communicative situations rather than explains outcomes (for example, Alvesson 1996; Knights and Willmott 1987; Rosen 1985); (b) refraining from directive statements regarding what people should do (revolt, liberate) but emphasizing the problematization of dominating beliefs and values (Deetz 1992); (c) recognizing pluralistic qualities, but still insisting that there are strong asymmetries between various interests and perspectives; and (d) treating ideologies as dominating without seeing them as a simple instrument or in the interest of an elite group, thus showing that elites may have internalized and may suffer from the effects of dominating sets of ideas (such as pollution or through work processes: Heckscher 1995).

Explanations of Ideologies
Harrison M. Trice and Janice M. Beyer

. . . People are "meaning-seeking animals" (Geertz 1973, 140). These meanings are embodied in their cultures as ideologies—shared, interrelated

Source: *The cultures of work organizations* by Harrison M. Trice and Janice M. Beyer, 33–34, 44–45, 201. Copyright © 1993 by Prentice-Hall, Inc. Reprinted by permission of Pearson Education, Inc., Upper Saddle River, NJ.

sets of beliefs about how things work; values that indicate what's worth having or doing; and norms that tell people how they should behave.

Ideologies tend to be rather general sets of ideas, but they are powerful in specific situations because they link actions and fundamental beliefs. Ideologies are not mere intellectual theorizing about the world and how it works. They are emotionally charged, fundamental belief systems that impel people to act in certain ways. Ideologies also fulfill two major social functions: (1) the sharing of beliefs, values, and norms incorporated in their ideologies binds groups of people together and thus promotes their social solidarity; (2) the rationalized understandings that ideologies provide help to sustain individuals in enacting their social roles (Apter 1964).

For the purpose of analyzing decision making in organizations, a definition of ideologies was developed specifically to apply to organizational and managerial behavior (Beyer 1981, 166). For the purpose of analyzing the broader topic of culture, this definition must be expanded to include related values and norms. Ideologies, in a cultural sense, can best be defined as *shared, relatively coherently interrelated sets of emotionally charged beliefs, values, and norms that bind some people together and help them to make sense of their worlds.* While usually closely interrelated in actual behavior, beliefs, values, and norms are distinct concepts. Ideological beliefs express cause and effect relations; for example, that certain behaviors will lead to certain outcomes. Values express preferences for certain behaviors or for certain outcomes. Norms express which behaviors are expected by others and are culturally acceptable ways to attain outcomes. . . .

Max Weber's analysis of *The Protestant Ethic* provides a classic example of this process. The beliefs of the Calvinist doctrine provided the basis for the growth of this ideology. It taught that the impulses and desires of human beings must be subjected to God's will in order for them to attain salvation, but that each individual's fate was predestined. The only way to demonstrate that one was among "the chosen" was to accumulate tangible evidence of God's favor through unremitting work in a worldly calling. Such beliefs dictated both hard work and determined renunciation of enjoying the results of that work. Money and wealth could be accrued as signs of God's favor—but not spent lavishly in pursuit of worldly enjoyments. Instead, the wealth so accrued provided capital for the accumulation of further wealth and the exploitation of natural resources (Sahlins 1974). Thus the Protestant ethic laid the foundations of modern capitalism. This belief system carried with it associated values favoring rugged individualism and individual success and norms prescribing hard work and achievement as acceptable routes to success. Powerful residues of these norms and values persist within many Western societies including the United States (Jackall 1988).

The Protestant ethic also illustrates three important features of ideologies. First, through norms, ideologies often compel people to action. When people believe behavior *A* will lead to outcome *B* and they prefer outcome

B to other possible outcomes for themselves and others, they are likely to feel compelled to exhibit behavior *A* and urge others to do so as well. Most Calvinists worked hard because this was the accepted way to demonstrate that they were among the chosen. The belief system was so strong that *not* to do so involved outcomes too threatening for most people to even consider. Second, the beliefs embodied in ideologies become imbued with strong emotions. People naturally cared very deeply about whether they would attain salvation and therefore wanted to believe that hard work and renunciations would ensure they were among the chosen. Third, ideologies provide consistent moral justifications for intended and past behaviors. . . .

There are two major explanations for the origins and role of ideologies in human culture: interest theory and strain theory (Geertz 1964, 52). Interest theory sees ideology as a weapon in a universal and unending struggle among social classes, each seeking to advance certain interests its members hold in common. In particular, ideology is a vehicle for the capture and exercise of political power and economic advantage. This view has been most elaborated in Marxian thought and scholarship, which holds that the dominant ideology is that of the ruling class. Strain theory takes a broader view of ideology. Its general tenets are that (1) social life inevitably produces ambiguities, conflicts, and other strains; and (2) that people use ideologies to deal with the anxieties arising from those strains. Its proponents argue that interest theory neglects these basic functions served by ideologies. Accordingly, strain theory emphasizes "the role that ideologies play in defining (or obscuring) social categories, stabilizing (or upsetting) social expectations, maintaining (or undermining) social norms, strengthening (or weakening) social consensus, relieving (or exacerbating) social tensions" (Geertz 1964, 53).

Another scholar who found interest theory too limiting was Reinhard Bendix, who pointed out that ideologies "can be explained only in part as rationalizations of self-interest; they also result from the legacy of institutions and ideas which is 'adopted' by each generation much as a child adopts the grammar of his native language" (Bendix 1970, 67). That historical legacies are part of the make-up of ideologies is often overlooked by the proponents of interest theory.

Because shared belief systems can crystallize within virtually *any* long-lasting human group—including nation states, social classes, professional groups, formal organizations, organizational subunits, and others—it seems unduly restrictive to limit the use of the term *ideology* to only those beliefs, held by certain social classes, that are used to further their domination of other social classes. The broader view of ideology consistent with strain theory is more useful for analyzing organizations and can subsume the narrower conception of interest theory within it (Beyer, Dunbar, and Meyer 1988).

Basic to strain theory is the idea that all human societies suffer from chronic malintegration. Anxiety is inevitably produced because "no social arrangement is or can be completely successful in coping with the functional problems it inevitably faces" (Geertz 1964, 54). All cultures are permeated with insoluble contradictions, ambivalence, and puzzles. Liberty conflicts with political order, stability with incessant and inevitable change, precision with flexibility, and so on. . . .

Ideologies lessen strain by fulfilling four functions: catharsis, morality, solidarity, and advocacy (Geertz 1964). The cathartic function is accomplished when emotional tension is lessened through projection of blame and anger onto symbolic enemies. The moral function applies when ideologies either deny chronic strain outright or else legitimize its existence in terms of higher values. Solidarity is realized when ideologies knit a group or social class together by creating a sense of community. Ideologies "lend dignity to everyday activities and elicit members' commitment by transforming formal organizations into beloved institutions" (Meyer 1982, 47). Finally, ideologies perform an advocacy function when they articulate strains, calling attention to them, often polarizing them, and in the process making it difficult to ignore and neglect them.

While serving these important functions, however, ideologies may also have dysfunctions. The projection of blame upon symbolic enemies that ideology provides may encourage bitterness toward other groups in society. The uplift generated by the legitimation of strains may create such a wide gap between reality and ideology that people despair and give up. Ideological commonality may produce not only solidarity, but internal schisms. And the clash of ideologies that serves to surface social problems may also make them so controversial as to preclude efforts to ameliorate them.

In more general terms, the most basic function of ideology is to create some semblance of order and ongoingness in an incomprehensible, often chaotic world. *Ideologies serve to make social situations comprehensive and meaningful. People naturally tend to simplify what they perceive; ideologies act to structure that simplification.* . . .

Most occupational groups develop ideologies that justify the work they do and the way they do it.

Ideologies in Organisation Studies
Ralph E. Stablein

The final category that I will use to examine the structure of debate in the organisational sciences is ideology. This concept does not have a generally accepted, well-defined meaning. According to Daniel Bell, "the word has been variously used to characterize ideas, ideals, beliefs, passions, values,

Source: "Structure of debate in organisational studies" by Ralph E. Stablein. Working paper, University of Otago (Dunedin, New Zealand, 1988). Reprinted with permission of Ralph E. Stablein.

weltanschauungen, religions, political philosophies, moral justifications" (1977, 298). My interest is in the particular ideologies of specific groups within organisation science as opposed to the broader "worldview" interpretations of the term. I will take the existence of a program, end, purpose or vision for organisation studies as the defining characteristic of an ideology. Following Gouldner (1979), an ideology can be expected to serve the material and ideal interests of the group which espouses it.

The relationship of ideology to ontology, epistemology and methodology is complex. Generally, an ideological group will adopt (explicitly or implicitly) common ontological, epistemological, and methodological stances. The end or vision of the group is usually endowed with ontological significance. At the epistemological level, the ideological group may constitute an epistemological community with its own understanding of what is a contribution to knowledge. However, this need not be the case. Different ideological groups may share their definition of knowledge but diverge on political commitments. At the methodological level, there is a tendency for leniency in judging the adequacy of research favourable to the group's position, and pious harshness in judging the quality of threatening work. . . .

Ideological debates are rooted in the goals and interests of the parties. Since these debates are driven by ends, all means are appropriate. The only nonlegitimate forms of debate would be those which the program of a group disallows. This yields a rather surprising conclusion. In so far as a debate invokes the ideological commitments of the disputants, anything goes if it serves the cause. Even "fudging" or fabricating the data is a legitimate tactic. Other tactical considerations, such as concern over maintaining credibility, may help control such practices but we really don't know given current review standards. That such "abuses" do occur is known. For example, faked research on the effects of drugs for severely retarded individuals may have been motivated by a sincere belief in the efficacy of such treatment (D. Greenberg 1987).

Generically, ideological combat is about winning. Given that the state monopolizes the means of force with reasonable effectiveness, the defining form of ideological debate in organisation studies is persuasive discourse. The primary tools are those of rhetoric. . . .

Turning to the ideological level in organisation studies four groupings are identifiable based on their program for organisation studies. I am labeling these ideologies: the scientistic, the humanistic, the managerial and the critical. The program of the scientistic camp in organisation studies is to construct a "scientific" discipline, generally along the natural science model. This group dominates the universities, most professional associations and some journals. It is concerned with developing a descriptive, as opposed to, a normative study of organisations. It is most fully developed as the psychologically oriented field of organizational behaviour. A current representative on the macro end on the spectrum would be population ecology.

The humanistic school is dominated by the organisational development movement. Its proponents include Lewin, Argyris, Bennis, etc. The program of the humanistic school is to develop the full potential of individual human beings. It is concerned with issues such as emotional maturity, open communication, and ethical decision-making as ends in themselves.

The managerial program is the development and appropriation of knowledge in the service of the managerial and capitalist elite. The emphasis is on practical prescription and active intervention in organisations to improve productivity, control, and ultimately, profitability.

The critical grouping is smallest of the four. It is also the only group to explicitly challenge the social, economic, political and organisational status quo. Representatives of the critical ideology would include Clegg and Dunkerley, Heydebrand, Nord, and Perrow. Sample issues would include the study of power, control, and exploitation in the organisation of the labour process.

Given the description of legitimate ideological debate outlined above one's immediate reaction may be to ban it from organisational studies. Unfortunately, this option is not available to us. Scholars are ideologically committed. There is no neutral, value-free position. The belief that there is, or can be, such a position is itself an ideological position of the scientistic camp. Because ideological positions generally include commitment to a set of ontological, epistemological and methodological positions, ideological debate tends to interpenetrate debate at the other levels. This makes disinterested debate at the other levels difficult, or some would hold impossible (e.g., the Frankfurt School which held that epistemology is ideology). In addition, ideological debate may be pursued under the guise [of] ontological, epistemological or methodological issues for tactical reasons. For example, the control of academic journals by the scientistic camp, requires debate [to] appear "unbiased" to gain access to journal space.

The first and most important implication of ideological debate in organisation studies is the simple recognition of its existence and inevitability. This will begin to clarify the issues in many debates. But acknowledging ideology will not make it go away. Gouldner (1970, 1985) suggests a remedy. He calls for constant critique and self-reflexiveness in the practice of social science. This requires a systematic application of the theories and findings we produce about organisations to our own organisation as a theory and findings producing enterprise. This process helps in the attempt to separate what we know from what we hold as an ideological commitment or background assumption.

Scientific Ethos
Harriett Zuckerman

Merton's initial statement held that "the institutional goal of science is the extension of certified knowledge," knowledge comprising "empirically confirmed and logically consistent statements of regularities (. . . in effect, predictions)" ([1942] 1973, 270). As a social institution, science is marked by an

> ethos . . . (or an) affectively toned complex of values and norms which are held to be binding on scientists. The norms are expressed in the form of prescriptions, proscriptions, preferences, and permissions. They are legitimized in terms of institutional values. These imperatives (or norms), transmitted by precept and example and reinforced by sanctions are in varying degrees internalized by the scientist, thus fashioning his scientific conscience. . . . Although the ethos of science has not been codified, it can be inferred from the moral consensus of scientists as expressed in use and wont, in countless writings on the scientific spirit and in moral indignation directed toward contraventions of the ethos ([1942] 1973, 268–269).

This compact paragraph lays out much of the theory: it holds that the institution of science has a distinctive set of norms and values; that these are legitimized by its principal goal, the extension of certified knowledge; that these are transmitted by socialization and reinforced by rewards and punishments; that the ethos or code of science can be inferred from what scientists write about science and from how they behave, particularly from scientists' responses to departures from the posited norms.[1]

Furthermore, "the mores (norms) of science possess a methodologic rationale, but they are binding, not only because they are procedurally efficient but because they are believed right and good" ([1942] 1973, 270). Here the double claim is made that the ethos of science contributes to the institutional goal of advancing knowledge and also has strong expressive significance.

What then are the norms of science that "are expressed in use and *wont* and in countless writings"? The ethos is composed of two sorts of norms: "technical" and "moral" or latterly, cognitive and social. "The technical (or

Source: "The sociology of science" by Harriett Zuckerman, in *The Handbook of Sociology*, edited by Neil J. Smelser, 514–516. Copyright © 1988 by Sage Publications, Inc. Reprinted by permission of Sage Publications, Inc.

1. This Durkheimian indicator of the significance of norms is often overlooked in writings about the ethos of science. This is particularly so for those claiming that since scientists often violate the norms, there can be no normative code to which they subscribe. Since social relations always involve interaction, social responses to violations are as pertinent as the violations themselves (see Zuckerman 1984).

cognitive) norm of empirical evidence, adequate and reliable, is a prerequisite for sustained true prediction; the technical norm of logical consistency, a prerequisite for systematic and valid prediction. The entire structure of technical and moral norms implements the final objective" of extending certified knowledge ([1942] 1973, 270). The moral or social norms were also treated briefly. Just four were proposed in the original statement.

1. The norm of *"universalism"* refers to the requirement that scientific contributions be judged according to "pre-established impersonal criteria." Social attributes of contributors such as their race, religion, class origins, or gender are deemed "irrelevant" in such judgments ([1942] 1973, 270–271). The norm of universalism also requires that scientists be rewarded in accord with the extent of their contributions to science ([1957] 1973).

2. The norm of *"communism,"* or as Barber re-termed it during the McCarthy era, "communalism" (1952, 130), prescribes that knowledge, which is the product of collective effort by the scientific community, must be shared—not kept secret. Indeed, the only way scientists can be sure that they will acquire property rights to their contributions is, paradoxically, to give them away to their scientific peers—that is, to publish them promptly ([1942] 1973, 273–275). As Hull (1985) observes, science is organized so as to make group goals and individual goals coincide; that is, that scientists are "forced" to make their work public or forgo priority and credit for it.

3. *"Disinterestedness,"* or the curbing of personal bias, involves institutional control over the motives for doing science so as to advance scientific knowledge. Put another way, the intrinsic reward of discovering new knowledge and sharing it will elicit other rewards, notably peer recognition. This prescription does not require scientists to feel altruistic—social arrangements depending wholly on altruism are notably unstable—rather, the reward and punishment systems of science generally make it in scientists' own interest to act in such a disinterested manner ([1942] 1973, 275–277).

4. Last, *"organized skepticism"* is "both a methodologic and an institutional mandate" that calls for "the suspension of judgment" until the requisite evidence is there. Once again, in this account of the normative structure of the institution of science, the emphasis is on its institutional arrangements. This calls for "organized" skepticism, for arrangements such as refereeing and other critical appraisals of work by competent peers; not necessarily for each scientist to feel uniformly skeptical. . . .

The ethos of science, as with norms generally, specifies shared expectations or ideals, how scientists should act in their work and vis-à-vis other scientists. No more than in other domains does every scientist uniformly live up to every norm on each and every occasion. In science, as in other institutions, there is often a "painful contrast" between normative expectations and actual behavior (Merton 1976, 40). This "painful contrast" does not mean that the norms of science do not exercise patterned control over behavior any more than occasional homicides mean that norms prohibiting murder are either absent or inconsequential. Sociologists seldom need to be reminded that norms and behavior are never perfectly correlated.

The Value-Oriented Bias of Social Inquiry
Ernest Nagel

We turn, finally, to the difficulties said to confront the social sciences because the social values to which students of social phenomena are committed not only color the contents of their findings but also control their assessment of the evidence on which they based their conclusions. Since social scientists generally differ in their value commitments, the "value neutrality" that seems to be so pervasive in the natural sciences is therefore often held to be impossible in social inquiry. In the judgment of many thinkers, it is accordingly absurd to expect the social sciences to exhibit the unanimity so common among natural scientists concerning what are the established facts and satisfactory explanations for them. Let us examine some of the reasons that have been advanced for these contentions. It will be convenient to distinguish four groups of such reasons, so that our discussion will deal in turn with the alleged role of value judgments in (1) the selection of problems, (2) the determination of the contents of conclusions, (3) the identification of fact, and (4) the assessment of evidence.

1. The reasons perhaps most frequently cited make much of the fact that the things a social scientist selects for study are determined by his conception of what are the socially important values. According to one influential view, for example, the student of human affairs deals only with materials to which he attributes "cultural significance," so that a "value orientation" is inherent in his choice of material for investigation. . . .

It is well-nigh truistic to say that students of human affairs, like students in any other area of inquiry, do not investigate everything, but direct their attention to certain selected portions of the inexhaustible content of concrete reality. Moreover, let us accept the claim, if only for the sake of the argument, that a social scientist addresses himself exclusively to matters which he believes are important because of their assumed relevance to his cultural values. It is not clear, however, why the fact that an investigator selects the materials he studies in the light of problems which interest him and which seem to him to bear on matters he regards as important, is of greater moment for the logic of social inquiry than it is for the logic of any other branch of inquiry. For example, a social scientist may believe that a free economic market embodies a cardinal human value, and he may produce evidence to show that certain kinds of human activities are indispensable to the perpetuation of a free market. If he is concerned with processes which maintain this type of economy rather than some other type, how is this fact more pertinent to the question whether he had adequately evaluated the evidence for his conclusion, than is the bearing upon the analogous question of the fact that a physiologist may be concerned with processes which maintain a constant internal temperature in the human body rather than with something else? The things a social scientist selects for study with a view to determining the conditions or consequences of their existence may indeed be dependent on the indisputable fact that he is a "cultural being." But similarly were we not human beings though still capable of conducting scientific inquiry, we might conceivably have an interest neither in the conditions that maintain a free market, nor in the processes involved in the homeostasis of the internal temperature in human bodies, nor for that matter in the mechanisms that regulate the height of tides, the succession of seasons, or the motions of the planets.

In short, there is no difference between any of the sciences with respect to the fact that the interests of the scientist determine what he selects for investigation. But this fact, by itself, represents no obstacle to the successful pursuit of objectively controlled inquiry in any branch of study.

2. A more substantial reason commonly given for the value-oriented character of social inquiry is that, since the social scientist is himself affected by considerations of right and wrong, his own notions of what constitutes a satisfactory social order and his own standards of personal and social justice do enter, in point of fact, into his analyses of social phenomena. For example, according to one version of this argument, anthropologists must frequently judge whether the means adopted by some society achieves the intended aim (e.g., whether a religious ritual does produce the increased fertility for the sake of which the ritual is performed); and in many cases the adequacy of the means must be judged by admittedly "relative" standards, i.e., in terms of the ends sought or the standards employed by that society, rather than in terms of the anthropologist's own criteria. . . .

It has often been noted, moreover, that the study of social phenomena receives much of its impetus from a strong moral and reforming zeal, so that many ostensibly "objective" analyses in the social sciences are in fact disguised recommendations of social policy. As one typical but moderately expressed statement of the point puts it, a social scientist

> cannot wholly detach the unifying social structure that, as a scientist's theory, guides his detailed investigations of human behavior, from the unifying structure which, as a citizen's ideal, he thinks ought to prevail in human affairs and hopes may sometimes be more fully realized. His

> social theory is thus essentially a program of action along two lines
> which are kept in some measure of harmony with each other by that
> theory—action in assimilating social facts for purposes of systematic
> understanding, and action aiming at progressively molding the social
> pattern, so far as he can influence it, into what he thinks it ought to be.
> (Burtt 1946, 522)

It is surely beyond serious dispute that social scientists do in fact often import their own values into their analyses of social phenomena. It is also undoubtedly true that even thinkers who believe human affairs can be studied with the ethical neutrality characterizing modern inquiries into geometrical or physical relations, and who often pride themselves on the absence of value judgments from their own analyses of social phenomena, do in fact sometimes make such judgments in their social inquirers.[2] Nor is it less evident that students of human affairs often hold conflicting values; that their disagreements on value questions are often the source of disagreements concerning ostensibly factual issues; and that, even if value predications are assumed to be inherently capable of proof or disproof by objective evidence, at least some of the differences between social scientists involving value judgments are not in fact resolved by the procedures of controlled inquiry.

In any event, it is not easy in most areas of inquiry to prevent our likes, aversions, hopes, and fears from coloring our conclusions. It has taken centuries of effort to develop habits and techniques of investigation which help safeguard inquiries in the natural sciences against the intrusion of irrelevant personal factors; and even in these disciplines the protection those procedures give is neither infallible nor complete. The problem is undoubtedly more acute in the study of human affairs, and the difficulties it creates for achieving reliable knowledge in the social sciences must be admitted.

However, the problem is intelligible only on the assumption that there is a relatively clear distinction between factual and value judgments, and that however difficult it may sometimes be to decide whether a given statement has a purely factual content, it is in principle possible to do so. Thus, the claim that social scientists are pursuing the twofold program mentioned in the above quotation makes sense, only if it is possible to distinguish between, on the one hand, contributions to theoretical understanding (whose factual validity presumably does not depend on the social ideal to which a social scientist may subscribe), and on the other hand contributions to the dissemination or realization of some social ideal (which may not be accepted by all social scientists). Accordingly, the undeniable difficulties that stand in the way of obtaining reliable knowledge of human affairs because of the fact that social scientists differ in their value orientations are practical difficulties. The

---

2. For a documented account, see Gunnar Myrdal, *Value in Social Theory*, London, 1958, pp. 134–52.

difficulties are not necessarily insuperable, for since by hypothesis it is not impossible to distinguish between fact and value, steps can be taken to identify a value bias when it occurs, and to minimize if not to eliminate completely its perturbing effects. . . .

Although the recommendation that social scientists make fully explicit their value commitments is undoubtedly salutary, and can produce excellent fruit, it verges on being a counsel of perfection. For the most part we are unaware of many assumptions that enter into our analyses and actions, so that despite resolute efforts to make our preconceptions explicit some decisive ones may not even occur to us. But in any event, the difficulties generated for scientific inquiry by unconscious bias and tacit value orientations are rarely overcome by devout resolutions to eliminate bias. They are usually overcome, often only gradually, through the self-corrective mechanisms of science as a social enterprise. For modern science encourages the invention, the mutual exchange, and the free but responsible criticisms of ideas; it welcomes competition in the quest for knowledge between independent investigators, even when their intellectual orientations are different; and it progressively diminishes the effects of bias by retaining only those proposed conclusions of its inquiries that survive critical examination by an indefinitely large community of students, whatever be their value preferences or doctrinal commitments. It would be absurd to claim that this institutionalized mechanism for sifting warranted beliefs has operated or is likely to operate in social inquiry as effectively as it has in the natural sciences. But it would be no less absurd to conclude that reliable knowledge of human affairs is unattainable merely because social inquiry is frequently value-oriented.

3. There is a more sophisticated argument for the view that the social sciences cannot be value-free. It maintains that the distinction between fact and value assumed in the preceding discussion is untenable when purposive human behavior is being analyzed, since in this context value judgments enter inextricably into what appears to be "purely descriptive" (or factual) statements. Accordingly, those who subscribe to this thesis claim that an ethically neutral social science is in principle impossible, and not simply that it is difficult to attain. For if fact and value are indeed so fused that they cannot even be distinguished, value judgments cannot be eliminated from the social sciences unless all predications are also eliminated from them, and therefore unless these sciences completely disappear. . . .

Moreover, the assumption implicit in the recommendation discussed above for achieving ethical neutrality is often rejected as hopelessly naïve — this is the assumption, it will be recalled, that relations of means to ends can be established without commitment to these ends, so that the conclusions of social inquiry concerning such relations are objective statements which make *conditional* rather than categorical assertions about values. This assumption is said by its critics to rest on the supposition that men attach value only to the ends they seek, and not to the means for realizing their aims. However, the supposition is alleged to be grossly mistaken. For the character of the means one employs to secure some goal affects the nature of the total outcome; and the choice men make between alternative means for obtaining a given end depends on the values they ascribe to those alternatives. In consequence, commitments to specific valuations are said to be involved even in what appear to be purely factual statements about means-ends relations.

We shall not attempt a detailed assessment of this complex argument, for a discussion of the numerous issues it raises would take us far afield. However, three claims made in the course of the argument will be admitted without further comment as indisputably correct: that a large number of characterizations sometimes assumed to be purely factual descriptions of social phenomena do indeed formulate a type of value judgment; that it is often difficult, and in any case usually inconvenient in practice, to distinguish between the purely factual and the "evaluative" contents of many terms employed in the social sciences; and that values are commonly attached to means and not only to ends. However, these admissions do not entail the conclusion that, in a manner unique to the study of purposive human behavior, fact and value are fused beyond the possibility of distinguishing between them. On the contrary, as we shall try to show, the claim that there is such a fusion and that a value-free social science is therefore inherently absurd, confound two quite different senses of the term "value judgment": the sense in which a value judgment expresses *approval or disapproval* either of some moral (or social) ideal, or of some action (or institution) because of a commitment to such an ideal; and the sense in which a value judgment expresses an *estimate* of the degree to which some commonly recognized (and more or less clearly defined) type of action, object, or institution is embodied in a given instance. . . .

4. There remains for consideration the claim that a value-free social science is impossible, because value commitments enter into the very *assessment of evidence* by social scientists, and not simply into the content of the conclusions they advance. This version of the claim itself has a large number of variant forms, but we shall examine only three of them.

The least radical form of the claim maintains that the conceptions held by a social scientist of what constitute cogent evidence or sound intellectual workmanship are the products of his education and his place in society, and are affected by the social values transmitted by this training and associated with this social position; accordingly, the values to which the social scientist is thereby committed determine which statements he *accepts* as well-grounded conclusions about human affairs. In this form, the claim is *factual* thesis, and must be supported by detailed empirical evidence concerning the influences exerted by a man's moral and social values upon what he is ready to acknowledge a sound social analysis. . . .

Another but different form of the claim is based on recent work in theoretical statistics dealing with the assessment of evidence for so-called "statistical hypotheses"—hypotheses concerning the probabilities of random events, such as the hypothesis that the probability of a male human birth is one-half. The central idea relevant to the present question that underlies these developments can be sketched in terms of an example. Suppose that, before a fresh batch of medicine is put on sale, tests are performed on experimental animals for its possible toxic effects because of impurities that have not been eliminated in its manufacture, for example, by introducing small quantities of the drug into the diet of one hundred guinea pigs. If no more than a few of the animals show serious after-effects, the medicine is to be regarded as safe, and will be marketed; but if a contrary result is obtained the drug will be destroyed. Suppose now that three of the animals do in fact become gravely ill. Is this outcome significant (i.e., does it indicate that the drug has toxic effects) or is it perhaps an "accident" that happened because of some peculiarity in the affected animals? To answer the question, the experimenter must *decide* on the basis of the evidence between the hypothesis H_1: the drug is toxic; and the hypothesis H_2: the drug is not toxic. But how is he to decide, if he aims to be "reasonable" rather than arbitrary? Current statistical theory offers him a rule for making a reasonable decision, and bases the rule on the following analysis.

Whatever decision the experimenter may make, he runs the risk of committing either one of two types of errors: he may reject a hypothesis though in fact it is true (i.e., despite the fact that H_1 is actually true, he mistakenly decides against it in the light of the evidence available to him); or he may accept a hypothesis though in fact it is false. His decision would therefore be eminently reasonable, were it based on a rule guaranteeing that no decision ever made in accordance with the rule would commit either type of error. Unhappily, there are no rules of this sort. The next suggestion is to find a rule such that, when decisions are made in accordance with it, the relative frequency of each type of error is quite small. But unfortunately, the risks of committing each type of error are not independent; for example, it is in general logically impossible to find a rule so that decisions based on it will commit each type of error with a relative frequency not greater than one in a thousand. In consequence, before a reasonable rule can be proposed, the experimenter must compare the relative importance to himself of the two types of error, and state what risk he is willing to take of committing the type of error he judges to be the more important one. . . .

Moreover, nothing in the reasoning of theoretical statistics depends on what particular subject matter is under discussion when a decision between alternative statistical hypotheses is to be made. For the reasoning is entirely general; and reference to some special subject matter becomes relevant only when a definite numerical value is to be assigned to the risk some investigator is prepared to take of making an erroneous decision concerning a given hypothesis. Accordingly, if current statistical theory is used to support the claim that value commitments enter into the assessment of evidence for statistical hypotheses in social inquiry, statistical theory can be used with equal justification to support analogous claims for all other inquiries as well. In short, the claim we have been discussing establishes no difficulty that supposedly occurs in the search for reliable knowledge in the study of human affairs which is not also encountered in the natural sciences.

A third form of this claim is the most radical of all. It differs from the first variant mentioned above in maintaining that there is a necessary *logical* connection, and not merely a contingent or causal one, between the "social perspective" of a student of human affairs and his standards of competent social inquiry, and in consequence the influence of the special values to which he is committed because of his own social involvements is not eliminable. This version of the claim is implicit in Hegel's account of the "dialectical" nature of human history and is integral to much Marxist as well as non-Marxist philosophy that stresses the "historically relative" character of social thought. In any event, it is commonly based on the assumption that, since social institutions and their cultural products are constantly changing, the intellectual apparatus required for understanding them must also change; and every idea employed for this purpose is therefore adequate only for some particular stage in the development of human affairs. Accordingly, neither the substantive concepts adopted for classifying and interpreting social phenomena, nor the logical canons used for estimating the worth of such concepts, have a "timeless validity"; there is no analysis of social phenomena which is not the expression of some special social standpoint, or which does not reflect the interests and values dominant in some sector of the human scene at a certain stage of its history. In consequence, although a sound distinction can be made in the natural sciences between the origin of a man's views and their factual validity, such a distinction allegedly cannot be made in social inquiry; and prominent exponents of "historical relativism" have therefore challenged the universal adequacy of the thesis that "the genesis of a proposition is under all circumstances irrelevant to its truth. . . ."

In brief, the various reasons we have been examining for the intrinsic impossibility of securing objective (i.e., value-free and unbiased) conclusions in the social sciences do not establish what they purport to establish, even though in some instances they direct attention to undoubtedly important practical difficulties frequently encountered in these disciplines.

Whose Side Are We On?
Howard S. Becker

To have values or not to have values: the question is always with us. When sociologists undertake to study problems that have relevance to the world we live in, they find themselves caught in a crossfire. Some urge them not to take sides, to be neutral and do research that is technically correct and value free. Others tell them their work is shallow and useless if it does not express a deep commitment to a value position.

This dilemma, which seems so painful to so many, actually does not exist, for one of its horns is imaginary. For it to exist, one would have to assume, as some apparently do, that it is indeed possible to do research that is un-contaminated by personal and political sympathies. I propose to argue that it is not possible and, therefore, that the question is not whether we should take sides, since we inevitably will, but rather whose side we are on. . . .

In the greatest variety of subject matter areas and in work done by all the different methods at our disposal, we cannot avoid taking sides, for reasons firmly based in social structure. . . .

I will look first, however, not at the truth or falsity of the charge [of bias], but rather at the circumstances in which it is typically made and felt. The sociology of knowledge cautions us to distinguish between the truth of a statement and an assessment of the circumstances under which that statement is made; though we trace an argument to its source in the interests of the person who made it, we have still not proved it false. Recognizing the point and promising to address it eventually, I shall turn to the typical situations in which the accusation of bias arises.

When do we accuse ourselves and our fellow sociologist of bias? I think an inspection of representative instances would show that the accusation arises, in one important class of cases, when the research gives credence, in any serious way, to the perspective of the subordinate group in some hierarchical relationship [where] the hierarchical relationship is a moral one. The superordinate parties in the relationship are those who represent the forces of approved and official morality; the subordinate parties are those who, it is alleged, have violated that morality.

. . . Similar situations, and similar feelings that our work is biased, occur in the study of schools, hospitals, asylums and prisons, in the study of physical as well as mental illness, in the study of both "normal" and delinquent youth. In these situations, the superordinate parties are usually the official and professional authorities in charge of some important institution,

Source: "Whose side are we on?" by Howard S. Becker. Reprinted from *Social Problems* 14, no. 3 (Winter 1967): 239–247, by permission. Copyright © 1966 The Society for the Study of Social Problems.

while the subordinates are those who make use of the services of that institution. Thus, the police are the superordinates, drug addicts are the subordinates; professors and administrators, principals and teachers, are the superordinates, while students and pupils are the subordinates; physicians are the superordinates, their patients the subordinates.

All of these cases represent one of the typical situations in which researchers accuse themselves and are accused of bias. It is a situation in which, while conflict and tension exist in the hierarchy, the conflict has not become openly political. The conflicting segments or ranks are not organized for conflict; no one attempts to alter the shape of the hierarchy. While subordinates may complain about the treatment they receive from those above them, they do not propose to move to a position of equality with them, or to reverse positions in the hierarchy. Thus, no one proposes that addicts should make and enforce laws for policemen, that patients should prescribe for doctors, or that adolescents should give orders to adults. We can call this the *apolitical* case.

In the second case, the accusation of bias is made in a situation that is frankly political. The parties to the hierarchical relationship engage in organized conflict, attempting either to maintain or change existing relations of power and authority. Whereas in the first case subordinates are typically unorganized and thus have, as we shall see, little to fear from a researcher, subordinate parties in a political situation may have much to lose. When the situation is political, the researcher may accuse himself or be accused of bias by someone else when he gives credence to the perspective of either party to this political conflict. I leave the political for later and turn now to the problem of bias in apolitical situations.

We provoke the suspicion that we are biased in favor of the subordinate parties in an apolitical arrangement when we tell the story from their point of view. We may, for instance, investigate their complaints, even though they are subordinates, about the way things are run just as though one ought to give their complaints as much credence as the statements of responsible officials. We provoke the charge when we assume, for the purposes of our research, that subordinates have as much right to be heard as superordinates, that they are as likely to be telling the truth as they see it as superordinates, that what they say about the institution has a right to be investigated and have its truth or falsity established, even though responsible officials assure us that it is unnecessary because the charges are false.

We can use the notion of a *hierarchy of credibility* to understand this phenomenon. In any system of ranked groups, participants take it as given that members of the highest group have the right to define the way things really are. In any organization, no matter what the rest of the organization chart shows, the arrows indicating the flow of information point up, thus demonstrating (at least formally) that those at the top have access to a more complete picture of what is going on than anyone else. Members of lower groups will have incomplete information, and their view of reality will be partial and distorted in consequence. Therefore, from the point of view of a well-socialized participant in the system, any tale told by those at the top intrinsically deserves to be regarded as the most credible account obtainable of the organizations' workings. And since, as Sumner pointed out, matters of rank and status are contained in the mores, this belief has a moral quality. We are, if we are proper members of the group, morally bound to accept the definition imposed on reality by a superordinate group in preference to the definitions espoused by subordinates. (By analogy, the same argument holds for the social classes of a community.) Thus, credibility and the right to be heard are differentially distributed through the ranks of the system.

As sociologists, we provoke the charge of bias, in ourselves and others, by refusing to give credence and deference to an established status order, in which knowledge of truth and the right to be heard are not equally distributed. "Everyone knows" that responsible professionals know more about things than laymen, that police are more respectable and their words ought to be taken more seriously than those of the deviants and criminals with whom they deal. By refusing to accept the hierarchy of credibility, we express disrespect for the entire established order. . . .

. . . It is odd that, when we perceive bias, we usually see it in these circumstances. It is odd because it is easily ascertained that a great many more studies are biased in the direction of the interests of responsible officials than the other way around. . . .

Why this disproportion in the direction of accusations of bias? Why do we more often accuse those who are on the side of subordinates than those who are on the side of superordinates? Because, when we make the former accusation, we have, like the well-socialized members of our society most of us are, accepted the hierarchy of credibility and taken over the accusation made by responsible officials.

The reason responsible officials make the accusation so frequently is precisely because they are responsible. They have been entrusted with the care and operation of one or another of our important institutions: schools, hospitals, law enforcement, or whatever. They are the ones who, by virtue of their official position and the authority that goes with it, are in a position to "do something" when things are not what they should be and, similarly, are the ones who will be held to account if they fail to "do something" or if what they do is, for whatever reason, inadequate.

Because they are responsible in this way, officials usually have to lie. That is a gross way of putting it, but not inaccurate. Officials must lie because things are seldom as they ought to be. For a great variety of reasons, well-known to sociologists, institutions are refractory. They do not perform as society would like them to. Hospitals do not cure people; prisons do not rehabilitate prisoners; schools do not educate students. Since they are supposed to, officials develop ways both of denying the failure of the institution to perform as it should and explaining those failures which cannot be hidden. An account of an institution's operation from the point of view of subordinates therefore casts doubt on the official line and may possibly expose it as a lie.

For reasons that are a mirror image of those of officials, subordinates in an apolitical hierarchical relationship have no reason to complain of the bias of sociological research oriented toward the interests of superordinates. Subordinates typically are not organized in such a fashion as to be responsible for the overall operation of an institution. . . . The lack of organization among subordinate members of an institutionalized relationship means that, having no responsibility for the group's welfare, they likewise have no complaints if someone maligns it. The sociologist who favors officialdom will be spared the accusation of bias.

And thus we see why we accuse ourselves of bias only when we take the side of the subordinate. It is because, in a situation that is not openly political, with the major issues defined as arguable, we join responsible officials and the man in the street in an unthinking acceptance of the hierarchy of credibility. We assume with them that the man at the top knows best. We do not realize that there are sides to be taken and that we are taking one of them.

The same reasoning allows us to understand why the researcher has the same worry about the effect of his sympathies on his work as his uninvolved colleague. The hierarchy of credibility is a feature of society whose existence we cannot deny, even if we disagree with its injunction to believe the man at the top. When we acquire sufficient sympathy with subordinates to see things from their perspective, we know that we are flying in the face of what "everyone knows." The knowledge gives us pause and causes us to share, however briefly, the doubt of our colleagues.

When a situation has been defined politically, the second type of case I want to discuss, matters are quite different. Subordinates have some degree of organization and, with that, spokesmen, their equivalent of responsible officials. Spokesmen, while they cannot actually be held responsible for what members of their group do, make assertions on their behalf and are held responsible for the truth of those assertions. The group engages in political activity designed to change existing hierarchical relationships and the credibility of its spokesmen directly affects its political fortunes. Credibility is not the only influence, but the group can ill-afford having the definition of reality proposed by its spokesmen discredited, for the immediate consequence will be some loss of political power.

Superordinate groups have their spokesmen too, and they are confronted with the same problem: to make statements about reality that are politically effective without being easily discredited. The political fortunes of the superordinate group—its ability to hold the status changes demanded by lower groups to a minimum—do not depend as much on credibility, for the group has other kinds of power available as well.

When we do research in a political situation we are in double jeopardy, for the spokesmen of both involved groups will be sensitive to the implications of our work. Since they propose openly conflicting definitions of reality, our statement of our problem is in itself likely to call into question and make problematic, at least for the purposes of our research, one or the other definition. And our results will do the same.

The hierarchy of credibility operates in a different way in the political situation than it does in the apolitical one. In the political situation, it is precisely one of the things at issue. Since the political struggle calls into question the legitimacy of the existing rank system, it necessarily calls into question at the same time the legitimacy of the associated judgments of credibility. Judgments of who has a right to define the nature of reality that are taken for granted in an apolitical situation become matters of argument.

Oddly enough, we are, I think, less likely to accuse ourselves and one another of bias in a political than in an apolitical situation, for at least two reasons. First, because the hierarchy of credibility has been openly called into question, we are aware that there are at least two sides to the story and so do not think it unseemly to investigate the situation from one or another of the contending points of view. We know, for instance, that we must grasp the perspectives of both the resident of Watts and of the Los Angeles policeman if we are to understand what went on in that outbreak.

Second, it is no secret that most sociologists are politically liberal to one degree or another. Our political preferences dictate the side we will be on and since those preferences are shared by most of our colleagues, few are ready to throw the first stone or are even aware that stone-throwing is a possibility. We usually take the side of the underdog. . . .

We are thus apt to take sides with equal innocence and lack of thought, though for different reasons, in both apolitical and political situations. In the first, we adopt the commonsense view which awards unquestioned credibility to the responsible official. (This is not to deny that a few of us, because something in our experience has alerted them to the possibility, may question the conventional hierarchy of credibility in the special area of our expertise.) In the second case, we take our politics so for granted that it supplants convention in dictating whose side we will be on. (I do not deny, either, that some few sociologists may deviate politically from their liberal colleagues, either to the right or the left, and thus be more liable to question that convention.)

In any event, even if our colleagues do not accuse us of bias in research in a political situation, the interested parties will. . . .

What I have said so far is all sociology of knowledge, suggesting by whom, in what situations and for what reasons sociologists will be accused of bias and distortion. I have not yet addressed the question of the truth of the accusations, of whether our findings are distorted by our sympathy for those we study. I have implied a partial answer, namely, that there is no position from which sociological research can be done that is not biased in one or another way.

We must always look at the matter from someone's point of view. The scientist who proposes to understand society must, as Mead long ago pointed out, get into the situation enough to have a perspective on it. And it is likely that his perspective will be greatly affected by whatever positions are taken by any or all of the other participants in that varied situation. Even if his participation is limited to reading in the field, he will necessarily read the arguments of partisans of one or another side to a relationship and will thus be affected, at least, by having suggested to him what the relevant arguments and issues are. . . .

We can never avoid taking sides. So we are left with the question of whether taking sides means that some distortion is introduced into our work so great as to make it useless. Or, less drastically, whether some distortion is introduced that must be taken into account before the results of our work can be used. I do not refer here to feeling that the picture given by the research is not "balanced," the indignation aroused by having a conventionally discredited definition of reality given priority or equality with what "everyone knows," for it is clear that we cannot avoid that. That is the problem of officials, spokesmen and interested parties, not ours. Our problem is to make sure that, whatever point of view we take, our research meets the standards of good scientific work, that our unavoidable sympathies do not render our results invalid.

We might distort our findings, because of our sympathy with one of the parties in the relationship we are studying, by misusing the tools and techniques of our discipline. We might introduce loaded questions into a questionnaire, or act in some way in a field situation such that people would be constrained to tell us only the kind of thing we are already in sympathy with. All of our research techniques are hedged about with precautionary measures designed to guard against these errors. Similarly, though more abstractly, every one of our theories presumably contains a set of directives which exhaustively covers the field we are to study, specifying all the things we are to look at and take into account in our research. By using our theories and techniques impartially, we ought to be able to study all the things that need to be studied in such a way as to get all the facts we require, even though some of the questions that will be raised and some of the facts that will be produced run counter to our biases. . . .

Values in Inquiry
Abraham Kaplan

The term "value"—"that unfortunate child of misery," as Weber (1949, 107) has called it—has two sorts of meanings (among many others). It may refer to the standards or principles of worth, what makes something have value, or it may refer to the worthy things themselves, the valuables, as it were (I shall be using the term "value" only in the first sense). Now while valuables have often before been felt to be uncertain, whether in possession or attainment, there has not often been any deep and pervasive doubt as to values, that is, as to whether such things are really valuable, really worth having and pursuing. It is this latter that is now very much in question. There have been various philosophers, like the Greek Sophists and the Cārvākas of India, who challenged the basis of the value judgments characteristic of their cultures; but by and large philosophers have been occupied with examining the specific varieties of value, and the conditions, personal or institutional, under which the values can be achieved. In modern times, however, and most notably in contemporary Anglo-American philosophy, there is an almost exclusive preoccupation with the basis of value judgments rather than with their content. We have still some sense of what is true, honorable, just, pure, lovely, or gracious, and we think of these things; but we do not any more really know what we are saying about things when we ascribe to them these excellences. . . .

The thesis I want to defend is that not all value concerns are unscientific, that indeed some of them are called for by the scientific enterprise itself, and that those which run counter to scientific ideals can be brought under control—even by the sciences most deeply implicated in the value process.

Bias

Let me use the term *bias* for adherence to values of such a kind or in such a way as to interfere with scientific objectivity, and let me use it without prejudging whether scientific objectivity requires that science be absolutely value-free. Then, by definition, bias is methodologically objectionable, but the question is still open whether values play a part in the scientific enterprise only as biases. I shall want to answer this question in the negative, and to insist further that this wish is not a matter merely of my own bias. . . .

I believe that it is the distinction between motives and purposes which underlies the appeal so often made to the difference between the role of the scientist and the role of the citizen, religionist, father, lover, or whatever. Yet

Source: *The conduct of inquiry* by Abraham Kaplan (San Francisco, CA: Chandler Publishing, 1964), 370–386.

each of these roles may define its own purposes, which are not to be confused with the motives that govern the choice of the role in question. There are right ways and wrong ways to do everything, whatever the reasons we may have for doing it.

Bias, then, is not constituted merely by having motives, that is, by subscribing to values which are somehow involved in the scientific situation. Everything depends on the conduct of the inquiry, on the way in which we arrive at our conclusions. Freedom from bias means having an open mind, not an empty one. At the heart of every bias is a prejudice, that is to say, a prejudgment, a conclusion arrived at prior to the evidence and maintained independently of the evidence. It is true that what serves as evidence is the result of a process of interpretation—facts do not speak for themselves; nevertheless, facts must be given a hearing, or the scientific point to the process of interpretation is lost. . . .

. . . Prejudice is betrayed in the determination to adhere to a certain belief no matter what evidence is brought forward. It is this determination or an approximation to it, and not merely having an interest in one conclusion rather than another, which constitutes bias. . . . In behavioral science, the scale of radicalism-conservatism may well be "the master scale of biases" (Myrdal 1944, 1038), affecting both the problems chosen for treatment and the conclusions drawn about whether and how they are to be solved. And everywhere in the scientific enterprise power structures develop, whose interests may have as much effect on the course of inquiry, or at least on the assessment of its outcome, as is exerted by comparable forces on the workings of their enterprises. The influence of the Academy may be as objectionable in science as it is in art. Even the culture as a whole has been a massive source of bias, as it no doubt continues to be; and for behavioral science it is especially true, as Boring put it (in Frank 1961, 195), that "what may be said of the big *Zeitgeist* may also be said of the little *Zeitgeist* of schools and of the egoist who has no following. They have their inflexible attitudes and beliefs, their loyalties that are prejudices, and their prejudices that are loyalties."

Every scientist is committed to resisting bias wherever he encounters it, and if we see that he is keen to detect the mote in his neighbor's eye, let us remember that he in turn is *our* neighbor, and beware of judging him. Fortunately, science does not demand that bias be eliminated but only that our judgment take it into account. It can be treated as we are accustomed to deal with errors of observation: we insulate ourselves from them where we can, and otherwise try to cancel their effects or at any rate to discount them. . . .

I believe that the profound significance for science of freedom of thought and its expression is this, that only thereby can we hope to cancel bias. The power structures in science can be relied on to serve the general welfare of the scientific community only if they are subject to some system, however, informal, of checks and balances, so that what is rejected by one journal or professional association may find acceptance in another. Perhaps even more important is what Derek Price has called the "invisible university" of our time, constituted by the personal exchange of ideas among highly mobile scientists. That free competition in the marketplace of ideas will invariably yield up the truth may be as much a myth as the more general belief that such a process is the source of every social good. The conflict between freedom and control is an existential dilemma for science, whatever it may be for society at large. Yet for science, at any rate, it seems to me that reason requires that we push always for freedom, freedom even for the thought which we enlightened ones so clearly see to be mistaken.

The question may now be considered whether values play any part in the scientific enterprise in ways which do not necessarily constitute bias. I believe that they do, and in a number of different ways.

Values as Subject-Matter

To start with, values occur as subject-matter for scientific investigation. In this capacity they do not in the least make for bias, because what is being inquired into is their existence, not their validity (Weber 1949, 39). We ask what values are held by various persons and groups, under what conditions and with what effect, and plainly, no answer that we give in itself commits us to sharing or rejecting those values. . . .

The fundamental point is that a proposition affirming something about values is different from a valuation—unless what is being affirmed is precisely the *value* of those values, that is, their validity or worth. Let me call such affirmations *value judgments*; they constitute a special class of judgments about values, namely, those for which making the judgment expresses the judger's own values. Plainly, not every statement which we make about someone's values says something about our own; the statement may be a "factual" one, as it is called, even if it is about values. The recurrent difficulty here is that it is not always easy to see just what a statement does say in this respect, and even the man making it may be unclear in his own mind. The language of behavioral science is marked by *normative ambiguity*, allowing for interpretation both as reporting a value and as making a valuation. This ambiguity is obviously present in statements about what is "normal" or "natural," but it may also be present in such less obvious cases as "lawful" or "rational." What is worse, normative ambiguity is only temporarily removed at best, by changing notations. . . .

Values in the Ethics of the Profession

Values occur in a second way in science without making for bias, as constituting the ethics of the profession; here, indeed, they work to eradicate bias, or at least to minimize it and to mitigate its effects. That certain professional pursuits have moral prerequisites is beyond question; I am saying, in the broadest sense of the term "moral," the same of scientific pursuits. In our society it is usually taken for granted that moral prerequisites will be satisfied by those entering politics, medicine, or the church, and that such prerequisites are absent or irrelevant for the army, business, and the law. Science, like the philosophy from which it sprang, has equivocal status. The love of wisdom or truth is a virtue, yet the first sin was eating of the fruit of the tree of knowledge, and the myth of Faust—that those who seek knowledge sell their souls to the Devil—is thought by many, especially today, to convey a dismal reality.

Yet the expression "a good scientist," as used by scientists themselves, seems to me rather more like "a good man" than like "a good Nazi": it embodies a valuation, conveying an appraisal rather than merely a characterization. Being a scientist in itself commits a man to the values embodied in being a good one. We might say that science is a calling and not an occupation only, or at any rate, that it cannot flourish if it is always an occupation only. And the difference between these two sorts of pursuit lies in this, that we choose an occupation while a calling chooses us; we are impelled to the calling from within, which is to say that we are committed to its values. To be sure, all purposive behavior has its own goals and therefore its own values. But in the case of an occupation the values enter only into the purpose (in the narrow sense introduced earlier), and not also into the motives. The values are operative only in the limited context of the purposive behavior, but the purpose which the behavior is to fulfill may have no intrinsic importance, calling for no emotional investments and not reaching beyond the peripheral regions of the personality.

But the passion for truth is just that—a passion: and the thirst for knowledge may be as insistent and provide as deep satisfactions as do needs less specifically human. To follow his calling, even to do his work, a scientist must have what Aristotle called the "intellectual virtues"; and he must not only have them, but also regard them as virtues, that is, seek and cherish them. In a word, they must be his values.

Thus, the scientific habit of mind is one dominated by the reality principle, by the determination to live in the world as it is and not as we might fantasy it. For the scientist, ignorance is never bliss. A robust sense of reality, in William James's phrase, is above all a willingness to face life with open eyes, whatever may confront our sight. The scientist is humble before the facts, submitting his will to their decision, and accepting their judgment whatever it might be. This humility of his is counterpoised by integrity and honesty, by the courage of his convictions, and—if I may paraphrase—by firmness in the truth as God gives him to see the truth, and not as it is given him by tradition, by the Academy, or by the powers that be. And there is a certain distinctive scientific temper, marked by judiciousness and caution, care and consciousness. How far all this view is from the model—or rather, the myth—of science as the work of a disembodied, unfeeling intellect! Surely these attributes of the scientist are all virtues, in the scientist's judgment, as well as in our own; and surely the possession of these virtues is a value to which the scientist has wholeheartedly committed himself. . . .

There is also a *metaprofessional ethics* (not to be confused with the "metaethics" which philosophers today profess), a set of values concerning, not the conduct of inquiry, but the contexts in which it is carried out. The metaprofessional values consist of the commitments to create and maintain conditions under which science can exist—for instance, freedom of inquiry, of thought, and of its expression. Such values are particularly important to the behavioral scientist, for it is he who suffers most from restrictions on those freedoms. . . .

Values in the Selection of Problems

Values enter into science, in the third place, as a basis for the selection of problems, the order in which they are dealt with, and the resources expended on their solution. Weber (1949, 21) seems to contrast "the social sciences" with "the empirical disciplines" in that the problems of the former "are selected by the value-relevance of the phenomena treated." But so may be the problems of any kind of subject-matter. The contrast, if any, is just that behavioral science deals with matters where the values involved are likely to be more conspicuous, and perhaps more widely shared, or more directly affecting many people. Whatever problems a scientist selects, he selects for a reason, and these reasons can be expected to relate to his values, or to the values of those who in one way or another influence his choice.

This obvious point is often obscured, I think, by a too facile distinction between so-called "pure" and "applied" science, as though values are involved only in the latter. In fact, much of what is called "applied" science can be seen as such only in a subsequent reconstruction: a theory is developed in the course of dealing with a problem of so-called "application," it is abstracted from such contexts, then afterwards referred back to them as "applied science." A great deal of science, in other words, is "applied" long before it is "pure." The fact that a scientist has reasons for his choice of problems other than a thirst for knowledge or a love of truth scarcely implies that his inquiry will be biased thereby. . . .

Values and Meanings

Values also plays a part in science, and especially in behavioral science, as determinants of the *meanings* which are seen in the events with which it deals. But here the confusion between act meaning and action meaning is especially dangerous.

Weber, for example, has argued (1949, 80) that behavioral science cannot even have a subject-matter except as marked out by certain values: "Knowledge of cultural events is inconceivable except on a basis of the significance which the concrete constellations of reality have for us in certain individual situations. In which sense and in which situations this is the case . . . is decided according to the value-ideas in the light of which we view 'culture' in each individual case." Interpretation he then defines (1949, 143) as the consideration of the "various possible relationships of the object to values." Very well; but the question is, whose values? Cultural events must have a significance, or they are only biophysical occurrences, but in this respect it is not, as he says, the significance which they have for us which matters. It is the significance for the actor (and those interacting with him) which makes an act a determinate action. . . .

With respect to action meaning, however, the situation is quite different. Here it is a matter of the sorts of conceptualizations we will apply, the formulations we will give to the problem, the hypotheses we will entertain, and the theories we will invoke. In all these we are making choices, and our values inescapably play a part. Here it is significance for us which is involved, though this involvement does not make our interpretation pejoratively "subjective." . . .

. . . The point is that in most of their application these ways of formulating both problems and solutions are to some degree metaphoric, conceptualizing their subject-matters as though they were something other than what they actually are. But our own metaphors always tend to present themselves to us as literal truths. They are the ways of speaking which make sense to us, not just as being meaningful but as being sensible, significant, to the point. They are basic to semantic explanation and thereby enter into scientific explanation. If there is bias here it consists chiefly in the failure to recognize that other ways of putting things might prove equally effective in carrying inquiry forward. But that we must choose one way or another, and thus give our values a role in the scientific enterprise, surely does not in itself mean that we are methodologically damned.

Values and Facts

But the judgment whether a particular choice is an effective one is itself in some degree a matter of our values. Whether a particular way of conceptualizing problems yields solutions for them is a question of fact, but values enter into the determination of what constitutes a *fact*. Here is the central issue in the question whether science ought to be, or even can be, value-free. I am not referring to the effect of values on the willingness to embark on an inquiry into a question of fact. Here, indeed, we are likely to encounter bias, as in the refusal of Galileo's colleagues to look through his telescope, or in the difference between British and American attitudes today toward psychic research or investigations of telepathy (or, for that matter, in my own felt need to disclaim any belief in such phenomena whenever I mention them). What is at stake here is the role of values, not in our decisions where to look but in our conclusions as to what we have seen.

Nature might better be spoken of as an obedient child than as a protective mother: she speaks only when spoken to, is often seen but seldom heard. Data come to us only in answer to questions, and it is we who decide not only whether to ask but also how the question is to be put. Every question is a little like the wife-beating one—it has its own presuppositions. It must be formulated in a language with a determinate vocabulary and structure, the contemporary equivalent of Kant's forms and categories of the knowing mind; and it follows upon determinate assumptions and hypotheses, on which the answer is to bear. How we put the question reflects our values on the one hand, and on the other hand helps determine the answer we get. If, as Kant said, the mind is the lawgiver to nature, it also has a share in facts, for these are not independent of the laws in terms of which we interpret and acknowledge their factuality. Data are the product of a process of interpretation, and though there is some sense in which the material for this process are "given" it is only the product which has a scientific status and function. In a word, data have meaning, and this word "meaning," like its cognates "significance" and "import," includes a reference to values. "The empirical data," says Weber (1949, 111), "are always related to those evaluative ideas which alone make them worth knowing and the significance of the empirical data is derived from these evaluative ideas."

There are behavioral scientists who, in their anxieties about bias, hope to exclude values by eschewing theories altogether, in the spirit (but not in the meaning!) of Newton's "I invent no hypotheses!" They restrict themselves to what they regard as "just describing what objectively happens." But this restriction expresses "the dogma of immaculate perception" all over again. What is thus being attempted simply cannot be done, or if it is done, the outcome is of no scientific significance. . . .

Nagel has argued (in Madden 1960, 193) that "there is no factual evidence to show that the 'content and form' of statements, or the standards of validity employed, are logically determined by the social perspective of an inquirer. The facts commonly cited establish no more than some kind of causal dependence between these items." This argument is sound if "logical determination" has the sense of entailment; indeed, no factual evidence can possibly be given for an entailment. But this is not to say that what is "no more than some kind of casual dependence" can have no methodological import. To ignore some of the evidence, for example, is illogical: even though ignoring it does not *entail* that the conclusions arrived at will be false or even improbable, the ignoring may well cause us to arrive at false conclusions. The more basic point, perhaps, is that even though values are not *sufficient* to establish facts it does not follow that they are therefore not *necessary*. The ultimate empiricism on which science rests consists in this, that thinking something is so does not make it so, and this negation applies even more forcibly, if possible, to wishing it were so.

Summary

As we have seen, the beliefs and values of ideologies, along with the other components of the philosophic context, frame or shape all other aspects of inquiry. And we have also been able to see that there are ideological alternatives and hence important choices.

What should we believe? What should we value? In what ways do our ideologies and values constrain and focus our choice of research questions, strategies, methods, and choice of meanings? If we are aware of these largely implicit preferences, to what degree might we neutralize their impact? Should we aspire to a value-free organizational science or not? Must inquiry always be both social and political? What are the consequences for organizational science if just one ideology dominates? Can serious inquiry embrace a variety of values—say, situationally pragmatic as well as universal ones? These and related questions require thoughtful choices—choices usefully conditioned by many other factors discussed in other parts of this book, such as schools of thought, which follows in Chapter 7.

Allegiances to Schools of Thought

The most difficult thing in science, as in other fields, is to shake off accepted views.

— *George Sarton*

Methodology is a function of the society that produces it—to work with any methodology is a political act.

—*Johan Galtung*

Theoretical-Methodological Subcultures

The last core assumptive component of the paradigmatic frame that we have termed "philosophic context" is schools of thought. Schools of thought—and there are usually several in most fields—are a theoretical-methodological community. They are "theoretical" in that they are centered around a coherent conceptual explanation of some observed or experienced phenomena. They are "methodological" in that there are preferred, and therefore common, research strategies, designs, and methods. They are a "community" in that there is a set of inquirers mostly known to one another who share (and sometimes actively defend) a common philosophic perspective and research modality as well as a phenomenological focus.

Schools of thought are in effect subcultures of inquiry within intellectual disciplines and fields. They share basic assumptions, as well as beliefs and values, about what is meaningful and therefore tend to adhere to particular rules (not often articulated) for choosing research topics, designing and doing research, compiling findings, and so on—that is, they share rules for making meanings (Lundberg 2001) and producing a communal store of texts and discourses. Because all intellectual terrains are inherently contestable, debates and similar contests for hegemony are almost always between schools of thought. While schools of thought can be ranked according to their status and prestige at a point in time, their popularity comes and goes, and they split and merge over time—sometimes because of explanatory merit, but sometimes because of personal rivalries, resource control, public opinion, and other institutional factors.

TABLE 7-1

Examples of schools of thought and associated problematic and interpretive frameworks

Major problematic	Interpretative framework	Illustrative major schools of thought/spokespersons
Rationality	Order	Classical organization theory, scientific management, decision theory/Taylor, Fayol, Simon
Integration	Consensus	Human relations, neo-human resources, functionalism, contingency theory, systems theory, corporate culture/Durkheim, Barnard, Mayo, Parsons
Market	Liberty	Theory of the firm, institutional economics, transaction costs, agency theory, resource dependency, population ecology, liberal organization theory/Williamson, Pfeffer, Hannan and Freeman
Power	Domination	Neoradical Weberians, critical-structural Marxism, labor process, institutional theory/Weber, Marx
Knowledge	Control	Ethnomethod, organizational culture-symbol, post-structuralist, post-industrial, post-Fordist modern, actor-network theory/Foucault, Garfinkel
Justice	Participation	Business ethics, morality and organizational behavior, industrial democracy, participation theory, critical theory/Habermas

SOURCE: Adapted from M. Reed (1996): 34.

The theoretical-methodological core of a school of thought is first articulated in a particular sociohistorical context, which if amenable allows the school to root and grow. Compelling theories and methods often require more than empirical confirmation and use. Usually they gain attention and adherents when they speak to a major problematic or a societal concern within an ascendant interpretive perspective—for instance, Argyris's humanistic theory of how typical organizations stultify personality came in the postwar affluent American 1950s; Deming's statistics-based model for increasing quality and productivity became popular when America felt Japan's competitive strength. Other examples of the problematic-interpretive framework context of major schools of thought are shown in Table 7-1. Schools of thought are typically identified by reference to some combination of the theory or methodology adduced, the geographical place where the theory initially was promoted and flowered, or an early or prominent spokesperson. Examples of prominent identifiers are shown in Figure 7-1. Reputable, articulate spokespersons attract and socialize disciples. Rapid developing or insight producing or highly visible schools of thought require both adherents and recognition—that is, allegiance.

A school of thought, once established, has both functional and dysfunctional consequences. On the one hand, a school of thought engenders research and theory refinements—that is, it provides justifications for

	Place	Person
Theory	Tavistock Institute/sociotechnical systems Aston/strategic contingencies theory Harvard Business School/human relations	Weber/bureaucracy Hannan & Freeman/population ecology House/path-goal theory
Method	Cornell University/participative action research Survey Research Center (Michigan)/survey feedback	Van Maanen/ethnomethodology Mitroff/stakeholder analysis G. Morgan/metaphors

FIGURE **7-1**   Examples of school of thought identifiers

explanatory claims, provides identity for researchers and their organizations, sometimes promotes cross-organization or cross-national research, and, often, is where real advances in knowledge occur. On the other hand, schools of thought contain the seeds of bias (see Kaplan, Chapter 6) and conformity, narrow the avenues of creativity, and may subtly foster strategies of either verification or falsification (see Chapter 8). The social products of schools of thought can take many forms: common social products are approximations of reality, a meaningful interpretation, a legitimating myth, an instrument for effecting change, and so on. Each school of thought develops criteria for deciding what constitutes a contribution to knowledge. This is accomplished through norms for what members regard as good research, through particular technical training and norm inculcation of new members, through review norms, sanctions that threaten recognition or status loss, and the like. A school of thought may be understood, like any subculture, as varying structurally from relatively rigid and unyielding (Kuhn 1970) to relatively permeable and open to modification (Toulmin 1953). All too often differences among schools of thought reflect the outcomes of power and politics, not inquiry. The pluralism of schools of thought that currently exists in the organization sciences dismays some. Pfeffer (1993), for example, opinions that, "the domain of organization theory is coming to resemble more of a weed patch than a well-tended garden. Theories . . . proliferate along with measures, terms, concepts. . . . It is often difficult to discern in what direction knowledge of organizations is progressing" (p. 616). Others, such as Fabian (2000), would justify allowing proliferation as long as the inevitable controversy is fully debated with an awareness of the philosophic differences influencing discourse.

In the single selection that follows, Richard Whitley shows the importance of sociohistorical context for the growth of organizational science theorizing as well as its expanding variety.

An Expanding Variety: Management Schools of Thought
Richard Whitley

One of the fields most affected by the changes sketched above, especially the decline of Fordism and expansion of higher education has been business and management studies. Indeed, its institutionalization as a research-based science in many university systems is a largely post-war phenomenon dependent upon the growth of academic positions and the success of science-based problem-solving (Locke 1989, 1996). . . .

Management research is explicitly concerned with producing useful knowledge and draws upon ideas and concepts from many social sciences in addition to formal modeling procedures. Conducted in universities, private management training institutions, consulting firms and by contract research agencies, it is heterogeneous in its organizational locations and subject to varied and changing evaluation standards. Similarly, research funds are often provided by a variety of groups and organizations, pursuing diverse goals and applying contrasting performance criteria. It is not too surprising then that intellectually and organizationally it resembles a fragmented adhocracy (Engwall 1995; Whitley 1984).

As discussed in this book, these kinds of scientific fields combine high levels of task uncertainty, i.e., about the nature, meaning, and significance of research results, and low levels of task and strategic interdependence with other researchers. Research in these sciences is rather personal, idiosyncratic, and open to varied interpretations. Typically, scientists do not have to produce results that contribute to others' research programmes in a clear and unambiguous manner, but rather make diffuse contributions to broad and fluid intellectual goals that reflect local exigencies and environmental pressures. The authority structures of fragmented adhocracies are pluralist and shifting, with dominant coalitions being formed by temporary and unstable alliances controlling resources, and by charismatic reputational leaders. Intellectual

Source: *The intellectual and social organization of the sciences*, 2nd ed., by Richard Whitley, xxxi–xxxvi, xxxix–xl. Copyright © 1984, 2000 by Richard Whitley. Used by permission of Oxford University Press.

problems, descriptions of phenomena, and research procedures are formulated in everyday language and communication between researchers is not highly standardized or formalized . . .

In general, however, such a narrowing of focus and domination of the reputational system by highly formalized and restricted intellectual approaches and techniques have not typified management studies as a whole. Despite the hegemonic claims of a single management science in the 1950s and later, this field has not become integrated around a common set of theoretical goals and research skills, but has rather developed multiple subfields with different goals, problems, and approaches. . . .

In fact, not only has the separation of the subfields of finance, marketing, strategic management, human resources management, etc., as distinct reputational organizations become more entrenched, but further differentiation of research areas within them seems to have taken place in the 1980s and 1990s. Additionally, the growth of management consultancy in the Americas, Europe, and parts of Asia, together with other organizations producing and disseminating various forms of knowledge about management, has broadened both the range of types of formal knowledge produced in many countries and the variety of knowledge producing organizations (e.g., Kipping and Amorin 1999/2000; Kipping and Armbruester 1999). As a result, increasing intellectual variety has been matched by organizational differentiation in this area.

At the end of the twentieth century, researchers in university undergraduate departments of management, graduate business schools and various combinations of the two pursue a wide range of research programmes that differ considerably in their orientation to managerial practice and their concern with explanatory goals. At the same time, a growing number of research institutes, consultancies, industry groups, and other organizations produce more market-oriented knowledge across a wide range of issues. While the degree of organizational and intellectual segmentation continues to vary between countries in this field as in others, the overall impression of business and management studies is of a great variety of intellectual programmes, methods, and standards, both within and between increasingly different kinds of organizations. It is no longer, if it ever was, a single instrumental science of the kind proclaimed by the founders of management science in the 1950s, but rather a wide ranging collection of specialized research areas that differ considerably in their intellectual goals and organizational locations. In particular, their closeness to, and dependence upon, managerial practices and elites, varies greatly as does the extent of coordination of research results around common purposes (Whitley 1988).

This continuing differentiation of intellectual objectives, research fields, and audiences has been fueled by the continuing expansion of university education in business and management studies, and changes in the structure and behaviour of big business in North America and parts of Europe. Considering first the impact of growth in university business education, this was especially marked in Europe during the 1980s and early 1990s (Engwall and Gunnarsson 1994; Engwall and Zamagni 1998), but also continued in the USA where the popularity of MBA programmes during the long 1990's economic boom remained considerable. Such growth in teaching posts and other resources reduces the ability of disciplinary elites to control research priorities and impose quality standards. It enables researchers to pursue their own interests without needing to coordinate their results with those of specialist colleagues and so encourages the proliferation of specialist subfields focusing on distinct problems and/or approaches.

In business and management studies in particular, the speed of expansion allowed academics to establish their own subspecialisms as separate reputational organizations without having first to overcome established ones. In the sciences, as elsewhere, rapid growth facilitates new entrants developing distinctive competencies and niches so that novel ideas, methods, and frameworks are not only able to gain a hearing but can also become the basis of separate identities and resource controlling organizations. As in many other scientific fields during the academic expansion of the 1960s and 1970s, the recent growth of business education provided the opportunity for new specialisms to become established as separate fields of study whose elites could award jobs and other rewards on the basis of contributions to their distinctive intellectual goals.

This can be seen quite clearly in the continuing debate over the status and structure of organization studies. As Knudsen (1999) has recently emphasized, in the 1960s when this area was most institutionalized in the Anglo-Saxon countries, it was dominated by structural contingency theory. This combined particular intellectual goals with a set of research techniques and strategies that enabled researchers to study quite specific problems in a fairly standardized manner with the assurance that their work would make a meaningful contribution to the field. In terms of the framework presented in this book, organization studies at that time displayed relatively low strategic and task uncertainty. Furthermore, given the limited number of active researchers in the field in the early 1970s, coordination of research results was quite easy, with personal connections being as important as more formal ones.

By the end of the 1980s, the field had fragmented into considerable variety of competing research programmes pursuing divergent goals with quite different methods and strategies, as bemoaned by Pfeffer (1993) amongst others. Not only had the structural contingency programme lost many of its adherents, and failed to overcome internal conflicts, but its whole intellectual approach and presuppositions came under sustained attack and were opposed by a number of contrasting perspectives on what organization studies should be about and how research should be conducted. In North America, it became replaced by a plethora of research programmes, such as population ecology, organizational economics, and the "new" institutionalism, which were able to establish their own specialisms in the major business schools and journals without seriously engaging intellectual and organizational conflict.

In much of Europe and elsewhere, debates tended to focus more on conceptual issues to do with the nature of the field as an intellectual enterprise, and its epistemological presuppositions. The organization of the field in most European countries has been less structured around separate research specialisms than in the USA because of differences in the organization of intellectual competition and institutional contexts. Rather, intellectual approaches have been developed by distinct schools of thought, often dominated by particular individuals or small groups, which rarely engage in sustained, continuing conflict over competing programmes and access to resources. Coordination of research results thus tends to be weak across such schools and specialisms. . . .

In sum, the combination of: (a) the continued expansion of business education in different kinds of higher education systems; (b) the decline of the post-war US Chandlerian enterprise operating in relatively predictable markets and focused on systematically driving down costs (Lazonick 1991); (c) the growth of international competition from different models of economic organization and behaviour; and (d) the transformation of capital markets with its attendant reorganization of US and UK business, has led to increasing variety in the types and organization of knowledge production in business and management studies. . . . Both the extent to which explanations of managerial practices and structures are sought, and the focus on managerial applications, will continue to vary considerably between and within specialist subfields, as well as between countries whose academic institutions differ in their responsiveness to market pressures and business elite influence.

Summary

At present, the phenomenological territory of the organizational sciences is remarkably broad. As models and theories have proliferated, more and different organizational sciences–related phenomena are attended to and methodological variety is increased. The variety of schools of thought—as theoretical-methodological subcultures—have likewise increased in number and become evermore differentiated.

The now wide variety of schools of thought in the organizational sciences appeal to and attract their own set of researchers. While allegiance to a school of thought can come about in many ways, two general ones seem widespread. One is simply that newcomers to organizational science research usually are trained and mentored by others with an investment of time and energy in some theoretic-methodological nexus. Acquisition of a research identity and research-related relationships go hand in hand with the acquisition of conceptual knowledge, research techniques, and know-how—inquirer socialization is almost always a function of a place, persons, and intellectual work organized around a school of thought. Allegiances are thus, in part, the products of socialization. In addition, allegiance comes about and is reinforced by the recognition and reputation accruing to those who extend and refine the theory and/or methods of a school of thought (of course, initiating work that has the potential for a new school of thought is an alternative path to visibility and prominence, although it is rare and reputationally risky). The more success one has within a school of thought, the more difficult it may be to shift allegiances—to choose alternative assumptions.

Given the range of perspectives on the variety of phenomena in the organizational sciences, there are many alternative schools of thought among which to choose. Inquirer socialization practices mean, however, that for most researchers the choice of which school of thought to have allegiance to is usually limited. Allegiances to a particular school of thought often carry with them implicit choices about ideology, ontology, epistemology, and images of human nature. Those adhering to a school of thought tend not to think about the choices available with these assumptions of the philosophic context of inquiry.

Serious inquirers most often "live" and work in and through their philosophically like-minded associates with whom they share a preferred set of methods, problems, and, importantly, a conceptual framework. These sets of associates comprise the membership of schools of thought both formally and informally organized.

Communication and coordination are enhanced within research projects and programs with common norms and similar identities. Contributing to—or becoming an articulate spokesperson for—the common theoretic-methodologic endeavor provides the recognition and reputation that motivates many inquirers. As schools of thought proliferate, interschool competitions (politely referred to as debates) inevitably occur, and, over time, the status of schools ascends and descends, influencing research careers, funding, and much else.

In the organizational sciences, there are many, many schools of thought.[1] This is likely to be the case well into the foreseeable future. This set of schools

---

1. Some indication of this variety can be garnered by perusal of handbooks in organizational studies, such as Clegg, Hardy, and Nord (1996), and handbooks in subfields, such as Nystrom and Starbuck's (1981) *Handbook of Organizational Design* and C. L. Cooper, Cartwright, and Earley's (2001) *International Handbook of Organizational Culture and Climate*.

of thought is at best loosely coupled with several semi-integrated para-digmatically centered nodes. For every phenomenon of interest there are likely to be competing schools of thought to choose among. Being aware that there are schools, that they differ in size, prestige, theoretical and/or methodological development, and so on should enhance one's choice of school. Few inquirers can go it alone for long; associates are always needed, and the exchange for assistance is allegiance—and allegiance means ac-ceptance of the assumptions guiding a school of thought.

Part 3

Centering Inquiry: Models and Theories

The truism that theory organizes knowledge should not be allowed to conceal the equally important truth that it changes the content of knowledge as well as the form.

—*Abraham Kaplan*

In the field of observations, chance favors only the mind that is prepared.
—*Louis Pasteur*

Conceptual frameworks attempt to capture patterns among observables at a point in time or over time. Let us unpack this sentence, for it says so much. "Conceptual" means both abstract and symbolic. "Frameworks" suggest both the systems and the sensemaking that frames provide. "Attempt to capture" indicates a tentative, never quite completed act. "Patterns" are regularities observed repeatedly. The term "observables" refers to reality *as it is known*, directly and/or indirectly. "At a point in time" and "over time" suggest that the conceptual framework tells us, on the one hand, about what seems to constitute a portion of the world and how it is configured or structured, and, on the other hand, how a portion of the world repeatedly seems to change.

In serious inquiry, conceptual frameworks take two general forms—models and theories. The sets of related ideas that comprise models and theories are at the heart and soul of inquiry, igniting and capturing knowledge through the research process. The aim of serious inquiry is to construct and confirm better and better understandings and explanations of what the world is like and how it works. Serious inquiry is thus all about producing ever clearer, more and more succinct, accurate, and valid conceptual frameworks.

In our map of inquiry (see Figure 2-3), models and theories are placed in the center, symbolizing their significance and function. Models and theories usually manifest to a considerable degree the framing assumptions and preferences of their philosophic context. Models and theories are reservoirs of knowledge—their appropriateness, form, and scope capture the findings and guide the question-asking and answering that is the research process. Research that is neither theory generating nor theory testing is usually spurious, even silly, and almost always wasteful.

The three chapters devoted to theories should serve as a measure of their centrality and importance. Chapter 8 clarifies what models and theories are, reminds us what they do for us, and emphasizes the scope of their phenomenological reach. The next chapter focuses our attention on the many forms theories may take, emphasizes their consequences, and surveys the ways we assess conceptual edifices. Chapter 10 then adopts a more dynamic perspective, examining how theories are developed and improved—the sine qua non of serious inquiry.

Theory is how we move to further research and improve practice. If manuscripts contain no theory, their value is suspect. Ungrounded theory, however, is no more helpful than are atheoretical data.

—*Notice to Contributors*, Administrative Science Quarterly

In order to talk about the nature of the universe and to discuss questions of whether it has a beginning or an end, you have to be clear about what a scientific theory is.

—*Steven Hawking*

Theories . . . are not inexorable inductions from facts. The most creative theories are often imaginative visions imposed upon facts. . . .

—*Stephen Jay Gould*

"Model" and "theory" are surely leading candidates for words used and misused in inquiry generally and in research more particularly. Much of the mystification and misunderstanding about science probably revolves around these two terms at the center of inquiry (see Figure 2-3). "Model" and "theory" are both often used inappropriately and/or inaccurately: they each seem to have several meanings; they often seem to be used synonymously; they have a negative connotation in popular culture (e.g., something is "merely a theory"); and, when they are ignored, the resulting research is likely to be insignificant (Daft 1985). Given this confusion about the conceptual frameworks at the heart of inquiry, this chapter is devoted to clarifying what models/theories are and are not, what their functions are, and what their scope can be.

"Model" has come to have three quite different meanings. The most common use of the term is to indicate a precursor of theory, either because a model is partial or simply a not-as-yet-very-well-verified beginning. "Model" is also used to refer to unformalized theory—for instance, ideas offered in a literary style rather than propositionally or mathematically. The third meaning is a technical one, in which model is the part of a theory that enables other parts to be interpreted. In all three meanings we note that a model is not a theory; models and theories are not synonymous. In all three meanings, models function metaphorically, suggesting by analogy the meaning of that which is to be explained.

A rather inclusive definition of "theory" is that it is a powerful, contingent, abstract analytical scheme—where "powerful" signifies highly accurate with respect to a well-defined scope of recurrent phenomena or experience (not unique events); where "contingent" means that the truth or falsity of the theory is derived from factual reality; where "abstract" points to theory as a symbolic construction referring to the materials of experience; where "analytical" signifies descriptive or explanatory generalizations about patterns of some phenomena or about how or why some phenomenon of interest happens; and "scheme" simply refers to the systematic forms or shape that a theory takes. This characterization of theory, we should quickly add, is concerned with empirical reality, not fiction or imagination.

> Thus, theory exercises compelling influence on research—setting problems, staking out objects and leading inquiry into asserted relations. In turn, findings of fact test theories, and in suggesting new problems invite the formulation of new proposals. Theory, inquiry and empirical fact are interwoven in a texture of operation with theory guiding inquiry, inquiry seeking and isolating facts, and facts affecting theory. The fruitfulness of their interplay is the means by which an empirical science develops (Blumer 1954, 3).

Theories and their precursor models are always tentative, never complete. They can always be more accurate, more valid, and better confirmed. Research is about model and theory improvement, and improvements can occur in many ways. The frame provided by a model or theory prompts exploration and discovery; with the frame provided by a theory we notice what was otherwise unobservable. The frame provided by a theory allows the interpretation of research findings and their unification.

While models provide meaningful contexts within which specific findings can be located as significant details, theories go further. As Kaplan (1964, 268) emphasizes,

> Every theory serves, in part, as research directive; theory guides the collection of data and their subsequent analysis, by showing us beforehand where the data are to be fitted, and what we are to make of them when we get them. The word "data," it cannot too often be emphasized, is an incomplete term, like "later than"; there are only data *for* some hypothesis or other. Without a theory, however provisional or loosely formulated, there is only a miscellany of observations, having no significance either in them-

selves or over against the plenum of fact from which they have been arbitrarily or accidentally selected.

And theoretic frames provide comprehension and understanding, explanation and sometimes prediction. Improving theory improves its heuristic, compiling, and meaning-making functions, which in turn improves theory, on and on.

Models and theories, regardless of their degree of improvement or their
form (see Chapter 9), may be differentiated in two fundamental ways. One
has to do with the reach or distance between the facts pertinent to the theory and the level of abstraction on which its conceptualization occurs.
Some theories are close to their phenomena; other theories, far. This distance is important simply because abstraction level translates into theoretic
scope: the higher the level of abstraction, the more inclusive the theory.
Conventionally, we speak of three levels and hence three degrees of scope:
general or macro, midrange, and micro. These levels of theoretic—and
phenomenological—scope may or may not be congruent; higher levels
may subsume lower ones, or the same facts may be explained differently at
different levels of theory. The second way models and theories may be differentiated has to do with time; for instance, does a conceptual framework
reach across time or not? does it explain its phenomena of interest for just
now or for all time? If the model or theory purports to be general or universal (and is abstract), we call it nomothetic; if the model or theory is about
something unique, singular, or concrete, we call it idiographic.

The selections that follow provide clarification and elaboration for many
of the key points we have sketched. In the first selection, Samuel Bacharach
provides us with an up-to-date vocabulary for discussing theory and then
goes on to provide useful distinctions as to what theory is and is not in the
organization sciences. Following Bacharach's selection is a selection by Sutton and Staw that leaves no doubt about what a theory is not. The com-
mentaries that follow, by Karl Weick and Paul DiMaggio, soften and nuance
theory work. Finally, another selection from Abraham Kaplan's classic book
compellingly lists what the functions of theories are—in other words, what
they do for us.

What a Theory Is and Is Not
Samuel B. Bacharach

A theory is a statement of relations among concepts within a set of boundary assumptions and constraints. It is no more than a linguistic device used
to organize a complex empirical world. As C. S. Hall and Lindzey (1957, 9)

Source: "Organizational theories: Some criteria for evaluation" by Samuel B. Bacharach, *Academy of Management Review* 14 (1989): 496–500. Copyright © 1989 by the Academy pointed out, the function of a theory "is that of preventing the observer from being dazzled by the full blown complexity of natural or concrete events." Therefore, the purpose of theoretical statements is twofold: to organize (parsimoniously) and to communicate (clearly).

Many current theories in organizational behavior fail to accomplish this purpose, primarily because they ignore certain generally accepted rules about theoretical statements. Just as a collection of words does not make a sentence, a collection of constructs and variables does not necessarily make a theory.

Students of theory construction have tried to develop a set of rules for the examination of the constructs and variables which are the units of theoretical statements (cf. Dubin 1969; Cronbach and Meehl 1955; Blalock 1968; Schwab 1980). They also have attempted to develop a set of rules for the examination of the relationships among these units (cf. Blalock 1969; B. Cohen 1980; Nagel 1961; Hempel 1965; Stinchcombe 1968; Popper 1959; Dubin 1976; Gibbs 1972). Nevertheless, the diversity of these perspectives suggests the need for a more specific examination of their rules as applied to organizational studies.

What Theory Is Not: Data, Typologies, and Metaphors

Description, the "features or qualities of individual things, acts, or events" (Werkmeister 1959, 484) must be distinguished from theory. As Hempel (1965) pointed out, the vocabulary of science has two basic functions: (a) to adequately describe the objects and events being investigated and (b) to establish theories by which events and objects can be explained and predicted. While descriptions may be the source material of theories, they are not themselves theoretical statements. In the organization and management literature, the two are often confused. Specifically, three modes of description must be distinguished from theory: categorization of raw data, typologies, and metaphors.

While some forms of descriptive analysis are often confused with theory, all researchers agree that categorization of data—whether qualitative or quantitative—is not theory. In this context, much of the work in organizational and management science should not be thought of as theory. Categorization characterizes much of the work in these fields, particularly in the realms of business policy/strategy and human resource strategy. One theme in the former case, for example, has been the search for empirical categorizations, or gestalts, of organizational environments and characteristics (e.g., D. Miller 1986; D. Miller and Friesen 1977). One characteristic in the latter case has been the search for a goodness of fit between empirically derived categorizations of business strategy and human resource strategy (e.g., Schuler and Jackson 1987; Wils and Dyer 1984). Some of these studies, both quantitative and qualitative, are often particularly rich and thus useful as grounds (Glaser and Strauss 1967) for theory building (e.g., Dyer and Holder 1989; D. Miller 1987; D. Miller and Friesen 1984). In and of themselves, however, they clearly fall in Hempel's (1965) realm of description, not theory.

Other descriptions—specifically, those based upon typologies—have been more abstract in organizing observations (e.g., Blau and Scott 1962; Etzioni 1975; Gouldner 1954). Typologists have implicitly emulated Weber's ideal construct, in that most typologies meet his classic definition of an ideal type . . . "a mental construct formed by the synthesis of many diffuse individual phenomena which are arranged, according to certain one-sidedly accentuated points of view, into a unified analytical construct" (Shils and Finch 1949, 90).

Yet even these abstractions should not be viewed as theory. The one-sided accentuation of which Weber spoke is found in most typologies. For example, in creating a typology of organizations, Blau and Scott (1962) emphasized the beneficiaries; Gouldner (1954), leadership style; and Etzioni (1975), compliance structure. While this one-sided accentuation achieves one of the goals of theory (i.e., eliminating some of the complexity of the real world), and while typologies are more abstract than a categorical description of raw data, such typologies are limited to addressing the primary question asked by descriptive researchers—the question of *what*, rather than the more theoretical *how*, *why*, and *when*.

In recent years, metaphors have become popular in organizational studies. Broadly speaking, a metaphor is a statement that maintains that two phenomena are isomorphic (i.e., they have certain properties in common) (Brodbeck, 1959). Unlike the case of categorical analysis of raw data (What are the phenomena?), or the case of typology (What is the most important aspect of the phenomenon?), the metaphor is used to ask how the phenomenon is similar to another (often unrelated) phenomenon. Some of the most well-known metaphors include the notions of organizations as "loosely coupled systems" (Weick 1976) and as "garbage cans" (M. D. Cohen, March, and Olsen 1972).

Metaphors are powerful literary tools. Robert Burns' comparison of his love to a red rose evokes strong emotional imagery. It does not need to evoke a series of analytical questions about love; the description itself suffices. To be of use in the development of theory in organizational behavior, a metaphor must go beyond description and be a useful heuristic device. That is, the imagery contained in the metaphor must assist the theorist in deriving specific propositions and/or hypotheses about the phenomenon being studied. In this context, metaphors are not theories but may well serve as precursors to theories, and should be judged on that basis. For example, if one chooses to view organizations as "nonconflictual zeppelins," it's his or her prerogative to do so. What must be evaluated is not whether organizations are in fact "nonconflictual zeppelins," but rather the propositions and hypotheses derived from the imagery. If one's image of organizations as "nonconflictual zeppelins" is to thrive, then it is because the quality of propositions and hypotheses generated by this image is better than the quality of those generated by other alternative images such as "garbage can models" or "loosely coupled systems."

What Theory Is

Building on the works of previous students of theory construction (e.g., Dubin 1969; Nagel 1961; B. Cohen 1980), researchers can define a theory as a statement of relationships between units observed or approximated in the empirical world. *Approximated* units mean *constructs*, which by their very nature cannot be observed directly (e.g., centralization, satisfaction, or culture). *Observed* units mean *variables*, which are operationalized empirically by measurement. The primary goal of a theory is to answer the questions of *how*, *when*, and *why*, unlike the goal of description, which is to answer the question of *what*.

In more detailed terms, a theory may be viewed as a system of constructs and variables in which the constructs are related to each other by propositions and the variables are related to each other by hypotheses. The whole system is bounded by the theorist's assumptions, as indicated by Figure [8-1].

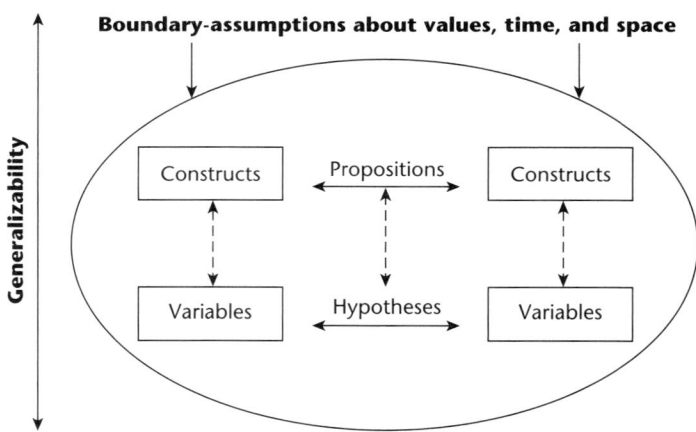

FIGURE **8-1**   Components of a theory

SOURCE: "Organizational theories: Some criteria for evaluation" by Samuel B. Bacharach. *Academy of Management Review* 14 (1989): 499, fig. 1. Copyright © 1989 by the Academy of Management. Reproduced with permission of the Academy of Management via Copyright Clearance Center.

Boundaries of Theories

The notion of boundaries based on assumptions is critical because it sets the limitations in applying the theory. As Dubin (1969) maintained, all theories are constrained by their specific critical bounding assumptions. These assumptions include the implicit values of the theorist and the often explicit restrictions regarding space and time.

Values are the implicit assumptions by which a theory is bounded. Theories cannot be compared on the basis of their underlying values, because these tend to be the idiosyncratic product of the theorist's creative imagination and ideological orientation or life experience. This may explain why perpetual debates such as those between Marxists and Structural Functionalists have made so little progress over the years. As Weber pointed out, the value-laden nature of assumptions can never be eliminated. Yet if a theory is to be properly used or tested, the theorist's implicit assumptions which form the boundaries of the theory must be understood. Unfortunately, theorists rarely state their assumptions. Thus, while Mintzman's (1970) extensive and fascinating discussion of the influence of Weber's personal reality on his theoretical product does not serve to expand or change Weber's theory, it does assist in explicating the implicit values which bound his theory.

An example of how a theorist's values may be manifest in a theoretical debate may be found in a classic debate over the concept of power. Parsons maintained that power is essentially the mobilization of resources and thus is not a zero-sum game. On the other hand, C. Wright Mills (1956) maintained that power is the control of resources, and thus is a zero-sum game. An argument may be made that this differential orientation toward power is based on these theorists' different values. Parsons, viewing society and organizations as functional and consensual systems, ignored the possibility of finite resources as a potential source of conflict. Rather, he saw resources as being capable of perpetual expansion. Mills, on the other hand, seeing society and organizations as stratified and conflictual entities, ignored the expansive nature of resources and instead emphasized finite resources and a zero-sum notion of power. The interaction between these two theorists is thus implicitly a collision of values.

The current debate over the application of the concept of culture to the organizational context also may be viewed as an example of the implicit debate over values if not ideology. During the early resurrection (by organizational theorists) of the concept of culture (Schein 1985; Deal and Kennedy 1982), most theorists chose to view it as an integrative normative device. In doing so they implicitly drew on the values that underlie functionalist theorizing by scholars such as Radcliffe-Brown (1949), Malinowski (1962), and Durkheim (1933). Therefore, their implicit functional orientation (placing emphasis on sustaining the organization as a whole) may make them vulnerable to criticism that they serve the interests of management. In more recent work from the conflict theory perspective, culture is viewed as an organizational mechanism for the normative coercion of the individual worker. For example, Kunda (1992), in studying a company that is often held up as a shining model of positive normative impact of culture, unveiled a story of oppression where others told a tale of productivity. While these two orientations toward culture are not inherently inconsistent, they do show the effects of different values on the construction of theories about organizations.

While values often can only be revealed by psychoanalytic, historical, and ideological studies of the theorist (e.g., Gay's work on Freud 1988; Mintzman's work on Weber 1970), spatial and temporal assumptions are often relatively apparent. Spatial boundaries are conditions restricting the use of the theory to specific units of analysis (e.g., specific types of organizations). Temporal contingencies specify the historical applicability of a theoretical system. Taken together, spatial and temporal boundaries restrict the empirical generalizability of the theory.

While most theories are limited by spatial and temporal restrictions, some are more bounded by one than the other. For example, some theories may be unbounded in time, but bounded in space. That is, these theories are only applicable to specific types of organizations, but can be applied over different historical periods. Other theories are unbounded in space (that is, they may be applicable to many types of organizations), but very much bounded in a specific temporal context. Finally, theories may be relatively unbounded in both space and time. Such theories have a higher level of generalizability than those bounded in either or both space and time, ceteris paribus. Of course, this generalizability requires a higher level of abstraction, which means that the theory sacrifices the level of detail needed to fit a specific situation. This leads to the paradox that some of the most detailed theories and elaborate studies about organizations are not generalizable enough to build a cumulative body of research on (e.g., Goffman's theory of total institutions). On the other hand, some of the most abstract and broad perspectives on organizations, while not necessarily rich in detail, have provided a critical basis for cumulative research (e.g., Hannan and Freeman's 1977, population ecology, and Kimberly and Miles' 1980, life-cycle theory).

Implied in the notion of generalizability are different levels on which one can theorize. This implicit continuum stretches from empirical generalizations (rich in detail but strictly bounded in space and/or time) to grand theoretical statements (abstract, lacking in observational detail, but relatively unbounded in space and/or time).

Variables, Constructs, and Relationships

Within these boundaries lies the stuff of theory. On a more abstract level, propositions state the relations among constructs, and on the more concrete level, hypotheses (derived from the propositions) specify the relations among variables. In this context, theorists must be specific in how they use the notions of constructs and variables. Theorists should not use these terms synonymously. Constructs may be defined as "terms which, though not observational either directly or indirectly, may be applied or even defined on the basis of the observables" (Kaplan 1964, 55). A variable may be defined as an observable entity which is capable of assuming two or more values (Schwab 1980). Thus, a construct may be viewed as a broad mental configuration of a given phenomenon, while a variable may be viewed as an operational configuration derived from a construct. Schwab listed a number of examples of such constructs and their related variables (e.g., performance: sales or return on investment; cohesion: rate of interpersonal interaction or member voting patterns; leader consideration: member perceptions of specific supervisory behavior).

Created within the context of specified boundaries and built from abstract constructs or their more concrete manifestations (variables), theoretical systems take the form of propositions and proposition-derived hypotheses. While both propositions and hypotheses are merely statements of relationships, propositions are the more abstract and all-encompassing of the two, and therefore relate the more abstract constructs to each other. Hypotheses are the more concrete and operational statements of these broad relationships and are therefore built from specific variables.

What Theory Is Not
Robert I. Sutton and Barry M. Staw

. . . Though there is conflict about what theory is and should be, there is consensus about what theory is not. We consider five features of a scholarly article that, while important in their own right, do not constitute theory. Reviewers and editors seem to agree, albeit implicitly, that these five features should not be construed as part of the theoretical argument. By making this consensus explicit we hope to help authors avoid some of the most frequent reasons that their manuscripts are viewed as having inadequate theory.

Source: "What theory is *not*" by Robert I. Sutton and Barry M. Staw, *Administrative Science Quarterly* 40 (September 1995): 372–378. Copyright © 1995 Johnson Graduate School of Management, Cornell University. Reprinted with permission.

Parts of an Article That Are Not Theory

1. References Are Not Theory

References to theory developed in prior work help set the stage for new conceptual arguments. Authors need to acknowledge the stream of logic on which they are drawing and to which they are contributing. But listing references to existing theories and mentioning the names of such theories is not the same as explicating the casual logic they contain. . . .

Calls for "more theory" by reviewers and editors are often met with a flurry of citations. Rather than presenting more detailed and compelling arguments, authors may list the names of prevailing theories or schools of thought without even providing an explanation of why the theory or approach leads to new or unanswered theoretical questions. . . . References are sometimes used like a smoke screen to hide the absence of theory. . . . Mark Twain defined a classic as "A book which people praise but don't read." Papers for organizational research journals typically include a set of such throw-away references. These citations may show that the author is a qualified member of the profession, but they don't demonstrate that a theoretical case has been built.

Authors need to explicate which concepts and causal arguments are adopted from cited sources and how they are linked to the theory being developed or tested. This suggestion does not mean that a paper needs to review every nuance of every theory cited. Rather, it means that enough of the pertinent logic from past theoretical work should be included so that the reader can grasp the author's logical arguments. . . .

2. Data Are Not Theory

Much of organizational theory is based on data. Empirical evidence plays an important role in confirming, revising, or discrediting existing theory and in guiding the development of new theory. But observed patterns like beta weights, factor loadings, or consistent statements by informants rarely constitute causal explanations. Kaplan (1964) asserted that theory and data each play a distinct role in behavioral science research: Data describe *which* empirical patterns were observed and theory explains *why* empirical patterns were observed or are expected to be observed. . . . Prior findings cannot by themselves motivate hypotheses, and the reporting of results cannot substitute for causal reasoning. . . . Just like theorists who use quantitative data, those who use qualitative data must develop casual arguments to explain *why* persistent findings have been observed if they wish to write papers that contain theory (Glaser and Strauss 1967). . . . Mintzberg (1979b, 584) summarized this distinction succinctly: "The data do not generate theory—only researchers do that."

3. Lists of Variables or Constructs Are Not Theory

A theory must also explain why variables or constructs come about or why they are connected. Weick (1989, 517) quoted Homans to make this point:

> Of particular interest is Homan's irritation with theorists who equate theory with conceptual definitions; he stated that "much official sociological theory consists in fact of concepts and their definitions; it provides a dictionary of a language that possesses no sentences. . . ."

As an empirically based field, organizational research is often enticed by tests showing the relative strength of one set of variables versus others on particular outcomes. We are attracted to procedures that show the most important influence on dependent variables, as though the contest will show who the winner is. Comparative tests of variables should not be confused with comparative tests of theory, however, because a predicted relationship must be explained to provide theory; simply listing a set of antecedents (or even a causal ordering of variables as in LISREL models) does not make a theoretical argument. The key issue is why a particular set of variables are expected to be strong predictors.

4. Diagrams Are Not Theory

Diagrams or figures can be a valuable part of a research paper but also, by themselves, rarely constitute theory. Probably the least theoretical representations are ones that simply list categories of variables such as "personality," "environmental determinants," or "demographics." More helpful are figures that show causal relationships in a logical ordering so that readers can see a chain of causation or how a third variable intervenes in or moderates a relationship. Also useful are temporal diagrams showing how a particular process unfolds over time. On occasion, diagrams can be a useful aid in building theory. For researchers who are not good writers, a set of diagrams can provide structure to otherwise rambling or amorphous arguments. For those researchers who are talented writers, having a concrete model may prevent obfuscation of specious or inconsistent arguments.

Regardless of their merits, diagrams and figures should be considered as stage props rather than the performance itself. As Whetten (1989) suggested, while boxes and arrows can add order to a conception by explicitly delineating patterns and causal connections, they rarely explain *why* the proposed connections will be observed. Some verbal explication is almost always necessary. The logic underlying the portrayed relationships needs to be spelled out. Text about the reasons why a phenomenon occurs, or why it unfolds in a particular manner, is difficult to replace by references to a diagram. . . .

5. Hypotheses (or Predictions) Are Not Theory

Hypotheses can be an important part of a well-crafted conceptual argument. They serve as crucial bridges between theory and data, making explicit how the variables and relationships that follow from a logical argument will be operationalized. But, as Dubin (1976, 26) noted, "A theoretical model is not simply a statement of hypothesis." Hypotheses do not (and should not) contain logical arguments about why empirical relationships are expected to occur. Hypotheses are concise statements about *what* is expected to occur, not *why* it is expected to occur.

Identifying Strong Theory

Though we have noted that it is easier to identify features of manuscripts that are not theory than it is to specify exactly what good theory is, our own prejudices about the matter are already evident. We agree with scholars like Kaplan (1964) and Merton (1967) who assert that theory is the answer to queries of *why*. Theory is about the connections among phenomena, a story about why acts, events, structure, and thoughts occur. Theory emphasizes the nature of causal relationships, identifying what comes first as well as the timing of such events. Strong theory, in our view, delves into underlying processes so as to understand the systematic reasons for a particular occurrence or nonoccurrence. It often burrows deeply into microprocesses, laterally into neighboring concepts, or in an upward direction, tying itself to broader social phenomena. It usually is laced with a set of convincing and logically interconnected arguments. It can have implications that we have not seen with our naked (or theoretically unassisted) eye. It may have implications that run counter to our common sense. As Weick (1995b) put it succinctly, a good theory explains, predicts, and delights.

What Theory Is Not, Theorizing Is
Karl E. Weick

Products of the theorizing process seldom emerge as full-blown theories, which means that most of what passes for theory in organizational studies consists of approximations. Although these approximations vary in their generality, few of them take the form of strong theory, and most of them can be read as texts created "in lieu of" strong theories. These substitutes for theory may result from lazy theorizing in which people try to graft theory

Source: "What theory is *not*, theorizing *is*" by Karl E. Weick, *Administrative Science Quarterly* 40 (September 1995): 385–390. Copyright © 1995 Johnson Graduate School of Management, Cornell University. Reprinted with permission.

onto stark sets of data. But they may also represent interim struggles in which people intentionally inch toward stronger theories. The products of laziness and intense struggles may look the same and may consist of references, data, lists, diagrams, and hypotheses. To label these five as "not theory" makes sense if the problem is laziness and incompetence. But ruling out those same five may slow inquiry if the problem is theoretical development still in its early stages. Sutton and Staw know this. But it gets lost in their concern with theory as a product rather than as a process. To add complication and nuance to their message, I want to focus on the process of theorizing. . . .

I begin with the issue of approximation. Most products that are labeled theories actually approximate theory. Merton (1967) has been most articulate about this point and suggests that approximations take at least four forms: (1) general orientations in which broad frameworks specify types of variables people should take into account, without any specification of relationships among these variables; (2) analysis of concepts in which concepts are specified, clarified, and defined but not interrelated; (3) post-factum interpretation in which ad hoc hypotheses are derived from a single observation, with no effort to explore alternative explanations or new observations; and (4) empirical generalization in which an isolated proposition summarizes the relationship between two variables, but further interrelations are not attempted. While none of these are full-blown theories, they can serve as means to further development. If they are serving this function, then it is imperative that the author make this clear. . . .

So part of what Sutton and Staw make clearer to me is how hard it is in a low-paradigm field, in which people are novice theorists, to spot which of their efforts are theory and which are not. This difficulty arises because theory work can take a variety of forms, because theory itself is a continuum, and because most verbally expressed theory leaves tacit some key portions of the originating insight. These considerations suggest that it is tough to judge whether something is a theory or not when only the product itself is examined. What one needs to know, instead, is more about the context in which the product lives. This is the process of theorizing. If we take a closer look at Sutton and Staw's five forms of "no theory," some seem closer to theory than others, and all five can serve as means to theory construction. . . .

Lists of variables are farther from a well-developed theory than are stories, but lists still can approximate a theory. The tacit message in a list is that items *not* on this list are less crucial determinants than those that are on it. Another tacit message of a list is that the more items on the list that are activated, and the stronger the activation of each, the more determinate is the relationship. Lists also convey the tacit message that causation is assumed to be simultaneous rather than sequential, that history is less crucial than contemporary structure, that relations among items are additive, and that items toward the top of the list are more important than items toward the bottom. I realize these informal theoretical messages may be inadvertent and simply wrong. But as long as there is an implied set of relations among items in the list, or one can infer such relations, there are the beginnings of a theory. . . .

To summarize my point about the five parts, the issue seems to be one of means and ends. And the questions is, Do you publish just ends, or do you publish what Runkel and Runkel called "interim struggles?" The process of theorizing consists of activities like abstracting, generalizing, relating, selecting, explaining, synthesizing, and idealizing. These ongoing activities intermittently spin out reference lists, data, lists of variables, diagrams, and lists of hypotheses. Those emergent products summarize progress, give direction, and serve as placemarkers. They have vestiges of theory but are not themselves theories. Then again, few things are full-fledged theories. The key lies in the context—what came before, what comes next? And this question of context can be phrased in terms of Sutton and Staw's five parts. If prior and subsequent steps in theorizing are merely more of the same— diagrams preceded this paper and diagrams will be the focus of the next paper—then the theorizing is less robust and promising than if people are moving from one of the five, through a second of the five, on to a third of the five. Furthermore, references and data seem to have less generality and seem to be farther from theory than do lists, diagrams, and hypotheses. If that is plausible, then it means that it is easier to reject papers that use the first two in lieu of theory than those that use the last three.

So where does this leave us? It says in part that if much of what we do consists of approximations, then, as Sutton and Staw say, we may expect too much of any one attempt at theorizing.

Comments on "What Theory Is Not"
Paul J. DiMaggio

. . . I would suggest that three additional issues render the problem of theory even more complicated than Sutton and Staw suggest.

1. There Is More Than One Kind of Good Theory

There are at least three views of what theory should be, and each of them has some validity. Each of them also has limitations.

Source: "Comment on 'What theory is *not*'" by Paul J. DiMaggio, *Administrative Science Quarterly* 40 (September 1995): 391–397. Copyright © 1995 Johnson Graduate School of Management, Cornell University. Reprinted with permission.

Theory as Covering Laws

A familiar position, which Sutton and Staw implicitly reject, is that theories should consist of covering laws: generalizations that, taken together, describe the world as we see (or measure) it. The fact that most social scientists to some extent embrace this approach renders Sutton and Staw's argument more radical than it sounds, for they reject some key tenets of behavioral science as it is usually practiced: a focus on explaining variance rather than regularities; the view of scientific process as a kind of R^2 sweepstakes; and the image of a world in which variables explain one another—all parts of the perspective that Abbott (1988) has derided as "ordinary linear reality." At the limit—a limit reached by economists who admit that they don't care if their assumptions are implausible, so long as their R^2s are high (Friedman 1953)—this view provides the "what" of theory that Sutton and Staw argue is insufficient unless accompanied by the how and why.

Theory as Enlightenment

A second view of theory, especially prominent in those neighborhoods of the social sciences influenced by the humanities, is as a device of sudden enlightenment. From this perspective theory is complex, defamiliarizing, rich in paradox. Theorists enlighten not through conceptual clarity (a postmodernist once told me that to define what she meant by "postmodernism" would be unfaithful to the theory), but, like R. Crumb's Zen master Mr. Natural, by startling the reader into satori. The point of theory, in this view, is not to generalize, because many generalizations are widely known and rather dull. Instead, theory is a "surprise machine" (Gouldner's 1970, unflattering assessment of Parsons' system), a set of categories and domain assumptions aimed at clearing away conventional notions to make room for artful and exciting insights.

Theory as Narrative

A third perspective on theory emphasizes narrativity: theory as an account of a social process, with emphasis on empirical tests of the plausibility of the narrative as well as careful attention to the scope conditions of the account. The minimalist version of this approach (Collins 1981, on "microtranslation") simply requires that hypotheses detailing regularities in relations among variables be accompanied by plausible accounts of how the actions of real humans could produce the associations predicted and observed. . . . the point of theory is to explain things, and explanation means accounting for variance: In this view, the distance between hypothesis and theory is vanishingly small, and if you need a lot of hypotheses to explain a lot of variance, then so be it. Similarly, because enlightenment theories are often intuitive, they may employ references or diagrams or graphic presentations of data as rhetorical devices to elicit epiphanies.

2. Good Theory Splits the Difference

One can go beyond simply recognizing the diversity of useful and plausible approaches to suggest that many of the best theories are hybrids, combining the best qualities of covering-law, enlightenment, and process approaches. One reason that theory construction is so difficult to teach is that these approaches, as we have seen, are driven by different purposes and embody different values. Consequently, the researcher who tries to combine them faces not a list of brightline standards, but a set of vexing choices.

Clarity vs. Defamiliarization

By defamiliarization, I refer to the process of enabling a native—of society, an organization, or an academic discipline—to see his or her world with new eyes. Arguably, good theory should accomplish this. But it must not go too far. The conventional justification for neologisms is that the old words carry too much baggage to convey new ideas or perspectives. At the same time, too many neologisms render a theory too strange for people to grasp. . . .

Focus vs. Multidimensionality

Most graduate programs highlight the importance of focus in theory: Take a strong position or a new model and push it as far as it will go. Sutton and Staw endorse this when they argue that hypotheses, especially disparate hypotheses drawn from different theoretical traditions, do not constitute theory. Graduate programs also highlight exegesis and teach students to pick apart a paper or study for the factors or variables it omits. Some theorists even view "multidimensionality"—the extent to which a theory includes reference to agency, culture, structure, and several other abstract categories in its rhetoric—as a decisive criterion of its adequacy (Alexander 1982). Alas, one person's multidimensionality is another's goulash; one author's focus, another's crude reductionism. Again, I side with Sutton and Staw in their general orientation toward what one might call "strategic reduction": abstracting away enough of the world's confusion to develop pointed explanations of organizational phenomena. But where one draws the line is still more art than science.

Comprehensiveness vs. Memorability

Theories that are both enlightening and focused tend to emphasize processes and associations that many readers find surprising. We are rewarded for deriving logical deductions from theoretical first principles that generate surprising predictions linking domains that are often considered separate; for example, demonstrating that people who receive little autonomy on the job give their kids little autonomy in the home (Kohn and Schooler 1978). The trouble is that the most interesting casual factors are often not the most important. . . .

Our collective preoccupation with theoretical novelty often leads organizational researchers to overlook crucial if banal patterns in their data (sometimes even omitting "dull" variables at the cost of misspecifying statistical models). Once again, one must find the point on the tightrope at which balance can be achieved.

3. Theory Construction Is Social Construction, Often after the Fact

Even if one constructs a careful hybrid theoretical strategy and finds the proper balance between the conflicting values that good theory may embody, that theory's fate will be determined in part by factors outside one's control. If the production of good theory requires the utmost care, theory's reception is ordinarily helter-skelter: a process of appropriation driven more by resonance than by reason, in which complex arguments are reduced to slogans and related to one another along binary dimensions more redolent of Levi-Strauss's tribal cultures than of graduate theory classes. And not only is theory created by its readers as well as its writers—it is then recreated by the authors who employ it.

The Value of Resonance

Here is an hypothesis (not a theory): The reception of a theory is shaped by the extent to which a theory resonates with the cultural presuppositions of the time and of the scientific audience that consumes it. . . .

I suspect that the same thing happens in organizational science, as cultural change enhances or corrodes our capacity to see aspects of the organizations we study, by limiting the metaphors we think with. If one observes progress of organization theory from the 1950s through the 1990s, it is intriguing to consider the relative impact on our theories of organizational change, on the one hand, and changes in broader preoccupations and cultural repertoires, on the other. . . .

Theories into Slogans

People read quickly. Unless their teaching or research leads them to attend to a paper or book with special care, they will pick from the field of ideas in any theoretical work those that resonate with preexisting expectations and assumptions and forget the rest. In many cases, they will further simplify the ideas they retain until those ideas fit neatly into preexisting schemas (Fleck 1979; D'Andrade 1995). The more widely a theoretical paper or book is read, the greater the proportion of readers who are not specialists in the subject matter it addresses. The greater the proportion of non-expert readers, the greater the extent to which its reception is determined by a cognitive field different than that of its authors, and the greater the extent to which its arguments are refashioned and simplified. . . .

Related to this is the tendency for the field to classify theories on the basis of primordial antimonies rather than coherent and multidimensional analytic categories.

Post Hoc Theory Construction

Theories are not just constructed, they are socially constructed after they are written. Theoretical ideas take on a life of their own. In some cases, sophisticated ideas are degraded. In other cases, half-baked ideas go back into the oven, coming out in more satisfactory form. To some extent, the quality of a theory is a function of the quality of the people who employ it. . . .

Conclusion

I have suggested two modest revisions to Sutton and Staw's argument. First, good theory is so difficult to produce routinely, in part, because "goodness" is multidimensional: the best theory often combines approaches to theorizing, and the act of combination requires compromise between competing and mutually incompatible values. Second, theory construction is a cooperative venture between author and readers: Theory reception rides on much more than scientific potential; in the short run, we tend to reduce theories to slogans; and in the long run, brilliant expositors can turn muddled theories into canonical masterpieces. If the first set of points, on tensions within theories, highlights the need for theorists to exercise judgment and pluck, the second suggests the importance of environment and luck.

Functions of Theories
Abraham Kaplan

Theory puts things known into a system. But this function is more than a matter of what the older positivism used to call "economy of thought" or "mental shorthand," and what today is expressed in terms of the storage and retrieval of information. It is true that the systematization effected by a theory does have the consequence of simplifying laws and introducing order into congeries of fact. But this is a by-product of a more basic function: to make sense of what would otherwise be inscrutable or unmeaning empirical findings. A theory is more than a synopsis of the moves that have been played in the game of nature; it also sets forth some idea of the rules of the game, by which the moves become intelligible. . . .

In providing meaning, the theory also attests to truth. A hypothesis may be as much confirmed by fitting it into a theory as by fitting it to the facts. For it then enjoys the support provided by the evidence for all the other hypotheses of that theory. Just as a law is not only confirmed by factual data but also helps give the data factual status, so a theory is not only supported by established laws but also plays a part in establishing them. We may say both that psychoanalytic theory, for example, is supported by the symbolic fulfillment of wishes in dreams, and that it provides a basis for the interpretation of dreams as wish fulfillments. In the same way, Darwin found support in the fossil record, but only by interpreting fossils as something other than antediluvian remains.

Theories in Process

Theory, therefore, functions throughout inquiry, and does not come into its own only when inquiry is successfully concluded. It has a greater responsibility than that of an accessory after the fact: it guides the search for data, and for laws encompassing them. "Theories in physics," it has been said, "are constructions which serve primarily to integrate or organize into a single deductive system sets of empirical laws which previously were unrelated. . . . In psychology, on the other hand, theories serve primarily as a device to aid in the formulation of empirical laws. They consist in guesses as to how the uncontrolled or unknown factors in the system under study are related to the experimentally know variables." It is not surprising that this view was expressed by a psychologist (K. Spence in [M. H.] Marx [1955, 178–179]). In his own field the role of theory in the process of inquiry is apparent to him; what he sees of another inquiry is not the process but only

Source: *The conduct of inquiry* by Abraham Kaplan (San Francisco, CA: Chandler Publishing, 1964), 302–306.

the product. How lush and lusty the grass looks, how green—from a sufficient distance! I do not believe that the role of theory in behavioral science is any different from what it is in physical or biological science. There are, of course, differences in the number, power, and weight of the theories which have been established concerning these different subject-matters; but everywhere, so it seems to me, theory works in essentially the same way.

What is important is that laws propagate when they are united in a theory: theory serves as matchmaker, midwife, and godfather all in one. This service is what is delicately known as the "heuristic" function of theory. To be sure, laws may also be produced by a kind of epistemic parthenogenesis, by direct inspection of the data, or by analogizing from a law already known—what I called "extensional generalization." But this becomes less and less likely as inquiry into a particular subject-matter proceeds. The more or less directly observable regularities are, almost tautologically, the first to be recognized; to go beyond them we must move from the observational materials to theoretical constructions. "At the present time, in the more highly developed sciences," says [N. R.] Campbell (1952, 88), "it is very unusual for a new law to be discovered or suggested simply by making experiments and observations and examining the results (although cases of this character occur from time to time); almost all advances in the formulations of new laws follow on the invention of theories to explain the old laws." This genesis is especially likely for the great breakthroughs in science. Conant (1952, 53) says flatly that "the history of science demonstrates beyond a doubt that the really revolutionary and significant advances come not from empiricism but from new theories." To be sure, theory will not generate new laws by explaining old ones till we have old ones to be explained. It is not part of my intent to urge that the time is ripe for behavioral science to abandon the direct search for laws of behavior and to occupy itself instead with developing theories of behavior. But where the behavioral scientist *is* occupied with theory, let him not settle for a purely Platonic relationship with what he already knows, in an elegant but possibly sterile system, but see to it, rather, that in the fullness of time the union is blessed.

It might well be said that the predicament of behavioral science is not the absence of theory but its proliferation. The history of science is undeniably a history of the successive replacement of poor theories by better ones, but advances depend on the way in which each takes account of the achievement of its predecessors. Much of the theorizing in behavioral science is not building on what has already been established so much as laying out new foundations, or even worse, producing only another set of blueprints. In an important sense, new scientific theories do not "refute" the old ones but somehow remake them; even scientific revolutions preserve some continuity with the old order of things. It is usual to speak here of "saving the appearances." In the classic example, the notion that the earth is flat has a grain of truth in it—the earth *looks* flat, and the hypothesis that it is in fact round must assign a sufficiently large radius of curvature to the earth to account for this look; it is crucial that plane geometry will fit to any desired degree of approximation a sufficiently small portion of the surface of a sphere.

This reconciliation, it might be urged, is again a matter of preserving the "integrity of the data." But laws, too, are carried over in some form. Sometimes the old laws are retained as special cases of the more general laws which play a part in the new theory. This mode of continuity is not the only one, however; old beliefs may be quite transformed by new knowledge—but transformed, not simply negated. Knowledge grows not only by accretion and the replacement of dubious elements by more sound ones, but also by digestion, the remaking of the old cognitive materials into the substance of new theory. Hierarchical theories are typically improved by replacing some of their postulates with others, or by formulating a new set from which we can deduce the old one and other significant consequences as well. In the case of concatenated theories the pattern is sometimes extended, but more often it is changed in ways that reveal it to be a fragment of a larger and usually quite different pattern. The realization that some of the so-called "nebulae" are not really nebulous but enormously distant galaxies of stars in their own right not only generated new conceptions of the stellar universe, but also changed significantly the conception of our own Milky Way. Similarly, Freud's discernment that there is really a commonality between the lunatic, the lover, and the poet not only disclosed the method in madness but also altered our understanding of the workings of the unfrenzied imagination.

In general, we may say that knowledge grows in two ways: by *extension* and by *intension*. Growth by extension consists in this, that a relatively full explanation of a small region (of behavior, or of whatever the subject-matter may be) is then carried over to an explanation of adjoining regions. It is in this perspective that most studies of the conditioned reflex, for example, are viewed: when conditioning is sufficiently understood we may move on to more complex types of learning, then to other sorts of behavior seen as the products of learning. Growth by extension is implicit in the models or metaphors of science as an edifice, a mosaic, an erector set, or a jigsaw puzzle—it is built up piece by piece.

In growth by intension a partial explanation of a whole region is made more and more adequate. This growth type is characteristic, it seems to me, of the contributions of Darwin, Marx, and Freud, for example; it is not so much that they definitively explained a limited subject-matter which was afterwards enlarged, but that they laid out lines for subsequent theory and observation to follow, so as to yield a better understanding of the broad-scale phenomena which were their primary concern. Growth by intension is associated with such metaphors for the scientific enterprise as developing a photographic negative, bringing binoculars to a sharper focus, or gradually illuminating a darkened room—progress is not piecemeal but gradual on a larger scale.

Both sorts of growth, I believe, are involved in every theoretical advance, and for both concatenated and hierarchical theories.[1] A new theory adds some knowledge, but it also transforms what was previously known, clarifies it, gives it new meaning as well as more confirmation. Before we had the new theory we did not quite know just *what* it was we knew. Paranoid systems and pseudoscientific doctrines, it has been pointed out (Hutten 1962), grow by extension only; they are essentially closed systems of thought even though additional beliefs can be annexed to them. In science, growth "is not simply adding on units to something already existing that remains unchanged in the process. The whole structure, the skeleton, changes with growth even though it remains recognizably similar to what it has been. The system of science would not be flexible unless its structure could change with increasing knowledge." The truism that theory organizes knowledge should not be allowed to conceal the equally important truth that it changes the content of knowledge as well as the form.

Summary

In this chapter, which has focused on what models and theories are and what they do for us, we once again note that there are many alternatives among which to choose and that they reflect alternative assumptive configurations of the philosophic context. Our two main contentions (neither of which is original with us)—that models and theories are at the center of inquiry and that theory improvement is the essence of inquiry—seem uncontestable.

The selections in this chapter enable us to understand better that models and theories may and do vary in many ways. If research is about theory improvement, then it behooves us to be as clear as possible about the theories guiding our research and the perspective and boundary conditions of the assumed philosophic context. Models and theories do differ in their purpose, degree of formalization, extent of confirmation, level of abstraction, and breadth of reach, as well as in how they are communicated and accepted. These features of theories not only contain important choices for theorizing but also raise real choices for the growth of knowledge—whether extensionally and intensionally. Once again, while there are norms and conventions for theory construction, there are trade-offs among theoretic purposes or levels.

Suggested in this chapter but not yet fully discussed are the many forms that theories can take and the processes of creating and verifying theories, subjects that will be taken up in Chapters 9 and 10, respectively.

1. Editors' note: see Kaplan in Chapter 9.

9   Patterns and Criteria of Theories

The truism that theory organizes knowledge should not be allowed to conceal the equally important truth that it changes that content of knowledge as well as its form.
        —*A. Kaplan*

You *have* to have a theoretical model. You can't do science without prejudice.
        —*M. Geller*

It is no doubt platitudinous to note that the aim of all serious inquiry is to develop a body of "verifiable" theory—theory that can be tested empirically and that is falsifiable. Minimal standards for such theory, regardless of the theory's intended purposes or desired scope, are that its ideas can be defined in an operationally, unambiguous manner and that the relationships among and between its ideas must also be specified unambiguously.

Relatively unappreciated is the impact of these minimal standards on the patterned form of a theory and vice versa. Theory is not only the sine qua non of inquiry, but the structure of a theory can act as both constraint and leverage. If the structure of a theory is appropriate and sound—that is, if its essential ideas have merit and the minimal standards for theory construction have been met—substantive errors will be gradually reduced through the ongoing interplay of theory and research. While there are strident advocates of one type of theory over another in the organizational sciences, their claims are seldom justified by insisting on a balance between the minimal standards noted above.

The importance of the structure of a theory—that is, its form or type—can be further appreciated by recalling how sophistication enhancement occurs (cf. Figure 1-2). Knowledge, we recall from Kaplan (1964) in Chapter 8, grows in two ways: by extension and intension. "Growth by extension consists of this, that a relatively full explanation of a small region (of behavior, or of whatever the subject-matter may be) is then carried over to an explanation of adjoining regions. . . . In growth by intension a partial explanation of a whole region is made more and more adequate" (p. 305). The alternative patterned configurations of theories will more or less allow for their extensional reach and/or their intensional development. The more general a theory, with the potential to be broadly inclusive, the more it will be difficult to falsify. Focused micro theories, in contrast, with the greater potential to be falsified, tend to be the most difficult to widen in scope.

The selections in this chapter cluster into two sets. The first four selections provide a variety of ways to classify patterned theoretic forms. The last two selections present criteria for judging theoretic adequacy.

The first selection, by Abraham Kaplan, outlines the two classic forms of theory structure—one deductive and hierarchical, the other composed of laterally connected, or "concatenated," propositions. Kaplan goes on to note several other less major classifications of theory types. In the second selection, Paul Reynolds presents clear examples of Kaplan's two major types and discusses their advantages and disadvantages, and also provides one other theory type common to the social sciences.

The third and fourth selections, by Roger Evered and Lawrence Mohr, respectively, provide expanded descriptions of theoretic differences that are gaining increasing attention in the organizational sciences. Evered carefully uses time to differentiate future, purpose-focused theories from present, gestaltic theories and from the more common past-oriented theories. Mohr, discussing what Nagel in 1961 termed "genetic" explanations, explicates process theory (Rescher 1996) and contrasts it to the much more familiar variance theory.

The last two selections shift from patterns of theory type to offer criteria for assessing any theory. Karl Weick reminds us of the three general goals that theories strive for—generality, simplicity, and accuracy—and notes Thorngate's postulate that a theory cannot achieve all three goals simultaneously. Weick provides many conceptual examples of the trade-offs involved when a theory focuses on one, two, or all three of these goals. Samuel Bacharach's selection describes two generally accepted criteria for evaluating a theory, falsifiability and utility.

Types of Theories
Abraham Kaplan

The system that constitutes a theory may be of two types. Where the two are distinguished they are often regarded as marking the earlier and later stages of theory formation. I prefer to view them as belonging to two different reconstructed logics. They represent not so much different theories as

Source: *The Conduct of Inquiry* by Abraham Kaplan (San Francisco, CA: Chandler Publishing, 1964), 298–301.

differences in the methodologist's rational reconstruction of theories. But even though each reconstruction were in principle applicable to all theories, in fact, I believe, some theories lend themselves more readily to the one and some to the other, so that, if we choose, we may speak of two sorts of theories without too gross a distortion.

A *concatenated* theory is one whose component laws enter into a network of relations so as to constitute an identifiable configuration or pattern. Most typically, they converge on some central point, each specifying one of the factors which plays a part in the phenomenon which the theory is to explain. (It has therefore been called a theory of the "factor type," as contrasted with the "law type" [Q. B. Gibson 1960, 117–119, 144–145]). This is especially likely to be true of a theory consisting of tendency statements, which attain closure only in their joint application. A law or fact is explained by a concatenated theory when its place in the pattern is made manifest. The "big bang" theory of cosmology, the theory of evolution, and the psychoanalytic theory of the neuroses may all be regarded as being of this type.

A *hierarchical* theory is one whose component laws are presented as deductions from a small set of basic principles. A law is explained by the demonstration that it is a logical consequence of these principles, and a fact is explained when it is shown to follow from these together with certain initial conditions. The hierarchy is a deductive pyramid, in which we rise to fewer and more general laws as we move from conclusions to the premises which entail them. Because of the fundamental role of deductive relations in hierarchical theories, these theories are especially suited to the postulational and even the formal style. Such a theory may then be described as consisting of: (1) a calculus, whose sentences contain names for the "theoretical entities" being dealt with and provide horizontal specifications of the meaning of these names; (2) a set of "coordinating definitions" giving the entities a vertical specification, a dictionary couched in observational terms; and (3) an interpretive model, a system of which the postulates of the calculus are true when they are interpreted as specified. (As I shall point out shortly, the process of coordination is emphasized in the instrumentalist conception of theories and the resultant model is emphasized in the realist conception.) The theory of relativity, Mendelian genetics, and Keynesian economics may be taken to exemplify hierarchical theories.

A somewhat similar distinction between two sorts of theories has been suggested by Einstein (1934, 53–54): "We can distinguish various kinds of theories in physics. Most of them are constructive. They attempt to build up a picture of the more complex phenomena out of the materials of a relatively simple formal scheme from which they start out. . . . Along with this most important class of theories there exists a second, which I call 'principle-theories.' These employ the analytic, not the synthetic, method. The elements which form their basis and starting-point are not hypothetically constructed but empirically discovered ones, general characteristics of natural processes, principles that give rise to mathematically formulated criteria which the separate processes or the theoretical representations of them have to satisfy. . . . The advantages of the constructive theory are completeness, adaptability and clearness, those of the principle theory are logical perfection and security of the foundations."

Quite another classification of theories is based on characteristics of content rather than of form. Every theory may be said to demarcate an *explanatory shell* for the phenomena with which it deals. The shell around a given event is, as it were, a sphere containing whatever is referred to in the theory of that event. The contents of the shell constitute what is, from the standpoint of the theory, an effectively "isolated system." Such a system consists of the things that are both necessary and sufficient for an explanation, according to the theory, of the event in question. On this basis, we may distinguish *macro* or *molar theories* from *micro* or *molecular theories* according to the radius of the explanatory shell, as compared with the extensiveness of the sorts of events being considered. The distinction is a matter of the range of the laws occurring in the theory, the set of individuals to which they refer. Thus macro economics might be concerned with the workings of an economy or an industry, micro economics with the behavior of individual participants in the economic process. Similarly, a molar psychology considers a person as a whole, while a molecular psychology may focus on the interplay of habits or neural connections within the personality or organism.

In many quarters the position has been taken that micro theories are intrinsically more satisfactory. "It is often felt that only the discovery of a micro-theory affords real scientific understanding of any type of phenomenon, because only it gives us insight into the inner mechanism of the phenomenon, so to speak. Consequently, classes of events for which no micro-theory was available have frequently been viewed as not actually understood" (Hempel and Oppenheim 1948, 147). Underlying this position is what might be called the *principle of local determination*: the radius of the explanatory shell can be made indefinitely small. This principle is not identical with doctrinal determinism, though it implies the latter: where statistical theories are unavoidable the explanatory shell cannot be smaller than would allow for a statistically stable population. Local determination is determinism conjoined to a denial of action-at-a-distance in space or time: whatever happens anywhere is capable of being explained by reference to what is to be found then and there.

This point of view may well be involved in what Whitehead has called the fallacy of "simple location." It is not immediately and inescapably apparent—to me, at any rate—that a person, for example, must be conceived as localized within his skin, any more than that money must be conceived in terms of the local properties of the coin or currency. At any rate,

I do not see that the principle of local determination is methodologically necessary, whatever metaphysical justifications for it might be given. Of course, economical explanations are to be preferred over those which introduce considerations that another theory can dispense with. But contracting the explanatory shell is by no means always a move in the direction of economy. It is not obvious that a neural explanation of Hamlet's behavior will inevitably be simpler than the Oedipal one. On the other hand, it is reasonable to expect that the former may be capable of explaining a great deal else besides. As with so many methodological disputes, I protest only against the denials each side would exact of the other, not against what each aspires to achieve for itself.

A classification of theories with which the preceding one is often confused is that into *field theories* and *monadic theories*. A theory may take as fundamental a system of relations among certain elements, explaining the elements by reference to these relations, or it may give primacy to the relata, explaining the relations by reference to the attributes of what they relate. (Leibniz's "monadology" is the most extreme antithesis to a field theory, since he repudiates relational propositions altogether: each of his monads mirrors within itself the whole universe.) Thus a theory of personality in terms of roles might be contrasted with a theory in which roles are explained by reference to sets of needs of the individual personalities participating in the social process. What makes a field theory depends, not on the range of the constituent laws, but on their scope — not on what things the laws are about, but on what the laws say about those things. Thus even a micro theory can be a field theory, as for instance when memory is dealt with in terms of reverberations in neural circuits rather than in terms of engrams: the stationary wave is a relational property of the system, not an attribute of any of its components. That field theories are necessarily more "scientific" is again a doctrine for which I do not see any methodological necessity, if this discrimination is separated from metaphysical preferences. There is no doubt, however, that the recent history of science, especially physics, puts field theories in a favorable light. What they can contribute to behavioral science remains to be seen.

Three Conceptions of Theory
Paul Davidson Reynolds

Scientific knowledge is basically a collection of abstract theoretical statements. At present there seem to be three different conceptions of how sets of statements should be organized so as to constitute a "theory": (1) set-of-laws,

Source: *A Primer in Theory Construction* by Paul Davidson Reynolds, 83–85, 90–98, 106–107. Published by Allyn and Bacon, Boston, MA. Copyright © 1971 by Pearson Education. Reprinted by permission of the publisher.

(2) axiomatic, and (3) causal process. The purpose of this chapter is to present examples of those different conceptions of theory and to consider the advantages and disadvantages of each for the purposes of science. . . .

The Set-Of-Laws Form

One approach is to accept only those statements that can be considered laws as part of scientific knowledge. A set of laws is then considered to be the theory. As mentioned in the previous chapter, all laws are directly supported by empirical research; this means that all concepts used in laws must have operational definitions that allow their identification in concrete situations.

In addition to the potential for measurement of all concepts, some scientists would prefer that only relational statements be called laws, and preferably those that posit a causal relationship rather than an association between concepts. They would rule out statements, such as:

All social systems have identifiable status hierarchies.

However, this restriction would rule out a number of statements that appear to be useful descriptions of phenomena, such as:

All livings things eventually die.

The statement does not state what will cause death, or even when it will occur, but only that the concept "dead" will at some time be an appropriate description of any living thing.

All of the laws described here will contain theoretical concepts that can be measured directly in concrete settings, and most will describe a causal relationship between two concepts. After discussing some examples, the set-of-laws conception of theory will be considered further.

Example: The Iron Law of Oligarchy (Michels 1959)[1]

. . . the majority of human beings, . . . , are predestined by tragic necessity to submit to the dominion of a small minority, and must be content to constitute the pedestal of an oligarchy (Michels 1959, 390).

In more modern terms, using the following concepts:

Social system — Any aggregate of individuals that are organized and have collective interests (i.e., collective goals).

1. It is clear that Michels considered this statement as a summary of a set of processes, discussed later in the chapter, and does not suggest that scientific knowledge be organized as a set of laws.

Democratic leadership — Control of all matters affecting a social system or its members, shared *equally* by all the members of the social system, either through direct vote or indirect control over the leaders.

Oligarchical leadership — Complete control of all matters affecting a social system or its members by a privileged clique, drawn from the membership.

The "iron law of oligarchy" now may be restated as follows:

> The only stable form of leadership, even in social systems initially utilizing a democratic leadership, is an oligarchical leadership, and an oligarchy will eventually develop in any social system.

Notice that the "iron law of oligarchy" is in the form of an existence statement. It does not refer to any concept or variable as causing the development of an oligarchy; it states only that all social systems will eventually develop an oligarchical form of leadership. . . .

Scientific knowledge in the form of a set of laws appears to be useful for providing a typology, providing predictions and explanations, and, if the statements are sufficiently precise, allowing the potential for control. However, they do not provide any "sense of understanding" with regard to any of the phenomena discussed. What social processes cause all organized collectivities to develop oligarchical leadership structures? What mental processes cause individuals on intermittent schedules to take longer to learn that certain behavior is rewarding and longer to learn that certain behavior is no longer rewarding, compared to those on continuous schedules? What group processes cause individuals more central in an interaction pattern to acquire higher prestige (rank) in a face-to-face group? These types of questions cannot be answered by a theory in the form of a set of laws. Therefore, if scientific knowledge is organized in the form of a set of laws, a scientist cannot achieve all the purposes of science, since he cannot provide a sense of understanding.

This conception of scientific knowledge has several other disadvantages. First, since laws are directly supported by empirical research, every concept used in a law must have at least one operational definition that allows identification of the theoretical concept in concrete settings. This prohibits the use of any unmeasurable concepts or hypothetical constructs in theoretical statements. As mentioned earlier, this would prohibit the use of many concepts currently employed in science, particularly dispositional concepts, which refer to the tendency of "things" to create certain effects, i.e., magnetism, authoritarianism, etc. One can only measure the consequences of a dispositional concept, i.e., attraction to iron, tendency to perceive in absolutes (good or bad), and the like, but not the actual concept itself.

Second, the statements that compose a set of laws are supposed to be independent, unrelated to one another. This has several disadvantages. It means that the final set of statements will be very large, since the relationship between every set of concepts requires a theoretical statement or law. Also, since the statements are considered to be independent, research in support of one statement or law cannot provide support for another statement or law. Compared with other ways of organizing theoretical statements, the set-of-laws form may require more research and therefore may be comparatively inefficient. However, this depends on which research strategy is being employed. . . .

In summary, the conception of scientific knowledge as a set of laws will allow scientists to achieve some of the goals of science—typologies, prediction and explanation, and if the laws are carefully specified, the potential for control. However, a sense of understanding is completely absent when laws are used to logically explain phenomena. The attempt to concentrate on developing a set of laws eliminates unmeasurable or hypothetical theoretical concepts from the repertoire of available concepts, results in a very large set of statements (that may be difficult to organize in a useful form) and a much larger program of research, since each law must receive empirical support independent of empirical support provided for any other law.

As a final comment, most of human knowledge, perhaps more than 90 percent, consists of statements that meet the criterion of laws or empirical generalizations, that is, a relationship between two observed concepts. This is particularly true of "practical knowledge," such as medicine, engineering, or administration, where "rules of thumb" are employed, often disguised as "judgment," without precise knowledge of the specific causal processes involved. . . .

The Axiomatic Form

An axiomatic theory is typically defined as an interrelated set of definitions and statements with several important features:

1. A set of definitions, including theoretical concepts, both primitive and derived (nominal), and operational definitions (to allow the identification of some abstract theoretical concepts in concrete settings).
2. A set of existence statements that describe the situations in which the theory can be applied, sometimes referred to as the *scope conditions* since they describe the scope of conditions to which the theory is considered applicable. (These statements are not required in a completely imaginary theory, such as in mathematics, that is not intended to be applied to concrete or "real" phenomena.)
3. A set of relational statements, divided into two groups:
   a. Axioms—A set of statements from which all other statements in the theory may be derived.

   b. Propositions—All other statements in the theory, all derived
      from combinations of axioms, axioms and propositions, or other
      propositions.
4. A logical system used to:
   a. Relate all concepts within statements, and
   b. Derive propositions from axioms, combinations of axioms and
      propositions, or other propositions.

Plane geometry is perhaps the most widely known axiomatic theory; in
fact, most mathematical theories are in this form.

It is extremely difficult to find examples of axiomatic theory relating to
social or human phenomena, and it is even harder to find those that are
simple enough for an introductory discussion. However, Hopkins (1964)
does present his statements in this form, and his material will serve as an
example.

Example: The Exercise of Influence in Small Groups (Hopkins 1964)

The crucial definitions in this theory are those of rank, centrality,
influence, observability, and conformity, all defined in the previous section.

The only scope condition is that the theory applies only to small interacting groups, where each member has the opportunity to form a personal
impression of every other member.

Hopkins selected nine statements as axioms:

A-1 If rank, then centrality.

A-2 If centrality, then observability.

A-3 If centrality, then conformity.

A-4 If observability, then conformity.

A-5 If conformity, then observability.

A-6 If observability, then influence.

A-7 If conformity, then influence.

A-8 If influence, then conformity.

A-9 If influence, then rank.

These axioms can be combined to produce new statements, or propositions. For example, axioms A-1 and A-2 may be combined to produce a new
proposition as follows:

A-1 If rank, then centrality.

A-2 If centrality, then observability.

——————————

Therefore: If rank, then observability.

Another set of axioms may be combined to produce the same proposition:

A-1 If rank, then centrality.
A-3 If centrality, then conformity.
A-5 If conformity, then observability.

———————

Therefore: If rank, then observability.

Using all possible combinations of axioms, it is possible to produce eleven propositions, some in as many as four ways (four different combinations of axioms). . . .

One of the most important problems in dealing with theories in axiomatic form is determining how to select the axioms. In other words, what criteria will be used to choose certain statements and call them axioms. Consistency is clearly required; no two axioms, or any combination of axioms, should make conflicting predictions. But, aside from the criterion of consistency, it is difficult to establish criteria for substantive theories.

In dealing with logical systems that are completely abstract and independent of any feature of the "real world," as in mathematics, a common criterion is to select the smallest set of axioms from which all other statements can be derived, reflecting a preference for simplicity and elegance. There is reason to think that this is inappropriate for a substantive theory, particularly when it makes it more difficult to understand the theory.

One criterion that is seriously entertained is to accept as axioms only those statements that have achieved the status of laws.[2] If this criterion is accepted, an axiomatic form of theory becomes a procedure for organizing and integrating a set of laws, which has merit. However, it will be remembered that any statement that becomes a law must have considerable empirical support *before* it is considered a law. This would mean that all the statements and the concepts contained in the statements used as axioms must have a direct correspondence to concrete settings. This would prevent the inclusion of hypothetical or unmeasurable concepts in an axiomatic theory, thereby eliminating one of its most useful advantages.

In dealing with axiomatic theory related to substantive matters, it seems appropriate to select as axioms that set of independent statements that makes the theory easiest to understand, no matter how large. Blalock (1969, 18) suggests that this is achieved if only those statements that describe a *direct causal* relationship between two concepts are employed as axioms. This is the criterion used by Hopkins (1964), and it seems to be a reasonable suggestion. However, if it is found that some other set of statements is more clearly understood (there is more shared agreement among the audi-

———————

2. Costner and Leik (1964) assume this criterion in their critique of the problems of testing theory in axiomatic form.

ence), the theorist should feel free to use it. This is consistent with Blalock's goal, which is to reduce the ambiguity in the description of theories.

As with the statements in the set-of-laws concept of theory, the statements in the axiomatic form of theory can be used to logically derive explanations and predictions. The concepts contained in the theory can also be used to classify and organize events. But, since the logical notion of explanation is utilized with this form of theory, it fails to provide a "sense of understanding."

However, the axiomatic form does have several advantages over the set-of-laws form of theory. First, since some statements can be derived from others, it is not necessary for all concepts to be measurable. Hence, unmeasurable or hypothetical concepts may be employed in developing the theory. Second, the number of statements that express scientific knowledge can be smaller. Instead of requiring a statement to describe a relationship between every pair of concepts, a set of axioms and the logical system may be used to generate a large number of statements. The set of axioms and the logical system may be less cumbersome than a large set of independent statements. Third, research may be more efficient. Because the theory is an interrelated set of statements, empirical support for any one statement tends to provide support for the entire theory and, hence, support for the other statements that compose the theory. . . . Fourth, the axiomatic form allows the theorist to examine *all* the consequences of his assumptions, or axioms. Often the careful formalization of a theory results in some surprises, or "unintended consequences," that derive from a certain conceptualization or paradigm.

Finally, the axiomatic form of theory is compatible with the causal process form of theory described in the next section. Frequently, the statements that compose an axiomatic theory can be organized in such a way as to provide a causal description of the process that relates changes in an independent variable with changes in a dependent variable. If this is done, they can provide a "sense of understanding." However, this is not always possible.

The lack of social science theories in axiomatic form suggests that it has either been impossible or inconvenient for social scientists to put their ideas into this format. However, almost all of the paradigms in social science appear amiable to the following form of theory, the causal process form.

The Causal Process Form

The causal process form of theory is an interrelated set of definitions and statements with the following features:[3]

1. A set of definitions, including those of theoretical concepts, using both primitive and derived (nominal) terms, and operational

3. Berger et al. (1962) discuss theoretical-construct models (pp. 67–101), which are identical to the causal process model discussed here. Blalock (1969) discusses causal mod-

definitions (that describe how to identify some of the theoretical concepts in concrete settings).
2. A set of existence statements that describe those situations in which one or more of the causal processes are expected to occur: or as it is sometimes described, when these processes will be "activated."
3. A set of causal statements, with either deterministic or probabilistic relations, that describe one or more causal processes or causal mechanisms that identify the effect of one or more independent variables on one or more dependent variables. Although different causal mechanisms may differ in impact on the dependent variables, all statements are considered of equal importance in terms of the presentation of the theory.

The major difference between this form of theory and the axiomatic form is that all statements are considered to be of equal importance, they are not classified into axioms and propositions, and the statements are presented in a different fashion, as a causal process. Intersubjective theoretical concepts are still required, hypothetical (unmeasurable) concepts are allowed, and scope conditions, describing when and where the causal process will occur, are necessary.

No matter what type of theory a scientist claims to be dealing with, when he explains "how" something happens he usually refers to a description of one or more causal processes. Therefore, it seems reasonable to openly acknowledge the description of a causal process as a theoretical form and consider its advantages. . . .

Example: The Effect of First Impressions on Cognitions

The following statement, taken from Secord and Backman (1964, 59) can be considered an empirical generalization:

> When an individual forms an impression of another person, information about the other received earlier has more effect on the final impression than information about the other received later.

One causal process that will explain this finding is composed of the following statements:

> *Scope Condition*: This process is expected to be activated at any time the individual forms, for the first time, an impression of a complex object, including other individuals.

---

els and puts them in the form of systems of linear equations. Both discussions are more sophisticated, and complex, than the discussion here.

Under this condition, the following causal process will be activated:

1. When a person develops a cognition of a complex object, an overall framework is developed before the details are completed.
2. Information received first is used to develop the overall framework of the new cognition.
3. Information received later is used to complete the details of the cognition.
4. Final impressions reflect the general outlines of the new cognition more than they reflect the details.

This process can be summarized by stating that initial information is used to develop a general outline that is refined as more details are acquired. However, the overall impression is a reflection of the general outlines, which are not significantly affected by the details. Hence, the overall impressions are influenced more by the initial information than by later information. . . .

In addition to achieving the four primary purposes of science, theory in causal process form shares several advantages with the axiomatic form of theory: it allows for hypothetical or unmeasurable concepts; it provides for more efficient research (since it is possible to test interrelated sets of statements); and, finally, carefully described causal processes allow the theorist to examine all of the consequences of his formulation, including the unintended consequences.

One of the most important advantages of the causal process form of theory is that this seems to be the way that most theories in social science, related to either social or individual phenomena, are developed. If this is the case, the transformation between the development of an idea and the causal process form is easier than the translation to either the axiomatic or set-of-laws form of theory.

One problem exists with the causal process form of theory: When do you stop? In other words, at what point can a theorist decide when all the steps, or statements, in a causal linkage have been specified? There seems to be no objective answer to this question, and perhaps the only solution is to require inter-subjective agreement among the relevant scientists. Only when a researcher and his colleagues agree that all the steps in a causal process have been identified is it time to stop working on the theory.

A Typology of Explicative Models
Roger D. Evered

Introduction

The primary business of the social sciences is to provide conceptual frameworks (e.g., theories) for *understanding and explaining human behavior*, with the hope that by improving our understanding of social/organizational/managerial phenomena we can facilitate desirable improvements within some particular social/organizational/managerial system. The task is particularly difficult in the context of rapid change, whether environmental, organizational or individual.

Throughout the literature on the philosophy of science (i.e., the epistemological and conceptual basis for scientific explanation) we find a continuing discussion on the nature of explanation (e.g., Kaplan 1964; Reichenbach 1951; Feigl and Brodbeck 1953). What has become increasingly clear, especially since the systematic development of the biological and social sciences, is that *a wide range of explanatory approaches are utilized for rendering observed facts intelligible*. Although many different modes of explanations have been presented and espoused regarding the question of what constitutes "explanation" and "understanding," so far there has been little attempt at generating typologies (e.g., Bunge 1970).

What do we mean by the term "explanation"? Etymologically, "to explain" means "to lay something out on a flat surface"; that is, to unfold, reveal, develop it. In everyday language, it means making sense of what appears to be strange and outlandish. In the scientific sense, to explain something means to render observable facts intelligible, meaningful and clear to a mind seeking understanding (C. Taylor 1970; Rescher 1970).

The function of an explanation is to remove some of the complexity, confusion and surprise associated with the real world events. An explanation helps to convert the unknown into the known, by making the seemingly unintelligible more intelligible. Events and acts are interpreted in terms of a credible and parsimonious framework, or some set of interconnected reasons, beliefs, or laws—in the context of other credible frameworks, reasons, beliefs, laws. And this interpretation is made in such a manner that our understanding of the events is enhanced. That is to say, we feel more enlightened as a consequence of the explanation.

Essentially an explanation is a response to a "why?" question that we have about some particular phenomena or observed event(s). As Braithwaite

Source: "A Typology of Explicative Models" by Roger D. Evered, *Technological Forecasting and Social Change* 9 (1976): 260–269. Copyright © 1976 American Elsevier Publishing Company, Inc. Reprinted with permission from Elsevier.

(1953) writes "What is demanded in a 'why?' question is intellectual satis-faction of one kind or another, and this can be provided, partially or com-pletely, in different ways."

This variety of ways of explaining events arises from—

a. the tremendous variety of the phenomena we encounter,
b. the variety of possible questions which may be posed from the same phenomenon,
c. the many different kinds of responses which can be given for any particular question,
d. the fact that what constitutes "intellectual satisfaction" for one person may not for someone else.

The purpose of this paper is to draw attention to the many different kinds of "explanation," and to provide a typology which relates them in an orderly way.

What Kinds of Questions Are We Interested In?

Most of the questions we have about social phenomena arise from our observations of events which strike us as novel or different or unfamiliar; that is, from our awareness of something changing, growing, developing, moving. In short the majority of our social/organizational/managerial ques-tions arise from the *phenomena of change*.

We want to understand how a particular situation came to be, how it might become something else, why and how it transitions into a different situation. We want to know why a certain individual acted in a particular way; why a particular department evolved the way it did; why an unex-pected crisis occurred in the organization; and why some familiar organiza-tion process no longer seems to be working. And in the managerial field, we want to know whether a particular action we have in mind will be effective; will generate the consequences we hope for; will lead to unexpected re-sponses from others; will improve or worsen the situation which we are cur-rently dealing with.

All of these questions (and the many others like them) require explana-tions which help us to make sense of the events and actions which make up our socio-organizational lives. We need explanatory frameworks which ex-press the transitional, generative, "becoming" nature of the social phenom-ena we are part of.

Managers, perhaps more than any other group, think in terms of this emergent process. They function by making decisions regarding actions to take within organizational settings. What they do is to try to create or produce something not currently existing; that is, *they are continuously gen-erating and regulating change*.

The Components of an Explanation

The simplest kind of explanation is a *description* of the phenomena using everyday English language. More elaborate explanations will employ more elaborate *symbolic languages* like mathematics. Descriptions which employ clearly defined constructs, which express relationships in operational terms and which permit the explanation to be verified are called *scientific* explanations. (Not all explanations, however, meet these criteria, particularly not the verifiability criteria.)

As stated above, an explanation is essentially a response to some "why?" question which someone has about particular phenomena or set of events.

The observed event(s) or fact(s) which stand in need of an explanation is often called the *Explicandum* (or explanandum); while those statements which purport to explain the explicandum are referred to as the *Explicans* (or explanans) (Braithwaite 1953; Carnap 1950; Hempel 1959). The explicandum (fact) is the *object* of explanation and the explicans (proposition) is the *basis* of explanation.

The explanation will, generally, incorporate the following:

a. A set of other, more familiar events, facts, acts (occurring either *anterior*, *concurrent*, or *posterior* to the events, facts, acts which need explaining [i.e., to the explicandum]);
b. One or more interrelationships or lawlike statements connecting the events, facts and acts;[4]
c. A language for expressing the necessary constructs, entities and relationships.

The dialogue between the explicandum (events needing to be explained) and the explicans (explanatory statement) can be viewed essentially as a device for resolving inconsistencies or discontinuities in the universe of observable events.

The Temporal Relationship Between the Explicandum and the Explicans

The essential dimension of the typology presented here is *the temporal relationship* between the events described in the explicandum and the events

---

4. It will be noticed that the explicans contains interrelational connective statements. If we insist that these connective statements be precise laws (i.e., nomological, or representable by logic statements), then we obtain Hempel's "covering law model of explanation." In Hempel's formulation the explicandum (he calls it the explanandum) is therefore logically deducible from the explicans (he uses explanans). That is, the explicans suffices as an explanation if the observed events can be deduced from the two sets of premises (i) a set of statements describing the initial conditions and (ii) a set of general laws.

employed as part of the explicans. As noted in (a) above, the former may be *anterior* to, *contemporary* with, or *posterior* to the latter.

We can readily appreciate these time distinctions by noting the various responses that are commonly given to a "why?" question. Each kind of response suggests a different form of explanation.

For example, the simple question, "Why did he decide to go to New York today?" may be responded with either—

1. *Because* (his boss asked him to and the President authorized it) (anterior events), or
2. *In order to* (talk with a client about a proposed project) (posterior events), or
3. *It fits.* (It seems reasonable and appropriate to do so in the light of the circumstances he now finds himself in. That's his job anyway. That is what most people familiar with the situation would expect. I'd be surprised if he didn't.) (contemporary events)

We can readily distinguish three broad classes of explanation which are invoked to explain the observed event, E (he decided to go to New York today).

1. Causal Explanations: Why E? *Because* C (C = Cause).
2. Teleological Explanations: Why E? *In order to* P (P = Purpose).
3. Gestaltic Explanations: Why E? *For these natural reasons*, R (R = Reasons).

In the causal case the explicans employs events which *precede* the observed events (of the explicandum;) in the *teleological case the explicans refers to events which occur later* than the explicandum events; while in the *gestaltic* case, the explicandum employs more-or-less concurrent or contemporaneous events.

The key distinction here is a temporal one. The set of explanatory events used in the explicans is located at different times (past, present and future), in relation to the explicanda (that which stands in need of explaining). The qualitative nature of this temporal distinction is shown in [Figure 9-1].

The same temporal distinction has been made by Grünbaum (1962) and by Rescher (1970). Grünbaum defines explanations "*a tergo*" as "the notion that occurrences at time *t* can be explained *only* by reference to earlier occurrences and *not also* by reference to later ones"; and explanations "*a fronte*" as "the notion that all phenomena occurring at a time *t* are to be understood by reference to later occurrences only." . . .

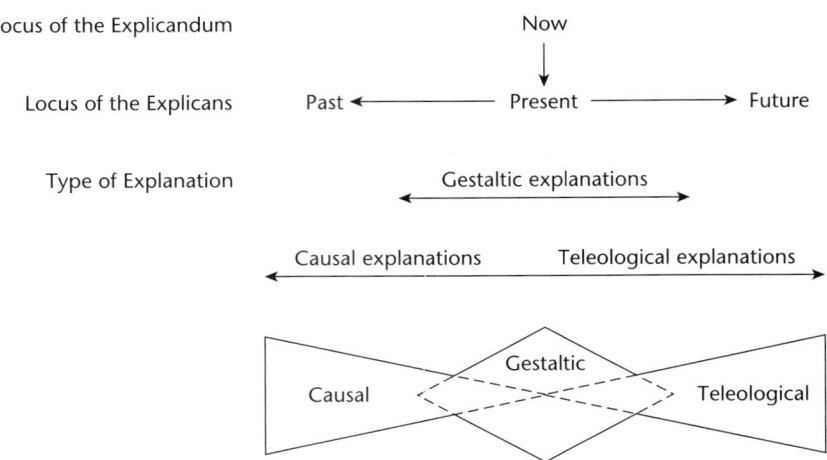

Locus of the Explicandum   Now

Locus of the Explicans   Past ◄──────── Present ──────────► Future

Type of Explanation   Gestaltic explanations

Causal explanations   Teleological explanations

Causal   Gestaltic   Teleological

FIGURE **9-1**   The temporal relationship between the *explicans* (that which explains) and the *explicandum* (that which needs explaining)

Variance and Process Theories
Lawrence B. Mohr

The basis of the distinction between process theory and variance theory is best conceptualized in terms of necessary and sufficient conditions as modes of explanation, or forms of theory. The variance theory is a type whose characteristics grow out of a foundation in the necessary and sufficient, whereas the characteristics of process theory grow out of a foundation in the necessary alone.

We imagine an outcome (Y) and a set of events and conditions considered as precursor (X), wishing to view the precursor as a powerful explanatory generalization in connection with the outcome, so as to have a law, or a theory of Y.

If the precursor set is a necessary and sufficient condition for the outcome, then this clearly constitutes a satisfactory theory. It fits into the category of variance theory.

If the precursor is merely a sufficient condition and strives to be nothing more, then it does not constitute a satisfactory theory of Y, for if Y occurs

TABLE 9-1

Characteristics of variance theory and process theory

Variance theory	Process theory
The basis of explanation is causality.	The basis of explanation is probabilistic rearrangement.
1. The precursor (X) is a necessary and sufficient condition for the outcome (Y).	1. The precursor (X) is a necessary condition for the outcome (Y).
2. A variance theory deals with variables.	2. A process theory deals with discrete states and events.
3. A variance theory deals with efficient causes.	3. A process theory deals with a final cause.
4. In variance theory, time ordering among the contributing (independent) variables is immaterial to the outcome.	4. In process theory, time ordering among the contributing events is generally critical for the outcome.

SOURCE: *Explaining organizational behavior* by Lawrence B. Mohr, 38, table 1. Copyright © 1982 by Jossey-Bass Inc., Publishers. Used by permission of Lawrence B. Mohr.

quite commonly without X (since X is not necessary), then one has not yet a good explanation. It lacks completeness. What makes Y occur when X does not? The precursor X may surely be considered a cause of Y, and it may be extremely important to know that X sometimes causes Y, but this falls somewhat short of providing a theory of Y. Strangulation, in these terms, is a cause of death but not a theory of death. If one seeks a more general cause or strives to add Xs in order to achieve completeness, then one's orientation moves toward a precursor that, taken as a whole, is both necessary and sufficient rather than merely sufficient. To try to cast an explanatory theory of a recurrent phenomenon in terms of the merely sufficient is to guarantee instability. By its very nature, the merely sufficient condition will be found to exert a strong influence in one context and little or no influence in another. . . .

Two propositions regarding variance theory and process theory are important for the present critique of theoretical development. The first . . . is that they may be and should be viewed as distinct types. For convenience in this discussion, the primary and secondary characteristics of variance theory and process theory are summarized in Table [9-1]. The second claim is that confusion of the types and the attempt to mix them constitute a significant impediment, one source of the frustration of theory. . . .

Variance Theory

In variance theory *the precursor (X) is a necessary and sufficient condition for the outcome (Y).* In other terms, if X, then Y, and if not-X, then not-Y. This kind of explanation is likely to be a most satisfying one if it is well supported and if it also is intuitively appealing, or makes sense, given what one already feels one knows. Unfortunately, it has thus far proved extremely difficult to find powerful explanatory relations of this kind in the social realm. Nevertheless, the form of the theory is so straightforward and appealing that it generally serves as a model and a goal. If one's explanation happens to be as yet incomplete, one hopes that one has a part of a theory, at least, and that the precursor set will be filled out more satisfactorily in the future. A large amount of empirical social research is carried out in this tradition.

The logic of experimental design (D. T. Campbell and Stanley 1963) is also that of the necessary and sufficient condition. The results of a true experiment are a variance theory in microcosm; instead of being an explanatory theory descriptive of the world in general, the results are descriptive only of what takes place for one set of subjects in one context. In an experiment, however, the precursor, instead of occurring naturally, is manipulated by the investigator. This fact suggests that the variance-theory format may be used conveniently in evaluating the effects of purposeful interventions. This use will become important when considering theories of the effectiveness of organizational designs or programs.

Because the precursor is necessary and sufficient, one of the prominent uses to which a variance theory can be put is prediction. Prediction without explanation is possible—quite common, in fact—but it is also true that an explanatory generalization can be both tested and applied by using the precursor to predict the outcome. In the same sense, if one can manipulate the precursor, then one has control over the outcome of interest. Prediction and control are powerful benefits, and the potential for attaining them helps to explain why variance theories are so commonly pursued.

. . . Variance theory is state-oriented (Simon 1969, 111–112); it deals in snapshots rather than movies. The functional relation among the independent causes is important (for example, it may be linear or nonlinear), but the time ordering among those causes is unimportant because each contributor has an independent effect. Each cause is always sufficient, with the others held constant, to produce a given impact on Y. The very idea of holding *constant* demonstrates the irrelevance of time. It does not matter for the volume of the gas, for example, whether temperature precedes pressure or vice versa. . . . But it is not essential to recognize time order in the necessary and sufficient explanation, and this fact allows a parsimony in the number of variables included and a simplicity in their arrangement without which it would be difficult to proceed.

Process Theory

In this section, the term *process theory* is given a highly specific meaning. At present, however, it is a common term with a variety of alternative meanings and connotations. The reader is therefore requested to put aside prior interpretations for the moment in order to allow the concept to be constructed here in its entirety for use in the present context. Loosely, a process theory is one that tells a little story about how something comes about, but in order to qualify as a theoretical explanation of recurrent behavior, the manner of the story telling must conform to narrow specifications.

Process theories are quite different from variance theories in all the respects just reviewed. Paradoxically, however, although process theories as they will be described here are monumentally important in science and are at least as common as variance theories, their characteristics have not been articulated to the same extent. They have, in fact, only barely been suggested (see Kaplan 1964, 109–111; Simon 1969, 107–118; Lave and March 1975). The variance-theory *outlook* dominates thinking about theory by scientists, philosophers, and the general public, even though the variance-theory *form* does not in practice dominate theory itself.

In process theory, the precursor (X) is a necessary condition for the outcome (Y). Again, we deal with some particular outcome, Y, as a descriptor of some focal unit, such as a person or object. The orientation is toward an explanatory theory of Y. Since the precursor, X, is necessary for Y, the basic logical statement involved is "If not-X, then not-Y." This statement, however, cannot be the most important thrust of a theory; to have an explanation, one must be heavily concerned with when Y does occur, not exclusively with when it does not. The precursor in a process theory contains three types of elements—(1) necessary conditions and (2) necessary probabilistic processes, which together form the core of the theory, and (3) external, directional forces that function to move the focal unit and conditions about in a characteristic way, often herding them into mutual proximity. Let us elaborate on these three components.

One crucial element of the precursor, as noted, is a set of necessary conditions or objects. These and the focal unit (for example, the person who may get malaria) are capable of changing over time and, particularly, of *combining* with one another in such a way as to yield the outcome. In the theory or story of malaria, for example, these necessary conditions are the malarial parasite, persons already harboring the parasite, and *Anopheles* mosquitoes. The combining of elements is of paramount importance. Process theory eschews efficient causality as explanation and depends instead on *rearrangement*—that is, on the joining or separation of two or more specified elements rather than on a change in the magnitude of some element. Whereas a variance theory explains a behavior or a characteristic of an object, a process theory explains the pairing or other rearrangement of mutually autonomous objects, such as the bets of the players and the number on the roulette wheel, whose individual courses are determined independently of one another by forces external to the core of the theory. One particular combination of the conditions and focal unit is defined, within the theory, *to be* the outcome. (For example, in the present context, the simple joining of the parasite and the focal person will be labeled "contraction of malaria," omitting all concern with the later appearance of symptoms.)

Because the precursor is not sufficient, there is no inherent force either within the focal unit or within the necessary conditions that makes them inevitably combine in such a way as to result in the state defined to be the outcome. Nothing about the prior malaria victim or the parasite is assumed to make the bite of another mosquito inevitable, and nothing about the mosquito makes it inevitable that it will later bite the focal person. Nevertheless, there must be something that leads to the occurrence of Y, even though it is not an efficient cause, or there can be no sense of explanation. If the joining of elements does not follow inevitably from any set of antecedent conditions, then it must occur by chance. What has not been sufficiently emphasized in this connection, however, is the degree of system, the regularity that may be then involved. The laws of chance, though based in randomness, do not necessarily imply disorder. On the contrary, those laws are *laws*; they can be used to construe powerfully some of our most profound insights into the nature and the order of things.

Thus, as the second element of the precursor, the role in process theory that is analogous to efficient cause is occupied by probabilistic processes—by random draws from simple or joint probability distributions of various shapes that are either explicit or implied. In part, it is occupied as well by the external directional forces, the third element, which are simply presumed to carry on in some generally accepted manner (for example, mosquitoes look for people and animals to bite), but the theoretical essence, the guarantor of the proper combinations of objects, lies in one or more probabilistic processes. For example, *Anopheles* mosquitoes bite people with and without malaria at random.

It is critical to recognize that from the viewpoint of the model, at least—and the model may attempt either to reflect faithfully or perhaps to simplify the physical world—*Anopheles* mosquitoes, no matter how many there are, need *never* bite any person without malaria. The fact that they do (and the rate at which they do) depends on the operation of the laws of chance. *Without those laws, there would be no basis for believing that new persons would ever contract the disease*, but given those laws, there is indeed a scientifically satisfactory explanation, and one that would be inadequate if it depended on efficient causality alone. In this way, probabilistic processes are crucial for explanation in certain theories and therefore become the basis for establishing a separate type of theory, the process theory. . . .

The view just elaborated is in sharp contrast to the usual view of probabilistic events in science and the philosophy of science. There, random processes are explanation. This is not at all to say that there is no ignorance, no missing variables or hidden causes. It is possible to suggest, however, that at least some occurrences that would automatically be ascribed to hidden causes might indeed be inherently probabilistic instead. The discussion of probabilistic occurrence is almost always conducted with a causal metaphysic as backdrop (for example, Hempel and Oppenheim 1948; Suppe 1977, 266–283; or the discussion of Bohr's views on quantum theory in Suppe 1977, 180–191), and in such a perspective, tendency statements, or nondeterministic hypotheses, will always be in a certain amount of conceptual trouble as theory. Tendencies are an admission that the causal picture is a bit obscure. The difficulty evaporates, however, when a probabilistic metaphysic itself is applicable. Not all recurring events are causal, especially because what is considered an event depends on how reality is construed. The explanation of a roulette's wheel's stopping with the ball on number 23 may be causal, subsumed by covering laws from Newtonian mechanics, but the explanation for the fact that somebody wins is not causal; it is inherently probabilistic. It depends on the ball's happening to come to rest on a number that happened to be covered by a bet, each phenomenon being governed by its own set of forces. Similarly for the genetic composition of the sperm that fertilizes a given egg: To the egg, it is a turn of the wheel.

Without external forces and probabilistic processes, alleged, tentative, or incipient process theories are anemic. They may be of value in clarifying the nature of certain developmental and other procedures that exist in the world, and they may eventually be developed into theory. In order actually to be theory, however, in the sense of being an explanation for a recurrent Y, a compelling flow of action is required. It is not sufficient merely to name a succession of necessary stages or events—for example, to say that organizational innovation proceeds through a process of unfreezing, moving, and refreezing (Zand and Sorensen 1975); one must also supply the external forces and probabilistic processes constituting the means by which that sequence of events is understood to unfold. Either the causes of the development inhere in the initial state (as the infant inherently becomes the adult), or the progression depends on encounters of the focal unit with factors that spring from elsewhere. Moreover, there is a tendency for the outcome in such incipient theories to be an individual behavior or characteristic rather than a combination. In such cases, merely interjecting probability does not help, for it is not a satisfactory explanation. One may always ask, "Why?" Why did this organization refreeze instead of retrogressing, as many do? Any seriously explanatory answer must be in terms of either some form of causality or some form of motivational reasoning. Probability simply begs the issue. Unless the precise probability is universal and immutable, the theoretical understanding of refreezing is not enhanced by reporting the probability—that is, the relative frequency—of its occurrence in a certain study or organization. When outcomes are successfully conceptualized as a combining of independently developing entities, however, probability becomes not only a meaningful response but generally the only response. It is, no doubt, often true that an outcome of interest is capable of being seen either as a characteristic that has a cause or as an encounter that is probabilistic, but to be a process-theory outcome it must somehow be conceptualized as the latter. Unfortunately . . . process-oriented ideas in organizational behavior, and in social science more broadly, tend to be primarily of the stage-naming variety. They are incomplete from the standpoint of theory in that they simply rehearse a series of steps; they lack the lines of action—either causal or probabilistic—that must be present to convey a sense of explanation.

Whereas in variance theory, use, testing, and theoretical modification proceed largely by direct prediction and control of outcomes, the procedure is more varied in process theory. Much emphasis is still on the future—that is, process theories can predict that an outcome will occur some proportion of the time. Similarly, they may be used to prevent the occurrence of phenomena (for example, diseases) or to enhance their occurrence (for example, the diffusion of innovations). But the fertility of a process model may also be extremely strong and significant in the direction of reconstruction of the past. The Darwinian theory of natural selection has been incredibly rich in increasing understanding by "predicting" what must be there or must have been there; it continues to inform and assist growth throughout the many branches of biology and in other sciences as well, such as geology. Similarly with the elementary laws of Mendelian genetics[,] they not only predict and explain proportions of progeny by type but have helped to establish the necessity of genetic linkage, recombination, and so forth. In fact, as will be evidenced in later chapters, there is a tendency to overemphasize prediction of outputs as a means of verifying and exploring what are really process-type theories in social science, probably because of the prevailing variance-theory orientation. Often, that is not what process theories do best, particularly with respect to a given trial. Output checking can be distracting and even misleading. It would be better simply to look into the process itself to see whether it occurs as alleged and, as Lave and March (1975) highlight so successfully, to concentrate on fertility, to look for implications of the model for phenomena other than the outcome.

With this introductory elaboration of process theory as involving the necessary but not sufficient precursor, let us now turn to the resultant characteristics, which stand in marked contrast to the characteristics of variance theory.

A process theory deals with discrete states and events. The predominant flavor of a process model is that of a series of occurrences of events rather than a set of relations among variables. With variance theory, one is permitted to extend the statement "If X, then Y" to cover the case of infinite, continuous

variables—"If less-or-more X, then less-or-more Y"—but a similar extension cannot be made with the process-theory statement. As noted earlier, to
say that X is necessary for Y is to say that if not-X, then not-Y. The extension
of this statement would read "If not-less-or-more-X [that is, if X], then not-
less-or-more-Y [that is, then Y]," which, as indicated by the bracketed expressions, ends in a violation of the nonsufficiency requirement. In other
words, the merely necessary cannot be transformed into a functional relation
between *variables*; it must simply deal with a given precursor (although possibly one that involves many events and processes) and a given outcome. (The
term *function* is still being used here in the strict sense of one and only one
value of Y for each value of X.) In general, if one desires an explanation for a
different state of Y, or for not-Y, one must produce a second process model.
It might be quite similar to the first one, but it might be quite different, or it
might not exist at all. . . .

A process theory states that X is necessary for Y. Does this at least provide, by extension, a process theory of not-Y? Not even that. The original
statement cannot be extended in variable-like fashion to the theoretical
statement that not-X is necessary for not-Y, because that again, and even
more clearly, would imply the unacceptable sufficiency conclusion "If X,
then Y." We do not say, for example, that the absence of prior victims, or of
mosquitoes, or of the parasite, is necessary in order that A not get malaria.
These are not the *only* ways to avoid the disease. The random processes are
such that many individuals may remain free of the parasite amid all the dangerous conditions simply because they happen not to get bitten, or at least
not by the right mosquito.

. . . *A process theory deals with a final cause.* The concept of efficient
cause is essential to the definition of variance theory, its true counterpart in
process theory being the probabilistic processes that account for combinations of objects. There is no inherent necessity to pursue Aristotelian terminology further, and in that light the present section is provided largely for
the sake of symmetry, yet the perspective in which it places the contrast between variance theory and process theory is important.

To say that X is necessary for Y is to say that Y is sufficient for X: If Y,
then X.[5] This by no means implies that Y is a theory of X, but it does suggest that Y may in some sense be taken as a cause. In using this terminology
I am asking the reader to set aside the common tendency to equate *cause*
with *efficient cause*. Since Y comes after X in time, to say that it is a cause
of X is plainly to use that term in an unusual sense.

5. Picking up a thread from the previous section, the statement "If Y, then X" cannot
be extended to "If more-or-less Y, then more-or-less X" without the unwanted implication
that X is sufficient for Y. The reason clearly is that "If more-or-less Y, then more-or-
less X" implies that "If not-more-or-less-X [that is, if X], then not-more-or-less-Y [that is,
then Y]."

It is by analogy with or extension of Aristotole's reasoning (1941, 241, 250–251) that one may say that process theory deals with a final cause. Basically, a final cause, to Aristotle and his interpreters, is an end point whose existence connotes the occurrences of certain prior events. Aristotle uses the term essentially, it seems to me, with implied reference to a state that gives the purpose (divine, human, or animal) for which events occur. He places special emphasis on the development of organisms, on the adult form as the final cause of the earlier stages. Clearly, however, the same reasoning can be applied to other natural processes, aside from organic development. Aristotle does not explicitly make this extension, but he appears to strive toward it and to avoid it only with difficulty. That is the sense in which the term *final cause* is used here. Thus, not only is the adult the final cause of the prior developmental process of the organism, but so is malaria the final cause of its precursor, a new species the final cause of its precursor in Darwinian theory, and so forth. All are natural processes consisting of steps that we know must have occurred if we see before us the phenomenon we have been calling the outcome.

In this sense, a process model involves *pull-type* causality: X does not imply Y, but rather, Y implies X.

In process theory, time ordering among the contributory events is generally critical for the outcome. It is not critical in the sense of a universal. It is not true, and does not follow deductively from the definition of process theory, that in any precursor consisting of two or more events, those events must be ordered in time. However, what comes out of a probabilistic process depends on what goes in, and what goes in almost always depends on what came out of a former one, so that their order must be faithfully rendered within the model.

Recall that in a variance theory the time ordering of two direct causes, X_1 and X_2, is immaterial in the sense that each has independent effect on Y with the other held constant. In a process theory it is rare for two events to have this kind of independent connection with the outcome. Rather, one tends to pick up where the other left off (for example, after acquiring the parasite, the mosquito then bites person A). In this circumstance, the order of events clearly matters; if the mosquito first bites A and then acquires the parasite, malaria does not occur in A.

As long as the necessary conditions are merely necessary, their role is that of ingredients. Ingredients alone do not convey a sense of explanation (for example, victims, mosquitoes, parasites; so what?). There must also be some instruction for mixing them—a recipe. Recipes generally mandate activities that occur over time and in a prescribed order. They do not necessarily have to; a martini, for example, can be arrived at by adding the vermouth first, then the olive, and then the gin, or indeed by adding all three at once. Nevertheless, the rarity with which it apparently does exist makes the flow of time a striking and pervasive feature of the process model as a theoretical form.

Thorngate's Criteria and Their Tradeoffs
Karl E. Weick

A person who can identify the inevitable tradeoffs in inquiry and relax gracefully having done so is a seasoned inquirer. One version of these trade-offs is found in Thorngate's (1976) postulate of commensurate complexity. This postulate states that it is impossible for a theory of social behavior to be simultaneously general, accurate, and simple. The more general a simple theory is, for example, the less accurate it will be in predicting specifics.

To grasp the implications of this postulate imagine the face of a clock (see [Figure 9-2]). At twelve o'clock is inscribed the word *general*, at four o'clock is inscribed the word *accurate*, and at eight o'clock is inscribed the word *simple*. The mnemonic device to store away these observations is simply the word GAS (or SAG). If we array this postulate across the clock face, we can see the dilemma inherent in any research. If you try to secure any two of the virtues of generality, accuracy, and simplicity, you automatically sacrifice the third one.

Consider some examples. Two o'clock research is general and accurate but is also difficult. Psychoanalytic theory (Fenichel 1945), Levinson's book on organizational diagnosis (Levinson 1972), and Bateson's (1972) work are good examples. Six o'clock research is accurate and simple, but its generality is suspect. Coalition theory (Komorita and Chertkoff 1973), much of which is tied to highly contrived situations, is a good example of this position. It's interesting that lab studies as well as case studies share positions at six o'clock. Both preserve accuracy and simplicity and sacrifice general relevance. The final position, ten o'clock research, combines generality and simplicity at the expense of accuracy. Concepts such as the organized anarchy, loose coupling, deviation amplification, and the Peter Principle illustrate this position.

Failure to accept the inevitable tradeoffs implied in the GAS formulation seems to be at the heart of many current research problems. Investigators act as if they can simultaneously accomplish all three aims in their explanations, and that delusion is at the heart of much trivial, inconclusive research. The solution would seem to be either robust compromises or alternation rather than attempts to accomplish all three. If one accepts the reality that at most only two of those three virtues can be realized, then many rules and

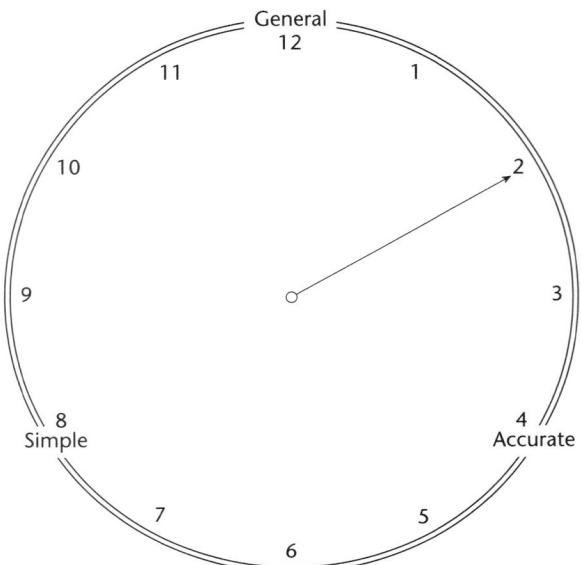

FIGURE **9-2**   Thorngate's clock

SOURCE: *The social psychology of organizing*, 2nd ed., by Karl E. Weick, 36, fig. 2.1. Copyright © 1979, 1969 by McGraw-Hill Higher Education. Reproduced with permission of The McGraw-Hill Companies.

constraints in inquiry take on a new interpretation. This can be illustrated if we look at three mixed positions: two o'clock research, six o'clock research, and ten o'clock research.

If one intentionally sets out to do *two o'clock research*, then Occam's Razor (Luchins and Luchins 1965) is sacrificed in favor of intentional overdetermination. The concept of *overdetermination* states that there are usually more factors that act to produce a single behavior than are really necessary to have it occur. The concept was first described by Freud in 1896 when he tried to account for symptoms of hysteria. Used in that context the idea meant essentially that a single bit of behavior served simultaneously to reduce tensions generated by several motives. . . .

The concept of overdetermination says that a given bit of behavior should be regarded and analyzed as expressing a maximum number of psychological factors. If a maximum number of psychological determinants are expressed in a minimum amount of behavior, then invoking a minimal explanation will exclude the majority of determinants that in fact are influencing the behavior. Thus an explanation that satisfies Occam's Razor should be disturbing, not satisfying. That feeling of disturbance coupled with a search for overdetermined explanations is more likely to occur if people self-consciously try to do two o'clock inquiry.

People who try to generate explanations that have generality and accuracy will probably enlarge questions rather than try to shrink them. Several of Steinbeck's (1941) attempts at speculative metaphysics illustrate this strategy. For example, the observation that prehistoric animals had the greatest amount of armor just before they became extinct becomes enlarged into a set of speculations about the equivalent armor in human societies and the question of whether that human armor has developed to a point where it too is at its maximum, hinting at extinction. This line of questioning exemplifies two o'clock research because it is grounded in concrete observations (the presence of armor prior to extinction), but the accurate observation is enlarged and generalized to other species.

Six o'clock inquiry is illustrated by recent arguments of noted investigators such as Cronbach (1975) and D. T. Campbell (1975) that case studies are better tools of inquiry than they first imagined. Cronbach describes "interpretation in context" and suggests that journalists (Behrens 1977) and playwrights may serve as more accurate models of what psychologists can realistically do than can physical scientists. Because many psychological findings are unstable over time, Cronbach concludes that we should try harder to make our interpretations specific to situations. This suggestion renders generality of secondary importance.

Campbell's (1975) recent second thoughts about case studies stem from his insight that investigators who use case studies can obtain the equivalent of degrees of freedom in statistical tests by using multiple theoretical implications. The argument is this:

> In a case study done by an alert social scientist who has thorough local acquaintance, the theory he uses to explain the focal difference also generates predictions or expectations on dozens of other aspects of the culture, and he does not retain the theory unless most of these are also confirmed. In some sense, he has tested the theory with degrees of freedom coming from multiple implications of any one theory (1975, 181–82).

Thus the intensive case study may have a capacity to reject theories. If people become compulsive about recording the thought experiments that emerge in a given setting from a given theory, and if they record both the implication and the test, then it is likely that they will not be so culpable when confronted by people who use more quantitative strategies.

Qualitative researchers need not blindly spot more quantitative opponents the advantage, even on the issue of confirmation. Lancelot White, a well-known physicist and historian of ideas, has argued that the truth value of any statement in science in the last analysis is evaluated by one criterion only: "how deeply acquainted with the phenomena, how non-defensive, how truly open to all facets of his experiencing, is the scientist who perceived the pattern and put it to test" (Rowan 1974, 95).

Lest all of this be interpreted as license for endless, groundless, needless case studies of organizations, it's important to realize that investigators must simultaneously proliferate their theoretical degrees of freedom as well as their observations. Many pseudo-observers, trying to imitate Woodward and Bernstein's Watergate coup, seem bent on describing everything and, as a result, describe nothing. It can be argued that the current upswing in social science enthusiasm for ethnography, thick description, grounded theory, and case studies is partly a symptom of the Watergate *Zeitgeist*. What's worrisome is that relatively little discernment seems to be applied to the zeal for description (Leonard 1977). Seemingly, the more that is contained in the description, the better the description is felt to be.

Two things are necessary to offset those trends. First, more than ever we need to invest in theory to keep some intellectual control over the burgeoning set of case descriptions (e.g., L. M. Smith and Pohland 1976). Second, those people who insist on doing case descriptions should be encouraged to adopt the model of theoretical degrees of freedom and to supply a contextual embedding along with at least partial theoretical interpretation of those descriptions they feel other people should take the time to read.

Many of my favorite concepts, ideas, and studies in organizational theory are a mixture of simplicity and generality and fall at the *ten o'clock position*. That these concepts also have modest accuracy (and sometimes irk people because of this) came as no particular surprise when I discovered it, although it was pleasant to see how neatly my experiences in the classroom could fit into the compact world of the GAS argument. The attractiveness of explanations such as the garbage can, organized anarchy, or the distinction between exit, voice, and loyalty (Hirschman 1970) is the fact that they are simple, easy to remember, portable, and seem to apply in a wide variety of situations. But when you really press these explanations in any specific situation, you find it hard to spot something that is nothing but a garbage can or loose coupling or specific exit versus voice alternatives. Qualifications and amendments become so detailed in the face of this imprecision that the original general and simple explanation soon disappears.

Once again, intentional effort devoted to ten o'clock inquiry need not be an embarrassment. It remains true that any explanation dreamed up by anyone will be true for some other person at some time at some place. All explanations, no matter how bizarre, are likely to be valid part of the time. It's simply up to the originator of the idea to be smart enough or lucky enough to find those sites where the theory is accurately supported.

The concept of ten o'clock research also provides a good excuse to examine other tabooed issues in science. For example, Ravetz, a historian of science, argues that the social sciences may be misplacing their energies by trying to ape the natural sciences. This theme, which is common enough, becomes more interesting when Ravetz then asserts that the so-called facts of social science may be of a different form than those facts associated with mature mathematical and experimental sciences. Rather than being simple, impersonal, elementary, and indubitable assertions, Ravetz feels that the typical product of a social scientist will more likely be aphorisms: "an expression of a deep personal understanding of its objects in a condensed and communicable form" (1971, 375) (e.g., "Everybody wants to be somebody; nobody wants to grow," or "What we do not understand we do not possess").

The idea that aphorisms could be bearers of knowledge has distinguished roots, including some of Francis Bacon's early writings:

> But the writing in Aphorisms hath many excellent virtues, whereto the writing in method [science] doth not approach. For first, it trieth the writer, whether he be superficial or solid; for Aphorisms, except they should be ridiculous, cannot be made but of the pith and heart of sciences; for discourse of illustration is cut off; recitals of examples are cut off; discourse of connection and order is cut off; descriptions of practice are cut off; so there remaineth nothing to fill the Aphorisms but some good quantity of observation; and therefore no man can suffice, nor in reason will attempt, to write Aphorisms, but he that is sound and grounded (cited in Stern 1963, 105).

The interesting characteristic of aphorisms is that knowledge is distilled rather than deduced, and that it has a developing character much like interpretations in context. Thus, it's conceivable that people doing ten o'clock research can argue that they're in the business of producing aphorisms rather than deduced knowledge; they might tailor their activities of inquiring accordingly, and might count it as a plus when people routinely think of their world as populated with such things as organized anarchies, seesaws, and octopuses.

In suggesting that aphorisms rather than deductions may be the form that social facts take, Ravetz is not blind to drawbacks associated with aphoristic knowledge. Aphorisms are not the conclusions of a tightly structured argument, which means that they are difficult to modify through criticisms of particular details, they do not go through the same rigorous processes of development and standardization as do other scientific results, which means they have been developed in a much less rigorous fashion. Aphorisms express private understandings, which means that their terms often have important nuances of meaning that are lost when the aphorisms are removed from their original context.

Aphorisms, pure and simple, don't have the permanence and objectivity of laws. But this doesn't mean that they are necessarily inferior. Aphorisms can move inquiry along; they can help people see facets of problems they hadn't seen before; they can force people to keep asking questions, possibly improving the quality of questions that get asked; and they have the obvious advantage of honesty. If a discipline proceeds as if it is mature when in fact it isn't, and if it proceeds as if it can generate facts when it can't, then remodeling itself to produce the best aphorisms possible is a potentially healthy way to redefine its identity.

Aphorisms are relevant to another taboo topic: speculation. Speculation involves consecutive logical thought that starts with premises or data and proceeds, through inferences, to arrive at conclusions or judgments. What sets speculation apart from reasoning is the fact that there is some uncertainty in the premises or some incompleteness in the data and, therefore, there is more tentativeness to the conclusions reached. But the important points to remember about speculation are that it is constrained activity, it unfolds in an orderly manner, and when the raw materials on which it operates are insufficient, premises or data are invented so that the process can continue and possibly arrive at a provocative conclusion.

Speculation brings feelings and intuitions into conscious awareness, a process that leads the speculator more deeply into the phenomenon about which he is speculating. Speculation exemplifies ten o'clock research. Accuracy is not a major constraint because the process of reasoning doesn't grind to a halt in the absence of information. It continues. This means that speculation is quite as credible a way to conduct inquiry as are many of the other strategies which have received a better press.

It's interesting that many writers have suggested that speculation actually predominates in social science. Consider the following comment by C. H. Cooley:

> It is perhaps not sufficiently understood that 19/20's of what men of science write, and what the public takes for science, is not such but an overflow of speculative discussion not necessarily less biased or more-grounded than any other matter of the kind. No doubt this has a scientific value in that from the flood of conjecture fruitful hypotheses may emerge, but in the meantime all men should know that it is conjecture (1931, 148–49).

In discussing tradeoffs I have argued that there is virtue in such things as speculation, armchair theorizing, aphorisms, overdetermined explanations, enlarged questions, complicated explanations, and journalism. Each of those recommendations was made without apology on the assumption that it's impossible for an explanation to be simultaneously general, accurate, and simple. To know what we are doing is to be realistic rather than arrogant about what can be accomplished at any one time in an inquiry.

This line of analysis has several implications. A sound research program would consist of a portfolio that contained explanations and investigations at all twelve positions on the clockface. If I'm right that much organizational theory converges on the ten o'clock position, then we have eleven other locations that need attention.

The argument implies that each individual should locate a position on the clockface, banish any unnecessary guilt that is tied to ideals that can't possibly be realized from that position, and somehow keep in touch with work at all of the other eleven positions, especially the one directly opposite the located position. If, for example, my style of scholarship falls at ten o'clock, then I should try especially hard to locate people at the four o'clock position, and I should be certain that I understand their work and maintain some contact with that work. Better still might be the solution in which I alternate my research style and systematically try to move among the various positions over the duration of a year or a career.

I think much of organizational research is uninformative and pedestrian partly because people have tried to make it general *and* accurate *and* simple. In trying to accommodate all three of these aims, none have been realized vigorously; the result has been bland assertions.

Furthermore, much of the low morale among social scientists may be traced to the fact that lay people don't seem to implement their findings or give social scientists sufficient credit and support for their work. If you look at the tradeoffs in the GAS model, you can see why these reactions by lay people are inevitable. Scientists want to do relevant research that also has generality. But a completely general explanation (twelve o'clock research) is hard to generate and may, in fact, be nonexistent. This means that the person who wants to be relevant has the following choice: the person can either be wrong as he moves from twelve o'clock toward the ten o'clock position, or he can be obscure as he moves from twelve o'clock to two o'clock. It's very unlikely that scientists who move in either direction will be regarded as saviors. It's good to know what you're doing.

Theory Evaluation Criteria
Samuel B. Bacharach

No evaluation of a theory is possible unless researchers first establish those broad criteria by which it is to be evaluated. Based on previous work (e.g., Popper 1959; Nagel 1961; Hempel 1965), the two primary criteria upon which any theory may be evaluated are (a) falsifiability and (b) utility [see Figure 9-3].

	Falsifiability	**Utility**
Variables	Measurement issues	Variable scope
Constructs	Construct validity	Construct scope
Relationships	Logical adequacy Empirical adequacy	Explanatory potential Predictive adequacy

FIGURE **9-3**   A framework for evaluating theories

SOURCE: "Organizational theories: Some criteria for evaluation" by Samuel B. Bacharach, *Academy of Management Review* 14 (1989): 502, fig. 2. Copyright © 1989 by the Academy of Management. Reproduced with permission of the Academy of Management via Copyright Clearance Center.

Falsifiability

Falsifiability determines whether a theory is constructed such that empirical refutation is possible. While the idealistic goal of science is the pursuit of universal truth, most philosophers of science would agree that theories can never be proven, only disproven (cf. Nagel 1961; Popper 1959). As Popper (1959, 41) maintains, "It must be possible for an empirical scientific system to be refuted by experience."

Theories are thus like the accused in an American courtroom—innocent until proven guilty. The problem with organizational studies is that theories are often stated in such a vague way that the theorists can rebut any discrediting evidence. Just as no person can be above the law, no theory ought to be constructed in such a way that it is forever exempt from empirical refutation. If researchers are to avoid wading through ever deeper piles of irrefutable statements disguised as theories, they must be able to discard such false theories. To be able to do this, they must try to construct theories that are coherent enough to be refuted.

Utility

Utility refers to the usefulness of theoretical systems. As Bierstedt (1959) pointed out, utility may be viewed as "the bridge that connects theory and research" (p. 125). At the core of this connection are explanation and prediction. That is, a theory is useful if it can both explain and predict. An explanation establishes the substantive meaning of constructs, variables, and their linkages, while a prediction tests that substantive meaning by comparing it to empirical evidence.

One problem of incomplete theoretical systems is that they are often used to make predictions, yet they do not provide explanations. In this context, Kaplan (1964) spoke of the ancient astronomers, who were able to make superb predictions, but were incapable of providing adequate explanations of observed phenomena. Thus, in organizational behavior, when researchers accept predictive statements as theory (e.g., the proposition: the greater the organizational size, the greater the horizontal differentiation; or its derived hypothesis: the greater the number of employees, the greater the number of departments), they sound a bit like the ancient astronomers. Only when theory shows how and why larger organizations have more departments will it be able to explain as well as predict.

The Falsifiability of Variables, Constructs, and Relationships

With an understanding of the components of theory at different levels of abstraction (variables, constructs, and the relationships that connect them) and the two main types of criteria (falsifiability and utility), researchers can begin to understand the way these criteria can be applied to theory. Because constructs and variables are the building blocks of hypotheses and propositions, theorists must first evaluate them before analyzing the relational properties of theories. If they are working with inappropriate constructs and variables, how these constructs and variables are assembled into hypotheses and propositions is irrelevant. All parts of a bridge may fit together perfectly, but if this bridge is constructed of "silly-putty," it is not a good idea to drive over it.

By beginning the analysis with variables and constructs, researchers are not excluding the possibility that theory building or evaluation is a process which begins with the examination of the relationships in hypotheses and propositions, or what Kaplan refers to as the paradox of conceptualization. As Kaplan (1964) noted, "The proper concepts are needed to formulate a good theory, but we need a good theory to arrive at the proper concepts" (p. 53). . . .

Summary

As in all the previous chapters, we see from the selections that there are a variety of alternatives—in this chapter, alternatives about theory forms or types and about criteria for evaluating theories. Our choices among these alternatives are influenced by our appreciation of the trade-offs involved. To enhance our knowledge about some phenomena of interest, should we aspire to deductive or probabilistic, past-, present-, or future-oriented, micro or macro explanations? Should our theory explain variance or describe processes? If we select a variance theory, should we structure it hierarchically or as a concatenated factor network? How formal should it be? Should our theory strive toward generality, simplicity, or accuracy? Will the theory be falsifiable? Useful? Each of these choices will impact all the others. As Weick states, "It is good to know what you're doing!"

For some phenomena, there is no one best theoretical type. Given the current modest state of theoretical development and an inquirer's preference for a particular paradigmatic frame, for theoretical development to make both better and better meanings and to move systematic knowledge into scientific knowledge (see Figure 1-2), inquirers must be aware of theoretic purpose and reach (as described in Chapter 8), possible theory types, and the theoretic criteria needed to create and improve theory. The centrality of theory for inquiry generally—along with the function of theory as the proximate frame for research—requires that we go beyond understanding alternative theoretic purposes, patterning, and worthiness, and appreciate how theories are generated and improved—the subject of the next chapter.

10 Theorizing

> There are and can be only two ways of searching into and discovering truth. The one flies from the senses and particulars to the most general axioms [laws], and from these principles, the truth of which it takes for settled and immoveable, proceeds to judgment and to the discovery of middle axioms [less abstract statements]. And this way is now in fashion. The other derives from the senses and particulars, rising by gradual and unbroken ascent, so that it arrives at the most general axioms [laws] last of all. This is the true way, but as yet untried.
>
> —*Francis Bacon*

> The whole of science is nothing more than a refinement of everyday thinking.
>
> —*Albert Einstein*

The title of this chapter, "Theorizing," is a verb and as such signals that our perspective has shifted from the static purposes and patterned forms of theories to the dynamics of theories over time—in particular, to the two major dynamic processes of theory creation and theory improvement.

Given the significance and centrality of theory to inquiry, attention to theorizing's twin processes is remarkably recent in the social and behavioral sciences as well as in organizational science. Until a couple of decades ago, the authors of theory construction manuals seldom referenced one another. As evidenced by the recent writings from which selections for this book have come, there is now, however, an active and well-informed cadre of social and organizational scientists explicating, discovering and inventing, and nuancing theory creation and improvement. Until recently, there has been a discontinuity between what theory construction manuals advised and how theories actually came to be (J. Berger and Zelditch 1993). This discontinuity can be traced to at least three confusions. One is the confusion between the statistical procedures of empirical generalization and the methods of theoretical science—empirical generalizations always specific to time and place and scientific laws that seek to be more universal. A second confusion was engendered by an excessive separation of methods from theory

(Willer and Willer 1973). Put somewhat differently, theory construction and its exposition requires quite different methods than theory verification (Suppe 1974). The third confusion was to separate the form and function of theory from its content—as if theory was a calculus simply awaiting data. These confusions can be traced in part to the emulation of the natural sciences by social and behavioral scientists without fully understanding the natural sciences or fully appreciating the phenomenological differences involved across scientific disciplines. Theory generation and theory improvement are both processes with alternatives—neither is written in stone; there is, as we have repeatedly noted, no one best way.

In the first epigraph to this chapter, the outline of the two basic strategies for theory construction was stated by Bacon hundreds of years ago. One strategy, which he refers to as the "Anticipation of the Mind," consists of inventing theories that are then tested by empirical research. The other strategy Bacon calls the "Interpretation of Nature"; it consists of deriving the "laws of nature" from a careful examination of all available data. Let us amplify each.

"Anticipation of the Mind" begins with an inductive jump, analytic leap, speculative escape, or constructive ascent from sense impressions or experienced concrete facts to a highly abstract symbolic system of axioms, premises, or precepts. With this inductively invented, abstract system in place, the next step is to logically deduce statements that are essentially theoretical predictions that can be empirically tested. If any propositions are not verified, then the axioms have to be reformulated and the deductive-then-testing process repeated. This strategy may be swift or slow—swift if the axioms achieve empirical support, slow if the cycle has to be repeated and repeated.

"Interpretation of Nature," in contrast, is a process of short inductions from data to constructs. Only when these low-level constructs are thoroughly grounded in data are interconstruct relations proposed and subjected to confirmation in data. With well-confirmed constructs and their relationships established, and only then, does the theory builder tentatively induce slightly higher-level constructs and somewhat more parsimonious—but always data-confirmed—statements. This strategy is obviously a slow one, but it is probably the surer one.

The two strategies as outlined are relatively pure. Many composites exist, of course, essentially mixing the ratio of deduction and induction. Those theories that induce constructs will always have "something" in mind (e.g., metaphors and aphorisms), and those theories that deduce from abstract premises will always have some sense of the data patterning in the phenomena of interest. Regardless, theory construction is a process of successive approximation, served by theory improvement.

With a more or less complete, more or less well-developed, more or less explicated theory, improvement proceeds. Theory improvement goes by many labels, such as theory verification, theory testing, theory validation, and theory confirmation. These labels mask that there are just two sorts of activity involved: (1) seeking data that corroborates and confirms one or more relationships of the theory; (2) seeking data that does not. In other words, acquiring data either to support or to falsify are the alternatives. Theory improvement takes research. With the data acquired and processed through research, the theory's "scope statements" (Walker and Cohen 1985) can be modified, for a theory is general only under specified conditions. If research finds exceptions or nonsupportive facts, the conditionals of the theory need to be respecified to delimit the theory's scope. If, however, research evidence repeatedly supports a theory, the theorist may want to relax conditional restrictions to make the theory more general (Zhao 1996). This reasoning aids us in understanding the advocacy of devices designed to produce more relevant data, such as utilizing multiple methods, crucial experiments, and replications (see Chapters 12 and 13).

The centrality and significance of theorizing—and the twin tasks of generating and improving theories—suggests that the selections of this chapter should receive extra attention. We can anticipate that, at the core of understanding theorizing, there will be choices about inductive and deductive processes—induction essential for theory generation, deduction necessary for most theory improvement.

Paul Reynolds, in the first selection, outlines the two basic—but somewhat oversimplified—strategies Bacon noted for developing a body of knowledge. One, which he terms "research-then-theory," begins with careful attention to data from which "laws of nature" are derived. The other, called "theory-then-research" begins with stating an explicit theory followed by the systematic testing of statements derived from the theory. Karl Weick, in the second selection, usefully summarizes how Reynolds' two strategies have been manifested in theory construction relevant to the organization sciences, showing how induction and deduction are intertwined and how theorizing may be enhanced by conscious attention to theorizing activities that embrace what he terms "disciplined imagination."

The next selection, by L. J. Bourgeois III, highlights the induction-deduction "dilemma" of theory building, arguing that both are needed, and suggests a beginning blueprint for theory construction that embraces both. The final selection, by Kenneth MacKenzie and Robert House, summarizes the classic Baconian method for improving theory by competitively testing competing theories. This "strong inference" strategy, in which theorists actively attempt to falsify competing theories, contrasts with the common—but necessarily much slower—strategy of verifying a theory until an anomaly is encountered, which returns us to the Baconian alternatives with which this chapter begins.

Two Contrasting Strategies
Paul Davidson Reynolds

Research-Then-Theory

This strategy is essentially as follows:

1. Select a phenomenon and list all the characteristics of the phenomenon.
2. Measure all the characteristics of the phenomenon in a variety of situations (as many as possible).
3. Analyze the resulting data carefully to determine if there are any systematic patterns among the data "worthy" of further attention.
4. Once significant patterns have been found in the data, formalization of these patterns as theoretical statements constitutes the laws of nature (axioms, in Bacon's terminology).

Under what conditions will this strategy, referred to as the Baconian approach, be an efficient strategy for developing a useful theory? Two conditions seem to be required. The first is a relatively small number of variables to measure during data collection. It is even more desirable if reliable measurement of these variables is both easy and inexpensive. Under such conditions, measuring "all" the characteristics of a situation or event is not a difficult task, because measuring "all" the characteristics results in a relatively small amount of data.

The second condition is that there be only a few significant patterns to be found in the data. It is then relatively easy to locate these few obvious patterns. In other words, if there are only a few causal relationships in a given situation, it may be easy to locate these relationships by examining the data.

Based on present knowledge of social phenomena, can we expect most social situations to meet these two conditions, a small number of important variables and a limited number of significant causal relationships?

NO.

If anything characterizes social science it is the lack of agreement as to what variables are important for characterizing an event or phenomenon. Hundreds of different variables are proposed and measured for investigating any particular event or entity; for example, there are easily thousands of personality variables that have been proposed for describing individuals.

This inability to get past the first step is perhaps the basic reason for be-

Source: *A primer in theory construction* by Paul Davidson Reynolds, 140–151. Published by Allyn and Bacon, Boston, MA. Copyright © 1971 by Pearson Education. Reprinted by permission of the publisher.

ing skeptical of the Baconian strategy for social science. In an absolute sense, there is an almost infinite number of ways to describe anything, and social scientists seem to have approached this with respect to many phenomena. But assuming that this problem is solved, what about the second condition, that there be a small number of causal relationships?

The second dominant feature of social phenomena is that there seems to be a relatively large number of subtle and inter-related causal relationships that influence most events. If this is the case, then it is going to be difficult to detect any systematic pattern among the masses of variables that are being analyzed in step three.

Classical statistical inference, unfortunately, does not provide an ideal means for finding such patterns in large masses of data. Assume that a statistical significance (value of Alpha) of 0.05 is selected as the level at which a relationship between two variables is considered "meaningful." This means that the probability that a scientist will infer that there is a systematic pattern in the data when the relationship is actually random is 1 in 20, if there is only *one* relationship under examination. If an investigator has hundreds of relationships under consideration, and a value for Alpha of 0.05 is adopted with a classical statistical test, then it is to be expected that 1 out of every 20 relationships will be significant at the 0.05 level, *even if there is a random relationship among the variables*. In short, when analyzing the patterns among a large number of variables, classical tests of statistical significance lose much of their value as measures of significance.

Thus the Baconian strategy appears to have two major drawbacks. First, the amount of data that can be collected is theoretically infinite, and the lack of agreement among social scientists as to what are *the* important variables has resulted in an endless list of characteristics to measure. Therefore, a scientist adopting this strategy couldn't get past the first step of listing all the important variables. Second, the problem of finding substantively interesting patterns among the resulting data is overwhelming; there are just too many potential relationships to give *all* of them serious consideration.

The question arises, if this strategy has so many disadvantages, why is it still being used? There is no question that it is still alive as a scientific strategy. A recent book on the experimental study of social processes initiates its theory chapter with a quote from Bacon (Burgess and Bushell 1969, 27). The answer seems to be that this strategy is associated with two assumptions about nature and its relationship to science: (1) that there is a "real truth" to be discovered in nature, in the form of discoverable patterns or regularities, and (2) that scientific knowledge should be organized as a set of laws, reflecting the "real truth." If an individual adopts these two assumptions, it seems reasonable to conclude that research-then-"set-of-laws" is the only strategy that will result in "real" science—discovery of the true "laws of nature."

There is actually no way to test empirically the first of these two assumptions, that there is a "real truth" to be discovered in nature. The fact that confidence in some laws is so strong that they are considered to be the truth is irrelevant to the general proposition that truth is there to be discovered. Since it is an untestable assumption (or unfalsifiable hypothesis) and cannot be evaluated directly, it is only possible to evaluate the usefulness of strategies based on such an assumption. In a later section, the utility of the research-then-theory strategy will be discussed in more detail.

The second assumption, that scientific knowledge should be organized as a set of laws, should actually be subsumed under the first assumption. For if you assume that these laws describe relationships that are "out there" in nature, then it is reasonable to assume that scientific knowledge should be organized in such a way as to reflect the true patterns in nature. . . .

One interesting feature of this strategy is the emphasis on acquiring *all* the ideas about the phenomenon from the data. Bacon (1863, 60–61) actually suggests that,

> . . . the mind itself be from the very outset not left to take its own course, but guided at every step, and the business done as if by machinery.

If the word "computer" replaces the word "machinery," this suggestion takes on a very modern tone. A number of methodological procedures have been developed for the use of social scientists that allow for the analysis of data to be done "as if by machinery"—by computer.

Factor analysis is a procedure that allows one to determine which variables "go together" in different situations. Once the procedure has indicated which measured variables are highly correlated, positively or negatively, the scientist can invent an abstract concept that will incorporate all of these operational procedures. Latent structure analysis (Lazarsfeld and Henry 1968) uses a similar strategy but assumes a lower level of quantification of the measured variables. Measurement or scaling models (Torgenson 1958) allow a person to collect a set of data and then, by examining the internal consistencies of the data, to determine what level of measurement (or quantification) can be attributed to a particular variable. Since many of these procedures would be impossible without modern-day computers, the "business" *must* be "done by machinery."

These mechanical techniques are not, in themselves, a reflection of the research-then-theory philosophy. But they are often used as if they will allow the "laws of nature" to be "discovered." However, a scientist may use these procedures for other purposes than implementing the Baconian strategy, science untouched by human minds; he may use them to "get ideas." More will be said about this in a following section.

As, a closing comment, it appears that this strategy is not unique to scientists.

. . . young filmmakers, who are . . . hooked on technology, love an approach in which the thinking out in advance is minimal—an approach in which you shoot a lot of footage and then try to find your film in it. . . . The filmmaker looks for the drama in life, and may occasionally find some, but he has to pan a lot of earth for a little bit of gold (Kael 1970, 117).

Theory-Then-Research

This strategy may be described as follows:

1. Develop an explicit theory in either axiomatic or process description form.
2. Select a statement generated by the theory for comparison with the results of empirical research.
3. Design a research project to "test" the chosen statement's correspondence with empirical research.
4. If the statement derived from the theory does not correspond with the research results, make appropriate changes in the theory or the research design and continue with the research (return to step 2).
5. If the statement from the theory corresponds with the results of the research, select further statements for testing or attempt to determine the limitations of the theory (the situations where the theory does not apply).

The major focus of this strategy is the development of an explicit theory through a continuous interaction between theory construction and empirical research.

The theory-then-research strategy is developed most explicitly by Popper in *Conjectures and Refutations* (1963), where he suggests that scientific knowledge would advance most rapidly through the development of new ideas (conjectures) and attempts to falsify them with empirical research (refutations).

If one assumes that there is no "real truth" or "laws of nature" to be discovered, but that science is a process of inventing descriptions of phenomena, then the "theory-then-research" approach becomes the preferred strategy. As the continuous interplay between theory construction (invention) and testing with empirical research progresses, the theory becomes more precise and complete as a description of nature and, therefore, more useful for the goals of science.

One important issue related to this strategy is the question of which statement from an axiomatic or causal process theory should be selected for comparison against empirical data. Several possibilities exist. One could

(1) select the statement that is most likely to be true, i.e., correspond with the empirical results, (2) select that statement that is most likely to be false, i.e., not correspond with the empirical results, or (3) select that statement that is most crucial to the theory, i.e., most important in the formulation. If we assume that the basic purpose of scientific activity is to develop useful theories, then it would appear that the questionable or crucial statements should be tested first. Otherwise a great deal of effort may be expended on a theory that later turns out not to be useful. If the most crucial statement is tested first, or, barring that, the statement that is most likely to be false, then it will become immediately obvious where the theory needs to be changed, and, if not supported, the existing theory may be modified or a new theory may be constructed in its place. Therefore, as a general rule, research should be designed to make it as difficult as possible for theories. This doesn't mean that the research should be sloppy; it means that the weakest part of a theory should be tested first.

There is one feature of this strategy that seems to impose superhuman self-discipline upon scientists. When a theory has failed to be supported by empirical evidence, it must be discarded or altered. In a sense this is the hardest part of the procedure, for it takes a great deal of time and intellectual investment to develop a theory, and scientists tend to become ego-involved with their theories. Rejecting such a product is often very difficult, like the alchemist in the cartoon who is convinced he can get gold from lead (if the lead is "absolutely" pure). Unfortunately, at present there is no way to force a person to lose confidence in a theory; the human mind is always able to invest a reason why a theory "should work" or is not wrong. Even after photographs of the earth taken from the moon, there is still a Flat Earth Society. The goal of an ego-free scientific strategy may never be attainable.

There is one unsolved problem with this strategy: Where does the initial idea come from? Any theory will provide guidance for the research activity, or data gathering, and this activity will be more efficient if guided by a theory. However, much research activity might be eliminated or made less expensive if the initial theory were not just an uninformed guess. . . .

Comparison of Strategies

These two strategies, research-then-theory and theory-then-research, cannot be evaluated by any objective means because each strategy reflects a different assumption about the relationship between the "real world" and scientific knowledge. The research-then-theory approach reflects the assumption that there are "real" patterns in nature and that the task of scientists is to *discover* these patterns, the laws of nature. . . .

The theory-then-research approach reflects the assumption that scientists impose their descriptions on any phenomenon that is studied. Scientific activity is the process of *inventing* theories (formalizing an idea in axiomatic or causal process form) and then testing the usefulness of the invention. . . .

These two approaches reflect different philosophies about the relationship between nature and scientific knowledge. It may be that the final result of using the theory-then-research strategy (when no better solution can be invented) will be the same as using the research-then-theory strategy, after all the laws have been discovered. In this case the theory-then-research approach has the advantage of providing an approximate answer until the final truth is reached. But there is no way to develop an empirical answer to this question or even to determine if there is ultimately only one set of patterns or laws to be discovered. As such, these views have the same status as philosophical or religious beliefs in that accepting one strategy or the other depends on what assumptions about nature one begins with. However, the two strategies may be compared in terms of their apparent usefulness for achieving a scientific body of knowledge.

The basic problem with implementing the research-then-theory approach is that it is almost impossible to define all the variables that might be measured for any phenomenon; the list of things to measure is infinite. But even if this is overlooked, the problem of selecting the significant causal relationships from among the infinite number of possible relationships is insurmountable. There are just too many relationships to give them all serious consideration. However, in actual application, this strategy may not be used in this fashion. The researcher will often select only those variables to measure that he thinks might be interesting, using his professional judgment or intuition to guide his choices. Similarly, when analyzing the data, he will tend to look at a relationship between variables that he feels might be significant, again using intuition or judgment to guide his activity. However, if the scientist is using unformalized rules to make decisions about the progress of his research, it will be very difficult for another to reproduce his results, and intersubjectivity will not be achieved, thereby decreasing the confidence of others in his results.

The most fundamental problem with implementing the theory-then-research strategy is in inventing the initial theory. There is a tendency not to develop a theory in fully formalized form before the first empirical data are collected. A scientist may actually start with a brief sketch of a theory and then do some preliminary studies to determine whether or not it is worth pursuing the idea. During the preliminary research, he may actually sift through his data for any interesting patterns that have appeared that might have a bearing on the theory or the phenomenon. Again, the procedure may not be adhered to in strict form, but the focus is on theory before research — look before you leap.

The two strategies may be considered in relation to the efficiency with which empirical research is conducted. However, this depends on which conception of a scientific theory is adopted. If scientific knowledge is to be organized as a set of laws, then it is clear that the research-then-theory strategy will lead to more efficient research, since a large number of laws or empirical generalizations may be discovered from the same set of data. The more laws that can be discovered, the lower the cost per law. In contrast, the theory-then-research strategy would be less efficient for discovering a set of laws. This strategy would suggest that each potential law be stated and then a research project designed to test that single law. A separate research project for each law would be more expensive than testing many laws at once.

On the other hand, if scientific theory is to be organized in axiomatic or causal process form, it would be inefficient to test a number of propositions not relevant to the theory while testing propositions relevant to the theory. A thorough test of one or a few propositions derived from the theory may provide all the information necessary to change or reject the theory. In addition, as mentioned earlier, since the theory is an interrelated set of statements, confidence in all the statements in the set is affected by a test of any one statement. Rather than completing one large project designed to test all the statements in the theory at once, it is better to have a number of smaller research projects, and, as each project is completed, the theory can be revised and improved and then retested in the next project. Thus, which strategy is more economical depends on the conception of how scientific knowledge should be organized.

Finally, it is possible to ask which of these strategies has been used by those individuals who have been most responsible for making great advances in the sciences, natural and social. It would appear that no "scientific revolution," or Kuhn paradigm, has been developed by a scientist using the research-then-theory or Baconian strategy in his research. This is perhaps the most damning evidence against this approach. Although this does not mean that the research-then-theory strategy will not lead to scientific revolutions in the future, it does suggest that it should be deemphasized, at least in the form Bacon suggested.

In summary, if one considers that scientific knowledge should be organized as a set of laws that reflects the patterns in nature that "really exist," then the research-then-theory strategy provides for more efficient research, but (1) it will not provide an approximate answer until the final solution is achieved, and (2) it has the disadvantages of a set-of-laws form of theory. On the other hand, if one assumes that scientists invent descriptions of the real world and then test the usefulness of their inventions, the theory-then-research strategy provides for (1) more efficient research if the axiomatic or causal process form of theory is employed, and (2) for some kind of organized scientific knowledge, which is gradually improved and becomes more useful as research continues.

Theory Construction
Karl E. Weick

Theorists often write trivial theories because their process of theory construction is hemmed in by methodological strictures that favor validation rather than usefulness (Lindblom 1987, 512). These strictures weaken theorizing because they de-emphasize the contribution that imagination, representation, and selection make to the process, and they diminish the importance of alternative theorizing activities such as mapping, conceptual development, and speculative thought.

Theory cannot be improved until we improve the theorizing process, and we cannot improve the theorizing process until we describe it more explicitly, operate it more self-consciously, and decouple it from validation more deliberately. A more explicit description is necessary so we can see more clearly where the process can be modified and what the consequences of these modifications might be.

Theorizing consists of disciplined imagination that unfolds in a manner analogous to artificial selection. To understand this analogy, we should first see descriptions of the theorizing process and how these descriptions often misrepresent the process. Second, we can learn how some of these misrepresentations can be correct if theorizing is viewed as disciplined imagination, where the "discipline" in theorizing comes from consistent application of selection criteria to trial-and-error thinking and the "imagination" in theorizing comes from deliberate diversity introduced into the problem statements, thought trials, and selection criteria that comprise that thinking. An elaboration of the theorizing process model is thus organized around the three components of problem statements, thought trials, and selection criteria.

Descriptions of Theory Construction

An understanding of the terms *theory*, *validation* and *quality of theory* is necessary for an understanding of the model. Theory is a dimension rather than a category (Mohr 1982, 6; Runkel and Runkel 1984, 129–130), which means that the more fully a generalization satisfies the criteria of a theory, the more it deserves the label *theory*. By theory we mean "an ordered set of assertions about a generic behavior or structure assumed to hold throughout a significantly broad range of specific instances" (Sutherland 1975, 9).

The dimensions implied by the definition are indicated by the terms *ordered*, *generic*, and *range*. As generalizations become more hierarchically ordered, behaviors and structures that are the focus of the generalizations become more generic, and as the range of specific instances that are explained becomes broader, the resulting ideas are more deserving of the label *theory*.

Verification and *validation* are used interchangeably to mean the demonstration, beyond pure chance, that the ordered relationship predicted by a hypothesis exists and thereby lends support to the hypothesis (adapted from Lastrucci 1963). Proof, in other words, consists of verification of a probabilistic statement. As Lastrucci (1963) noted,

> Thus, for example, to say that the theory of inherited characteristics has been "validated" by demonstrating it in a given number of predictable instances is tantamount to saying that the expressed relationship is a reliable one. To an increasing extent, scientists tend to avoid implications of causality by thinking of verification as an expression of high reliability (pp. 236–237).

Finally, a good theory is a plausible theory, and a theory is judged to be more plausible and of higher quality if it is interesting rather than obvious, irrelevant or absurd, obvious in novel ways, a source of unexpected connections, high in narrative rationality, aesthetically pleasing, or correspondent with presumed realities. Each of these outcomes is more likely when theorists develop fuller problem statements, create more diverse thought trials, and apply multiple selection criteria more consistently to these thought trials.

Previous Descriptions

Given these background assumptions, we can now look more closely at what has been said previously about the actual activities that go on during theory construction. Unfortunately, the literature on this topic is sparse and uneven, and tends to focus on outcomes and products rather than process. For example, Freese (1980), in constructing his review of formal theorizing for the *Annual Review of Sociology*, discovered the "incredible anarchy" of "language, conceptions, proposals, interpretations, and results of formal theorizing" (p. 189). Freese's attempt to impose some order on this anarchy is impressive and recommended reading. Other suggestions of process are found in sources such as Reynolds (1971), Blalock (1969), Johnson, Dandekar and Ashworth (1984), and Merton (1967). Representative previous descriptions of process include the work of Homans, Kaplan, and Freese.

Homans (1964) described theory construction as the concurrent development of concepts, propositions that state a relationship between at least two properties, and contingent propositions whose truth or falsity can be determined by experience (a noncontingent proposition is a straightforward mathematical deduction). Of particular interest is Homans' irritation with theorists who equate theory with conceptual definitions; he stated that "much official sociological theory consists in fact of concepts and their definitions: it provides the dictionary of a language that possesses no sentences" (p. 957). As Homans makes clear, researchers cannot make deductions from concepts alone even though Parsons repeatedly tried to do so. The lesson to be learned is that any process must be designed to highlight relationships, connections, and interdependencies in the phenomenon of interest.

Kaplan (1964) contrasted knowledge growth by intention with knowledge growth by extension (p. 305). This contrast, which resembles Bartlett's (1958) distinction between interpolation and extrapolation, suggests two different processes of theory building. Intention is used when a partial explanation of a whole region is made more and more adequate. This strategy is illustrated by the work of Darwin and Freud but it also seems applicable to the work of Bateson, J. D. Thompson, and Selznick. Theorizing in this mode lays out the lines that will be followed in subsequent theory and observation. Representative metaphors are developing a photographic negative, bringing binoculars into sharper focus, or gradually adding light to a darkened room.

Knowledge growth by extension is used when a relatively full explanation of a small region is then carried over to an explanation of adjoining regions. This strategy is illustrated by the expansion of studies of conditioning into a concern with more complex forms of learning. The work of Perrow on normal accidents, Bruner on narrative rationality, and Staw on escalation illustrate this strategy. Representative metaphors include a mosaic built piece by piece, science as an edifice that is constructed much like an erector set, and a puzzle that is gradually solved as more pieces are put into place.

Freese (1980) made a related distinction in which he distinguished between two strategies: (a) the strategy of developing generalizations in open systems through the use of inductive abstraction, a strategy evident in the work of Blau or Thibaut and Kelley; (b) the strategy of developing predictions in hypothetical or artificial closed systems, as represented in the work of Harrison White or Ken MacKenzie.

Closest in spirit to the current model is Bourgeois (1979).[1] He suggested that seven steps are involved in building theories of the middle range and he presented these steps as chapter headings in a thesis. They include, (1) partitioning of the topic under investigation, (2) method of theory construction, (3) review of literature, (4) construction of theory-induction from empirical base, (5) extension of theory-deduction into propositions, (6) metaphysical elaboration, and (7) conclusion.

Although this list suggests that theory building is virtually indistinguish-

1. Editors' note: See the Bourgeois selection later in this chapter.

able from problem solving, there are some important subtleties. First, Steps 3, 4, and 5 occur concurrently rather than sequentially. Second, Step 6, metaphysical elaborations, is described as a receptacle for the intuitions that surface during the theory-building task. These intuitions consist of "conceptualizations that might not fit the categories delineated or forced by the imposed rigor of the general theory building" (p. 445). This wisdom of the theoretician, expressed in discursive form, consists of speculative ideas and deductions that may be untestable; these may be crucial outcomes of the theorizing process. Third, Bourgeois insisted that the process continuously should weave back and forth between intuition and data-based theorizing and between induction and deduction. He concluded with five prescriptions such as "read some of the old masters," "ground your theory on data," and "take advantage of serendipity."

Toward a Method of Theorizing
L. J. Bourgeois III

Most of the current generation of organizational researchers attempt to either extend or verify extant theory through empirical investigation; in contrast, few undertake an exercise in theory construction. One might reasonably attribute part of the imbalance to the preponderance of empiricism in most doctoral-level training. This is, one could conjecture that the scarcity of theoretical literature reflects a lack of teaching emphasis on how to use theoretical tools. This paper represents an attempt at beginning a catalog of such tools.

After discussing the type of theory to which this effort is directed, I will address such methodological issues as how to organize the theory-building effort, where to conduct it (e.g., in observation or in reflection), what types of information to rely on, and whose examples to follow. . . .

In preparing an inventory of procedures to use in the construction of middle-range theories, I found in surveying the literature that the outlining of method comes in three basic forms: It is the subject of a book (Blalock 1970; Merton 1968a; Wallace 1971), or, more frequently, it is mentioned in prefaces or introductions as a framework for the substantive material that follows (Glaser 1968; March and Simon 1958; Price 1968a). However, as Hage points out (1972, 2), few, with the exceptions of Blalock (1969) and Glaser and Strauss (1967), provide techniques for constructing theories. What follows, then, is both a preliminary cataloging of techniques and a reference document that will direct the reader to lengthier treatments.

Theory-Building Format

Let me first speculate on the form that a theoretical piece should take. Unlike empirical work, theoretical pieces—owing to their paucity—have few good models to follow. As a result, the following is based somewhat on my intuition. I will contrast the suggested outline with that of the usual empirical thesis, which usually follows the following format:

1. problem statement
2. review of theoretical and empirical literature
3. method
4. results
5. discussion, implications, conclusion.

The theoretical work, however, might look as follows:

1. partitioning of the field (topic) under investigation
2. method of theory construction
3. review of literature
4. construction of theory—induction from empirical base
5. extension of theory—deduction into propositions
6. metaphysical elaboration
7. conclusion.

At first glance, it appears that a theoretical work might merely be an inflated version of steps 1, 2, and 5 of the empirical model, but closer scrutiny of the "how to" literature (cited above) indicates that considerably more rigor than this may be required. As will be shown in the ensuing discussion, the biggest conflict for the theory builder comes in reconciling the *order* in which steps 3, 4, and 5 of the theoretical model are undertaken. They are not discrete processes, although the output may lead a reader to infer a sequential ordering of thought. The processes underlying these three steps entail a rather sticky swim through the morass created by their simultaneous interactions. Additionally, a theoretical work normally entails the concurrent juggling of a larger number of constructs and spanning a longer hierarchy of abstractions; in contrast, an empirical study tends to apply a large number of measurements to a smaller number of variables than might be found in a theoretical piece. One way out, in terms of written presentation, is to take the route that Peery (1974) did and first state the general theoretical propositions (he had four) and then devote one section to each, subsuming steps 3, 4, and 5 under each generalization and confining the discussion to the relevant literature, inductions, and extensions applicable to or derived from it.

A final word on format: The inclusion of the sixth step listed above, "metaphysical elaboration," is my own notion. This kind of writing does not appear often in management journals, nor does it get much mention in any of the literature on theory building. I have included it to provide a receptacle for the occasional intuitions that surface into consciousness as one pursues the theory-building task, conceptualizations that might not fit the categories delineated or forced by the imposed rigor of the general theory building. In other words, it could be the theory builder's chapter for philosophizing, for expressing those ideas and deductions that cannot, because of their speculative and perhaps untestable nature, be properly subjected to the rigor of analysis that middle-range theory building requires. It would be the "wisdom" of the theoretician, expressed in a more discursive form.

The product of theorizing is usually a set of relational statements that range from discursive essays to highly formalized propositional or conceptual inventories. Examples of the former are Cyert and March (1963), Etzioni (1961), and Weick (1969). Propositional inventories are statements of the type "if x, then y" or "the more of x, then the more of y," which assume that important relationships have already been explored through the empirical work of others, and are frequently built on a review and synthesis of often unconnected earlier empirical work. Examples include such works as Hage (1965), March and Simon (1958), Peery (1974), and Price (1968b). Conceptual inventories assume plausible relationships between variables but tend to lack systematic evidence. They rely more on case examples, illustrations, and the like. The prime example of this type of work is James D. Thompson's (1967).

Modes of Human Reasoning

How does one come to arrive at the construction or derivation of these propositions? Does one build on assembled empirical evidence or on conceptual logic and wisdom? As an answer, Kerlinger contrasts two "ways of knowing": the method of intuition or a priori method, which relies on rationalistic propositions that are "agreeable to reason" and self-evident, and the method of science, wherein beliefs are "determined by some external permanency—by something upon which our thinking has no effect" (1964, 6), i.e., by observable phenomena. By valuing knowledge that agrees with experience over that which agrees with reason, Kerlinger seems to settle the scientific philosopher's dilemma (see below) in favor of empiricism. Lewin, on the other hand, argues that pure empiricism may result in mere counting, measuring, and classifying observable phenomena without making contact with the facts that lie "below the surface" (1965, 202).

Neither empiricism nor cerebral logic, however, should drive out intuitive insight. Arguing along this vein, Pirsig posits the classical versus romantic modes of human understanding (1974, 66–67). The classical mode is his term for the rational process of discovering or creating a world of underlying form as opposed to surface appearance, comparable to the logician versus empiricist. It proceeds by use of reason and laws; it is straightforward, unadorned, unemotional, economical. This is the manner in which the theoretical piece must be built and communicated. The romantic mode, on the other hand, is what step 6 above provides. It relies on inspiration, imagination, creation, and intuition more than on observation of facts. That intuition and data-based theorizing should go hand in hand is supported by Glaser and Strauss, who devote an entire chapter to the topic (1967, chap. 11).

These dichotomies parallel the induction/deduction dilemma discussed below, and the theory building versus theory testing divergence in academe today. (See Wallace [1971, 16–25] for a discussion of the interrelations between these segments of the scientific process.) The dilemma for the scholar occurs if these modes of thinking are seen as mutually exclusive, a position suggested by Blalock: "The resolution of this particular difficulty appears to require a division of labor between those who would construct the abstract theories and those who wish to test them" (1969, 5).

It is hoped that any such dichotomies indicate merely predispositions and not mutual exclusions. Lewin's description of the "Galilean Period" of social science, in which theory building and testing occur either simultaneously or in leapfrog manner in a systematic exploration for truth, is appealing and encouraging (1965, 202).

The Deduction/Induction Dilemma

The dilemma described here was prefaced in the discussion on the sequence of mental processes involved in the production of steps 3, 4, and 5 in a theoretical research paper. The dilemma arises not out of the question of "how does one arrive at 'knowing'?," but "how does one begin the search?" The question finds its genesis in the fact that there is no pure induction or deduction. *Inductive* inferences start with observations of a set of phenomena, after which one arrives at general conclusions—i.e., reasoning from particular experiences to general truths. *Deduction* starts with general knowledge and predicts a specific observation. The "arrival" at knowledge involves no dilemma because "the solution of problems too complicated for common sense to solve is achieved by long strings of mixed inductive and deductive inferences that weave back and forth between the observed (event) and the mental hierarchy" (Pirsig 1974, 99).

So the issue is: Does one start by going to a mountain top and meditating, or by inundating oneself in facts and literature (i.e., others' accumulated observations)? None of the sources I have encountered advise starting by deduction from "grand" theories. Most state an imperative for theory grounded in data. But given that one must get exposure to data, should one go out with an idea of what one is looking for? Glaser suggests not; rather, one should begin without any preconceived hypotheses (1968, 4). Blalock, in contrast, suggests that building deductive (testable) theories that will combine with the inductive theories sufficiently complex to give new insights, one must begin with simple models (which may not mirror the real world) and add new variables and complications a few at a time, resulting in the construction of more realistic theories by what amounts to an inductive process (1969, 3–4).

Merton's approach to the dilemma is to recognize it for what it is and discuss both sides of the issue. Should one read others' thoughts on a subject first or should one pursue one's own line of reasoning? Erudition has been known to stifle creativity if for no other reason than that it consumes inordinate amounts of valuable time, but not checking with predecessors runs the risk of rediscovery—again, a consumption of resources. Taking the dilemma by the horns, Merton suggests that one selectively read the writings relevant to one's own work, or, alternately, turn first to one's own ideas and then check on the antecedent literature before publishing one's results (1968a, 33). I suggest that the theoretician might combine both approaches. That is, start with preconceived notions, develop them a bit, then check the literature for support and (perhaps, grudgingly) make modifications where necessary.

A related dilemma involves how far back to take the literature review. Merton discusses the value not only of exposing oneself to the literature in anticipation of "the search" in order to be able to exercise better judgment by comparing what one reads and what one sees together, but also of reading the classics in one's field. This suggestion is particularly thorny because, as a science midway between the humanistic and physical sciences, social science can neither reject the "ancients" in favor of the "moderns" nor rely totally on recent work. That is, one cannot rely on old masters (as one should in philosophy or English literature) because scientific discovery tends to make the ancients obsolete. However, setting an arbitrary cutoff date (as Peery [1974] does in his literature search in order to make an already exhaustive review more manageable) runs the risk of losing the vital functions served by studying classical theory (Merton 1968a, 35–37). Of the functions Merton lists, perhaps the most important for our purpose are: (1) Occasionally, one finds one's independent ideas are merely a *rediscovery* of a classical "prediscovery." Though initially deflating, the result is usually the satisfaction of having confirmation of one's own ideas by the powerful mind of an old master. (2) It validates one's own ideas by citing the independent agreement of the earlier master. And perhaps most important, (3) classics produced by penetrating theoretical minds provide a model for intellectual work.

Theory-Building Blueprints

In summary, then, some beginning blueprint items for theory construction would include:

1. Read some of the "old masters."
2. Ground your theory on data (Glaser 1968, 4; Glaser and Strauss 1967).
3. Generate the theory through comparative analysis of empirical laws and substantive theories (Glaser 1968, 7–10; Martindale 1960, 73–75).
4. Codify your theory, either through propositional statements of the if-then variety (Blalock 1970, 82) or the employment of a paradigm (Merton 1968a, 69–72).
5. Take advantage of serendipity (Merton 1968a, 157-162) and record intuitive insights as they arise (Glaser and Strauss 1967, 251–257).

The above list is frightfully short, but notwithstanding Blalock's assertion that "there seem to be very few really useful guidelines that the practicing social scientist can use in constructing specific theories and then moving in some systematic way to explanation of a more general nature" (1970, 85), one can be heartened by the successful attempts of the authors cited in this article.

Strong Inference
Kenneth D. MacKenzie and Robert House

Strong inference research is based on the assumptions that: (a) all theories, no matter how good at explaining a set of phenomena, are ultimately incorrect and consequently will undergo modification over time (Kuhn 1970); and (b) the fate of the better theories is to become explanations that hold for some phenomena in some limited conditions. These assumptions are expressed by two quotations:

> A theory which cannot be mortally endangered cannot be alive (W. A. H. Ruston).

> A good theory is one that holds together long enough to get you to a better theory (D. O. Hebb).

Source: "Paradigm development in the social sciences" by Kenneth D. MacKenzie and Robert House, *Academy of Management Review* 13 (1978): 13–16. Copyright © 1978 by the Academy of Management. Reproduced with permission of the Academy of Management via Copyright Clearance Center.

These assumptions are further illustrated in modern physicists' challenge of the unrestricted range of application of classical mechanics, or in biochemists' dispute over what is to count as living (Cunningham 1973). A guiding principle of the strong inference research strategy is the Popperian position that pursuit of knowledge is more efficient when scientists deliberately set out to disprove theories, or seek rejections, than when they attempt to assemble proof for theories. Such attempts to disprove theories not only reflect the tradition of scientific skepticism but also focus the investigator on a different set of variables than do attempts to prove theories. Dubin (1969) makes the distinction between research directed at proving a theory and research directed at *improving* a theory. He points out that research directed at improving a theory causes the researcher to focus:

> particularly on the deviant cases and nonconforming results that do not accord with the predictions made by the hypotheses of his theoretical model. It is from the evidence contained *in the deviant cases* that the insights come on the basis of which the extant theory is improved by *reformulating* it to generate predictions that will encompass all the data, including those initially considered deviant (1969, 234, emphasis ours).

Dubin argues that none of the advantages of the theory-proving orientation are lost by the theory-improving orientation. Opportunities are enhanced for theory modification and, therefore, for growth and improvement of the theory. Churchman (1968, 1971) calls for construction of a counter-perspective to one's view in order to flush out into the open one's basic assumptions and tacit restrictions. His ideas are useful in generating instances of deviant cases which are so important to theory construction.

If it is assumed that all theories will undergo modification over time, successful attempts at disproving them are contributions to knowledge, in that such disproof facilitates identification of the specific aspects of the theory that are erroneous, or the boundaries within which the theory holds. Thus, attempts to disprove a theory constitute one of the most efficient processes whereby knowledge can be discovered. This process is illustrated in an experiment on the effects of seeking confirming evidence versus seeking disconfirming evidence as a means of discovering valid hypotheses.

Wason (1960) instructed subjects to infer a mathematical rule from a set of numbers. He then observed the process by which the subjects arrived at their conclusions. A greater proportion of subjects who systematically eliminated alternative rules by seeking disconfirming evidence (counter examples) discovered the appropriate rule than subjects who sought confirming evidence. Subjects who sought disconfirming evidence also discovered the appropriate rule in fewer trials than subjects who sought confirming evidence.

Wason's experiment simulates in the most pure form a scientific problem in which the variables are unknown and in which evidence has to be used to refute or support an hypothesis. Those subjects indicating a disposition to refute rather than to vindicate assertions and to tolerate the distress of negative results made more rapid progress. This disposition to refute and an orientation toward focusing on deviant cases evidence what we call the "strong inference attitude." The strong inference approach is a natural result of such an attitude.

The Strong Inference Approach

The strong inference approach consists of the following steps. A substantial amount of time and effort is invested in conceptualizing a theory of a given set of phenomena in such a way that the theory resolves previous anomalies and/or explains important issues in the area of inquiry. The emphasis is on development of well defined concepts and deductive-nomological theory. In the absence of an initial theory that appears to the investigator to be adequate to guide research, initial work frequently begins with exploratory investigation, literature review, or sheer speculation. After development of a tentative theory, strong inference research usually involves development of research technology, i.e., experimental designs, measurement instruments, and criteria for the rejection of hypotheses. Here the emphasis is on development of bridging principles and transformations required to link empirical observations to the concepts expressed in the explanandum sentence. Research is then directed at identifying counter examples to the theory's most fundamental predictions. Identification of clear counter examples requires the theorist to reexamine the theory as it was originally stated. Such identification requires scientists to specify the transformation to be used and the criteria of acceptance to be applied. If counter examples are found, either a fundamentally new theory is advanced, or the initial theory is reformulated in such a way that the reformulation accounts for the counter examples. The more fundamental the counter examples, the more fundamental the revision of the theory.

Failure to identify clear counter examples of the obvious and fundamental predictions of the theory establishes tentative credibility of the theory in the eyes of scientists, but does not end the process of theory building. Failures to reject the theory are not considered confirmation. Rather, the theory is considered "not yet" invalidated and is considered tentatively to be useful. A "not no, yet" result stimulates new attempts to produce a rejection. After attempts to reject the basic propositions of the theory have failed, more subtle and less fundamental predictions of the theory may be stated and attempts may be made at identifying clear counter examples of these predictions. By focusing on counter examples, the researcher concentrates energy on improvement of the theory. Extensions, improvements, and refinements of the theory are made by identification of such counter examples. Clear counter examples to the theory's predictions not only call those predictions into question, but also may call into question the more fundamental propositions. Thus, each counter example requires the researcher to reconsider the credibility placed on even the earlier successful predictions of the theory, since prior successful predictions may be sample specific, or they may be based on faulty methodology.

The strong inference process can be linked to the construction of a logical tree whose trunk represents the basic propositions of the theory. The objective is to grow the tree by careful nurturing and pruning. A major emphasis is placed on conceptualization of a cumulating series of interrelated studies and on careful formulation of competing hypotheses and the criteria of clear counter examples. Predictions are derived from the propositions, and studies are designed in an attempt to disprove them. A series of contingency statements is made before the studies are conducted, indicating the branch, or branches, of the logical tree to be followed, contingent on the outcome of the initial round of studies. The potential outcomes of each study are compared. The studies with potential to eliminate the largest number of predictions and answer the greatest number of questions are conducted first.

If the result of the first series of studies is not inconsistent with this theory, one has more specific information about the theory. As a result, the theory can be made less crude or more fine. If the experimenter feels that she or he can still reject the theory using a different research design, it should be tried. If the results are inconsistent with the theory, the theory must be changed. After the change, the researcher repeats the steps to construct the first branches out of this new base. These branches on the same level are called *outward growths*. Outward growths represent: (a) the domain of the theory, i.e., the populations and range of variables for which the theory makes accurate predictions; and (b) the kinds of predictions that can be derived validly from the propositions of the theory at that level. Those branches leading from other branches, but which apply under a more restricted range, are *upward* growths. The process of strong inference starts at the base and proceeds upwards and outwards by asking questions and making predictions that lead to more specificity about the theory or its mechanisms. Rejections are used to prune the strong inference tree by cutting back "dead" branches. In this process, the branches in question may have been allowed to grow from a conceptually incorrect branch. A branch may be theoretically irrelevant, and such growth must be weeded out from the proper branches in the main tree; thus, pruning and weeding often result in a reorganization of the tree.

A failure to reject adds a twig or a leaf. Every rejection raises questions, and consistent rejections allow one to chop off branches. The goal of strong inference is to produce a theory. This is done best by pruning and weeding because it is wasteful to expend resources following clearly false leads, no matter how attractive they may seem.

The planning phase of a strong inference strategy provides the intellectual framework for theory building. The strong inference plan is a tentative deductive nomological explanation. But this explanation need not be static or rigid. New information may suggest rerouting to a lower level branching point, or it may suggest entirely new branches. For example, suppose that an early study indicated taking Branch A as an alternative explanation and excluding Branch B. Suppose also that a later study indicated findings contrary to the first one. These suggest a problem with the methodology of one of the two studies or the existence of new variables not specified at the outset. Such a sequence would require backtracking to the initial decision point where Branches A and B parted, specifying new laws or bridge principles to account for the findings of the second study, and recycling the effort.

Strong inference planning is likely to cut down the number of investigations required, by providing a framework for arraying all relevant, available information and evaluating the potential payoff of alternatives that can be eliminated by the next study. While failures to disprove the theory are comforting, less is likely to be learned from them than from successful disproofs because they do not help identify where the theory made erroneous predictions. Identification of erroneous predictions helps identify invalid propositions within the theory, inadequate conceptualization of the theoretical variables and their relationships, and boundary conditions beyond which the theory does not make valid predictions. If multiple, mutually exclusive, hypotheses are advanced, failure to disprove one hypothesis results in elimination of one or more of the other hypotheses. Disproof of one hypothesis results in further support for counter hypotheses. Thus, attempts to disprove these hypotheses constitute advances in the state of knowledge, regardless of the outcome of the study. Strong inference planning also can be used to coordinate the efforts of a set of research efforts, even if the scientists are separated geographically. The strong inference strategy is considered by Platt (1964) as the most efficient means of developing reliable theory.

Summary

In theorizing, as in inquiry generally, there are alternatives, and choice involves trade-offs. How shall we proceed to generate theory? The general choice is between inventing a theory and then testing it or discovering a theory inductively. How shall we improve theory? Again speaking generally, the choice is between finding either confirming or falsifying data. The trade-offs among these choices have less to do with the strategies of theory generation and improvement and more to do with the sophistication of conceptualization in a given field at the time, resource availability (e.g., time, money, equipment, colleagues), and the competencies and inclinations of the theorist.

If there are no correct procedures for theorizing, perhaps the best we can do is to follow the fruitful suggestions contained in this chapter's selections. Serious inquiry assumes that regularities exist in the phenomena of interest in different forms and degrees. The purpose of theoretical work, along with the research that underpins it, is to state or discover such regularities, the extent to which they exist in some portion of organizational life, and the conditions under which they are maintained and modified. Given that there are different forms and degrees of patterned phenomena, there are many ways to conceptualize and then study them. Theorists should probably resist highly codified methods for theory generation and improvement. Regardless of how a theory is generated or improved, the ultimate criterion is: does it lead us to better theory?

Part Four

The Research Process

We have delayed introducing any extended treatment of the process of research because of our contention that the series of choices involved, activity by activity, reflects both the distal frame that is philosophic context and the more immediate frame of relevant theory. As previously described in Chapter 2 (see Table 2-1), the research process is an ordered sequence of activities. As McGrath (1982, 71) usefully notes, it is locally directional (questions are formed before the research design; data acquisition must come before data analysis; etc.) but systematically circular (it starts with a question and gets back to it with an answer). The research process is an ordered sequence of activities that is often messier than portrayed. Research activities constitute a "context of discovery" that seldom resembles the reconstructed logic of justification (Kaplan 1964) mandatory for research reports.

The five chapters that follow do not map neatly on to the activity stages of the research process. Recall that this book is not a technical manual; because the relevant literature is quite large and growing swiftly, we will be content to mostly emphasize the alternative activities available throughout the research process. The larger and more accessible the literature about research activity, the more we will simply frame its alternatives. There are, in each of the chapters that follow, several points of emphasis:

- Chapter 11 suggests that research questions are invented/created, not discovered or simply found.
- Chapter 12 explores the difference between research strategy and research design—terms that are often used synonymously.
- The phrase "research methods" has, we believe, too many meanings. To some scholars it means statistics; to others it means the

analytical techniques currently in vogue within a school of thought. To some investigators, the term bundles together designs and methods, to others it refers to both data acquisition and data analysis methods. We propose that there are two distinct classes of methods—methods for acquiring data (Chapter 13) and for making sense of data (Chapter 14). We further indicate that both kinds of methods are neither research strategies nor designs (Chapter 12).

- In Chapter 13 we emphasize that data management is not only different from data acquisition but deserves more attention than it often gets. In this chapter we also will note a sample of major data-related problems that confound the research process.
- Chapter 15 expands the usual goal of research—"dissemination of findings"—by presenting alternative purposes research-based knowledge may be used for.

While there are alternative activities at every stage of the research process to choose among, there are also two action choices for each activity. We speak of who decides and who performs a selected activity. Research reports and textbook examples of research projects typically simplify these "who" choices with reference to the "researcher"—implying an individual. In reality, however, the solo researcher is almost always a myth. More typically, for many or most of the research process activities, there is a "team"—two or more others who participate, formally or informally. One way to appreciate this point is to ask for each of the activities listed in Table 2-1: Who decides? Who performs? Put this way, we can readily see the possibilities for participation by research associates, supervisors, colleagues, informants, sponsors, mentors, gatekeepers, and so on.

11 Inventing and Framing Research Questions

Nothing is interesting if you're not interested.

    —*Unknown*

Thus the task is not so much to see what no one yet has seen, but to think what nobody yet has thought about that which everybody sees.

    —*Arthur Schopenhauer*

All animals are able to think, and many can use tools. What sets humans apart is our ability to deceive ourselves.

    —*Anonymous*

As has been repeatedly noted throughout this book, inquiry is focused by means of questions. Regardless of their scope—from broad, general, "orienting questions" to narrow, precise "hypotheses" that question the data-based relationships specified by a model or theory—posing questions initiates the research process. While selecting and stating one or more questions about some phenomena, issue, topic, or problem is generally acknowledged by serious inquirers to be the crucial activity in conceiving a research project, it is surprisingly little discussed. All too often research manuals either ignore question formulation altogether or downplay it as question finding—as if questions are somehow simply there waiting to be discovered—rather than the active, creative, inventive activity it really is.

The importance of questions and questioning as a basically creative act is emphasized by Roger Schank in the initial selection that follows. Schank also usefully reminds us of the basic forms questions can take and how they may be generated. The form of basic questions and approaches for their generation is also discussed in the second selection, by Lundberg. He offers one of the few catalogs of question-generation devices available. These two selections provide quite different provocative and suggestive "how to do it" lists. Common to them is their playful quality.

In the next two selections by well-known organizational scholars Paul Lawrence and Karl Weick, we find arguments for, and some discussion of, problem-oriented and theory-oriented approaches to question formulation. These two (mostly) contrasting approaches probably describe what the vast majority of organizational scientists do.

In the final two selections, methods for generating and criteria for assessing the value and worth of research questions are offered. Lundberg and Davis both transcend their disciplines in their articles. Lundberg presents six question-generating ploys, and Davis argues that important research questions are the "interesting" ones—those that overturn commonly held beliefs. His classification of interesting question types may be as close to a question generator as there is.

The Importance of Questions
Roger Schank

Is creativity something mystical? No. Creativity is a function of questions. Questions are not mystical. They come from confusion or curiosity or failure or success. Moreover, the questions that begin the creative process are rarely more than reasonable next steps along a normal chain of thinking. Asking why an apple fell on your head or what material might conduct electricity in a vacuum is not an especially mystical process. But failing to ask such questions eliminates the possibility of discovery.

Our knowledge is biased by the questions we ask. It is futile to search for answers unless we are asking the right questions. Often one cannot even understand the answers that others have discovered unless one has posed the question oneself. You cannot simply tell people the answers to questions they haven't asked. They won't be able to hear the answers. People must learn to ask questions, to really want to know the answers, before they can begin to make use of the answers. . . .

The hard part of creativity is generating good questions, and this is why scientists value a good question more than a good answer. A good question leads to great discoveries and creative solutions. Creative people have a great many more questions than answers.

Answers make us able to go on with business, whereas questions force us to pause and consider what we are doing. For a society in a hurry, answers are more important than questions. For a society concerned with innovation, questions are more important than answers. But wait, you say, don't the questions that we pose eventually lead to answers? Ultimately, aren't answers what we want?

Source: *The creative attitude: Learning to ask and answer the right questions* by Roger Schank, 169–175, 181–184, 188–192. Copyright © 1988 by Roger Schank. Reprinted with the permission of Scribner, an imprint of Simon & Schuster Adult Publishing Group, and Brockman, Inc.

Surprisingly, the answer to this is no. Of course, if there were a specifiable number of answers to the questions of the universe, if there were one and only one meaning to life, if there were one and only one true religion, if there were one and only one true morality, then what we would need would be those answers. We would want to know the facts and be done with it. But life isn't so simple. Today's truths are tomorrow's old-fashioned opinions. We live in a constantly changing world, a world in which, if we depend upon others for the answers, we can be sure of getting yesterday's answers. . . .

What we really require is new ways of looking at things. Innovation requires new perspectives. A question invites a new perspective. How can we learn to ask good questions? How can we alter the attitudes in us that prevent us from asking new questions?

. . . Having all the answers is one way of feeling good about the world and about yourself. But that is not what this book is about. Creativity doesn't always feel good, partially because it's difficult, partially because it's risky and open to criticism, and partially because not every answer is easy to live with. . . .

Many people have a tremendous fear of questions, especially questions that raise taboo subjects or repressed ideas. . . .

. . . A good question is an irritant. But it is always a potentially valuable irritant. It's like a grain of sand that gets inside a clam's shell, and a clam inside its shell is a great metaphor for someone with a closed mind, or a mind that doesn't ask itself questions or face questions from others. Imagine all the questions that children in this country will never ask because of their parents' overzealous moral and religious beliefs, provincial attitudes, taboos, and superstitions. . . .

Most people don't realize that questions occur to them constantly as they read or see, and most of these questions remain unanswered. Adults tend to inhibit their questions all the time, which may make them adult but probably doesn't make them any smarter.

On the other hand, children have no self-editing mechanism to stop them from asking the questions that occur to them. Asking questions is an inherently playful activity, and children are inherently playful. Think of the last time you talked with a four-year-old who had just discovered the effect on adults of the word *Why?*

What Are the Questions to Ask?

In order to discover what might be anomalous about an event or an action, we have to have been asking ourselves a set of questions about the nature of that action. Anomalies appear when the answers to one or more of those questions are unknown. It is then that we seek to explain what was going on. It is then that we can begin to create an explanation.

People have powerful models of the world. Through these models, which are based on the accumulated set of experiences that a person has had, new experiences are interpreted. When the new experiences that a person perceives fit nicely into the framework of expectations that have been derived from experience, an understander has little problem understanding.

But new experiences often do not correspond to what we expect. In that case, we must reevaluate what is going on. We must attempt to explain why we were wrong in our expectations. We must do this or we will fail to grow as a result of our experiences. Learning requires expectation failure—the recognition that there is an anomaly—followed by the explanation of that expectation failure. . . .

Generating Questions

There really aren't that many different kinds of questions to ask. If this seems an odd thing to assert, consider that most of our questions about the world are transformations of three basic questions, which, in turn, correspond to three basic types of things that we try to explain:

Reason Questions: Why did he do that? Used for explaining the reasoning of others. . . . These questions are posed in many different forms. For example, you can ask of a terrorist incident, Why did they do that? or you can ask, What do terrorists hope to gain from their actions?

Event Questions: What caused that event to take place? Used for explaining the causal chain of events leading up to an event. These questions can include ones such as, Why did Swale die? Why did World War II start? or Why did the Mets fail to win the pennant?

Outcome Questions: What will happen? Used for explaining why something happened the way it did as opposed to another way, so that the event can be correctly predicted next time. These questions can concern a variety of different events that people care to predict. The answers to them are not causal chains. That is, we don't care to know that a horse lost because another one won. We want to know our error in reasoning so that we can bet on a better choice in the next race. Thus we might ask, Why did that stock go up? and really mean, How can I find another one like that one? or we might ask, Why did the Giants lose? and really mean, How do I know they won't lose next time?

Even though there are only three types of questions to ask about an anomaly, there are thousands of ways of *transforming* or reformulating those questions. It is the transformation of the question from one which merely wonders into one that points the way to a helpful answer that constitutes the trick in asking questions. Questions are usually unanswerable without being transformed.

Transforming Questions

Our original question about people's reasons for doing things, Why did he do that? can be transformed into the following questions that one ought to ask in order to better understand why someone is doing something:

What good does he think will come from his action?
What's his plan?
What's his goal?
What does he believe about the world that would make him have such a goal?

These are neither a standard nor a unique set of useful transformations. They are some of the possible useful transformations. Transformations are as limitless as are the possible contexts of an anomaly.

The question Why did things turn out that way? can be transformed into the following questions:

Who gains from this event?
Who loses?
Could this event have been a mistake?
What could have been done to make it come out differently?
What circumstances could have been changed that would have made it turn out differently?
What exactly were the chains of events and states that led up to this event, so that it could happen again?

The question "How will things turn out?" can be transformed into the following questions:

What pattern of actions and states has occurred before that is identical to this one?
What usually occurs when this action occurs?
What could happen after this action occurs?
Did this kind of thing work the last time?

Anyone could protest that the preceding list is a bit arbitrary. But that is my point, almost. There is no unique, correct list of questions to ask. These are simply the kinds of questions one must ask when one is faced with an anomaly. It is for each of us to transform these general types of questions into truly effective questions using some of the paths and techniques suggested in this book. . . .

Where Questions Come From

Questions can come from many places. One standard source of questions is the remindings of old events that you wonder about and don't fully understand. . . .

Other types of questions are derived from an attempt to follow the course of the story while gathering the basic facts and data that are there to be derived from the story. These are the basic journalistic sort of who-what-when-where questions. We know how to ask these very well and do not need to be taught to ask them. They are a part of our normal everyday understanding capability.

Another set of questions come into play when the expectations generating the normal run-of-the-mill questions begin to break down. These questions specifically address the possible reasons that a given expectation may have failed. . . .

Questions in the Understanding Cycle

Understanding is not an all or nothing affair. Understanding is gradual, on occasion partial, and most important, subject to wide variation depending upon one's interest. Understanding is a mixed-mode process, involving focusing on only a portion of what one is reading, mulling on that portion, wondering about it, and then returning to the text with new ideas and questions that will serve to control the subsequent understanding of the remaining text. Understanding depends upon explanation, and explanation depends upon the ability to formulate questions. Questions, explanations, and remindings are part of the basic understanding cycle, and are also the basic tools of creative thought. Creativity depends upon the ability to formulate the right question at the right time. We have to want to know something in order to learn anything at all. We have to ask a question in order to get an answer. . . .

Questions arise from the fundamental desire to know. And wanting to know implies having an active knowledge-seeking mechanism that can be frustrated when it is not fed frequently enough. In other words, we also wish to eliminate boredom.

Boredom is a paucity of questions, or if questions are present, a paucity of information from which one could derive answers. One advantage of boredom is that it may begin the process of generating more questions simply because one is bored, without any outside stimulus. In any case, it should be clear that the capacity to be bored and the capacity to ask creative questions are very much related. . . .

Conclusion

Creativity means asking questions. To become more creative one must learn to generate questions. In order to answer those questions, one must learn to transform those questions into ones that are answerable and whose answers themselves bring new questions to mind. It is that simple, and it is that difficult.

Question Creation in Organizational Research
Craig C. Lundberg

New research questions seem to result from examining our assumptions and a combination of passive observation, putting questions to nature and active observation. Weick (1974b) argues that what is vital for stimulating research is the transformation of our assumptions into questions. By assumption he means that which we "know" is there in reality. Thus, for example, instead of studying the relationship of an individual's utility function to another construct, one could ask: is it the case that individuals have utility functions? If utilities don't exist, what, if anything, is guiding preference ordering and decisioning? Suppose that what occurs is that goals get progressively clarified in decisioning. If anything like this is going on in people, researchers are missing it; and the reason they are missing it is because they assume that individuals have utilities.

Observation is neither a mysterious nor an erudite process. Basically, it boils down to keeping one's eyes and ears open and making a record. Passive observation occurs by chance or spontaneously. Active observation is induced by some sort of preconceived idea, however roughhewn it may be (Bernard 1957, 7). Questions put to nature then stimulate active observation. One must poke into all sorts of silly things and risk looking foolish, even stupid, at times. Active observation often comes down to a simple playfulness, having fun with ideas, theories and oneself. Weick (1974b), for example, prescribes the following ways to discover new questions of organizations: fondle building blocks, burn caribou bones, count statues, communicate non-verbally, and construct flimsy objects. Playfulness is necessary to counteract the fact that we are all brought up to think we know our own minds and what they are up to at any given moment (Hebb 1974, 77).

While we obviously cannot list the questions put to nature, we can speak to their form. There seem to be six basic question forms as follows:

What is an X?

X is asserted. Is it so?

Where does X occur; what is the distribution of X?

What are the similarities and differences between X_1 and $X_2 \ldots X_n$?

What is associated with X?

What causes X, or what does X cause?

In these questions, X is a descriptor of some phenomenon. Actually, these questions indicate two quite different kinds of research work. The first four define descriptive efforts (the identification and classification of various elements). The last two define theoretical work (discovering the relationships among elements).

Before discussing hypothesis creation, there are four prerequisites for such activity: acquiring a "knowledge of acquaintance" of the phenomena, really knowing the subject, possessing an ingrained paradigm, and the ability to "galumph." Acquiring and reacquiring a knowledge of acquaintance (Roethlisberger et al. 1954, 7), that is a firsthand familiarity, of one's focal phenomenon offers a grasp of it, useful for countervailing more abstract and analytical knowledge. Possessing a thorough knowledge of the subject may appear obvious, although it is often side-stepped by the more eager researcher. There is an old saying that a discovery is an accident finding a prepared mind. Clearly creative insight occurs more frequently with a thorough knowledge of one's subject area than as a bolt from the blue. The third prerequisite, possessing an ingrained paradigm, is less well appreciated. What is suggested here is the ability to think unconsciously in accord with a fundamental model. For example, many sociologists are structural functionists, whether they are aware of it or not. Perhaps in organization behavior the paradigm is that of a cybernetic open system. "Galumphing" (S. Miller 1973), the last prerequisite, is the psychological process of voluntarily placing obstacles in one's own path, where such deliberate complication of a process becomes interesting for itself and not under the dominant control of goals. Galumphing as a prerequisite to hypothesis creation implies a strict avoidance of task-oriented efficiency.

When a question put to nature is formalized by specification of constructs or concepts and their supposed relationship, this conjecture is called a hypothesis, and hypothesis formulation or generation can come about in many ways. In the listing which follows, the emphasis will be on approaches other than theory testing. The approaches will be discussed in three sets: first, those that are most clearly exploratory efforts; then those approaches that exhibit an intentional search; and lastly, those efforts that extend antecedent research, that is, by the coupling of one project to another.

Exploratory Approaches

The first approach is probably improperly termed exploratory, for it concerns happenstances or *accidents*. Accidents are not just the unexpected, but include those events resulting from a failure or a blunder in a process which provides an opportunity for seeing some phenomenon in another way. Accidents have been dignified in science by the term "serendipity."

The *paradoxical incident* offers another opportunity for arriving at an interesting hypothesis. Something is noted that does not make sense according to our general understanding of social events; that is, it appears paradoxical and efforts to account for it can lead to new discoveries. For example, the problem of performance decline was unsatisfactorily "explained" by motivation models and this led to the recognition of activation/arousal.

The *intensive case study* is an approach long acknowledged as a fruitful source of hypotheses. The case need not be an unusual or exceptional one, for it seems that almost any case studied intensively might serve. The early history of organizational behavior, i.e., its "human relations" phase, held numerous examples. One wonders what the impact on the field would be if another period of such case studies occurred.

The *analyzing of a practitioner's or craftsman's rule of thumb* is another source of hypotheses. The procedural rule of thumb is assumed to work, and the research task is to think of theoretical explanations for its effectiveness. Of course, they may be as suggestive by their failures as by their successes. Many prominent ideas in the field, e.g., "satisficing," came about in this way.

The last truly exploratory approach can be labeled *"thinking around."* This refers to the activity of letting go of one's focus on whatever problem or specific phenomenon one is working on and permitting oneself to speculate and fantasize about any related matters that come to mind. A deliberate cessation of effort to solve a problem often leads unexpectedly to a new perception. More pertinent to the discussion, it sometimes leads to the discovery of new problems or questions that are likewise surprising.

Intentional Search Approaches

Prior research efforts often provide the opportunity for hypothesis creation from their *byproducts*. Anyone who searches his or her own research or the research of others will find unexpected behaviors or patterns. How often research reports contain phrases which begin "In addition . . ." or "It was also noted that . . ." These incidental observations or those recorded by others can often be mined for new questions or hypotheses. Similarly, there are methodological by-products, such as the idea of using a technique in a different context or with a different problem, or new ways of assessing or controlling variables in the often hard and ingenious work of research.

The *intentional use of analogy* is another approach. Here one simply takes the properties, patterning or functioning of some familiar subject and asks whether some other topic exhibits any similarity. Well-known examples include the computer as an analogy to cognitive processes, the biological analogies to organizational growth and development, and the economic transaction as an analogy to social exchange.

Less in evidence in organizational behavior is the approach called *hypothetico-deductive*. This approach involves putting together two or more common sense principles or empirical findings and deriving from their conjunction some predictions of interest. This hypothesis generating procedure has become increasingly popular and possible with the advent of computer simulation.

The *contextual twist* is one approach that seems underappreciated in organizational behavior. Thinking about replicating a study in a very different context can often point to new interactions or condition general findings. Moving research into the laboratory from the field or vice versa, as well as replicating a project in a different business function, industry, institution or culture, can be provocative of new ideas.

Seldom do research findings lend themselves to single explanations. Thus, another source of hypotheses is by thinking through the possible *additional interpretations* of any set of data. A closely related technique for provoking new hypotheses is to try to *account for conflicting results*. Another creative method is to attempt to *account for the exceptions to general findings*. Still another approach related to these efforts of developing new hypotheses by examination of prior work is to attempt to *reduce observed complex relationships* to simpler component relationships.

Finally, in the cataloguing of intentional search approaches to hypothesis creation, *the manipulation of scientific statements* must be mentioned—specifically, the two forms of questions listed earlier, defined as theoretical, and their more complex kin. Scientists tend to put their knowledge in the form of statements, and any untested statements are hypotheses. The manipulation of statements of association simply involves substituting some new factor or variable for one already established (including the specification of new conditioning variables). For "causative" statements, manipulation could consist of reversing the statement (e.g., satisfaction and productivity), substituting variables, the postulation of intervening variables, etc. This approach, called the manipulation of statements, is close to the next set of approaches to be discussed, the explicit coupling of research to research.

Extending-Coupling Approaches

Research often evolves from research. The two prior sections have emphasized the more obviously creative approaches. This section notes approaches to hypothesis generation which most explicitly build on previous research, forming a well-defined line of investigation (Cartwright 1973). In general, this means extending research by *making a finding (or technique) interactive with the findings, observations or capabilities of others* (W. B. Webb 1961). Actually these approaches can be rather quickly identified. Independent variables can be substituted, added to, controlled better or differently, or reduced in number. Similarly, dependent variables may be replaced, added to or otherwise modified (i.e., altering the level of measurement or refining the selected behavior). There are also the obvious surplus or additional relationship variables, the so-called intervening variables. The point here is that these changes in statements deliberately reflect other research and therefore "couple" prior research to that being initiated.

An Amendment on Implementing New Research Ideas

Assuming the discovery of a new and interesting idea for either a question to put to nature or for a hypothesis: then what? While experienced researchers will exhibit stylistic uniqueness, the following advice seems to have wide acceptance.

Any new idea must be examined in light of a critical requirement—for while any new idea may produce a doable or even a successful research project, to increase the probability that it will result in a valuable project, one must ask of it, will the results be generalizable? That is, in how many and what kind of specific circumstances will the relationship expected to be confirmed in the research be likely to hold? This is the requirement of "extensity." If the idea produces findings applicable to a vast heterogeneity of events in time and space, the findings are likely to have a great value.

If a question or hypothesis seems to possess extensity, two activities are urged: professional encounter and the mental experiment. The professional encounter takes the two forms of talking with colleagues and searching the relevant literature. Such talk can generate leads to other investigators working on the same or similar problems, pertinent parts of the literature, alternative explanations, etc.

An extensive literature search, an arduous and often dull task which is often done inadequately, is more than collecting citable references. It is also a place to test questions and hypotheses without going into the field or the laboratory. How does this occur? One way is to go to the classical pieces of research in one's field, which may or may not have any apparent relationship to one's focus, and then read those research reports carefully once again, trying to see whether the phenomenon that one is interested in was in fact in that previous research. It just didn't happen to be of direct interest. Second, if one takes key terms and asks what the synonyms are and then goes to the literature and looks up those synonyms, one may find all kinds of things hidden away that would not have been otherwise noticed, especially what Blumer calls additional "sensitizing concepts" (Blumer 1954, 5).

The second activity urged is called the mental experiment. It consists of putting one's feet up and staring at the ceiling and imagining the research project in some detail—envisioning in a detailed and descriptive way what is involved and what one finds. The phrase "mental experiment" is appropriate because the project is best fantasized as an experiment: if I did or didn't do something, what phenomena would appear? This kind of mental work lets one get a better hold, not only on the phenomena but also on the processes and the implicit model.

The last suggestion relates to time. There is a great pressure to rush into print these days, particularly among younger researchers. This can be dangerous. A caricature of an older style of scholarship makes the point. Here a researcher talked to colleagues, carefully and thoroughly looked at the literature, thought through one after another mental experiment and then, and only then, wrote down a set of notes, roughly defining the research, probably slighting methodology and the finer details, concentrating on the phenomena and the questions. The key activity at this point is to put those notes away for a while. Go on and do something else; then after the passage of time, pull out the notes and read them with somewhat fresher eyes as well as pass them around to colleagues. Then, if it still seems reasonable and makes sense, formalize the research proposal.

Concluding Comments

Organizational behavior research today is fast becoming complex, costly, and overly formalized. Some redirections in research training and a renewed emphasis on hypothesis creation are called for. While it is likely that we cannot all construct basic paradigms or initiate crucial experiments, we can at least try to be less trivial. When it comes to doing research that is enduring and critical, we can, paraphrasing Webb, learn as much as we can, believe in new ways, more effectively discover new ideas, seek as great extensity in our variables as we can, and never lose sight of the phenomenon (W. B. Webb 1961). Doing research in organizational behavior is just like doing science in general; and that, according to Bridgman, is simply "doing one's damnedest with one's mind" (Bridgman 1954, 460).

Problem-Oriented Research
Paul R. Lawrence

. . . Let me state the point in a declarative way and then elaborate. *The better work in our field has come from problem-oriented research rather than from theory-oriented research.* What does this mean?

I have come to believe that we behavioral scientists have made a serious mistake in our practice of the scientific process as we have borrowed it from the physical sciences. In borrowing methods from these "hard sciences" I believe we made a major, even if totally understandable, mistake. The physical sciences start their discovery process with a theory orientation. They first ask what is known and from this they formulate their questions about what needs to be known. They move from the known to the unknown because that is the only logical and practical way for them to proceed. We behavioral scientists have, rather unthinkingly, copied this practice. It is the discovery process we were taught as doctoral students and that we teach to our own doctoral students. We teach each other that all journal articles must start with a theory review if there is to be any hope of their publication. We have come to believe that the theory orientation is not just one path to discovery, but it is the only path. In doing this, we have ignored a very fundamental difference between the subject matter of chemistry and physics and our subject matter, human behavior. The objects of study of chemists and physicists, physical and chemical substances, have no voices. On the other hand our subjects most definitely do have voices. Their subjects cannot tell them about their problems, whereas ours most emphatically can. This is a profound difference that, unfortunately, we have been conditioned to ignore. By largely ignoring this difference I think we are throwing away a means of significantly upgrading the quality of our research. We are discarding a marvelous way to find and identify where knowledge is missing, a way that is simply not available to the hard sciences. Our subjects can tell us what needs to be studied—where our theories and knowledge are inadequate. This single insight has important implications about the way to do research.

My suggestions for how best to do behavioral research follow logically from this insight about our subjects:

> Step one: Select an important emerging human problem to study, a selection based on careful listening and observations; be explicit about the value choices involved.

Source: "The challenge of problem-oriented research" by Paul R. Lawrence, *Journal of Management Inquiry* 1 (1992): 140–142. Copyright © 1992 by Sage Publications, Inc. Reprinted by permission of Sage Publications, Inc.

Step two: Do some initial field scouting of the problem to make an initial assessment of the key parameters.

Step three: Examine relevant theory to use promising hypotheses and conceptualizations.

Step four: Be eclectic in research design, choice of data collection techniques, and analytic methods.

Step five: Collect data systematically.

Step six: Analyze and generalize.

Step seven: Present results so that they are useful for action by responsible problem solvers as well as accessible to the academic community.

Each of these points needs some elaboration.

The research process I recommend always starts with the choice of a significant emerging problem. To prepare for this, one needs to broadly observe both current affairs and history. One has to be a good listener, to interact as thoughtfully as possible with managers and employees. Personally, I have found that if one focuses on the anticipation of important problems, it can be done. For example, the issue of U.S. business competitiveness was already conspicuous in 1979 when I began to research it. By 1983, when *Renewing American Industry* (with David Dyer, Free Press) was published, it was still ahead of the crest of interest in the problem.

Many of the major human and social problems in the 1990s that behavioral scientists can contribute to solving are not new or hard to anticipate. Under the heading of improving business competitiveness, for instance, I would cite, for example, such problems as (a) shortening new product development cycles, (b) enriching the exchange process with suppliers and customers, (c) improving the resolution of intergroup and interlevel conflict, (d) developing supportive relations between business and government, (e) developing goal setting and reward systems that lead to unified effort, and (f) developing the creative potential of a more diverse work force. Beyond strictly business problems, I believe applied behavioral scientists can also contribute to understanding such broader issues as managing for consistently healthy national economies, managing especially weak sectors such as health care and education, managing population growth, and managing the integration of the Communist bloc nations into the global economic and political system. This is a staggering agenda. I believe applied behavioral scientists have made some significant contributions in the past 50 years to making the world work better, especially in making organizations more productive, innovative and humane. But those contributions pale in comparison with the future agenda. At least applied behavioral scientists need never be bored.

Remember that the choice of a research question always involves values. When a choice is based on a generally perceived problem, the values involved, it can be argued, are apt to be widely shared rather than strictly personal.

I, obviously, believe research methods should be selected only after the research question has been chosen and initial scouting has taken place. Methods should be selected from the full apparatus of systematic behavioral inquiry, to achieve a proper fit with the research question. To do this requires that we challenge ourselves to be open to new methods as we move to new problems. I subscribe to the idea that developing richly documented research cases is an especially useful way of exploring poorly mapped phenomenon. The use of larger samples and more quantitative methods is usually more appropriate for testing hypotheses that have grown out of exploratory research. I have tended to alternate between both of these research modes. The work with Arthur Turner, *Industrial Jobs and the Worker* (Division of Research, Harvard Business School, 1965), was a large sample study. It was preceded by an intensive case study of organizational change (*The Changing of Organizational Behavior Patterns*, Division of Research, Harvard Business School, 1958), and followed by *Organization and Environment* (with Jay Lorsch, Division of Research, Harvard Business School, 1967) that combined qualitative and quantitative modes. Longitudinal studies are usually desirable for capturing organizational dynamics. In some special circumstances, action research methods, in spite of their difficulties, could be appropriate.

Simultaneously with choosing methods, one needs to examine relevant research literature for ideas that will help in formulating hypotheses and conceptualizing the research question; but note, this is the third step, not the first. For instance, Jay Lorsch and I had largely completed our data collection for *Organization and Environment* before we started digging into the relevant theory. This was true even though, for conventional reasons, we started our book by citing the theory. Based on my experience, theory is not the best guide in selecting the research question; it is a good guide in framing the research question.

The analysis and presentation of research should always, I believe, be user friendly. The primary user I have in mind is, of course, the practitioner, the organizational manager, or the policymaker. Whether research is in fact used by practitioners is the first quality test I would apply: Whether it has contributed to theory is the second important test.

What are the special advantages of a problem-oriented approach to research? I see seven:

1. A problem-oriented approach to research is more apt to develop not only usable findings but findings that are actually used—for two basic reasons. The existence of a major problem means that

there is apt to be a ready market for the findings. Some people out there are hurting and asking for help. Second, it means the findings are more likely to be conceptualized in a way that meshes with the language and thinking of the practitioner. Less translation is likely to be required.

2. A problem-oriented approach tends automatically to link micro- and macrolevels of analysis, that desired but often elusive research goal. The linkage happens because problems almost always require both micro- and macrolevels of analysis.

3. Problem-oriented research is practical because it is possible to iden- tify important problems.

4. Problem-oriented research makes it easier to gain access to study sites and usually easier to secure funding.

5. A problem-oriented approach will usually identify some perfor- mance indicators as dependent variables. It will rather automatically be normative research.

6. Problem-oriented research is more likely to discover new and better organizational forms and other social inventions. This is true be- cause such research normally tries to identify a sample that contains not only sites with the focal problem but comparative sites that are of special interest because they are free of the problem. The problem-free condition might well be found to be due to valuable social inventions that otherwise might have been overlooked.

7. Finally the chief advantage of problem-oriented research is the one we started with earlier—the fact that problems are a powerful way of identifying gaps in our theory or, at least, gaps in our ability to apply available knowledge. It is exactly because the subject of our research is human behavior, that the existence of human problems is the very best guide to where knowledge is missing. It follows from this, that when research findings are generated that do address a problem, they are likely also to fill an important gap in our basic knowledge. Research always involves risk, but I believe that starting with a problem is the surest way to end up making an important contribution to theory. This is simply not the way it works in the physical sciences.

What are the negatives of problem-oriented research? It has been argued that a problem-oriented approach is apt to lead to findings that do not con- nect neatly with the generalizations that have been built up over the years in any one discipline of the behavioral sciences. This is a valid criticism, if the findings are articulated for only a narrow specific application. This situation would, however, reflect a weak research design and presentation. But even when broadly framed, problem-oriented research might well not meet the publication standards of some prestigious disciplinary journals. Also such research might not connect neatly with the promotion standards of many schools. To address these issues, I would simply suggest we treat the standards as the problem and change them so that they recognize and reward high-quality problem-oriented behavioral research. This may sound utopian, but my guess is that if we begin to practice problem-oriented research, the significant results I predict will themselves bring about radical changes in the standards.

But first we—all of us—must get over any lingering hang-ups about problem-oriented, normative research. Ours is an applied discipline—let's be proud of it. We belong to the behavioral, not the physical sciences, and our methods should reflect that fact. Let's get over our identity crisis. Let's listen for our subjects' voices identifying important problems where knowledge is needed. Let's aggressively and boldly study these important problems. If we do that, I would anticipate a strong upsurge in the quality and effectiveness of our organizational research. As a final note I would add that it is also simply more fun and more personally gratifying to generate research that is useful and constructive in the real world.

A Theory-Focused Approach
Karl E. Weick

My attempt to provide a compact, personally grounded description of a theory-oriented approach is divided into three parts. These include (a) the understanding of theory that drives my approach, (b) the activity of choosing problems, and (c) alternative ways to contrast how Lawrence and I work. Advantages and disadvantages of a theory-based approach will be evident throughout.

The Understanding of Theory That Drives My Approach

Although the ways in which I understand theory are most evident in my previous discussions of theorizing about organizational communication (Weick 1987b) and theory construction as disciplined imagination (Weick 1989), two quotations anticipate the main points I want to make about theory itself.

The first quotation, which appears in Kaplan's (1964) influential *Conduct of Inquiry*, reminds readers that, "theory is of practice, and must stand or fall with its practicality, provided only that the mode and contexts of its

Source: "Agenda setting in organizational behavior" by Karl E. Weick, *Journal of Management Inquiry* 1 (1992): 172–178. Copyright © 1992 by Sage Publications, Inc. Reprinted by permission of Sage Publications, Inc.

application are suitably specified" (p. 296). Although that statement may seem to make trouble for a theory-based approach, I don't think it does at all. Business organizations are certainly not the only settings where practice occurs, nor are they the only place where practicality is an operative criterion. Instead, all theories are about practice and practicality, and the trick is to discover those settings and conditions under which they hold true. This is the crucial insight in McGuire's (1983) work on contextualism, and it is implicit in the final phrase from Kaplan, which counsels investigators to specify those modes and contexts where the theory does apply.

A theory-based approach is often a continuing effort to find those contexts where a theory holds true. The question is not, Is the theory true? It is. All theories are true. Everything possible to be believed is an image of truth (McGuire 1985, 575). The question is, Where is the theory true? In what context do events go together the way the theory predicts?

The second quotation elaborates what I think a theory-based approach involves. It is Peter Vaill's (personal communication, 7/2/75) description of art as "the attempt to wrest coherence and meaning out of more reality than we ordinarily deal with." Theory has too seldom been treated as an art form, in the provocative ways suggested by Nisbet (1962). That alone is enough to keep Vaill's statement exactly as it is. However, I want to make that implication explicit by substituting the word theory for the word art, so the revised statement reads, "theory is the attempt to wrest coherence and meaning out of more reality than we ordinarily deal with."

To me, the goal of a theory-based approach is to find patterns that edit particulars into a more compact summary that allows people (including theorists) to anticipate and thread their way through the complexities of everyday social life. For example, the summary statement, "people act their way into meaning," comes in part from my observation of the pattern in which people who agree to work on an assignment, with some reservations, act intensely to create an interesting assignment that justifies their compliance and makes it a meaningful act (Weick 1964).

For me, the particular is a pretext to look for a pattern that is more generalizable, more abstract, something that applies to people in general (e.g., Meehl 1972). This baldly instrumental treatment of the particular makes sense if you assume that people are all pretty much alike (Marceil 1977). By contrast, I suspect that problem-focused research doesn't look on the particular as a pretext for anything and is much more deliberate in its treatment of the particular as a unique end in itself. In problem-focused work, the particular is a context rather than a pretext and consists of a self-contained story, tied together by its own logic. Different logics will generate different stories, and different stories will suggest different remedies.

The view of theory that lies behind my attraction to these two quotations, can be summarized as follows. Theories abbreviate stories and get rid of data (I am indebted to John Van Maanen for this imagery). People differ passionately in their reactions to what is discarded from the stories and what is retained. Furthermore, some stories are so compelling, so plausible, so narratively rational, that the inevitable editing produced by theory would set back understanding. Exemplary problem-focused research can produce narrative particulars that embody the universal.

But when stories are incomplete and something is missing, we need theories to fill those gaps. So, we tend to find the best theories where we have the worst stories, and vice versa. Said differently, theory-focused research is an exercise in sense making (Weick 1989, 519). For example, the story of airline deregulation is a puzzling incomplete saga until a theorist such as Bob Cole speculates that the history of airline deregulation recapitulates the history of capitalism (personal communication, June 1988). That suggestion turns an incomplete rendering of something concrete into a more complete rendering of something abstract. And it guides the curious listener back to the concrete events of airline deregulation to see whether they are consistent or inconsistent with the abstraction.

That exercise in abduction (Scheff 1990) is something that Lawrence and I both do. Where we differ is that I am in no hurry to move from the abstract to the concrete, and when I do, a little concreteness (e.g., one lab study) goes a long way. I suspect that Lawrence has the opposite set of preferences, namely, a little abstraction goes a long way, and he prefers to spend his time close to the phenomenon rather than close to the library.

A brief gloss of the distinction between map and territory (Bateson 1979; Korzybski 1958) completes my description of the view of theorizing that drives my work. Theory work is language work and consists in part of efforts to refine and enrich the representations that people impose on territories to make sense of them. Viewed as language work, theorizing classifies, proposes analogies, codifies everyday understanding, and discredits synonyms. Theories partition the world into mechanistic and organic systems. Theories propose that interaction resembles exchange, that a loosely coupled system resembles baseball, that organizations resemble populations. Theories propose new maps such as "normal accidents," which then single out features that had previously gone unnoticed. Theories show that the construction and creation of reality are not synonymous, and to treat them as such is to miss the core of social sense making (Isaac 1990, 26).

If theorizing about organizations is an exercise in cartography, then it is important to remember that there is no one best map; there are many different projections, and it makes no sense to try to discover the preexisting map. Furthermore, if we cannot achieve the one true picture of the world, we must also face the even more unsettling possibility that we can never even be sure if we're closer to it or not. Theories of organizations not only represent the territory but, when taken seriously, may enact and construct the territory (MacIntyre 1985). In the case of organizations, if the map is not the territory, that may be the fault of the territory and not the map, which inverts the usual understanding of this phrase.

Choice of the Problem

This section was triggered by Lawrence's statement that he defines problems as areas where human failures, discomforts, and pain occur, with his interest being to learn how human affairs can work better. I certainly do not disagree with that statement or its values, but I am not driven by the same imperatives. Pain, compassion, and betterment are less central as drivers for me, and more central are such things as incompleteness, novelty, counterintuitive implications, puzzlement, and fascination. Those triggers seem to be more cognitive, more internal, more tied to existing explanations, and more comparative than is true for Lawrence. To begin working, I do not need a problem. All I need is some kind of difference, something that attracts attention. An interesting phrase (e.g., "small wins"), a diagram (Maruyama's cause map of sanitation), an inversion (e.g., what if people accomplish impossible tasks because of loose coupling, not in spite of it), a puzzle (e.g., how could two 747 airliners collide on the ground with catastrophic results), a borrowed category (e.g., narrative rationality)—any of these inputs, when glossed, enlarged, instantiated, and tied into existing theories of attention, postdecisional behavior, systems, and interaction, become for me what a problem becomes for Lawrence.

My trigger is "what if," not "now what?" Lawrence's impetus to begin a study is the question, What does the world find troubling? My impetus to begin a study is the question, What do I find interesting? We seem to differ partly because my internal world is a more conspicuous source of questions than is true for Lawrence, who pays more attention to things around him. We also seem to differ because curiosity is more central for me, whereas compassion is more central for Lawrence.

This latter contrast between problem choice based on curiosity versus problem choice based on compassion paves the way for us to consider the question of problem choice more systematically. W. B. Webb (1961) argued that investigators routinely choose problems on the basis of six criteria, none of which are as sound or as significant as the three additional criteria of knowledge (choose problems in areas where you have a thorough understanding), dissatisfaction (choose problems that reflect a healthy, active opposition to existing knowledge and methodology), and generalizability (choose variables and situations that are universal and common rather than unique and rare).

The six criteria of problem choice that people commonly use are these:

1. *Curiosity*: Am I interested? Curiosity is a charming urge but no guarantee of nontrivial problem choice.
2. *Confirmability*: Can I get an answer? Confirmability precludes choice of mysterious new areas and is the criterion most likely to result in pedestrian problems.
3. *Costs*: How much? Cost is uncorrelated with value.
4. *Compassion*: Will it help? [W. B.] Webb (1961) cites the following passage from H. G. Wells' book *Meanwhile*: "The disease of cancer will be banished from life by calm, unhurrying, persistent men and women working with every shiver of feeling controlled and suppressed in hospitals and in laboratories. . . . Pity never made a good doctor, love never made a good poet, desire for service never made a discovery" (p. 225).
5. *Cupidity*: What's the payoff for me? What is good for your promotion or publicity is not necessarily good for others.
6. *Conformity*: What is the current hot topic? Some things people are currently doing are quite worthwhile and some are quite ridiculous.

These criteria, plus those of knowledge, dissatisfaction, and generalizability (W. B. Webb 1961, 225), can be used in several ways to distinguish between a problem-focused and theory-focused approach. I have already suggested that compassion may be a more central basis of problem choice in problem-focused research and that curiosity may be more influential when theory-based research is involved (e.g., in my case the curiosity is reflected in questions such as, What would happen if ethnomethodology were applied to organizational theory, if cultural transmission were studied in the laboratory using the common target game, if Bartlett's serial reproduction task were run in reverse?).

I suspect that both Lawrence and myself are equally driven by knowledge and dissatisfaction, although Lawrence's knowledge and dissatisfaction are focused on the world and mine are focused on theory. Generalizability is of primary importance for me and possibly less central for Lawrence. The remaining four criteria—confirmability, cost, cupidity, conformity—seem of lesser salience for both of us.

The point is that people who focus on problems and on theories may choose the things they do for different reasons. The word *choose*, however, may mislead because it suggests a more formal and deliberate process than that which actually operates. Ziman (1987) suggests that the process operates at the level of rationality in everyday life (p. 97), and often "may be no more than a serendipitous intimation that an unconsidered problem, with a possibly significant solution, lies just behind some curious observation or anomaly" (p. 96). Furthermore, it is crucial to remember that the implied sequence of choosing a problem to do research, is often reversed because the process of research usually becomes the occasion to clarify, formulate, and reformulate the question being investigated. . . .

I suspect also that personal biography affects not only the form of inquiry but also its content. In thinking about why I chose to study psychology, and what personal question I might be trying to answer by this choice of field, I was struck by the frequency with which I seem to study what happens when people don't understand what is going on. My proximate concern is not deja vu (I've already experienced that), but rather "vuja dé" (I have never been here before and I have no idea where I am). Consider the evidence. I study interpretation, sense making, equivocality, stress, dissonance, and crisis behavior, all of which are associated with the question, What is going on here? I advise people to become more complicated so they can sense more of the complications in their worlds. I sound like a cartographer manqué because I keep looking for maps, and my favorite story is one in which people find their way out of the Alps using a map of the Pyrenees. I define technology as material relations that exceed human comprehension. Seemingly ineffective organizational acts such as "hypocrisy," "ambivalence," and "galumphing" surprise us by having unexpected benefits. Small stuff can be satisfying and sensible. And events only make sense after the fact.

It is all well and good to say I'm interested in how people cope with complexity, but that interest is anything but idle curiosity. Apparently, I never survived my first encounter with bewilderment, and my professional life represents one long Ziegarnik effect to gain some closure on that raw, open-ended initial experience.

Small wonder that I keep looking for ideas, tactics, and determinants of sensemaking at a microlevel of analysis. My work is no less problem-focused than is Lawrence's. It's just that the problems I focus on are more private, closer in, and more hidden by theory-based overlays. But the question, what does it all mean, is certainly not my question alone, which explains why I feel my analyses have generality. Also, because the problem is close in, I also have no shortage of data. Everything I do is empirical. However, I am also deeply mindful of the sentiment attributed to Freud that the only trouble with self-analysis is countertransference.

So what's the point? A theory-based approach, as I practice it, is triggered by incompleteness and puzzles in theory rather than by injustices and pain in people. A concern with theory in no way precludes the latter. It's just that my instantiation of a theory-based approach gives less prominence to injustice and pain than other theorists might. The work is driven more by curiosity than by compassion. And yet, when I look for patterns in actual problems I chose to work on, the work converges on a theme that perpetually charms me as a person—namely, What is going on? And my recurrent answer is, You'll know once you act.

No big deal. But then, as Bergson said, "a true philosopher says only one thing in his life-time, because he enjoys but one contact with the real" (cited in Wagner 1983, 115).

Alternative Ways to Contrast the Two Approaches

Although there are clear differences between the approaches that Lawrence and I exemplify, I am not convinced that the contrast is best labeled problem focused versus theory focused. Having just concluded the previous section with the suggestion that my theorizing is driven by personal concerns with sense making, I can cite other examples of my work that are problem oriented just as Paul can cite examples of his work that are theory oriented. Among the problems I have addressed are why did the Tenerife disaster occur (Weick 1990a); what does it mean to have a career in an organization with no hierarchy (Weick and Berlinger 1989); what are the costs of coping with overload on military battlefields (Weick 1985a); how can schools become more responsive to local conditions (Weick 1982); and why are computer-driven analyses misleading (Weick 1985b)? We all work with theories and problems, and cycle between them, although we seem also to linger at one or the other of these poles and hurry to get back to the pole we find more attractive. Theories have problems just as problems have theories.

I think the contrast between our two approaches can be understood more meaningfully using other dimensions than problem versus theory. I want to suggest four possibilities briefly: Myers-Briggs Type Indicator (MBTI), insider-outsider, divergent-convergent, extension-intention.

If a theory-based approach involves an intuitive-thinking style, then the opposite of this style is sensation-feeling or a particular humanist in the categories of Mitroff and Kilmann (1978). Although they repeatedly contrast the conceptual theorist with the analytic scientist, the difference between those two styles is relatively minor, consisting largely of a preference for sensation or imagination. A more significant contrast occurs if a preference for thinking versus feeling as ways to process data is added. Recall that compassion versus curiosity seemed to distinguish sharply between the problems that Lawrence and I chose to study. Thus if it were the case that Lawrence's type is sensation-feeling (SF) then the contrast between our approaches would be more substantial than if he were any one of the other three types—intuitive-feeling (NF), intuitive-thinking (NT), or sensation-thinking (ST). In any case, adding this dimension to the theory-problem difference seems to suggest more about our distinctive approaches to agenda setting than does use of those global categories alone.

The same enrichment of the contrast seems to occur if we pose our differences as those between an insider (Lawrence) and an outsider (Weick). Debate over the relative merits of perspectives from the inside or the outside, and over whether outside is even a perspective, have raged for some time (e.g., Merton 1972). . . .

The distinction between divergent and convergent research styles has been made by several investigators (e.g., Hudson 1966), but McGuire's (1985, 564) recent attempt to contrast the convergent style of Carl Hovland with the divergent style of Leon Festinger provides at least half a distinction between Lawrence and myself, because I was schooled in and continue to use many of Festinger's ideas.

Several distinctions in McGuire reflect previous content. The divergent style is driven by theory rather than the phenomenon, a difference we have tracked from the start, but what McGuire adds are such additional nuances as (a) the theory is applied to as many phenomena as possible (e.g., commitment is organizing), (b) more care is taken in defining the independent variable than the dependent variable (e.g., I worry about the subtle difference between ambiguity, uncertainty, and equivocality, whereas Lawrence worries about subtle differences in measures of effectiveness), (c) small Ns predominate (e.g., a little data goes a long way), and (d) interaction effects are trouble (e.g., general simple explanations are my goal). Although McGuire's distinctions are narrowly drawn, because they are phrased in terms of laboratory methodology, they hint at patterns that should be found across more diverse methodologies.

The distinction between knowledge growth by extension (Weick) and intention (Lawrence) is Kaplan's (1964, 305), and suggests a difference in approach that often may be confounded with the theory-problem distinction. Knowledge growth by extension occurs when a relatively full explanation of a small region is carried over to an explanation of adjoining regions, as when studies of conditioning are enlarged into studies of more complex learning. The metaphor is of science as a mosaic that is built piece by piece. It is exemplified when I take small understandings of commitment, minimal social situations, jazz orchestra rehearsals, or knot tying under stressful conditions and then complicate those understandings so they generalize to other settings.

Lawrence, however, seems to develop a partial explanation of a whole region and then makes it more and more adequate, a pattern that is labeled "knowledge growth by intention" and is visible in the work of Freud and Darwin. The metaphor is one of bringing things into sharper focus or gradually adding light to a darkened room. It is this contrast that is perhaps most visible in our differing agendas. I tend to enlarge the small things we know well, Lawrence tends to define the large things we know poorly.

Although other contrasts could be cited (e.g., Lawrence strives for accurate-simple explanations, whereas I strive for general-simple explanations), the point is that our two approaches are a good deal more subtle and complex in their differences than is conveyed by a simple contrast between a theory-focused approach and a problem-focused approach. I would argue that whatever merits these approaches have, whatever hit rates they generate, whatever interest they generate in readers, and whatever help they give theorists and practitioners lies in those subtleties. And it is the complexities of each of the two approaches that enable both of us to sense some of the complexities that surround us.

The question for research agendas in the 1990s is, Are current research approaches sufficiently subtle and complex to sense and make sensible the subtleties and complexities of organized social action in an increasingly interdependent and turbulent global environment? The answer seems obvious. No one pattern of subtlety and complexity is anywhere near sufficient. The only way we can generate the requisite complexity to grasp the complexity that surrounds us is to become an inquiring community in which there is respectful complementarity, integration, listening to one another, an ethic of mutual helpfulness, and nonstop conversation. I know that sounds bland, difficult, perhaps even maudlin. But I'm not convinced that chronic ethnocentric conflict between warring paradigms has done much to help us consolidate organizational studies into a shared body of knowledge. We need to be subtle and complex in diverse ways if we want to comprehend significant differences in organizational life. But we also need to match this differentiation with the integration that comes when we articulate connections, themes, and patterns that tie those differences into coherent, memorable guidelines.

An agenda that simultaneously strengthens the community, differentiates the phenomenon, and integrates the representations is what I think we need to work toward. Neither Lawrence nor I were able to craft agendas that fully meet these requirements, but our approximations and the way we arrived at them, provide at least a starting point for others to articulate the approaches and trade-offs they feel will advance the field and coalesce the community.

Ploys for Question Generation
Craig C. Lundberg

If you want to understand what a science is you should look in the first instance not at its theories or findings and certainly not at what its apologists say about it; you would look at what the practitioners of it do.
(Clifford Geertz)

Source: "Finding research agendas: Getting started Weick-like" by Craig C. Lundberg, *The Industrial-Organizational Psychologist* (1999): 32, 34–38. Used by permission of the Society for Industrial and Organizational Psychology, Inc.

What are the ways by which scholars initiate significant organizational research? How might an organizational inquirer go about discovering research foci that are likely to result in substantial advances in understanding? These are obviously very important and at the same time very difficult questions. Following the advice in our epigraph, this article will suggest some tentative answers by examining the agenda-finding practices of one influential and widely acknowledged creative scholar—Karl E. Weick. . . .

Notice an Anomaly, and Try to Explain It

Anomalies are unexpected and hence surprising events. That they have occurred at all is puzzling, and by definition they do not lend themselves readily to known explanations. Focusing on an anomaly, whether personally observed or described by others, raises the question, how could that happen? If sufficiently bothered by this question, then sense-making efforts follow—garnering additional facts, valuing some facts differently, arranging and rearranging the facts of the situation until new understandings suggest themselves, until there is an explanation of how the event could have happened. One example of a triggering, anomalous event is to notice that in spite of the technically sophisticated systems and the considerable expertise of all the parties involved, two 747 airliners collided on the ground with catastrophic results (Weick 1990a). Another example occurred in the events surrounding the death of all but three of a 13-man team of professional smoke jumpers in a Montana forest fire (Weick 1993a). While obviously a situation of considerable risk, what was puzzling was why such an experienced crew disregarded their foreman's order, panicked, and ran.

Notice the Level of Analysis That Dominates the Explanation of Something, and Try an Explanation at Another Level

The phenomena of interest in the organizational sciences ranges from the intra-psychic to the societal. The theorizing about some particular unit of analysis usually reflects the level at which the phenomena is first conceived. This ploy simply asks if the prevalent level of theorizing might be augmented by explanations at some other level; that is, could useful explanations also be made that are more fine-grained or more inclusive than those that currently exist? For example, while organizational theory at one time was devoted to structural variables about collectivities (e.g., centralization, formalization, and hierarchy), organizations can also be conceived in terms of patterned alliances among members, that is, collectivities as sets of interpersonal relationships (Weick 1979). Shifting the level of analysis typically provides provocative insights, for example, the environment changes from the structural antecedent to an outcome in the above example. A variant of this ploy takes an idea developed for one unit of analysis and applies it to another unit at a different level, for example, using the mind to explain high reliability organizations by means of collective mental processes (Weick and Roberts 1993). In a recent example, Weick and Quinn (1999) reframe organizational change as episodic or continuous by viewing it from either a macro or micro level of analysis, respectively.

Notice (or Create) Language That May Enrich Explanation and Explore It

This ploy is based on the view that research is basically theory work (i.e., theory brackets and frames phenomena, defines what is data, is confirmed or disconfirmed, etc.), and theory work in turn is language work (i.e., language as symbols and rules for symbol arranging and manipulation). Words common to one field or endeavor may be suggestive of new insights when used in a different context. For example, "bricolage," which means making do with whatever resources are at hand, when applied to organizationally relevant learning, suggests that organizations may already know what they need to know to survive, which counteracts the assumptions of accumulation in the organizational learning literature (Weick 1993b). Another example is "galumphing," a type of play observed among baboons where there is a deliberate complication of process not controlled by goals. When applied to persons, it has implications for dealing with novel problems (Weick 1979). A variant of this stratagem is to take seriously the ideas in unfamiliar combinations of words. "Loose-coupled systems," once a throwaway phrase in a talk by J. G. March, suggested to Weick (1976) that organizations might usefully be conceived in terms of the degree of their internal coupling—now a standard idea in organizational theory.

Notice Common or Simple Activities or Things and Exploit Them as Metaphors

This ploy rests upon the notion that metaphors are not only one of the oldest, most deeply imbedded, even indispensable ways of knowing in the history of human consciousness (Nisbet 1969), but are the basis of some of the most central bodies of theory in the social sciences (Galt and Smith 1976). Metaphors let us explore analogically from one thing to another. All sorts of things, events, and activities may serve as metaphors. For example, a carpenter's contour gauge is suggestive of the several properties of medium; and when these are used to describe leadership as a medium, many useful implications appear, for example, followers use the leader as a contour gauge, leaders who are good mediums will have shorter time horizons, and so forth (Weick 1978). For another example, a laboratory experiment using three-person groups playing the common target game over and over with one member being occasionally replaced is used to show the perpetuation of arbitrary traditions (Weick and Gilfillan 1971) and later used to tease out properties of organizational learning (Weick 1993b). We note that science for Weick is metaphorically a mosaic, that is, built piece by piece, rather than accumulating a pile of findings as science is often popularly understood.

Notice the Context of an Explanation, and Apply the Explanation to Another Context

This ploy works in two ways. One way is to take our understandings from one situation and ask if they help to explain a different situation. For example, the interpersonal dynamics in love relationships have much to say about long-term, self-managing organizational teams (Weick 1992). Other examples are to see the close parallel between theory building, something we know little about, and evolutionary processes, something we know a lot about (Weick 1989), or the parallels between technology and sensemaking (Weick 1990b). The other way this stratagem works is to take understandings of some things or events and then complicate those explanations so that they generalize to other settings. One now-famous example was the creation of a cause map for a jazz orchestra, which prompted a method (an etiograph) for representing complex cause maps with loops, which then enabled a test of the proposition that system fate is not in the content of the variables but in the structure of causality among them—a finding generalizable to all organizations (Bougon, Weick and Binkhorst 1977).

Notice Commonly Accepted Knowledge or Practices, and Pursue Possible Counterintuitive Explanations

This ploy quite clearly is an application of Davis's (1971) proposition of what's "interesting." [1] While many others have seemingly used it, Weick does so often. As before, we will restrict ourselves to just a few examples. Where almost all stress-management advice argues for removing or avoiding stressors, Weick (1975), noting the futility of this, shows that training under very stressful conditions is more effective because then the normal regression toward simplified thinking under the next stress means the person will regress to what in others would be a relatively unstressful cognitive condition. A second example concerns learning. Many organizational learning theorists posit

1. Editors' note: See Davis later in this chapter.

a parallel between individual learning and organizational learning. Weick (1991), however, disconnects this parallel when he points out, appropriately, that individual learning is a different response to the same stimulus, and organizational learning is the same response to a different stimulus.

The six question-generating ploys of Weick sketched above, while admittedly attributions and probably not exhaustive of Weick's creative gambits (the late Lou Pondy attributes two others to Weick, that is, take a well accepted aphorism and turn it around; take everyday life and embellish it seriously) seem to be quite different than those conventionally advocated. We now turn to the explication of these differences as well as what seems to be themal to the Weickian ploys.

Stepping Back

The conventional advice for finding research agendas speaks to the discovery of problems, either by listening closely to what practitioners say are problems or by specifying the intellectual problems of how extant knowledge might be refined or extended. In contrast, Weick believes "problems" of all types are designed, not discovered (Weick 1995a). Each of the ploys noted above begins by "noticing," an intentional behavior guided by the cognitive framing, punctuation, and bracketing of the researcher. This noticing is presumably not emotionally neutral. In contrast to the empathy with practitioners facing pragmatic problems (i.e., compassion) that seemingly motivates problem-oriented researchers or the pragmatic pseudo-neutrality (i.e., curiosity, confirmability, conformability) of theory-extending researchers, Weick appears to be bothered by practices and explanations that gloss over factual complexity or gloss over cause and effect, thought and action, structure and process, and the like (Weick 1979, 1983, 1995a).

While Weick has relied on phrases that incorporate the word "problem" for example, "problem finding" (Weick 1992), "problem statement" (Weick 1989), it is clear that his ploys do not identify problems per se but surface questions—questions about what is actually going on, how one thing might resemble another, how representations might be enriched or refined, where explanations might apply, what might be alternative explanations, and so forth. . . . .

Whereas a "problem" implies discrete solutionability, questions lead to sensemaking variety. In research agenda finding, the variety of Weick's opening ploys begins to outline the requisite variety in the equivocality of multiple realities. Said differently, to make sense out of the equivocal, the more ways we can come to questions and the more questions we can ask, the more we will eventually understand. For Weick (1995a), understanding means sensemaking—how managers and scholars make sense of situations, more or less collectively with more or less coordination, and, how to make sense out of sensemaking. In this way, Weick discredits organizational phenomena as either disordered, indeterminate, or chaotic and thus essentially incomprehensible, or as fully ordered and determinate, merely awaiting discovery with the right approach. Rather, he seems to advocate an image of organizational sciencing that is rich in the multiplicity of meanings that can be imposed on equally complex phenomenological situations—if we are risky and playful enough.

That's Interesting!
Murray S. Davis

It has long been thought that a theorist is considered great because his theories are true, but this is false. A theorist is considered great, not because his theories are true, but because they are *interesting*. Those who carefully and exhaustively verify trivial theories are soon forgotten; whereas those who cursorily and expediently verify interesting theories are long remembered. In fact, the truth of a theory has very little to do with its impact, for a theory can continue to be found interesting even though its truth is disputed—even refuted!

Since this capacity to stimulate interest is a necessary if not sufficient characteristic of greatness, then any study of theorists who are considered great must begin by examining why their theories are considered interesting—why, in other words, the theorist is worth studying at all. But before we can attempt even this preliminary task we must understand clearly why some theories are considered interesting while others are not. In this essay, I will try to determine what it means for a theory to be considered "interesting" (or, in the extreme, "fascinating").

Students who follow to the letter all of the injunctions of current textbooks on "theory-construction," but take into account no other criterion in the construction of their theories, will turn out work which will be found dull indeed. Their impeccably constructed theories will go unnoted—or, more precisely, unfootnoted—by others. But should these students also take into account that criterion, to be detailed below, which distinguishes "interesting theories" from "uninteresting theories" they will find that their theories will make their readers literally "sit up and take notice." Their theories will then be discussed among colleagues, examined in journals, confirmed or denied in dissertations, and taught to students as the most recent instances of "progress" in their profession.

Source: "That's interesting: Toward a phenomenology of sociology and a sociology of phenomenology" by Murray S. Davis, *Philosophy of the Social Sciences* 1 (1971): 309–313, 315–327. Copyright © York University, Toronto and contributors 1971. Reprinted by permission of Sage Publications, Inc.

I will confine my inquiry to *social theories* which have been considered interesting, giving special attention to famous *sociological theories*. I suggest, however, that the level of abstraction of the analysis presented here is high enough for it to be applicable equally well to theories in all areas of social science and even to theories in natural science. But this generalization of the following discussion will have to await further investigation.

Interesting Non-propositions

I will further restrict this paper to analysing the "interesting" component of those theories which Kant has called "synthetic *a posteriori* propositions"—assertions which refer to the empirical world and are not merely matters of definition. But these propositions, of course, are not the only ingredients of the scientific enterprise that may be found interesting, though they are the most important. Space, however, forbids consideration here of the various types of non-propositions that are also capable of evoking interest. Thus I will not be dealing with (1) "Findings" which confirm or disconfirm hypotheses, (2) "Clues" which indicate the way a problem can be solved, (3) "Aesthetic Descriptions" which refine perception, (4) "Analogies" which render the unfamiliar in terms of the familiar, and (5) "Models" which simplify the integration of complex relationships.

The Interesting and the Routine

The interesting is something which affects the attention. *Webster's Third* defines "interesting" as "engaging the attention." The question naturally arises: "Where was the attention before it was engaged by the interesting?"

It is hard to answer this question because, by definition, one is usually not attentive to what one is usually not attentive to. But, for those who wish to understand human behaviour, it is very important to answer this question because most people spend most of their lives in this state they are not attentive to. Harold Garfinkel (1967) has called this state of low attention or low consciousness "the routinized taken-for-granted world of everyday life." Since the interesting, by definition, is that which engages the attention more than the non-interesting, perhaps the former can be used to make manifest the latter. I will attempt to use what is found interesting to disclose what is routinely taken-for-granted.

If the defining characteristic of anything which some audience considers interesting is that it stands out in their attention in contrast to the routinized taken-for-granted world of their everyday life, then the defining characteristic of a theory which some audience considers interesting is that it stands out in their attention in contrast to the web of routinely taken-for-granted propositions which make up the theoretical structure of their everyday life.

In other words, a new theory will be noticed only when it denies an old truth (proverb, platitude, maxim, adage, saying, common-place, etc.). (The actual process by which a theory comes to be considered interesting today is, of course, much more complicated because of the present fragmentation of the audience who does the considering into lay and professional groups. This important complication will be taken up in a later section.)

The Interesting in Theory and in Practice

All *interesting* theories, at least all *interesting* social theories, then, constitute an attack on the taken-for-granted world of their audience. This audience will consider any particular proposition to be "worth saying" only if it denies the truth of some part of their routinely held assumption-ground. If it does not challenge but merely confirms one of their taken-for-granted beliefs, they will respond to it by rejecting its value while affirming its truth. They will declare that the proposition need not be stated because it is already part of their theoretical scheme: "Of course." "That's obvious." "Everybody knows that." "It goes without saying."

The "taken-for-granted world" includes not only this theoretical dimension but also a practical dimension as well. A theory will be considered truly interesting only if it has repercussions on both levels. On the latter level, an audience will find a theory to be interesting only when it denies the significance of some part of their present "on-going practical activity" (Garfinkel 1967) and insists that they should be engaged in some new on-going practical activity instead. If this practical consequence of a theory is not immediately apparent to its audience, they will respond to it by rejecting its value until someone can concretely demonstrate its utility: "So what?" "Who cares?" "Why bother?" "What good is it?"

An analysis of the rhetorical structure of social research reveals how it is made to seem "interesting" on both theoretical and practical levels. The "standard form" of the books and articles in which this research is presented is the following: (1) The author articulates the taken-for-granted assumptions of his imagined audience by reviewing the literature of the particular sub-tradition in question ("It has long been thought . . ."), (2) he adduces one or more propositions which deny what has been traditionally assumed ("But this is false . . ."), (3) he spends the body of the work "proving" by various methodological devices that the old routinely assumed propositions are wrong while the new ones he has asserted are right ("We have seen instead that . . ."), and finally (4) in conclusion, he suggests the practical consequences of these new propositions for his imagined audience's on-going social research, specifically how they ought to deflect it onto new paths ("Further investigation is necessary to . . .").

An analysis of the cognitive content of social research reveals much more about the nature of that which is interesting and, equally important, that which is not. Theoretically, it is worth investigating those social theories that have been considered interesting because of what they reveal about the common-sense everyday layman's view of the world, which they are attacking. Practically, it is worth investigating those social theories that have been considered interesting so that we can learn to assert interesting theories ourselves. If we come to understand the process by which interesting theories are generated, we will not have to continue to do what has been done up till now—leave the "interesting" to the "inspired" . . .

The Common Element of All Interesting Propositions

All of the *interesting* propositions I examined were found to involve the radical distinction between seeming and being, between the subject of phenomenology and the subject of ontology. An *interesting* proposition was one which first articulated a phenomenological presumption about the way a particular part of the world had looked, and then denied this phenomenological presumption in the name of "truth," that is, in the name of a more profound, more real, more ontological criterion. Put more precisely, an *interesting* proposition was one which attempted first to expose the ontological claim of its accredited counterpart as merely phenomenological pretence, and then to deny this phenomenological pretence with its own claim to ontological priority. In brief, an *interesting* proposition was always the negation of an accepted one. All of the *interesting* propositions I examined were easily translatable into the form: "What seems to be X is in reality non-X," or "What is accepted as X is actually non-X."

The Species of Interesting Propositions

While all interesting propositions were found to have in common the same dialectical relation between the phenomenological and the ontological, they were found to be distinguished on the logical level. The variety of interesting propositions fell into twelve logical categories which involved either the characterization of a single phenomenon or the relations among multiple phenomena. These twelve logical categories constitute an "Index of the Interesting."

The Index of the Interesting

The Characterization of a Single Phenomenon

Organization

a. What seems to be a disorganized (unstructured) phenomenon is in reality an organized (structured) phenomenon.

Example: Ferdinand Tonnies' assertion in *Community and Society* that the relations among people within all societies were considered at the time he wrote to be manifold and indeterminate, can in fact be organized around two main types (*Gemeinschaft* and *Gessellschaft*).

b. What seems to be an organized (structured) phenomenon is in reality a disorganized (unstructured) phenomenon.
   Example: Karl Marx's assertion in *Capital* that the economic processes of bourgeois society, which were considered at the time he wrote to be organized in one way, are in fact not organized in that way (but rather organized in another way). . . .

Composition

a. What seem to be assorted heterogeneous phenomena are in reality composed of a single element.
   Example: Sigmund Freud's assertion throughout his *Collected Works* that the behaviour of children, primitives, neurotics, and adults in crowds, as well as dreams, jokes, and slips of the tongue and pen, which were considered at the time he wrote to be unassociated in any way with one another, are in fact all various manifestations of the same instinctual drives.

b. What seems to be a single phenomenon is in reality composed of assorted heterogeneous elements.
   Example: Max Weber's assertion in *Economy and Society* that the stratification system, which was considered at the time he wrote to be monolithic is in fact composed of the three independent variables of economic class, status prestige, and political power. . . .

Abstraction

a. What seems to be an individual phenomenon is in reality a holistic phenomenon.
   Example: Emile Durkheim's assertion in *Suicide* that suicide, which was considered at the time he wrote to be a behaviour characteristic of an individual, is in fact (more crucially) a process characteristic of a society.

b. What seems to be a holistic phenomenon is in reality an individual phenomenon.
   Example: Sigmund Freud's assertion in "Thoughts for the Times on War and Death" that war, which was considered at the time he wrote to be a social phenomenon, is in fact (more crucially) a psychological phenomenon. . . .

Generalization

a. What seems to be a local phenomenon is in reality a general phenomenon.
   Example: Karl Mannheim's assertion in *Ideology and Utopia* that the ideological limitation and distortion of thought processes, which was considered at the time he wrote to effect only the bourgeois class, in fact effects all social classes.
b. What seems to be a general phenomenon is in reality a local phenomenon.
   Example: Malinowski's assertion in *Sex and Repression in Savage Society* that the Oedipus Complex, which was considered at the time he wrote to be a human universal, in fact does not occur in all societies. . . .

Stabilization

a. What seems to be a stable and unchanging phenomenon is in reality an unstable and changing phenomenon.
   Example: Karl Marx's assertion in *Capital* that the social organization of bourgeois society, which was considered at the time he wrote to be permanent, is in fact about to be suddenly and dramatically transformed.
b. What seems to be an unstable and changing phenomenon is in reality a stable and unchanging phenomenon.
   Example: Georg Simmel's assertion in "Conflict" that any conflict-ridden social organization, which was considered at the time he wrote to be on the verge of transformation, may in fact be capable of continuing indefinitely as it is (in a steady-state of conflict). . . .

Function

a. What seems to be a phenomenon that functions ineffectively as a means for the attainment of an end is in reality a phenomenon that functions effectively.
   Example: Robert Merton's assertion in *Social Theory and Social Structure* that the political machine, which was considered at the time he wrote to be an inefficient institution for obtaining community goals, is in fact an efficient institution for obtaining community goals.
b. What seems to be a phenomenon that functions effectively as a means for the attainment of an end is in reality a phenomenon that functions ineffectively.

Example: Herbert Marcuse's assertion in "Repressive Tolerance" that the tradition of tolerance in America, which was considered at the time he wrote to be a value that fostered the goal of a liberated society, is in fact a value that hindered the goal of a liberated society. . . .

Evaluation

a. What seems to be a bad phenomenon is in reality a good phenomenon.
Example: R. D. Laing's assertion in *The Politics of Experience* that schizophrenia, which was considered at the time he wrote to be a bad thing, is in fact a good thing.
b. What seems to be a good phenomenon is in reality a bad phenomenon.
Example: Friedrich Nietzche's assertion in *On the Genealogy of Morals* that Christian morality, which was considered at the time he wrote to be a good thing, is in fact a bad thing. . . .

The Relations Among Multiple Phenomena

Co-relation

a. What seem to be unrelated (independent) phenomena are in reality correlated (interdependent) phenomena.
Example: August Hollingshead's assertion in *Social Class and Mental Illness* that social class and mental illness, which were considered at the time he wrote to be uncorrelated, are in fact correlated.
b. What seem to be related (interdependent) phenomena are in reality uncorrelated (independent) phenomena.
Example: Emile Durkeim's assertion in *Suicide* that suicide and such other phenomena as psychopathological states, race, heredity, and climate, which were considered at the time he wrote to be correlated, are in fact uncorrelated. . . .

Co-existence

a. What seem to be phenomena which can exist together are in reality phenomena which cannot exist together.
Example: Denis de Rougemont's assertion in *Love in the Western World* that love and marriage, which were considered at the time he wrote to be compatible, are in fact incompatible.
b. What seem to be phenomena which cannot exist together are in reality phenomena which can exist together.

Example: Sigmund Freud's assertion in "Notes on a Case of Obsessional Neurosis" that love and hate, which were considered at the time he wrote to be incompatible, are in fact compatible (in the psychological state of "ambivalence"). . . .

Co-variation

a. What seems to be a positive co-variation between phenomena is in reality a negative co-variation between phenomena.
   Example: David Caplovitz's assertion in *The Poor Pay More* that expenditures for many goods and services, which were considered at the time he wrote to decrease at the lower income levels, in fact increase at the lower income levels.
b. What seems to be a negative co-variation between phenomena is in reality a positive co-variation between phenomena.
   Example: Alexis de Tocqueville's assertion in *The Old Regime and the French Revolution* that a social group's desire for revolution, which was considered at the time he wrote to decrease as their standard of living goes up, in fact increases as their standard of living goes up. . . .

Opposition

a. What seems to be similar (nearly identical) phenomena are in reality opposite phenomena.
   Example: Marshall McLuhan's assertion in *Understanding Media* that radio and television, which were considered at the time he wrote to be similar media, are in fact opposite media (one being a "hot" medium; the other being a "cool" medium).
b. What seems to be opposite phenomena are in reality similar (nearly identical) phenomena.
   Example: Eric Hoffer's assertion in *The True Believer* that the psychological motivations of those who join opposing social movements, which were considered at the time he wrote to be opposite, are in fact similar. . . .

Causation

a. What seems to be the independent phenomenon (variable) in a causal relation is in reality the dependent phenomenon (variable).
   Example: Howard Becker's assertion in *Outsiders* that the peculiar behaviour of some individuals, which was considered at the time he wrote to cause other people to label them "deviants," is in fact caused by other people labeling them deviants.

b. What seems to be the dependent phenomenon (variable) in a causal relation is in reality the independent phenomenon (variable).
Example: Max Weber's assertion in *The Protestant Ethic and the Spirit of Capitalism* that the religion of a society, which was considered at the time he wrote to be determined by the economy of the society, in fact determines the economy of the society. . . .

Discussion: Non-interesting Propositions

We have seen that an audience finds a proposition "interesting" not because it tells them some truth they did not already know, but instead because it tells them some truth they thought they already knew was wrong. In other words, an interesting proposition is one which denies some aspect of the assumption-ground of its audience, and in *The Index of the Interesting* we have categorized the various aspects of this assumption-ground which can be denied. Since this is the defining characteristic of an "interesting proposition," it can also be used as a criterion to determine whether or not a particular proposition is interesting.

If the criterion by which an audience judges a particular proposition to be interesting is that it denies some aspect of their assumption-ground, then the criterion by which they will judge a particular proposition to be non-interesting is that it does *not* deny some aspect of their assumption-ground. There are three ways in which a proposition can fail to deny some aspect of the assumption-ground of its audience and therefore there are three general types of propositions which will be found non-interesting by their audience.

First, an audience will consider a proposition to be non-interesting if instead of denying some aspect of their assumption-ground, the proposition affirms some aspect of their assumption-ground (e.g., "Husbands often influence their wives' political behaviour").[2] In effect, the proposition is saying to its audience: "What seems to be the case is in fact the case." "What you always thought was true is really true." Phenomenology is Ontology. The audience's response to propositions of this type will be: "That's obvious!"

Second, an audience will consider a proposition to be non-interesting if instead of denying or affirming some aspect of their assumption-ground, the proposition does not speak to any aspect of this assumption-ground at all (e.g., "Eskimos are more likely than Jews to . . ."). In effect, the proposition is saying to its audience: "What is really true has no connection with what you always thought was true." Phenomenology is unrelated to

2. However, a person might find interesting a proposition which affirms one of his assumptions if this assumption has been strongly attacked by others. New supports for old suppositions are welcomed by those whose beliefs have been recently weakened ("Just as I always thought!").

Ontology. The audience's response to propositions of this type will be: "That's irrelevant!"

Third, an audience will consider a proposition to be non-interesting if, instead of denying some aspect of their assumption-ground, the proposition denies the whole assumption-ground (e.g., "Social factors have no effect on a person's behaviour"). In effect, the proposition is saying to its audience: "Everything that seems to be the case is not the case at all." "Everything you always thought was true is really false." Phenomenology is completely contrary to Ontology. The audience's response to propositions of this type will be: "That's absurd!"

Summary

As we have seen, research questions can be invented and framed in many alternative ways. The specification or framing of questions will be a function of their breadth or scope and precision, from loosely to carefully stated about phenomena that range from the very general to the very narrow. In part this will reflect the state of conceptualization available and ascribed to—that is, the more elaborated a theory, the more focused and precise the questions it stimulates. Questions will also vary along a mundane to interesting continuum, with theory-testing and theory-extending questions probably less interesting, and those (rarer) questions that potentially overturn or replace extant theory most interesting of all. There are many mundane criteria for assessing the value of a question, and several other criteria for thinking through the mundane. Many alternative means of creating or inventing research questions exist—from intentional search to playful serendipity, from attending to problems to noticing the unnoticed. While there is no formula for question formulation, there are several guides that can enhance our efforts.

If theory creation and improvement is at the heart of serious inquiry, then the focus, form, and worth of questions are crucial for the research process. The sorts of alternatives noted in this chapter thus require the most thoughtful choices possible. Question formulation not only initiates the research process, it also constrains subsequent choices about research strategy, methodologies, and much else. With one or more theoretic and/or pragmatic questions, the process of planning how to answer them may begin—to which we now turn.

12   Planning for Answers: Strategies and Designs

"Would you tell me, please, which way I ought to go from here?" Alice
asked the Cheshire Cat. "That depends a good deal on where you
want to get to," said the Cat. "I don't much care where . . ." said Alice.
"Then it doesn't matter which way you go," said the Cat.
> —*Louis Carroll*

Thus, the task is not so much to see what no one yet has seen, but to
think what nobody yet has thought about that which everybody sees.
> —*Arthur Schopenhauer*

Everyone knows the story about the emperor and his fine clothes: Although the townspeople persuaded themselves that the emperor was ele-
gantly costumed, a child, possessing unspoiled vision, showed the citizenry
that the emperor was really naked. The story is instructive in several ways:
that some of reality is subject to social definition, that collective delusions
can be undone by fresh perspectives, and that intentions, conscious and
unconscious, have much to say about what may be observed.

Research is analogous to that story: it makes it possible for people to see
what is actually there to be seen but that formerly was unacknowledged. We
found in Chapter 10 that theory improvement requires data, and in Chapter 11 that data is gathered to provide answers to questions. Data-based answers to theoretically relevant questions—that is, research findings—come
from intentional systematic search for which planning helps.

Plans for acquiring the right amount of the right kind of data combine
strategies and designs. *Research strategies* are plans that specify what kind
of data is needed and where they may be found. *Research designs* are plans
that specify how to obtain the desired data in the preferred places (methods for data gathering and data analysis and interpretation are dealt with
in the next two chapters).

The literature on research planning is both skewed and awkward. Research manuals often skip over general planning to focus on methodology.
If research strategy and design happen to be discussed, the focus is often
on those strategies and/or designs that are currently in favor in a field or

within a school of thought. These biases are compounded by inconsistent labeling; thus, research designs become tactics and approaches, irritating at best, more often confusing. The strategy and design literature is disappointing in two other ways. Discussions of strategy and design are legitimately in the "context of discovery," but Kaplan (1964) reminds us that they are all too often described in a postresearch, "context of justification" manner. Finally, the strategy and design literature often promulgates false dichotomies and debates, perhaps the most prominent and enduring of which is the qualitative versus quantitative debate.

The selections that follow begin with a portion of a "classic": Joseph E. McGrath's insightful classification of eight research strategies (settings), how they relate to one another, and the degree to which each strategy achieves goals of population generalizability, measurement precision, and contextual realism. McGrath takes pains to point out and illustrate that all research strategies fail to optimize all three goals simultaneously—in other words, *no* strategy is without flaws! So McGrath argues, as do we with this book, that there is no one best research strategy and that there are important choices to be made and trade-offs to be considered.

The second selection, by Eugene F. Stone, is a masterful tutorial. Stone carefully describes six major research strategies and lists in detail the advantages and disadvantages of each. Again we shall see that no single strategy is appropriate for all research purposes and that there are trade-offs among the many design alternatives. Stone, like McGrath, counsels employing multiple strategies when researching any phenomena through a series of research projects.

The final three selections all counter design beliefs promulgated by statistical methods. Louis R. Pondy and Mary Linda Olson point out that statistics have subtly conditioned researchers to focus on modal cases and to ignore the extreme cases in any distribution. This, they argue, prompts us to overlook the uniqueness of observed cases as well as clarify the boundary conditions of generalization. William F. Dukes shows how statistics-induced large sample sizes tend to supplant sample sizes chosen based on the purpose of the research. He shows how even a sample of one can legitimately contribute to studies of uniqueness and of generality. He also usefully reminds us that sampling should more often be about situations than persons. While Duke writes as a psychologist about samples of persons and their situations, his argument can be applied to all types of units of analysis.

A third statistics-induced concern is with mixing levels of analysis. This, however, is a design as well as a data analysis issue. Appa Rao Korukonda, in the last selection, tackles a question of growing importance to organizational science researchers: When is it reasonable to gather and/or analyze data from more than one level of analysis in the same study? Korukonda suggests that considering multiple levels theoretically is possible and sometimes even desirable given the nature of some organizational science phenomena—a position recently touted as a design advantage (Klein and Kozlowski 2000; Rousseau 1985).

Research Strategies and the Three-Horned Dilemma
Joseph E. McGrath

The research process can be viewed as a *series of interlocking choices*, in which we try *simultaneously to maximize several conflicting desiderata*. Viewed in that way, the research process is to be regarded not as a set of problems to be "solved," but rather as a set of dilemmas to be "lived with;" and the series of interlocking choices is to be regarded not as an attempt to find the "right" choices but as an effort to keep from becoming impaled on one or another horn of one or more of these dilemmas. . . .

The upshot of such a view of research is, of course, rather unpolyanna. Not only is there no one true method, or correct set of methodological choices that will guarantee success; there is not even a "best" strategy or set of choices for a given problem, setting, and available set of resources. In fact, from the dilemmatic point of view, *all research strategies and methods are seriously flawed*, often with their very strengths in regard to one desideratum functioning as serious weaknesses in regard to other, equally important, goals. Indeed, *it is not possible, in principle, to do "good"* (that is, methodologically sound) *research*. And, of course, to do good research, *in practice*, is even harder than that. (We are a very long way from converting "dilemmatics" into "dilemmetrics," much less into a full-fledged "dilemmatology." And there is no "dilemmagic" that will make the problems go away!). . . .

Research Strategies and the Three-Horned Dilemma

Classes of Strategies

Methodological strategies are generic classes of research settings for gaining knowledge about a research problem. There are (at least) eight readily distinguishable research strategies (see Figure [12-1]). They are related to each other in intricate ways, some of which are reflected in Figure [12-1]. They can be viewed as eight "pie slices" within a circumplex; but also as four quadrants, each with a related pair of strategies. The circular space is defined in terms of two orthogonal axes: (a) the use of obtrusive versus unobtrusive operations, and (b) concern with universal or generic behavior systems versus

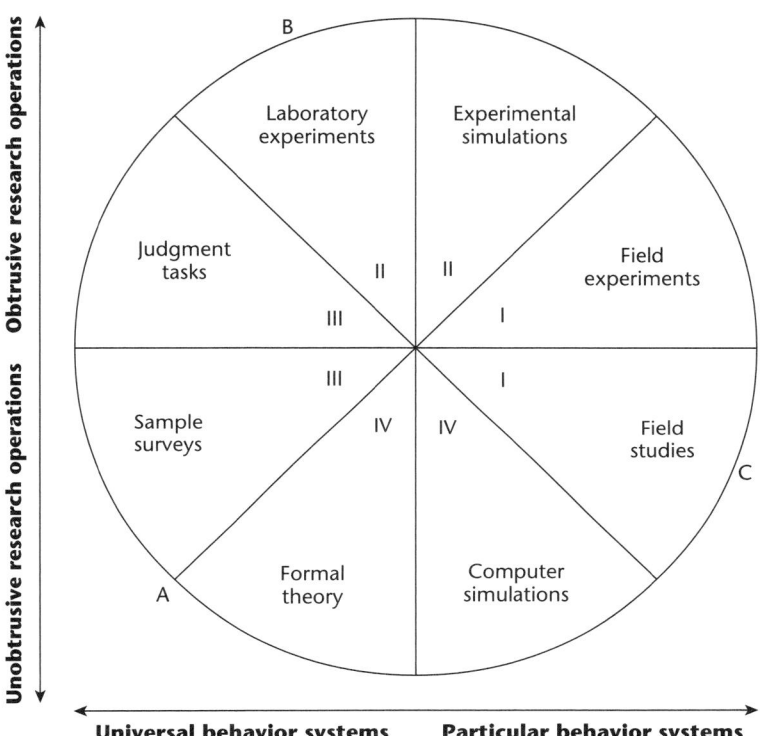

FIGURE **12-1**   Research strategies

SOURCE: "Dilemmatics: The Study of Research Choices and Dilemmas" by Joseph E. McGrath, in *Judgment Calls in Research*, edited by Joseph E. McGrath, Joanne Martin, and R. A. Kulka, 73, fig. 3.2. Copyright © 1982 by Sage Publications, Inc. Reprinted by permission of Sage Publications, Inc.

NOTE: I = settings in natural systems; II = contrived and created settings; III = behavior not setting dependent; IV = no observation of behavior required; A = point of maximum concern with generality over actors; B = point of maximum concern with precision of measurement of behavior; C = point of maximum concern system character of context.

concern with particularistic or concrete behavior systems. But within that two-dimensional space there are three "maxima," points at which each of three mutually conflicting desiderata are realized at their highest values (marked A, B, and C in the figure, and to be discussed presently). Thus, the "2-space" circumplex maps the territory of a *three-horned dilemma*!

Three Conflicting Desiderata

All research evidence involves some population (here, A, for Actors) doing something (here, B, for Behavior) in some time/place/thing setting (here

C, for Context). It is *always desirable (ceteris paribus) to maximize*: (A) *generalizability* with respect to populations, (B) *precision* in control and measurement of variables related to the behavior(s) of interest, and (C) existential *realism*, for the participants, of the context within which those behaviors are observed. But, alas, *ceteris is never paribus*, in the world of research. In Figure [12-1], the maxima for A, B, and C are shown at widely spaced points in the strategy circle. The very choices and operations by which one can seek to maximize any one of these will reduce the other two; and the choices that would "optimize" on any two will minimize on the third. Thus, the research strategy domain is a three-horned dilemma, and *every* research strategy either avoids two horns by an uneasy compromise but gets impaled, to the hilt, on the third horn; or it grabs the dilemma boldly by one horn, maximizing on it, but at the same time "sitting down" (with some pain) on the other two horns. Some of these dilemmatic consequences will be discussed later, as we examine the research strategies in each of the four quadrants of the strategy circumplex.

Quadrant I Strategies.   Quadrant I contains two familiar and closely related strategies: field studies (FS) and field experiments (FX). Both are characterized by—and distinguished from the other six strategies by—taking place in settings that are existentially "real" for the participants. They differ in that field studies are as unobtrusive as they can be, while field experiments are a one-step compromise toward obtrusiveness in the interest of increasing precision with respect to behavior, B. Note that desideratum C (realism of context) is at a maximum in the field study octant. However, both desideratum B (precision with regard to measurement, manipulation, and control of behavior variables) and desideratum A (generalizability with regard to populations) are far from their maxima. The field study, thus, seizes the "C" horn of the dilemma boldly, but must "sit" upon relatively uncomfortable levels of the "A" and "B" horns. (This is no mere hyperbole: To *lack* precision and generalizability is a serious matter even if you *have* realism.)

Quadrant II Strategies.   Quadrant II contains two other familiar research strategies: laboratory experiments (LX) and experimental simulations (ES) (the latter not to be confused with computer simulations, which are to be considered in Quadrant IV). The Quadrant II strategies are distinguished from the Quadrant I strategies in that they involve deliberately contrived settings, *not* existentially "real" for the participants. They differ from each other in that laboratory experiments reflect an attempt to create a generic or universal "setting" for the operation of the behavior processes under study, while experimental simulations reflect an attempt to retain some realism of *content* (what has been called "mundane realism"), even though they have given up realism of *context*. (Whether this is a worthwhile attempt to compromise is a matter for argument, as is the chance of actually attaining "realism.")

Note that the octant of the laboratory experiment contains the point of "maximum" for desideratum B (precision with regard to measurement of behavior), although it is a very low point with respect to desiderata A and C. Note, also, that the experimental octant, along with the neighboring field experiment octant, lies in between the B and C maxima—neither very high nor very low on either of them. But, at the same time, those octants lie as far as possible from the maximum for desideratum A (generalizability with regard to populations). Thus, these strategies fit snugly between horns B and C, but get fully impaled on the A horn. So: The field study maximizes C (realistic content) but is very low on A and B; and the laboratory experiment maximizes B (precision) but is very low on A and C; field experiments and experimental simulations are moderately high on B and C, but disastrously low on A.

The Three-Horned Dilemma

These unintended, and often unattended, consequences of choices of research strategies begin to give substance to our earlier remarks that, from the "dilemmatic" view of the research process, the very strengths of each strategy, plan, or method with respect to one desideratum is often its main weakness with respect to another desideratum. To maximize on one desideratum (boldly grabbing that horn) is to have relatively unfavorable levels of the other two (that is, to get part way impaled on both of the other two horns). Conversely, to optimize between two desiderata (snugly fitting between those two horns) is to guarantee a minimum on the third desideratum (that is, to get impaled, to the hilt, on the third horn).

There is no way—in principle—to maximize all three (conflicting desiderata of the research strategy domain). . . .

Quadrant III Strategies. The pair of research strategies located in Quadrant III—the sample survey (SS) and the judgment study (JS)—are contrasted with both the Quadrant I and the Quadrant II strategies in regard to both context and population sampling. Quadrant I deals with behavior in a "real" context—one that exists for the participants independently of the study and its purposes. Quadrant II deals with a contrived context, but deals with behavior as it occurs within—and intrinsically connected to—that context. In other words, for laboratory experiments and experimental simulations, the context has *experimental* reality though not *existential* reality for the participants. In Quadrant III, it is the intent of the investigator that the context should *not* play a part in the behavior of concern. In the case of judgment studies, the investigator tries to mute or nullify context—by "experimental control" of "all" extraneous conditions at what the investigator hopes will be neutral or innocuous levels. In the case of sample surveys, the investigator tries to neutralize context by asking for behaviors (often, responses to questions) that are unrelated to the context within which they are elicited (often, doorstep or telephone).

In regard to population sampling: Quadrant I studies are stuck with the "real" populations that already inhabit the settings studied; and Quadrant II studies often are stuck with whatever participants they can lure to the lab. The two strategies of Quadrant III both take sampling far more seriously, but in two different ways. The sample survey maximizes concern with effective sampling of the population units to be studied (be they individuals, or organizations, or dyads, or other social units). The judgment study typically uses only a few population units—construed as "judges" of stimuli, not as "respondents" to stimuli—presumably under the assumption that those judges are somehow "generic" judges. But at the same time, judgment studies typically focus much care on appropriate sampling—usually systematic rather than representative sampling of the stimuli to which the judges are to respond.

The judgment study (like the experimental simulation) is an uneasy compromise between two desiderata (B and A) with desideratum C (realism of context) at a minimum. The sample survey maximizes A (population generalizability), but does so by buying relatively low levels of B (precision) and C (realism of context). Judgment studies sit down hard on the C horn of the dilemma, while snuggling moderately between A and B horns. Sample surveys deal effectively with the A horn, but rest uncomfortably, partly impaled on the other two (B and C) horns.

Quadrant IV Strategies.   The two strategies of Quadrant IV differ from the strategies of the other three quadrants in that they are *not empirical*. There are no Actors. No Behavior occurs. There is no behavior Context. Rather, these two strategies are *theoretical*. One, here called formal theory (FT), refers to all attempts at general theory—in the sense of universal versus particular, but not necessarily in the sense of broad versus narrow content. The other, computer simulations (CS), refers to all attempts to *model* a particular concrete system (or set of concrete systems)—not necessarily using a computer, or even formal mathematics, though such is almost always the case in actuality. Formal theories, like sample surveys, maximize population generalizability (A) though they are quite low on realism on context (C) and on precision of measurement (B). Computer simulations (like experimental simulations and judgment studies) are compromises that try to optimize two desiderata (A and C), but do so at the price of minimizing the third (B). Thus, as with the empirical strategies, these theoretical strategies require either handling one "horn" well but sitting on the other two, or fending off two horns while paying a price on the third. . . .

Some Concluding Comments about Research Strategies

Many discussions of research strategies are carried out in terms of a much smaller set of strategies, often only two: lab versus field, survey versus lab, lab versus field study versus field experiment, empirical versus theoretical, or experiment versus simulation (meaning, variably, either experimental simulation or computer simulation). Furthermore, the set of strategies that is discussed is often a mixed bag (from the present point of view) of strategies, designs, and methods. For example, the set might include: lab experiment versus natural observation versus questionnaires; or case studies versus surveys versus correlational studies (meaning studies using archival data). It is important, I think, to make explicit all of the classes of strategies, so that we can consider their relations to one another. It is also important, I think, to draw clear distinctions between strategies or settings, study designs, and methods of measurement/manipulation/control. Those different levels or domains of the research process are beset by different problems, or dilemmas; they demand different kinds of choices, and they offer different kinds of alternatives from among which to choose. It is not that they are independent, those different domains; it is just that they are different.

Another problem with many discussions of research strategies is that they proceed from a shaky syllogism. That syllogism goes as follows: "I can point out numerous flaws, indeed fatal flaws, in strategy A (which I am opposing). Since strategy A is bad, therefore strategy B (which I am touting) must be "good." It is relatively easy, for example, to point out the many limitations and flaws—indeed fatal flaws, if you like—in laboratory experiments. But if lab experiments are "bad," it does *not* follow that some other strategy (most often Field Studies, occasionally one of the other classes of strategies) must, therefore, be "good." One can equally easily point out the flaws, some fatal, of field studies or of any of the other strategies. Doing so does not make lab experiments "good," either. Indeed, what is the case—and this is the central message of the dilemmatic viewpoint—is that *all* research strategies are "bad" (in the sense of having serious methodological limitations); none of them are "good" (in the sense of being even relatively unflawed). So, methodological discussions should not waste time arguing about which is the right strategy, or the best one; they are *all* poor in an absolute sense. Instead, such discussions might better engage in questions of how best to *combine* multiple strategies (*not within* one study, but over studies within a program) so that information can be gained about a given problem by *multiple means that do not share the same weaknesses*. This central theme—of using multiple methodological probes to gain substantive convergence by methods that compensate for one another's vulnerabilities—will occur again in discussion of the other two levels, design and methods.

Basic Designs: Features and Assessment
Eugene F. Stone

Laboratory Experiments

Description of the Strategy

A laboratory experiment is a research strategy characterized by the following attributes: (a) the researcher creates a setting for the study of some phenomena; (b) the experimenter has control over the assignment of experimental subjects to treatment and control conditions . . . ; (c) the experimenter has control over virtually all independent variables that may have an impact on the dependent variable; and (d) the experimenter manipulates one or more independent variables of interest.[1] Each of these points is more fully developed below.

Laboratory experiments take place in laboratories as opposed to organizations or other naturally occurring systems. A laboratory may be defined as any setting in which the experimenter has a high degree of control over the stimuli to which experimental subjects are exposed and the conditions associated with the observation of behavior (Zelditch and Hopkins 1961). In creating this setting the experimenter's objective is not to duplicate some naturally occurring behavioral system (e.g., a work organization), but rather to highlight selected aspects of such a system (Runkel and McGrath 1972). . . .

Stated somewhat differently, a laboratory experiment should be designed so as to mirror one or more conditions found in some criterion setting and to have none of the features that would never be found in the criterion setting (Fromkin and Streufert 1976). A criterion setting is one for which the results of our research are assumed to have relevance. . . .

In the laboratory experiment the experimenter has control over the assignment of subjects to treatment and control conditions. It was noted earlier . . . that the most effective method for minimizing the effects of nuisance variables is the random assignment of subjects to various groups associated with a study's design. Since the experimenter has control over the assignment of subjects, the minimization of nuisance variable variance is better accomplished with laboratory experiments than with any other research strategy. It should, however, be noted that it is *impossible* to design an experiment in

Source: "Empirical research strategies" by Eugene F. Stone, *Research Methods in Organizational Behavior*, 118–138. Copyright © 1978 by Scott, Foresman and Company. Used by permission of Eugene F. Stone-Romero.

1. See Carlsmith, Ellsworth, and Aronson (1976), Fromkin and Streufert (1976), and Runkel and McGrath (1972).

which no variables other than the manipulated independent variables affect the experiment's results (Carlsmith, Ellsworth, and Aronson 1976). At best, the influence of nuisance (confounding) variables can be held to a minimum through adequate experimental design.

In laboratory experiments the researcher manipulates one or more independent variables while controlling for the effects of virtually all other independent variables. . . .

Advantages and Disadvantages of the Strategy

As is the case with all research strategies, laboratory experiments have both advantages and disadvantages. Among the advantages of laboratory experiments are:

a. Measurement is generally more precise with laboratory experiments than with other research strategies because measurement in the laboratory takes place under highly controlled conditions. This minimizes the degree of error variance in measures (caused by such factors as filling out the questionnaires in environments with many distractions) and minimizes the extent to which the systematic variance of confounding variables influences our measures.
b. Causality can be inferred from the results of a laboratory experiment since threats to internal validity can be reduced or eliminated through the use of control groups. . . .
c. The experimenter controls the assignment of subjects to treatment and control conditions.
d. The independent variable(s) of a study can be precisely and unambiguously defined by the experimenter through the manipulations used to produce them.
e. Laboratory experiments can be replicated (i.e., results of one study reproduced in a later study) because experimenters other than the one first reporting an experiment's results can, with generally little difficulty, closely approximate the laboratory setting, manipulations, measures, etc., of a study they are attempting to replicate.

Among the disadvantages of laboratory experiments are:[2]

a. Some phenomena cannot be studied in the laboratory (e.g., natural disasters and the behavior that accompanies them).
b. A number of variables cannot be manipulated by experimenters (age, race, intelligence, etc.).

2. See Festinger (1953), Fromkin and Streufert (1976), and Weick (1967).

c. There are ethical and moral concerns with the manipulations associated with some experiments (i.e., subjects may experience psychological and/or physical harm).

d. The generality (i.e., external validity) of results produced through laboratory experimentation may be limited, that is, the range of criterion settings may be restricted.[3]

e. A number of artifacts (i.e., demand characteristics, evaluation apprehension, and experimenter expectancy effects) may influence the results obtained from laboratory experiments.[4]

f. Laboratory settings may lack "realism" (i.e., a high degree of correspondence between laboratory setting and naturally occurring organizational settings).

g. The strength of independent variables produced by experimental manipulation is, in general, very low when compared to the strength of these same variables in "real-life" situations.

h. It is difficult to successfully manipulate more than three or four independent variables in any given experiment.

i. Performing laboratory experiments successfully requires highly skilled and creative experimenters (in Weick's [1967] term, "artisans").

j. Subjects may substitute their own tasks for those they are asked to perform by the experimenter.

k. An independent variable that is shown, through laboratory experimentation, to influence a dependent variable may have little or no impact on the same variable in a field setting because the independent variable may have little or no prominence in a setting where a myriad of other independent variables impact upon subjects.

l. Subjects may react more to the perceived harm (e.g., esteem losses and degradation) that accompanies some experimental manipulations than they do to the study's real independent variable(s). . . .

3. Some critics of laboratory experimentation take the position that the findings of laboratory experiments are totally devoid of external validity and are not in general relevant to the solution of real-world problems. We reject this rather extreme view in favor of the position expressed by Fromkin and Streufert (1976) that instead of laboratory experiments never or seldom yielding data relevant to the solution of real-world problems, such studies *"merely impose identifiable limitations upon the range of criterion situations to which a particular set of laboratory findings may be applied"* (p. 442).

4. Editors' note: For more on experimenter effects, see the Rosenthal selection in Chapter 13.

Simulation [5]

Description of the Strategy

Simulations are research strategies with the following features:[6] (a) the simulation settings are created so as to replicate, to varying degrees, the attributes of naturally occurring systems; (b) participants (i.e., subjects) are exposed to a number of "real-world-like" events; (c) participants are free to behave within the constraints of the established rules of the simulation; (d) participation in the simulation is generally for protracted time periods; (e) depending upon the type of simulation ("free" vs. "experimental") the researcher exerts varying degrees of control over the assignment of subjects to various simulation conditions and the stimuli to which the participants are exposed; and (f) the dependent variables of the simulation are the behaviors exhibited by the participants.

The simulation setting is created so as to mirror important dimensions of some naturally occurring system. As in the case of the laboratory experiment, the simulation setting is deliberately structured for the purposes of a study. Unlike the setting of the laboratory experiment (which is created so as to have properties common to *generic class* of systems), the setting of the simulation is designed so as to be like a specific class of behavior systems (Runkel and McGrath 1972). . . .

The simulated environment is created in such a way as to maximize the degree of mundane realism associated with a study. At the same time the researcher often maintains a high degree of control over the events to which participants are exposed. Thus, simulation may be looked upon as a strategy falling somewhere between the laboratory experiment on the one hand and the field study on the other (Crano and Brewer 1973). . . .

Simulation participants are exposed to a number of events that parallel those found in naturally occurring systems. In the *experimental simulation* (cf. Fromkin and Streufert 1976) the nature and timing of these events is completely determined by the researcher. In the free simulation, on the other hand, events and their timing are determined by both researcher-established simulation rules and the behavior of simulation participants. The experimental simulation thus more closely resembles the laboratory experiment than the *free simulation* as far as degree of control is concerned. . . .

---

5. The presentation associated with the simulation strategy is limited to those studies in which human behavior (as opposed to computer-simulated behavior) is the focus. Those interested in computer simulation of individual, group, and organizational behavior should consult such sources as Abelson (1968), Borko (1962), K. J. Cohen and Cyert (1965), Green (1963), Roby (1967), and S. S. Tompkins and Messick (1963).

6. See Crano and Brewer (1973), Fromkin and Streufert (1976), and Runkel and McGrath (1972).

Depending upon the form (i.e., free vs. experimental) taken by the simulation, causal hypotheses may be tested using this research strategy. The greater the degree to which the simulation approximates the experimental form (e.g., allows the researcher to randomly assign subjects to various conditions and control the stimuli to which subjects are exposed), the greater the potential for the testing of causal hypotheses. Where a study takes the form of a free simulation, the assessment of causality is more risky since the behavior of participants is determined not only by the rules established by the researcher, but also by interactions among the subjects.

The dependent variables of a simulation are the measured behaviors of study participants. (Behavior here implies not only observable acts, but also expressed attitudes, opinions, etc.) The measurement of such behavior may take a number of forms (observation, questionnaires, interviews, etc.). . . .

Advantages and Disadvantages of the Strategy

Included in the advantages of the simulation strategy are:

a. Realism is high because the setting mirrors some "real-world" setting and the events that take place in the simulation are "real-world-like";
b. Subject involvement generally tends to be high;
c. Causal hypotheses may be tested in simulations that are of the experimental variety;
d. Demand characteristics (Orne 1962) are generally lower in simulations than in laboratory experiments;
e. Control over extraneous sources of variance is generally higher than in field studies, especially in the case of the experimental simulation; and
f. Simulations allow for the manipulation of independent variables. The researcher's ability to manipulate independent variables is, of course, greater in experimental than free simulations.

Among the disadvantages of the simulation strategy are:

a. Simulations are expensive. This expense results mainly from the costs associated with creation of the setting for the simulation;
b. To the extent that the simulation is of the free (as opposed to the experimental) variety the study's independent variables are harder to identify, the possibility of confounding factors in influencing dependent variables increases, and the opportunity to test causal hypotheses decrease; and
c. The high degree of participant involvement in the simulation increases the risk of subjects being psychologically harmed in the

course of the study (cf. for example, Haney, Banks, and Zimbardo 1973, or Milgram 1963, 1965). . . .[7]

Field Experiments

Description of the Strategy

A field experiment is a research strategy characterized by the following features: (a) the research takes place in a natural setting (i.e., one that subjects do not perceive as having been set up primarily for the conduct of research); (b) the experimenter manipulates one or more independent variables while exerting as much control as the situation permits over other, possibly confounding variables; and (c) the effect of the manipulations on one or more dependent variables is systematically observed.

Field experiments take place in naturally occurring systems rather than in settings that subjects perceive as having been created specifically for research purposes (T. D. Cook and Campbell 1976). . . . The study of "natural" groupings of subjects in naturally occurring social systems *may* lead to greater generalizability of research findings (Meyers and Grossen 1974; Lin 1976).

A researcher employing this strategy manipulates one or more independent variables and attempts to exert as much control as is possible over nuisance variables. . . . Control over nuisance variables is accomplished by the use of experimental designs (e.g., the Solomon Four Group and the post-test-only control group designs), the use of quasi-experimental designs (e.g., the time-series design), or through less effective means (e.g., statistically removing the effects of suspected confounding variables from discovered independent-dependent variable relationships). . . .

The reader should note that organizational field experiments need not (and generally do not) employ true experimental designs. Both quasi-experimental and pre-experimental designs are commonly used in field experiments. A study to test the effects of changes in job design on workers' attitudes (Lawler, Hackman and Kaufman 1973), for example, used a one group pretest-posttest pre-experimental design. And a study to test the effects of participation in decision making on employee absenteeism (Lawler and Hackman 1969) employed a time-series design. To the extent that an investigation deviates from a true experimental design the results of a study become progressively more difficult to interpret unambiguously.

In field experiments the effect of the independent variable on the dependent variable is systematically observed. . . .

---

7. It should be pointed out that several of the disadvantages of laboratory experimentation (e.g., items *a* and *c*) also apply to simulations—especially to those of the experimental variety.

Advantages and Disadvantages of the Strategy

The advantages of a field experiment are as follows:

a. Assuming that the researcher employs an experimental design or one of the better (in terms of control) quasi-experimental designs, causal inferences from field experimental data may be justified;
b. As a consequence of the fact that field experiments involve studying phenomena in "natural settings" the external validity of results of such studies may be greater than that of data from laboratory experiments;
c. The manipulation of independent variables (as opposed to the simple measurement of their values) allows the researcher to clearly identify antecedents of observed effects. Stated differently, the independent variables have greater construct validity (cf. T. D. Cook and Campbell 1976);
d. Randomization of individuals, groups, and organizations is sometimes possible, allowing for improved control of nuisance variables;
e. Field experiments are useful for not only the development of theory, but also for the solution of applied problems;
f. If the investigator chooses to do so, both the short- and long-term effects of manipulated variables can be addressed using the field experimental strategy;
g. The logic of the field experiment can be applied in the analysis of many naturally occurring changes (cf. D. T. Campbell 1969; T. D. Cook and Campbell 1976). The strength of the independent variable in naturally occurring experiments is often greater than the strength of researchers' manipulations; and
h. Field experiments allow for the testing of "broad" hypotheses dealing with complex social processes in lifelike situations (Kerlinger 1973). In the case of the Latham and Kinne (1974) study, for example, the effect of goal setting on a number of performance criteria was assessed. In a laboratory experiment the focus of the study would generally have been much narrower (e.g., a study by Chapanis [1964] dealing with the effects of differing levels of task feedback on task productivity).

Among the disadvantages of field experiments as research strategies are:[8]

a. The degree of control associated with most field experiments is insufficient to allow for unequivocal claims of causality;

8. See T. D. Cook and Campbell (1976), Festinger (1953), Scott (1965), and Seashore (1964).

b. The manipulation of variables in field settings may result in legal and/or ethical problems;

c. The precise measurement of dependent variables possible in laboratory settings, in general, cannot be attained in field settings;

d. Field experiments are generally much more expensive to conduct than laboratory experiments;

e. The greater the strength of the manipulation employed by the experimenter the greater the degree to which the "naturalness" of the original setting is disrupted (Runkel and McGrath 1972);

f. In general, too few units agree to participate in a field experiment for randomization to be an effective control procedure;

g. The intentional manipulation of one variable in field experiments often results in the unintentional manipulation of others;

h. Field experimenters must be highly skilled "social operators" to gain and maintain access to social systems they desire to study (Kerlinger 1973);

i. To the extent that a field experiment requires the researcher to maintain prolonged contact with a system, the experimenter's objectivity in studying the system may suffer;

j. If the researcher acts as the change agent (i.e., the person effecting the change), his or her presence may alter the values of the variables measured in the study;

k. Gaining access to social systems generally requires the approval of "top management personnel" in such systems. "Lower-level" participants may come to associate the researcher with top management, and, therefore, data from the lower-level personnel supply may be biased;

l. Organizational officials are often reluctant to withhold desirable treatments from no-treatment control groups;

m. Even if randomization of individuals, groups, work units, etc., is initially effective, processes occurring within the system studied (interunit transfer of personnel, merger, etc.) may destroy its effectiveness;

n. Some individuals, groups, or other units may refuse to accept the treatment they are scheduled to receive;

o. Control groups not receiving what is perceived to be a desirable treatment may resent their status and experience a "resentment treatment" (T. D. Cook and Campbell 1976); and

p. If individuals in groups that are supposed to be experiencing different treatments communicate with one another the purity of the various treatments may suffer. . . .

Although field experiments are difficult to perform successfully their value as a research strategy should not be underestimated. Only through the field experiment can findings of rigorous, well-controlled laboratory experiments be tested for their applicability to naturally occurring systems.

Those contemplating the use of the field experimental strategy should carefully study a number of published works on the subject.[9] One source (i.e., T. D. Cook and Campbell 1976) offers a thorough treatment of field experiments in organizational settings.

Field Studies

Description of the Strategy

The field study strategy can be characterized in the following way:[10] (a) the research is ex post facto in nature . . . , no independent variables are manipulated by the researcher; (b) intact, naturally occurring systems are the object of study; (c) variables are systematically measured; (d) the investigator attempts to minimize his or her intrusion upon the system being studied; and (e) the focus of such research may be exploratory, descriptive, or hypothesis testing.

The field study strategy comes under the general heading of ex post facto research, which . . . is non-experimental in nature. (D. T. Campbell and Stanley 1966, label such research as "pre-experimental.") The researcher has no control whatsoever over the independent variable(s) of the study. Instead, the investigator relies upon self-reports of subjects or some other (non-manipulation based) measure of the extent to which subjects have received some treatment as a mode for assigning independent variable values to subjects. . . .

Field studies deal with intact, naturally occurring systems as opposed to those created for research purposes (as, for example, the setting of a laboratory experiment). As Scott (1965, 262) has said, field studies are used to study "human beings 'on the hoof'—as opposed to studies of *ad hoc* groups conducted in the laboratory. . . ."

Field studies employ systematic means for obtaining and recording the value of studied variables. Other research strategies (e.g., the case study) involve far less systematic data-gathering techniques. In most instances field study data are obtained through questionnaires or interviews. . . .

A key consideration of the researcher employing the field study strategy is to intrude as little as possible upon the system being studied. The consequence of this is that the investigator ends up collecting a weaker form of data than could be collected from more intrusive methods (e.g., a field experiment). Collecting data at only one point in time means that only

9. See, for example, Campbell (1969), T. D. Cook and Campbell (1976), Festinger (1953), Scott (1965), and Seashore (1964).

10. See Bouchard (1976), Kerlinger (1973), Runkel and McGrath (1972), and Scott (1965).

correlational or cross-sectional analyses . . . of the data are possible. If the investigator collects data longitudinally the data base is strengthened but there is an increased probability that data collection efforts will modify the system under study (Runkel and McGrath 1972). It should be noted there that even in instances of "one-shot" data collection efforts in field studies, intrusiveness is never eliminated.

Field studies have several purposes.[11] One variant of the field study has as its goal the gaining of familiarity with a system (e.g., a work organization). Increased familiarity might enable the researcher to define a research problem or develop hypotheses about some process associated with the system. A second variant of the field study has as its objective the description of a system. This might include measurement of a number of characteristics of system elements (e.g., organizational members) or recording the frequency of certain system occurrences (e.g., rates of message flow among organizational units). The final variant of the field study has as its aim the "testing of hypotheses." The term hypothesis testing is used loosely here since as D. T. Campbell and Stanley (1966) have noted, data from correlational and/or cross sectional studies are relevant for hypothesis testing only in that they expose causal hypotheses to opportunities for disconfirmation. . . .

Advantages and Disadvantages of the Strategy

The field study strategy has a number of advantages, including:[12]

a. Field studies are high on realism since they are conducted in naturally occurring systems;
b. The intrusiveness of this strategy is relatively low compared with that of others (e.g., the field experiment);
c. Data on a large number of variables can be obtained from subjects;
d. Complex phenomena can be studied;
e. Socially significant (i.e., applications-oriented) problems are amenable to study by this strategy;
f. Field studies are often valuable for their heuristic qualities; and
g. The strengths of independent, intervening, and dependent variables are generally greater than would be found in a laboratory experiment.

Disadvantages of the field study strategy include:

a. The cooperation of organizations is often difficult to obtain;
b. The effects of any given variable upon another are difficult, if not impossible, to assess with data from field studies. Causal inferences from field study data, therefore, are highly tenuous;

11. See Katz (1953), Kerlinger (1973), and Selltiz et al. (1976).
12. See Bouchard (1976), Kerlinger (1973), and Scott (1965).

    c. Data from most field studies are likely to contain unknown sampling biases;

    d. There are usually limits on the number of variables that can be measured in a field study. As a result, many variables that may be relevant to a phenomenon under study are simply ignored by the researcher;

    e. Independent variables are not manipulated in field studies;

    f. Measurement is not as precise as it is in the laboratory because of increased error variance and the influence of confounding variables;

    g. Field studies are generally very expensive to conduct and, as has been recently noted (Bouchard 1976, 367), "with the development of sophisticated instrumentation and more extensive and powerful research designs . . . [the field study] will get even more expensive"; and

    h. The "dross rate" or proportion of irrelevant data yielded by measures (cf. E. J. Webb et al. 1966) may be high in field studies (for a conflicting view see Bouchard 1976).

It should be noted here that despite all the problems associated with field studies, "most of what we know today about organizations and the behavior of their members is known on the basis of field studies" (Scott 1965, 261). But as Runkel and McGrath have observed so aptly, ". . . with the field study strategy the investigator ends up learning a lot about complex and meaningful behavior systems, but he [or she] does not know with high confidence just what he [or she] has learned" (1972, 94). Fortunately for those interested in organizational behavior phenomena, recent years have seen an increase in the practice of testing propositions stemming from field studies in the laboratory and vice-versa. . . .

Sample Surveys

Description of the Strategy

The sample survey strategy involves research in which (a) data are collected from members of a sample that represents a known population; (b) a systematic technique (e.g., questionnaires or interviews) is used to collect data; (c) the researcher manipulates no independent variables; (d) data are sought directly from respondents; (e) subjects provide data in natural settings; (f) responses of subjects are assumed to be largely unaffected by the context in which they are elicited; (g) influences of confounding variables are "controlled" statistically; and (h) the purpose of the research may range from exploration of phenomena to hypothesis testing.

The sampling strategy used in the sample survey allows the researcher to generalize a study's results to a known population. . . . A researcher using the sample survey strategy collects data directly from respondents in a systematic fashion. The setting in which the data are obtained is natural and assumed to not influence the values of the measured variables. . . . Data collection takes place in settings that are natural and assumed to have no measurable impact upon the levels of measured variables. . . . The sample survey is a form of ex post facto research. The researcher manipulates no independent variables. Instead, such variables are simply measured by the researcher. . . . If the investigator suspects that confounding influences may be present in the data obtained from a survey then the potentially confounding variables are measured and statistical techniques (partial correlation, hierarchial correlation, etc.) are used to "control" their effects. . . . As was the case with the field study strategy, a researcher doing a sample survey might be concerned with gaining familiarity with a population, describing a population, or the testing of hypotheses. . . .

Apart from the purposes mentioned above, the sample survey may also be used to predict future conditions (e.g., the outcome of an election or consumer buying behavior), to evaluate social programs (e.g., assess the effects of a guaranteed income program), or to develop social indicators (e.g., data upon which to base the unemployment rate, the consumer price index, and the wholesale price index). (Warwick and Lininger (1975) provide detailed coverage of the various purposes served by the sample survey.)

Advantages and Disadvantages of the Strategy

Among the advantages associated with the sample survey strategy are:

a. The sample is chosen in such a way as to allow for generalizations to a defined population;
b. Results are accurate because of large sample sizes and generally low sampling error;
c. Random sampling procedures reduce or eliminate problems of sample bias;
d. Data collection takes place in "natural" settings;
e. Data are obtained directly from respondents;
f. Surveys often yield data that suggest new hypotheses;
g. If mailed questionnaires are used to collect data, the per subject cost of data is relatively low (compared, for example, to interview data); and
h. A variety of systematic data collection methods (e.g., interviews, questionnaires, and observation) can be used alone or in combination.

Disadvantages of this strategy include:

a. Decreased willingness of people to respond to sample survey probes. As Warwick and Lininger have observed: "Sample surveys and even the 1970 census in the United States have been plagued by refusals and omissions because of suspicions, fear, and other forms of resistance, particularly in central city areas" (p. 5);

b. Most surveys are "one-shot" (as opposed to the panel type in which repeated measures are taken on the same sample). As a result their capacity for generating data with which to test causal connections among variables is limited;

c. In terms of total costs, the sample survey is an extremely expensive research strategy because of large administrative and/or personnel costs;

d. The standardized response formats of many sample survey measures (e.g., questionnaires and structured interviews) may force respondents to subscribe to statements they don't fully endorse. (Note that this is more an indictment of the measurement mode than it is of the sample survey research strategy.);

e. If questionnaires are used to collect data, the proportion of returned questionnaires may be low;

f. Questionnaire and/or interview measures may be "poor" indicants of the constructs studied by a researcher using the sample survey strategy. Information gleaned from sample surveys generally is "shallow" in nature;

g. Control over nuisance or confounding variables is poor. If such variables are controlled at all it must be through statistical means; and

h. No independent variables are manipulated by the researcher using this strategy. As a result, causal inferences from sample survey-generated data are difficult to justify.

The Case Study

Description of the Strategy

The case study approach to research can be described as follows: (a) the researcher intensely examines a single unit (e.g., person, group, or organization); (b) data are often collected by multiple means; (c) no attempt is made to exercise experimental or statistical controls; (d) phenomena are studied in natural settings; and (e) the strategy is suited more to the generation of hypotheses than their testing.

Whereas other research strategies such as the sample survey involve the study of multiple elements of a defined population, the case study restricts attention to but one. The element may be a person, group, organization, or a larger entity. . . .

Results of a case study are useful inductive or hypothesis generating vehicles; they are not appropriate for deductive or hypothesis testing purposes.

Not only is generalization (i.e., external validity) problematic with the case study, but the certainty of what one has really discovered (internal validity) using this research strategy is also dubious. As D.T. Campbell and Stanley (1966) have observed in their seminal work on research design: "Basic to scientific evidence . . . is the process of comparison, of recording differences, or of contrast. Any appearance of absolute knowledge, or intrinsic knowledge about singular isolated objects, is found to be illusory upon analysis" (p. 6). . . .

The case study allows for "flexibility" in data collection. The researcher has considerable discretion over not only the type of data gathered, but also over sources from which information is obtained. . . .

While such methods allow for the gathering of data in natural settings, they also open the possibility for the investigator to alter the setting under study and vice versa. While some would argue that the case study minimally interferes with the natural setting under study, this appears to be an overly optimistic view of the strategy.

Several purposes might be served by the case study approach; these include (Shontz 1965): (a) presentation of "evidence" on what the researcher considers to be a rare, remarkable, or atypical instance of some phenomenon; (b) exemplifying or illustrating a concept that would be difficult to describe using solely abstract theoretical language; (c) demonstrating the use of a technique (e.g., the conduct of a "team building" exercise); (d) establishing a pool of data that may be useful at a future point in time; (e) challenging existing modes of thought by showing case study evidence that cannot be explained adequately by existing theory; and (f) "confirming" theories or hypotheses by the presentation of supporting case study data.

Advantages and Disadvantages of the Strategy

Advantages of the case study strategy are:

a. The full complexity of the unit under study can be taken into consideration;
b. Data collection is flexible;
c. The case study is a useful vehicle for the generation of hypotheses and insights;
d. Data are collected in natural settings; and
e. Case studies are generally less expensive research strategies than others (e.g., laboratory experiments, field experiments, field studies, and sample surveys).

Included in the set of disadvantages of the case study strategy are:

a. It is the least systematic of all research strategies;
b. Causal inferences from case study data are impossible since there are no controls over confounding variables;
c. Data collection may alter the setting under study;
d. Hypothesis testing is not possible using case study data;
e. Results of case studies are likely to have substantial amounts of bias because of nonsystematic collection, condensation, and inter-pretation of data;
f. Generalization from a case study's findings is not possible; and
g. Case studies are more time-consuming than other strategies (e.g., laboratory experiments, and field studies).

Integration of Research Strategies

A researcher contemplating the study of some phenomenon can employ one or more of several different research strategies. Each strategy has a unique set of advantages and disadvantages. Case studies while useful in the formulation of hypotheses are of little use in the testing of hypotheses. Lab-oratory experiments are ideal strategies for maximizing internal validity but leave unanswered questions of external validity. No strategy is more appro-priate than others for *all* research purposes!

A researcher investigating any phenomenon would be well advised to carry out not a single study or a series of studies employing one research strategy, but instead a series of studies using multiple strategies. What is be-ing advocated here is a programmatic approach to research.[13]

13. For more on programmatic research see Evan (1971, 4), Fromkin and Streufert (1976, 457), and Runkel and McGrath (1972, 103).

Taking Extreme Cases Seriously
Louis R. Pondy and Mary Linda Olson

A species of bamboo tree exists that blooms only every 120 years, a fact less notable for its truth than for its detection and interpretation by botanists. The "120 year bamboo clock" (Gould 1977a) is an extreme case of strategies of sexual reproduction, a deviation away from the perennial norm. But the *strategy* has another component. When *Phyllostachys bambu-soides* blooms, it covers the forest floor with six inches of seeds, so many that they are not totally consumed by feeding animals, and *P. bambusoides*,

Source: "Theories of extreme cases" by Louis R. Pondy and Mary Linda Olson, paper presented at the American Psychological Association Symposium (San Francisco, CA, 1977).

therefore, survives yet another generation. By considering this and other extreme cases (e.g., 17 year locusts), biological scientists have developed a deeper, more general understanding of reproductive processes and adaptive mechanisms.

What concerns us about the above example is that we can imagine how some social scientists would have approached the study of bamboo reproduction. In our worst fears, they would have taken a random sample from among species of bamboo, and estimated the mean reproductive cycle to be, say, 1.017 years, which, although true, would conceal the more significant truth about the variety of reproductive mechanisms and the general principles underlying their nature.

Spurred on by this example, our intent is to ask, "What kind of science would we have if we were to take extreme cases seriously rather than regarding them as mere statistical deviants away from the modal case, if they were to influence the content of our theories fully as much as more typical instances?" In exploring this question, we have adopted what George Kelly (1964) has called the "invitational mood" rather than the indicative mood of purely descriptive inquiry; that is, we preface our assertions with "suppose . . ." and adopt a provisional "as if" attitude toward our subject matter. Suppose we were to take extreme cases seriously. Suppose the key to understanding a phenomenon were to lie as much in its off-beat manifestations as in its empirically most common ones. Suppose our research methods were blinding us to the significance of deviant cases. If we were to treat these suppositions as if they were true, how would it change how we do science?

It is difficult to pinpoint the origins of these questions, although it is clear that they reflect nagging personal doubts about the fruitfulness of our social and organizational inquiry. The seeming impossibility of applying general theories of organization structure, or change, or leadership in specific circumstances surely contributed to those doubts, as did the failure to make those theories meaningful to practitioners. Equally persuasive was our inability, after reading typical large sample, cross-sectional comparative studies of certain social phenomena, to reconstruct what some specific instance of the phenomena must be like, or to develop an intuitive, qualitative feeling or understanding of the individual instances that make up the phenomenal class. Surely not all members of the class were characterized by the mean values of the measured attributes. Visits over the last several years to numerous zoos, conservatories, aquaria, and museums of natural history flooded us with the immense variety of living organisms that make up our world. How is it possible that our theories have failed to document or even be aware of an equivalent variety in human social organization? Is it conceivable that humans exhibit *less* variety than supposedly more primitive forms of life? Whatever the origins, questions about extremity, variety, and individuality of organizational phenomena have occurred to us, and we pursue them here.

Consistent with the Whorfian hypothesis, having invented for ourselves the concept of "extreme cases," we began seeing the concept used elsewhere. Vaill (1977) had developed a series of hypotheses about "high performing systems." Mitroff (1974) studied the behavior of scientists examining the first moonrocks. Sears (1977) reported on Terman's work with gifted children. Kuhn's (1970) theory of scientific revolutions could be seen as an extreme case theory of scientific progress, characterized by (to paraphrase Derek Ager) "long periods of boredom punctuated by short periods of terror" (quoted in Gould 1977b). House (1976) is working on a theory of charismatic leadership. Theories of creativity and of mental illness can be thought of as extreme instances that do not fit the modal pattern of mental functioning . . .

What has become obvious to us in trying to puzzle through what makes an extreme case worth studying is that each instance is in some sense unique. This does not mean that an extreme case shares nothing with other cases, but only that it does not share everything (Kaplan 1964). Nor are we suggesting that uniqueness is the only defining property of extreme cases. But the essential uniqueness of every case means that it must be understood in its own right prior to comparison with other cases. Newell and Simon (1972, 10), in arguing that we should develop "a theory of the individual" propose to . . .

> . . . model the behavior of a single individual in a single task situation. Full particularity is the rule, not the exception. Thus, it becomes a problem to get back from this particularity to theories that describe a class of humans, or to processes and mechanisms that are general to all humans.

Although Newell and Simon adopt an idiographic method of research ("efforts that deal with the individual in all his uniqueness," ibid.), they still aim at generalization across cases, *but only after understanding each case in its own right*! (That suggests that the classification of any case as modal or extreme prior to understanding it at an idiographic level is premature.) Idiographic methods are contrasted with nomothetic methods which "deal with an individual only as an intersection of statistically defined populations" (ibid.) and aim at discovering general laws that apply to all individuals. What is emerging from this inquiry into extreme cases is the necessity that idiographic methods precede nomothetic inquiry. Gordon Allport said it 35 years ago as well as it can be said:

> Acquaintance with particulars is the beginning of all knowledge— scientific or otherwise. In psychology the font and origin of our curiosity in, and knowledge of, human nature lies in our acquaintance with concrete individuals. To know them in their natural complexity is an essential first step. Starting too soon with analysis and classification, we run

the risk of tearing mental life into fragments and beginning with false cleavages that misrepresent the salient organizations and natural integrations in personal life (1942, 56).

Or, more recently, Donald Campbell (1974):

Qualitative, common-sense knowing of wholes and patterns provides the enveloping context necessary for the interpretation of particulate quantitative data. . . . (Q)uantification both builds upon and is cross-validated by, the scientist's qualitative knowledge. . . . If we are to be truly scientific, we must reestablish this qualitative grounding of the quantitative in action research.

The function of theory in idiographic inquiry is, in Geertz's phrase, "not to generalize across cases but to generalize within them . . . to ferret out the unapparent import of things" (Geertz 1973, 26).

Our argument grows complex at this point, and it would be well to take stock of the ground we have covered, and to supply some of the steps now realized to be missing. (1) We have left open the question of whether extremeness is an artifact of our methods of description, or a characteristic of human behavior. We shall argue that both mechanisms contribute to uniqueness. (2) We have argued that extreme cases exhibit uniqueness; they are different from modal cases in some significant way not captured by modal descriptions. A possible counter-argument is that *all* cases are unique, so that singling out extreme cases contributes nothing unless we can specify the ways in which extreme cases are unique. We shall make some educated guesses about the dimensions of uniqueness of extreme cases. (3) Some further clarification is necessary on the difference between generalization and comparative analysis.

These three topics are taken up in order, and the paper concludes with a proposal for a two-stage research strategy that places extreme case analysis in what we believe is its most effective role.

Sources of Extremeness

In one sense extremeness is an artifact of our attempt to explain common variance across large samples of persons or organizations. The practice of comparative statistical analysis rests on John Stuart Mill's presumption of the essential uniformity of phenomena (Hamilton 1976) and on his belief that our certainty of understanding that uniformity would increase by studying ever larger populations of cases so that individual idiosyncrasies would cancel out (Kaplan 1964). Such an assumption of uniformity is both reasonable and functional within the physical sciences: not to assume that the oxygen gas in Priestly's lab in Cambridge was identical to that in Lavoisier's lab in Paris would have stalled chemistry in its tracks. But we need to re-examine that assumption of uniformity in the social sciences. We need to bring Mill's system of logic back out into the open air where we can rethink its working assumptions, as Hamilton (1976) has begun to do.

Indeed there are persuasive reasons for believing that the greater neural capacity of human beings gives them a capacity for variety an order of magnitude larger than that of lower animals.

Again, Gordon Allport seems to have got hold of the nub of the matter:

> The individuality of man extends infinitely beyond the puny individuality of plants and animals, who are primarily or exclusively creatures of tropism or instinct. Immense horizons for individuality open when billions of cortical cells are added to the meager neural equipment of lower species. Man talks, laughs, feels bored, develops a culture, prays, has a foreknowledge of death, studies theology, and strives for the improvement of his own personality. The infinitude of resulting patterns is plainly not found in creatures of instinct. For this reason we should exercise great caution when we extrapolate the assumptions, methods, and concepts of natural and biological science to our subject matter. In particular, we should refuse to carry over the indifference of other sciences to the problem of individuality (1955, 22).

There is a subtle point to be made here. The natural variety of human behavior looks extreme only against the backdrop of an assumption of essential uniformity and statistical methods aimed at describing uniform modal behavior. So to say that we should develop theories of extreme cases can be interpreted to mean, when the assumption of uniformity is lifted from us, that we should attempt to understand human behavior in all its individual variety, not merely in its modal tendencies. Extremeness seems to be a combination of the natural tendencies in humans toward individuation and our methods for detecting uniformity rather than variety.

Dimensions of Uniqueness

We have argued that one important attribute of extreme cases (at this stage perhaps we ought to say what *appear* to be extreme cases *from the viewpoint of modal theories*) is that they have essential elements of uniqueness. But we have not described some of the ways in which extreme cases are likely to be unique. We undertake that task in this section, and we also suggest what implications the forms of uniqueness might have for how we theorize about extreme cases. Three dimensions of uniqueness are singled out:

1. Modal case theories are typically theories about systems in equilibrium, systems that have reached some stable state after being

worked on by external forces that have come into balance. Because the external forces are common to the systems in a given field, they are likely to reach a *common* equilibrium. But extreme cases are likely to be unique because they are in a state of disequilibrium (for example, in the process of change) and because the forces acting on the person or organization are internal rather than external and therefore not common to neighboring systems. So extreme cases are likely to be unique in that they are undergoing change due to the working of internal forces and therefore are in a state of disequilibrium.

2. As we have argued previously, extreme cases tend to exhibit non-patterned variety. Systems tend to be modal in only a few ways, but there are many distinctive ways to be extreme or unique. Therefore, extreme case theories need to have a greater capacity than modal case theories to describe such non-patterned variety. One such example is Weick's (1969) evolutionary theory of organizing. Significantly, Weick's organizing model places great stress on the group or organization generating or enacting its own environment, thus making possible the non-patterned variety we have argued characterizes extreme cases.

3. Persons, groups and organizations that are modal in their behavior probably share frames of reference, or definitions of the situation. That is, they tend to look at the world in the same way. Therefore, the scientist can take those frames of reference as given, and inquire within them. But extreme cases are likely to exhibit unique frames of reference, so that their frames of reference themselves become objects of inquiry. A method of inquiry that imposes one definition of the situation, as in a pre-set interview schedule or questionnaire, will necessarily fail to capture the subject's own characteristic frame. We need to be much more receptive to methods of research that reveal subjective points of view, for example, participant observation, if we are to understand extreme cases.

Extreme Cases and the Meaning of Generalization

Edmund Leach (1971) has made the distinction between comparative analysis and generalization. By comparative analysis, Leach means the establishment of empirical regularities, but by generalization he means the creation of a new abstraction that captures the essence of all cases, within a new way of representing the phenomena in question. In this process of generalization, extreme cases play the important function of providing boundary conditions that a new abstraction must meet. In particular, he uses variations across cultures in kinship ties to develop a new and more general concept of kinship relations that transcends mere biological functions, but also mirrors cultural beliefs about the reproductive process:

> Just as the Trobriands are an extreme case in the sense that the father has no consanguineous ties with his wife's children but is bound only to their mother as an affine, so also the Lakher are an extreme case in the sense that the mother has no kinship ties with her husband's children but is bound only to their father as an affine (p. 14).

> We should note that in both the "extreme" cases the affinal alliance between the lineage of the father and the lineage of the mother is expressed in enduring and elaborately defined economic obligation. The requirement that a married Trobriand son should contribute *urigubu* harvest gifts to his father has its counterpart in the payment due from a Lakher male to his mother's brother and his mother's brother's sons. Both sets of payments have their basis in a contract of marriage and are in no way connected with any recognition of common bodily substance (pp. 15–16).

A comparative analysis of kinship ties would merely have documented the statistical distribution of kinship patterns and correlated them with other cultural practices, but not sought some higher level abstraction. As we see it, the extreme cases serve as the fulcrum around which the lever of generalization pivots. So we are arguing that not only should extreme cases be understood in terms of their own uniqueness, but they play a (perhaps "the") central role in the kind of generalized creative induction that makes up science at its best.

Conclusion—A Two Stage Model for Research

We have argued throughout this paper that we ought to take extreme cases seriously, not dismiss them as statistical error within a large sample approach to nomothetic inquiry. And we have implied that extreme cases should be studied intensively using, for example, ethnographic techniques of participant observation that [try] to get at the meaning of the situation from the subjective perspective of the participants themselves. All this implies a commitment to a different kind of research strategy and research skills, not the least being a commitment to live longer with and understand better the persons, groups, and organizations under study.

But this small sample strategy leaves unspecified how the extreme cases should be identified. What is troublesome about much case study research is that the cases selected for intensive investigation seem to have been arbitrarily selected. For example, the cases included in March and Olsen's (1976) *Ambiguity and Choice in Organizations* have the flavor of being extreme, but it is totally unclear what mode they are deviant from. What we would propose to remedy this dilemma is a two-stage model for research. In the first stage, typical large sample research would be conducted, and on the basis of modal analysis, a small sample of extreme cases would be selected for the kind of idiographic analysis or "thick description" (Geertz 1973) that we advocate as the second stage of research. The failure of March and Olsen's (1976) strategy is that it has an atrophied stage one, and the failure of most other research in organizational behavior is that it has an altogether missing stage two. By joining the two stages, we believe that better research can result from our collective efforts.

$N = 1$
William F. Dukes

In the search for principles which govern behavior, psychologists generally confine their empirical observations to a relatively small sample of a defined population, using probability theory to help assess the generality of the findings obtained. Because this inductive process commonly entails some knowledge of individual differences in the behavior involved, studies employing only one subject ($N = 1$) seem somewhat anomalous. With no information about intersubject variability in performance, the general applicability of findings is indeterminate.

Although generalizations about behavior rest equally upon adequate sampling of both subjects and situations, questions about sampling most often refer to subjects. Accordingly, the term "$N = 1$" is used throughout the present discussion to designate the *reductio ad absurdum* in the sampling of subjects. It might, however, equally well (perhaps better, in terms of frequency of occurrence) refer to the limiting case in the sampling of situations—for example, the use of one maze in an investigation of learning, or a simple tapping task in a study of motivation. With respect to the two samplings, Brunswik (1956), foremost champion of the representative design of experiments, speculated:

> In fact, proper sampling of situations and problems may in the end be more important than proper sampling of subjects, considering the fact that individuals are probably on the whole much more alike than are situations among one another (p. 39).

As a corollary, the term $N = 1$ might also be appropriately applied to the sampling of experimenters. Long recognized as a potential source of variance in interview data (e.g., Cantril 1944; Katz 1942), the investigator has recently been viewed as a variable which may also influence laboratory results (e.g., McGuigan 1963; Rosenthal 1963)[14]. . . .

Despite the limitation stated in the first paragraph, $N = 1$ studies cannot be dismissed as inconsequential. A brief scanning of general and historical accounts of psychology will dispel any doubts about their importance, revealing, as it does, many instances of pivotal research in which the observations were confined to the behavior of only one person or animal. . . .

A few studies, each in impact like the single pebble which starts an avalanche, have been the impetus for major developments in research and theory. Others, more like missing pieces from nearly finished jigsaw puzzles, have provided timely data on various controversies.

[An] historical recounting of "successful" cases is, of course, not an exhortation for restricted subject samplings, nor does it imply that their greatness is independent of subsequent related work. . . . In actual practice . . . idiographic research is extremely rare.

Rationale for $N = 1$

The appropriateness of restricting an idiographic study to one individual is obvious from the meaning of the term. If uniqueness is involved, a sample of one exhausts the population. At the other extreme, an N of 1 is also appropriate if complete population generality exists (or can reasonably be assumed to exist). That is, when between-individual variability for the function under scrutiny is known to be negligible or the data from the single subject have a point-for-point congruence with those obtained from dependable collateral sources, results from a second subject may be considered redundant. . . .

A variant on this typicality theme occurs when the researcher, in order to preserve some kind of functional unity and perhaps to dramatize a point, reports in depth one case which exemplifies many. . . .

In other studies an N of 1 is adequate because of the dissonant character of the findings. In contrast to its limited usefulness in *establishing* generalizations from "positive" evidence, an N of 1 when the evidence is "negative," is as useful as an N of 1,000 in *rejecting* an asserted or assumed universal relationship. . . .

While scientists are in the long run more likely to be interested in knowing *what is* than *what is not* and more concerned with how many exist or in what proportion they exist than with the fact that at least one exists, one negative case can make it necessary to revise a traditionally accepted hypothesis.

Still other $N = 1$ investigations simply reflect a limited opportunity to ob-

14. Editors' note: See Rosenthal selection in Chapter 13.

serve. When the search for lawfulness is extended to infrequent "nonlaboratory" behavior, individuals in the population under study may be so sparsely distributed spatially or temporally that the psychologist can observe only one case, a report of which may be useful as a part of a cumulative record. . . .

Not all $N = 1$ studies can be conveniently fitted into this rubric; nor is this necessary. Instead of being oriented either toward the person (uniqueness) or toward a global theory (universality), researchers may sometimes simply focus on a problem. Problem-centered research on only one subject may, by clarifying questions, defining variables, and indicating approaches, make substantial contributions to the study of behavior. Besides answering a specific question, it may (Ebbinghaus' work [1885] being a classic example) provide important groundwork for the theorists.

Regardless of rationale and despite obvious limitations, the usefulness of $N = 1$ studies in psychological research seems, from the preceding historical and methodological considerations, to be fairly well established. (See Shapiro (1961) for an affirmation of the value of single-case investigations in fundamental clinical psychological research.) Finally, their status in research is further secured by the statistician's assertion (McNemar 1940) that:

> The statistician who fails to see that important generalizations from research on a single case can ever be acceptable is on a par with the experimentalist who fails to appreciate the fact that some problems can never be solved without resort to numbers (p. 361).

Mixing Levels of Analysis
Appa Rao Korukonda

Within recent years much has been written about the sins of mixing levels of analysis in organization theory (e.g., Pfeffer 1982). Since Robinson's (1950) classic article on ecological correlation, distortions introduced by moving back and forth between different levels of analysis have been emphasized in one form or another (See, for example: Glick 1985; J. L. Hammond 1973; Lang, Dollinger and Marino 1987; Langbein and Lichtman 1978). There has thus been a concerted effort to sensitize researchers to what essentially are a potential pitfall and a key methodological concern in the conduct of research in social sciences.

Most of this exhortation, however, has proceeded from the almost axiomatic belief that it is inherently wrong to mix levels of analysis and has fallen short of analytical or philosophical exposition of why and when it

Source: "Mixing levels of analysis in organizational research" by Appa Rao Korukonda, *Canadian Journal of Administrative Sciences* 6 (June 1989): 1–7. Copyright © Administrative Sciences Association of Canada.

might be wrong. The consequences of this growing tide of assertion without analysis have been quite unfortunate. [The] level of analysis argument has been used as a catch-all, as some kind of a universal criterion to which all scientific endeavor should conform. . . .

While the arguments in favor of consistency of level of analysis have certain clear merits, one wonders whether an overriding sensitivity to this issue in all phases of research might not blind us to a rich variety of theoretical perspectives. For example, Rousseau (1985), in a recent article has called upon organizational researchers to examine the role of level in theory development and acknowledge "the multi-level character of the field and its subject." This paper is an attempt in that direction. . . .

The Level of Analysis Issue

Concerns with the level of analysis issue in organizational research have been sparse and somewhat diffuse with the result that no precise, all-encompassing statement of these issues is available in the literature. However, a review of the literature suggests that although the level of analysis argument is mainly employed to indicate methodological and data analytic techniques such as aggregation and disaggregation, there are other aspects of the issue that need to be considered. It appears that, on the whole, level of analysis issues impact on five major facets of organization research. These are: (1) Epistemological Beliefs (2) Labeling of Phenomena (3) Observation-Inference Fallacy (4) Reification (5) Discovery vs. Justification. . . .

Epistemological Beliefs

Epistemology is theory of knowledge. The level of analysis employed reflects an underlying epistemological belief. Thus it must be emphasized that there is no "appropriate" or "inappropriate" level of analysis for discourse about a given phenomenon. . . .

Thus, the level of analysis adopted reflects deep-rooted epistemological beliefs about where to look for the causes of social and organizational phenomena. Two polar positions such as the individualist and structuralist beliefs highlight this diversity clearly. Individualist thinking, reflected in the writings of Weick (1969), Collins (1981), Argyris (1972) and others, maintains that it is necessary to translate descriptions and analyses of macro-constructs into their micro equivalents. This position is stated quite forcefully by Collins:

> The ultimate empirical validation of sociological statements depends upon their microtranslations. By this standard, virtually all sociological evidence as yet presented is tentative only (1981, 988).

By contrast, structuralists argue, with equal force, that the individualist position is logically untenable and could lead to reductionism. This position is stated succinctly by Pfeffer:

> ... in arguing that social entities must be studied in terms of their under-lying processes, one embarks on a process of reductionism from which there is no logical stopping. Concepts such as attitudes, conflict, values, goals and so forth, which are regularly used in individual-level explana-tions of behavior, are themselves hypothetical constructs and in many cases aggregates of even more molar behaviors. Thus the process of ar-guing that behavior must be understood in terms of its microprocesses can lead to the study of behavior in almost biological terms (1982, 21).

The point of the foregoing discussion is that debates such as those be-tween individualists and structuralists ... cannot be resolved by appeal to some self-evident and "appropriate" level of analysis. Arguments about the "appropriate" level of analysis can be traced to deep-rooted epistemologi-cal beliefs. One's choice of a particular level of analysis represents an en-during belief in the potency of that level to explain phenomena. This belief is neither right nor wrong and should be recognized as such. Level of analy-sis is incidental to such discussions and not the central issue by itself.

Labeling of Phenomena

A favorite level of analysis argument among many organization theorists has to do with artificial labeling of phenomena. This fallacy owes its origins to the fact that constructs in social sciences are a result of artificial, perhaps arbitrary, labeling of phenomena. Pfeffer articulates this concern as follows:

> The problem with this heuristic [which says that the level at which the dependent variable is defined should determine the level of analysis] is that it potentially does not tell us anything at all. Any set of characteris-tics can be aggregated to any level and called a property of the collectiv-ity. . . . In a similar fashion one could argue that the level of strike activ-ity in an industry is an indicator of an industry-level property (Britt and Galle 1974) even though strikes occur for the most part at the level of the firm or plant (1982, 15).

Pfeffer's argument about definitions and conceptual constructions being the end-product of labeling of phenomena across levels of analysis is valid. But whether such labeling serves no purpose or "does not tell anything at all" is open to debate. Consistent with the referential theory of meaning is the argument that the label itself acts as a metaphor and creates "meaning by understanding one phenomenon through another in a way that encour-ages us to understand what is common" (Morgan 1983b).

Many organizational level constructs are derived from their analogues at the individual level and vice versa. Take for example, a construct such as innovation at the organization level. Our conceptualization of organizational innovation is derived from the individual-level imagery we associate with the word innovation (for example, non-conformity to established norms). We could use the authoritarian orientation among the group's members to represent the "authoritarian context" of a group (Blau 1960). Similarly, we could speak of bureaucratic thinking at the individual level to represent lack of flexibility and rule-bound behavior.

Spanning across levels of analysis is necessary in order to create metaphors and facilitate theoretical insights. Jaynes argues that metaphor is an inevitable part of a living language:

> Because in our brief lives we catch so little of the vastness of history, we tend too much to think of language as being solid as a dictionary, with a granite-like permanence, rather than as the rampant restless sea of metaphor which it is. Indeed, if we consider the changes in vocabulary that have occurred over the last few millennia, and project them several millennia hence, an interesting paradox arises. For if we ever achieve a language that has the power of expressing everything, then metaphor will no longer be possible. I would not say, in that case, my love is like a red, red rose, for love would have exploded into terms of its thousands of nuances, and applying the correct term would leave the rose metaphorically dead (1976, 51–52).

Although presented in somewhat of a poetic vein, Jaynes' argument for developing theory is obviously relevant. A discipline that has no need for metaphor has exhausted its theoretical and conceptual possibilities. "Relaxed meaning" (Bidwell 1979)—or a leap across levels, species and phenomena—lies at the heart of generating conceptual and theoretical insights. Thus, although perfect analogy is unattainable in many cases, moving across levels of analysis in labeling phenomena does appear to be useful for guiding and structuring perceptions—especially in the developmental stages of a discipline.

Observation—Inference Fallacy

One could measure the variables at an aggregate level and use the observed relationship to draw unwarranted inferences at a lower level—or vice versa. In a classic article on "ecological fallacy" Robinson (1950) demonstrated the pitfalls of drawing inferences from the group to the individual level of analysis. The term "ecological fallacy," though initially used to refer to the practice of moving down levels of analysis, has since been used in a broader sense to refer to the "fallacy of the wrong level," or the "fallacy" of cross-level movement in either direction (Galtung 1967; Rousseau 1985).

Detailed statistical treatment of ecological inference is available in the literature (e.g., Hannan 1971; Langbein and Lichtman 1978) and will not be discussed here. There is no question that one should be aware of the level of analysis issue while drawing inferences. Robinson (1950) showed, for example, that the correlation between race and illiteracy which was as high as .95 at the level of states dropped down to .20 at the level of individuals. It is erroneous to rely on the state level data and draw conclusions about the literacy of a given individual based on his/her race.

Ecological fallacy is not a mere statistical phenomenon. Sometimes this fallacy can be traced to the presence of apparent similarities in constructs at two different levels. Thus, for example, finding a positive relationship between professionalization and innovation at the organizational level does not automatically mean that at the individual level a person with a professional background is likely to be more innovative than one without such a background. This fallacy could result from the fact that the professionalization construct is operationalized differently at the two levels. At the individual level it could be measured as the extent of professional education and training received. By contrast, an empirical referent of the construct at the organizational level could be the percentage of employees with a professional background. Thus, although the constructs are "similar" at the two levels, this similarity does not extend much beyond surface description.

The possibility of observation-inference fallacy, however, should not blind us to legitimate and logical conclusions that can be drawn at one level based upon observations at a different level. For example, if it is determined that a particular pest has the effect of lowering the yield of a mango tree, we should probably have no hesitation in saying that this pest will have the same effect on a mango garden. This particular conclusion will be valid to the extent that the underlying assumption about a collectivity-level phenomenon (yield of the mango garden) being the aggregate of an individual level phenomenon (yield of a single tree) is valid. In this case, this assumption will mean that (i) the total yield is the sum of the yields of the individual trees, and (ii) the mechanism by which the pest will affect the yield is the same for a collection of trees as it is for an individual tree. These two are the issues to be addressed by a theory of composition and a theory of process respectively.

In organizational sciences, the observation-inference fallacy is the result of presumed violation of one or both of these assumptions. Often, individual effects, group effects and interaction effects all play a role in social phenomena. For example, it is a matter of common experience that one-on-one dealings are qualitatively different than collectivity-level dealings. A manager might be able to convince the employees individually about a proposed change but still face collective resistance (Shaw 1977). Similarly, [N. M.]

Webb (1980) found that working in mixed-ability groups was beneficial for high-ability and low-ability students whereas medium ability students learned most in uniform-ability groups. Here we cannot describe group effects as a simple aggregate of individual effects, nor can we assume away contextual effects and say that group level processes are derivable from individual level processes alone.

The point of the mango plant example, however, is that where there is a strong theoretical reason to suspect that similar or related mechanisms operate at both the levels, or where the phenomenon at the higher level is, by definition, an aggregate of individual-level phenomena (or vice versa), level of analysis should not act as a barrier to gaining new insights or drawing cross-level inferences. . . .

Blanket labels, such as the term "fallacy," have a tendency to be universally incriminating. However, the Observation-Inference fallacy is really a question of specifying the underlying theories of process and composition. As Langbein and Lichtman (1978) point out, theory—not technique—is the key to cross-level inference. Uslaner makes a similar argument: "grouping variables does not always result in less precise estimates of the effects of one variable on another; if the relationship is properly specified, there may be no bias at all. In some cases there may even be a gain in precision" (1978, 5).

Reification

In the context of level of analysis, reification may be described as the fallacy of imputing material qualities to constructs at one level based on the meanings associated with the terms at a higher or lower level. The reification argument is used to mount an attack on collectivity-level notions such as goals and needs which are derived from a view of organizations as supraindividual abstract concepts. Silverman, for example, describes the problem of reification as follows: "To use the concepts of organizational needs and of a system's self-regulating activities in any way other than as a heuristic device is inadmissible since it implies that the power of thought and action may reside in social constructs—this is sometimes known as the problem of reification" (1970, 3).

It can be seen at once that reification is yet another manifestation of the level of analysis argument. The underlying concern here, however, is one of ontology. The extent to which this is a valid concern remains questionable. To criticize organization level concepts as failing to pass tests for cognition, intention, etc. is perhaps tantamount to applying the wrong tests. As Donaldson argues,

> Concepts are constructs, i.e., artificial and manmade efforts to understand the buzzing world of phenomena. Particle Physics is the study of

vapor trails in chambers, whether the particles exist in an ontological sense is an irrelevant question. Constructs in science do not have to pass tests for tangibility ("Can you see it, touch it, smell it") to be legitimate elements in a scientific argument. Realism is an extra-scientific doctrine which is not implied in sociological theories which posit a social world independent of the immediate perceptions of individuals. Researchers who characterize organizations as having collectivity-level properties of structure such as centralization or formalization (e.g., Pugh and Hickson 1976a; Hage 1980) are not thereby attributing ontology to their constructs (1985, 50).

Anthropomorphism, or the attribution of human-like qualities to collectivities, cannot thus be faulted on grounds of reification. For example, in his book entitled *Stakeholders of the Organizational Mind*, Mitroff (1983a) uses the notion of stakeholders to describe a wide range of forces that impinge on any social system, be it a large organization or a single individual. The issue of whether organizations possess a mind is irrelevant to examining the usefulness of Mitroff's argument and represents the extra-scientific criterion Donaldson is referring to.

By way of illustrating this argument further, let us look at the following example. In a recent article, L. R. James, Joyce and Slocum state rather forcefully that ". . . no organization has ever had, or ever will have, an attitude. An attitude *must* be an individual-level phenomenon. . . ." (1988, 130) [emphasis added]. But do we have any more evidence about the "reality" of attitudes at the individual level than at the collectivity level? It is easy to lose sight of the fact that concepts and constructs are invoked, by definition, to explain phenomena. Such definition is the starting point of research. . . .

Discovery vs. Justification

Discovery of hypotheses, laws and theories belongs in the context of discovery whereas the criteria for acceptance or rejection of a truth claim belong in the context of justification. However, confusion between the discovery and the justification of knowledge appears widespread even among such philosophers of science as John Dewey and Hegel (see, e.g., Bergman 1957). For the unsuspecting researcher, level of analysis offers a ready trap and a source of such confusion. As we shall show, consistency of level of analysis is an issue of concern in the logic of justification alone.

Logic of discovery is in reality a misnomer since discovery as a scientific activity is neither programmable nor method-bound. It has been suggested that science and discovery involve "doing the damnedest with one's mind." As [S. D.] Hunt (1983) argues, somewhat less forcefully, many, if not most, major scientific discoveries are flashes of perceptual insight and are not the result of following some rigorously prescribed procedure. . . .

As we can see from the above, level of analysis is really not an issue in the context of discovery. This does not mean that assumptions in theory have to be accepted on faith. Their ultimate validation is an empirical question, not logical, philosophical or metaphysical. Thus, in our example, the appropriate criterion for examining the validity of the homeostasis assumption is whether we can predict organizational phenomena better with this assumption than without it.

In the context of justification, level of analysis concerns are valid to the extent that they call for consistency between empirical referents and theoretical conceptualizations. The differential relevance of level of analysis concerns to the contexts of discovery and justification can be illustrated by a simple example. In the testing of a theory of organizational life cycles, it is obviously inadmissible to measure the age of an organization as the mean age of its employees. It is admissible to measure the age in terms of time since the organization was founded. Nonetheless, the fact that this theory is generated on the basis of observation of the human life cycle (i.e., at an individual level of analysis) should not make it less valid as a theory of organizations. . . .

Summary and Conclusions

In summary, we have looked at the five most common manifestations of the level of analysis issue in organizational research. We have seen that arguments for consistency of levels of analysis cannot be justified on grounds of epistemology, artificial labeling of phenomena or reification. We have seen further that mixing levels of analysis could be a source of fallacy if inferences are drawn across levels based on (i) level-specific data, and (ii) apparent similarity of constructs; however, the observation-inference fallacy is not universal and should serve only to highlight the need for appropriate definitional and process schema rather than condemn all cross-level inference. Finally, we have examined this issue within the context of discovery as opposed to the context of justification and found that level of analysis is an issue of concern in the logic of justification alone.

Summary

With one or more research questions in hand, researchers begin to plan. First, they select an appropriate research strategy, which consists of choosing the sort of data desired and determining where it can be found. Second, they select an appropriate research design, which consists of choosing how to acquire the preferred amounts and types of data. As McGrath and Stone have carefully shown, there are many alternative types of strategies and designs—none perfect for all research questions, each holding pros and cons to be traded off to partially satisfy strategy desiderata and design criteria. In addition, there are choices regarding the levels of analysis of data, attention to common or exceptional observations/cases, and the number of cases. Project by project we choose as best we can, depending on future projects and other researchers to compensate for our plans.

13   Acquiring and Handling Data

Methodology is a function of the society that produces it—to work
with any methodology is a political act.

    —Johan Galtung

Man is an animal suspended in webs of significance he himself has
spun.

    —Clifford Geertz

You observe a lot watching.

    —Yogi Berra

"Data" is information believed to be relevant for responding to one's research questions. Given choices about an appropriate research design, investigators next face several important questions about gathering and managing a study's data: What information needs to be acquired? How much
data is needed? How might it be acquired? How do we make it amenable for
storage and analysis? In short, what data, what shall the sample be, what
methods, and what form? Because there are many alternative responses
to these questions, choices and trade-offs abound. When we add concerns
about available resources, costs, access to information, skill requirements for
data gathering, preferences for eventual analysis of the data, data quality,
and so on, we begin to see three things very clearly. There is no one best way
of acquiring data; these choices are very important, often crucial, to a study's
success; and these choices are always intertwined.

At present there is a very large, often detailed, and easily accessible literature about data acquisition, and no summary of it will be attempted here.
Consistent with this book's thesis, we will merely note the array of methods
among which a researcher can choose, point to the many sources of data
distortion to be aware of, and, through some of this chapter's selections,
proffer comment on several of the major considerations behind methodological choices. In contrast to the literature on data acquisition, the literature on data processing and management (see Figure 2-1), or data handling,

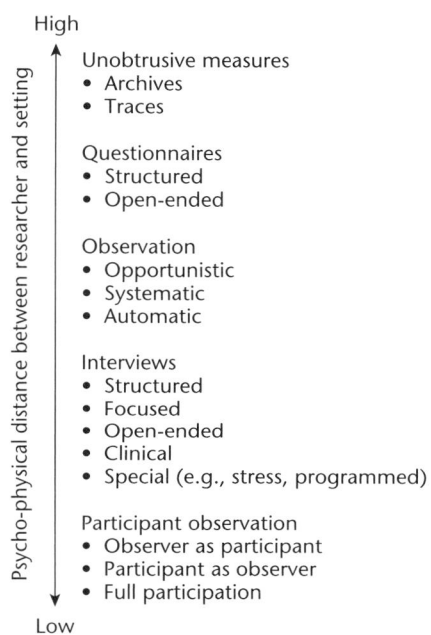

High

Unobtrusive measures
• Archives
• Traces

Questionnaires
• Structured
• Open-ended

Observation
• Opportunistic
• Systematic
• Automatic

Interviews
• Structured
• Focused
• Open-ended
• Clinical
• Special (e.g., stress, programmed)

Participant observation
• Observer as participant
• Participant as observer
• Full participation

Low

Psycho-physical distance between researcher and setting

FIGURE **13-1**   Data acquisition methods

is relatively sparse and scattered. Thus, we can draw attention only to the many steps involved in data handling and the choices inherent in them.

With regard to data gathering methods, the key choice is whether to use one or more methods (and, if several, in what mix). Interestingly, the array of methods is quite small. As shown in Figure 13-1, there are just five general types of data acquisition methods—although there are two or more variants of each. We note that the listing in Figure 13-1 does not indicate the variety of data recording alternatives, such as notes, forms, photos, film, audio tapes (again choices). Choices among alternative methods (the general ones and their variants) will reflect several considerations, such as the responses to the questions with which this chapter began; the choice of research design, research resources, skills, and preferences; and the state of development of the relevant current theory. The importance, complexity, and difficulty of selecting appropriate methods cannot be overstated. It is no surprise then that many researchers, feeling overwhelmed, simply select methods currently popular in their school of thought or let such factors as convenience, cost, or time dominate.

Given the many considerations that have to be factored into the choice of an appropriate data-gathering methodology, optimal choices are unlikely. Problematic data quantity and quality are therefore a constant threat to the eventual discovery of meaningful findings. One major source of data distortion is overreliance on a single method (for the reasoning behind this assertion see the Martin selection later in this chapter). Even with what seems to be a very appropriate method or mix of methods and with the benefits of triangulation they provide, many other types of possible distortion exist, and these can also influence data quality. Some distortions may be associated with the research, others associated with respondents (here "respondents" will refer to all of the roles of those providing data— informants, subjects, participants, as well as respondents). Researchers may subtly influence respondents and hence the quality of the data in many ways. For example, having or assuming information about respondents before gathering data may condition researchers to hold dysfunctional attitudes toward respondents, to project certain response expectancies, and make attributions to respondents that create conscious or unconsciously preferred data responses. Other outcome confirmation effects can occur through subtle research communications, such as verbal conditioning and other modeled behaviors. Respondents by themselves may also unconsciously distort their responses. For example, respondents may vary considerably in their susceptibility to research outcome confirmation effects. Data quality may be distorted by respondent perceptions of research creditability, by respondents' needs for approval and recognition, how they respond to the reward characteristics inherent in a methodology, and, of course, how they deal with the stress and anxiety of being in a data gathering situation. Safeguards against data distorting features, beyond an awareness of them, consist of practices that embrace researcher sensitivity, consistency, and redundancy. Such practices include systematic self-reflection, careful pilot testing of methods, careful investigator training, using multiple investigators, keeping a research project journal of questions, feelings, and insights, and regular sharing with colleagues.

The "raw" data derived by most methodologies almost always has to be transformed into "usable" data; it has to be put into a form amenable to analysis and a form accessible for storage and retrieval. Data handling is relatively ignored in the research literature compared to the stages before and after it in the research process (see Figure 2-1). Why this is so is unclear. Perhaps it is because data handling seems minor or straightforward or technically simple; we contend, however, that it is equally important to all other steps in the research process and, similarly, also full of consequential choices and trade-offs. The sequence of the five main activities of data handling are as follows:

1. Editing Data
   a. Handle blanks and outliers
   b. Clarify and decipher

2. Coding, Sorting, Indexing Data
3. Categorizing Data
   a. Data reduction
   b. Data aggregation
4. Storing Data
   a. Form
   b. Security
5. Retrieving Data

The seven selections in this chapter may usefully be viewed as two re-lated sets. The first set of three selections brings attention to three basic considerations that are reflected in data acquisition methods: precise con-struct formulation, field settings characteristics, and phenomenological representativeness. The second set of four selections offers a sampler of common—even pervasive—issues related to data and data gathering.

In the first selection, Chimezie A. B. Osigweh, Yg. reminds us that meth-ods cannot compensate for imprecise ideas. Careful concept formulation before data acquisition enhances methodological selection and theoretical improvement. Thomas Bouchard, in the second selection, reminds us of the characteristics of field settings—settings in which the majority of data gath-ering methods are applied—and how these characteristics impact the na-ture of research findings. In the last selection of this set, Thomas Lee reminds us of another basic consideration in the choice of method: the reliability and validity of our constructs always influences the representativeness of the phenomena of interest. Methods that provide reliable and valid findings therefore are always the preferable ones.

The next four selections alert us to several basic issues that affect the meaning of findings derived from data acquisition methods. First, Joanne Martin artfully rebuts the false quantitative-qualitative methods dichotomy (*data* are quantitative or qualitative, not methods) as well as the touted su-periority of any particular methodology. Martin thus promotes both hybrid methods and multimethods. Podsakoff and Organ, in the next selection, alert us to the several distortion possibilities in self-reports—a common as-pect of data acquired through several prominent social and organizational science methodologies. They nicely summarize the data distortions related to problems of common method variance, consistency, and social desirabil-ity. Data distortions are also the consequence of researcher expectations and researcher presence, the focus of the Robert Rosenthal selection. While discussed in terms of one research design—experiments—Rosenthal's points are probably more or less applicable to all research designs and data-gathering methods. The final selection in our sampler of issues, by Philip Bobko, reminds us of the data distortions (and theory distortions) that occur from seeing orthogonal constructs as bipolar.

Concept Formulation Before Methods
Chimezie A. B. Osigweh, Yg.

This article is concerned with the almost routine practice of creating, reconceptualizing, or defining concepts for organizational science (e.g., Rice et al. 1985; Stevenson, Pearce and Porter 1985; Venkatraman and Grant 1986; Weiss and Miller 1987). It addresses the tendency of researchers to derive concepts loosely and fallibly, thus, muddying the understanding of them and the ability to develop and test specific hypotheses using the concepts (J. P. Campbell, Daft and Hulin 1982; Fry and Smith 1987; Mitchell 1985; Reichers 1985; Steers 1989). One primary source of the fallibility, addressed by this article, is concept "misformation." Here, the term concept *misformation* is used to mean the malformation of concepts and the misinformation that results.

The solution to misformation offered in this article is straightforward: Its basic logic requires specifying what concepts are not, in order to better define meaning boundaries. The solution calls for, and the article describes, an approach to forming concepts that are at once general and precise. The aim is to advance organizational science by providing a rigorous approach to the formation of concepts.

Particular attention is given to how to minimize the problem of concept stretching (broadening the meaning beyond reason) while maximizing the potential for concept traveling (fitting precisely a variety of applications). . . .

Need for Precise Concepts in Organizational Science

The need for developing precise concepts in organizational science (Miner 1984; Osigweh 1989) cannot be overstated. Concepts are the building blocks of science upon which propositions are based, and scientific knowledge exists "only when our propositions are organized in systematic way, so that we can perceive their interrelations" (Copi 1954, 167). Concepts suggest first-order questions that need to be researched and aspects of situations that need to be investigated. If any of the concepts that form a proposition are ill-defined, an ambiguous research proposition or an ill-conceived emphasis on certain aspects of an organizational phenomenon may result. Also, imprecise concepts make it difficult to produce knowledge that is cumulative (Achinstein 1968; Bagozzi and Fornell 1982; Schutz 1971).

By contrast, precisely formed concepts are thoroughly discriminating

Source: "Concept fallibility in organizational science" by Chimezie A. B. Osigweh, Yg. *Academy of Management Review* 14 (1989): 579–585, 588–589, 591–592. Copyright © 1989 by the Academy of Management. Reproduced with permission of the Academy of Management via Copyright Clearance Center.

and, thus, are excellent for data-gathering purposes. They do not misinform their users as to the empirical import of the theoretical propositions containing them; so, they do not misguide the efforts of researchers and practitioners using them. They assist organizational scientists in the continuing development of their discipline as a science. . . .

Unless research is based on such well-defined concepts, no one knows which "meanings" are valid (e.g., for each new situation) and which are not, regardless of the concepts level of abstraction. I maintain that concept misformation in general, and concept stretching in particular, is directly responsible for the lack of organizational knowledge that spans different contexts.

. . . In short, I have argued that the development of clear definitions for concepts is important to improving organizational research and theory building.

Concepts, Concept Traveling, and Concept Stretching

As in other sciences, some of the concepts involved in organizational science propositions can be explained or defined on the basis of others. For example, motivation can be defined in management as the process that energizes, channels, and sustains behavior (Locke et al. 1981; Pinder 1984; Steers and Porter 1983; Wexley and Yukl 1984), just as in physics the concept of density is defined as mass per unit volume. This definition of concepts by means of others serves to reveal interrelationships among them. It illustrates their concern with common subject matter, while allowing the concepts to be integrated with the scientific propositions containing them. It underpins the fact that concepts add to the skeletal framework of organizational science as a science. Further, it suggests that concepts are not only building blocks of science, as formerly discussed, but are also *meaning-laden* classifications that may or may not be variables. . . .

. . . The above description of concepts and some of their roles in science can help define a concept by specifying some of what it is not. A concept is *not* an unclassifiable mental construction; it can be decomposed taxonomically. It is *not* just an attribute of some phenomenon that cannot in itself be decoupled. It does *not* only refer to a variable. It is *not* without meaning; a concept is meaning-laden, *not* meaningless.

This further suggests that . . . those defined should have definitions sufficiently precise to enable them to "travel" in the light of the numerous variables and circumstances that characterize our field. *Concept traveling*, in this sense, means that the concept is precise enough to allow researchers to define it in the same way, and so to test it in a wide range of situations — that is, that the concept is a universal. Consider the concept, puzzle. The jigsaw puzzle, crossword puzzle, or Rubik's cube come to mind. Each creates essentially the same image anywhere: (a) a maze of activities that *cannot* be correctly solved outside settings or mental frameworks that prescribe following certain paths or specific combination of paths; (b) an exercise of figures, numbers, or behaviors that *cannot* be engaged in or successfully disengaged in, except through a specific order or steps, procedures, or systems of thought processes; (c) activities that when completed *cannot* fail to yield exact answers, known solutions, or ultimates that could be exactly predicted beforehand. Puzzle, viewed in this way, is a traveling concept.

Few scholars would disagree that universal categories or concepts are needed that can be understood simultaneously at any time and place and that can be validly tested in a wide range of situations. Yet, when concepts are broadened in order to extend their range of applications, they may be so broadly defined (or, *stretched*) that they verge on being too all-embracing to be meaningful in the realm of empirical observation and professional practice. For example, according to one definition, *participation* (in organizational management, or participative management) "encompasses efforts to broaden employees' involvement and control" (Stokes 1978, 6). So defined, the meaning of participation can include joint consultation on productivity standards, worker ownership, union representation on corporate boards, collaboration to improve the psychological and physical work environment, handling of routine personnel problems, and anything else that evokes the idea of democracy in the workplace. (I shall return to this concept later to illustrate how else it can be defined.)

Because concept stretching in organizational science results in amorphous, unclear conceptualizations, what appears to have been a gain in extensional coverage (breadth) often has been matched and even surpassed by losses in connotative precision (depth). . . .

. . . In short, no harm is done if precise organizational science concepts are of the traveling kind, as those that are (precise) universals should be. However, a quagmire sets in when conceptual stretching leads to concepts that are not precise, thereby producing universal concepts that cannot accurately travel.

Theoretical Versus Empirical Concepts

To understand how to properly develop concepts requires researchers to make a distinction between two types of concepts: theoretical and empirical.

Theoretical or universal concepts (Hempel 1965; Kaplan 1964) are defined by their systemic meaning (Kaplan 1964), in the sense that each meaning derives from the part that the concept plays in the theory. Hempel (1965, 189) described them as open concepts because they reflect the availability of different operational criteria for application to different contexts. As a result, their meanings are not fully defined by reference to observable things and their characteristics. . . .

Consider the concept of efficacy. Whether it is used in democratic theory in political literature (e.g., Pateman 1970), appears in a theory of citizen education in international relations (Alger 1978, 1980), or is found in an investigation of organizational problem solving (e.g., Osigweh 1983), the concept is nevertheless defined in terms of three distinct elements. The first element is the belief that one can do, the second is the confidence in one's ability, and the third is the sense of effectiveness in controlling one's life or environment (Alger 1978, 17–18; Osigweh 1983, 30, 41; Pateman 1970, 45–46). Now, it may well be that this concept, and each of the others mentioned, is more precisely defined in the discipline in which it originated, but each (with or without the possible exception of efficacy) has been borrowed from somewhere else because it seems to apply to some organizational phenomenon. Obviously, then, with such borrowings, care must be exercised to be sure that all meanings attached to the concept actually apply. . . .

In contrast to theoretical concepts, observational or empirical concepts (Bagozzi 1984; Hempel 1965) have meanings that can be used in concrete as well as abstract contexts. They can be positioned or repositioned, upward or downward, on a ladder of abstraction. They are terms derived from inferences that are made from observables, despite their being highly abstract concepts. Their meanings can be used in relation to direct observables or to describe distant observations. Examples are communication, puzzle, group, decision, problem, conflict, and participation.

That observational concepts can be positioned or repositioned upward or downward on a ladder of abstraction is illustrated by the concept, participation. When participation is defined . . . as embracing all efforts to broaden a worker's control and involvement in organizational affairs (Stokes 1978, 6), the concept is (positioned upward and) pushed too high as a general or abstract construct. However, when participation is used to mean a subordinate's involvement in the decision-making process with guidance from superiors (Lowen 1968), the emphasis on the specific notion of making decisions repositions the concept downward or to a less general and abstract level. Then, the concept does not include every conceivable employee-oriented program, but zeroes in on those dealing with the more specific domain of decision making. This illustration further reveals a source of difficulty. Because *empirical* or *observational concepts* can be moved up (ladder climbing) or down (ladder descending) on the ladder of abstraction, the researcher in organizational science is confronted with the quagmire of how to retain *extensional* (breadth or denotation) gains by ladder climbing, while minimizing losses in *connotative* (intention or depth) precision. The latter objective is critical because it in turn affects both the empirical testability and practical applicability of the concept in organizational settings.

The *extension* of a concept refers to the class of things to which it applies, or the totality of objects which it identifies. The *connotation* of that

same term refers to the sum total of characteristics or collection of properties that anything must possess to be denoted by that term.

Climbing and Descending a Ladder of Abstraction

How, then, can an organizational concept be formed while maintaining
an appropriate level of abstraction? I propose that the ladder of abstraction
may be climbed in organizational research by using one of two procedures.
The first and more desirable procedure involves extending the breadth of a
concept while reducing its properties or connotation (Figure [13-2a]). A
precise universal (or traveling) concept retains its precision while maintaining its universality or general character. The concept is general in the sense
that it represents a large class. But it is also precise, because its differentiae
are few.

As an example, consider Quick and Quick's (1984) use of the concept of
organizational stress. They view organizational stress as dealing with the generalized, patterned, unconscious mobilization of the body's natural energy resources when confronted with any demand in the course of organizational
life (Quick and Quick 1984, 3). This description is broad and underscores the
concept's extension. Then they specify the concept's connotation in terms of
three sets of attributes: demands originating from *inside* (role demands, task
demands, physical demands, interpersonal demands) and *outside* the organization (marriage/spousal demands, children/parenting demands, social
responsibilities, self-imposed responsibilities) and in terms of *individual resources* for managing these demands (knowledge, skills, and abilities; social
support system; biological life history; psychological life history) (Quick and

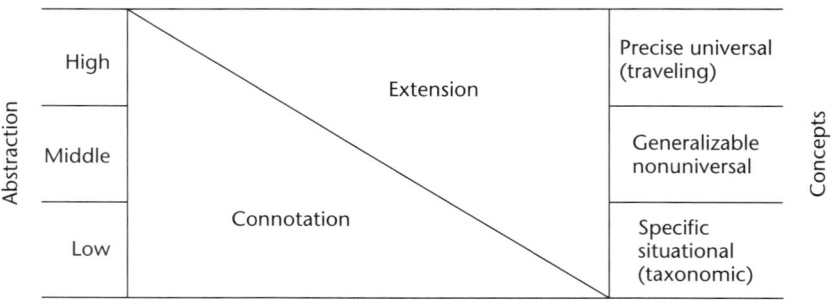

FIGURE **13-2a**   Climbing/descending the abstraction ladder (widened extension,
restricted connotation)

SOURCE: "Concept fallibility in organizational science" by Chimezie A. B. Osigweh, Yg., *Academy
of Management Review* 14 (1989): 585, fig. 1a. Copyright © 1989 by the Academy of Management.
Reproduced with permission of the Academy of Management via Copyright Clearance Center.

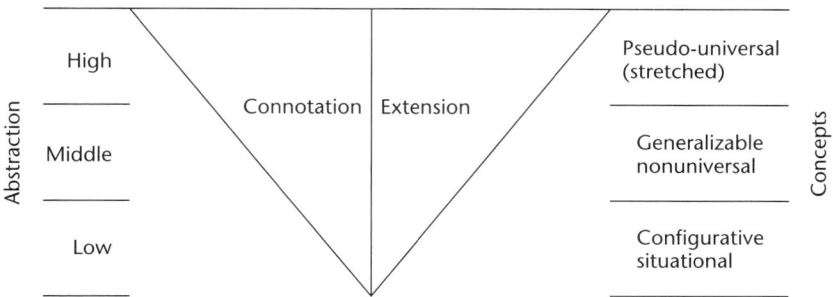

FIGURE **13-2b** Climbing/descending the abstraction ladder (widened extension, increased connotation)

SOURCE: "Concept fallibility in organizational science" by Chimezie A. B. Osigweh, Yg., *Academy of Management Review* 14 (1989): 585, fig. 1b. Copyright © 1989 by the Academy of Management. Reproduced with permission of the Academy of Management via Copyright Clearance Center.

Quick 1984, 3–5). Because it points to attributes that are more specific than those provided by another definition examined later on, this description is more helpful in targeting organizational stress for research.

The second and less desirable procedure involves extending the concept's denotation, while also expanding its connotation (Figure [13-2b]). The result is a large class or highly inclusive concept, possessing a large number of differentiae that cannot boast of being precise. Due to its all-embracing nature, the construct may be described as general, but only in the sense that it is a mere generality.

As an example, consider an unsuccessful definition of the concept, organizational stress. A recent national study describes the concept's extension as one "concerned principally with the adverse health/mental health effects of the psychosocial aspects of work" (Association of Schools of Public Health 1988, 96). As in the preceding example, the extension is broad, but so is the connotation. First, there are six sets of attributes, not three: the "psychosocial coverage connotes a category of problems encompassing a wide array of *social*, *behavioral*, and *biological* conditions with diverse and often unknown etiologies . . . sometimes connoting *causal factors*, sometimes *outcomes*, and sometimes *intermediary processes*" (Association of Schools of Public Health 1988, 96). Second, a zealous researcher who is attempting to isolate the specific attributes constituting the six sets may find well over 150 factors to choose from, which will clearly cloud any resulting research. . . .

Emerging from the foregoing discussion are two maxims for climbing (and descending) a ladder of abstraction. Simply stated, the abstraction ladder should be ascended in a way that retains precision by decreasing the number of attributes and properties of a concept. On the other hand, descending the abstraction ladder (i.e., from precise universal to specific situational constructs) requires adding to the attributes that characterize the concept.

An Approach to Concept Formation

In light of the foregoing discussion, let me present an approach that is based on the notion of *omnis determinatio est negatio*, which for simplicity's sake shall be called the *negation approach*. This approach, inspired by readings of several philosophers, such as John Dewey and George Hegel, can advance concept formation in organizational science by further explaining the process and further guiding organizational researchers in its use.

As a phrase, *omnis determinatio est negatio* refers to the ability to determine things by negation. The approach itself may be understood by examining two principles of concept formation encompassed by it. First is the *with-negation principle*. According to this principle, concepts should be defined by specifying what they are not. Doing this delimits the concept while clearly charting its meaning boundaries, in the sense that its attributes are well defined, even if its scope is large. Thus, regardless of how broad (extension), the concept is nonetheless determinate, and empirical universals are more likely to be produced at the point where [middle abstraction level] categories become [high abstraction level] concepts in the ladder-climbing process.

Second is the *without-negation principle*. According to this principle, concepts may be defined without explicitly specified boundaries or termination points. Concepts created in this way are indeterminate. They are "no-opposite" concepts, in the sense that they have no ends or delimiting points. Thus, their properties are more confusing than precise, and the class concepts derived during ladder climbing possess little empirical value. Although, at the point in which [middle abstraction level] concepts are transformed into [high abstraction level] categories, these without-negation concepts do become universals, they can be described as philosophical or pseudouniversals, literally pointing to everything. Supraempirical, they are perfect examples of concept stretching. They persist only because they derive from following a line of least resistance. Attempting to say what something is, while not bothering to say what it is not, is a natural line of least resistance, in the sense that it is an intuitive tendency that everyone possesses.

In short, the negation approach proceeds from an assumption similar to the Hegelian thesis-antithesis premise that every determination involves a negation. Simply stated, the approach says that the extension of a concept involves determination by negation, with concepts determined with negation being determinate, while those determined without negation are indeterminate. The principles or rules of with and without negation suggest that [high abstraction level] concepts that are derived, via a with-negation process during ladder climbing are turned into empirical universals, while those that are derived without negation become conceptually stretched, philosophical universals.

Since philosophical universals nurture indefiniteness and elusiveness, the search for them translates to a self-nullification of the research effort, from a theoretical and observational or empirical standpoint. Hence, I propose that the cut-off point beyond which the search for universal inclusiveness becomes theoretically self-nullifying, while the empirical or observational content of the class concept literally vaporizes, is the point at which the concept cannot be determined with negation. Indeed, the with-negation principle enables one to recognize that a concept is what it is because it is not something else. Accordingly, knowledge about any group of concepts must begin by understanding what they are not. . . .

Conclusion

Concept formation in organizational science research is important because concepts are meaning-laden classifications that serve as building blocks of science. Yet organizational science, a developing field consisting of management scholars who are interested in the study of organizations, has devoted little attention to concept formation issues. As a result, "misformed" concepts prevail. The imprecise nature of these concepts has added to our field's lag in development as a science. For example, the theories and theoretical propositions that are built upon our concepts are "not so useful" (Miner 1984), because of their "limited applicability" (Fry and Smith 1987) and "internal validity" problems (J. Greenberg 1987; Mitchell 1985). Besides, the search for traveling concepts inadvertently becomes a concept-stretching endeavor that produces concepts that are universals only in name, because they are supraempirical; they are too philosophical to be empirically observed or tested.

Indeed, precise organizational concepts are not only possible but also necessary if organizational science is to progress. Further, precise organizational concepts are possible not only at the low level of abstraction but also at the middle and high levels as well. Thus, this work may be viewed: first as a plea that more organizational researchers confront concept formation issues in organizational science, and second, as a proposal and point of departure for minimizing concept misformation, particularly the concept-stretching difficulty, in organizational research.

Characteristics and Difficulties of Settings
by Thomas Bouchard Jr.

Given the context in which this chapter appears it would seem to be unnecessary to spend time justifying the use of field methods as a means of studying human behavior. Yet, it is necessary because field researchers have not developed adequate intellectual justification for their role among either their experimental or applied colleagues. The experimentalist disparages field research and calls for rigor while the applied practitioner ridicules the sterility of the laboratory and calls for relevance. The field researcher finds himself hard put to meet one demand without sacrificing the other. Thus his dilemma. In our opinion creative field research should constitute a synthesis of these apparently conflicting demands. How is this to be done? By testing as rigorously as possible in the field setting the relevance and generality of laboratory-derived concepts. Consider the following example.

In 1941, Barker and his colleagues (R. G. Barker, Dembo and Lewin 1941) conducted a laboratory experiment which was to become known to almost every student who would subsequently take a course in the behavioral sciences. They found that the frustration of children leads to regressive behavior. More than twenty years later, as part of a field study, a student of Barker's analyzed the records of children's everyday behavior. He reported (Fawl 1963):

> The results . . . were surprising in two respects. First, even with a liberal interpretation of frustration fewer incidents were detected than we expected. . . . Second . . . meaningful relationships could not be found between frustration . . . and consequent behavior such as . . . regression . . . and other theoretically meaningful behavior manifestations (p. 99).

This example illustrates the different kinds of knowledge that can be obtained by the two types of studies, the different conclusions they may lead to, and the inherent limitations of each. The laboratory study clearly demonstrated a causal link between frustration and aggression. The field study demonstrated that the phenomenon had very little generality and helped specify the conditions under which the law held (e.g., when the child was forced to remain in the noxious setting and his potential repertoire of responses was so limited that he could not turn to a new class of activities). It also told us something about the frequency of frustrating events in the environment: they were far more infrequent than expected. More than anything

Source: "Field research methods" by Thomas Bouchard Jr., in *Handbook of Industrial and Organizational Psychology*, ed. Marvin D. Dunnette, 363–368 (1976). Used with permission of Marvin D. Dunnette.

else, this example shows us that a workable theory of human behavior will consist not only of a series of if-then laws, but will also contain numerous boundary specifications.

Laboratory experiments seldom deal adequately with boundary conditions or context factors and, therefore, lend themselves to unjustified and often erroneous extrapolations (cf. Berlyne 1964; Chomsky 1968). Field settings, on the other hand, allow us to explore boundary conditions in ways which may serve to enhance or delimit laboratory findings and thereby increase our understanding of the various lawful processes under investigation by both types of researchers (McGrath 1964).

Special Characteristics of Field Settings

Each of the factors to be discussed below is a special characteristic of field settings which is either unavailable or extremely difficult to manipulate in laboratory settings. They are the primary factors a field researcher should be sensitive to and capitalize on in the course of conceptualizing, designing, and carrying out a field study.

The first three—intensity, range, and frequency and duration—are boundary factors. Their greater magnitude in field settings often allows a researcher to explore and perhaps specify the form and limits of a relationship just as a physical scientist specifies a melting point, a boiling point, etc. The analogy to the physical sciences can be pushed further. Just as the point at which a material changes state is of great theoretical interest in the physical sciences, the point at which a behavioral function changes dramatically is of great interest to behavioral scientists. For example, the point of disobedience in the Milgram (1965) studies was characterized by a variety of symptoms of great theoretical, as well as practical, interest. The next three factors, natural time constants, natural units, and complexity, are context or structural factors. They are important features of the natural environment that the experimentalist typically destroys in order to study a phenomenon under controlled conditions. The last two factors, setting effects and representativeness, while not strictly advantages of only field settings, allow the field researcher to ask and test broader kinds of questions than are often asked in the laboratory.

Intensity

An important independent variable may display a range of intensity in the field that could not be generated in the laboratory because of ethical and other restrictions. Firings, layoffs, demotions, and transfers can produce levels of stress that would be unethical for an experimenter to simulate in a laboratory setting. Yet, they occur with great frequency in the world of work.

Range

Phenomena in the field often show a far wider range of variation than could be simulated in the laboratory. Cross-cultural studies can often extend the range even further (Roberts 1970; Udy 1962, 1965; Whiting 1968). Examples that come to mind are: group size, span of control, degree of centralization, complexity, and time span of discretion. Laboratory studies cannot study even in principle the effects of some physical spaces (cf. Sommer 1969).

Frequency and Duration

Laboratory studies encompass a relatively short time span. Human beings have the capacity to buffer wide ranges of stimulation when exposed to them for only short periods (Block 1968; Sommer 1968), and experiments may simply fail to provide conditions which cross the response system threshold. Thus, an effect may be shown in the field, but not in the laboratory. Trigger effects are also related to the threshold problem. A small stimulus (trigger) may elicit an effect if predisposing stimuli have occurred repeatedly or for long periods of time.

Natural Time Constants

System theorists (Berrien 1968; Buckley 1967) have sensitized researchers to the fact that some phenomena have natural life spans and that the temporal structure of events is often critical to the outcome of particular manipulations (cf. Savas 1970). Only field studies allow us to study long temporal structures and to search for natural time units.

Natural Units

The field setting is not passive. "Intrinsic orders exist 'out there' and . . . these regularities will organize and drive events even though our theories take no notice of them" (Gutman 1969, 162). The field researcher is in a position to seek natural units of behavior, units which occur in conjunction with particular environments. R. G. Barker (1968, 1969) calls these eco-behavioral entities (cf. J. G. Kelly 1969; Menzel 1969).

Setting Effects

Studies conducted in certain settings are highly likely to have different outcomes in other settings. Hovland (1959) has suggested that setting effects probably have a strong influence on studies of attitude change. For example, subjects might be open to influence in an educational context, but be much harder to influence in other contexts. This is a simple interaction effect. It is not absurd to assume that there are many higher-order interactions. Field settings are extremely complex. A large number of forces are at work in any given situation. Some of them may be powerful, but subtle and hidden from an observer who does not have an understanding of the antecedent events. Self-selection may have populated the setting only with individuals who have demonstrated a capacity to adapt to the influence of the variable under study. Field settings are open and dynamic in the sense that individuals are continually moving in and out of them.

Thus, a relationship found at time T_1 may not be found at time T_2. All of these factors threaten the validity of any interpretation of an event. Thus, if an effect can be shown to hold in both the lab and the field it can be considered robust and generalizable. Failure to demonstrate an effect in the field should lead a researcher to suspect (among other things) a treatment X organismic variable interaction due to self-selection, the existence of avoidance or neutralizing mechanisms, or a more powerful main effect due to uncontrolled variables that masks the expected relationship.

Representativeness

While laboratory studies are reasonably strong on representativeness of subjects (e.g., $N = 10$ or more) they are notoriously weak on representativeness of treatments (Feldman and Hass 1970; K. R. Hammond 1954). A conceptual variable and its empirical realization are not the same thing. Many psychological processes have been demonstrated using only one experimental manipulation. Given the complexity of social-psychological manipulations, a failure to observe an expected effect in the field can be considered a threat to the interpretation of an analogous laboratory study. An example of this problem is the risky-shift phenomenon.

The conceptual variable—tendency of an individual to make riskier decisions in a group than as an individual—had been operationalized in most early studies with only one instrument, the choice dilemma questionnaire. What had appeared to be a striking but simple phenomena became complex when additional measures of the conceptual variable were introduced (Dion, Baron, and Miller 1971; Clark 1971; Vinokur 1971).

Each of the points discussed above illustrates why we must be careful in extrapolating from the small amount of rigorous and carefully worked-out experimental knowledge generated in the laboratory. Indeed there are strong grounds for arguing that with respect to practical issues of wide social concern it is perhaps better to extrapolate or generalize from data gathered in field settings, even if direction of causation remains unknown, than to make use of principles based on rigorously conducted laboratory studies (Meehl 1971; Willems and Raush 1969). This is not to imply that scientific knowledge and rigorous procedures should not be used when they are applicable (S. W. Becker 1970; Bouchard 1971; D. T. Campbell 1969), but rather to emphasize that the context of discovery has hardly been mined while the context of justification has been overburdened with trivial investigations (cf. Argyris 1968; McGuire 1967; Ring 1967).

Special Difficulties with Field Studies

The points discussed below are meant to alert the field researcher to the kinds of problems which make it difficult to conduct field studies or draw valid inferences from them. The list is not exhaustive, but is rather selective.

Causal Ambiguity

The study of groups subsequent to their arrival in a situation usually makes it impossible to determine the direction of causation when relationships between variables are found. Kornhauser (1965), for example, compared the mental health of workers at different job levels and found that workers in the lower-skilled jobs were in poorer mental health. He concluded that their occupational situation caused this condition. A plausible alternative explanation is that there is a social class difference (Dohrenwend and Dohrenwend 1969), perhaps mediated by genetic factors (Goldberg and Morrison 1963; R. J. Turner and Wagenfeld 1967). The same error underlies the argument of many of those who favor job enlargement because "simplified jobs lead to poorer mental health." The argument may be correct, but correlational studies will never confirm or deny it. Similar interpretive problems plague all studies which contrast groups at different levels of the occupational hierarchy. Hulin and Blood (1968) present an excellent analysis of this particular problem.

A number of researchers have suggested that some of the problems caused by self-selection can be handled by specialized sampling procedures, matching, or covariance analysis (cf. Scott 1965; Price 1968b). These procedures are very likely to result in systematic unmatching (Meehl 1970). For example, a researcher may be interested in the relationship between the size of an organization and the personality characteristics of managers. He knows that managers in large organizations have higher IQs than do managers in small organizations so he matches high-IQ managers in small organizations against managers in large organizations. Unfortunately, the managers of small organizations are no longer representative of the population in which the researcher is interested. They lack what Brunswick (1956) called ecological validity (see also Feldman and Hass 1970). The contrast is between managers of small organizations with high IQs versus unselected managers of large corporations. Such a contrast does not yield data with any generality. Note also that a covariance design is mathematically identical to the matching design and does not overcome the problem, nor does the use of a large number of covariates (Meehl 1970). Meehl (1970) has concluded "that the ex post facto design is in most instances so radically defective in its logical structure that it is in principle incapable of answering the kinds of theoretical questions which typically give rise to its use" (p. 402).

$N = 1$

Many field studies involve only one organization or subject. While the one-case study is generally sterile scientifically (D. T. Campbell and Stanley 1966) it need not be (Dukes 1965; Davidson and Costello 1969; Edgington 1972; Forehand and Gilmer 1964). Carefully documented cases which make use of standard instruments may be useful as part of a cumulative record. Data collected in a single case may be compared with previously reported data on the same or different cases. Variation in the performance of one case as a function of environmental variation may be so systematic and regular as to make all alternative interpretations implausible. A well-chosen single case may seriously threaten a traditionally accepted hypothesis. The single case may also represent the sampling of a response to a rare, extreme, and unique event and thereby improve ecological sampling. Brunswick (1956) has argued that "In fact, proper sampling of situations and problems may in the end be more important than proper sampling of subjects, considering the fact that individuals are probably on the whole much more alike than are situations among one another" (p. 39).

We do not advocate the use of $N = 1$ except in exceptional circumstances. The judicious choice of contrasts is still our most powerful methodological strategy (D. T. Campbell and Stanley 1966; Platt 1964), but research in organizational psychology is in its infancy and the role of tacit knowledge (Polanyi 1958) is large.

Cost — Time — Money

Field work of any sort is expensive. With the development of sophisticated instrumentation and more extensive and powerful research designs, it will get even more expensive (R. G. Barker 1968, 1969; Sells 1966; Schwitzgebel 1970). One major complaint about field studies is the high-dross rate. That is, a great many "irrelevant" events occur and are recorded before something significant happens and, therefore, much time and money is supposedly spent for very little useful information. We consider this an unwise argument. The fact that important events are rare has been shown to have profound theoretical and empirical implications (Dyck 1963; Fawl 1963; Gump and Kounin 1960). In R. G. Barker's (1969) terms "data that are dross for one investigator are gold for another" (p. 39). There is every reason to believe that social science research of any significance is going to get more expensive, not less (Deutsch, Platt and Senghaas 1971), and it is time to destroy the myth of social science research as cheap.

In summary, field research, like any other enterprise, is beset by both pitfalls and advantages. However, its advantages put it in the position of being the place where the generality, applicability, and utility of psychological knowledge are put to the test. The role of the field researcher is thus an important one from the standpoint of both social utility and scientific advance. His work can enhance the usefulness of scientific theory for applied work and counter erroneous extrapolation and generalization at the theoretical level. The field researcher is the mediator of a relevant social-psychological science.

The Representativeness of Phenomena
Thomas W. Lee

In the larger world of social science, conceptualization and measurement of economic, sociological, and psychological constructs are universally accepted as playing key roles in the judgment of the quality of research (Blalock 1982; Nunnally 1978). In the smaller world of organizational science, the closely related ideas of reliability and validity have been similarly accepted as critical to the evaluation of research (Schwab 1980). Although management researchers consider the concepts of reliability and validity to be important, there is a very real dichotomy between qualitative and quantitative researchers in how they apply these concepts. . . .

Any study's conceptualizations, measurement processes, and interpretations should be chosen carefully and systematically, and should be *representative* of the phenomena of interest. The clarification of the utility of these concepts is critical to the expansion of the application of qualitative research in organizational science and to the blending of qualitative and quantitative designs. . . .

Traditional Views on Reliability

In its simplest meaning, *reliability* refers to the consistency and stability of "scores." These scores are assumed to result from some "measurement process." *Consistency* is most often thought to mean repeatability. If one

Source: *Using qualitative methods in organizational research* by Thomas W. Lee, 145–157, 168–170. Copyright © 1999. Reprinted by permission of Sage Publications, Inc.

were to replicate a certain hypothetical measurement process numerous times, for example, consistency would be demonstrated if the obtained scores occurred within some acceptable margin of error. *Stability* is most often thought to mean the obtained scores' consistency over time. Furthermore, these scores can represent a continuous, finely calibrated, and random variable (e.g., job satisfaction). Alternatively, these scores can represent the presence or absence of some categorical state, condition, or class (e.g., a CEO's staying or leaving). Between continuous and dichotomous variables, scores can also represent the ordering of categorical states (e.g., employees' salaries arranged in increments of $10,000). The measurement process can take the form of a standard, off-the-shelf, well-researched paper-and-pencil attitude instrument; of observations made during an ethnography of some employees' experiences; of the videotaping of verbal comments made during an interview; and so on.

In a more technical meaning, *reliability* refers to the strength of the shared systematic variance, usually conceptualized as some statistical association, between a theorized entity (e.g., a latent trait from a structural equation model) and an overt indicator of that theorized entity (e.g., scores resulting from a measurement process). Psychometricians often describe this shared variance (or association) through the theories of true and error scores, domain sampling, or "true scores and parallel tests" (Ghiselli 1964, 218–251; Ghiselli, Campbell and Zedeck 1981, 195–222). Despite these formal, theoretical approaches to understanding reliability, similar conclusions are reached for definitional formulas and for their corresponding empirical estimates (e.g., user-friendly formulas). In other words, the more formal definitions and various theoretical approaches produce similar empirical estimates of reliability. For example, coefficient alpha usually assesses the internal consistency of scores, and test-retest coefficients usually assess the scores' stability over time. It is important to emphasize that the standard conceptualization of reliability (i.e., shared variance indexed by a statistical association) can be applied to scores obtained from, for example, numerically based standard paper-and-pencil tests, researchers' recorded interpretations made during intensive participant observer studies (i.e., field notes), or the verbal comments of interviewees. Note that each of these techniques constitutes a measurement process, and its outcomes can be taken as "scores."

Some level of confusion may occur when reliability is thought to apply to the measurement procedures themselves, rather than to the scored outcomes from these measurement procedures. Reliability does *not* apply to the data gathering methods themselves—to observations or interviews per se, or to standard paper-and-pencil job attitude instruments. Reliability *does* apply to the *properties of the scores' inferences*. Conceptually, then, it is quite appropriate to ask whether scores (e.g., interviewees' comments elicited by a researcher; observations recorded via field notes) from a qualitative study are consistent (e.g., repeatable under hypothetically identical or highly similar conditions) and stable (e.g., a researcher's interpretation of an employee's social construction of the firm's political situation remains relatively constant over time, presuming the situation itself also stays relatively constant). Whereas it would not be appropriate to conclude that a given survey instrument is reliable, it would be appropriate to conclude that the empirical estimates of reliability indicate reliable properties of the resulting scores. . . .

Comment

It is important to reiterate that *reliability* refers to the shared systematic variance between a researcher's phenomenon of interest and its scored measurement. As one part of judging the quality of any study, the strength and nature of that conceptual association should be considered. I have suggested above that reliability is sometimes mistakenly interpreted as being interchangeable with its empirical estimates. As a result, it can *appear* that traditional notions of reliability do not apply to qualitative research. I would argue that reliability is a universally meaningful concept in the evaluation of both qualitative and quantitative organizational research.

Traditional Views on Validity

Whereas reliability is defined as the total amount of shared systematic variance, which includes any systematic error (or bias), validity is often defined as the shared "true" variance between an underlying concept and its empirical scores. In particular, true variance is defined to exclude systematic bias and to include only the "theoretically meaningful" systematic variance between an underlying idea and its overt representations. Thus, theory, some system of logic, or a clear specification for a focal concept is critical in determining what is and what is not true variance. Moreover, *true variance* can refer to a continuous relationship or a dichotomous association. In more exploratory, inductive studies, which seek to identify an underlying construct or process, validity remains a meaningful concept. The presence of validity would certainly be more difficult to infer and to document, however, because its theoretical basis would be less developed.

Based on the traditional psychometric definition, there is only one kind of validity. Accordingly, management researchers should strive to study true variance, both qualitatively and quantitatively. (These definitional relationships allow for the old—and correct—adages, "Reliability sets an upper bound to validity" and "Scores can be no more valid than their reliability.")

Although most formal presentations conclude that validity concerns explaining (or understanding) the shared true variance between an underlying concept and its manifest indicators, most descriptions imply various kinds of validity. Somewhat akin to mixing the conceptual definition of reliability with its empirical estimates, the implication of multiple kinds of validity reflects the erroneous mixing of a single conceptual definition—widely accepted as shared true variance—with its various empirical indices. Although it may appear to be only a semantic issue, there is substantial utility in defining one kind of validity that has multiple, though imperfect, forms. Whereas certain forms of validity may indeed not fit a given qualitative study's context or analytic situation, the larger concept of validity—shared true variance—holds merit for all management studies.

Below, the common forms of validity are summarized. . . .

Criterion-Related Validity

Evidence for criterion-related validity may be established if a statistical association is demonstrated between a predictor variable and some meaningful criterion. Most commonly, the statistical association is indexed by a Pearson product-moment correlation coefficient, but other statistics could be applied just as well (e.g., point-biserial correlation).

Two issues arise. First, it is *assumed* that the criterion itself is already reliably measured and meaningful. The criterion can be theoretically meaningful or deemed intrinsically valuable, as is often the case, for example, with job performance, accident rates, and absenteeism. Second, the predictor variable can be measured either before or simultaneous with the measurement of the criterion. If the predictor is measured before (at Time 1) the criterion (measured at Time 2), the design is called *predictive validity*. If the predictor and criterion are measured simultaneously, the design is called *concurrent validity*. Note that in order for comparable inferences to be drawn from predictive and concurrent validity designs, strong assumptions must be made that the effects of employees' natural maturation and job experience are unimportant or have already occurred. In sum, the inference of criterion-related validity is based on an empirical relationship.

Content Validity

Instead of the term *content validity*, some authors prefer to use the alternative label *content-oriented test construction*. As that name implies, evidence for this form of validity may be established if the procedures followed in constructing a measure (often called the test plan) are judged to derive "clearly and in a compelling fashion" from a meaningful conceptual domain. In contrast to the empirical orientation of criterion-related validity, the inference of content validity is based on the *qualitative judgment* that (a) the conceptual domain, (b) the test plan designed to map that conceptual domain, and (c) the resulting measurement instrument overlap substantially.

Empirical data about reliability, item difficulty, and population norms can facilitate the judgment, but content validity is an essential qualitative judgment about content coverage.

Convergent and Discriminant Validity

Evidence for convergent validity may be established if scores from several measurement procedures that purport to measure the same (or very similar) concept are "highly" correlated. That is, scores from multiple measures of the same (or very similar) concept should converge. In contrast, evidence for discriminant validity may be established if scores from several measurement procedures that purport to measure different concepts are uncorrelated. Scores from multiple measures of different concepts should diverge. Scores from different measurement procedures for different concepts should diverge even more. In addition, there should be some indication that the convergent (or highly correlated) scores meaningfully differ from the divergent (or weakly correlated or uncorrelated) scores. Although exploratory or confirmatory factor analysis can clarify matters, it is ultimately a matter of qualitative judgment as to what constitutes sufficient convergence and sufficient divergence.

Construct Validity

In perhaps its most abstract form, construct validity is a continuous, ongoing process of accumulating evidence that suggests scores from a measurement procedure reflect its intended construct. In other words, do scores actually measure what a researcher claims they do, and not something else? As such, construct validity subsumes all the forms of validity discussed above, and the argument can more readily be made that there is only one kind of validity, albeit with many forms.

Although a continuous, ongoing process of accumulating evidence, construct validity can be established only through the presentation of a substantial body of data. Nonetheless, when "sufficient evidence" has been accumulated remains a subjective judgment. Some recent examples are illustrative. Mowday, Steers, and Porter (1979) define the conceptual domain for their construct of interest, organizational commitment, and carefully describe the procedures they used in constructing their measurement instrument. They then present data from nine samples of employees that support judgments for internal consistency, test-retest reliability, convergent validity, discriminant validity, and predictive validity. In similar fashion, Pierce, Gardner, Cummings, and Dunham (1989) define the conceptual domain for their construct of interest, organization-based self-esteem, and carefully describe their test construction procedures. They then present data from seven studies and empirical evidence that supports judgments for internal consistency, stability over time, convergent validity, discriminant validity, incremental validity, predictive validity, and concurrent validity.

In a somewhat different fashion, Van Dyne, Graham, and Dienesch (1994) attempt to redefine, measure, and validate their construct of interest, organizational citizenship behavior. These researchers carefully describe their construct domain, measurement procedures, and theory-based hypotheses about the construct's "nomological network" (a set of theoretically relevant variables). Across six independent data sets, they report evidence suggesting internal consistency, test-retest reliability, and the empirical relationships between organizational citizenship behavior and the set of theoretically relevant variables.

Across these three examples, it should be noted that the central issue is not whether construct validity was demonstrated. Rather, the key issue is the qualitative judgment that sufficient evidence has been gathered for construct validity to be demonstrated.

Generalizability and Other Forms of Validity

Primarily from experimentally oriented research, *internal validity* refers to the judgment that an experiment's procedures are sufficient to justify rejection or provisional acceptance of its hypotheses. For example, if an experiment's focus is on work effort, does the experimental task in fact reflect the effects of effort, and not some alternative factor (e.g., prior experience)?

External validity refers to the judgment that an experiment's results can be generalized to a larger population or to an alternative population. For instance, does the experiment's random sampling of college students allow generalization of the study's results to the larger U.S. workforce?

Although less often seen, *ecological validity* refers to the judgment that a study's or an experiment's features include or reflect the major features of the context in which the phenomenon of interest is found. Whereas the absence of these features implies ecological invalidity, their presence implies ecological validity. For example, if interest centers on when a firm decides to sell a new retail product, does the study's design features include the major contextual characteristics that surround those decisions (e.g., Staw, Barsade and Koput 1997)? Because of its heavy emphasis on context, as well as its judged importance, ecological validity is particularly important to the evaluation of most qualitative research.

Comment

It cannot be overemphasized that *validity* refers to the shared true variance between a researcher's phenomenon of interest and its scored measurement. As another part of judging the quality of any study, the strength and nature of that conceptual association should be considered. Akin to reliability, validity is sometimes mistakenly taken to be interchangeable with one (or more) of its forms. As a result, it only appears that traditional views on validity do not apply to qualitative research. Again, I would argue that the concept of validity is universally meaningful to the evaluation of both qualitative and quantitative organizational research.

As suggested above, there are numerous empirical estimates of reliability and validity. Although heavily influenced by these empirical estimates, as well as accompanying rhetorical arguments, decisions about reliability and validity ultimately rest upon the researchers' and readers' judgment about sufficient or systematic true variance between an underlying notion and its objective indicators. . . .

Conclusion

Both qualitative and quantitative researchers look for and evaluate various signs of their studies' soundness. Nonetheless, there is a mistaken idea among many management scholars that these signs are fundamentally different for both groups. The focus of this chapter has been that these signs are in fact very similar. It is sometimes said, for example, that quantitative researchers adopt a proactive view, whereas qualitative researchers adopt a reactive view. More specifically, the former attempt to control for error statistically or experimentally, whereas the latter attempt to account for or explain away error. In fact, all organizational studies involve proactive and reactive concerns about error. Both camps endeavor to anticipate problems and eliminate them before they occur, and both try to identify problems before, during, and after data collection and to discount their significance.

A few qualitative researchers hold that social construction of organizational life is so pervasive that agreement among participants is negligible. As a result, consistency, stability, and shared systematic variance between an idea and its manifest observations are so inherently slight that traditional notions about reliability and validity, though nice ideas, do not hold value for their research. The world changes too quickly, it is too subjective, and everyone socially constructs differently. This extreme position is somewhat comparable to that of those few quantitative researchers in management who dogmatically hold that the vast preponderance of laboratory research is irrelevant and that only field studies are meaningful. Under such an extreme view, discussion about reliability and validity in qualitative research may indeed seem pointless. Moreover, those qualitative researchers who hold such an extreme view would appear constrained to describe individual circumstances and precluded from the traditional scientific goal of accumulating knowledge. From a certain point of view, these researchers would also seem precluded from "doing organizational science." That is, they appear restricted to journalistic accounts of organizational life. Though potentially insightful, their work would not be science as defined by the larger managerial discipline, common definitions of science, or standard practice.

Finally, it should be acknowledged that determinations about reliability and validity are inherently judgmental. Moreover, what signs are judged may appear to differ between qualitative and quantitative studies, but their basic content is the same. Researchers' judgments are not restricted to qualitative studies and precluded from quantitative research. Any study's conceptualizations, measurement processes, and interpretations should be judged as carefully made, systematically addressed, and representative of the study's intended underlying construct (or idea or theory).

Ultimately, the burden falls on the organizational researcher to present a compelling case for the reliability and validity within his or her study. In particular, the researcher should design into the research project as many checks and tactics as practically feasible. Moreover, it is imperative that some discussion of the results of these checks be included in any qualitative research report. In the absence of such text, discourse, or discussion, such a research report may not merit journal space. . . .

Breaking Up the Mono-Method Monopolies
Joanne Martin

During the last ten years, efforts have been made to improve the breadth and quality of empirical approaches to the study of organizations (e.g., Burrell and Morgan 1979; Van Maanen 1979; Mitroff and Mason 1982; Hackman 1982; Morgan 1986). Partially in response to such efforts as these, organizational researchers are discussing methods and methodology more openly than before. Often, one of two positions is argued. The first, a simple mono-method argument, proposes that one type of method is generally better than another. The second, a complex mono-method approach, argues that one type of method is better than another for the purpose of addressing a particular theoretical issue. Because these two positions have been advocated frequently, this chapter explores both seriously.

After some introductory definitions, this paper presents versions of the simple and complex mono-method approaches. Each of these one-sided positions is then rebutted. In conclusion, a more complex alternative is proposed—the methodological chameleon.

Source: "Breaking up the mono-method monopolies in organizational analysis" by Joanne Martin, in *The Theory and Philosophy of Organizations*, edited by John Hassard and Denis Pym, 30–33, 38–43. First published in 1990 by Routledge. Copyright © 1990 by John Hassard and Denis Pym. Used with permission of the publisher.

Qualitative vs. Quantitative: A False Dichotomy

In order to discuss these issues, labels are needed to describe the different types of methods available. In order to facilitate discussion of previous work, this paper uses the terms quantitative and qualitative.

The label quantitative is used here to refer to methods that primarily seek to express information numerically—in terms of amounts or counts. To use Daft's terminology, quantitative methods rely on low variety research languages, such as analytic mathematics (e.g., calculus, dynamic equilibrium models), linear statistics (e.g., correlations, regressions), and categorization (e.g., frequencies, percentages, cross-tabulations) (Daft 1980, 623–4). Although associating the label "quantitative" with specific techniques can sometimes be misleading, statistical analyses of experimental, survey, and archival data are generally considered quantitative.

Qualitative methods, according to Van Maanen, are best defined in terms of axiom-like beliefs of the researcher (e.g., the importance of detailed observation; first-hand witness; studying normal, ordinary behaviour; sensitivity to meanings and contexts) (Van Maanen, Dabbs and Faulkner 1982, 16). Qualitative methods rely on high-variety research languages, such as verbal expression (e.g., open-ended interviews, reports of observations) and non-verbal modes of communication (e.g., photographs, videotapes, illustrations). A broad variety of specific techniques are used in a qualitative way, including participant observation, videotaping, formal and informational interviewing, ethnomethodology, historical and conversational analysis.

Two caveats should be noted in order to avoid the confusion often associated with these labels. First, some methods are difficult to classify. For example, some kinds of qualitative data can be counted and texts can be systematically content-analysed (e.g., E. J. Webb et al. 1972; Downey and Ireland 1979). Thus it is essential to conceptualize the qualitative *vs.* quantitative distinction not as a dichotomy, but as a continuum, with mixed methods at the midpoint of the scale. Secondly, these definitions are not meant to imply that quantitative research is objective, while qualitative research is subjective. Any research—whether qualitative or quantitative—must include subjective elements.

Arguments about the relative merits of method choices are often phrased in terms of the inherent superiority of qualitative—or quantitative—types of methods. The next section of this paper describes two common forms of these arguments: the simple mono-method approach and the complex mono-method approach. Quantitative and qualitative versions of each of these arguments are described. Although these arguments have been elaborated and enacted by the practicing researchers in more moderate and complex terms, this chapter uses extreme examples in order to clarify and highlight the essences of these positions.

The Simple Mono-method Approach

This position is mono-method in that it considers well-executed quantitative methods to be inherently superior to well-executed qualitative methods or vice versa. It is simple because that superiority is said to hold across a broad spectrum of organizational research questions. There are currently quantitative and qualitative versions of the simple mono-method approach.

The Quantitative Version

According to this point of view, well-executed quantitative methods are seen as superior to well-executed qualitative approaches, irrespective of the topic being studied. An example is Blau's influential critique of the case-study approach to organizations (Blau 1965). In order for knowledge of organizational phenomena to expand, Blau argued that researchers should collect quantitative data from large numbers of organizations, rather than focus qualitatively on a single setting. The prevalence of this point of view is demonstrated by the steady increase in the proportion of quantitative papers accepted by the *Administrative Science Quarterly* between 1959 and 1979 (Daft 1980).

Because this position dominates the field, it is usually not necessary to state it explicitly. Instead, the quantitative version of the simple mono-method approach usually remains a tacit assumption, the truth of which need not be explicated to those who are already true believers. It surfaces primarily when newcomers are being indoctrinated (as in some methodology textbooks) and when someone has the temerity to use qualitative methods.

The Qualitative Version

Because the organizational field is dominated by quantitative methods, qualitative researchers are often asked to, or feel it helpful to, defend their unorthodox method choices. Understandably, some of these discussions are one-sided arguments for the superiority of qualitative over quantitative methods, as if the point were, "My method is better than your method."

These defenses often begin by extolling the advantages of qualitative approaches, citing for example the richness of the data, the strengths of a holistic approach that eschews decompositions, and the ease with which contradictions and paradoxes can be explored. A classic example of the qualitative version of the simple mono-method approach begins, "Although questionnaires and interviews have their value, systematic observation has a number of advantages for organizational analysis. . . ." (Light 1979, 552).

Some proponents of qualitative research take their argument one step further by denigrating quantitative research. Those who take the stance that reality is a socially constructed phenomenon are particularly likely to express discontent with all forms of quantitative methods: "The large-scale empirical surveys and detailed laboratory experiments that dominate much social research . . . become increasingly unsatisfactory and, indeed, inappropriate" (Morgan and Smircich 1980, 498).

As these examples illustrate, some proponents of the simple mono-method position sound like lawyers presenting one side of a case. They catalogue the merits of their preferred method and the demerits of the unchosen alternatives, as if it would be unintelligent to give the opposition (such as a critical editor, reviewer, or reader) ammunition by admitting the strengths of the opposite point of view. This contentious approach to methodological discussions reinforces the simple mono-method position and makes it less likely that adherents of this approach will appreciate research findings obtained using non-preferred methodologies. Thus, the simple mono-method approach impedes the sharing of knowledge about organizational phenomena.

The Complex Mono-method Approach

Many theoretical problems are characteristically addressed with either quantitative or qualitative methods. For example, a review of articles published in key organizational journals during the last decade yielded a list of sixteen frequently studied topics (J. P. Campbell, Daft, and Hulin 1982). Most of these topics were addressed predominantly with one or more quantitative methods. Studies of macro-level issues, such as organizational structure, technology, and size, generally relied on archival data. Goal-setting and expectancy theory were usually studied using experimental laboratory methods. Surveys were the preferred mode of assessing job attitudes. In contrast, organizational culture is usually studied using qualitative methods (e.g., Jelinek, Smircich and Hirsch 1983).

The complex mono-method position justifies these observed affinities between substantive areas and method choices by arguing that quantitative or qualitative methods are better for addressing particular kinds of theoretical problems . . . [like the] study [of] culture. This . . . example was chosen because methodological disagreements are surfacing in this domain. Similar disputes, however, have focused on other substantive issues, such as decision-making, organizational symbolism, and cognitive approaches to the study of organizations. . . .

The Research Dilemma: Inevitable Trade-offs

McGrath presents a systematic analysis of the inevitable trade-offs that underlie the choice of any one method (McGrath 1982). He examines eight "pure" or idealized techniques: laboratory experiments, experimental simulations, field experiments, field studies, computer simulations, formal theoretical exercises, sample surveys, and judgment tasks. While some of these techniques fall on the "mixed" or "variable" midpoint of the qualitative-quantitative continuum, others are defined by McGrath in terms that are clearly quantitative (such as laboratory experiments) or qualitative (non-experimental field studies). Each of the eight techniques is classified according to the extent to which three criteria are maximized: controlled and precise measurement of behavior, generalizability across subjects and detailed knowledge of contexts.

McGrath argues that method choices which maximize any one of these criteria will necessarily minimize the other two; and that the choices that would "optimize" on any two will minimize on the third. For example, non-experimental field studies, as defined by McGrath, are as unobtrusive as possible. They take place in settings that are existentially real for participants. Thus, realism of context is maximized, at the cost of precision and generalizability. In contrast, laboratory experiments involve deliberately contrived settings. Realism of context and generalizabilily are sacrificed in order to maximize precision of measurement. Although space limitations make it impossible to summarize the rest of McGrath's analysis of the trade-offs involved in method choices, these two examples illustrate his fundamental conclusions—any method has inherent weaknesses; no method is perfect. Moreover, one method's strengths are another method's weaknesses.

If method choices do have complementary strengths and weaknesses, the simple and complex mono-method positions are misguided. The simple version ignores the weaknesses of the preferred method and does not allow the accumulation of knowledge to benefit from the strengths of the non-preferred methods. The complex mono-method position suffers from similar problems. If research on any one topic, such as culture, relies on any one method, such as ethnography, the inherent weaknesses of the method will cause blindspots in knowledge about that topic. Thus, both the simple and the complex mono-method positions inhibit the development of knowledge.

These conclusions have implications for the behavior of researchers. First, the simple mono-method approach should be discarded. One-sided "my method is better than your method" discussions are oversimplified and, to the extent that they are persuasive, are dangerously misleading. The complex mono-method approach is equally misleading, although within the narrower constraints of a single topic area. It too should be abandoned. Instead, multiple methods should be used to address topic areas, so that the weaknesses of one method would be compensated for, over time, by the strengths of other methods. Multi-method approaches have been frequently advocated and, less frequently, practiced. If the argument above is correct, it is important to understand why such eminently sensible practices are avoided. . . .

Triangulation and Hybrid Methods

Perhaps the most familiar of the multi-method techniques is triangulation. According to classic definitions, a successful triangulation study uses different methods to come up with the same answer to a single theoretical question (cf. D. T. Campbell and Fiske 1959). McGrath's analysis suggests a different, perhaps equally desirable, outcome. Because different methods must address somewhat different aspects of a problem, they will yield divergent answers. Rather than invalidating each other, such conflicting results may offer insight into different aspects of the problem.

Even if researchers see the risk of divergent results as a desirable outcome, there are a number of practical reasons why they may avoid triangulation. It is conceptually and technically difficult, time consuming, and costly (cf. Jick 1979). Even when these problems are resolved, it is often impossible to publish the results in a single journal article, so that discrepant findings can be discussed in the context of detailed information about the methods used. Journals have stringent space limitations and, in a few cases, have well-developed preferences for either quantitative or qualitative methods. Thus, the hard-earned insights gained from triangulation are often buried in a footnote which begins, "A survey concerning these issues was also administered . . . ."

Advocates of triangulation often stress the advantages of selecting "pure" methods which are as different as possible (e.g., Runkel and McGrath 1972). A second multi-method approach uses a quite different strategy. Rather than using several different methods, the researcher develops a hybrid method which has a blend of strengths and weaknesses uniquely suited for addressing a specific topic.

Because organizational researchers must be able to relate the results of their work to what goes on in organizations, they have developed a variety of hybrid techniques. For example, laboratory experiments have used full-time employees as subjects, adapted stimulus materials from organizational archives, and structured the experimental context to approximate subjects' normal working environments (e.g., Fox and Staw 1979; Salancik 1978; Staw and Ross 1980; Zucker 1979). Materials from a qualitative observational study of culture have been used to create a standardized survey, designed to assess systematically knowledge of, and commitment to, some aspects of an organization's culture throughout all levels of the institution (Siehl and Martin 1984). Unobtrusive measures and systematic sampling procedures have been used to integrate quantitative techniques into the traditionally qualitative case-study approach (D. T. Campbell and Stanley 1963; E. J. Webb et al. 1972; McClintock, Brannon and Maynard-Moody 1979; Van Maanen, Dabbs and Faulkner 1982). . . .

Hybrid methods such as these involve trade-offs, because some advantages of the "pure" forms of these methods are sacrificed. It is often difficult to make these choices, particularly if the trade-offs are to be uniquely suited for addressing a specific problem. Even if the choices can be made appropriately, to the researcher's satisfaction, others must also be convinced. In addition to these difficulties, there are broader reasons why multi-method approaches are often avoided. These are discussed below.

Garbage Cans and the Scarcity of Multi-method Competence

Researchers who choose triangulation or who develop hybrid methods are making method choices in a well-reasoned, self-conscious manner. In accord with the procedure described in research textbooks these researchers are defining a theoretical problem and then letting the nature of that problem dictate their careful choice of an appropriate method. However the sequence of research decisions described in the textbooks may not be an accurate description of how researchers actually make method choices.

Instead, the research decision-making process may resemble the garbage can model of managerial decision making (M. D. Cohen, March and Olsen 1972), so that the sequential assumptions of the research textbook model are suspended (Martin 1982). Instead of theoretical problems always dictating the choice of a method, method choices may be determined by the availability of resources, the preferences or limited skills of a researcher, or even the likelihood that particular results may be found. Indeed, the textbook sequence may be reversed, so that methodological preferences dictate what theoretical problem is studied. For example, some of the projects of Michigan's Institute for Survey Research, such as the Detroit Area Study, can be characterized as a method (survey) in search of a theoretical problem to address.

There is considerable evidence that the garbage can model is more accurate than the textbook model in its portrayal of how method choices actually are made (e.g., E. J. Webb and Ellsworth 1975; Ellsworth 1977; T. D. Cook and Campbell 1979; Knorr 1979; McGrath, Martin and Kulka 1982). If this is so, it may be very difficult to convince researchers to make method choices in the complex, well-reasoned, self-conscious manner that is a prerequisite for the multi-method approaches advocated above.

A second difficulty is that triangulation and, to a lesser extent, hybrid methods require that a researcher becomes a jack-of-all-trades, adept in several different methods. Most researchers are adequately trained in one, or at best a few, methods. Multi-method approaches may require changes in skills and attitudes that are unlikely, perhaps impossible.

Methodological Chameleons

There is another alternative. Researchers could become more appreciative of, and more able to judge the merit of, studies in their field of interest that use unfamiliar or non-preferred methods, so that the results of these studies could be integrated into their own work. Researchers could learn to be tolerant of different methods, coming to prize and encourage divergent conclusions that emerge from divergent method choices. This open-minded stance is rare. Even in an openly interdisciplinary, multi-method field such as organizational behavior, theoretical integration of results obtained using different methods is proceeding in a slow, crude and inefficient fashion (Roberts, Hulin and Rousseau [1978]).

Methodological open-mindedness may be rare because some people feel that a complex or simple mono-method position is the only intellectually honest alternative—that one method is, in fact, superior. This tendency may be particularly strong among those who believe in a single epistemological point of view and feel that point of view justifies a simple or complex mono-method approach to research (Burrell and Morgan 1979). All too often, methodologies are discussed as if they were scientific religions—each one labeling itself the one true faith.

Methodological—and perhaps even epistemological—conflicts could be overcome by drawing from existentialism. As atheists, the existentialists disavowed belief in all ideologies except that which asserted that no ideology was valid. Regarding the void left by the absence of any kind of faith, existentialists felt themselves faced with a brutal choice: to commit suicide or to act as if they believed in something. Those that chose the latter alternative often aspired to act in accordance with some of the ethical principles of religious ideologies, even though they had discarded some of the basic premises of religion, such as a faith in God (cf. Camus 1948; Hartt 1963).

It is possible to take an "existential" approach to method choices by admitting that no alternative is free of flaws or inherently superior to the others. The researcher who believes this is faced with a choice. He or she could stop doing research, or he or she could continue to do research within the constraints of a quantitative or qualitative preference, but with full awareness that those constraints have no monopoly on truth; alternative types of methods may well be equally valid (and equally invalid).

A researcher who adopts this position would be a methodological chameleon. While conducting a study, the researcher would act like—perhaps even temporarily become—an advocate of one of the mono-method positions. When reading completed studies, even his or her own, the researcher would evaluate the results with the skepticism of a methodological atheist, with no belief in the supremacy of any mono-method position. In this state of mind, the existential methodologist could draw on research results using any well-executed method.

The image of a chameleon may not capture the quality and intensity of commitment required by this existentialist stance. It is exceedingly difficult to adopt an existential approach to research. We seem to need to believe in the superiority of the method we use, perhaps because otherwise we might have to question the worth of doing research at all. Like religious faiths, mono-method justifications are comforting, making multi-method-appreciators, if not practitioners, an all-too-rare phenomenon.

Breaking Up the Monopolies

In our efforts to improve the breadth and quality of empirical studies of organizations, researchers have begun to invest more time and energy in discussing methodology. This is good. Unfortunately, the tone of that discussion has, all too often, taken the form of a one-sided justification of a given method choice: either a simple or a complex version of a mono-method argument.

This chapter argues that we should refrain from this type of argument and, instead, actively work to break up mono-method monopolies. The difficulties inherent in this task should not be minimized. Methodological existentialists are rare, in part for the understandable reasons outlined above. These problems are exacerbated by the difficulties of designing and publishing triangulated studies, inventing effective hybrid methods, and overcoming the lack of self-consciousness that is often inherent in the garbage can approach to making method choices.

Nevertheless, if we could overcome these difficulties, the benefits of breaking up the mono-method monopolies would be considerable. As individual researchers, we would have a better understanding of the phenomena we study. If we could—in our own research or in our reading—draw on the insight of a variety of quantitative and qualitative studies, our theories might be less riddled with blind spots caused by mono-method monopolies. Expanding and deepening our knowledge of organizations is, after all, the business we are in, and there are those who would argue that breaking up monopolies is good for business.

Issues with Self-Reports
Philip M. Podsakoff and Dennis W. Organ

A casual inspection of published research in organizational behavior or management shows the self-report to be well-nigh ubiquitous as a form

Source: "Self-reports in organizational research" by Philip M. Podsakoff and Dennis W. Organ, *Journal of Management* 12 (1986): 531–536, 541–542. Copyright © 1986 by the Southern Management Association. Reprinted with permission of the Southern Management Association.

of data collection (cf. Dipboye and Flanagan 1979; Gupta and Beehr 1982; Mitchell 1985; Sims 1979). Coincident with ubiquity, however, is the apparently widespread suspicion that self-report methodology is the soft underbelly of the organizational research literature (cf. J. P. Campbell 1977). It seems that organizational researchers do not like self-reports, but neither can they do without them. On the assumption that self-reports are here to stay, a dispassionate assessment of this research procedure is needed.

Concern about the problems of self-report research is—or at least should be—shared by practitioners in management or staff positions. Many of the findings disseminated to the management community draw from self-report research. In addition, managers rely heavily on their own self-report research in employee opinion surveys, program evaluation, and human resource planning.

The authors have themselves struggled over the years with the dilemma posed by use of self-reports in organizational research. From the beginning, we were aware that the questionnaire, at best, provides "soft" data, perhaps better than mere opinions with no data at all, but vastly inferior to most other kinds of data. The problem is more serious in some instances than in others, at times so serious that findings are rejected out of hand. But many organizational research issues stubbornly resist reformulation in terms of other approaches. Those who recommend carrying the research into the laboratory and manipulating the variables of interest do, of course, have the textbooks of scientific method on their side, but such a strategy often seems to change profoundly the very nature of the issue that prompted our interest in the first place.

Therefore, like many researchers, we have found ourselves in the position of having to use self-reports while knowing that this invited serious problems. The sensible approach seemed to be to either reduce the magnitude of the problem as much as possible, or, failing that, to assess the problems inherent in the data. But no structured guide exists for using self-reports in the most defensible fashion. In our own research, we have tried a number of devices in more or less trial-and-error style, seeking as we went along a more clearly defined notion of just what the relevant problems were, how to relate them to the broader context of research problems, how to measure them, and how to deal with them. We believe that an account of our odyssey, however insufficient as a researcher's guide, may nonetheless begin constructive discussions of the issue. . . .

Uses of the Self-Report

The uses of self-reports for data gathering break down roughly into the following categories:

1. Obtaining demographic or otherwise factual data (such as age or sex of respondent, years of tenure, etc.), that are, in principle, verifiable from other sources.
2. Assessing the effectiveness of experimental manipulations.
3. Gathering personality data (trait anxiety, need for achievement, locus of control, and so forth).
4. Obtaining descriptions of a respondent's past or characteristic behavior (e.g., asking supervisors about their "structuring" behaviors), and/or seeking respondents' intentions of future behavior (e.g., to quit), or how they would behave under certain hypothetical conditions (i.e., various role-playing exercises).
5. Scaling the psychological states of respondents, such as job attitudes, tension, or motivation.
6. Soliciting respondents' perceptions of an external environmental variable (the supervisor's behavior, formalization of organizational processes, climate).

Problems That Arise

The categories identified above are not mutually exclusive in every case and probably not exhaustive, but they offer a basis for preliminary discussion. Of the six categories noted, the first two appear to offer the least difficulty. Demographic data obtained by self-reports are usually independently verifiable from other sources; often the data can be checked in the aggregate or against archival information. Moreover, although persons may report erroneous information, the practical problems so posed seldom offset the convenience and economy of collecting such data by self-reports (Gupta and Beehr 1982). In any case, self-report items designed to gather such data are often included because the commitment has already been made to use self-reports for other types of variables.

Manipulation checks basically provide reassurance to the experimenter and his/her colleagues that the independent variable "registered"; otherwise they seldom figure importantly in the conclusions drawn from the research.

Categories 3 through 6 present greater problems. Self-report measures of such variables are, in the strictest sense, not verifiable by other means. There may well be other better measures of such variables, but there is no direct means of cross-validating people's descriptions of their feelings or intentions. Only in the most limited cases—as when we ask someone how many days he or she has been absent, or how many grievances he or she has filed—can the answers be verified, even in the aggregate.

What soon becomes obvious upon examining Categories 3 through 6 is that when using self-reports to scale such variables, we are generally not asking people to report a specific fact or a finite event. We are asking persons to go well beyond that and to engage in a higher-order cognitive process—a process that involves not only recall but weighting, inference, prediction, interpretation, and evaluation. Many times during a brief interval, we are requiring the respondents to work at a fairly high level of abstraction. Thus, the data we obtain are already quite a few steps removed from the level of discrete stimuli and responses.

Nonetheless, despite the rarified form of response to a scale measuring a personality, environmental, or attitudinal variable, the result is still a measure. If the use of this measure is to correlate it with some other measure derived by some other means, the only real problem is establishing the validity of the self-report measure. In principle, this is true of any measure, and there are a variety of methods by which to adduce evidence of validity. For example, the validity of a self-report measure of job characteristics can be established if it discriminates among officially graded job levels, the training or intelligence of people who perform such jobs, or the ratings of such jobs by independent experts. (On the whole, however, our research community has probably been somewhat negligent in documenting validity evidence of self-report measures, particularly with respect to discriminant validity; Schwab 1980).

The most severe problems arise when measures of two or more variables in Categories 3, 4, 5, and 6 are collected from the same respondents and the attempt is made to interpret any correlation(s) among them. This is the well-known problem of *common method variance* (D. T. Campbell and Fiske 1959; D. W. Fiske 1982). Because both measures come from the same source, any defect in that source contaminates both measures, presumably in the same fashion and in the same direction. The problem is not eliminated by evidence of validity. One measure may be shown to correlate highly with alternative indices of its referent and the other measure may likewise be shown to correlate with what it should correlate with. But the correlation between the two measures, when both are obtained from same-source self-reports, need not include any variance common to both of their domains (see Figure [13-3]). Thus, a self-report measure of job characteristics and a self-report measure of job satisfaction may each overlap with the variance in their respective domains. But that does not guarantee that the overlap in variance of the measures themselves, when taken from the same sources, includes any of the overlapping variance they share with their referent domains. The correlation could erroneously lead us to infer a substantive relationship.

Thus, the most critical problem in the use of self-reports is identifying the potential causes of artifactual covariance between self-report measures of what are presumed to be two distinctly different variables. When the same persons provide us with self-report measures of two or more different constructs, what could account for any correlations we find, other than a real underlying relationship?

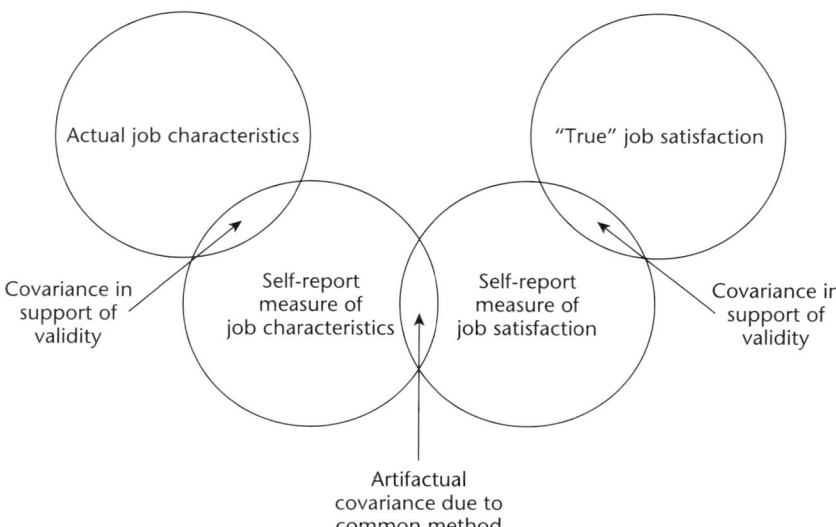

FIGURE **13-3**   **Problem of common method variance.**   Although the measures of job satisfaction and job characteristics can both be shown to have validity (in the sense of overlapping with their intended domain), the overlap between the measures themselves does not ensure that the domains of interest are interrelated in a substantive sense.

SOURCE: "Self-reports in organizational research" by Philip M. Podsakoff and Dennis W. Organ, *Journal of Management* 12 (1986): 534, fig. 1. Copyright © 1986 by the Southern Management Association. Reprinted with permission of the Southern Management Association.

Perhaps the most general problem is the *consistency motif*. That is, given what we know from decades of research on cognitions and attitudes, respondents apparently have an urge to maintain a consistent line in a series of answers, or at least what they regard as a consistent line. This creates problems because, first of all, many people have lay theories of how personality, behavior, psychological states, and organizational environments are interrelated (Eden and Leviatin 1975; Lord et al. 1978; Phillips and Lord 1986; Staw 1975). This would be less of a problem if we were asking people to report discrete events, the perception and recall of which are less vulnerable to distortion. But in self-report research, we often ask for summary judgments. When we do so, we are inviting respondents to array their judgments consistent with prevalent lay theories (e.g., the relationship between leader style and group morale).

Furthermore, research by Chapman and Chapman (1967, 1969), Jenkins and Ward (1965), and Berman and Kenny (1976) shows that even the most astute subjects are prey to illusory correlations when exposed to a series of events. Not only do respondents have lay theories about how organizational phenomena ought to be related, they also overestimate the strength of the empirical relationships they have observed between classes of events. Perhaps this is because they do have lay theories; confirming cases are given disproportionate weight in overall impressions and are the most likely to be recalled.

Aggravating the consistency motif problem is the fact that self-report measures of different variables are often found to contain items similar in content. That is, a scale purporting to measure job satisfaction may refer to considerate treatment from the supervisor, and another measure given to the same person may ask questions designed to measure the supportiveness given by the supervisor. Little wonder that respondents will answer consistently to what are essentially the same questions from different scales.

Note that the most frequently studied topics within Categories 3, 4, 5, and 6 contain matters about which organizational participants, as well as researchers, are likely to have fairly strong sentiments. Few people are indifferent to how leaders behave, how the job is designed, or how much stress they experience. How a person reports on such matters can obviously be affected by his or her mood, whatever its cause (e.g., a bad night's sleep, a cold, rainy weather, tax time approaching). Thus, when we obtain self-report measures from a person at one sitting for several variables, there certainly is the risk that transient mood state will contribute a consistent but artifactual bias across the measures.

Most researchers who contemplate the use of self-reports have heard of the *social desirability* problem (cf. Arnold and Feldman 1981; J. B. Taylor 1961; K. W. Thomas and Kilmann 1975), so labeled because questionnaire items may prompt responses that will present the person in a favorable light. To the extent that this problem causes only an upward shift in the distribution of responses, it is not a serious concern, at least in the interpretation of correlations involving the scale. Even if the effect of socially desirable responses were to compress the range of responses around the end of the scale, the damage would occur mainly in the attenuation of correlations (because of restricted variance in scale scores).

Unfortunately, the social desirability problem goes further than merely adding bias to the responses. Not only are some responses to some items more socially desirable than others, certain reasons for responses are also more ego flattering than others. Thus, suppose I answer a self-report measure of stress by indicating that I experience severe job-related tensions. I am apt to respond to other items that implicate poor supervision, irrational policies and procedures, incompetent subordinates—as opposed, perhaps, to my own inability to work constructively with others or my own lack of planning. Social psychological research in self-attribution (cf. Mitchell, Green and Wood 1981) has clearly shown that we are not indifferent to the reasons we ascribe for our failures or our problems.

Answers to two sets of self-report items may also display artifactual co-variation because the behavior of responding is, to some extent, under the control of various cues in the stimulus setting. These cues may be quite subtle, even to the extent that the respondent is unaware that they affect his or her behavior. For example, if the subject responds to items in two or more scales while at work in the middle of the afternoon, his or her responses could be influenced by a report he or she has just read or written, a prior conversation, or hunger. The problem here is not the effect of such stimuli on responses to any one scale taken by itself; any measure, self-report or otherwise, will pick up some irrelevant variance. The problem is that such stimuli could affect responses to two or more different scales in the same fashion, resulting in a potentially misleading correlation. And lest the reader think we have descended to the nittiest nitpicking, remember that our research thrives on correlations in the .20–.40 range, when found statistically significant. Therefore, systematic overlapping variance of 4%—not very much—can give misleading signals. . . .

Summary and Recommendations

The following recommendations are offered for future research using self-report measures. These recommendations represent an ordering of the procedures that we feel should be used.

1. Ideally, researchers should obtain multiple measures of the conceptually crucial variables from multiple sources using multiple methods. (Conceptually crucial variables are those whose functional relationship is central to theoretical interpretation of the study.) Using structural equation modeling techniques, researchers could assess the relationships among the variables with and without common method variance (CMV), and therefore increase our knowledge of the effects of this phenomenon.
2. If it is not possible to obtain all of the conceptually important variables from multiple sources, researchers should attempt to obtain the independent and criterion variables from different (i.e., procedurally independent) sources, thus avoiding the potential confounding effects of CMV.
3. If conceptually appropriate, data should be aggregated to a larger unit of analysis, using part of each unit to estimate the independent or predictor variable and another part to estimate the criterion or dependent variable. (Even if aggregation is conceptually appropriate, within- vs. between-groups analysis of variance may be necessary to demonstrate that the aggregation process is justified.)
4. If all subjects have to be used for all measures, conceptually crucial variables should be taken at different times, preferably with different scaling formats and in different settings.

5. The scale trimming procedure should be employed to eliminate obvious overlap in items on the independent and criterion measures scales.
6. Failing all else, researchers should at least report results from a test of the single-factor hypothesis as an explanation of the inter-correlation of the variables of interest. The results of such a test cannot be interpreted unequivocally, but may provide a useful note of information to the reader.

Observer Effects
Robert Rosenthal

In a recent experiment conducted by John Laszlo, three experimenters conducted the same basic experiment in person perception employing a total of 64 subjects. In this study, all three experimenters made computational errors. For the most accurate experimenter, 6 percent of his computations were in error. The other experimenters erred 22 and 26 percent of the time. The magnitudes of the errors were quite small, but for all three experimenters, a majority (75 percent overall) of the errors tended to favor the experimental hypothesis, though the frequency of these biased errors did not reach statistical significance. In spite of the apparent regularity of the occurrence of such errors, little attention has been given to real or alleged numerical errors in the scientific literature of psychology (Hanley and Rokeach 1956; Wolins 1962).

Conceptualization of Observer Effects

. . . By "observer effects" or "observer error" we have referred to over-statement or understatement of some criterion value. When two observers disagree in an observation, each may be said to err with respect to the other. Both may be said to err with respect to some third observation which may, for various reasons, be a more or less usefully employed criterion. Given a population of observations, we may choose to define some central value (such as the mean or mode) as the "true" value and regard all observations not falling at that value as being more or less in error as a direct function of their distance from the central value.

Observer errors or effects may be distinguished from observer "bias" by the fact that observer errors are randomly distributed around a "true" or "criterion" value. Biased observations tend to be consistently too high or

Source: *Experimenter Effects in Behavioral Research* by Robert Rosenthal, 13–15, 305–308, 401–402, 407–410. Copyright © 1966 by Meredith Publishing Company. Used by permission of the author.

too low and may bear some relation to some characteristics of the observer (Roe 1961), the observation situation (Pearson 1902), or both.

In considering the act or sequence of acts constituting the observation in the scientific enterprise, we may distinguish conceptually among locations of error or bias. The error of "apprehending" occurs when there is some sort of misrecording between the event observed and the observer of the event. We may include here such diverse sources of apprehending error as differing locations of observers (Gillispie 1960) or angles of observation (George 1938), imperfections in the sensory apparatus, central relay systems, cortical projection areas, and the like. The error of recording may be distinguished conceptually from the apprehending error. In the case of recording error, we assume first an errorless act of apprehending followed by a transcription of the event (to paper, to the ear of another observer, or to another instrument) which differs from the event as correctly apprehended. In actual practice, of course, when an event or observation is recorded in error with respect to some criterion, we cannot locate the error as having occurred either in apprehending, in transcribing, or in both processes. There is no certain method for isolating an apprehending error unconfounded with a recording error, though introspective reports may be suggestive. . . .

Finally, throughout this chapter the assumption has been made that the classes of errors discussed occurred without the intent of the observer. . . .

The Control of Observer Effects

A powerful, necessary, though insufficient, tool for the control of observer error is our awareness of the phenomenon. The role of various mechanical apprehenders and recorders in the reduction of observer error has been noted earlier. As Boring (1950) pointed out, these mechanizations do not replace the human observer; rather they postpone human observation to some other, more convenient time and circumstance of reapprehension and rerecording. If mechanization reduces observer error—and it very likely does—there remain still subsequent errors of "re"-observation. . . .

The most critical control of observer error is probably woven into the fabric of science by the tradition of replication. Frequent replication of observations serves to establish the definition of observer errors. It does not, however, eliminate the problem, since replicated observations made under similar conditions of anticipation, instrumentation, and psychological climate may, by virtue of their intercorrelation, all be in error with respect to some external criterion (Pearson 1902). . . . Perhaps the great contribution of the skeptic, the disbeliever, in any given scientific observation is the likelihood that his anticipation, psychological climate, and even instrumentation may differ enough so that his observation will be more an independent one. Error, in the sense of discrepancy, will then have a greater chance of being revealed. Which of two contradictory sets of observations will be regarded as error-free depends on sets of criteria subsequently adopted by the assessing community. . . .

The Generality and Assessment of Experimenter Effects

As behavioral scientists, what should be our reaction to the evidence presented in this book? Three different reactions to the presentation of some of the data from this book have actually been observed: (1) the *incredulous*, (2) the *gleeful*, (3) the *realistic*. The *incredulous* reactor (who may not have read this far) feels vaguely that all of this is just so much nonsense and that if it is not completely nonsense, at least it does not apply to him. The *gleeful* reactor (who may have read this far, but may read no further) has "known all along that experiments in the behavioral sciences were riddled with error." He does not do or like empirical research. He is gleeful because, paradoxically, he reads into the experimental evidence presented in this book his justification for his epistemology that knowledge of the world comes through revelation rather than observation. After all, if observation is subject to observer influence, is he not justified in his eschewal of observation? The *realistic* reactor (and the choice of terms is intentionally positively evaluative) has read this far more or less critically and has wondered a bit whether some of his own research might have been affected by his own expectancies or more enduring attributes.

Much of what follows is for that reader who, although skeptical by training, is not incredulous; who, although interested, is not overdeterminedly gleeful; who, although reminiscing about his own research, is not contemplating giving up the scientific enterprise. It is for the reader who agrees with Hyman and his co-authors (1954) when they say: "Let it be noted that the *demonstration* of error marks an advanced state of a science. All scientific inquiry is subject to error, and it is far better to be aware of this, to study the sources in an attempt to reduce it, . . . than to be ignorant of the errors concealed in the data" (p. 4). . . .

One type of experimenter effect, that of his hypothesis or expectancy, has received our special attention in this book. For this special case of experimenter effect we can sketch out the evidence bearing on the question of its generality. . . . Does any of the work reported, then, have any real relevance to the "real" experimenter? The *gleeful* reactor mentioned earlier may too quickly say "yes." The *incredulous* reactor may too quickly say "no." In his discussion of the generality of interviewer effects, Hart (obviously a *realistic* reactor) put it this way:

> Generalization of our conclusions to researchers of greater maturity and sophistication than these subjects has to be made, therefore, with due and proper caution. It would be dangerous, however, though consoling,

for the mature and sophisticated interviewer to assume that he is not equally subject to the operation of the same error-producing factors affecting the varied group of interviewers covered by the studies we are here reporting. As a matter of fact, the available evidence suggests that, while the sophisticated interviewer may be less subject as variable errors of a careless sort, he is probably equally subject to certain biasing errors (1954, pp. ix–x).

Indeed we can go further than Hart. If anything, our data suggest fairly strongly that more professional, more competent, higher status experimenters are more likely to bias the results of their research than are the more amateurish data collectors. . . .

Earlier we asked the question of the generality of the effects of the experimenter on the results of his experiment. We are now in a position to conclude, at least for one type of experimenter effect (that of his hypothesis or expectancy), that the phenomenon may well be a fairly general one. This conclusion seems warranted by the variety of experimenter, subject, and situation or context domains sampled and by the fact that expectancy effects have been shown to occur in other than experimental laboratories.

Conclusion

The social situation that comes into being, when an experimenter encounters his research subject is one of both general and unique importance to the social sciences. Its general importance derives from the fact that the interaction of experimenter and subject, like other two-person interactions, may be investigated empirically with a view to teaching us more about dyadic interaction in general. Its unique importance derives from the fact that the interaction of experimenter and subject, *un*like other dyadic interactions, is a major source of our knowledge in the social sciences.

To the extent that we hope for dependable knowledge in the social sciences generally, we must have dependable knowledge about the experimenter-subject interaction specifically. We can no more hope to acquire accurate information for our disciplines without an understanding of the data collection situation than astronomers and zoologists could hope to acquire accurate information for their disciplines without their understanding the effects of their telescopes and microscopes. For these reasons, increasing interest has been shown in the investigation of the experimenter-subject interaction system. And the outlook is anything but bleak. It does seem that we can profitably learn of those effects that the experimenter unwittingly may have on the results of his research.

. . . A variety of suggestions have been put forward which show some promise as controls for the effects of the experimenter in general and for the

TABLE 13-1
Strategies for the control of experimenter expectancy effects

1. Increasing the number of experimenters:
   decreases learning of influence techniques
   helps to maintain blindness
   minimizes effects of early data returns
   increases generality of results
   randomizes expectancies
   permits the method of collaborative disagreement
   permits statistical correction of expectancy effects

2. Observing the behavior of experimenters:
   sometimes reduces expectancy effects
   permits correction for unprogrammed behavior
   facilitates greater standardization of experimenter behavior

3. Analyzing experiments for order effects:
   permits inference about changes in experimenter behavior

4. Analyzing experiments for computational errors:
   permits inference about expectancy effects

5. Developing selection procedures:
   permits prediction of expectancy effects

6. Developing training procedures:
   permits prediction of expectancy effects

7. Developing a new profession of psychological experimenter:
   maximizes applicability of controls for expectancy effects
   reduces motivational bases for expectancy effects

8. Maintaining blind contact:
   minimizes expectancy effects

9. Minimizing experimenter-subject contact:
   minimizes expectancy effects

10. Employing expectancy control groups:
    permits assessment of expectancy effects

SOURCE: *Experimenter Effects in Behavioral Research* by Robert Rosenthal, 402, table 24-1. Copyright © 1966 by Meredith Publishing Company. Used by permission of the author.

effects of his expectancy in particular. In Table [13-1] these suggestions are summarized as ten strategies or techniques. . . .

Expectancy Effects in Everyday Life

The concept of expectancy has been of central importance for many psychological theorists (e.g., Allport 1950; G. A. Kelly 1955; Rotter 1954; Tolman 1932), and A. P. Goldstein (1962) has reviewed the role of expectancy as a construct of interest to psychologists. Expectancy as a determinant of behavior has most often been investigated with an eye to learning the extent to which an individual's expectancy might determine his own subsequent behavior. The construct of expectancy as employed in this book has been more specifically interpersonal. The question, for us, has concerned the extent to which one person's expectancy of another's behavior might serve as determinant of that other's behavior.

In everyday life people do have expectations of how others will behave. These expectations usually are based on prior experience, direct or indirect, with those other people's behavior. Scientist and layman seem agreed that predictions of future behavior are best based on past behavior. If this assumption were untenable there would be no behavioral sciences. If past behavior were unrelated to future behavior, then there could only be the humanist's interest to prompt us to study behavior, not the scientist's. But if expectations are only based upon history how do they influence future events?

It is unpleasant to have one's expectations disconfirmed, though that is not always the case. An unexpected inheritance need not lead to negative feelings. But often it is more pleasant to have one's expectations confirmed than disconfirmed. The evidence for this comes from experiments in which the expectancy is of an event that will befall the "expecter" (Aronson and Carlsmith 1962; Carlsmith and Aronson 1963; Festinger 1957; Harvey and Clapp 1965; Sampson and Sibley 1965). The "expecter" seems to behave in such a way as to confirm his expectancy about what will befall him or how he will act (Aronson, Carlsmith and Darley 1963). It seems to be not too great an extension to think that if one's expectancy is not of one's own behavior but of another's, one will also behave in such a way as to influence that other to behave in an expected way. Whatever its basis, whether to achieve greater cognitive order, stability, predictability, or to maintain cognitive consonance (Festinger 1957), there appears to be a motive to fulfill one's interpersonal expectancy. . . .

The fact that there appear to be two components to the accuracy of interpersonal predictions, hypotheses, or expectations has implications for research methods in expectancy effects. If we simply ascertain people's expectations of others' behavior and correlate these with the others' subsequent behavior, the two components of experiential accuracy and self-fulfilling accuracy will be confounded. If we take the appropriate safeguards, however, we can eliminate the self-fulfilling accuracy component (as in asking people to "predict" behavior that has already occurred). We can also randomize the experiential accuracy component by "assigning" expectancies at random, and that is the strategy adopted in much of the research described in this book. What we do not yet know, and what is worth the learning, is the magnitude of expectancy effects, of the self-fulfilling type, in important everyday social interactions. . . .

The complexity and subtlety of the communication of one's expectancy of another's behavior to that other is well emphasized by reference to that experiment in which expectancy effects were transmitted from the experimenter through his research assistant to the subject (Rosenthal et al. 1963).

It appeared from that experiment that in the two-person interaction between subject and research assistant there was a nonpresent third party, the primary experimenter. This nonpresent other appeared to communicate his expectancy through the research assistant but without having simply made the assistant a passive surrogate for himself. The research assistant, while serving as a "carrier" for the nonpresent influencer, was still able to exert his own influence in an additive manner to the influence of the nonpresent participant. This interpersonal influence, once-removed, is no all-or-none phenomenon. The more a person is able to influence others subtly, the more effectively he is able to make other people carriers of his subtle, unplanned influence. How far this chain of subtle interpersonal influence can extend, complicating itself at each link, is not known, nor is the pattern of interpersonal communication of which the chain is woven. . . .

On Removing Measurement Bipolarity
Philip Bobko

What, incidentally, is the opposite of "democracy"? How about "aristocracy," "autocracy," "dictatorship," "people's republic"? (Pei 1978, 4)

There is an increasing awareness in organizational theorizing of basic philosophical premises and assumptions implicit in the collection and interpretation of organizational data. These assumptions often are prescientific stipulations about the nature of individuals or society (Israel 1972; Landy 1982). For example, the choice in studying individuals as biological organisms versus conscious, goal-directed entities is bound to affect scientific measurement and design, as well as consequent theoretical interpretations (Israel 1972).

The present concern is with implicit assumptions of bipolarity—both in measurement processes and organizational theory construction. Images of opposition, bipolarity, and thesis/anti-thesis are embedded in the fabric of Western scientific thinking (Capra 1975; Humphreys 1968; Taggart and Robey 1981). Answers are assumed to be "right" or "wrong;" organizations are assumed to be "highly structured" or "loosely coupled;" tasks are seen to be "creative" or "routine." Indeed, many psychometric scales are formatted and scored in bipolar fashion.

The present analysis attempts to demonstrate that the removal of assumptions of bipolarity can enhance the progress of measurement and theory construction in organizational science. . . .

As a preliminary example, consider the personality constructs of masculinity (M) and femininity (F), which initially were conceived as bipolar opposites. As such, measurement was employed with masculinity and femininity on the same scale, but 180° apart. A radical departure from this approach questioned the assumption that masculinity and femininity are necessarily negatively related (Bem 1974; Constantinople 1973). Subsequent research measured the two constructs on separate scales. This resulted in the emergence of a new construct: androgyny. Persons who could encompass both masculine and feminine attributes were labeled androgynous, and now androgyny is embedded in many personality networks. Current operationalizations of androgyny consider the interaction of M-F (the "congruence" of previously bipolar adjectives) and M + F (the "intensity" of total gender awareness) (Bobko and Schwartz 1984). In summary, the removal of traditionally held dualistic assumptions may pave the way for the emergence of new constructs and operationalizations of new measures.

In the organizational literature, Hickson (1966) indicated that theories on the structure of organizations repeatedly reduce to a bimodal pattern of role expectations: that is, high role specificity (or precision) versus low specificity. This results in a theoretical view in which "new ideas may be inhibited" and "a linear relationship between degree of role prescription and other behavior variables is almost universally taken for granted" (1966, 224). Hickson argues that an awareness of this bimodal convergence may refocus attention on "fresh ideas" such as role pressures, role ambiguity, and role conflict.

Research on optimal levels of worker participation suggests another example in which assumptions of bipolarity may have restricted theorizing. Early experiments in participation assumed a dimensionalization of authority that placed supervisor control and worker control in bipolar opposition (Tannenbaum and Schmidt 1958). As a result, the strategy for increasing worker participation was to take authority from the supervisor and give it to the workers—a zero-sum image of authority. In contrast, Sennett (1980) suggests that such constructions of authority conceal complex psychological dynamics and that more effective and humane authority relations may include more visible supervisory control, more acknowledged worker dependence, and more worker autonomy. Thus, subordinates perceive the greatest autonomy when they are most clear about which behaviors are to be controlled.

A Vector Analogue

Metaphorically, the notion of bipolarity may be conceptualized in a linear, unidimensional vector space. A concept (A) and its bipolar opposite (A_{opp}) may be represented as two vectors, separated by 180° (see

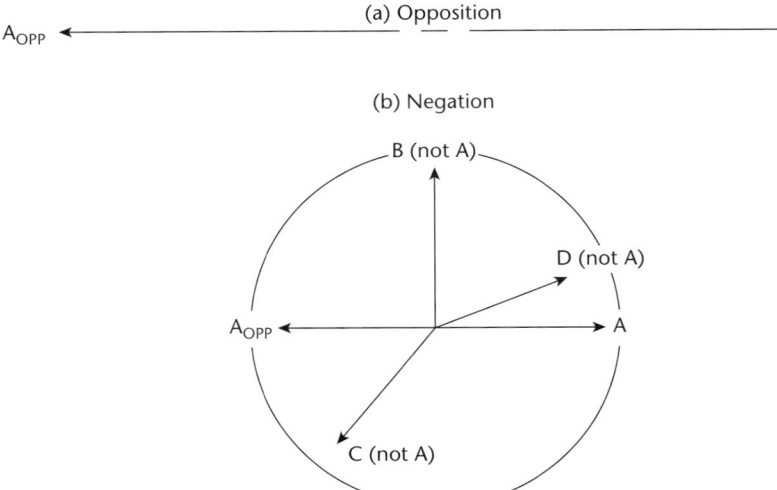

FIGURE **13-4**   Vector representations of opposition and negation

SOURCE: "Removing assumptions of bipolarity" by Philip Bobko, *Academy of Management Review*
10 (1985): 101, fig. 1. Copyright © 1985 by the Academy of Management. Reproduced with permission of the Academy of Management via Copyright Clearance Center.

Figure [13-4a]). However, this representation is rather myopic. For example,
all linear combinations of vectors A and A_{opp} will form a resultant vector
somewhere along the already existing one-dimensional horizontal line defined by A and A_{opp}. In order to break out of this confine, it is necessary to
introduce other constructs that are not A, but also are not the opposite of A,
say B or C (see Figure [13-4b]). By allowing other non-A points in addition
to A_{opp}, the pictorial representation is enhanced by moving from one to two
dimensions. In so doing, new constructs can be generated that have different
orientations from previous constructs (e.g., D as a resultant combination of
A and B). The crucial point is that the negations of A form a potentially
richer set of possibilities than the sole consideration of A and its bipolar opposite. In one sense, the forcing of responses in bipolar format is a form of
an "either-or fallacy" (L. Brown 1966) in the theory of logic. That is, one in-
duces a person to accept position A by having that person deny the opposite
of position A. This process is fallacious. It rules out (1) the possibility of
"non-A" being different from "opposite of A" or (2) the possibility of some
resolution/integration of A and the opposite of A.

   To complete the metaphor, let A and B represent nonbipolar representations of masculinity and femininity (see Figure [13-4]). Then the new combination D, which encompasses both masculinity and femininity, is labeled

androgyny. Or perhaps let A and B represent satisfaction and dissatisfaction, respectively. Then, the new orientation vector D may represent "total intensity surrounding work life" or some other construct integrating both satisfaction and dissatisfaction. For example, the high arousal pattern of extreme satisfaction and extreme dissatisfaction may provide an indirect measure of organizational commitment—a measure associated with high levels of caring and large expenditures of effort.

. . . Example: People and Production

As noted earlier, removal of the bipolar formatting of masculinity and femininity was a precondition for conceptualizing and measuring androgyny. Similar perspectives have been applied to Little's (1972) theory on the specialization of environmental experience. A central idea in this theory is that individuals are selectively attentive/oriented to two aspects of their environment: persons and things.

Both Little's original scales and current scaling revisions (Frost and Barnowe 1982) confirm the essentially orthogonal, nonbipolar relationship between orientations toward people and orientations toward things. These approaches therefore are adaptable to constructs that integrate "person" and "thing" orientations. By splitting each dimension at the median, a fourfold typology has been generated: thing specialists, person specialists, generalists, and nonspecialists. This discrete, four-level independent variable of cell membership has been related to managerial values (Drechsler et al. 1979) and students' decisions to major in business curricula (Barnowe, Frost, and Jamal 1979).

This approach to attitudes is remarkably similar to other two-factor orientations in organizational science: for example, the leader behavior dimensions of consideration and initiating structure (Fleishman 1967) or the dimensions of "concern for people" and "concern for production" in Blake and Mouton's (1964) managerial grid. In all cases, the break from bipolarity allows the emergence of integrative, holistic constructs. For example, the classic "9,9" cell of Blake and Mouton's grid has been equated with the construct of "team management". . . .

Conclusion

It has been argued that the removal of bipolarity enhances explanations of organizational phenomena from both metric and theoretical perspectives. In addition, attempts at overlaying bipolar constructs (for example, "true" versus "false") on self-referential statements lead directly to a lack of consistency. It is the very nature of humans, however, to reflect upon themselves, their organizational structures, and their social realities. Bipolar explanations and evaluations therefore will be inadequate representations of social theory, because they cannot logically capture the seeming paradoxes of self-exploration. As Mitroff notes, "Contradictoriness is one of the essential characteristic properties of man, groups, organizations, and institutions. An organization can be both big and small, weak and strong, beautiful and ugly, and so on all at the same time" (1983b, 393).

The removal of bipolarity allows a regained freedom to enhance knowledge about social and organizational structures. This enhanced knowledge will not add, in a linear sense, to previous results. Rather, as in the earlier example of androgyny, qualitatively new explanations will emerge. That is, the concept of androgyny is conceptually unrelated to someone being *either* masculine or feminine. Similarly, it may be too restrictive to ask whether a worker is satisfied or dissatisfied; whether a manager is concerned for people or production; whether an organization is concerned with quality or quantity. In a nonbipolar view, focus is on the inherent integration of these constructs: on the ability to tolerate job ambiguity; on the willingness to exercise integrative management; on the understanding that quantity and quality can be positively interdependent. The nonbipolar research attitude is holistic and complex. It focuses on interrelationships, not on discrete facts.

However, it is important to remember that *bipolar* explanations also have enhanced constructions of organizational phenomena. The present nonbipolar approach, by definition, cannot deny the potential utility of a bipolar system. Otherwise, the nonbipolar approach would be "guilty" of having a bipolar statement (about bipolarity). However, the nonbipolar system cannot deny the possibility of having a bipolar statement, and so on. Thus, a linear analysis of bipolarity versus nonbipolarity leads to vicious circles. Both perspectives need to be embraced by organizational science.

Summary

Since all research is data dependent, it goes without saying that data acquisition and data handling are very important steps in the research process. The criteria for selecting one or combining a few data acquisition methods, therefore, have to be based on the type, amount, and quality of data to be gathered. And, since no one method will be perfect for any research project, choice of method is always significant and always somewhat problematic. Thus the suggestion is for being methodologically open-minded, for employing more than one method when feasible or employing hybrid methods. Given the modest array of data acquisition methodologies utilized in the organization sciences, the field seems ripe for methodological innovation. Because of the large available literature detailing the usage of alternative data acquisition methodologies, this chapter has emphasized more basic considerations: how choice of methods will usefully reflect the properties of the concepts being investigated, and the settings where their data are acquired. In addition, we have brought attention to several (but certainly not all) features of methodologies that impede meaning-making from acquired data.

This chapter has also, hopefully, drawn needed attention to the importance of not only transforming the raw data acquired into a form that enhances its storage and retrieval, but turning it into research findings—the subject of the next chapter.

14   Data Sensemaking

The most exciting phrase to hear in science, the one that heralds new discoveries, is not "Eureka" (I found it) but rather "hmm . . . that's funny."

—*Isaac Asimov*

It is true that what serves as evidence is the result of a process of interpretation—facts do not speak for themselves; nevertheless, facts must be given a hearing, or the scientific point of the process of interpretation is lost.

—*Abraham Kaplan*

As noted several times in earlier chapters, the aim of serious inquiry is, ultimately, to improve theory through the creation of meaningful knowledge. Because data by themselves neither elucidate nor explain, we must work with them to find their meanings. This chapter focuses attention to the activities—analysis and interpretation—of making sense of data. While analysis is the ordering and assessment of data, analysis alone does not provide answers to research questions—interpretation of analysis is always required. Interpretation takes the results of analysis and makes inferences about the relationships studied to appreciate and explain them.

To wrest meanings from data—that is, to create meaningful new knowledge—is both social and technical. It is social simply because researchers do it—researchers with varying expertise, theoretical and subculture allegiances, and data sensemaking experience—and because knowledge is both produced in and reproduces human communities. Data sensemaking is technical in the sense that it is composed of a sequence of four general activities: data exploration (getting a feel for the data); examining the quality of the data (testing the goodness of the data); substantiating patterning by testing the relationships among the data (analysis); and seeking meanings and implications of the analyzed data by comparing results with the demands and expectations of theory (interpretation). Because these activities, just like all other aspects of inquiry, can be accomplished in alternative ways, many choices and trade-offs exist for the data sensemaking of the research process.

Data sensemaking begins with the researcher's doing some careful description and preliminary ordering of his or her data. The description of the data includes information regarding where the data was collected and who the respondents were, and an estimate is made about the representativeness of the phenomena that are being studied. The amount and type of data are also carefully described, and any data gaps or instances of skewed data are noted. Where feasible, the data are subjected to descriptive statistics: for each type of data—by variable if possible—a measure of central tendency, range, and dispersion is calculated.

Exploratory data analysis follows: the data is ordered, as feasible, by means of an intercorrelation matrix or by chronology, similarity, or contextual dependency. In all of this exploratory work, the researcher has to be alert to spurious relationships among the data, such as multicollinearity (independent variables are correlated), as well as to biases that arise from attending too closely to data collected early on, from having preferred data, or from formatting the data for presentation.

Data sensemaking next moves on to a two-part examination of data quality. First, the researcher asks how well the data represents the phenomena of interest, or how well the actual sample of data resembles the sample that emerging conceptualization or relevant theory demands. Then the researcher asks about the quality of the data themselves, examining their reliability and validity (for quantitative data depending, of course, on the number and types of variables, such as nominal, interval, or ordinal).

Data, we recall, are the factual information that reflect the conceptually related constructs of a research project. Testing the strength of these relationships (both those that emerge from the data and those inspired by some relevant theory) is the province of analysis. Analysis, in essence, provides an indication of whether some conceptually specified relationship exists in the data and how well it is confirmed by the data in hand. It probably goes without saying that analysis has to be systematic and thorough. For quantitative data, analysis is usually the statistical testing of the significance of hypothesized relationships. There are, at present, a large number of such tests, and new additions continue to appear. Qualitative data analysis requires repeatedly comparing and contrasting data, being ever alert to the time and place of their observation in terms of antecedents and consequences, dependence on surrounding context, and categorical similarity.

Data-supported relationships are typically referred to as research results or findings, but findings, like the data themselves, are just inputs to creating meaningful knowledge. Meaning creation requires interpretation, the final step of data sensemaking. Sometimes, although rarely, research findings are just described and are taken at face value and understood literally. Most often, however, research findings are rendered believable and general—they are given meaning—with mindful reference to context and theory. Data may be given meaning by referencing the context in which the data were collected or all other similar contexts and, theoretically, by referencing just the model or theory guiding the study, or competing theories about the same general phenomenon. Meaning is also typically sought by comparisons between one's own research findings and conclusions and those of other researchers. Interpretation often has an almost playful quality, at least initially, when metaphors and other heuristics are applied to suggest alternative meanings. Generalization, however, is necessarily done cautiously. Interpretive work is, like all data sensemaking, susceptible to several kinds of potential bias, such as simple overstatement, unconscious political agendas, and the overemphasis of positive findings.

Serious inquiry presumes that the task of a research project goes beyond acquiring data, noting patterns, and indicating the frequency and strength of patterned relationships. In the context of the organizational sciences meaningful findings are those that reflect, on the one hand, how people in organizations appreciate, view, and attribute meanings to their individual and collective experiences and, on the other hand, how some set of inquirers currently comprehends and explains the whats and hows of organizational life. In data sensemaking and in the selections in this chapter there are several points of thematic emphasis: sensemaking is more than the manipulation of data or numbers; sensemaking is always in some part socially constructed, never simply objective; sensemaking itself is evolving; and sensemaking will reflect the preferences of and allegiances to subcultures of inquiry practice.

In the first selection, Gergen and Semin remind us of a now familiar point: social scientists' understanding of their phenomena of interest is based on particular sets of assumptions. They also argue persuasively that, in the ways that they go about creating and talking about their understandings, scientists are neither special nor privileged in relation to those they study.

Chatfield, in the second selection, provides guidance for using statistical tools in data exploration, thus bringing needed attention to an early stage of data sensemaking that is all too often underappreciated.

Terence Mitchell's selection examines a popular type of organizational science study, cross-sectional correlational survey research, through the lens of a checklist of types of validation. His critique and suggestions for improving such research holds much useful advice for enhancing the analysis of related approaches.

The next two selections, both by psychologists, focus on statistical analysis. Rosnow and Rosenthal encourage us to be careful of which statistical tools we employ and to guard against using them unthinkingly as we justify our analysis. Labovitz's selection argues against slavishly using any conventional levels of statistical significance (for instance, the ubiquitous .05). In his selection he offers a number of criteria for selecting an appropriate significance level. In the final brief selection, Fred Kerlinger gently clarifies several general premises for the interpretative phase of data sensemaking.

Toward Understanding Scientific Understanding
Kenneth J. Gergen and Gün R. Semin

The focal concern . . . is with people's everyday understanding of the world, and more directly, their understandings of themselves and others. Yet, as we focus on this critical domain, it is also apparent that we as scientists are engaged in the very process that is central to our concerns. We are in the process of generating everyday understanding within the profession, and the results of our work may play a vital role in fashioning the future contours of life, both within the science and within the culture more generally. Thus a range of interesting and important questions present themselves. What is the status of lay understandings; how are they generated; how are they to be assessed; and how do they influence or insinuate themselves into science? Are the processes we as scientists hope to elucidate in the arena of daily life identical to those we employ within the science: If so, what does this say about the traditional advantage accorded to the scientist over the layman? If the processes are different, in what ways is this so, and what implications does this have for both science and social policy?

There are well-wrought answers to these questions that have emerged and become progressively sharpened over the years. A massive range of research has attempted to elucidate lay understandings. . . .

In many of these cases, the research places scientists in a clearly advantageous role; scientists function so as to elucidate the previously unarticulated conceptualization of the layperson, thus exposing the foundations of social life. At least implicitly, scientific understandings are superior; they appear as true reflections of what the layperson understand only feebly. And, as a result, a top-down educational system—where knowledge flows from science to society—is provided additional justification.

Yet certain participants in this dialogue have begun to speak in new ways, both persistent and disquieting. For them the difference between everyday understanding and scientific beliefs is less compelling than heretofore. In certain respects the scientist may even be placed in a position of dependency on the social milieu more generally. What is suggested is a broad-scale reconsideration of scientific practice along with existing processes of education. At stake then is the traditional conception of human understanding, of science and of education. . . .

Let us proceed by outlining first what may be regarded as the traditional view of human understanding, and the relationship between lay and scientific accounts. We shall then consider what many regard to be critical problems inhering in the traditional position. This will set the stage for examining two alternative orientations, both attempting to answer criticisms inherent in the traditional view, and offering disparate and challenging perspectives on everyday understanding.

Understanding as Cognitive Representation

That understanding is a process occurring in the mental world of the individual is a view widely shared at least since the Enlightenment. It is a view to which both empiricist and rationalist thinkers—each with their own particular emphasis—have contributed over the centuries. It is also a view that resurfaces in the present century in logical empiricist philosophy. Interestingly, while psychology as a profession has been largely committed to a logical empiricist view of science, theories of knowledge as mental representation were not readily forthcoming. While behavioural scientists believed in their own powers of reason and observation, so keen were they to ground their theories in observables that propositions about the mental states (or cognitive representations) of persons were hazarded only as hypotheticals (if at all), and couched in formalities tied closely to an observation language. The theories of Thorndike, Hull, Spence, Tolman, Skinner and Watson are all apposite.

In this regard, perhaps the most significant effect of the more recent "cognitive revolution" was to reinstate the traditional commitment to knowledge as individual representation of the external world. . . . Traditional languages of "ideas," "thoughts," "categories," "attributions" and "representations" are converted to and homogenized by the pervasive metaphor of the mind as a form of computer computational device. . . .

It is useful to elucidate these assumptions as they apply to the problem of everyday understanding—both in science and in society. At the outset, there is a shared commitment to the view that the cognitive world is in some way sensitive to, correspondent with or reflective of events within the objective world. In this sense, knowledge or understanding of the real world is carried within the cognitive system, and it is in the degree that this system is correspondent with the world that one can speak of correct understanding or accurate knowledge.

A second generally binding assumption is that the cognitive system plays a major role in the production of behaviour. Ideally, behaviour should be guided by accurate representation on the cognitive level. One should build up knowledge of the world, and act on the basis of this knowledge. To the degree that cognition is correspondent with reality and behaviour is dictated by cognition, we may speak of behaviour as adaptive (or, in Darwinian terms, as possessing survival value).

A third rudimentary corollary is that language, as a form of behaviour, is guided by cognition. If the categories in language reflect or are systematically linked to the features of the cognitive system, and this system is tied to the real world, we may speak of the communication of knowledge or understanding. In any case, language itself represents a secondary or derivative process. It is useful as a conveyance of knowledge, but does not constitute knowledge itself. . . .

In effect, cognition functions in both cases to represent the world and to enable the individual to act effectively. Research in both cases typically relies on the subject's language as an inferential guide to the locus of knowledge and action within. In effect, language operates as a conduit or vehicle for expressing the state of the individual's cognition.

Embedded within this minimal array of agreements is also a set of assumptions concerning the relationship of everyday understandings at the lay level with those of the scientist. First, at the level of real world representation, it is generally presumed that, while similar in their reliance on cognitive structures, the observational skills of the scientist . . . are more rigorous and systematic than those of the lay person . . . It follows that the cognitive system of the scientist is more accurately reflective of real-world properties than that of the lay person. . . .

A similar advantage to the scientist is often traced to the linkage between cognition and behaviour. . . . The lay person is under little constraint to evaluate the goodness of fit between inner representation and outer reality; the process is haphazard and piecemeal. In contrast, the central activity of science is that of hypothesis-testing. Thus the everyday understanding of the scientist is linked systematically to his/her behaviour and subjected to empirical test.

A third advantage accorded to the scientist can be traced to the link between cognition and language. . . . The layman is not obliged to formulate his/her ideas for expression in language. And if converted to linguistic currency, there is little pressure to communicate with others in a clear and consistent manner. In contrast, it is held, the major challenge for the scientist is to communicate his/her ideas in as transparent and rigorous a manner as possible. . . .

From these latter assumptions, in turn, one can derive the major challenges for programmes of science and education. To wit: (1) It is essential for the scientist to assay the everyday understandings of the lay person, for knowledge of these understandings is the key to predicting human conduct. (2) It is essential to compare everyday understandings on the lay level with those generated by science. Because in this way it is possible to determine domains of deficiency on the lay level—areas in which the lay population fails to understand the world in a competent way and thus fails the task of adaptation. (3) The educational process should be used to transmit scientific understanding to the lay level. In this manner, understanding in daily life will be improved and choices rendered more effective.

A Tradition in Trouble

For most readers the preceding account may seem both modest and unnecessary. In one form or another this network of assumptions has been with the profession (if not the culture) for many years, and is in little need of such simplistic clarification. However, this preliminary sketch is useful because it enables us, first, to isolate various ways in which the assumptive structure is proving unwieldy and, second, to understand more clearly the quest for alternatives. . . .

Let us consider four of these problems as they have emerged within recent debates.

The Generation of the Representational System

Whereas it is traditionally assumed that the optimally functioning cognitive system stands in a reflective relationship to objective reality, it has become increasingly difficult for investigators to specify how, in any simple way, this could be possible. Within experimental psychology Chomsky's (1959) critique of Skinnerian theory of language development served as a signal invitation to reconsideration, because, as his critique compellingly demonstrated, knowledge of language could not simply be the product of external inputs. For the richness and flexibility of language use to be understood, it was essential to consider the innate potentials (knowledge) of the language-user. This conclusion was magnified in a broad number of nativist accounts of animal learning and in J. J. Gibson's (1966, 1979) work on perceptual affordances. In each case it was argued that organisms bring to situations dispositions determining the individual's sensitivity to or strategies for searching the environment.

On the one hand, these various lines of thinking and research contributed importantly to the cognitive revolution. They all pointed to the essential capacities of the individual to organize, select, attend to or otherwise act upon the environmental givens. It is not the environment as such that determines the individual's beliefs or understandings, but what the individual brings to the environment in terms of cognitive predilections. Yet, while favouring a shift of attention to the cognitive level (and more specifically to top-down functioning), such conceptions simultaneously laid to rest the traditional empiricist assumption that the internal world is a replica of the external world. Precisely how cognitive structures (ideas, concepts, categories) were "built up" from environmental inputs became problematic. These concerns with the bottom-up conception of knowledge now resonate throughout the literature on social understanding. . . .

The Internal Determination of the Real

Confronted by the array of problems inhering in a representational or bottom-up conception of knowledge, many psychologists (aided by a host of AI specialists) have turned their attention to the top-down alternatives— theories emphasizing the inherent capacities of the person to organize, store and retrieve, information. Rather than reality driving the conceptual system, the conceptual system is said to determine what is taken as real. Thus, depending on the availability or salience of a given schema, the environment is scanned for certain information and memory-biased (Wyer and Srull 1985) so as to sustain or maintain the schema. . . .

Yet, as many begin to see, by avoiding the Scylla of everyday understanding as built up or produced by the environment, theorists run headlong into the Charybdis of knowledge as internally generated. . . .

The Identification of Internal Structure

A central question for many investigations of everyday understanding is the methodology of measurement. Of critical concern is how to determine whether one's measures are valid indications of internal states of individual understanding. As we have seen, it is generally assumed that understanding is more or less propositional in nature, or at least minimally, that its structure can be revealed through language. Yet these presumptions are without justification save through western dualistic tradition that views the mind as present and revealed within language (or, as Derrida has put it, a "metaphysics of presence"). Further, even those who accept the dualistic presumption are beset by considerable doubt concerning the validity of any given interpretation of the language. There are not only the classic problems treated by hermeneutic theorists such as Gadamer and Ricoeur, problems concerning the capacities of the interpreting agent to "see beyond the forestructure." Is it possible, they ask, to understand another's words (the text) in any other way than by duplicating or sustaining the array of understandings one brings to the text (the vicious form of the hermeneutic circle)?

There are also problems in determining whether and how speakers understand their own mental states, that is whether they can report accurately on what they know. . . . Rather scientists must work cooperatively with their subjects toward a "dialogic consensus." In effect, there is little to warrant the traditional claim that specimens of language furnish accurate or transparent indications of the internal world.

The Influence of Understanding on Action

A final array of problems arises in determining how and under what conditions understanding, as a set of cognitive states, determines action. At a basic level, the problem shares much with the preceding issue—whether cognitive states are or can be expressed in language. Present-day psychology inherits a tradition in which this presumption is a significant entry into the commonsense make-up of scientific procedure. However, the presumption that cognition influences action shares all the problems of a dualistic worldview—as confronted by philosophers from Descartes to Ryle and Rorty (see Gergen's summary, 1989). Yet, even when the presumption is accepted, psychologists have not rested sanguine with its implications. There are perennial problems in determining how intentions (as cognitive activities) can be translated into bodily movements, whether attitudes as cognitive states determine behaviour, and whether actions are not often driven by motivational sources beyond conscious comprehension. . . . Individuals may not understand the motivational sources underlying their actions; and, if this is so, then their actual states of cognition may have little to do with their behaviour. In the worst case, individuals may only furnish rationalizations for acts whose sources they cannot comprehend. . . .

The Initial Examination of Data
C. Chatfield

The development of Statistics continues apace as increasingly sophisticated techniques become readily available. Yet my experience suggests that all is not well. There is a disturbing tendency for techniques to be used by people who do not fully understand them and the standard of statistical argument in scientific journals can best be described as variable. This paper attempts to shift attention away from complicated methods by concentrating on the "simple" but important stage of a statistical analysis which I will refer to as the initial examination of data, or initial data analysis (abbreviated IDA). The idea is that one should begin an analysis with an informal, exploratory look at the given data in order to get a "feel" for them. The aim is to clarify the general structure of the data, obtain simple descriptive summaries, and perhaps get ideas for a more complicated analysis.

Source: "The initial examination of data" by C. Chatfield, *Journal of the Royal Statistical Society* 148 (1985): 214–219, 227–230. Copyright © 1985 Royal Statistical Society. Used with permission of the Royal Statistical Society.

In principle, most statisticians have long recognized the importance of IDA, so why is this paper needed? In practice one has only to look at the literature to see that the methods are still generally undervalued, often neglected, and sometimes actively regarded with disfavour. Reasons for this are discussed and countered.

The paper reviews IDA with the aid of some examples, takes a broad view of its ingredients and objectives, and aims to encourage its more systematic use. The implications for the teaching of Statistics are then considered. . . .

The Objectives of IDA

The two main objectives of IDA are *data description*, and *model formulation*. The first is "well known," but the second is not always explicitly recognized despite its importance (see Section "Model Formulation").

However even some aspects of data description are also not always widely appreciated. Of course one should usually begin by scrutinizing, summarizing and exploring a set of data. What is less well appreciated is that the IDA may be all that is necessary. This arises in two types of situation.

(a) The objectives are limited to finding descriptive statistics. This usually applies to the analysis of entire population, as opposed to sample, data, and may also apply to the analysis of very large samples where the question is not whether differences are "significant" (they nearly always are in large samples) but whether they are interesting. In addition IDA is all that is possible when the data quality is too poor to justify inferential methods which perhaps depend crucially on unfulfilled "random error" assumptions. . . . An IDA may also be sufficient when comparing new results with previously established results. Thus whereas inference is primarily useful for one-off random samples, IDA can additionally be applied to "dirty" data and to the analysis of several related data-sets.

(b) The results from the IDA indicate that no inferential procedure is either desirable or necessary. This applies particularly when significance tests are envisaged. . . .

The above remarks explain why I have avoided the term "Preliminary" Data Analysis in that one important message from this paper is that an IDA may be sufficient by itself. However it should also be said that it is not always easy to decide when a descriptive analysis is adequate by itself (Cox and Snell 1981, 24).

Historical Background

Before 1900, Statistics was mainly restricted to what is now called Descriptive Statistics. Despite, or perhaps because of, this limitation, Statistics made useful contributions in many scientific areas (e.g., Florence Nightingale's work on hospital data). Yet the need for a more formal apparatus was apparent so that statistical inference developed throughout this century, albeit in a rather restricted direction. By the 1960's, most statistics textbooks were primarily concerned with the special inference problem of estimation and testing for an *assumed* family of models for a *single* set of data. This narrow view of Statistics (e.g., Cox and Hinkley 1974, 1) spread into teaching so that practical aspects of analysing data were often neglected. Within the last decade or so, practising statisticians have begun to question the relevance of some Statistics courses and much published research. The latter has been described as "theories looking for data rather than real problems needing theoretical treatment" (Moser 1980). Partly as a result there are signs that interest in data-analysis has been rekindled, helped by improvements in computing facilities and by the publication of Tukey (1977). However there has been little effect on research journals, and Statistics teaching is still often dominated by formal mathematics. . . .

Preliminary Questions

Before rushing into any data analysis, an essential preliminary is to formulate the problem and clarify the objectives of the investigation. When asked for advice, the statistician should ask questions to get sufficient background to the problem and may find that the true objectives are completely different to those initially suggested. Of course a statistician should ideally be "in at the start" and advise on data-collection but this often does not happen.

The statistician should also find out what prior information is available, and assess the questions of costs. A literature search may be invaluable in giving previous results for comparison or even making the investigation unnecessary.

Data Scrutiny and Data Description

The analyst should start an IDA by assessing the structure and quality of the data and I will refer to this as *data scrutiny*. It is unfortunate that this important topic is omitted from many text books. As regards structure, the analysis will depend crucially, not only on the number of observations, but also on the number and type of variables (e.g., Cox and Snell 1981, Sections 1.7 and 2.1).

It is particularly important to find out how the data were collected (e.g., Cox and Snell 1981, Section 1.8). With some highly structured data sets, arising perhaps from complicated designs where the analysis is determined *a priori*, it is not obvious how, or if, one should carry out an IDA, apart from some data-quality checks. . . . Regrettably, a more common situation is that the data have been collected with little or no statistical guidance. Fortunately

IDA is particularly useful for "messy" data and for revealing data-collection inadequacies. . . .

Turning to data quality, the possible presence of errors, outliers and missing observations should be investigated and decisions made as to what to do about them (e.g., Chatfield and Collins 1980, Section 3.1). A computer can readily be programmed to check for consistency, credibility and completeness, and the human eye is also very efficient at spotting suspect values in a data array when printed in strict column formation in a suitably rounded form. Despite careful checking, it is important to realise that some errors may still get through, particularly with large-scale data sets. Outliers (e.g., Barnett and Lewis 1978) can create severe problems and the inexperienced analyst is advised that tests on outliers are less important than advice from "people in the field" and that analyses can be repeated with and without suspect observations.

It is also advisable to find out how easy it is to actually record the data (try weighing a live pig!) and whether too much or too little precision is available. The true recording accuracy may only become evident on arranging the data in rank order, or on looking at the distribution of the final recorded digit (see Preece [1981] who gives some fascinating examples). A non-uniform distribution may, for example, reveal problems in reading a scale or that the given data have been transformed or converted from some other units.

After assessing and processing the data, IDA will usually continue with what is often called "Descriptive Statistics." This should also be seen as a continuation of data scrutiny as further outliers may be revealed. Summary statistics should be calculated for the data as a whole and for important subgroups. I often prefer the range to the standard deviation as a descriptive measure for groups of roughly equal size. Measures of skewness and kurtosis are rarely enlightening, and skew, bimodal and other "funny" distributions may be better presented graphically or described in words.

Appropriate graphical procedures should be selected from the wide variety available (e.g., Chambers et al. 1983). To assess the distribution of a single variable, stem-and-leaf plots provide a useful variant to histograms, although the choice of class interval is more restricted. Box plots, or box-and-whisker plots, are particularly useful for comparing several groups of observations. . . .

Some "obvious" general rules are that summary statistics should be suitably rounded (probably using Ehrenberg's two-effective-digits rule), that graphs should have a clear title with labeled axes, and that the presentation of tables needs extra care (Ehrenberg 1982, Chapters 15–17). The fact that it seems necessary to spell out these much-ignored points is a sad commentary on the state of the art.

The possibility of modifying the data should be borne in mind throughout the investigative stages. In particular, a transformation can sometimes work wonders in deciphering the data. Some robust methods of estimation (e.g., Hoaglin et al. 1983) may eventually become part of IDA, but only when we have more experience of their use in practice and when they can be routinely implemented by computer packages.

Handling Multivariate Data

Lack of space prevents a thorough treatment of this important topic. Summary statistics for each variable will be supplemented by correlations as appropriate. Two-way tables and scatter diagrams can be very useful although it is sometimes misleading to collapse higher-dimensional data onto two dimensions. Thus traditional descriptive statistics may only tell part of the story in 3 or more dimensions. . . .

More modern graphical techniques include the useful Andrews curves (e.g., Everitt 1978) and the more controversial Chernoffs faces (Chatfield and Collins 1980, 50).

It seems natural to suggest that IDA could also include the group of data-analytic techniques comprising principal component analysis, many forms of cluster analysis, multi-dimensional scaling (e.g., Chatfield and Collins 1980, Chapter 10) and correspondence analysis (e.g., Greenacre 1984). The adjective "data-analytic" could reasonably be applied to any statistical technique, but I follow modern usage (e.g., Barnett 1982, 287/307) in applying it to techniques which do not depend on a formal probability model except perhaps in a secondary way. Their role is to provide information-rich summaries of the data as well as to help in the search for structure and the generation of hypotheses. The techniques are generally much more sophisticated than earlier data-descriptive techniques and should not be undertaken lightly. Thus their inclusion in IDA may be regarded as optional but potentially fruitful. In particular, plotting the first two principal components can be helpful in identifying clusters and outliers. . . .

The Informal Use of Inferential Methods

This section suggests that IDA might also include the informal use of methods which would normally be regarded as part of classical inference. In my experience, statisticians often use techniques without "believing" the results but rather using them in an informal exploratory way to get further understanding of the data and fresh ideas for future progress.

As an example, consider multiple regression. I have rarely used this technique in a "textbook" way for prediction because of such problems as correlations between the "independent" variables, and doubts about model assumptions. Indeed the technique is widely misused (Preece 1984). However I have occasionally found it useful for descriptive/exploratory purposes in indicating which explanatory variables, if any, are potentially "important."

As a second example, consider significance tests. They are also widely overused and misused (Cox 1977) and I rarely use them in a purely confirmatory way. However I sometimes use them in an exploratory way, even when the required assumptions are known to be invalid, in the hope of getting some informal guidance on the possible existence of an interesting effect. It is often possible to assess whether the resulting P-value is likely to be an under- or over-estimate and whether the result is clear one way or the other.

Model Formulation

Suppose now that the objectives of our investigation are not confined to data description. Then we may for example wish to generate and test hypotheses, build a model and analyse the data using an appropriate inferential procedure. The model-builder's main problem is often not how to fit an assumed model—to which there is often a nice straightforward reply—but rather to formulate the model in the first place.

The general principles of model formulation are covered in books on scientific method even though they are rather neglected in statistics textbooks (but see Cox and Snell 1981, Chapter 4; Gilchrist 1984). The principles include the need to collaborate with appropriate experts, to incorporate as much background theory as possible, to look at the data and recognize their important features, to check that a model formulated on empirical and/or theoretical grounds is capable of reproducing the main characteristics of the data, and to look for improvements as necessary. We are primarily concerned with the role of IDA particularly for giving the analyst a feel for the data, for picking out the more important features of the data, and in generating hypotheses.

Apart from models formulated entirely on *a priori* theoretical grounds, most models are based on IDA to some extent. Completely empirical models are rare and the more usual intermediate case arises when a class of models is entertained *a priori*, but the IDA is crucial in selecting reasonable primary and secondary assumptions. For example in regression the general approach is determined *a priori*, but a scatter diagram should indicate the shape of the curve (linear, quadratic or whatever) as well as giving guidance on secondary assumptions (normality, homogeneous variance, etc.). Thus IDA is vital in selecting a sensible model and inhibiting the sort of "crime" where, for example, a straight line is fitted to data which is clearly non-linear.

In a similar vein, time-series analysis should start by plotting the observations against time, to show up important features such as trend, seasonably, discontinuities and outliers. The time-plot will normally be augmented by more technical indicators such as correlograms and spectra, but is the first essential prerequisite to building a model.

IDA can also be very useful as a preliminary to many types of significance test, both in generating hypotheses and in suggesting reasonable secondary assumptions. In addition, IDA may indicate that a significance test planned beforehand is either unnecessary or undesirable. This arises when (a) the results are "clearly significant" or "clearly not significant," (b) the differences even if "significant" are not large enough to be "interesting," (c) the data are unsuitable for formal testing because of data contamination, a lack of randomization, gross departures from the "usual" secondary assumptions, inadequate sample sizes or whatever. These findings, whether "positive" or "negative," give further aid in model formulation.

The formulation of a preliminary model from an IDA is the first step in the iterative formulation/criticism cycle of model-building. An important general question is whether IDA and inference are compatible on the same set of data—see Cox and Snell (1981, Section 3.7). While it is desirable to have some idea how to analyse data before you collect them, it is unrealistic to suppose that the analysis can be completely decided beforehand and it would be stupid to ignore unanticipated features noticed during the IDA. On the other hand, there is no doubt that if features are spotted and then tested on the same set of data, their statistical significance needs adjustment. In a similar vein the fit of a regression predictor to new data is nearly always worse than its fit to the original data (Copas 1983). Thus it is preferable to confirm effects on two or more sets of data. However, when data are difficult or expensive to obtain then some assessment of significance in the original data set can still be valuable. As this sort of thing is done all the time (rightly or wrongly!), more guidance is badly needed. . . .

Concluding Remarks

This paper argues that more emphasis should be given to IDA and that a broader view should be taken of its ingredients and objectives. IDA is valuable not only for scrutinizing and summarizing data, but also in model-formulation. The examples demonstrate in particular that IDA may obviate the need for more sophisticated statistical techniques. In presenting the case for IDA, I am not, of course, suggesting we abandon classical inference, but rather that the teaching of Statistics should provide a more balanced blend of IDA and inference. Then future generations of statisticians will be able to have the best of both worlds.

Validity and Correlational Research
Terence R. Mitchell

> . . . *unfortunately, a not uncommon phenomenon in the literature today is a "study" in which the authors sent a non-pretested, non-scaled questionnaire to a convenient sample of uncertain nature in which little or no thought was given to the reliability of the measurement or the meaningfulness of responses. Nonetheless, numbers are obtained and are subjected to the staggering array of sophisticated computer assisted statistical techniques and "results" are obtained and generalized to a population of which the initial sample had very little relationship* (J. P. Campbell, Daft and Hulin 1982, 61).

The focus of this passage seems to be the large body of survey/correlational research that appears in the organizational literature. Such research is done in the field, involves no manipulations, is cross-sectional, and makes associational inferences. . . .

Background Literature

The distinction between "experimental" and "correlational" research was highlighted in a classic article by Cronbach (1957). Cronbach pointed out that these two methods used different types of samples, measures, analyses, and inferences. It was his hope that a rapprochement would evolve so that both treatment differences and individual differences could be integrated in theories and research.

Whether that rapprochement has occurred is still debatable and a topic for another paper. What is clear and obvious, however, is the extent to which methodological expertise has focused on one set of procedures over the other. Perhaps the fact that they were dealing with "causal" issues made experimental topics seem more crucial. Or perhaps the clarity and insight of this tradition was easier to put on paper. In any case, sophistication in judging the validity of experimental research designs seems greater than for correlational research designs. However, some important standards for correlational research may be inferred by an examination of the literature on experimental research. . . .

T. D. Cook and Campbell (1976, 1979) . . . developed a set of concepts that also were helpful for evaluating correlational research. These four concepts—internal validity, construct validity, statistical conclusion

Source: "An evaluation of the validity of correlational research conducted in organizations" by Terence R. Mitchell, *Academy of Management Review* 10 (1985): 192–198, 200–205. Copyright © 1985 by the Academy of Management. Reproduced with permission of the Academy of Management via Copyright Clearance Center.

validity, and external validity—serve as the basis for the checklist developed in the current paper. . . .

Survey of Current Research

Results

[Table 14-1] presents the findings. The data were broken down further by journal, but various analyses failed to show any large or meaningful differences. Therefore, the data are presented at the global level.

First, in terms of sampling issues, the data paint a fairly bleak picture. Over 80 percent of the studies used a convenience sample, and only about 10 percent of the studies compared respondents with nonrespondents. Of

TABLE 14-1
Overall results

CASES: TOTAL = 126 (*JAP* = 37; *OBHP* = 28; *AMJ* = 61)

1. Sample:[a] random, cluster, stratified, convenience (Yes 21; No 105)
2. Response rate: range = 30–94% (not available for 67 studies)
3. Respondents vs. nonrespondents: Yes 11; 115 No
4. Type of method:[b] AQ = 58; MQ = 34; DQ = 21; PI = 19 (6 studies used more than one method)
5. Reliability:[c] alpha = 88; NA = 26; TR = 7; IR = 10; SH = 6 (11 studies used more than one method)
6. Citations of reliability and/or validity: Yes 100; No 26
7. Construct validity tests: Yes 33; No 93
8. Type of construct validity: multiple measures = 19; factor analysis = 13; discriminate validity = 1
9. Did *A* & *B* measures use similar format: Same 52; Different 74
10. Test for method variance: Yes 84; No 42
11. Significant correlations: Yes 65; No 22; NA[d] 39
12. Issue of method variance addressed: Yes 81; No 45
13. Holdout sample or cross-validation: Yes 7; No 119

SOURCE: "An evaluation of the validity of correlational research conducted in organizations" by Terence R. Mitchell, *Academy of Management Review* 10 (1985): 200, exhibit 1. Copyright © 1985 by the Academy of Management. Reproduced with permission of the Academy of Management via Copyright Clearance Center.

NOTE: *JAP* = *Journal of Applied Psychology*; *OBHP* = *Organizational Behavior and Human Performance*; *AMJ* = *Academy of Management Journal*.

[a] Yes = a good sample: random, clustered or stratified; No = convenience sample.

[b] AQ = administered questionnaire; MQ = mailed questionnaire; DQ = delivered questionnaire; PI = personal interview.

[c] NA = not reported; TR = test/retest; IR = interrater; SH = split half.

[d] For a few of the articles (N = 3) for which no complete intercorrelation matrices were provided, some correlations showed method variance.

equal importance, over half of the studies did not even report a response rate. This occurs most of the time when questionnaires are administered personally or interviews are done. The researchers in most cases simply call their sample (those who show up) their population, and the concept of sampling loses its meaning altogether.

In terms of measurement procedures, questionnaires clearly dominate interviews. The reliability reported also is quite discouraging. Over half the studies used alpha, and only 17 studies (14 percent) reported test-retest or interrater reliabilities. No reliability at all was reported by 26 studies (21 percent).

The citation information indicates that at least the researchers cited studies that had used the measures before. Only 26 of the 126 studies (21 percent) failed to give information about instrument reliability or validity from previous studies. However, because the data suggest that most studies rely on alpha as an indication of reliability, citations of past research probably were referring to alpha as the reliability estimate. Also, few studies reported either convergent or discriminant validity. Therefore, the past citations of measurement validity likely referred to face validity or concurrent or predictive validity. To some extent this represents a self-reinforcing cycle of dependence on inadequate measures.

The information on construct validity also is rather discouraging. Only 33 of the studies (26 percent) provided information on construct validity, and most of those used multiple measures (19) or factor analysis (13), which provided evidence for convergent validity. Only one study looked at discriminant validity specifically.

The tests for method variance were more prevalent, and this seems to be an issue to which most authors and reviewers are sensitive. First, 59 percent of the studies used as and bs that were assessed by measures using different formats. Second, 67 percent of the studies reported the intercorrelations among various "independent" and "dependent" variables. And in most cases in which there were significant correlations an appropriate statistical procedure was used to correct for it. That is, partial correlations or stepwise regressions were used to remove the multi-colinearity.

Finally, only seven of the studies looked at holdout samples or used cross-validation procedures. Both of these procedures reflect on statistical conclusion validity, and the cross-validation can represent external validity as well.

Discussion

These data are rather unsettling. They suggest that the typical cross-sectional correlational study uses a convenience sample with an administered questionnaire. No response rate is reported, and no comparisons are made between respondents and nonrespondents. The literature on reliability and validity is often cited, but the actual reliability and validity demonstrated is very weak. Alpha predominates as a measure of reliability, and construct validity is infrequently checked. Researchers do seem to be sensitive to the dangers of method variance, but the use of cross-validation or holdout samples is almost nonexistent. . . .

Strategies for Doing Better Research

Sample.   Three issues concern the sample. First and most obvious, is the response rate. It should be reported (48 studies failed to do this). Also, if the response rate is low, various follow-up procedures (e.g., a second mailing, a phone call, a reminder memo, or a postcard) should have been arranged already.

A second issue is whether the sample is representative of anything—even the organization from which it was drawn. Most studies (83 percent) failed to obtain random samples, making it difficult to determine the identity of the population represented by the sample. What is almost universally missing from survey studies is any mention of norms for the measures, for the organization, or for the occupation involved in the study, even though normative data are available for many of the most frequently used measures (e.g., the Leader Behavior Description Questionnaire, the Least Preferred Coworker Scale, the Job Descriptive Index, the Job Diagnostic Survey, and many more). There also may be normative data on the organization as a whole to which the sample can be compared. Biographical data probably are readily available (age, income, education, gender), and some data are gathered by unions and the government on various occupational groups. The point is that gathering these data can be done in most cases by simply having the investigator do a little more work, and these data can be very helpful in understanding what sort of group is being studied.

Much of the above information also could be useful for the third sample issue: making comparisons between respondents and nonrespondents. Some additional thinking before gathering data again can be helpful. Find out the variables for which measures can be obtained for the organization as a whole (e.g., number of people at different job levels, number of people in different divisions or departments) or for every individual within the organization (e.g., the descriptive data mentioned above). Ask these questions on the questionnaire (e.g., job level, age, income) and then compare the sample with the population.

When differences exist between the population and the sample or between respondents and nonrespondents, various corrective procedures are available. For example, if the respondents have 10 percent more college educated people than the nonrespondents, 10 percent of the college educated respondents can be randomly dropped. There also are statistical procedures available for making comparisons between sample and population characteristics. If these procedures show that the sample is not significantly different from the population, one can proceed with the other analyses without changing the constitution of the sample or empirically adjusting the data.

Also, the researcher can actively think about and measure those variables that might be correlated with the variables being tested for associational effects (A^s and B^s). If, for example, in the hypothetical charisma study one believes that respondents may be older (or younger) than nonrespondents and that age may be related to charisma, one should make sure to measure age. These data can help both the investigator and the reader understand the results.

Finally, a possible strategy for gathering non-respondent data is to include a postcard with all questionnaires requesting that, if the recipient is not going to fill out the questionnaire, he/she check the items on the postcard and drop it in the mail. A few critical biographical questions or one or two scales can be included. These data, though incomplete, are better than nothing.

Measures.   Obviously, more information is desired about the reliability and validity of the measures. At the minimum, for the sample issues better reporting is needed. Most studies do cite the source of the measure, but few specifics are given for the type of reliability or validity or its strengths.

In conducting the research, the ideal situation would be to get multiple measures of each construct using different methods and to obtain test-retest reliability for each measure. However, such thoroughness usually is unattainable. But something can be done with limited cost. In most cases test-retest data can be collected on a small sample (e.g., 15 to 20 people). If test-retests are impossible, the questionnaire can be designed so that some items are repeated. In a long questionnaire, in which multiple constructs are measured with multiple items, such a procedure could be used.

Some things can be done to help minimize problems with method variance and construct validity. If multiple constructs are assessed, measures with different formats should be used. If multiple measures of the same construct cannot be used in the questionnaire, perhaps convergent validity data can be obtained in other ways. For example, if a number of people are working at the same job, half of them could fill out one type of measure for describing the job and the other half could use a different measure. Also, just as a small additional sample can help with reliability, it can help with validity. A small group can receive a longer questionnaire with multiple measures of multiple constructs.

One could also do some things to reduce other aspects of method variance discussed by D. W. Fiske (1982). For example, [constructs] A^s and B^s might be gathered at different times or with different experimenters or in different rooms. Anything that changes the test or the *test context* should reduce method variance.

Another suggestion is to split the sample used for reliability or validity purposes. More specifically, if a sample of about 200 people can be measured only once, randomly assign them to 4 groups of 50 each. Each subgroup might receive a different questionnaire composed of a somewhat different combination of A^s and B^s, potential confounds, reliability or validity checks, and so on. Although some commonality should exist for all four groups, this strategy also can generate data on almost all the other aspects of validity addressed here.

Analyses and Inferences.   Most investigators seem to be sensitive to problems of multicolinearity because of a lack of independence of constructs, measures, or both. However, little emphasis is placed on convergent or discriminant validity. To demonstrate discriminant validity, the investigator needs to think of and measure variables to which A^s and B^s should be unrelated or related in an opposite direction from the predicted relationships for A^s and B^s. It does not take many of these to provide such a demonstration, but again it does require that these factors be thought about before the data are gathered.

Finally, to increase confidence in both the stability of the finding and its generalizability, more holdout samples and cross-validation is necessary. In many studies the sample clearly is large enough for holdout samples to be used—but this is infrequently done. If the sample is small, a replication with another sample would be desirable.

In summary, many things can be done to improve the current state of affairs, and most of the above strategies are within the investigator's control—they simply require more work or more preliminary thinking. However, in some cases some of these strategies simply may not be possible. What may be done in these circumstances?. . . .

It is clear that much published work does not conform to some fairly standard guidelines for doing acceptable cross-sectional correlational research. Correlational research of the variety described can be and is a powerful research tool. The purpose of this paper is not to compare the strengths and weaknesses of cross-sectional correlational studies with those of other strategies or to suggest how various research strategies can be combined—such as the use of longitudinal surveys allowing cross-lag analyses or highly articulated theories allowing for path analysis. These are topics for a different paper. Rather, it is hoped that the checklist and suggestions presented in this paper will help investigators deal with the complexities and practical problems inherent in the use of correlational methodology. More thorough reporting, innovative measurement, and preresearch planning [are] needed. And the use of meta-analysis where feasible can add to knowledge in the area. Correlational methodology is a valuable research tool. With the recognition of where and how it can be done better, it will continue to serve an important function in organizational research.

Concerns About Statistical Data Analysis
Ralph Rosnow and Robert Rosenthal

"Think Yiddish, write British" might be an apt slogan for the dominant discursive pattern of the intuitions and inductive inferences that characterize the scientific outlook in psychology during the entire 20th century. As is true in other fields, the inventive ways that psychological researchers think frequently seem to resemble the hunches and intuitions, the illogical as well as logical inferences, of an astute Jewish grandmother. Indeed, it has been observed that the progress of science, as much as the saga of human discoveries in all fields, is not a history of stunning leaps of logic but is often the outcome of "happy guesses" and "felicitous strokes of talent" in ostensibly unrelated situations (Grinnell 1987, 24). The creative process in psychological science, as in all scientific disciplines, might be compared to the energy that excites a neuron in the human nervous system. The energy used to excite the neuron is nonspecific. The same ion flow occurs whether one hits one's finger with a hammer, burns it on the stove, or has it bitten by a dog. As long as the excitation is there, the result will be the same—ignition. In science, it also seems to make little difference as to what circumstances provide the inspiration to light the fuse of creativity. As long as the situation is sufficiently stimulating to excite thought in the scientist, there will be "ignition."

In contrast, the rhetoric of psychological science, the tightly logical outcome of this "thinking Yiddish," tends to be consistent with the traditions of British empiricist philosophy. As much as in all fields of science, journal articles and research monographs that describe the way in which the scientific method was used to open up the psychological world fail to communicate the day-to-day drama of the interplay of discovery and justification, in which speculative ideas based on facts, theories, intuitions, and hunches exert a constant influence on each other (cf. Knorr-Cetina 1981; Mahoney 1976; Mitroff 1974). One reason for this situation may be that language, insofar as it is limited (Polanyi 1967), imposes limitations on the ability of scientists to justify what they feel that they know. Another plausible reason is that the world's richness of information often exceeds our capacity to process it directly. As a result, the knower's representation of what is "out there"

Source: "Statistical procedures and the justification of knowledge in psychological science" by Ralph Rosnow and Robert Rosenthal, *American Psychologist* 44 (1989): 1276–1282. Copyright © 1989 by the American Psychological Association. Reprinted with permission.

is, like any model of reality, reduced and distorted to fit in with his or her own available schematisms (McGuire 1986).

In this article, we are concerned with various specific aspects of the rhetoric of justification, which in part draws on the strict logical consequences of statistical data analysis to shore up facts and inductive inferences. Despite the great range of procedures employed, there are some common problems of methodological spirit and methodological substance that although they have been addressed before, nevertheless endure. By exposing these problems again, we hope it may be possible to weaken their influence. In modern philosophy, a nautical analogy may be used to compare the progress of science to a boat that must be reconstructed not in drydock but at sea, one plank at a time. The aspects of statistical data analysis that we discuss might be thought of as the connecting tools that help us hold fast our facts and inductive inferences. In our reliance on statistical data-analytic tools used to reinforce the empirical foundation of psychological science, we want to choose the right tools for the job and to use them properly.

We begin by discussing four matters pertaining to the methodological spirit, or essence, of statistical data analysis. They are (a) the over-reliance on dichotomous significance-testing decisions, (b) the tendency to do many research studies in situations of low power, (c) the habit of defining the results of research in terms of significance levels alone, and (d) the over-emphasis on original studies and single studies at the expense of replications. We then turn to a consideration of some matters of methodological substance, or form. These are primarily problems in the teaching and usage of data-analytic procedures. The issues to be considered here are the use of omnibus or multivariate tests, the need for contrasts or focused tests of hypotheses, and the nearly universal misinterpretation of interaction effects.

Matters of Methodological Spirit

Dichotomous Significance-Testing Decisions

Far more than is good for us, psychological scientists have for too long operated as if the only proper significance-testing decision is a dichotomous one, in which the evidence is interpreted as "anti-null" if p is not greater than .05 and "pro-null" if p is greater than .05. It may not be an exaggeration to say that for many Ph.D. students, for whom the .05 alpha has acquired almost an ontological mystique, it can mean joy, a doctoral degree, and a tenure-track position at a major university if their dissertation p is less than .05. However, if the p is greater than .05, it can mean ruin, despair, and their advisor's suddenly thinking of a new control condition that should be run.

The conventional wisdom behind the approach goes something like this: The logic begins, more or less, with the proposition that one does not want to accept a hypothesis that stands a fairly good chance of being false (i.e., one ought to avoid Type I errors). The logic goes on to state that one either accepts hypotheses as probably true (not false) or one rejects them, concluding that the null is too likely to regard it as rejectable. The .05 alpha is a good fail-safe standard because it is both convenient and stringent enough to safeguard against accepting an insignificant result as significant. The argument, although not beyond cavil (e.g., Bakan 1967), affords a systematic approach that many researchers would insist has served scientists well. We are not interested in the logic itself, nor will we argue for replacing the .05 alpha with another level of alpha, but at this point in our discussion we only wish to emphasize that dichotomous significance testing has no ontological basis. That is, we want to underscore that, surely, God loves the .06 nearly as much as the .05.[1] Can there be any doubt that God views the strength of evidence for or against the null as a fairly continuous function of the magnitude of p?

Gigerenzer (1987; Gigerenzer and Murray 1987; Gigerenzer et al. 1989), in discussions that examined the emergence of statistical inference, reminded us that the notion of dichotomous significance testing was initially developed out of agricultural experimentalists' need to answer questions such as, "Is the manure effective?" It is perhaps harder to object to the necessity of an accept-reject approach when the experimental question is phrased in precisely this way. However, the composition of the data base of psychological science, certainly, is substantively different, as would seem to be the phraseology of the research questions that psychological experimentalists try to answer. Indeed, Fisher at one point (largely as a reaction against the criticisms of Neyman and E. S. Pearson) voiced his strong objections to the idea of a fixed, dichotomous decision-level approach and instead argued for a cumulative, more provisional conception of statistical data analysis in science (as discussed in Gigerenzer 1987, 24)—an idea that we will discuss in more detail.

To be sure, determining the particular level of significance of the data at which a null hypothesis will be rejected is essentially a personal decision, and by extension a decision by the field at a given historical moment. It is well known that in other scientific fields there is a strong tradition of rejecting the null hypothesis at an alpha level other than 5%. In using the Bonferroni procedure, scientists further redefine the alpha level so as to protect against post hoc selection of the largest effects (e.g., Harris 1975; Morrison 1976; Myers 1979; Rosenthal and Rubin 1984). The essential idea at this point in our discussion is that, from an ontological viewpoint, there is no sharp line between a "significant" and a "nonsignificant" difference; significance in statistics, like the significance of a value in the universe of

1. Editors' note: See Labovitz in the next selection for more on this point.

values, varies continuously between extremes (Boring 1950; Gigerenzer and Murray 1987).[2]

Working with Low Power

Too often, it seems that psychologists do significance testing with low power as a consequence of ignoring the extent to which, in employing a particular size of sample, they are stacking the odds against reaching a given p value for some particular size of effect. One reason for this situation may be that even though the importance of the implications of the mechanics of power analysis for practice were recognized long ago by psychological statisticians, these mechanics were dismissed in some leading textbooks for a time as too complicated to discuss (e.g., Guilford 1956, 217). However, as a consequence of a series of seminal works by Cohen beginning in the 1960s (e.g., J. Cohen 1962, 1965), the concept resurfaced with a vengeance in psychological science.

No matter the reasons why a sense of statistical power was never fully inculcated in the scientific soul of laboratory experimental psychology, it cannot be denied that this situation has led to some embarrassing conclusions. Consider the following example (the names have been changed to protect the guilty): Smith conducts an experiment (with $N = 80$) to show the effects of leadership style on productivity and finds that style A is better than B. Jones is skeptical (because he invented style B) and replicates (with $N = 20$). Jones reports a failure to replicate; his t was 1.06, $df = 18$, $p > .30$, whereas Smith's t had been 2.21, $df = 78$, $p < .05$. It is true that Jones did not replicate Smith's p value. However, the magnitude of the effect obtained by Jones ($r = .24$ or $d = .50$) was *identical* to the effect obtained by Smith. Jones had found exactly what Smith had found even though the p values of the two studies were not very close. Because of the smaller sample size of 20, Jones's power to reject at .05 was .18 whereas Smith's power *(N* of 80) was .60 — more than three times greater. . . .

Thus, the generally greater weight attached to the avoidance of Type I errors relative to Type II errors increases the smaller the effect size (i.e., r value), the smaller the N, and of course, the more stringent the p value. Although it might be argued that psychologists working in laboratories usually have plenty of power to detect even small effects because in laboratory experimentation error terms are often very small, we see that working si-

2. Interestingly, Enrico Fermi, the great physicist, thought $p = .10$ to be the wise operational definition of a "miracle" (Polanyi, 1961), and recent findings would lead us to believe that a similar standard might seem reasonable as a kind of "last ditch threshold" (i.e., before accepting the null hypothesis as true) to many psychological researchers (Nelson, Rosenthal and Rosnow 1986).

multaneously with a small effect, a small sample, and a binary decisional $p = .05$ might be compared to trying to read small type in a dim light: It is harder to make out the material. How much power is needed? J. Cohen (1965) recommended .8 as a convention for the desirable level of power. With a "small" effect (i.e., $r = .10$, $d = .20$), a power of .8 would require us to employ a total N of approximately 1,000 in order to detect various effects at $p = .05$, two-tailed (J. Cohen 1977). With a "medium" effect (i.e., $r = .30$, $d = .63$), it would mean a total N of approximately 115 sampling units, and with a "large" effect (i.e., $r = .50$, $d = 1.15$) a total N of approximately 40 sampling units, to detect various effects at $p = .05$, two-tailed.[3] Given a typical medium-sized effect (J. K. Brewer 1972; Chase and Chase 1976; J. Cohen 1962, 1973; Haase, Waechter and Solomon 1982; Sedlmeier and Gigerenzer 1989), it would appear that psychological experimenters seemingly choose to work, or are forced to work by logistic constraints, in "dimly lit" rather than in "brightly lit" situations. This is not universally true in all fields, as we will show.

Defining Results of Research

The example of Jones and Smith would lead us to believe (quite correctly) that defining the results of research in terms of significance levels alone fails to tell the whole story. In his classic *Design of Experiments*, Fisher (1960) stated further that

> convenient as it is to note that a hypothesis is contradicted at some familiar level of significance such as 5% or 2% or 1% we do not ever need to lose sight of the exact strength which the evidence has in fact reached, or to ignore the fact that with further trial it might come to be stronger or weaker (p. 25).

He did not give specific advice on how to appraise "exact strength" of the evidence, but the use of statistical power analysis, effect-size estimation procedures, and quantitative meta-analytic procedures (to which we refer later) enables us to do this with relative ease.

We have looked into power, and we now take another look at significance testing and effect-size estimation in the framework of a study with plenty of power overall. Before turning to this illustration, it may be worth reviewing the logic that insists that effect sizes be computed not only when p values in experimental studies are viewed as significant but also when they are viewed

3. Small, medium, and large effects of d are conventionally defined as .2, .5, and .8, respectively, but we see that in actually a somewhat larger effect of d is required when claiming correspondence with a medium or large effect of r (cf. Rosenthal and Rosnow 1984, 361).

as nonsignificant. There are two good arguments for this recommended practice.

First, computing population effect sizes guides our judgment about the sample size needed in the next study we might conduct. For any given statistical test of a null hypothesis (e.g., t, F, χ^2, Z), the power of the statistical test (i.e., the probability of not making a Type II error) is determined by (a) the level of risk of drawing a spuriously positive conclusion (i.e., the p level), (b) the size of the study (i.e., the sample size), and (c) the effect size. These three factors are so related that when any two of them are known, the third can be determined. Thus, if we know the values for factors (a) and (c), we can easily figure out how big a sample we need to achieve any desired level of statistical power (e.g., J. Cohen 1977; Kraemer and Thiemann 1987; Rosenthal and Rosnow 1984).

Second, it is important to realize that the effect size tells us something very different from the p level. A result that is statistically significant is not necessarily practically significant as judged by the magnitude of the effect. Consequently, highly significant p values should not be interpreted as automatically reflecting large effects. In the case of F ratios, a numerator mean square (MS) may be large relative to a denominator MS because the effect size is large, the N per condition is large, or because both values are large. On the other hand, even if considered quantitatively unimpressive according to the standards defined earlier, it could nevertheless have profound implications in a practical context. . . .

Overemphasis on Single Studies

The final matter of methodological spirit to be discussed concerns the importance of replication, a concept to which psychological journal editors, textbook writers, and researchers pay considerable lip service. In practice, however, the majority of editors, as much as most researchers, seem to be biased in favor of single studies at the expense of replications. Sterling (1959) found not a single replication in his classic review of experimental articles in four psychological journals during one year, and this practice does not appear to have changed much in more recent years (Mahoney 1976).

Is it possible there are sociological grounds for this monomaniacal preoccupation with the results of a single study? Might those grounds have to do with the reward system of science, in which, in our perceptions, as much as in the realities of many academic institutions, merit, promotion, and the like depend on the results of the single study, which is also known as the "smallest unit of academic currency"? The study is "good," "valuable," and above all, "publishable" when $p < .05$. Our discipline might be farther ahead if it adopted a more cumulative view of science. The operationalization of this view would involve evaluating the impact of a study not strictly on the basis of the particular p level, but more on the basis of multiple criteria, including its own effect size as well as the revised effect size and combined probability that resulted from the addition of the new study to any earlier studies investigating the same or a similar relationship. This, of course, amounts to a call for a more meta-analytic view of doing science.

The name, meta-analysis, was coined by Glass (1976) to refer to the summarizing enterprise, although the basic quantitative procedures for combining and comparing research results were known some years earlier (Mosteller and Bush 1954; Snedecor 1946). Because numerous texts and articles are available on this subject . . . we will mention only two, more or less secret, benefits to the research process of conducting meta-analytic reviews of research domains: the "new intimacy" and the "decrease in the splendid detachment of the full professor."

First, this new intimacy is between the researcher and the data. We cannot do a meta-analysis by reading abstracts and discussion sections. We have to look at the numbers and, very often, compute the correct ones ourselves. Meta-analysis requires us to cumulate *data*, not *conclusions*. Reading an original-study article is quite a different matter when one needs to compute an effect size and a fairly precise significance level—often from a results section that provides no information on effect sizes or precise significance levels. The *Publication Manual of the American Psychological Association* (American Psychological Association [APA], 1983)[4] insists that when reporting inferential statistics, authors give the symbol, degrees of freedom, value, and probability level. The APA manual does not require that an exact significance level or the estimated effect size be reported, but what a boon it would be for meta-analysts if all journal editors required that authors also report all of their analyses and findings to even this limited extent.

Second, closely related to the first benefit is a change in *who* does the reviewing of the literature. Meta-analytic work requires careful reading of research and moderate data-analytic skills. One cannot send an undergraduate research assistant to the library with a stack of 5×8 cards to bring back "the results." With narrative reviews that seems often to have been done. With meta-analysis the reviewer must get involved with the data, and that is all to the good because it results in a decrease in the splendid detachment of the full professor.

There are other benefits of replications that are well known to scientists. The fact that the results can be repeated ensures the robustness of the relationships reported. The results also can be repeated by uncorrelated replicators (i.e., truly independent experimenters) in different situations, which ensures the further generality of the relationships. In spite of the recognized methodological and epistemological limitations, the importance

4. Editors' note: Requirements that are still in force today.

of replications is supported by quite different methodological theories as essential in a pragmatic sense (e.g., Bakan 1967; M. B. Brewer and Collins 1981; Houts, Cook, and Shadish 1986; Rosenthal and Rosnow 1984; Rosnow 1981).

Matters of Methodological Substance

Omnibus Tests

The first problem of methodological substance concerns the over-reliance on omnibus tests of diffuse hypotheses that although providing protection for some investigators from the dangers of "data mining" with multiple tests performed as if each were the only one considered, do not usually tell us anything we really want to know. As Abelson (1962) pointed out long ago in the case of analysis of variance (ANOVA), the problem is that when the null hypothesis is accepted, it is frequently because of the insensitive omnibus character of the standard F-test as much as by reason of sizable error variance. All the while that a particular predicted pattern among the means is evident to the naked eye, the standard F-test is often insufficiently illuminating to reject the null hypothesis that several means are statistically identical.

For example, suppose the specific question is whether increased incentive level improves the productivity of work groups. We employ four levels of incentive so that our omnibus F-test would have 3 dfs in the numerator or our omnibus chi square would be on at least 3 dfs. Common as these omnibus tests are, the diffuse hypothesis tested by them usually tells us nothing of importance about our research question. The rule of thumb is unambiguous: Whenever we have tested a fixed effect with $df > 1$ for chi square or for the numerator of F, we have tested a question in which we almost surely are not interested.

The situation is even worse when there are several dependent variables as well as multiple degrees of freedom for the independent variable. The paradigm case here is canonical correlation, and some special cases are multiple analysis of variance (MANOVA), multiple analysis of co-variance (MANCOVA), multiple discriminant function, multiple path analysis, and complex multiple partial correlation. Although all of these procedures have useful exploratory data-analytic applications, they are commonly used to test null hypotheses that are scientifically almost always of doubtful value (cf. Huberty and Morris 1989). Furthermore, the effect size estimates they yield (e.g., the canonical correlation) are also almost always of doubtful value. Although we cannot go into detail here, one approach to analyzing canonical data structures is to reduce the set of dependent variables to some smaller number of composite variables and to analyze each composite serially (Rosenthal 1987).

Contrast Analysis

Whenever we have $df > 1$ for chi square or for the numerator of an F-test, we would argue that contrasts become the appropriate data analytic procedure given the usual situation of fixed effect analyses (Rosenthal and Rosnow 1984, 1985; Rosnow and Rosenthal 1988). Briefly, contrasts are 1 df tests of significance for comparing the pattern of obtained group means to predicted values, with predictions made on the basis of theory, hypothesis, or hunch. Among the practical advantages of contrasts are that they can be easily computed with a pocket calculator, can be computed on the data in published reports as well as with original data, and most important, usually result in increased power and greater clarity of substantive interpretation. . . .

Discussions of contrasts have been primarily within the context of ANOVA, but their use is not restricted to this situation (cf. Bishop, Fienberg and Holland 1975; Rosenthal 1984; Rosenthal and Rosnow 1984, 1985). For example, Donald Rubin (in Rosenthal and Rosnow 1985, 48–49) has shown how contrasts can also be used when the obtained values are cast as frequency counts in a $2 \times C$ contingency table, in which the classes in one classification are ordered and the classes in the other classification are expressed as a proportion (see also Snedecor and Cochran [1967, 247]). Although most current textbooks of statistics describe the logic and the machinery of contrast analysis, one still sees contrasts employed all too rarely. That is a real pity given the precision of thought and theory they encourage and (especially relevant to these times of publication pressure) given the boost in power conferred with the resulting increase in .05 asterisks.

Interaction Effects

The final matter to be discussed concerns what are probably the universally most misinterpreted empirical results in psychology, the results of interaction effects. A recent survey of 191 research articles employing ANOVA designs involving interaction found only 1% of the articles interpreting interactions in an unequivocally correct manner (Rosnow and Rosenthal 1989). The mathematical meaning of interaction effects is unambiguous, and textbooks of mathematical and psychological statistics routinely include proper definitions of interaction effects. Despite this, most of the textbooks in current usage and most psychological researchers reporting results in our primary journals interpret interactions incorrectly. The nature of the error is quite consistent. Once investigators find significant interactions they attempt to interpret them by examining the differences among the original cell means, that is, the simple effects. However, it is no secret that these condition means are made up only partially of interaction effects; main effects may contribute to simple effects even more than interactions (e.g., Lindquist 1953). The origin of the problem, as Dawes (1969) suggested, may in part be a consequence of "the lack of perfect correspondence between the meaning of "interaction" in the analysis of variance model and its meaning in other discourse" (p. 57). Whatever its etiology, however, the error of looking only to the uncorrected cell means for the pattern of the statistical interaction is deeply rooted, indeed. . . .

Researchers claiming to speak of an interaction must avoid the pitfall described in the anecdote of the drunkard's search. A drunk man lost his house key and began searching for it under a street lamp, even though he had dropped the key some distance away. When he was asked why he did not look where he had dropped it, he replied, "There's more light here!" This principle teaches that looking in a convenient place but not in the right place will never yield the key that will answer the question.

A Final Note

We have examined a number of aspects of the rhetoric of justification, which in part depends on statistical data analysis to shore up facts and inductive inferences. In particular, we have exposed several problems of methodological spirit and substance that have become deeply rooted in psychological science. Because of the unifying influence of the institutionalization of the classical procedure, we have sought in this discussion to review some ways of improving it rather than to argue for an alternative procedure for statistical inference (e.g., Goodman and Royall 1988). Much of what we have said has been said before, but it is important that our graduate students hear it all again so that the next generation of psychological scientists is aware of the existence of these pitfalls and of the ways around them.

Guidelines for Selecting a Level of Significance
Sanford Labovitz

The following is neither an exhaustive nor all inclusive classification scheme of criteria on which to select a significance level. However, it appears to represent the major dimensions that should be either explicitly or implicitly considered by researchers. There is no attempt to integrate the entire list, [or] to rank order the criteria in terms of importance. To do either seems premature. Note that none of the criteria should be considered in isolation—each should constitute just one of several guidelines in selecting a significance level.

Source: "Criteria for selecting a significant level: A note on the sacredness of .05" by Sanford Labovitz, *The American Sociologist* 3 (August 1968): 220–222. Copyright © 1968 by Transaction Publishers. Reprinted by permission of the publisher.

Eleven more or less independent criteria are delimited.

1. *Practical consequences.* The practicality of the problem refers to the gravity of available kinds of error on the basis of value orientations. Testing whether prefrontal lobotomy or sedation is the better method for curing patients is a grave choice if we value vitality and recognize the long lasting and extreme effects of lobotomy. In this example, a small error rate (level of significance) of perhaps .001 or less would be chosen so that it would be extremely difficult to reject the null hypothesis of no difference and accept lobotomy over sedation. On the other hand, if we were testing the difference between two types of sedation, perhaps a larger error rate would be chosen (.05), if there were few drastic or long range effects for either one.

2. *Plausibility of alternatives.* A test of hypothesis should not be considered in isolation. Unless the inquiry is in an area where virtually nothing is known, the available rationales and empirical evidence (from other studies) should be considered in interpreting a significance test. Suppose the results are directly opposed to existing theory and empirical evidence, or even "common sense." That is, the evidence against the conclusion is large, and there is no theoretical or empirical support for the finding. Under these conditions, it would probably be best to choose a small error rate (.01 or .001), because in all the studies opposing the conclusion we are bound to find a few negative results on the basis of chance alone. We would hesitate to so easily reject the null hypothesis, when rejection is such a deviant result. On the other hand, if the evidence supports the conclusion, a larger significance level would be more appropriate, since now we are usually more willing to reject the null hypothesis of no difference.

3. *Power of the test—sample size.* The power of a test varies directly with sample size, that is, as N increases there is a greater probability of correctly rejecting the null hypothesis (in comparison to a specific alternative hypothesis). Moreover, the standard error varies inversely with sample size. Consequently, with a large N a small difference is likely to be statistically significant, while with a small N even large differences may not reach the predetermined level. Therefore, small error rates (.01 or .001) should usually accompany large N's and large error rates (.10 or .05) should be used for small N's.

4. *Power of the test—size of true difference.* The power of a test not only varies with sample size (and level of significance), but also with the size of the "true" difference, e.g., the magnitude of the difference between means. Therefore when the true difference is large, the probability of correctly rejecting the null hypothesis is also large, except if the sample size is small enough to offset this condition. A small error rate probably should be used when the difference is expected to be substantial. This conclusion is based on the rationale that if a large difference is expected and only a small difference is obtained, the null hypothesis of no difference should not be rejected.

5. *Type I vs. type II error*. As pointed out by Skipper et al. (1967), most textbooks emphasize the criterion of minimizing the probability of errors described as type I (rejecting a true null) and type II (failing to reject a false null). These errors, to some extent, vary inversely with one another. Consequently, minimizing one type of error tends to increase the other. To illustrate, a .05 significance level yields fewer type II errors than the .01.

To digress on tests of hypotheses, a large significance level (.05) makes it easier to reject the null hypothesis and accept the original hypothesis set up by the researcher. The original hypothesis usually states a difference (and perhaps specifies the direction), while the null usually is stated in terms of no difference. Therefore, a large error rate increases the probability of accepting the researcher's hypothesis, but it also increases the probability of doing so incorrectly (type I error). However, with a large error rate, there is a low probability that the original hypothesis is both correct and we failed to accept it. If we feel that the original hypothesis should not be accepted until a high level of certainty is reached, then many true original hypotheses are likely to be lying around that are not accepted (type II error). Which error is best? Aside from our personal feelings on how a science should develop, at this point, the other alternatives listed should help solve the apparent dilemma.

6. *Convention*. Skipper et al. (1967) strongly argue against using conventional levels of significance such as .05 and .01. For the most part their conclusion seems justified, and the other criteria listed further indicate the limitations of using a conventional level. It is listed as a separate criterion primarily because (1) these conventions are used in sociology, and (2) they may be positively evaluated as yielding some consistency among research results. If most results are applied to a similar standard, readers have some idea of the comparability of results from one study to another. However, the disadvantages of a conventional level (such as not considering available evidence or the nature of the problem) well out-weigh this factor. As a final remark, the selection of a conventional level may not rest on any sound rationale, but on such incidental factors as the particular field of social science, where an individual received his degree, or the journal under consideration.

7. *Degree of control in design*. It is well known that R. A. Fisher generally selected the .05 level in his agricultural experiments. These experiments were based on complex (e.g., Latin square or factorial) designs that offered a high degree of control over the effects of extraneous factors. The effects of "other factors" were handled by randomizing plots of ground, rows and columns of products, etc. Under such highly controlled conditions Fisher seemed justified in using the larger error rate of .05 instead of .01 or lower. If other factors are controlled, the results of the experiment are likely to be due to the experimental variable or chance differences and not due to extraneous factors. Stated otherwise, a large amount of control in an experiment reduces alternative interpretations so that a larger level of significance can be

tolerated. In designs of low control, perhaps a more stringent error rate should be selected (.01) since the alternative chance differences could be due to extraneous factors as well as to the independent variable. Consequently, under low control conditions we should make it more difficult to reject the null hypotheses of no difference.

8. *Robustness of test.* Robustness is the ability of a statistical test to maintain its logically deduced conclusion when one or more assumptions have been violated. For example, Student's *t* and analysis of variance have been demonstrated to be robust under the conditions of non-normality and heterogeneity. However, under these conditions the actual .02 level of significance may be met at the .01 level and the .10 at the .05. Consequently, depending on the statistical test in question, when the data do not meet all the assumptions, a small error rate should be chosen and interpreted as a larger one, e.g., .01 is interpreted as .02 or .05. On the other hand, if the data reasonably meet the assumptions, then a large error rate can be used with confidence.

9. *One-tail vs. two-tail tests.* As stated in most introductory statistics books, it is easier to reject the null hypothesis in a directional (one-tail test) as opposed to a non-directional (two-tail test) hypothesis. The z-score equivalents for a one-tail test are lower than those for two tail (e.g., 1.65 as compared to 1.96 at the .05 level). It is reasoned that knowledge of the direction of the hypothesis should give the researcher the advantage of more easily rejecting the null and accepting the original hypothesis.

However, the notion of one-tail vs. two-tail is largely a myth, because it is based on the rationale that we either have absolutely no idea of the direction of the hypothesis or we have absolute knowledge of the direction. Either extreme alternative is an unlikely occurrence. It is most probable that we have some idea of the direction of the hypothesis, but there is a small to large amount of uncertainty in our reasoning. Consequently, we should neither accept the z-score equivalent of the one-tail or two-tail test, e.g., 1.96 or 1.65, but an intermediate score between the two values. At the .05 level if we are largely certain of the direction (that is, it is supported by previous research or sound rationale), then we should select a z-score closer to 1.65. If, on the other hand, there is a large degree of uncertainty, a z-score nearer to 1.96 would be more appropriate. This is the equivalent of saying that we should choose a larger or smaller error rate depending upon our degree of confidence in the direction of our hypothesis.

10. *Confidence interval.* A confidence interval not only provides a probability band containing some statistical measure or difference, but actually provides tests of hypotheses. Therefore, the difference between a test and an interval is not clear cut. The importance of considering the confidence interval as a criterion in selecting a level of significance depends on whether or not the problem requires a small or large interval. For a smaller interval a

larger error rate is necessary (.05), while for larger intervals (in which there is more confidence that they contain the parameters) a smaller error rate is necessary (.01).

11. *Testing vs. developing hypotheses.* If testing a well reasoned and developed hypothesis that will distinguish between two theories, it seems logical to select a small level of significance. This is based on the notion that we want to be fairly sure if one theory is to be selected over another. On the other hand, if we are just exploring a set of interrelations for the purpose of developing hypotheses to be tested in another study, a larger error rate will tend to yield more hypotheses—any of which may be subsequently validated. Therefore, in this exploration stage perhaps the .10 or .20 level would be sufficient.

Caution should be used not to fall into the trap of thinking that the few "significant" relations out of many possible ones have truly reached the designated level. Out of twenty interrelations we are likely to find one significant at the .05 level on the basis of chance alone. However, we do not fall into this trap if the "significant" relations are subsequently tested. . . .

A Few Precepts for Interpretation
Fred N. Kerlinger

Scientists, in evaluating research, can disagree on two broad fronts: data and the interpretation of data. Disagreements on data focus on such problems as the validity and reliability of measurement instruments, the adequacy and inadequacy of research design and methods of observation, and the adequacy and inadequacy of analysis. Assuming a certain degree of competence and adequacy, however, we find that major disagreements ordinarily focus upon the interpretation of data. Most psychologists, for example, will agree on the data of reinforcement experiments. Yet they disagree vigorously on the interpretation of the data of the experiments. Such disagreements are in part a function of theory. . . . We cannot labor interpretation from theoretical standpoints. We must be content with a more limited objective: the clarification of some common precepts of the interpretation of data within a particular research study or series of studies.

Adequacy of Research Design, Methodology, Measurement, and Analysis

One of the major themes of this book has been the appropriateness of methodology to the problem under investigation. The researcher usually has

Source: *Foundations of behavioral research*, 2nd ed., by Fred N. Kerlinger, 618–622. © 1973. Reprinted with permission of Wadsworth, a division of Thomson Learning: www.thomsonrights.com. Fax 800 730-2215.

a choice of research designs, methods of observation, methods of measurement, and types of analysis. All of these elements must be congruent; they must all fit together. One does not plan, for example, a factorial design with nominal data, nor does one use an analysis appropriate to frequencies with, say, the continuous measures yielded by an attitude scale. Most important, the design, the methods of observation and measurement, and the statistical analysis must all be appropriate to the research problem.

An investigator obviously must carefully scrutinize the technical adequacy of the methods, the measurement, and the statistics. The adequacy of data interpretation crucially depends upon such scrutiny. A frequent source of interpretative inadequacy, for example, is neglect of measurement problems. It is urgently necessary, in all social scientific and educational research, to pay particular attention to the reliability and validity of the measures of the variables. Simply to accept without question the reliability and validity of psychological measuring instruments is a gross error. The researcher must be especially careful to question the validity of his measures, since the whole interpretative framework can collapse on this one point alone. If an educational investigator's problem includes the variable anxiety, and the statistical analysis shows a positive relation between anxiety and, say, achievement, the investigator must ask himself and the data whether the anxiety measured is the type of anxiety germane to the problem. He may, for example, have measured test anxiety when the problem variable is really general anxiety. Similarly, he must ask himself whether his measure of achievement is valid for the research purpose. If the research problem demands application of principles but the measure of achievement is a standardized test that emphasizes factual knowledge, the interpretation of the data can be erroneous.

In other words, we face here the obvious, but too easily overlooked, fact that adequacy of interpretation is dependent on each link in the methodological chain, as well as on the appropriateness of each link to the research problem and the congruence of the links to each other. This is clearly seen when we are faced with negative or inconclusive results.

Negative and Inconclusive Results

Negative or inconclusive results are much harder to interpret than positive results. When results are positive, when the data support the hypotheses, one interprets the data along the lines of the theory and the reasoning behind the hypotheses. Although one carefully asks critical questions, upheld predictions are evidence for the validity of the reasoning behind the problem statement.

This is one of the great virtues of scientific prediction. When we predict something and plan and execute a scheme for testing the prediction, and things turn out as we say they will, then the adequacy of our reasoning and our execution seems supported. We are never sure, of course. The outcome, though predicted, may be as it is for reasons quite other than those we fondly espouse. Still, the fact that the whole complex chain of theory, deduction from theory, design, methodology, measurement, and analysis has led to a predicted outcome is cogent evidence for the adequacy of the whole structure. We make a complex bet with the odds against us, so to speak. We then throw the research dice or spin the research wheel. If our predicted number comes up, the reasoning and the execution leading to the successful prediction would seem to be adequate. It we can repeat the feat, then the evidence of adequacy is even more convincing.

But now take the negative case. Why were the results negative? Why did the results not come out as predicted? Note that any weak link in the research chain can cause negative results. They can be due to any one, or several, or all of the following: incorrect theory and hypotheses, inappropriate or incorrect methodology, inadequate or poor measurement, and faulty analysis. All these must be carefully examined. All must be scrutinized and the negative results laid at the door of one, several, or all of them. If we can be fairly sure that the methodology, the measurement, and the analysis are adequate, then negative results can be definite contributions to scientific advance, since then and only then can we have some confidence that our hypotheses are not correct.

The Interpretation of Unhypothesized Relations

The testing of hypothesized relations is strongly emphasized in this book. This does not mean, however, that other relations in the data are not sought and tested. Quite the contrary. The practicing researcher is always keen to seek out and study relations in his data. The unpredicted relation may be an important key to deeper understanding of theory. It may throw light on aspects of the problem not anticipated when the problem was formulated. Therefore researchers, while emphasizing hypothesized relations, should always be alert to unanticipated relations in their data. . . .

Such unpredicted findings must be treated with more suspicion than predicted findings. Before accepting them, they should be substantiated in independent research in which they are specifically predicted and tested. Only when a relation is deliberately and systematically tested with the necessary controls built into the design can we have much faith in it. The unanticipated finding may be fortuitous or spurious.

Proof, Probability, and Interpretation

The interpretation of research data culminates in conditional probabilistic statements of the "If p, then q" kind. We enrich such statements by qualifying them in some such way as: If p, then q, under the conditions r, s, and t. Ordinarily we eschew causal statements, because we are aware that such statements cannot be made without grave risk of error.

Perhaps of greater practical importance to the researcher interpreting data is the problem of proof. Let us flatly assert that nothing can be "proved" scientifically. All one can do is to bring evidence to bear that such-and-such a proposition is true. Proof is a deductive matter, and experimental methods of inquiry are not methods of proof. They are controlled methods of bringing evidence to bear on the probable truth or falsity of relational propositions. In short, no scientific investigation ever proves anything. Thus the interpretation of the analysis of research data can never use the term proof in the logical sense of the word. Interpretation, rather, must concern itself with the evidence for or against the validity of tested hypotheses.

Fortunately, for practical research purposes it is not necessary to worry excessively about causality and proof. Evidence at satisfactory levels of probability is sufficient for scientific progress. Causality and proof were discussed in this chapter to sensitize the reader to the danger of loose usage of the terms. The understanding of scientific reasoning, and practice and reasonable care in the interpretation of research data, while no guarantees of the validity of one's interpretations, are helpful guards against inadequate inference from data to conclusions.

Summary

This chapter has focused attention on the several stages of mindful data sensemaking in serious inquiry. Because data cannot speak for themselves, researchers create meaningful knowledge by showing how project data not only are informed by theory and contexts but inform theory and contexts as well. All too often the more or less statistically sophisticated analytical findings of a research project are viewed as the end product of inquiry. We have cautioned against this view, emphasizing that for findings to be meaningful they have to be interpreted not only in terms of time, place, and people (i.e., communities and subcultures of practitioners and scientists) but also in terms of existing theory. As has been noted, the analysis and interpretation of project data can be done in many ways, and there is not one best way. How to get a feel for one's data, how to establish how good the data are, how to see and clarify relationships in the data, and how to make both analytic and interpretative sense of one's findings—each of these sensemaking activities may be accomplished in more than one way. Important choices will be made, with every choice a matter of judgment conditioned by theoretic priorities and preferences, ideally eschewing habit, technique, or formula. Sensemaking for theory advancement is, after all, at the core of serious inquiry.

15   Sharing Research Contributions

At the end of reasons comes persuasion.
>   —*Ludwig Wittgenstein*

I grasp the meaning of your words only by the way of what I myself would have meant by them, but I am not you: I can understand what you say only if I know you, but I come to know you only if I understand what you say.
>   —*Abraham Kaplan*

Still you know, words mean more than we mean to express when we use them: a whole book ought to mean a great deal more than the writer meant.
>   —*Lewis Carroll*

A piece of writing was shown not long ago to an illustrious personage who smiled and said: "These words must be greatly astonished to find themselves together, for assuredly they had never met before."
>   —*Father Bouhours*

This chapter presumes that the research cycle is nearing completion—that there is new meaningful knowledge to share. Where might new knowledge go, how can it be shared, how might it be used? These questions are seldom adequately discussed in the organizational sciences.[1] All too often, serious inquirers think that a report of research results, shared in formal talks and academic publications, ends their work. Relatively little attention goes to the how, what, and when of sharing their discoveries or to the ways that various possible audiences will use new knowledge. Such considerations, however, are probably of great consequence for a field where the phenomena of

---

1. Editors' note: The notable contemporary exception is Cummings and Frost's (1985) *Publishing in the Organizational Sciences.*

interest are organizationally important. The aim of this brief chapter therefore is to review the real complexities of knowledge sharing by standing back and taking a broader perspective.

If the unexamined answer to the question of what happens to new knowledge is the sharing of a research report, we note that research reports are viewed simply as outputs of the research process. A broader view is obtained by asking, "How can new knowledge discovered in serious inquiry be used?" There are three general responses. One has been implied throughout this book: new knowledge is shared to improve theory. A second way knowledge can be used is through instruction: new knowledge is shared to inform those who wish to be up to date in some field of learning. A third way is that shared new knowledge can be used to improve the effectiveness of practice; that is, how people in organizations do what they do. Each of these three general types of new knowledge use implies different knowledge consumers, each with different criteria for knowledge use, each served by different kinds of agents or middlemen in the knowledge-sharing process.

Knowledge sharing intended for theory improvement—primarily through research reports—targets serious inquirers, who may be other researchers generally or, more typically, those researchers who share the school of thought of the knowledge producer. Acceptance of new knowledge is usually but not always paradigm bound, evaluated in terms of the significance of the questions pursued and the appropriateness of the research design, the data gathering methodology, the amount and quality of the data acquired, the rigor of the analysis, and so on—all of which need to be fully and candidly described. Research reports are shared through talks, seminars, colloquia, and other forms of oral presentation, and through written working papers, published articles, and monographs. Presentations and written reports, however, are subject to the influence of gatekeepers who control these knowledge-sharing methods, such as reviewers, editors, school-of-thought opinion leaders, academic conference program chairs, and institutional senior scholars.

Knowledge sharing intended for instructional use—primarily through textbooks and teacher-training seminars and workshops—obviously targets educators. Educators as consumers, however, serve secondary audiences, who are those who ultimately use the new knowledge, such as post-docs, teachers of all kinds, and students at many educational levels. Acceptance of new knowledge by educators almost always turns on its being understandable within, and relating to, existing knowledge frameworks. New knowledge is viewed as confirming, amplifying, or correcting a stream of thought or as an expansion at the "frontier of knowledge." New knowledge for educational use usually requires one kind of transformation, from scientifically precise specifics into believable generally asserted propositions. Adoption of new knowledge by the relevant secondary audiences in turn depends on the

Table 15-1
Major new knowledge dissemination alternatives

Purpose	Knowledge users	Criteria for use	Middleman role
Theory improvement	Serious inquirers	Paradigm conformity; rigor	Gatekeepers (e.g., academic editors)
Instruction	Educators	Relates to existing knowledge	Summarizers and synthesizers (e.g., text writers)
Improve organization performance and practice	Practitioners	Face validity; contextual relevance	Knowledge brokers (e.g., consultants)

summarizing and synthesizing skills of the educational middlemen in the knowledge sharing process, such as science journalists, textbook editors and writers, curricular designers, teacher trainers, as well as the marketing skills of publishers and their agents.

Knowledge sharing intended for the improvement of organizational performance and practices—primarily through advice for new behavioral rules—targets organizational members, especially practitioners in leadership positions. Acceptance of new scientific knowledge in the form of advice to organizational members usually depends on its contextual relevance and face validity, and on its being in an organizationally acceptable language and more or less consistent with the managerial beliefs of the organization's dominant coalition. For advice to fall within the comfort zone of organizational members means, of course, that scientific knowledge has to be modified. Between researchers and practitioners are knowledge brokers who select, compile, and translate new knowledge into rule-modified advice. Familiar knowledge-broker roles are consultants, policy analysts, and staff specialists.

The three knowledge-sharing processes (summarized in Table 15-1) constitute alternative types of knowledge dissemination, all consistent with the scientific value of making new knowledge public. As previously noted, when new knowledge is viewed as the output of the research processes in the form of research reports, it is easily accessible to, as well as usually understandable by, other serious inquirers. When new knowledge is viewed as inputs by the multiple nonscientific audiences of potential knowledge users, however, there are two distinctly different models for how knowledge should be diffused. One model, the "social engineering model," has new scientific knowledge bundled and translated by middlemen, who then pass it along to those who use it. The other is the "enlightenment model," in which new scientific knowledge piles up over time until some threshold of thematic appreciation is reached and it is incorporated naturally into practical new policies and decisions. Social engineers "push" transformed basic knowledge along to applied consumers; "enlightened" consumers take configurations of basic knowledge and "pull" them into new applied practices. We should note that there are those scholars who sidestep knowledge sharing completely, advocating the education of practitioners in the research process so that they are helped to help themselves.

Many factors affect the diffusion and adoption of new knowledge created by serious inquirers by nonscientific audiences. Some factors are partially within the control of researchers: the form, style, and timing of the research report; the medium for communicating the new knowledge; the nature and length of the communication channel; and no doubt several others. Some factors, however, are outside a researcher's influence. When diffused, both the middleman and the ultimate users of new knowledge can—some would say *will*—modify it. Explanations for nonadoption and/or distortion are linked to just a handful of scientific new knowledge features. One such feature of scientific new knowledge is the level of generality found in the research report. Most nonscientific audiences, however, prefer knowledge that is relevant for a specific context; they prefer a very local relevance. A second feature is that new scientific knowledge is always probabilistic, always tentative, always subject to being changed by new discoveries. Most nonscientific audiences, however, prefer advice that is sure or nearly so. Finally, a third feature is that significant new knowledge often seems counterintuitive to lay conceptions of how the world works or is couched in terms where the rigor of the work is emphasized. Nonscientific audiences, however, gain comfort from familiar and more casual formulations.

This short chapter has begun to focus attention to the processes by which new knowledge is shared. We have emphasized that its value depends on the purposes to which it is put and, concomitantly, on the middlemen who modify it, as well as those who ultimately use it. The dissemination of new knowledge is only partly under the control of the researcher, but its adoption is even less so. Nevertheless, the alternatives of form and style, communication medium and channel, the completeness of the research report, and similar considerations are matters of the researcher's choice, each with resulting trade-offs for the impact of new knowledge on models and theories, education, and organizational practice.

Part 5

Living Inquiry

Life is a rough draft published in final form.
  —*Ambrose Bierce*

Only where love and need are one,
And the work is play for mortal stakes,
Is the deed ever really done
For Heaven and the future's sakes.
  —*Robert Frost*

We have entitled the last part of this book "Living Inquiry" to signal our return to the human and social themes of Part 1—the inquirer is a learner and sensemaker who draws upon, collaborates with, and contributes to one or more colleagues and human communities; inquirers, individually and collectively, over time enhance the sophistication of their endeavors; serious inquiry requires artful trade-offs among philosophic, theoretic, and research choices; and inquiry is both a craft and a calling. We also note that inquiry is "living" because it evolves. The "storybook image of science" (Mitroff 1974)—in which scientists are emotionally and value neutral, impersonal and objective, technically precise and formulaic in practice—now seems both laughable as well as naive. People invent questions and find answers. People frame theories and improve them. People hold assumptions and change them. The accumulating legacy of inquirers is not only new knowledge and personal and professional growth but also enhancements in the process of inquiry itself.

Just one chapter follows. Chapter 16 offers a sampler of major considerations that can, and often do, combine to shape our choices about which research projects to pursue and about research career trajectories. Together these selections focus our attention on ways of thinking about how we might progress in our inquiry journeys, project by project and over a career, and how we weave together the processes of professional and personal development with the more or less patterned streams of relationships and activities of inquiry.

The chapter that follows reminds us that inquiry is continuously emotional, social, and often political: professional socialization and personal acculturation are entwined and ongoing; technical prowess is interlaced with bricolage, creativity, and serendipity; research-related associates, competencies, and identities proliferate; work and life circumstances overlap and interweave; and insights, mood, and energy pulsate as knowledge and science progress.

One finger can't lift a pebble.
>   —*Hopi saying*

A man needs a little madness or else he will never dare to cut the rope and be free.
>   —*Zorba (Nikos Kazantzakis,* Zorba the Greek*)*

A mind that is stretched to a new idea never returns to its original dimension.
>   —*Oliver Wendell Holmes*

It is good to have an end to journey toward; but it is the journey that matters, in the end.
>   —*Ursula K. Le Guin*

Inquiry in the organizational sciences produces knowledge, which can, when incorporated in redesigned structures, systems, policies, and practices, alter human circumstances from institutions to industries and from organizations to work groups. Such knowledge and the processes and circumstances that produce it also create personal experiences and personal knowledge that can change inquirers. This happens simply because research is done by whole persons and is essentially a social process. Becoming an inquirer—conducting research projects and embracing a scholarly career—will change a person. It does seem, however, that the more self-reflective an inquirer is about his or her findings and about how they are arrived at, the more the many philosophic and technical choices made can also be viewed as choices about the degree to which the person might change.

The opportunities for personal change as well as professional development from research experiences will probably reflect the degree of a project's philosophic conventionality, theoretic significance, and the "objectivity" of its methods. A positivist attempting to fine-tune a widely accepted theory through quantitative analysis, for example, may be relatively untouched by the presumed impersonality of this type of work. In contrast, a researcher attempting to generate a grounded theory of some new phenomenon by interpreting patterned behaviors observed in a long-term, intensive immersion in an unfamiliar field setting may more likely come to question many of his or her previous assumptions and beliefs. Projects and careers thus hold opportunities for personal and professional change, with the degree of change depending on whether researchers allow their experiences to influence their competencies, values, attitudes, relationships, assumptions— their identity as an inquirer, their identification with inquiry.

We have chosen the metaphor of a "journey" to draw attention to the processes of professional and personal development that are woven together with the more or less patterned streams of interactions and activities of scholarship. Inquiry-related journeys are generally cyclical, broadly directional, and of varying duration. Research projects and research careers are two such journeys. While each of these may be characterized in outline, these journeys will, in various degrees, be individually unique—the path taken by every scholar represents choices along the way at many, many crossroads. One cycle of the research process (see Part 4) constitutes a research project. Research projects may be viewed as punctuating the trajectory of a scholarly career.

Research projects are both patterned and time-bound. Each project, however, has its own more or less unique phenomenological, intellectual, and institutional history and context. Every project also carries the stylistic stamp of its researchers simply because all serious inquirers bring their own unique personality, training, and previous experience, as well as their current relationships, allegiances, and resources, to the project. Every project therefore overlaps with other parts of a researcher's life (intimate relationships, teaching, institutional and community service, recreation), occurs somewhere along a career path, and, sometimes, links to other ongoing projects. Projects are both figure and ground—figure to the ground of life and career; ground to the activities of research.

Because inquirers come to particular projects with a variety of research-related competencies and life experiences, they will—project by project— have some configuration of needs, expectations, aspirations, and attitudes toward the project itself, as well as about the project's impact on their research career. Competencies, hopes, previous scholarly experiences, and other factors will significantly condition choices about project-related activities and how they are experienced. All projects are multidimensional; there are always cognitive and emotional, social and technical, political and ethical, and other dimensions, all competing for attention and energy at every stage of the research process, all presenting choices among alternatives.

Compared to the research project journey, the journey of an inquiry career is both longer and less patterned. If research projects are knowledge-producing combinations of ordered activities (i.e., the research process), a set of research relationships, resources and settings, inquiry careers may be viewed as a sequence of research projects bundled with a set of projects for living—for instance, raising a family or maintaining health. Inquiry careers are distinguished by their opportunities for continuing professional socialization, researcher identity formation, and personal growth—all linked to enhanced competencies for carrying out research projects.

The inquiry career journey rhythmically manifests a ratio of learning and performing as inquirers learn how to perform research-related tasks proficiently; to know and influence power structures; to establish and use professional networks; to enhance their know-how about the ethos, goals, and values of employing and professional associations; to reflect (and sometimes challenge) the history, cultural myths, and traditions of their field; to shift allegiances with schools of thought and philosophic contexts; to assess and act on the goals and values of particular career paths, and much else. Inquiry career journeying will always reflect the person's personality and training, and his or her evolving circumstances (such as intellectual fashions, position requirements, rewards and recognitions, discipline stratification and status, and environmental and organizational munificence).

What should one consider when thinking about inquiry's journeys and the choices these considerations hold? The selections that follow point to four major considerations: professional activities other than research; the professional relationships of inquirers; the socialization of researchers and resulting research identities; and those emotions and ideals associated with doing exemplary work. Although many other considerations no doubt bear on inquiry journeying, we suggest that these are always pertinent.

In the first selection, Linda Ford, a graduate student just beginning to do independent research, reflects briefly on how her tacit personal and emotional learning intertwines with her professional training. She describes how her intellectual and research-skill acquisitions foster self-awareness and personal growth so that she can not only do research but has also become a researcher—and knows it.

Shulamit Reinharz, in the second selection, speaks to the socialization process and how it shapes the formation of one's professional identities project by project over a research career. She notes that researcher identities are both created as well as adopted through choices about the resolution of multiple ongoing tensions—between unlearning an outsider's conception and accepting an insider's understanding of a field, between being attracted to and rejecting certain socialization experiences, between overcoming disillusionment with and becoming committed to one's discipline, and between becoming socialized and retaining one's individualism.

In the third selection, James Hunt and John Blair direct our attention to the professional activities that contribute more or less directly to scholarly knowledge. They list and group these activities, then create four general sets or archetypes and discuss their career consequences. Hunt and Blair argue that choosing to do or not to do various scholarly activities will impact both the type and level of scholarly attainment.

The fourth selection, by Connie Gersick, Jean Bartunek, and Jane Dutton, is extracted from their exemplary research study about how a sample of female and male organizational scholars acquired and used their professional relationships. They show what such relationships allow—help, harm, learning, emotional support, and collaborative work—and further alert us to the differential effects of gender and status vis-à-vis power and control, inclusion and exclusion, and exchanges. Professional relationship choices are portrayed as both significant career ends and means.

Our last two selections begin with an interview of the indomitable Henry Mintzberg conducted by Charlie Galunic, which is prefaced with a list of Mintzberg's startling advice for putting passion back in organizational studies. Mintzberg has firm opinions and does not mince words: "There is no good science without passion"; "Be passionate about what you do or get out." Galunic has Mintzberg expand on his pithy advice as well as comment on its implications for academic institutions and practices. Throughout the interview, Mintzberg's theme is that deciding to be a passionate inquirer is a major choice with many real consequences.

The final selection is taken from remarks prepared by James March for a faculty seminar at his retirement. Reflecting on his career, March argues eloquently for maintaining the rigorous in the face of the relevant—not only within universities but throughout our lives. He reminds us that we can choose to seek the vision that higher education represents and to make serious inquiry a true calling.

Learning and Knowing
Linda Ford

Since I started working on my independent study in research about two years ago, I've learned a great deal about lots of things. Much of that learning, while not directly related to research was absolutely essential to my ability to engage actively with the subject. The "learning" took many forms, some very personal and emotional and some more intellectual. And the "doing" also took many forms, some active and outwardly reaching and some more inwardly searching. While the product of that learning is represented in the paper I've written, it seems worthwhile to pause briefly to reflect on the process.

First, I want to describe the emotional learning which had to take place to enable me to learn about research in a meaningful way. This entails changes in my self-perception, my attitudes and beliefs about reality and knowing, and in my feelings. While all of these are interrelated, I'll try to separate them somewhat to describe what happened. Also, they are all related to the more intellectual learnings I'll describe later.

When I first attempted to work on the research paper, I would have been quite comfortable describing my approach as positivist (although I didn't know that was the word for it). Reality was what I could touch and feel. While each person could form a subjective interpretation of reality, I was quite sure that we all live in the same reality. The way we can know about that reality is to measure things that are objectively observable. Then we can explain, predict, and control things in the world. Through several personal experiences, conversations, and readings, I began to believe that such phrases as "the social construction of reality" might be meaningful, that an individual's experience of an event could be completely different from another individual's experience of the same event, that knowing could come from many sources, some internal to me and some external. This awareness led me to be more open to learning about research which explores things I can't see or touch. I began to read about research strategies which aimed at understanding, not explanation, at uncovering meanings instead of observing behaviors, at exploring the person's experience of events instead of just the events. It became more important to me to consider the effect of the researcher on what she was observing or participating in and the consequences of the research results to those being observed.

I began to feel a sense of increased responsibility to use research in a socially responsible way—to want my research to empower and enable those who contribute to the research as subjects (or co-researchers in a collaborative inquiry). That feeling had its roots not only in my new approach to the personal nature of reality and its meanings for individuals, but also in my changed self-perception. Somewhere along the road, a gradual shift occurred in the mindset I had in reading research studies. Two years ago, I read studies as a student looking for "the answer." Now I read them as a peer, critiquing constructively, evaluating critically, and listening actively. Without that shift, I could not think in the first person about research. The key issues of values and ethics and meaning didn't come alive for me until I began to be able to think of "my" research. So, my relationship to the subject of research changed because my relationship to myself, to the nature of reality, and to the social system in which I live changed.

All of those changes opened the way for me to learn a variety of things related to research. I learned that learning and knowing are related but different. This definition isn't exactly *Webster's*, but for me, learning involves taking things in from the outside, whereas knowing is what happens inside. I may know because I've learned or simply because I find what was inside all along. The intuitive or tacit part of knowing is now real for me in a way that it wasn't before. Connected to that is that I've begun to know that there are many ways to know, many ways to learn, many ways to create, and many frameworks in which to place all of that.

So, I guess I've collected a little philosophy and epistemology along the way. And, through all of that, I've learned a little about myself in the world. I now know that I'm a self-aware, self-reflective, responsible, empowered actor in a social arena. That may seem obvious, but for me, it was just a set of words with no personal meaning. Now I KNOW it. That is, it lives inside me. And, I learned that research is exciting, challenging, and dynamic. That it can be personally engaging and rewarding. And that I may have something to contribute to that someday. . . .

Socialization and Identity Creation
Shulamit Reinharz

One product of this study is the isolation of a tripartite set of criteria by which to evaluate social research. All projects should generate knowledge within the three components engaged in a research project: person, problem, and method. In this scheme, self-knowledge (person) is a necessary and publicly relevant product of social research. When I began my socialization [as a survey researcher] I adopted the textbook notion of research, which integrates problem and method and considers the researcher-as-person as irrelevant or as a potential source of bias. . . . I revised the model to include *person*, problem, and method; in the experiential action study, the model further expanded to include person, team, problem, and method. Each subsequent project led me to recognize additional contextual features. The experiential analytic method that extends participant observation and that is my current resting point contains many desirable components of a valid, humanizing method for social research. I hesitate to propose experiential analysis, however, as the final answer to the search for method. Rather it is a personal but generalizable resolution that has its own problems. The context for its discussion here is "the search," which I have characterized as the dynamic force within the socialization process. It is interesting to contrast my distillation of "the search" as the key element of the socialization process based on my reflexive study with the conclusion of the Bucher and Stelling (1977) study that the experience of socialization is "working at constructing . . . identities" (p. 270). People being socialized search for a way to do the work of their identities, and in the doing they express their understanding and need for continuing the search.

Source: *On Becoming a Social Scientist* by Shulamit Reinharz, 370, 372–374, 377–382. Copyright © 1979 by Transaction Publishers. Reprinted by permission of the publisher.

. . . Since contemporary society is characterized by "frequent and momentous passage from status to status" (H. Becker and Strauss 1956, 263), then identity will change repeatedly throughout the life of an individual even if basic personality does not. The question is, How does the change occur? How do people acquire not only knowledge and skills, but attitudes and values as well? Why is it that some aspects change and others do not? How is it that the self is modified so that new attributes are not only situational but long-lasting? How are new "cognitive and normative frames of reference by which the individual defines and interprets life" (Gottlieb 1960, 5) internalized? . . .

These results [from socialization research] reflect the methods that were used—primarily, analysis of survey questionnaire responses. They mention conflicts both during training and later on the job but do not suggest that identity formation is the very coming to terms with those conflicts. An experiential method, on the other hand, uncovers epistemological and ontological components to identity formation and change (see H. Becker and others 1961; Olesen and Whittaker 1968; Bucher and Stelling 1977).

The Olesen and Whittaker (1968) study, based on participation with and observation of an entire nursing school class from entry to graduation, found that the students created "a constantly shifting phenomenological milieu in which the student came to ask herself continually where she stood in relation to her fellows, how she was doing vis-à-vis a beloved former self and a desirable future self, how and under what circumstances she should become as a nurse" (p. 291). In other words, socialization into a profession, as studied experientially, requires a true change of identity in that one acquires a new, although gradually approached, way of going about the business of knowing and being.

In accord with these latter studies, my own investigation suggests the importance of conceptualizing socialization not as a process of transfer but as one of development and conflict. Examples of the transfer model of socialization definitions are the following: Socialization is the "intergenerational transmission of culture" (Williams 1975, 1), or socialization is "both cognitive learning and at least minimal internalization of appropriate norms" (Moore 1969, 868). These are views from the socializers' perspective. The implication of the conservative transfer model is that there is a fixed body of skills, attitudes, values, and behavior patterns that students, recruits, novices, and others being socialized must adopt as their own. Students must attempt to acquire that which already exists. The process is complete when the student has incorporated the attitudes and values to such an extent that they are experienced as internal, or belonging to the new member. In this model, before socialization occurs the novice refers to "the profession's" values; after socialization occurs, he refers to them as "mine." Socialization is, therefore, the *cognitive* mastery of knowledge and skills plus *affective* internalization of the parent culture's norms and values, manifested in appropriate attitudes. Moore (1969, 869) states three tests of the quality of the introjection of norms: "compliance with norms—even if contrary to other immediate self-interests—in the absence of sanctions; manifestations of moral outrage at the misbehavior of others; and manifestations of guilt following personal misbehavior." Such an analysis presupposes a profession or occupation into which one is being socialized where compliance is possible because there is unanimity, uniformity, and consistency in its norms and visibility in its activity. In a consensus model such as Moore's (1969), "misbehavior," which might in fact be creative rebellion, must succumb to self-imposed constraints in deference to the culture being internalized.

In his study of the socialization of prison staff, Blum (1976) has shown that formal training is in conflict with the real conditions of the job, so that those who have "successfully" internalized the formal norms are physically endangered. Here again, socialization (the acquisition of an identity and a method of action) requires the personal resolution of the inherent conflicts, not the simple adoption of the given definitions. Defining socialization in terms of denying the self in order to reduce conflict reflects and abets a society in which selves and autonomous thought are endangered.

The process of socialization by which skills, values, and attitudes are transferred and internalized, and by which the personality is transformed, occurs (to my mind) by way of the resolution of problems. Sometimes these problems are encountered during formal training and sometimes shortly after taking the first job (Lortie 1959). What are these problems? The problem for many professions is the discrepancy between the idealized lay image and the reality of the practice—the self is transformed as the initiate comes to terms with the discrepancy (see also Hughes 1958). The problem in sociology is aggravated by the lack of consensus as to what sociology is and should be doing. As new members resolve the discrepancy during their socialization, they simultaneously create an innovation for the profession. Socialization is not merely the transfer from one group to another in a static social structure, but *the active creation of a new identity through a personal definition of the situation.* As these resolutions are made, the initiate ventures into more and more public exposure of private views and is confirmed by significant others. The newly forming self emerges by way of *the private resolution of dissonance, the intimate interaction with significant others, and the public confirmation of the new self through various ritualized events. It might be stated that socialization occurs through the process of experiencing and reducing cognitive dissonance with regard to the nature of the new identity* (see also Festinger 1957). . . .

The three research projects I have described illustrate the process by which I grappled with the dilemmas in sociological research methods and attempted to construct tentative resolutions and revolutions. This aspect of my socialization process has progressed almost to the point of accepting a research method that will enable me to assume the identity of a social scientist. Accepting a discovered or transmitted method and internalizing a professional identity are therefore simultaneous processes. Although one outcome of my search for method was an innovation or extension (experiential analysis), my companion discovery was that many "methods problems" are not resolvable but are dilemmas that must be experienced and endured. Being a sociologist will always mean becoming a sociologist and struggling with the continuously unmasked difficulties or inconsistencies in the field.

The basic dilemma of my socialization was the tension between becoming a member of the group and retaining my individuality and critical perspective. Could I become sufficiently, rather than completely, socialized? Socialization seemed to imply conformity. How much resistance is possible without diluting the identification? Is there room for deviance and innovation in the socialization process?

As the newcomers adopt and master appropriate skills and values, the peer group of fellow students and faculty supervise the transformation from recruit to member. It must always be kept in mind, but is frequently overlooked, that the recruit does not begin socialization abruptly or in a vacuum. Rather, students bring with them a set of anticipations, private agendas, and a web of social relations. The transformation of the "raw" student to the "fully cooked" member during training makes it possible for departments to exchange and therefore guarantees the social cohesiveness and continuity of the discipline (Stinchcombe 1975; Diesing 1971). The ultimate test of socialization is not merely the quality of the student's research but also the student's incorporation into the discipline's social network. Participation and acceptance into the network reflect the evaluation of the student by the "exchange managers" and "keepers of the myth" necessary for this exchange. The novice risks his or her incorporation into the network by revealing the socialization experiences of dissonance, uncovered anomalies, and disillusionment. Ultimately, identity transformation involves personal work: learning not to be bothered, not to wonder, and not to worry.

Becoming a sociologist means joining a team or clan and demonstrating "loyalty to the collectivity" (Moore 1969, 876) if one hopes to receive the benefits of membership. The discipline as a "collective other" continuously checks the newcomer's behavioral products to determine appropriateness and adequacy. The persistent possibility of failure perpetuates continuing occupational commitment. But fear of failure is accompanied by guilt of betraying the investment made by the elder: "The creation of this obligation solidifies occupational attitudes and loyalties. . . . The person feels he must remain what he has become in order not to let down his sponsor" (H. Becker and Carper 1956, 298). The specific personalized commitment to the socializers is generalized to an overall loyalty to the group in which the socializers are imbedded and through which the rewards are produced. These processes underscore stability rather than innovation, experimentation, or other forms of productive deviance, such as eclecticism.

Socialization is complicated for those novices who recognize that there is conflict concerning the definition of sociology, the role model for the sociologist, and the proper role performance with regard to research activities. The struggle of the initiate is the choice between addressing the myths (Stinchcombe 1975), anomalies (Ritzer 1975), and ambiguities (Hughes 1958) (thus risking embarrassment) and sustaining the irrational conventions necessary to assure the functioning of sociology as a social institution (thus risking alienation). Seeley (1964, 175) expressed this conflict as follows: "For whatever brave show sociologists might put on for others, and particularly for one another, doubts would not die down (and have not yet) [for me] as to what sociology 'is'; and given some definition of what it is, as to whether such an enterprise is possible; and given its possibility, of positive, zero, or negative utility."

This book traces the stages of my attempt to rid myself of my lay, idealized version of sociology after it had been deflated by my rude awakening as a result of survey research. Alternative models were also inadequate and incomplete. My socialization crisis was resolved only by rejecting the teleological image that posits a fixed identity definition as the culmination of the socialization process. Instead, I attempted to create my own identity definition and then socialize myself into it. My own definition centered on the values of a humanistic sociology that are operationalized in the research method of experiential analysis.

The identity change of professional socialization is propelled by the resolution of tension between *attraction* to certain goals and *rejection* of certain experiences, within an environment that balances control with intellectual freedom. My tension derived from my concern with the dilemmas of sociological method. Socialization into sociology was a process of *overcoming*, not just *becoming*. The overcoming of disillusionment through heightened commitment to the original belief has been documented (Festinger, Riecken, and Schachter 1956), but disillusionment can also be overcome by a commitment to change. My commitment to change the discipline rather than to change my own belief gave me room for exploration and creativity, while allowing me to become a member of a new collective identity. The very conflicts and discrepancies encouraged my self-reliance. Instead of conceiving of socialization as the mastery of what was given (ritualism), I attempted to fashion my socialization around what was needed (innovation).

This view proposes that socialization be redefined as a system of reciprocal impact between the parent culture and the novice. As Olesen and Whittaker (1968) conclude, "Socialization is a mutual dialogue" (p. 299). The "mutual modification model" considers trainees as changing that which is socializing them. Here is where the revolution in a discipline can take place (T. R. Young 1974) if the profession is modified by those who enter it. Just as parents are trained by their infants (Lewis and Rosenblum 1974), so too are all social systems affected by newcomers' input. Socialization is an opportunity not only for failure of the initiate but also for renovation of the culture. The parent generation is jeopardized as it socializes the young, since each new generation will not only master but also modify the culture if social controls are not excessive nor the reward system overly confining.

According to the dynamic interactionist model I have sketched, the parent culture is changed by the newcomer, and the individual *forms* rather than *adopts* an identity. The interaction of the incoming novice and the receiving culture can be reconceptualized as a dialectic process that yields a synthesis both for the culture and the individual. In this dialectic, reciprocal, or processual model, socialization is reconceptualized as unending rather than teleological. Socialization is not a leap from one given state to another but a continuous experience of negotiation between the individual and the culture.

To deny the continuity of socialization is to deny the fact that conflicts within a discipline compel the person being socialized to reexamine the position he has adopted. The teleological view of the fixed professional identity coincides with the view of the student's task as limited to acquiring skills, values, and attitudes. Instead, the socialization process as experienced seems to involve resolving, rejecting, embracing, synthesizing, and revising. The former view represents an overly socialized conception of the student (Wrong 1961), oblivious to the ambivalence and dissonance.

. . . The major task of socialization is the unlearning or rejection of a lay conception and an acceptance of the "insiders'" understanding of what the profession is. I have tried to show that in sociology this process is particularly difficult, because sociology contains several alternative models in addition to the simplified, distorted, or stereotyped lay conception. Because the parent culture has many competing models, the novice must choose an identity to adopt. The novices rid themselves of the lay conception and move toward the insiders' model by changing their attitude toward themselves and toward the profession. "The shift in choice of models by the student, his definite steps or his drifting into the path that leads to one model rather than others, is a significant part of his . . . education" (Hughes 1958, 123). Commitment emerges from the need to work out the puzzle of competing definitions.

As I have stated, professional identity formation is not only a struggle to become but a struggle to overcome. The problems inherent in the discipline "out there" are experienced as a problem of the self "in here" as internalization proceeds. Joining a discipline means changing one's self-definition. The ambiguities and contradictions imposed by conflicting models of sociology and the insoluble dilemmas that the novice experiences in the formative stages of socialization are either put aside as one becomes a full member or linger, ready to be ignited with each new experience. The problem of seeing sociology as in need of methodological reexamination continues to be both personal and political, since the definition of what a profession is reflects the given balance of power in that profession at any given time. Adult socialization does not end with initiation into a new role, for within that role there is continuous resocialization, change, and development of deeper ramifications and complexities. It is evident that I will always be becoming a sociologist (or social scientist/practitioner of some sort), just as I have always been becoming one. My fascination with the dilemmas of method rather than my acceptance of what is given will take a variety of forms as my socialization into new roles continues. My critical attitude toward the profession's claims, my debunking of the certitude with which methods and their products are presented, and my wish that the social sciences be rehumanized will most likely remain part of my personal perspective. These parts of my self contribute to an emerging professional identity and will remain while I develop temporary resolutions.

Scholarly Activities: Career Archetypes and Consequences
James G. Hunt and John D. Blair

Picture the situation of Professor Smith. He is an assistant professor of human resource management at a well-known state university who has been there four years and came there upon completing his doctorate. He recently co-authored a highly regarded scholarly book with Professor Jones, a renowned scholar in the management field. Professor Smith is very competent, played the lead role in the research leading to the book and is the book's first author. Professor Jones and he are attending a cash bar at a national meeting of the Academy of Management. The book has been displayed at their publisher's booth at the meeting and has elicited much interest.

Professor Smith is dismayed to overhear a conversation at the cash bar referring to the new book by Jones. A little while later he is further chagrined when a new acquaintance, seeing from Smith's name tag that he is at the same university as Jones, asks him if he has read Jones' book. Smith wonders why he is receiving no credit for the book even though he was the first, and presumably senior, author.

In another case, Professor Jaynes is an associate professor of management at Old Overshoe University. She has published three solid selling textbooks in the last four years. She is also quite active in the Organizational

Source: "Content, process and the Matthew Effect" by James G. Hunt and John D. Blair, *Journal of Management* 13 (1987): 191–198, 203, 205–206, 208–209. Copyright © 1987 by the Southern Management Association. Reprinted with permission of the Southern Management Association.

Behavior (OB) Division of the Academy of Management. Professor Smythe is also an associate professor of management, but at Old Ivy League University. She too has published three solid selling textbooks over the last four years and is as active as Professor Jaynes in the OB Division of the Academy of Management. Professor Jaynes is disappointed to find out that Professor Smythe was nominated ahead of her for an officership in the OB Division. The nominating committee simply felt that Smythe was a better scholar.

In a third case, Professor Smith-Jones is a full professor of strategic management and has written a best selling textbook. He currently serves on the editorial boards of three of the most highly regarded journals in his field. In addition, he is on the governing board of his national scholarly association and is the President-Elect of his regional association. Yet, his colleagues and the doctoral students in the department seem to defer in scholarly matters more to an associate professor than to him. This is upsetting to Smith-Jones since the other professor is not actively involved professionally and holds none of the elected offices he does. However, the other professor publishes several journal articles a year and has just completed a scholarly monograph with a well known publisher, but that is unlikely to sell very many copies.

We argue in the first case that a phenomenon called the "Matthew Effect" (Merton 1968b) is robbing Professor Smith of his just due. In the second and third cases Professors Jaynes, Smythe, and Smith-Jones are each performing a mixture of what we call "content" and "process" activities.

In the second case, a generalized version of the Matthew Effect is also operating so that an individual from a more prestigious institution (with the same writing accomplishments) is perceived to be a better scholar and thus, Professor Smythe, not Jaynes, receives the nomination.

In the third case, there is confusion over what is really content and what is process with Professor Smith-Jones believing he should receive scholarly (i.e., content) credit for his professional activities and textbook writing—an opinion not shared by his colleagues.

It is our contention that the feelings of confusion and inequity described above are common. Further, we believe that lack of understanding of the sources of these phenomena is also common. Thus, we feel that the Matthew Effect and the differences in content and process have substantial impact on short and long term outcomes or consequences for those in the academic field of management, and perhaps for other members of academia. . . .

Core Concepts

Content and Process Activities

Content activities are those activities in which an individual or group of individuals makes a direct contribution to (the content of) scholarly knowledge. We define process activities as those activities in which an individual or group of individuals facilitates (or provides a process for) the acquisition or generation of new scholarly knowledge or facilitates the professional activities of those involved in such knowledge acquisition or generation. In other words, process activities make an indirect contribution to scholarly knowledge.

Content and process activities are both necessary to advance scholarly knowledge. One advances new knowledge directly, whereas the other helps link the scientific community. As we shall show shortly, at the extremes the two activities are clearly separable (e.g., writing a scholarly article accepted for publication vs. serving on a professional association committee to revise the association's by-laws). However, in the middle the activities tend to blend together and provide ambiguous information in content or process terms (e.g., editor of a scholarly journal or chair of an academic program for a scholarly association). Such over-lapping is especially likely to cause confusion in the minds of many and lead them to expect content credit for process activities. Indeed this happened in the third example above. Although both kinds of activities are necessary and valued for the creation and dissemination of scholarly knowledge, content activities (as we term them) are valued more (J. Cole and Cole 1973, 41–46). . . .

The Matthew Effect

As an important contribution to the sociology of science, Robert Merton (1968b, 1973) developed the concept of and conducted research on what he called the Matthew Effect. Merton coined the name of this effect from the Gospel according to St. Matthew: "For unto every one that hath shall be given, and he shall have abundance; but from him that hath not shall be taken away even that which he hath" (Gospel of St. Matthew, XXV, 29).

According to Merton (1968b, 58), the Matthew Effect consists "in the accruing of greater increments of recognition for particular scientific propositions to scientists of considerable repute and the withholding of such recognition from scientists who have not yet made their mark." In other words, those that have, get more; and those that do not have much to start with, do not get much—no matter what their effort or results (advantage produces advantage). Merton (1973, 459) points out that a similar effect (using the Biblical quotation, though not the label) has even been discussed in the physical sciences where, for example, in dehydration of alcohols, hydrogen is eliminated preferentially from the adjacent carbon atom that is poorer in hydrogen (Fieser and Fieser 1957).

Merton and subsequent researchers (e.g., S. Cole 1970; J. Cole and Cole 1973) used the Matthew Effect in the context of studying (a) the kinds of recognition and visibility that scientists received based on their scientific contributions and (b) the way in which scientific ideas are diffused and communicated and the implication for the allocation of scientific resources. Pfeffer, Salancik and Leblebici (1976) have shown results in the awarding of NSF grants that appear consistent with the above diffusion and allocation aspects of the Matthew Effect.

An interesting issue for us in this article is what credit or recognition relatively unknown coauthors get when they publish together with much better known scientists as Smith did when he wrote the book with Jones in our first example. This probably is the best known or most easily recognized aspect of the Matthew Effect. This is an individual level outcome. Diffusion of scientific knowledge as influenced by disproportionate attention to the work of already eminent researchers can also have systemic effects beyond the recognition going to an individual or its impact on his or her career.

The Matthew Effect argues that particularistic (judged on the basis of particular personal or social attributes) as opposed to universalistic (judged on the basis of a universal set of standards with regard to scholarly achievement) criteria (e.g., Bedeian and Field 1980; Parsons 1951) operate in the evaluation and dissemination of a scientist's work. Such particularistic factors as a scientist's rank or reputation in the scholarly community will influence the initial reception of new ideas, the degree and speed of dissemination of that work, and the extent to which resources flow to given individuals or institutions with greater reputations (J. Cole and Cole 1973). . . .

Content and Process Activities and Archetypes

Content and Process Activities

. . . Table [16-1] shows examples of content and process activities in order to convey their flavor. Although one might think initially of a single content/process activity continuum for individuals, we believe it more realistic to think of each individual as having a separate score or standing on (a) content activities, (b) process activities and (c) activities that are a mixture of content and process. In other words, an individual academic can be classified or perceived separately as falling from high to low on content activities, from high to low on process activities, and from high to low on activities that are a mixture of content and process.

It is important to note that all of the content and process activities in Table [16-1], and those to be discussed in this article, are "cosmopolitan" as opposed to "local" in nature; that is, they are activities that are oriented externally toward a community of scholars rather than oriented internally to a given academic institution (cf. Gouldner, 1957). . . .

TABLE 16-1

Examples of content and process activities

Primarily content activities:	Writing a scholarly article/book that is published Writing a scholarly proceedings paper that is published Presenting a scholarly conference paper
Activities that are a mixture of process and content:	Editing a scholarly journal Writing a practitioner article/book that is published Editing a practitioner journal Writing a textbook that is published Editing a scholarly conference proceedings Reviewing a scholarly article/book proposal Reviewing a scholarly grant proposal Discussant for a conference paper Reviewing conference papers Coordinating/organizing a scholarly conference Reviewing practitioner book proposals Reviewing textbook proposals Chairing a scholarly conference session
Primarily process activities:	Serving as president/chair of a scholarly association/division Serving on a scholarly association governance board Editing a scholarly association newsletter Serving on a scholarly association ad hoc committee Serving on a scholarly association site selection task force Handling advertising for scholarly conference/journal publishers Serving on a scholarly association placement committee Serving on a scholarly association membership committee Serving as a scholarly association secretary/treasurer

SOURCE: "Content, process and the Matthew Effect" by James G. Hunt and John D. Blair, *Journal of Management* 13 (1987): 196, table 1. Copyright © 1987 by the Southern Management Association. Reprinted with permission of the Southern Management Association.
NOTE: For illustrative purposes, these activities are roughly ordered in terms of our judgment as to the estimated content in each activity. A more complete list of activities and their relative ordering should be determined empirically.

Content and Process Archetypes

Here we argue that it is possible to categorize individuals in terms of a high or low value on each type of activity. This classification could reflect either actual levels of activity or, more importantly for us here, perceptions by others of differential levels of activity. The archetype matrix is shown in Figure [16-1] and is a four-fold categorization of individuals in terms of their scores on each type of perceived activity.

Process activities

	High	Low
High	Type I Involved scholar	Type II Distant scholar
Low	Type III Association loyalist	Type IV Local (or marginal cosmopolitan)

Content activities

FIGURE **16-1**   Academic archetypes based on process and content activities

SOURCE: "Content, process and the Matthew Effect" by James G. Hunt and John D. Blair, *Journal of Management* 13 (1987): 197, fig. 1. Copyright © 1987 by the Southern Management Association. Reprinted with permission of the Southern Management Association.

Earlier we argued that there were content activities, process activities, and an activity category with mixed content and process components. This latter category further complicates the perceptions by others of the kind of activities in which an individual academic is engaged. Mixed content and process activities in this matrix include a spillover perceptual effect. In this spillover, actual mixed activities fall into a content or process perception category according to whether they are perceived as primarily content or process. These perceptions will be affected by the interaction of a given background variable with the actual activity. For example, we argue below that the mixed activity of editing a scholarly journal would be seen as a content activity if the individual were at a high prestige institution, but would be perceived as a process activity if the individual were at a low prestige institution.

Highly active individuals may be involved in a range of activities that are perceived as either content or process activities, and individuals will have different patterns of perceived activity levels. In Figure [16-1] we have provided summary labels that we feel capture the essence of these different types of management academics. In our typology, an individual can range from the high-high Involved Scholar (Type I) to the low-low Local (or Marginal Cosmopolitan) (Type IV).

Involved Scholar (Type I).   Here is a person perceived as high on both content and process activities. We might envision an individual with an extensive journal/scholarly book publication record who also has been very active in one or more scholarly associations. The person is likely to have held office and perhaps has even been elected as president or equivalent. The involved scholar may also serve on editorial boards or as editor of a scholarly journal.

Distant Scholar (Type II).   We see the distant scholar as one who is perceived as concentrating on content activities at the expense of activities involving process. We could expect such a person would have a very extensive record of journal publications and perhaps scholarly books and very few scholarly association activities, with the possible exception of paper presentations (a content activity).

Association Loyalist (Type III).   The association loyalist is the academic who is perceived as high on process activities and yet low on content activities. This person is often the backbone of professional and scholarly associations. Loyalists serve in many process roles such as treasurers or chairs of committees, and there are even those who were formerly active in terms of content who now spend virtually all of their time in process activities. Since they frequently view such roles as the reward for content activities or because their process activities put them in constant contact with high content people, they may easily confuse process roles for content activities. Perhaps more crucially, we expect that they may think that process recognition is actually recognition of their scholarly contributions, which it may well not be.

Local (or Marginal Cosmopolitan) (Type IV).   This individual is perceived as low on both content and process activities (as we have defined them) regardless of how active he or she may be on local teaching, administration, or committee work. The person may well attend scholarly meetings on a regular basis (e.g., a department chair involved in recruiting) or be involved in such activities as consulting or managerial training away from his or her institution. Even so, the perceived lack of cosmopolitan content and process activities leads us to use the term *local* or at most, *marginal cosmopolitan....*

A Content/Process Consequences Model

[Another] purpose of this article was to use the previous discussion to develop a general content/process consequences model, as shown in Figure [16-2]. The model contains: (a) background variables for an individual;

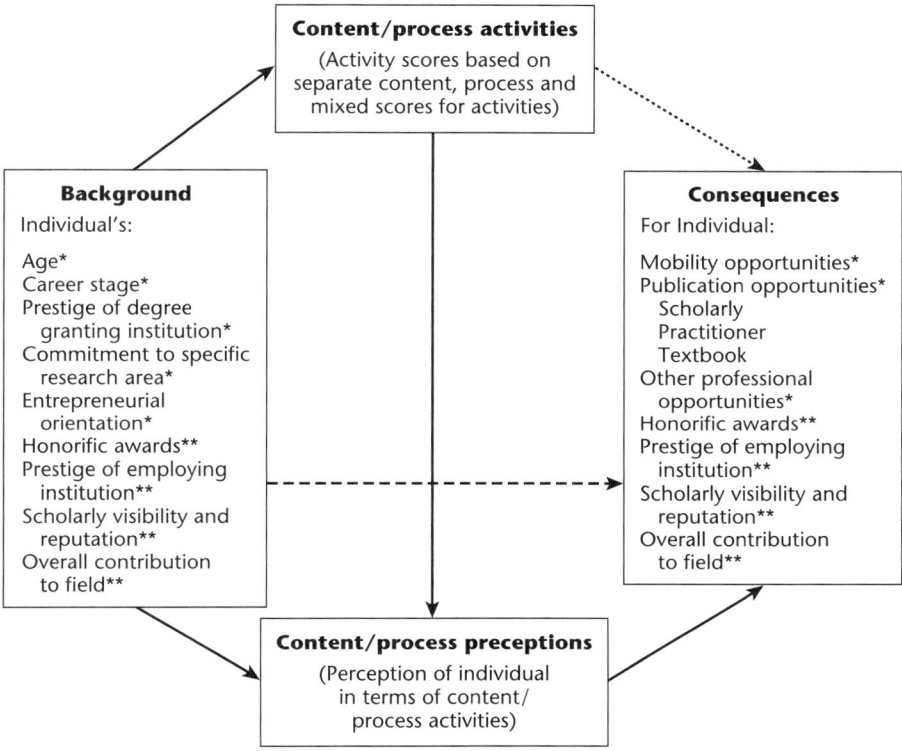

FIGURE **16-2**   Content/process consequences model

SOURCE: "Content, process and the Matthew Effect" by James G. Hunt and John D. Blair, *Journal of Management* 13 (1987): 203, fig. 4. Copyright © 1987 by the Southern Management Association. Reprinted with permission of the Southern Management Association.

(b) actual content and process activities for that individual; (c) others per-ceptions of an individual's content and process activities; and (d) the conse-quences for an individual hypothesized to result from content and process activities and perceptions as moderated by background factors.

Note that in this dynamic model, background variables precede content/ process activities. Even so, for conceptual clarity, background variables rather than content/process activities have been treated here and earlier as the moderator, or what Emory (1980, 97) calls a "secondary independent variable."

The content and process variables are those already shown in Table [16-1]. The background variables for individuals are suggestive and were derived both from the sociology of science literature and a priori from our experience and from that of others with whom we have discussed these issues. Variables included under the perceptions by others of the individual in terms of content and process activities in Figure [16-2] are the same as the actual content and process activities in Table [16-1]. The difference is that these variables deal with the perceptions by colleagues of others as opposed to the actual activities in which a person is engaged. . . .

Implications

First is the question of what a less renowned individual should do concerning the specific Matthew Effect (where the more renowned individual receives undue credit). Assuming the opportunity exists, should a lesser known person co-author with a better known person when (if the Matthew Effect is operating) the lesser known person's contribution will be undervalued?

This is not an easy decision. On the one hand, the undervaluation of credit is troublesome for the lesser known. However, co-authoring with a better-known person may make the difference between receiving less credit than deserved and receiving no credit at all, because the piece is either not written or not accepted for publication if written. The more renowned person may enhance publication possibilities because of the renown or because of additional publication expertise and experience. The piece is also likely to be more widely cited and better disseminated if done with a better known person.

The decision may be easier where there are more than two people involved. The less renowned person may become either an *et* or an *al* when the piece is referred to. Many less renowned individuals may decide that the credit undervaluation is too great in this case and choose to forego the collaboration or restrict collaboration to no more than two individuals.

Second, according to a process extension of the Matthew Effect, one should probably keep in mind that ". . . because the work [content activity] is difficult, scientists [in our case, academics] will find an unlimited number of ways to avoid it even while they are supposedly working" (J. Cole and Cole 1973, 71). Frequently, because of the difficulty (and uncertainty) of being successful at content activities, academics substitute process activities for content ones—or they confuse mixed content and process activities.

Third, to paraphrase Kerr (1975), "Do not do A while hoping for B." Management academics should not perform process or mixed content/

process activities while hoping for content perceptions or credit. Both are valued, but each is different, even though a number of activities (e.g., editing a scholarly journal or writing a textbook) fall in the mixed content/process category. Though both are valued, it has been contended earlier that content activities are more valued. Also, we believe that content activities are significantly more rewarded in terms of the kinds of consequences in our model.

Fourth, our earlier discussion suggests that it is not possible to substitute for a lack of content activities by emphasizing process ones at any single time period. However, it is consistent with previous discussion to argue that content activities at an earlier time period could shade the perception of later mixed activities so that they were perceived as content ones (a person received content credit for them).

Fifth, people are good at different things and need to be realistic and accurate in their self-assessment. Some individuals may be particularly good at process activities and gain particular satisfaction from doing them. If these people are also good at content activities, then they need to consider such satisfying involvement in process activities along with the kinds of consequences indicated in the model above. Then they need to balance their activities accordingly. Of course, they must not forget the third point above—"Do not do A while hoping for B!"

Sixth, if an individual is very good at process activities, but not as good at content activities, then the person can achieve intrinsic satisfaction through emphasizing process activities. Such an individual may even make a greater contribution to the field by doing what he or she does best. For example, this person's process activities may greatly facilitate the content work of others. However, as an academic, this person probably will not fare particularly well on the consequences indicated in the model.

Seventh, an argument can be made that it is appropriate for people to do different things at different points in their career. For example, consistent with earlier discussion, there should be advantages to performing content activities early and process or mixed activities later because of an expected content spillover to later process or mixed activities.

Finally, we believe the Matthew Effect is very real and consequential, although J. Cole and Cole (1973) have demonstrated the effect not to be as powerful and far reaching for the physical sciences as Merton (1968b) suggested. However, Merton (1973) indicated that he believed it more powerful for less well developed disciplines, and it has been argued that Management is one of these less well developed disciplines (Pfeffer 1982). . . .

Summary and Conclusions

Content and process activities are both necessary to advance scholarly knowledge. One advances new knowledge directly; the other helps link the scholarly community and therefore contributes indirectly. Although both content and process activities are valued, content activities are valued more. At the extremes, the two kinds of activities are clearly separable (e.g., publishing a scholarly book vs. serving on a professional association committee to revise the association's financial records).

However, in the middle they tend to blend together into mixed content/process activities (e.g., serving on the editorial board of a scholarly journal or chairing the academic program for an association). Such overlapping is especially likely to cause confusion in the minds of many people so that they expect content credit (expect people to perceive the activities in content terms) for mixed content/process activities.

The relationship between the actual performance of these mixed content and process activities is hypothesized to be moderated by such background variables as institutional prestige and career stage. As an example, following our generalizing of the Matthew Effect, a person from a high prestige institution performing mixed content/process activities is likely to be perceived as higher on content (receive more content credit) for a given level of these activities than a person from a low prestige institution.

The combination of content/process activities or perceptions leads to four content/process archetypes consisting of the Involved Scholar (high content/high process); the Distant Scholar (high content/low process); the Association Loyalist (low content/high process); and the Local (or Marginal Cosmopolitan) (low on both activities). Members of the management professoriate are believed to perceive individuals as falling primarily into one of these archetypes, not only based on what they have actually done, but also depending upon the person's background factors. In turn, others' perceptions of individuals in terms of these archetypes are believed to influence for an individual such consequences as career mobility and publication possibilities. . . .

Relationships Among Scholars
Connie J. G. Gersick, Jean M. Bartunek, and Jane E. Dutton

RESEARCHER: Why are these relationships important to you?

1A. Because I have to work with [these people]! You know, we have decisions we have to make here. . . . Because they're going to vote on my tenure. . . . If there's something rolling that's damaging toward me, and Sid adds to it—that's just fuel to the fire. . . . That's why it's important, and also, you don't like to have the negative. You know, you see

Source: "Learning from academia" by Connie J. G. Gersick, Jean M. Bartunek, and Jane E. Dutton, *Academy of Management Journal* 43 (2000): 1026–1031, 1033–1034, 1038–1042. Copyright © 2000 by the Academy of Management. Reproduced with permission of the Academy of Management via Copyright Clearance Center.

these people on a regular basis! . . . Sid just treats me like a child, and I don't respond well to that! (Junior female faculty member [JRF2], speaking of colleagues in her home department).

1B. Sometimes you lose confidence. And then you get with this group. And you're rejuvenated! You're excited again! They value what you do! They think what you do is interesting! They ask you the right questions! They—they're sort of everything! (Same junior woman [JRF2], of her professional association).

2. I haven't chosen this relationship to be important to me. It just—is. She's always there, in the back [of my mind]. . . . She has had such an impact on my thought of how I should run my life—how I should be a female faculty member. (Junior female faculty member [JRF3], of her dissertation chair).

3. Because I think . . . the most positive and most negative relationships . . . spell out the career. (Junior male faculty member [JRM1], of colleagues in his home department).

To join a profession is to plunge into a community of people. Much more than the meeting rooms and offices where we work, our relationships with individuals and groups constitute the environment in which we live our professional lives. Such environments can be nurturant sources of learning, inspiration, and enjoyment, or they can be destructive sources of frustration and injury. They send us powerful messages about who we are and how we are valued. They shape our expectations about what our careers can be, or ought to be.

Commensurate with the relevance and impact of these forces, there is a considerable literature on the importance of workplace relationships for individuals' careers. One of the most influential streams in that literature is the study of social networks (e.g., Brass 1985; Burt 1992; Granovetter 1973; Ibarra 1992, 1997; Uzzi 1997). Drawing essentially on a social exchange model, network researchers have typically construed relationships as resources instrumental for career mobility over which organization members actively compete (Podolny and Baron 1997; Ibarra and Smith-Lovin 1997). Scholars (e.g., Ibarra 1997) have focused on such key derived questions as: How do people acquire and use relationships to benefit their careers? Why do men fare better than women in the competition for network relationships and career gains? How do women catch up? . . .

For a variety of reasons, scholars have begun to call for more complex, exploratory research on relationships (Gargiulo 1993; Ibarra and Smith-Lovin 1997), for better attention to variation in relational content and context (Podolny and Baron 1997) and most recently, for coverage of negative as well as positive relationships (Labianca, Brass and Gray 1998). One of the most serious critiques of current research is that, despite consistent findings of gender differences, "no comprehensive perspective on networks and women's careers has been offered" (Ibarra and Smith-Lovin 1997, 359). We believe this theoretical problem ties directly to the need for additional complexity in research exploring how and why relationships matter. . . .

Contributions and Limits of the Network Approach

Organizational researchers have consistently described workplace relationships as providing two types of benefits: instrumental career help and emotional support. Career development researchers, for example, discuss *instrumental assistance*, such as advice, contacts, coaching, protection, and advocacy, and *emotional support*, such as counseling, friendship, and role modeling (Kram 1988), that "helps participants develop self-esteem and professional identity" (D. A. Thomas 1993, 170). In view of this research, many network scholars have assumed that relationships are beneficial for career success and that individuals pursue relationships strategically. Empirical work characteristically starts by asking organization members to identify the set of individuals from whom they get (pre-specified) positive resources such as task advice, strategic information, "buy in," social support, and mentoring. Stepping back from the interpersonal dynamics of career development, network studies have focused on identifying ties within pre-specified types of relationships. Scholars have emphasized the importance of organization members' portfolios of strong and weak ties (Granovetter 1973; Uzzi 1996), their centrality, and the pattern of ties among others in their networks (Burt 1992). Ultimately, ties with the right others, in the right configuration, improve individuals' access to organizational influence and career mobility. . . .

Research on network gender differences is subtle and useful, especially in explicating the consequences of differential networks for men and women. However, existing research has tended to focus on the structure of relationships and not on the meaning of the ties that compose networks. It has focused on relationships as resources, tending to allude to negative relationships without examining them or their importance directly. This omission leaves significant dynamics regarding ties, their meanings, and career consequences unexamined. . . .

Methods

Participants

The three of us interviewed a sample of 37 faculty members (10 junior women, 9 senior women, 9 senior men, and 9 junior men) from six management schools divided evenly among East Coast, West Coast, and Midwest locations. . . . To ensure some distance between ourselves and our inter-viewees, we restricted the sample to faculty outside the organizational be-havior and organization theory areas. None of the participants were people we knew well at the time of the study. The research participants' fields in-cluded marketing, management communication, finance, business law, com-puter science, strategy, and accounting. We stratified the sample in order to explore whether interviewees' experiences differed by rank and gender, us-ing a mix of school directories and referrals to locate at least nine participants in each of the four cells we wanted to cover.

Data Collection and Analysis

Our research was explicitly exploratory and therefore employed quali-tative and inductive methods (Glaser and Strauss 1967; Ragin 1994). Each author conducted 12–13 interviews of 45 to 90 minutes with people di-vided almost equally between junior (untenured) and senior (tenured) fac-ulty men and women. The interviews consisted of three sets of questions. In part 1, we requested background information about the interviewees' ca-reer histories. Parts 2 and 3 were designed to uncover what relationships an interviewee saw as central and why they were so perceived. This approach departed from previous studies in which researchers have asked for names of individuals from whom participants seek prespecified benefits. We were careful to keep our questions open-ended, to avoid biasing replies.

In part 2, we gave the interviewees ten blank cards and asked them to use these cards to record the names of persons or groups important to them as part of their professional lives. They could name people from the past or pres-ent, and they could use fewer than the ten cards. They then told us who was identified on each card and the type of relationship they had. In part 3, we asked them to choose, from the set of ten, the two relationships that, for bet-ter or worse, made the most difference in their professional lives. We asked the interviewees why these two relationships were important and requested an example of an encounter—a story—that illustrated each relationship's importance to them. All interviews were tape-recorded and transcribed. The transcripts provided the foundation for our analysis. . . .

Results

We present our findings in two main parts. First, we summarize the rela-tionships most frequently identified on the ten cards and indicate the reasons that these relationships were depicted as important. This general overview illustrates how the participants' significant professional relationships ex-tended beyond the individual, strategically chosen, positive instrumental ties prominent in previous research. We then flesh out this material and develop a more nuanced comparison of the men's and women's experiences by describing the stories participants told.

Part 1: Overview of Interviewees' Relational Environments

The interviewees named several different kinds of ties on the ten cards. Although 32 percent of the participants mentioned mentors and 32 percent named dissertation chairs, the most frequently chosen relationships were not clearly developmental ones. Sixty-eight percent of our interviewees chose coauthors; 57 percent chose people described as both friends and colleagues; 54 percent chose colleagues; 51 percent chose professional societies; and 32 percent chose friends. On the average, participants named 7.6 relationships, choosing 3.38 men, 1.46 women, and 2.22 groups as important in their professional lives. There were no significant differences based on gender or status in the numbers of men or groups chosen. As in previous research, women (mean = 1.95) chose significantly higher numbers of women than did men (mean = 0.94, F1, 33 = 6.19, p = 0.02).

Next, participants named the two relationships that had the biggest impacts on their professional lives. They most often chose colleagues (51 percent of our sample chose at least one colleague), people who were simultaneously friends and coauthors (46 percent of our sample chose at least one such person), senior faculty members from their graduate programs (chosen by 30 percent of our sample), and influential senior faculty from their current institutions (chosen by 22 percent of our sample). Of course, these categories sometimes overlapped; an influential senior faculty member might also be a friend and coauthor, for example. Thirty-five percent of the participants singled out at least one group as highly significant in their professional lives. Groups mentioned included employing universities, schools within universities, departments within schools, colleague groups, graduate schools, professional societies, and outside networks. . . . Participants primarily cited positive reasons for a person's or group's importance to them, but these accounts intertwined noninstrumental and instrumental explanations. For example, one interviewee noted her admiration for a colleague's intellectual capacity, and another interviewee described looking forward to the interest and amusement he experienced in one of his significant relationships. The categories of reasons include both services that identified others provided, such as mentoring, support, and validation, and feelings induced by relationships, such as safety, pleasure, and satisfaction. . . . Evident [is] the importance both of friendship and of simply being known in relationships of long duration.

Although many of the reasons reported . . . support the constructions of workplace relationships developed in past research (e.g., D. A. Thomas 1993), three categories depart from existing assumptions. The most prevalent reason for a relationship's importance, given by 39 percent of our sample, was *collegiality*. These descriptions concerned relationships in which respondents worked side-by-side with identified others, in pairs or in larger groups. Participants' statements conveyed a sense of the others as compatible partners with whom they jointly created value—not as instrumental resource-holders they tapped for assistance toward gaining private ends. The data indicate that good colleagues, in and of themselves, represent a central reward of professional life; we discuss this point further below.

Another twist on traditional conceptions of the role of choice in relational network building is evidenced in the 16 percent of relationships described as important because of their *power and control over* the participant or over the resources that he or she needs. These reasons . . . emphasize the participant's dependence on or vulnerability to the other person and remind us that power over another draws attention to a relationship (S. T. Fiske 1993). This category captures a less discretionary reason for the importance of a relationship than implied by the attraction of positive mentoring, admiration, validation, friendship, safety, and pleasure (Podolny and Baron 1997).

The final category suggests a very different view of why relationships matter than is typically implied in the literature. Eight percent of the people chosen were not described as helpful providers of resources, but as *negative influences* [e.g.,] a male junior faculty member, discussing a male peer, describes combative sparring that worsened in arguments over the critical resource of faculty recruitment . . . [and] a senior woman describes a relationship as a troubling source of doubt about whether she belonged and could succeed in her professional work setting. Such reasons for the importance of a relationship, although numerically few, are important, because negative experiences tend to have disproportionate effects on attitudes and behavior (Labianca et al. 1998; S. E. Taylor 1991). . . .

In summary, the interviewees' accounts reflected both traditional views of relationships as vehicles for resource acquisition and past findings that men are less likely than women to include women in their relational worlds. However, participants departed from the traditional picture by describing relationships more as ends-in-themselves than as means, by indicating that relationships are not necessarily consequential by choice, by depicting the importance of negative relationships, and by describing their ties to groups, not just to individuals, as significant relationships. Finally, these accounts showed men and women to be similar in their stated reasons for relationships' importance.

Part 2: The Stories of Relationships

The stories we gathered flesh out this skeletal view, and they evidence gender and rank differences in how relationships affected our research participants' lives. Our analysis is based on the four basic plots that each appeared in 20 percent or more of the stories, dealing with help, harm,

TABLE 16-2

Number of stories by plot type and interviewee gender and status[a]

Interviewee gender and status	n	Number of stories in total data set	Number of stories in analyzed data set	HELP		HARM		EMOTIONAL SUPPORT		JOINT WORK	
				Total data set	Analyzed data set	Total data set	Analyzed data set	Total data set	Analyzed data set	Total data set	Analyzed data set
Men											
Senior	9	30	18	15	10	1	0	14	8	10	6
Junior	9	29	18	19	12	6	2	2	1	5	3
Women											
Senior	9	37	18	14	7	12	5	6	4	7	3
Junior	10	27	20	11	11	7	5	10	8	5	5
Total number[a]		123	74	59	38	26	12	32	21	27	17

SOURCE: "Learning from Academia" by Connie J. G. Gersick, Jean M. Bartunek and Jane E. Dutton, Academy of Management Journal 43 (2000): 1033, table 2. Copyright © 2000 by the Academy of Management. Reproduced with permission of the Academy of Management via Copyright Clearance Center.

[a] Stories often had more than one plot, so the total number of plots is likely to be more than the total number of stories.

emotional support, or joint work/collegiality. (We later modified these categories, as we show below.) Table [16-2] presents the numbers of stories that included each plot, classified by participants' gender and status. This table shows both the total number of stories told ($n = 123$) and the two stories per participant we used for our statistical analyses ($n = 74$).

The most common stories involved *help*. In these stories, a protagonist needed some type of help—career resources or advice, for instance, or help in getting through a situation of acute risk or difficulty. In response, someone provided help or resources in a way the protagonist recognized as positive. A second type of story involved *harm*. In these stories, the protagonist (the research participant) needed help (as above), and the identified other responded with problematic, unfair, or damaging treatment that the protagonist experienced as harmful. A third type of story involved *emotional support*. In these stories, people described situations in which they felt able to be themselves, able to have fun, relax, or exchange emotional support in a relationship. In contrast to the first two types of story, these stories described mutual sharing. The fourth type of story dealt with *joint work*. In these stories, the protagonist and the identified other were described as taking a professional initiative together, such as writing a professional paper or organizing a conference, or as enriching each other's work in ongoing ways. In both the emotional support and the joint work stories, the emphasis was often more on an initiative being taken together than on one person experiencing a predicament and the other responding. . . .

Discussion

We began this study with a desire to understand better how relationships affect professional life and particularly, how men's and women's experiences compare. As expected, the research participants described instrumental, helping relationships as important. We found, though, that the more mutual bonds of collegueship were even more prominent in their accounts than the helping theme and that negative relational experiences were powerful forces in many of the interviewees' professional lives. Although gender and status made little difference in people's stated reasons for why relationships were important to them, the relational worlds described by women included significantly less career help and significantly more harm than the relational worlds described by men.

In reviewing the literature to get help interpreting our findings, we gained valuable insights and also found some gaps to which our findings are pertinent. The importance of this study is not that it contradicts existing research—it does not. But because it illuminates critical areas that have been neglected, it suggests a fresh theoretical context for existing findings and for future inquiry. In large part, network research has been designed to explore relationships in managerial careers and has primarily framed relationships as a positive means to the end of career mobility. Two central themes in our findings fall outside that paradigm. First is the prominent portrayal of relationships as valued ends in themselves. We believe this theme may reflect the nature of our research setting. As we argue below, both careers and relationships may have distinctive meanings for professionals—meanings underappreciated in network research focused on managers. The second theme is the impact of negative relationships on professionals' careers and identities; this theme emerged more obviously for women but was present for men as well. We believe these themes together suggest a view of relationships, careers, and the links between them that is more complex than the currently prevailing view. . . .

Relationships and Careers

Relationships as Ends in Themselves.   Our findings are saturated with interviewees' depictions of relationships as ends in themselves, from the preeminence of collegiality as a reason for relationships' importance, to the across-the-board significance of stories about joint work and colleagueship. We believe this valuing of relationships reflects not a unique tendency of academics to appreciate each other, but the centrality of peers in professional work and careers. As the interviewee in excerpt 1b, presented in the very beginning of this article said, a good colleague group is "sort of everything." Since colleagues help to define what counts as good and interesting in one's field they heavily influence one's potential to obtain day-to-day respect and enjoyment at work.

Where Relationships Fit into Careers.   Kanter's comparison of bureaucratic and professional careers shows how this distinction matters for network research and theory. In particular, she focused on career logics—people's reasoning about how to pursue success, given what success involves. In bureaucratic (managerial) careers, "defined by a logic of *advancement*, . . . 'career' consists of . . . movement from job to job, changing title, tasks, and often work groups in the process" (Kanter 1989, 509; emphasis in original). For studying managerial careers, it makes theoretical sense to focus on relationships as means and to treat mobility as the chief end goal and hierarchical rank as the key dependent variable. In contrast, the logic of professional career structures is "defined by craft or skill, with . . . 'reputation' the key resource for the individual . . . [Reputation and skill are] intermingled [through] the determination of career fate by fellow professionals" (Kanter 1989, 510). The customary network focus on relationships as a means and on hierarchical movement as an end does not fit the professions well. Here, "winning" also includes being able to choose one's group, to attract desired colleagues from outside, to influence which recruits are chosen and promoted, and to be welcomed into groups one would like to join. In professional settings, inclusion in desired groups is crucial in and of itself. Such inclusion is inherent in the meaning of achieving tenure or of being promoted to partnership. Implicitly, winning implies an ability to exert control over one's reputation and enjoyment of work by controlling the membership of one's group. Relationships are both means *and* ends; measures of hierarchical rank must be supplemented with measures of reputation and group membership to capture professional career outcomes.

Gender Differences: Inclusion, Exclusion, and the Logics of Reputation and Skill. The importance of inclusion in a desired group implies the existence of boundaries between insiders and outsiders and raises the comparable importance of exclusion. . . .

Scholars of both networks and career development have remarked that men and women live in different worlds (e.g., Ibarra and Smith-Lovin 1997). The stories we heard from both men and women faculty members echoed this observation, suggesting that the world of men is more inside the center of the profession and that the world of women is more outside that center. Paralleling Kanter's (1989) distinctions among the career logics of different occupations, our findings suggest that these worlds foster overlapping but different emphases, or sublogics, within the overall professional logic of reputation and skill. The first sublogic, evident in the stories told by the men we interviewed, involves the game of reputation, in which insiders help each other strategize on how to win. The second sublogic, evident in the women's stories, involves the test of skill, in which, outsiders struggle to prove their fitness to "play the game" at all.

Considering patterns of the help and harm stories as a whole and comparing their frequency and content for men and women is instructive. Men's help stories most often described instrumental assistance and meticulous career strategizing about the right relationships and projects to pursue. . . .

Men's few harm stories were about nasty tactics, cheating in the career game, and fights over group membership. The others described in their harm stories treated them, albeit offensively, like competitors in the game. Within this approach, negative encounters may be framed as part of the play, to be put behind one. Men explicitly told us that these incidents were over. The prominence and quality of emotional support stories from senior men may complete this picture of inclusion, indicating both the pressures it involves (needing relief from "fortune hunters") and the rewards of elite membership.

The contrasting and complementary picture told in women's stories portrays struggles with exclusion from the club. In line with previous research (Burt 1992; A. G. Cohen and Gutek 1991; Tharenou, Latimer and Conroy 1994; Umberson et al. 1996), the women interviewed here told significantly fewer stories about receiving career help than did the men. In addition, they often expressed gratitude for relationships in which they found acceptance, could consider both personal and professional dilemmas, and were valued and/or rescued from destructive treatment. . . . The quest for inclusion that McGowan and Hart (1990) noted as typical of women's professional identity formation seems clear in our data.

There are hints in our interviews that exclusion—perhaps by making people feel disqualified from "play"—simulates a logic greater than the logic of strategizing for reputation. We hypothesize that exclusion instead fosters an emphasis on gaining inclusion by proving one's skill. The women's help stories . . . convey a notable lack of strategizing for reputational gain. Interactions with others at key moments—when preparing a pivotal paper, for instance—raise doubts about status, converting the episode into a test of whether or not the interviewee belongs. . . .

Unlike the men, who universally asserted that negative events were behind them, the women we spoke to were more likely to describe the lingering effects of the harm described in their stories. For example, [a] senior woman . . . said, "These wounds haven't healed." The tenacity of negative effects may be another contrast between framing a negative encounter as part of an (impersonal) game and framing it as a (personal) assertion that one does belong.

Mintzberg on Passion in Science
Charlie Galunic

Putting the Passion Back In

Henry Mintzberg, OMT Distinguished Scholar Address, Cincinnati, August 1996

Screw tenure. Better to be able to look yourself in the mirror than to hang your head in the faculty club.

Publish only when you have something to say. You will be even happier as a reader.

Say it all at once, right, altogether. Take a chance at becoming famous instead of fractured.

Never set out to be the best. It's too low a standard. Set out to be good. Do *your* best.

Create knowledge. Discover something new; most everyone else is re-digesting what is old. Something new is probably staring you in the face right now (like Fleming with the mold). That little boy did not have the courage to *say* that the king wore no clothes; he had the courage to *see* it. After that, saying it was easy.

Write for the thoughtful practitioner. Falling over the cliff of academic irrelevance is no better than sliding down the slope of easy practicality. Stay up on that ridge; it's an exhilarating place to be, less dangerous than either side. Your reasonable colleagues will respect you for it.

Get close to action. Not "*the*" action, just action.

Surprise yourself. Then maybe you can surprise others.

Be passionate about what you do or get out.

CG (CHARLIE GALUNIC): Your distinguished scholar address was entitled "Putting the Passion Back In," a lively and often critical reflection on the state of organizational and management scholarship, accompanied by seven points of advice. Let's begin with your main theme: passion. In what way is our field passionless? Moreover, why do you think we have become passionless?

HM (HENRY MINTZBERG): Can you love numbers? Can you love statistical tests? Can you love tenure? Can you love referee reports? We have been overwhelmed by narrow thinking and narrow thinkers, angles more often than theories. Just look at so many of the doctoral programs—lockstep, like kindergarten. Put your head down and publish, we tell them, maybe you'll enjoy life when you retire. Ask yourself how people get into doctoral programs. Do we test for brilliance or for imagination? They are not the same thing. The way most exams (GMAT included) are designed, you get rewarded for giving it back correctly. There is one kind of doctoral student that terrifies me. The one who has done everything perfectly, right up to application time. That means he or she has been correct all the time. A correct thesis is a boring thesis. I choose dentists for doing things right; I choose doctoral students for doing things differently. We desperately need different theses. What makes us think we will get creative thinkers when we are so busy training technicians and statisticians? I am harping on doctoral students because our field is no better or worse than its raw material. But there is no need to worry: we suffer the same failings of most other "scientific" fields I know.

CG: Passion and Science, in some ways, are strange but necessary bedfellows—both are required in our task but are in danger of overwhelming each other. In particular, some would argue that passion should remain a personal issue and that our institutions should promote good science. What is your advice for this difficult balancing act?

HM: There is no good science without passion. Of course, there is lots of passion without science at all. What we need is not a tradeoff, but plenty of both. Two points: first, true science is not about numbers and testing and proof, etc., not *per se*; it's about discovering the world. Science is nothing without creativity. Show me a brilliant doctoral student without imagination and I'll show you a waste of everyone's time. We should get rid of students who want to replicate their professors' work and we should get rid of the professors who make them do this. Second, go back to the big debates in science—we had our own little one, over Pfefferdigms—and find me an objective actor. We don't find truth in proof, we move towards it in scientific shoot-outs. That, by the way, is why I said in the talk that I am a great believer in the flat earth theory. Really. They never built an airport runway in Holland based on the round earth theory. The other was a good enough approximation. But I like to climb mountains, and let me tell you, it would be a pretty dull sport if the earth was truly round. Columbus did not discover "truth" on his trip; he discovered a closer approximation to reality. (Did he realize that the earth bulges at the Equator?) Theories are not true; they are simplifications on pieces of paper. The only real test of a theory is its usefulness. The flat earth theory remains useful for some things.

CG: One of your arguments for why the field needs more passion revolved around the importance of organizations to society. In particular, you suggested that we have failed to attract enough attention and importance to organizational and management issues in society. Can you expand on this importance and on what the field needs to do?

HM: We need to get our people out of the archives and into the painting studios. Then maybe others will come to our museums. Let me explain by example. The worst place in the world to find a thesis topic is in a library. So what do we do? We lock our doctoral students up in the library for a few years and then say "go find a thesis topic." Even the ones who worked in the other world have forgotten it. So they do yet another test on some boring angle developed by someone who never met a manager who was not a dean. We don't need push in our field— shoving our angles unto practice. That is nothing but another kind of bureaucracy: imposing solutions on problems. We desperately need pull. We need to find the burning questions and address them. Let me give you a delightful example. Amidst all the papers presented in Cincinnati with unreadable titles (the abstracts should have read: "See Title"), was one called "Jolted by Gabriel: How becoming a father changed my career." You see, academics can't escape the world completely. (I hope the paper was as good as the title!) Gross titles, like ugly metaphors, are signs of weak scholarship—in the true sense of the word. There are all kinds of great questions out there; organizations are fascinating places. And let me add that even if we as academics make such a fuss about practicing "science," management itself is not a science, nor an applied science; it is a practice (that in part, sometimes, uses science). We can do without the pretensions of the economists in our field. That is the last discipline we should be using as a model.

CG: Your talk attacked the institution of tenure. What are your main arguments against tenure? What system of appraisal would you put forward instead?

HM: Tenure does the opposite of its intention. Created to protect free speech, it acts to gag free speech, because the radicals get assessed by those already in place, which all too often means conservatives. Let's ensure there are legal protections on freedom of expression; then let's make sure that radical ideas are assessed by people creative enough to appreciate the good ones. And let's get rid of five-year reviews, which are an abomination that encourage published trivia instead of serious scholarship. We can do a tentative review after a few years to ensure that there is activity, not necessarily publication in great quantity, and then a serious review after, say, seven or eight years. And while we are at it, how about forbidding doctoral students from publishing. They are there to develop, not to produce. Would you allow a medical student to operate on you?

CG: Your advice on "saying it all at once" was intriguing, a practice more common to other fields in the social sciences and humanities. What will make longer works necessarily better? And how do we confront the tendency for academics to compete on speed and volume of output?

HM: We get graded on number of publications. We get known on quality of publications. How many people don't you know who have published dozens of articles, not one of which you can recall? Yet publish one really interesting article and people remember you forever. This grading does not promote good scholarship. I don't want to look for one good idea in three journals. By the way, the New England Journal of Medicine has a constraint of only a few pages; articles in law journals can be huge. There are different routes to nirvana, although any establishment that thinks "long is bad" is itself bad. Good is good, period. No matter how long or short. When I see page constraints in journals, I want to laugh. Who says 20 pages or whatever is sufficient? There's a prestigious British medical journal that gives its page length preferences, and then warns authors that longer will be tough. I have no problem with that, especially since, in this journal, shorter is tough too! Research is about being creative, insightful. Norms are standards: bureaucracy again.

CG: The rest of your seven points of advice are essentially personal, directed at the individual academic. In what other ways, however, could our institutions and structures change to promote your goals?

HM: We could start by getting rid of the conventional MBA programs. You don't turn teeny-boppers into managers in a classroom. Then the void could be filled with real managers, intelligent ones. That way the professors who have nothing to say to them—which means they have nothing to say to the world beyond themselves—would be replaced by ones with ideas that can be made into something. That's where "pull" comes from—people out on the firing line who have to deal with managerial and organizational issues every day. It's the dialogue that's most constructive.

CG: Finally, some people would associate you as much with the Business Policy and Strategy community as with [Organization Management Theory]. Given your purview of both areas, what distinguishes them and what can they learn from each other?

HM: They are just a continuum in my view. Put the hard-nosed, business-minded, micro applications to macro (strategy) problems on one side and the hard-nosed, research-minded, (equally) micro applications to micro (people) problems on the other. I think organization theory belongs in the middle, about strategy, and structure, etc., hopefully significantly soft-nosed and macro in application. That's where I belong too. Hence, another, reason why I am happy to have been granted this honor.

A Scholar's Quest
James G. March

My topic is not what the future holds, nor what the implications of any future might be for business schools. Forecasting the future seems to me to be a fool's fantasy, and I have few illusions about the role of the old in shaping the decisions of the young. If I have anything to say, it is not about the decisions this school, or any school, should make but rather about how we think about taking action in our lives.

Modern portrayals of human action are overwhelmingly in a calculative and consequentialist tradition. Consequentialist reasoning is the basis for most of modern social and behavioral science, and preeminently for eco-

Source: "A scholar's quest" by James G. March. Reprinted from the *Stanford Business School Magazine* (1996) with permission. Available on the Stanford Graduate School of Business, Business School Magazine website: http://www.gsb.stanford.edu/community/ bmag/sbsm0696/ascholar.htm; retrieved 1/17/05.

nomics. Action is seen as choice; and choice is seen as driven by anticipations, incentives, and desires.

These ideas trace their roots at least to the Greeks, owe substantial parts of their modern manifestation to the formulations of Jeremy Bentham, and derive much of their contemporary power from the geniuses of L. J. Savage and John von Neumann.

It is no surprise that schools of applied economics (or business) teach such a consequentialist theology as a sacred doctrine and also address their own problems of decision and strategy in the same spirit. They evaluate their alternatives in terms of expected consequences, implement strategies with expected outcomes that appear attractive, and seek to manage the actions of others by assuming they are similarly guided.

Such practices honor ideas that are of enormous importance in human development. It is inconceivable that we would abandon them. Nevertheless, the ideas have their limitations. John Stuart Mill characterized Bentham, the patron saint of modern consequentialist thought, as having the "completeness of a limited man."

In particular, Mill wrote that "Man is never recognised by [Bentham] as a being capable of . . . desiring for its own sake, the conformity of his own character to his standard of excellence, without hope of good or evil from other source than his own inward consciousness."

Mill's comments on Bentham might as easily be applied to us. Our comfortable sense of completeness leads us, as it led Bentham, largely to exclude from our visions of human behavior a second grand tradition for understanding, motivating, and justifying action.

This tradition sees action as based not on anticipations of consequences but on attempts to fulfill the obligations of personal and social identities and senses of self, particularly as those obligations and senses are informed by the ethos and practices of great human institutions. It is a tradition that speaks of self-conceptions and proper behavior, rather than expectations, incentives, and desires.

This second vision has become somewhat obscured in contemporary life, and particularly in the halls of business schools; but it has a long and distinguished pedigree.

It is captured classically in many major works of literature and philosophy but particularly in that great testament to the human spirit, Don Quixote. When challenged to explain his behavior, Quixote does not justify his actions in terms of expectations of their consequences. Rather, he says, "I know who I am"—"Yo se quien soy."

Quixote seeks consistency with imperatives of the self more than with imperatives of the environment. He exhibits a sanity of identity more than a sanity of reality. He follows a logic of appropriateness more than a logic of consequences. He pursues self-respect more than self-interest.

As Quixote's misadventures illustrate quite vividly, following a sense of self has its own confusions and limitations, but it celebrates a non-consequentialist view of humanity. Great enthusiasms, commitments, and actions are tied not to hopes for great outcomes but to a willingness to embrace the arbitrary and unconditional claims of a proper life.

Quixote reminds us that if we trust only when trust is warranted, love only when love is returned, learn only when learning is valuable, we abandon an essential feature of our humanness—our willingness to act in the name of a conception of ourselves regardless of its consequences.

The words are obviously a bit peculiar for this setting. But I think they have some mundane implications for those of us who claim to be educators. Our involvements in education undoubtedly have many consequences that we value, but we also pursue and venerate knowledge and learning as a manifestation of faith in what it means to be a human being.

When we recognize ourselves as sharing a human identity that is intertwined with traditions of scholarship, we are led to view business schools in ways that are somewhat less consequentialist than are the ways that have become familiar to contemporary discussions.

Recently, our metaphors of business schools have become indistinguishable from metaphors of markets. The problems of business schools are pictured as problems of creating educational programs (or public relations activities) that satisfy the wishes of customers and patrons rich enough to sustain them.

It is a conception that yields useful insights and is not to be dismissed thoughtlessly. But it fails to capture the fundamental nature of the educational soul.

A university is only incidentally a market. It is more essentially a temple—a temple dedicated to knowledge and a human spirit of inquiry. It is a place where learning and scholarship are revered, not primarily for what they contribute to personal or social well-being but for the vision of humanity that they symbolize, sustain, and pass on.

Kierkegaard said that any religion that could be justified by its consequences was hardly a religion. We can say a similar thing about university education and scholarship. They only become truly worthy of their names when they are embraced as arbitrary matters of faith, not as matters of usefulness. Higher education is a vision, not a calculation. It is a commitment, not a choice. Students are not customers; they are acolytes. Teaching is not a job; it is a sacrament. Research is not an investment; it is a testament.

And when someone says, as they certainly will and do, that all this is romantic madness, that any such foolishness requires a consequential justification, perhaps one that discovers an evolutionary advantage in traditions and faith, the proper answer is Quixote's: "For a knight errant to make himself crazy for a reason merits neither credit nor thanks. The point is to act foolishly without justification."

The complications of confronting the ordinary realities of day-to-day life often confound such lofty sentiments, and I would not pretend that it is possible or desirable to ignore consequences altogether.

But in order to sustain the temple of education, we probably need to rescue it from those deans, donors, faculty, and students who respond to incentives and calculate consequences and restore it to those who respond to senses of themselves and their callings, who support and pursue knowledge and learning because they represent a proper life, who read books not because they are relevant to their jobs but because they are not, who do research not in order to secure their reputations or improve the world but in order to honor scholarship, and who are committed to sustaining an institution of learning as an object of beauty and an affirmation of humanity.

I do not know whether any such thing is imaginable, much less possible. But if it is, then perhaps we can say that we, like Quixote, know who we are. And that would not be entirely bad.

Summary

While general patterns may be discerned for project and career journeys, all such journeys are to some degree unique simply because they are replete with choices along the way. Just as choices about philosophic and theoretical foundations coupled with the many choices in the research process are consequential for the creation and improvement of scientific knowledge, professional and career considerations are likewise consequential for who we become as inquirers.

As the cyclic work of research is repeated project by project over the course of one's career, satisfactions and frustrations come and go; reputations are enhanced or not; competencies, preferences, and allegiances evolve; socialization continues; and contributions are made. As we journey through inquiry, we consider much that allows choice. We learn about, aspire to, and choose to enact professional activities related to our research. We choose to seek, develop, and work within some professional relationships and not others. We choose the challenge of some projects and not others, more or less opening ourselves to continuous socialization as inquirers and creating new research identities. We choose to devote more or less time and energy to our work, aware of how these investments may impact its quality. These sorts of career-related choices, as well as those about finding an appropriate balance between work and nonwork and how to live, combine to produce differential attainment of research productivity, recognition, and satisfaction and shape the trajectory of one's inquiry career.

To become a truly serious inquirer, as the selections above suggest, goes beyond becoming more competent and sophisticated with the craft of inquiry. To fully engage in inquiry means to embrace it as a calling that can and probably will change us. To be mindful about a career in inquiry means making choices not only about what one does but also about who we are and the stands we take as professional persons.

This chapter reminds each of us involved in inquiry—if we are really involved—that we risk changing who we are. Being mindful of the sorts of choices outlined above probably helps who we become. Reflecting upon our inquiry experiences also probably helps. Perhaps someday each of us might be able to state something about ourselves as inquirers like Louis (1991, 365) does: "My approach to organizational inquiry is . . . also my approach to living. It is clear to me that I am an instrument of my inquiry; and the inquiry is inseparable from who I am."

Reprise

We shall not cease from exploration and the end of all our exploring
will be to arrive where we started and know the place for the first time.
    —*T. S. Eliot*

In this book, we have characterized serious inquiry as a mindset that
embraces an awareness of and the judicious choice among many linked and
interdependent philosophic, theoretic, and research alternatives. Inquiry
has been portrayed as important and inspirational, as a reflective craft and
a calling. Conducting inquiry inevitably involves each of us with a community of scholars whose assumptions, values, beliefs, and practices influence
us and our choices about inquiry. Inquiry is a calling that requires much of
us: our intelligence, energy, and emotions; our courage and commitment;
our diligence and discipline. Some would even say that inquiry calls forth the
best of being human. Inquiry's gifts of knowledge widen and deepen our
understandings of ourselves, our organizations, our society, and our world.

As we contemplated the project that was to become this book, we had
a number of hopes. Our intentions were:

- To bring attention to inquiry in general and, especially, in the organizational sciences. We, frankly, hoped to entice our readers into
  joining—or renewing their commitment to—the community of
  serious inquirers.
- To demystify inquiry and dispel many of the misconceptions about
  it, as well as to encourage more careful, more critical, and bolder
  thinking about serious inquiry.
- To offer a perspective on the territory of inquiry that would bring
  order to its major components and that would also enable us to appreciate and discriminate among the variety of alternatives that exist
  in every aspect of serious inquiry.

- To provide access and leads to the literature of inquiry and research to enhance our sophistication as inquirers and to help us become better consumers of and contributors to the research literature.
- To encourage each of us to widen our understanding and appreciation of the philosophic context, theoretic forms, and research orientations and practices so that, in the words of our introductory chapter's epigraph, we can "identify the inevitable tradeoffs in inquiry and relax gracefully."

Looking back over the odyssey of *Foundations for Inquiry*, we can see that its contributions are seldom either unique or new; rather, they are a matter of emphasis. Our primary thesis has been that every aspect of inquiry holds choices that require thoughtful trade-offs among alternatives. In addition, we have also emphasized that:

- The essence of inquiry concerns learning and sensemaking in the pursuit of knowledge;
- Inquiry is usefully conceived of as a series of nested frameworks (our now familiar trio of philosophic context, theoretical, and research process frames);
- An enhanced understanding of phenomena will accrue when inquirers use a variety of perspectives for thinking about and studying them;
- Inquiry becomes increasingly sophisticated through a combination of researcher development, accumulation of knowledge, and the advancement of science as an institution;
- Some aspects of inquiry have been relatively underdiscussed or glossed over and need more attention—for instance, question formulation, ideological influence, theory development, and the differentiation of methods for data acquisition from methods for data analysis and interpretation;
- Although inquiry is a very serious process, it can benefit from a playful approach and passionate engagement.

How then might you continue the odyssey begun with this book? We invite our readers to consider creating two sorts of personal agendas. The first is an intellectual agenda, aimed at becoming more informed about the many facets of inquiry. We encourage you to read beyond your own research projects and outside your field, to read original sources when possible, to read beyond research design and methods, to be ever alert to the nuances of word usage and the influence of language conventions, and to read your own work more critically. The second is a self-socialization agenda. We encourage you to learn from your continuing research experiences as well as vicariously from the research-related experiences of others—consider how they enhance your repertoire of research competencies, how they shape your evolving researcher identities, how they create and draw on your network of research colleagues, and whether and how you allow your passion to infuse your work as a serious inquirer. These agendas can advance your pursuit of the trio of fundamental questions that give direction to each of your own odysseys:

- How does serious inquiry get accomplished?
- What constitutes the nature of scientific progress?
- How might we make sense of and use the variety of perspectives and practices of inquiry in the organizational sciences?

It is our sincere hope that this book has been a hermeneutic experience that leads you to revisit its selections, that inspires you to delve further into its complexities, that occasionally replaces frowns of puzzlement with smiles of appreciation. If inquiry is, ultimately, all about asking probing questions and constructing plausible tentative answers, then each of us should feel free to ask questions about the territory and processes of inquiry itself. We would argue that every issue, every perspective, every practice is unfinished and open for reasoned discussion. If there is no one best anything about inquiry, and if overzealous, idiosyncratic standards of what is good work in inquiry are fragmenting, dysfunctional, and costly to our collective scientific enterprise, then each of us should continue to seek to better understand, more fully appreciate, and carefully elucidate those choices and trade-offs that lead to philosophic, theoretic, and research progress.

References

Abbott, A. 1988. Transcending ordinary linear reality. *Sociological Theory* 6: 189–196.

Abelson, R. P. 1962. Testing a priori hypotheses in the analysis of variance. Unpublished manuscript. Yale University, New Haven, CT.

———. 1968. Simulation of social behavior. In *Handbook of social psychology*. Vol. 2. Edited by G. Lindzey and E. Aronson, 274–356. Reading, MA: Addison-Wesley.

Abercrombie, N., S. Hill, and B. S. Turner. 1980. *The dominant ideology thesis*. London: Allen and Unwin.

Achinstein, P. 1968. *Concepts of science*. Baltimore: John Hopkins University Press.

Aldrich, H., and D. A. Whetten. 1981. Organization-sets, action-sets, and networks: Making the most of simplicity. In *Handbook of organization design*. Vol. 1. Edited by P. C. Nystrom and W. H. Starbuck, 385–408. New York: Oxford University Press.

Alexander, J. 1982. *Theoretical logic in sociology: Positivism, presuppositions, and current controversies*. Vol. 1. Berkley: University of California Press.

Alger, C. F. 1978, Summer. Extending responsible public participation in international affairs. *Exchange: Journal of International Education and Cultural Exchange* 15: 17.

———. 1980. Enhancing the efficacy of citizen participation in world affairs. In *Citizenship and education in modern society*. Edited by C. F. Alger, J. A. Banks, A. Edel, H. A. Giroux, W. D. Hawley, W. Ophuls, R. S. Sigel, and E. A. Wynne, 195–237. Columbus: Ohio State University, Mershon Center.

Allport, G. W. 1937. *Personality: A psychological interpretation*. New York: Holt.

———. 1942. *The use of personal documents in psychological science*. New York: Social Science Research Council.

———. 1950. The role of expectancy. In *Tensions that cause wars*. Edited by H. Cantril. Urbana: University of Illinois Press.

———. 1955. *Becoming: Basic considerations for a psychology of personality*. New Haven: Yale University Press.

Alvesson, M. 1987. *Organizational theory and technocratic consciousness: Rationality, ideology, and quality of work*. Berlin: Walter de Gruyter.

———. 1990. Organizations: From substance to image? *Organization Studies* 11: 373–394.

———. 1993. *Cultural perspectives on organizations*. Cambridge: Cambridge University Press.

———. 1996. *Communication, power and organization*. Berlin: Walter de Gruyter.

Alvesson, M., and H. Willmott, eds. 1992. *Critical management studies*. London: Sage.

———. 1996. *Making sense of management: A critical analysis*. London: Sage.

American Psychological Association. 1983. *Publication manual of the American Psychological Association*, 3d ed. Washington, DC: Author.

Angus, I. 1992. The politics of common sense: Articulation theory and critical communication studies. In *Communication yearbook*. Vol. 15. Edited by S. Deetz, 535–570. Newbury Park, CA: Sage.

Apel, K. O. 1979. *Toward a transformation of philosophy*. Translated by G. Adey and D. Frisby. London: Routledge and Kegan Paul.

Apter, D. E., ed. 1964. *Ideology and discontent*. New York: Free Press.

Argyris, C. 1968. Some unintended consequences of rigorous research. *Psychological Bulletin* 3: 185–197.

———. 1972. *The applicability of organizational sociology*. London: Cambridge University Press.

Aristotole. 1941. Physica [physics]. In *The basic works of Aristotle*. Edited by R. McKeon, 218–397. New York: Random House.

Armstrong, J. S. 1980. Advocacy as a scientific strategy: The Mitroff myth. *Academy of Management Review* 5: 509–512.

Arnold, H. J., and D. C. Feldman. 1981. Social desirability response bias in self-report choice situations. *Academy of Management Journal* 24: 377–385.

Aronson, E., and J. M. Carlsmith. 1962. Performance expectancy as a determinant of actual performance. *Journal of Abnormal Social Psychology* 65: 178–182.

Aronson, E., J. M. Carlsmith, and J. M. Darley. 1963. The effects of expectancy on volunteering for an unpleasant experience. *Journal of Abnormal Social Psychology* 66: 220–224.

Association of Schools of Public Health & the Association of University Programs in Occupational Health and Safety, under a cooperative agreement with the National Institute for Occupational Safety and Health. 1988. *Proposed national strategies for the prevention of leading work-related diseases and injuries: Part 2.* Washington, DC: The Association of Schools of Public Health.

Astley, W. G., and A. H. Van de Ven. 1983. Central perspectives and debates in organization theory. *Administrative Science Quarterly* 28: 245–273.

Bacon, F. 1863. *The works of Francis Bacon: Novum Organum.* Vol. 8. Translated by J. Spidding, R. L. Ellis, and D. D. Heath. Cambridge, England: Riverside Press.

Bagozzi, R. P. 1984. A prospectus for theory construction in marketing. *Journal of Marketing* 48: 11–29.

Bagozzi, R. P., and C. Fornell. 1982. Theoretical concepts, measurements, and meaning. In *A second generation of multivariate analysis, vol. 2, Measurement and evaluation.* Edited by C. Fornell, 24–38. New York: Praeger.

Bakan, D. 1967. *On method: Toward a reconstruction of psychological investigation.* San Francisco, CA: Jossey-Bass.

Barber, B. 1952. *Science and the social order.* Glencore, IL: Free Press.

Barker, R. G. 1968. *Ecological psychology.* Stanford, CA: Stanford University Press.

———. 1969. Wanted: An eco-behavioral science. In *Naturalistic viewpoints in psychological research.* Edited by E. P. Willems and H. L. Raush, 31–43. New York: Holt, Rinehart and Winston.

Barker, R. G., T. Dembo, and K. Lewin. 1941. Frustration and regression: An experiment with young children. *University of Iowa Studies in Child Welfare* 18: no. 386.

Barker, S. F. 1969. Logical positivism and the philosophy of mathematics. In *The legacy of logical positivism.* Edited by P. Achinstein and S. Barker, 229–257. Baltimore, MD: Johns Hopkins Press.

Barnard, C. I. 1938. *The functions of the executive.* Cambridge, MA: Harvard University Press.

Barnes, B. 1977. *Interests and the growth of knowledge.* London: Routledge & Kegan Paul.

Barnes, B., and S. Shapin, eds. 1979. *Natural order: Historical studies of scientific culture.* Beverly Hills, CA: Sage.

Barnett, V. 1982. *Comparative statistical inference,* 2d ed. Chichester, UK: Wiley.

Barnett, V., and T. Lewis. 1978. *Outliers in statistical data.* Chichester: Wiley.

Barnowe, T., P. Frost, and M. Jamal. 1979. When personality meets situation: Exploring influences on choice of business major. *Journal of Occupational Psychology* 52: 167–176.

Bartlett, F. 1958. *Thinking.* New York: Basic.

Bateson, G. 1972. *Steps to an ecology of mind.* New York: Ballantine.

———. 1979. *Mind and nature.* New York: Dutton.

Becker, H., and J. W. Carper. 1956. The development of identification with an occupation. *American Journal of Sociology* 61: 289–298.

Becker, H., B. Geer, E. C. Hughes, and A. L. Strauss. 1961. *Boys in white: Student culture in medical school*. Chicago: University of Chicago Press.

Becker, H., and A. Strauss. 1956. Careers, personality, and adult socialization. *American Journal of Sociology* 52: 253–263.

Becker, S. W. 1970. The parable of the pill. *Administrative Science Quarterly* 15: 94–96.

Bedeian, A., and H. Field. 1980. Academic stratification in graduate management programs: Departmental prestige and faculty hiring patterns. *Journal of Management* 6: 99–115.

Behling, O. 1980. The case for the natural science model for research in organization behavior and organization theory. *Academy of Management Review* 5(4): 483–490.

Behrens, J. C. 1977. *The typewritten guerillas*. Chicago: Nelson-Hall.

Bell, D. 1977. Ideology. In *The Harper dictionary of modern thought*. Edited by A. Bullock and O. Stallybrass, 298–299. New York: Harper and Row.

Bem, S. 1974. The measurement of psychological androgyny. *Journal of Consulting and Clinical Psychology* 42: 155–167.

Bendix, R. 1970. Industrialization, ideologies, and social structure. In *Comparative perspectives on formal organizations*. Edited by H. A. Landsberger, 58–74. Boston: Little, Brown.

Benson, J. K. 1977a. Innovation and crises in organizational analysis. In *Organizational analysis, critique and innovation*. Edited by J. K. Benson, 5–18. Beverly Hills, CA: Sage.

———. 1977b. Organizations: A dialectical view. *Administrative Science Quarterly* 22: 1–21.

Bentz, V. M., and J. J. Shapiro. 1998. *Mindful inquiry in social research*. Thousand Oaks, CA: Sage.

Berger, J., B. P. Cohen, J. L. Snell, and M. Zelditch Jr. 1962. *Types of formalization in small-group research*. Boston: Houghton Mifflin.

Berger, J., and M. Zelditch, eds. 1993. *Theoretical research programs: Studies in the growth of theory*. Stanford, CA: Stanford University Press.

Berger, P. L. 1963. *Invitation to sociology: A humanistic perspective*. Garden City, NY: Doubleday.

Berger, P. L., and T. Luckmann. 1966. *The social construction of reality*. Garden City, NY: Doubleday.

Bergman, G. 1957. *Philosophy of science*. Madison: University of Wisconsin Press.

Berle, A. A., Jr., and G. C. Means. 1932. *The modern corporation and private property*. New York: Macmillan.

Berlyne, D. E. 1964. Emotional aspects of learning. *Annual Review of Psychology* 15: 115–142.

Berman, J. S., and D. A. Kenny. 1976. Correlational bias in observer ratings. *Journal of Personality and Social Psychology* 34: 263–273.

Bernard, C. 1957. *An introduction to the study of experimental medicine.* New York: Dover Publications.

Bernstein, R. J. 1976. *The restructuring of social and political theory.* Philadelphia: University of Pennsylvania Press.

Berrien, F. K. 1968. *General and social systems.* New Brunswick, NJ: Rutgers University Press.

Beyer, J. M. 1981. Ideologies, values, and decision-making in organizations. In *Handbook of organizational design: Remodeling organizations and their environments.* Vol. 2. Edited by P. C. Nystrom and W. H. Starbuck, 166–202. New York: Oxford University Press.

Beyer, J. M., R. L. Dunbar, and A. D. Meyer. 1988. Comment: The concept of ideology in organizational analysis. *Academy of Management Review* 13(3): 483–489.

Bidwell, C. E. 1979. The school as a formal organization: Some new thoughts. In *Problem-finding in educational administration.* Edited by G. L. Immegart and W. L. Boyd, 87–121. Lexington, MA: Lexington.

Bierstedt, R. 1959. Nominal and real definitions in sociological theory. In *Symposium on sociological theory.* Edited by L. Gross, 121–144. New York: Harper and Row.

Bishop, Y. M., S. E. Fienberg, and P. W. Holland. 1975. *Discrete multivariate analysis.* Cambridge, MA: MIT Press.

Blake, R., and J. Mouton. 1964. *The managerial grid.* Houston, TX: Gulf Publishing.

Blalock, H. M. 1968. The measurement problem: A gap between the languages of theory and research. In *Methodology in social research.* Edited by H. M. Blalock Jr., and A. B. Blalock, 5–27. New York: McGraw Hill.

———. 1969. *Theory construction: From verbal to mathematical formulations.* Englewood Cliffs, NJ: Prentice-Hall.

———. 1970. *An introduction to social research.* Englewood Cliffs, NJ: Prentice-Hall.

———. 1982. *Conceptualization and measurement in the social sciences.* Beverly Hills, CA: Sage.

Blau, P. M. 1960. Structural effects. *American Sociological Review* 25: 178–193.

———. 1965. The comparative study of organizations. *Industrial and Labour Relations Review* 28: 323–38.

Blau, P. M., and R. W. Scott. 1962. *Formal organizations.* San Francisco: Chandler.

Block, J. 1968. Some reasons for the apparent inconsistency of personality. *Psychological Bulletin* 70: 210–212.

Blum, L. 1976. Sources of influence in the socialization of corrections workers. Ph.D. diss., University of Michigan.

Blumer, H. 1954. What is wrong with social theory? *American Sociological Review* 19: 3–10.

———. 1969. *Symbolic interactionism: Perspective and method.* Englewood Cliffs, NJ: Prentice-Hall.

Bobko, P., and J. Schwartz. 1984. A metric for integrating theoretically related but statistically uncorrelated constructs. *Journal of Personality Assessment* 48: 11–16.

Boring, E. G. 1950. *A history of experimental psychology,* 2d ed. New York: Appleton-Century-Crofts.

Borko, H. 1962. *Computer applications in the behavioral sciences.* Englewood Cliffs, NJ: Prentice-Hall.

Bouchard, T. J., Jr. 1971. Abandon all hope ye who enter here. *Contemporary Psychology* 16: 324–325.

———. 1976. Field research methods: Interviewing, questionnaires, participant observation, systematic observation, unobtrusive measures. In *Handbook of industrial and organizational psychology.* Edited by M. D. Dunnette, 363–413. Chicago: Rand McNally.

Bougon, M., K. E. Weick, and D. Binkhorst. 1977. Cognition in organizations: An analysis of the Utrecht Jazz Orchestra. *Administration Science Quarterly* 22(4): 606–639.

Bourgeois, L. J. 1979. Toward a method of middle-range theorizing. *Academy of Management Review* 4: 443–447.

Braithwaite, R. B. 1953. *Scientific explanation.* Cambridge: Cambridge University Press.

Brass, D. J. 1985. Men's and women's networks: A study of interaction patterns and influences on organizations. *Academy of Management Journal* 28: 327–343.

Braverman, H. 1974. *Labor and monopoly capital.* New York: Monthly Review Press.

Brewer, J. K. 1972. On the power of statistical tests in the *American Educational Research Journal. American Educational Research Journal* 9: 391–401.

Brewer, M. B., and B. E. Collins, eds. 1981. *Scientific inquiry and the social sciences: A volume in honor of Donald T. Campbell.* San Francisco: Jossey-Bass.

Bridgman, P. W. 1954, Spring. The prospect for intelligence. *Yale Review* 34: 444–461.

Britt, D. W., and O. Galle. 1974. Structural antecedents of the shape of strikes: A comparative analysis. *American Sociological Review* 39: 642–651.

Brodbeck, M. 1959. Models, meaning, and theories. In *Symposium on sociological theory.* Edited by L. Gross, 373–403. New York: Harper and Row.

Brown, L. 1966. *General philosophy in education.* New York: McGraw-Hill.

Brown, R. H. 1977. *A poetic sociology*. Cambridge: Cambridge University Press.

———. 1978. Bureaucracy as praxis: Toward a political phenomenology of formal organization. *Administrative Science Quarterly* 23: 362–382.

Brunswik, E. 1956. *Perception and the representative design of psychological experiments*. Berkeley: University of California Press.

Bucher, R., and J. Stelling. 1977. *Becoming professional*. Beverly Hills, CA: Sage.

Buckley, W. C. 1967. *Sociology and modern systems theory*. Englewood Cliffs, NJ: Prentice-Hall.

Bunge, M. 1970. *Causality*. New York: World Publishing Co.

Burawoy, M. 1979. *Manufacturing consent*. Chicago: University of Chicago Press.

———. 1985. *The politics of production: Factory regimes under capitalism and socialism*. London: Verso.

Burgess, R., and D. Bushell Jr. 1969. *Behavioral sociology*. New York: Columbia Press.

Burns, T., and G. M. Stalker. 1961. *The management of innovation*. London: Tavistock.

Burrell, G. 1996. Normal science, paradigms, metaphors, discourses and genealogies of analysis. In *Handbook of organizational studies*. Edited by S. R. Clegg, C. Hardy, and W. R. Nord, 642–658. London: Sage.

Burrell, G., and G. Morgan. 1979. *Sociological paradigms and organizational analysis*. London: Heinemann.

Burt, R. 1992. *Structural holes*. Cambridge, MA: Harvard University Press.

Burtt, E. A. 1946. *Right thinking: A study of its principles and methods*. New York: Harper and Brothers.

Calas, M., and L. Smircich. 1996. From the "woman's" point of view: Feminist approaches to organization studies. In *Handbook of organization studies*. Edited by S. Clegg, C. Hardy, and W. Nord, 218–257. London: Sage.

Callon, M., J. Law, and A. Rip, eds. 1986. *Mapping the dynamics of science and technology*. London: Macmillan.

Campbell, D. T. 1969. Reforms as experiments. *American Psychologist* 24: 409–429.

———. 1974. Qualitative knowing in action research. Kurt Lewin Award Address, Society for the Psychological Study of Social Issues, New Orleans, LA.

———. 1975. "Degrees of freedom" and the case study. *Comparative Political Studies* 8: 198–193.

Campbell, D. T, and D. W. Fiske. 1959. Convergent and discriminant validation by the multitrait-multimethod matrix. *Psychological Bulletin* 56: 81–105.

Campbell, D. T., and J. C. Stanley. 1963. *Experimental and quasi-experimental designs for research*. Chicago: Rand McNally.

———. 1966. *Experimental and quasi-experimental designs for research*. Chicago: Rand McNally.

Campbell, J. P. 1977. The cutting edge of leadership: An overview. In *Leadership: The cutting edge*. Edited by J. G. Hunt and L. L. Larson, 221–233. Carbondale: Southern Illinois University Press.

Campbell, J. P., R. L. Daft, and C. L. Hulin. 1982. *What to study: Generating and developing research questions*. Beverly Hills, CA: Sage.

Campbell, N. R. 1952. *What is science?* New York: Dover Publications.

Camus, A. 1948. *The plague*. New York: Modern Library.

Cantril, H. 1944. *Gauging public opinion*. Princeton, NJ: Princeton University Press.

Capra, F. 1975. *The tao of physics*. Boulder, CO: Shambhala Publications.

Carlsmith, J. M., and E. Aronson. 1963. Some hedonic consequences of the confirmation and disconfirmation of expectancies. *Journal of Abnormal Social Psychology* 66: 151–156.

Carlsmith, J. M., P. C. Ellsworth, and E. Aronson. 1976. *Methods of research in social psychology*. Reading, MA: Addison-Wesley.

Carnap, R. 1950. *Logical foundations of probability*. Chicago: University of Chicago Press.

Cartwright, D. 1973. Determinants of scientific progress: The case of research on the risky shift. *American Psychologist* 28: 222–231.

Chambers, J. M., W. S. Cleveland, B. Kleiner, and P. A. Tukey. 1983. *Graphical methods for data analysis*. Belmont, CA: Wadsworth.

Chandler, A. D. 1977. *The visible hand: The managerial revolution in American business*. Cambridge, MA: Belknap Press.

Chapanis, A. 1964. Knowledge of performance as an incentive in repetitive, monotonous tasks. *Journal of Applied Psychology* 48: 263–267.

Chapman, L. J., and J. P. Chapman. 1967. Genesis of popular but erroneous psychodiagnostic observations. *Journal of Abnormal Psychology* 73: 193–204.

———. 1969. Illusory correlations as an obstacle to the use of valid psychodiagnostic signs. *Journal of Abnormal Psychology* 74: 271–280.

Chase, L. J., and R. B. Chase. 1976. A statistical power analysis of applied psychological research. *Journal of Applied Psychology* 61: 234–237.

Chatfield, C., and A. J. Collins. 1980. *Introduction to multivariate analysis*. London: Chapman and Hall.

Chio, V. C. M. 1992. Rethinking control and domination: The substantive and constitutive role of management theory and language. Presented to the AESA conference, the University of Massachusetts at Amherst.

Chomsky, N. 1959. Review of Skinner's 'Verbal Behaviour.' *Language* 35: 26–58.

———. 1965. *Aspects of the theory of syntax*. New York: Mouton.

———. 1968. *Language and mind*. New York: Harcourt, Brace and World.

———. 1987. *The Chomsky reader*. Edited by J. Peck. New York: Pantheon Books.

Churchman, C. W. 1968. *The systems approach*. New York: Delacorte Press.

———. 1971. *The design of inquiring systems*. New York: Basic Books.

Clark, R. D., III. 1971. Group-induced shift toward risk: A critical appraisal. *Psychological Bulletin* 76: 251–270.

Clegg, S. R. 1989. *Frameworks of power*. London: Sage.

Clegg, S. R., and D. Dunkerley. 1980. *Organization, class, and control*. London: Routledge and Kegan Paul.

Clegg, S. R., C. Hardy, and W. R. Nord, eds. 1996. *Handbook of organization studies*. London: Sage.

Cohen, A. G., and B. A. Gutek. 1991. Sex differences in the career experiences of members of two APA divisions. *American Psychologist* 46: 1292–1298.

Cohen, B. 1980. *Developing sociological knowledge: Theory and method*. Englewood Cliffs, NJ: Prentice Hall.

Cohen, J. 1962. The statistical power of abnormal-social psychological research: A review. *Journal of Abnormal and Social Psychology* 65: 145–153.

———.1965. Some statistical issues in psychological research. In *Handbook of clinical psychology*. Edited by B. B. Wolman, 95–121. New York: McGraw-Hill.

———. 1973. Statistical power analysis and research results. *American Educational Research Journal* 10: 225–229.

———. 1977. *Statistical power analysis for the behavioral sciences*, 2d ed. New York: Academic Press.

Cohen, K. J., and R. M. Cyert. 1965. Simulation of organizational behavior. In *Handbook of organizations*. Edited by J. G. March, 305–334. Chicago: Rand McNally.

Cohen, M. D., J. G. March, and J. P. Olsen. 1972. A garbage-can model of organizational choice. *Administrative Science Quarterly* 17(1): 1–25.

Cole, J., and S. Cole. 1973. *Social stratification in science*. Chicago: University of Chicago Press.

Cole, S. 1970. Professional standing and the reception of scientific discoveries. *American Journal of Sociology* 76: 286–306.

Collins, R. 1981. On the microfoundations of macrosociology. *American Journal of Sociology* 86: 984–1014.

Conant, J. B. 1952. *Modern science and modern man*. Garden City, NY: Columbia University Press.

Constantinople, A. 1973. Masculinity-femininity: An exception to the famous dictum? *Psychological Bulletin* 80: 389–407.

Cook, K. S., and R. M. Emerson. 1984. Exchange networks and the analysis of complex organizations. In *Research in the sociology of organizations*. Edited by S. B. Bacharach and E. J. Lawler, 1–30. Greenwich, CT: JAI Press.

Cook, S. D. N., and J. S. Brown. 1999. Bridging epistemologies: The generative dance between organizational knowledge and organizational knowing. *Organization Science* 10: 381–400.

Cook, T. D., and D. T. Campbell. 1976. The design and conduct of quasi-experiments and true experiments in field settings. In *Handbook of industrial and organizational psychology.* Chap. 7. Edited by M. D. Dunnette. Chicago: Rand McNally.

———. 1979. *Quasi-experimentation: Design and analysis issues for field settings.* Chicago: Rand McNally.

Cooley, C. H. 1902. *Human nature and the social order.* New York: Scribner's.

———. 1931. *Life and the student.* New York: Knopf.

Cooper, C. L., S. Cartwright, and P. C. Earley, eds. 2001. *International handbook of organizational culture and climate.* Chichester, UK: Wiley.

Cooper, R., and G. Burrell. 1988. Modernism, postmodernism and organizational analysis: An introduction. *Organization Studies* 9/1: 91–112.

Copas, J. B. 1983. Regression, prediction and shrinkage. *Journal of the Royal Statistical Society* B 45: 311–354.

Copi, I. M. 1954. *Symbolic logic.* New York: Macmillan.

———. 1986. *Introduction to logic.* New York: Macmillan.

Costner, H. L., and R. K. Leik. 1964. Deduction from "axiomatic theory." *American Sociological Review* 29: 819–835.

Cox, D. R. 1977. The role of significance tests. *Scandinavian Journal of Statistics* 4: 49–70.

Cox, D. R., and D. V. Hinkley. 1974. *Theoretical statistics.* London: Chapman and Hall.

Cox, D. R., and E. J. Snell. 1981. *Applied statistics.* London: Chapman and Hall.

Crano, W. D., and M. B. Brewer. 1973. *Principles of research in social psychology.* New York: McGraw-Hill.

Cronbach, L. J. 1957. The two disciplines of scientific psychology. *American Psychologist* 12: 671–684.

———. 1975. Beyond the two disciplines of scientific psychology. *American Psychologist* 30: 116–127.

Cronbach, L. J., and P. E. Meehl. 1955. Construct validity in psychological tests. *Psychological Bulletin* 52: 281–302.

Cummings, L. L., and P. J. Frost, eds. 1985. *Publishing in the organizational sciences.* Homewood, IL: Irwin.

Cunningham, F. 1973. *Objectivity on social science.* Toronto, Ontario, Canada: University of Toronto Press.

Cyert, R. M., and J. G. March. 1963. *A behavioral theory of the firm.* Englewood Cliffs, NJ: Prentice-Hall.

Czarniawska-Joerges, B. 1988. *Ideological control in nonideological organizations.* New York: Praeger.

Cziko, G. A. 1989. Unpredictability and indeterminism in human behavior: Arguments and implications for educational research. *Educational Researcher* 18: 17–25.

Daft, R. L. 1980. The evolution of organization analysis in ASQ, 1959–1979. *Administrative Science Quarterly* 25: 632–636.

———. 1983. Learning the craft of organizational research. *Academy of Management Review* 8: 539–546.

———. 1984. Antecedents of significant and not-so-significant organizational research. In *Method and analysis in organizational research*. Edited by T. S. Bateman and G. R. Ferris, 3–14. Reston, VA: Reston Publishing.

———. 1985. Why I recommended that your manuscript be rejected and what you can do about it. In *Perspectives on publishing*. Edited by L. L. Cummings and P. J. Frost, 164–182. Homewood, IL: Irwin.

Daft, R. L., and A. Y. Lewin. 1990. Can organization studies begin to break out of the normal science straitjacket? An editorial essay. *Organization Science* 1: 1–19.

D'Andrade, R. 1995. *The development of cognitive anthropology*. New York: Cambridge University Press.

Davidson, P. O., and C. G. Costello. 1969. *N = 1: Experimental studies of single cases*. New York: Van Nostrand.

Davis, M. S. 1971. That's interesting: Toward a phenomenology of sociology and a sociology of phenomenology. *Philosophy of Social Science* 1: 309–344.

Dawes, R. M. 1969. "Interaction effects" in the presence of asymmetrical transfer. *Psychological Bulletin* 71: 55–57.

Dawes, R. M., and R. H. Thaler. 1988. Anomalies cooperation. *Journal of Economic Perspectives* 2: 187–197.

Deal, T. E., and A. A. Kennedy. 1982. *Corporate cultures*. Reading, MA: Addison-Wesley.

Deetz, S. A. 1985. Critical-cultural research: New sensibilities and old realities. *Journal of Management* 11(2): 121–136.

———. 1992. *Democracy in the age of corporate colonization: Developments in communication and the politics of everyday life*. Albany: State University of New York Press.

———. 1994. The new politics of the workplace: Ideology and other unobtrusive controls. In *After postmodernism: Reconstructing ideology critique*. Edited by H. Simons and M. Billig, 172–199. Newbury Park, CA: Sage.

———. 1995. *Transforming communication, transforming business: Building responsible and responsive workplaces*. Cresskill, NJ: Hampton Press.

———. 1998. Discursive formations, strategized subordination, and self-surveillance: An empirical case. In *Foucault, management and organization theory: From panopticon to technologies of self*. Edited by A. McKinlay and K. Starkey, 151–172. London: Sage.

Deetz, S. A., and D. Mumby. 1990. Power, discourse, and the workplace: Reclaiming the critical tradition in communication studies in organizations. In *Communication yearbook*. Vol. 13. Edited by J. Anderson, 18–47. Newbury Park, CA: Sage.

Denzin, N. K., and Y. S. Lincoln, eds. 1994. *Handbook of qualitative research.* Thousand Oaks, CA: Sage.

Deutsch, K. W., J. Platt, and D. Senghaas. 1971. Conditions favoring major advances in social science. *Science* 171: 450–459.

Dewey, J. 1933. *How we think.* Lexington, MA: D. C. Health.

Diesing, P. 1971. *Patterns of discovery in the social sciences.* Chicago: AVC.

Dion, K. L., R. S. Baron, and N. Miller. 1971. Why do groups make riskier decisions than individuals? In *Advances in experimental social psychology,* vol. 5. Edited by L. Berkowitz, 306–377. New York: Academic Press.

Dipboye, R. L., and M. F. Flanagan. 1979. Research settings in industrial and organizational psychology: Are findings in the field more generalizable than in the laboratory? *American Psychologist* 34: 141–150.

Dohrenwend, B. P., and B. S. Dohrenwend. 1969. *Social status and psychological disorder.* New York: Wiley.

Donaldson, L. 1985. *In defense of organization theory: A reply to critics.* Cambridge: Cambridge University Press.

———. 1990. The ethereal hand: Organizational economics and management theory. *Academy of Management Review* 15: 369–381.

Douglas, J. D. 1970. *Understanding everyday life.* Chicago: Aldine.

Downey, H. K., and R. D. Ireland. 1979. Quantitative versus qualitative: The case of environment assessment in organizational studies. *Administrative Science Quarterly* 24: 630–638.

Drechsler, H., P. Frost, T. Barnowe, and I. Chafetz. 1979. Specialization and values as inputs to decision making of mining managers. *Relations Industrielles* 34: 241–256.

Drucker, P. F. 1954. *The practice of management.* New York: Harper and Row.

Dubin, R. 1969. *Theory building.* New York: Free Press.

———. 1976. Theory building in applied areas. In *Handbook of industrial and organizational psychology.* Edited by M. D. Dunnette, 17–40. Chicago: Rand McNally.

Dukes, W. F. 1965. N = 1. *Psychological Bulletin* 64: 74–79.

Durkheim, E. 1933. *The division of labor in society.* New York: MacMillan.

———. 1951. *Suicide.* New York: Free Press.

———. 1964. *The rules of sociological method.* New York: Free Press.

Dyck, A. J. 1963. The social contacts of some Midwest children with their parents and teachers. In *The stream of behavior.* Edited by R. G. Barker, 78–98. New York: Appleton-Century-Crofts.

Dyer, L., and G. W. Holder. 1989. *Toward a strategic perspective of human resource management: Evolving roles and responsibilities.* Washington, DC: Bureau of National Affairs.

Ebbinghaus, H. 1885. *Über das Gedächtnis.* Leipzig: Duncker & Humblot.

Eden, D., and V. Leviatin. 1975. Implicit leadership theory as a determinant of the factor structure underlying supervisory behavior scales. *Journal of Applied Psychology* 60: 736–740.

Edgington, E. S. 1972. N = 1 experiments: Hypothesis testing. *Canadian Psychologist* 13: 121–134.

Edwards, R. 1979. *Contested terrain: The transformation of the workplace in the twentieth century*. New York: Basic Books.

Ehrenberg, A. S. 1982. *A primer on data reduction*. Chichester, UK: Wiley.

Einstein, A. 1934. *Essays in science*. New York: New York Philosophical Library.

Ellsworth, P. C. 1977. From abstract ideas to concrete instances: Some guidance for choosing natural research settings. *American Psychologist* 32: 604–615.

Elsbach, K. D. 1994. An interview with John Van Maanen. *The Organization and Management Theory Newsletter* of the Academy of Management.

Emery, F. E., and E. J. Trist. 1965. The causal texture of organizational environments. *Human Relations* 18(1): 21–32.

Emory, C. W. 1980. *Business research methods*. Rev. ed. Homewood, IL: Irwin.

Engwall, L. 1995. Management studies: A fragmented adhocracy? *Scandinavian Journal of Management* 12: 225–235.

Engwall, L., and E. Gunnarsson, eds. 1994. *Management studies in an academic context*. Uppsala: Acta Universitatis Upsaliensis.

Engwall, L., and V. Zamagni, eds. 1998. *Management education in historical perspective*. Manchester, UK: Manchester University Press.

Etzioni, A. 1961. *A comparative analysis of complex organizations*. New York: Free Press.

———. 1975. *A comparative analysis of complex organizations*. Rev. and enl. ed. New York: Free Press.

Evan, W. M., ed. 1971. *Organizational experiments*. New York: Harper and Row.

Evered, R. D. 1976. A typology of explicative models. *Technological Forecasting and Social Change* 9: 259–277.

Evered, R. D., and M. R. Louis 1979. Organizational inquiry from the outside or the inside: Two epistemological perspectives. Paper presented at the meeting of the Academy of Management, Atlanta, GA.

Everitt, B. S. 1978. *Graphical techniques in multivariate analysis*. London: Heinemann Educational Books.

Fabian, F. H. 2000. Keeping the tension: Pressures to keep the controversy in the management discipline. *Academy of Management Review* 25: 350–371.

Fawl, C. L. 1963. Disturbances experienced by children in their natural habitats. In *The stream of behavior*. Edited by R. G. Barker, 99–126. New York: Appleton-Century-Crofts.

Feigl, H. 1970. The "orthodox" view of theories: Remarks in defense as well as critique. In *Minnesota studies in the philosophy of science*. Vol. 4. Edited by M. Radnor and S. Winokur, 3–16. Minneapolis: University of Minnesota Press.

Feigl, H., and M. Brodbeck, eds. 1953. *Reading in the philosophy of science.* New York: Appleton-Century-Crofts.

Feldman, C. F., and W. A. Hass. 1970. Controls, conceptualization, and the interrelation between experimental and correlational research. *American Psychologist* 25: 633–635.

Fenichel, O. 1945. *The psychoanalytic theory of neuroses.* New York: Norton.

Festinger, L. 1953. Laboratory experiments. In *Research methods in the behavioral sciences.* Edited by L. Festinger and D. Katz, 136–172. New York: Dryden Press.

———. 1957. *A theory of cognitive dissonance.* Stanford, CA: Stanford University Press.

Festinger, L., H. Riecken, and S. Schachter. 1956. *When prophecy fails.* Minneapolis: University of Minnesota Press.

Feuer, L. S. 1975. *Ideology and the ideologists.* New York: Harper and Row.

Fieser, L., and M. Fieser. 1957. *Introduction to organic chemistry.* Boston: Heath.

Fineman, S. 1993. Organizations as emotional arenas. In *Emotion in organizations.* Edited by S. Fineman, 159–169. London: Sage.

Fischer, F. 1990. *Technocracy and the politics of expertise.* Newbury Park, CA: Sage.

Fisher, R. A. 1960. *Design of experiments,* 7th ed. Edinburgh, Scotland: Oliver & Boyd.

Fiske, D. W. 1982. Convergent-discriminant validation in measurements and research strategies. In *New directions for methodology of social and behavioral science: Forms of validity in research.* Edited by D. Brinberg and L. H. Kidder, 77–92. San Francisco: Jossey-Bass.

Fiske, S. T. 1993. Controlling other people: The impact of power on stereotyping. *American Psychologist* 48: 621–628.

Fleck, L. 1979. *Genesis and development of a scientific fact.* Edited by T. J. Trenn and R. K. Merton. Translated by F. Bradley and T. J. Trenn. Chicago: University of Chicago Press.

Fleishman, E. 1967. The development of a behavior taxonomy for describing human tasks: A correlational-experimental approach. *Journal of Applied Psychology* 51: 1–10.

Forehand, G. A., and B. V. Gilmer. 1964. Environmental variation in studies of organizational behavior. *Psychological Bulletin* 62: 361–382.

Forester, J. 1983. Critical theory and organizational analysis. In *Beyond method.* Edited by G. Morgan, 234–257. Beverly Hills, CA: Sage.

Foucault, M. 1980. *Power/knowledge.* Edited by Colin Gordon. New York: Pantheon Books.

Fox, F. V., and B. M. Staw. 1979. The trapped administrator: Effects of job insecurity and policy resistance on commitment to a course of action. *Administrative Science Quarterly* 24: 449–472.

Frank, P. G., ed. 1961. *The validation of scientific theories*. New York: Beacon Press.

Freese, L. 1980. Formal theorizing. *Annual Review of Sociology* 6: 187–212.

Friedman, M. 1953. *Essays in positive economics*. Chicago: University of Chicago Press.

Friedrichs, R. 1970. *A sociology of sociology*. New York: Free Press.

Fromkin, H. L., and S. Streufert. 1976. Laboratory experimentation. In *Handbook of industrial and organizational psychology*. Edited by M. D. Dunnette, 415–465. Chicago: Rand McNally.

Frost, P. J. 1980. Toward a radical framework for practicing organizational science. *Academy of Management Review* 5: 501–507.

———. 1987. Power, politics, and influence. In *Handbook of organizational communication*. Edited by F. Jablin, L. Putnam, K. Roberts, and L. Porter, 503–548. Newbury Park, CA: Sage.

Frost, P. J., and T. Barnowe. 1982. Specialization theory: Convergence on the measurement of people's orientation to persons and things. Paper no. 638. Faculty of Commerce and Business Administration, University of British Columbia.

Frost, P. J., and G. Morgan. 1983. Symbols and sensemaking: The realization of a framework. In *Organizational symbolism*. Edited by L. R. Pondy, P. J. Frost, G. Morgan, and T. C. Dandridge, 207–236. Greenwich, CT: JAI Press.

Fry, L. W., and D. A. Smith. 1987. Congruence, contingency, and theory building. *Academy of Management Review* 12:117–132.

Gadalla, I. E., and R. Cooper. 1978. Towards an epistemology of management. *Social Science Information* 17: 349–383.

Gage, N. 1989. The paradigm wars and their aftermath: A "historical" sketch of research and teaching since 1989. *Educational Research* 18: 4–10.

Galt, A. H., and L. J. Smith. 1976. *Models and the study of social change*. New York: Wiley.

Galtung, J. 1967. *Theory and methods of social research*. New York: Columbia University Press.

———. 1977. *Methodology and ideology: Essay in methodology*. Copenhagen: C. Ejlers.

Garfinkel, H. 1967. *Studies in ethnomethodology*. Englewood Cliffs, NJ: Prentice Hall.

Gargiulo, M. 1993. Two-step leverage. *Administrative Science Quarterly* 38: 1–19.

Gay, P. 1988. *Freud: A life for our times*. New York: Norton.

Geertz, C. 1964. Ideology as a cultural system. In *Ideology and discontent*. Edited by D. E. Apter, 47–76. New York: Free Press.

———. 1973. *The interpretation of cultures*. New York: Basic Books.

George, W. H. 1938. *The scientist in action: A scientific study of his methods*. New York: Emerson.

Georgiou, P. 1973. The goal paradigm and notes toward a counter paradigm. *Administrative Science Quarterly* 18: 291–310.

Gergen, K. J. 1982. *Towards transformation in social knowledge.* New York: Springer-Verlag.

———. 1989. Social psychology and the wrong revolution. *European Journal of Social Psychology* 19: 463–484.

Gerth, H., and W. C. Mills. 1958. *From Max Weber: Essays in sociology.* New York: Oxford University Press.

Ghiselli, E. E. 1964. *Theory of psychological measurement.* New York: McGraw-Hill.

Ghiselli, E. E., J. P. Campbell, and S. Zedeck. 1981. *Measurement theory for the behavioral sciences.* San Francisco: Freeman.

Gibbs, J. P. 1972. *Sociological theory construction.* Hinsdale, IL: Dryden.

Gibson, J. J. 1966. *The senses considered as perceptual systems.* Boston: Houghton Mifflin.

———. 1979. *The ecological approach to visual perception.* Boston: Houghton Mifflin.

Gibson, J. L. 1966. Organizational theory and the nature of man. *Academy of Management Journal*, September: 232–245.

Gibson, Q. B. 1960. *The logic of social enquiry.* London: Routledge and Kegan Paul.

Giddens, A. 1976. *New rules of sociological method.* London: Hutchinson.

———. 1979. *Central problems in social theory.* London: Macmillan.

Gigerenzer, G. 1987. Probabilistic thinking and the fight against subjectivity. In *The probabilistic revolution.* Edited by L. Kruger, G. Gigerenzer, and M. S. Morgan, 11–33. Cambridge, MA: Bradford/MIT Press.

Gigerenzer, G., and D. J. Murray. 1987. *Cognition as intuitive statistics.* Hillsdale, NJ: Erlbaum.

Gigerenzer, G., Z. Swijtink, T. Porter, L. Daston, J. Beatty, and L. Krüger. 1989. *The empire of chance: How probability changed science and everyday life.* Cambridge: Cambridge University Press.

Gilchrist, W. 1984. *Statistical modelling.* Chichester, UK: Wiley.

Gillispie, C. C. 1960. *The edge of objectivity.* Princeton, NJ: Princeton University Press.

Gioia, D. A., and E. Pitre. 1990. Multiparadigm perspectives on theory building. *Academy of Management Review* 15: 584–602.

Glaser, B. G. 1968. *Organizational careers: A sourcebook for theory.* Chicago: Aldine.

Glaser, B. G., and A. L. Strauss. 1967. *The discovery of grounded theory.* Chicago: Aldine.

Glass, G. 1976. Primary, secondary, and meta-analysis of research. *Educational Researcher* 5:3–8.

Glick, W. H. 1985. Conceptualizing and measuring organizational and psychological climate: Pitfalls in multilevel research. *Academy of Management Review* 10: 601–616.

Goffman, E. 1959. *The presentation of self in everyday life*. New York: Doubleday.

Goldberg, E. M., and S. L. Morrison. 1963. Schizophrenia and social class. *British Journal of Psychiatry* 109: 785–802.

Goldstein, A. P. 1962. *Therapist-patient expectancies in psychotherapy*. New York: Pergamon Press.

Goldstein, K. 1938. *The organism*. New York: American Book.

Goodman, S. N., and R. Royall. 1988. Evidence and scientific research. *American Journal of Public Health* 78: 1568–1574.

Gottlieb, D. 1960. *Processes of socialization in the American graduate school*. Ph.D. diss., University of Chicago.

Gould, S. J. 1977a. The 120-year bamboo clock. *Natural History* 86(April): 8–16.

———. 1977b. Evolution's erratic pace. *Natural History* 86(May): 10–16.

Gouldner, A. W. 1954. *Patterns of industrial bureaucracy*. New York: Free Press.

———. 1957. Cosmopolitans and locals: Toward an analysis of latent social roles. *Administrative Science Quarterly* 2: 281–306.

———. 1970. *The coming crisis of Western sociology*. New York: Basic Books.

———. 1979. *The future of the intellectual and the rise of the new class*. New York: Continuum.

———. 1985. *Against fragmentation: The origins of Marxism and the sociology of intellectuals*. New York: Oxford University Press.

Gramsci, A. 1971. *1929–35 selections from the prison notebooks*. Translated by Q. Hoare and G. N. Smoth. New York: International.

Granovetter, M. S. 1973. The strength of weak ties. *American Journal of Sociology* 78: 1360–1380.

Gray, J. L. 1979. The myths about behavior mod in organizations: A response to Locke. *Academy of Management Review* 4: 121–129.

Green, B. F. 1963. *Digital computers in research: An introduction for behavioral and social scientists*. New York: McGraw-Hill.

Greenacre, M. 1984. *Theory and applications of correspondence analysis*. London: Academic Press.

Greenberg, D. 1987. Publish or perish—or fake it. *U.S. News and World Report*, 8 June.

Greenberg, J. 1987. A taxonomy of organizational justice theories. *Academy of Management Review* 12: 9–22.

Grinnell, F. 1987. *The scientific attitude*. Boulder, CO: Westview Press.

Grünbaum, A. 1962. Temporally-asymmetric principles, parity between explanation and prediction, and mechanism versus teleology. *Philosophical Science* 29: 146–170.

Guba, E. G., and Y. S. Lincoln. 1994. Competing paradigms in qualitative research. In *Handbook of qualitative research*. Edited by N. K. Denzin and Y. S. Lincoln, 105–117. Thousand Oaks, CA: Sage.

Guilford, J. P. 1956. *Fundamental statistics in psychology and education*. New York: McGraw-Hill.

Gump, P. V., and J. S. Kounin. 1960. Issues raised by ecological and "classical" research efforts. *Merrill-Palmer Quarterly* 6: 145–152.

Gupta, N., and T. A. Beehr. 1982. A test of the correspondence between self-reports and alternative data sources about work organizations. *Journal of Vocational Behavior* 20: 1–13.

Gutman, D. 1969. Psychological naturalism in cross-cultural studies. In *Naturalistic viewpoints in psychological research*. Edited by E. P. Williams and H. L. Raush, 162–176. New York: Holt, Rinehart and Winston.

Haase, R. F., D. M. Waechter, and G. S. Solomon. 1982. How significant is a significant difference? Average effect size of research in counseling psychology. *Journal of Counseling Psychology* 29: 58–65.

Habermas, J. 1971. *Knowledge and human interest*. Translated by T. McCarthy. Boston: Beacon.

———. 1975. *Legitimation crisis*. Translated by T. McCarthy. Boston: Beacon.

———. 1984. *The theory of communicative action: Reason and the rationalization of society*. Vol. 1. Translated by T. McCarthy. Boston: Beacon.

———. 1987. *The theory of communicative action: Lifeworld and system*. Vol. 2. Translated by T. McCarthy. Boston: Beacon.

Hackman, R. series ed. 1982. *Studying organizations: Innovations in methodology*. Beverly Hills, CA: Sage.

Hage, J. 1965. An axiomatic theory of organizations. *Administrative Science Quarterly* 10: 289–320.

———. 1972. *Techniques and problems of theory construction in sociology*. New York: Wiley.

———. 1980. *Theories of organizations: Form, process and transformation*. New York: Wiley.

Haire, W. F. 1962. *Organizational theory in industrial practice*. New York: Wiley.

Hall, C. S., and G. Lindzey. 1957. *Theories of personality*. New York: Wiley.

Hall, E. T. 1976. *Beyond culture*. New York: Doubleday.

Hamilton, D. 1976. A science of the singular? Unpublished paper. Center for Instructional Research and Curriculum Evaluation, University of Illinois, Urbana.

Hammond, J. L. 1973. Two sources of error in ecological correlations. *American Sociological Review* 38: 764–777.

Hammond, K. R. 1954. Representative versus systematic design in clinical psychology. *Psychological Bulletin* 51: 150–159.

Haney, C., W. C. Banks, and P. G. Zimbardo. 1973. Interpersonal dynamics in a simulated prison. *International Journal of Criminology and Penology* 1: 69–97.

Hanley, C., and M. Rokeach. 1956. Care and carelessness in psychology. *Psychological Bulletin* 53: 183–186.

Hannan, M. T. 1971. *Aggregation and disaggregation in sociology.* Lexington, MA: Heath.

Hannan, M. T., and J. Freeman. 1977. The population ecology of organizations. *American Journal of Sociology* 82: 929–964.

Hanson, N. R. 1969. Logical positivism and the interpretation of scientific theories. In *The legacy of logical positivism.* Edited by P. Achinstein and S. Barker, 57–84. Baltimore, MD: Johns Hopkins Press.

Harris, R. J. 1975. *A primer on multivariate statistics.* New York: Academic Press.

Hart, C. W. 1954. Preface to H. H. Hyman, W. J. Cobb, J. J. Feldman, C. W. Hart, and C. H. Stember, *Interviewing in social research.* Chicago: University of Chicago Press.

Hartt, J. N. 1963. *The lost image of man.* Baton Rouge: Louisiana State University Press.

Harvey, O. J., and W. F. Clapp. 1965. Hope, expectancy, and reactions to the unexpected. *Journal of Personality and Social Psychology* 2: 45–52.

Hauge, F. E. 1994. When history leads to multiplicity: A perspective on theory proliferation. Paper presented at the meeting of the Western Academy of Management, Santa Fe, NM.

Hebb, D. O. 1974. What is psychology all about? *American Psychologist* 29: 71–79.

Heckscher, C. C. 1995. *White-collar blues: Management loyalties in an age of corporate restructuring.* New York: Basic Books.

Heidegger, M. [1927] 1962. *Being and time.* Translated by J. Macquarrie and E. Robinson. New York: Harper.

Heider, F. 1958. *The psychology of interpersonal relations.* New York: Wiley.

Hempel, C. G. 1959. The logic of functional analysis. In *Symposium on sociological theory.* Edited by L. Gross, 271–307. New York: Harper and Row.

———. 1965. *Aspects of scientific explanation and other essays in the philosophy of science.* New York: Free Press.

———. 1969. Logical positivism and the social sciences. In *The legacy of logical positivism.* Edited by P. Achinstein and S. Barker, 163–194. Baltimore, MD: Johns Hopkins Press.

Hempel, C. G., and P. Oppenheim. 1948. Studies in the logic of explanation. *Philosophy of Science* 15: 135–175.

Hendricks, J., and C. B. Peters. 1973. The ideal type and sociological theory. *Acta Sociologica* 16: 31–40.

Herriegel, E. 1953. *Zen and the art of archery.* New York: Pantheon.

Hickson, D. 1966. A convergence in organization theory. *Administrative Science Quarterly* 11: 224–237.

Hirschman, A. O. 1970. *Exit, voice, and loyalty.* Cambridge, MA: Harvard University Press.

Hoaglin, D. C., F. Mosteller, and J. W. Tukey, eds. 1983. *Understanding robust and exploratory data analysis.* New York: Wiley.

Hodge, H., G. Kress, and G. Jones. 1979. The ideology of middle management. In *Language and control.* Edited by R. Fowler, H. Hodge, G. Kress, and T. Trew, 81–93. London: Routledge and Kegan Paul.

Homans, G. C. 1961. *Social behavior: Its elementary forms.* New York: Harcourt, Brace and World.

———. 1964. Contemporary theory in sociology. In *Handbook of modern sociology.* Edited by R. E. L. Farris, 951–977. Chicago: Rand McNally.

Hopkins, T. K. 1964. *The exercise of influence in small groups.* Totowa, NJ: The Bedminster Press.

House, R. J. 1976. A 1976 theory of charismatic leadership. Paper presented at the Southern Illinois University Fourth Biennial Leadership Symposium, Carbondale, IL.

Houts, A. C., T. D. Cook, and W. Shadish Jr. 1986. The person-situation debate: A critical multiplist perspective. *Journal of Personality* 54: 52–105.

Hovland, C. I. 1959. Reconciling conflicting results derived from experimental and survey studies of attitude change. *American Psychologist* 14: 8–17.

Huberty, C. J., and J. D. Morris. 1989. Multivariate analysis versus multiple univariate analyses. *Psychological Bulletin* 105: 302–308.

Hudson, L. 1966. *Contrary imaginations.* New York: Schoken.

Hughes, E. C. 1958. Professional and career problems of sociology. In *Men and their work.* Edited by E. C. Hughes, 157–175. New York: Free Press.

Hulin, C. L., and M. R. Blood. 1968. Job enlargement, individual differences, and worker responses. *Psychological Bulletin* 69: 41–55.

Hull, D. 1985. Openness and secrecy in science: Their origins and limitations. *Science, Technology and Human Values* 10: 4–13.

Humphreys, C. 1968. *Zen Buddhism.* New York: Macmillan.

Hunt, S. D. 1983. *Marketing theory: The philosophy of marketing science.* Homewood, IL: Irwin.

Husserl, E. 1962. *Ideas.* Translated by W. R. Boyce Gibson. New York: Collier.

———. 1965. *Phenomenology and the crisis of philosophy.* Translated by Q. Lauer. New York: Harper Torchbooks.

Hutten, E. H. 1962. *The origins of science; an inquiry into the foundations of Western thought.* London: Allen and Unwin.

Hyman, H. H., W. J. Cobb, J. J. Feldman, C. W. Hart, and C. H. Stember. 1954. *Interviewing in social research.* Chicago: University of Chicago Press.

Ibarra, H. 1992. Homophily and differential returns: Sex differences in network structure and access in an advertising firm. *Administrative Science Quarterly* 37: 422–447.

———. 1997. Paving an alternative route: Gender differences in managerial networks for career development. *Social Psychological Quarterly* 60: 91–102.

Ibarra, H., and L. Smith-Lovin. 1997. New directions in social network research on gender and organizational careers. In *Creating tomorrow's organization: A handbook for future research in organizational behavior*. Edited by C. L. Cooper and S. Jackson, 359–383. Sussex, England: Wiley.

Isaac, J. C. 1990. Realism and reality: Some realistic considerations. *Journal for the Theory of Social Behavior* 20: 1–32.

Israel, J. 1972. Stipulations and constructions in the social sciences. In *The context of social psychology*. Edited by J. Israel and H. Tajfel, 123–211. Orlando, FL: Academic Press.

Jackall, R. 1988. *Moral mazes: The world of corporate managers*. New York: Oxford University Press.

James, L. R., W. F. Joyce, and J. W. Slocum Jr. 1988. Comment: Organizations do not cognize. *Academy of Management Review* 13: 129–132.

James, W. [1890] 1918. *The principles of psychology*. Vol. 1. New York: Dover.

Jaynes, J. 1976. *The origin of consciousness in the breakdown of the bicameral mind*. Boston: Houghton Mifflin.

Jelinek, M., L. Smircich, and P. Hirsch. eds. 1983. Special issue on organizational culture. *Administrative Science Quarterly* 20: 331–338.

Jenkins, H. M., and W. C. Ward. 1965. Judgment of contingency between responses and outcomes. *Psychological Monographs: General and Applied* 79 (entire issue no. 594).

Jermier, J. 1985. When the sleeper wakes: A short story extending themes in radical organization theory. *Journal of Management* 11(2): 67–80.

Jick, T. 1979. Mixing qualitative and quantitative methods: Triangulation in action. *Administrative Science Quarterly* 24: 602–611.

Johnson, T., C. Dandeker, and C. Ashworth. 1984. *The structure of social theory*. New York: St. Martin's.

Kael, P. 1970. The current cinema. *The New Yorker*, 14 February.

Kanter, R. M. 1989. Careers and the wealth of nations. In *Handbook of career theory*. Edited by M. B. Arthur, D. T. Hall, and B. S. Lawrence, 506–521. New York: Cambridge University Press.

Kaplan, A. 1964. *The conduct of inquiry*. San Francisco: Chandler.

Katz, D. 1942. Do interviews bias poll results? *Public Opinion Quarterly* 6: 248–268.

———. 1953. Field studies. In *Research methods in the behavioral sciences*. Edited by L. Festinger and D. Katz, 56–98. New York: Dryden.

Keat, R., and J. Urry. 1975. *Social theory as science*. London: Routledge and Paul.

Kelly, G. A. 1955. *The psychology of personal constructs*. New York: Norton.

————. 1964. The language of hypothesis: Man's psychological instrument. *Journal of Individual Psychology* 20: 137–152.

Kelly, J. G. 1969. Naturalistic observations in contrasting social environments. In *Naturalistic viewpoints in psychological research*. Edited by E. P. Willems and H. L. Raush, 183–199. New York: Holt, Rinehart and Winston.

Kerlinger, F. N. 1964. *Foundations of behavioral research*. New York: Holt, Rinehart.

————. 1973. *Foundations of behavioral research*. 2d ed. New York: Holt, Rinehart and Winston.

Kerr, S. 1975. On the folly of rewarding A while hoping for B. *Academy of Management Journal* 18: 769–783.

Kimberly, J. R. 1980. Data aggregation in organizational research: The temporal dimension. *Organization Studies* 1: 367–377.

Kimberly, J. R., R. H. Miles, and Associates. 1980. *The organizational life cycle*. San Francisco: Jossey-Bass.

Kipping, M., and C. Amorim. 1999/2000. Consultancies and management schools. *University of Reading Discussion Papers in Economics and Management*, series A, vol. 12. no. 409.

Kipping, M., and T. Armbruester. 1999. The consultancy field in western Europe. *CEMP Report*, no. 6. University of Reading, Department of Economics.

Klein, K. J., and S. W. J. Kozlowski, eds. 2000. *Multi level theory research and methods in organizations*. San Francisco: Jossey-Bass.

Knight, F. H. 1965. *Risk, uncertainty and profit*. New York: Harper and Row.

Knights, D., and H. Willmott. 1985. Power and identity in theory and practice. *Sociological Review* 33: 22–46.

————. 1987. Organizational culture as management theory. *International Studies of Management and Organization* 17(3): 40–63.

Knorr, K. D. 1979. Tinkering toward success: prelude to a theory of scientific practice. *Theory and Society* 8: 22–43.

Knorr-Cetina, K. D. 1981. *The manufacture of knowledge: An essay on the constructivist and contextual nature of science*. Oxford, England: Pergamon.

Knudsen, C. 1999. Pluralism, scientific progress and the structure of organization science. Presented to the 15th EGOS Colloquium, University of Warwick.

Koestler, A. 1978. *Janus*. New York: Random House.

Kohn, M., and C. Schooler. 1978. The reciprocal effects of the substantive complexity of work and intellectual flexibility: A longitudinal assessment. *American Journal of Sociology* 84: 24–52.

Kolakowski, L. 1968. *The alienation of reason: A history of positivist thought*. Garden City, NY: Doubleday.

Komorita, S. S., and J. M. Chertkoff. 1973. A bargaining theory of coalition formation. *Psychological Review* 80: 149–162.

Kornhauser, A. 1965. *Mental health of the industrial worker: A Detroit study*. New York: Wiley.

Korukonda, A. R. 1989. Mixing levels of analysis in organizational research. *Canadian Journal of Administrative Sciences* 6: 1–8.

Korzybski, A. 1958. *Science and sanity*. 4th ed. Lakeville, CT: International Non-Aristotelian Library Publishing.

Kraemer, H. C., and S. Thiemann. 1987. *How many subjects? Statistical power analysis in research*. Beverly Hills, CA: Sage.

Kram, K. E. 1988. *Mentoring at work: Developmental relationships in organizational life*. New York: University Press of America.

Kuhn, T. S. 1962. *The structure of scientific revolutions*. Chicago: Chicago University Press.

———. 1970. *The structure of scientific revolutions*. 2d ed. enl. Chicago: Chicago University Press.

Kunda, G. 1992. *Engineering culture: Control and commitment in a high-tech corporation*. Philadelphia: Temple University Press.

Labianca, G., D. J. Brass, and B. Gray. 1998. Social networks and perceptions of intergroup conflict: The role of negative relationships and third parties. *Academy of Management Journal* 41: 55–67.

Lakatos, I., and A. Musgrave, eds. 1970. *Criticism and the growth of knowledge*. Cambridge: Cambridge University Press.

Landy, F. 1982. Models of man: Assumptions of theorists. In *Theory and practice of organizational psychology*. Edited by N. Nicholson and T. Wall, 103–121. Orlando, FL: Academic Press.

Lang, J. R., M. J. Dollinger, and K. E. Marino. 1987. Aggregation bias in strategic decision-making research. *Journal of Management* 13: 689–702.

Langbein, L. I., and A. J. Lichtman. 1978. *Ecological inference*. Beverly Hills, CA: Sage.

Lastrucci, C. L. 1963. *The scientific approach*. Cambridge, MA: Schenkman.

Latham, G. P., and S. B. Kinne. 1974. Improving job performance through training in goal setting. *Journal of Applied Psychology* 59: 187–191.

Latour, B., and S. Woolgar. 1979. *Laboratory life: The social construction of scientific facts*. Beverly Hills, CA: Sage.

Laudan, L. 1977. *Progress and its problems*. Berkeley: University of California Press.

Lave, C. A., and J. G. March. 1975. *An introduction to models in the social sciences*. New York: Harper and Row.

Lawler, E. E., and J. R. Hackman. 1969. Impact of employee participation in the development of pay incentive plans: A field experiment. *Journal of Applied Psychology* 53: 467–471.

Lawler, E. E., J. R. Hackman, and S. Kaufman. 1973. Effects of job redesign: A field experiment. *Journal of Applied Social Psychology* 3: 49–62.

Lazarsfeld, P. F., and N. W. Henry. 1968. *Latent structure analysis*. Boston: Houghton Mifflin.

Lazega, E. 1992. *Micropolitics of knowledge: Communication and indirect control in workgroups*. New York: Aldine de Gruyter.

Lazonick, W. 1991. *Business organization and the myth of the market economy*. Cambridge: Cambridge University Press.

Leach, E. R. 1967. An anthropologist's reflections in a social survey. In *Anthropologists in the field*. Edited by D. G. Jongmans and P. C. Gutking, 75–88. Atlantic Highlands, NJ: Humanities Press.

———. 1971. *Rethinking anthropology*. New York: Humanities Press.

Leblebici, H. 1985. Transactions and organizational forms: A reanalysis. *Organization Studies* 6: 97–116.

Lee, A. S. 1989a. Case studies as natural experiments. *Human Relations* 42(2): 117–137.

———. 1989b. A scientific methodology for MIS case studies. *MIS Quarterly* 13(1): 33–50.

———. 1991. Integrating positivist and interpretative approaches to organizational research. *Organization Science* 2: 342–365.

Leonard, J. 1977. The anarchy of blab. *New York Times Book Review*, 1 May.

Leontiades, M. 1980. *Strategies for diversification and change*. Boston: Little Brown.

Levinson, H. 1972. *Organizational diagnosis*. Cambridge, MA: Harvard University Press.

Lewin, K. 1931. The conflict between Aristotelian and Galilean modes of thought in contemporary psychology. *Journal of General Psychology* 5: 141–177.

———. 1951. *Field theory in social science*. New York: Harper.

———. 1965. Formalization and progress in psychology. In *Theories of personality*. Edited by G. Lindzey and C. S. Hall, 201–215. New York: Wiley.

Lewis, M., and L. Rosenblum, eds. 1974. *The effect of the infant on its caregiver*. New York: Wiley.

Light, D., Jr. 1979. Surface data and deep structure: Observing the organization of professional training. *Administrative Science Quarterly* 24: 551–560.

Lin, N. 1976. *Foundations of social research*. New York: McGraw-Hill.

Lincoln, Y. S. 1985. *Organizational theory and inquiry: The paradigm revolution*. Beverly Hills, CA: Sage.

Lindblom, C. E. 1987. Alternatives to validity: Some thoughts suggested by Campbell's guidelines. *Knowledge: Creation, Diffusion, Utilization* 8: 509–520.

Lindquist, E. F. 1953. *Design and analysis of experiments in psychology and education*. Boston: Houghton Mifflin.

Little, B. 1972. Psychological man as scientist, humanist, and specialist. *Journal of Experimental Research in Personality* 6(2): 95–118.

Locke, E. 1977. The myths about behavior mod in organizations. *Academy of Management Review* 2: 543–553.

———. 1979. Myths in "The myths of the myths about behavior mod in organizations." *Academy of Management Review* 4: 131–136.

———. 1989. *Management and higher education since 1940*. Cambridge: Cambridge University Press.

———. 1996. Rewriting the discovery of grounded theory after 25 years. *Journal of Management Inquiry* 5: 239–245.

Locke, E., L. Saari, K. Shaw, and G. Latham. 1981. Goal setting and task performance. *Psychological Bulletin* 90: 125–152.

Lord, R. G., J. F. Binning, M. C. Rush, and J. C. Thomas. 1978. The effect of
   performance cues and leader behavior on questionnaire ratings of leadership
   behavior. *Organizational Behavior and Human Performance* 21: 27–39.

Lortie, D. 1959. Laymen to lawmen: Law school, careers, and professional socialization. *Harvard Educational Review* 29: 363–367.

Louis, M. R. 1991. Reflections on an interpretive way of life. In *Reframing organizational culture*. Edited by P. J. Frost, L. F. Moore, M. R. Louis, C. C.
   Lundberg, and J. Martin, 361–365. Newbury Park: Sage.

Lowen, A. 1968. Participative decision making: A model, literature critique,
   and prescriptions for research. *Organizational Behavior and Human Performance* 8: 68–106.

Luchins, A. S., and E. H. Luchins. 1965. *Logical foundation of mathematics for
   behavioral scientists*. New York: Holt, Rinehart and Winston.

Lukács, G. 1971. *History and class consciousness*. Translated by R. Livingstone.
   Cambridge, MA: MIT Press.

Lukes, S. 1974. *Power: A radical view*. London: Macmillan.

Lundberg, C. C. 1981. On the paradigm orthodoxy of the organizational sciences: Consequences for theory and research-toward an alternative strategy of inquiry. *Proceedings of the eighteenth annual meeting of the Eastern Academy of Management*. Binghamton, NY: Eastern Academy of
   Management.

———. 2001. Working with culture: A social rules perspective. In *The international handbook of organizational culture and climate*. Edited by C. L.
   Cooper, S. Cartwright, and P. C. Earley, 325–346. Chichester, UK: Wiley.

Lyotard, J. F. [1979] 1984. *The postmodern condition: A report on knowledge*.
   Translated by Geoff Bennington and Brian Massumi. Manchester, UK: Manchester University Press.

MacIntyre, A. 1985. How psychology makes itself true or false. In *A century of
   psychology as science*. Edited by S. Koch and D. E. Leary, 897–903. New
   York: McGraw-Hill.

MacIver, R. 1942. *Social causation*. New York: Harper and Row.

Madden, E. H., ed. 1960. *The structure of scientific thought*. Boston: Houghton
   Mifflin.

Mahoney, M. J. 1976. *Scientist as subject: The psychological imperative*. Cambridge, MA: Ballinger.

Malinowski, B. 1962. *Sex, culture, and myth*. New York: Harcourt, Brace & World.

Mangham, I. L., and M. A. Overington. 1983. Dramatism and the theatrical metaphor. In *Beyond method: Strategies for social research*. Edited by G. Morgan, 219–233. Beverly Hills, CA: Sage.

Marceil, J. C. 1977. Implicit dimensions of idiography and nomothesis: A reformulation. *American Psychologist* 32: 1046–1055.

March, J. G., and J. P. Olsen, eds. 1976. *Ambiguity and choice in organizations*. Bergen, Norway: Universitetsforlaget.

March, J. G., and H. A. Simon. 1958. *Organizations*. New York: Wiley.

Marsden, R. 1993. The politics of organizational analysis. *Organization Studies* 14: 92–124.

Martin, J. 1982. The garbage can model of the process of making research decisions. In *Judgement calls in research*. Edited by J. E. McGrath, J. Martin, and R. A. Kulka, 69–102. Beverly Hills, CA: Sage.

———. 1990. Breaking up the mono-method monopolies in organization research. In *The theory and philosophy of organization: Critical issues and new perspectives*. Edited by J. Hassard and D. Pym, 30–43. London: Routledge.

Martindale, D. 1960. *The nature and types of sociological theory*. Boston: Houghton Mifflin.

Maruyama, M. 1974. Paradigms and communication. *Technological Forecasting and Social Change* 6: 3–32.

Marx, K. [1844] 1964. *Economic and political manuscripts of 1844*. Translated by M. Miligan. New York: International.

———. [1867] 1967. *Das Kapital*. Vol 1. Berlin: Dietz.

Marx, M. H., ed. 1955. *Psychological theory*. New York: Macmillan.

Maslow, A. H. 1954. *Motivation and personality*. New York: Harper and Brothers.

Masterman, M. 1970. The nature of paradigm. In *Criticism and the growth of knowledge*. Edited by I. Lakatos and A. Musgave, 59–89. Cambridge: Cambridge University Press.

Mathew, B. 1993. *Power and history in information technology environments: Genealogy of managerial practices*. Ph.D. diss., University of Pittsburgh, PA.

Mayo, E. 1933. *The human problems of an industrial civilization*. New York: Macmillan.

McClintock, C. C., D. Brannon, and S. Maynard-Moody. 1979. Applying the logic of sample surveys to qualitative case studies: The case cluster method. *Administrative Science Quarterly* 24: 612–630.

McGowen, R. R., and L. E. Hart. 1990. Still different after all these years: Gender differences in professional identity formation. *Professional Practice Psychology: Research and Practice* 21: 118–123.

McGrath, J. E. 1964. Towards a "theory of method" for research on organizations. In *New perspectives in organization research*. Edited by W. W. Cooper, H. J. Leavitt, and M. W. Shelly III, 533–556. New York: Wiley.

———. 1982. Dilemmatics: The study of research choices and dilemmas. In *Judgement calls in research*. Edited by J. E. McGrath, J. Martin, and R. A. Kulka, 69–80. Beverly Hills, CA: Sage.

McGrath, J. E., J. Martin, and R. A. Kulka, eds. 1982. *Judgment calls in research*. Beverly Hills, CA: Sage.

McGuigan, F. J. 1963. The experimenter: A neglected stimulus object. *Psychological Bulletin* 60: 421–428.

McGuire, W. J. 1967. Some impending reorientations in social psychology: Some thoughts provoked by Kenneth Ring. *Journal of Experimental Social Psychology* 3: 124–139.

———. 1983. A contextualist theory of knowledge: Its implications for innovation and reform in psychological research. In *Advances in experimental social psychology*. Vol. 16. Edited by L. Berkowitz, 1–47. New York: Academic Press.

———. 1985. Toward social psychology's second century. In *A century of psychology as science*. Edited by S. Koch and D. E. Leary, 558–590. New York: McGraw-Hill.

———. 1986. A perspectivist looks at contextualism and the future of behavioral science. In *Contextualism and understanding in behavioral science: Implications for research and theory*. Edited by R. L. Rosnow and M. Georgoudi, 271–301. New York: Praeger.

McNemar, Q. 1940. Sampling in psychological research. *Psychological Bulletin* 37: 331–365.

Mead, G. H. 1956. *On social psychology*. Chicago: University of Chicago Press.

Meehl, P. E. 1970. Nuisance variables and the ex post facto design. In *Minnesota studies in philosophy of science*, IV. Edited by M. Radner and S. Winokur, 373–402. Minneapolis: University of Minnesota Press.

———. 1971. Law and the fireside inductions: Some reflections of a clinical psychologist. *Journal of Social Issues* 27: 65–100.

———. 1972. Second-order relevance. *American Psychologist* 27: 932–940.

Menzel, E. W., Jr. 1969. Naturalistic and experimental approaches to primate behavior. In *Naturalistic viewpoints in psychological research*. Edited by E. P. Willems and H. L. Raush, 78–121. New York: Holt, Rinehart and Winston.

Merton, R. K. [1942] 1973. The normative structure of science. Chap. 13 in *The sociology of science*. Chicago: University of Chicago Press.

———. [1957] 1973. Priorities in scientific discovery. Chap. 14 in *The sociology of science*. Chicago: University of Chicago Press.

———. 1967. *On theoretical sociology*. New York: Free Press.

———. 1968a. *Social theory and social structure*. New York: Free Press.

———. 1968b, January. The Matthew Effect in science. *Science* 159: 56–63.

————. 1972. Insiders and outsiders: A chapter in the sociology of knowledge. *American Journal of Sociology* 78: 9–47.

————. 1973. *The sociology of science.* Chicago: University of Chicago Press.

————. 1976. The sociology of social problems. In *Contemporary social problems.* Edited by R. K. Merton and R. Nisbet, 3–43. New York: Harcourt Brace Jovanovich.

Meyer, A. D. 1982. How ideologies supplant formal structures and shape responses to environments. *Journal of Management Studies* 19(1): 45–61.

Meyers, L. S., and N. E. Grossen. 1974. *N. E. Behavioral research: Theory, procedure, and design.* San Francisco: W. H. Freeman.

Michels, R. 1959. *Political parties.* Translated by Eden and Cedar Paul. New York: Dover Press.

Milgram, S. 1963. Behavioral study of obedience. *Journal of Abnormal and Social Psychology* 67: 371–378.

————. 1965. Some conditions of obedience and disobedience to authority. *Human Relations* 18: 57–76.

Miller, D. 1986. Configurations of strategy and structure. *Strategic Management Journal* 7: 233–250.

————. 1987. The genesis of configuration. *Academy of Management Review* 12: 686–701.

Miller, D., and P. H. Friesen. 1977. Strategy making in context: Ten empirical archetypes. *Journal of Management Studies* 14: 259–280.

————. 1984. *Organizations: A quantum view.* Englewood Cliffs, NJ: Prentice-Hall.

Miller, P., and T. O'Leary. 1989. Hierarchies and American ideals: 1900–1940. *Academy of Management Review* 5: 250–265.

Miller, S. 1973. Ends, means, and galumphing: Some leitmotifs of play. *American Anthropologist* 75(1): 87–98.

Mills, C. W. 1956. *The power elite.* New York: Oxford University Press.

Miner, J. B. 1984. The validity and usefulness of theories in an emerging organizational science. *Academy of Management Review* 9: 296–306.

Mintzman, A. 1970. *The iron cage: An historical interpretation of Max Weber.* New York: Knopf.

Mintzberg, H. 1979a. *The structuring of organizations.* Englewood Cliffs, NJ: Prentice-Hall.

————. 1979b. An emerging strategy of "direct" research. *Administrative Science Quarterly* 24: 582–589.

Mitchell, T. R. 1985. An evaluation of the validity of correlational research conducted in organizations. *Academy of Management Review* 10: 192–205.

Mitchell, T. R., S. G. Green, and R. Wood. 1981. An attributional model of leadership and the poor performing subordinate. In *Research in organizational behavior.* Vol. 3. Edited by L. L. Cummings and B. M. Staw, 197–234. Greenwich, CT: JAI Press.

Mitroff, I. I. 1974. *The subjective side of science*. New York: American Elsevier.

———. 1983a. *Stakeholders of the organizational mind*. San Francisco: Jossey-Bass.

———. 1983b. Archetypal social systems analysis: On the deeper structure of human systems. *Academy of Management Review* 8: 387–397.

Mitroff, I. I., and R. H. Kilmann. 1978. *Methodological approaches to social science*. San Francisco: Jossey-Bass.

Mitroff, I. I., and R. Mason. 1982. Business policy and metaphysics. *Academy of Management Review* 7: 361–370.

Mitroff, I. I., and L. R. Pondy. 1978. Afterthoughts on the leadership conference. In *Leadership: Where else can we go?* Edited by M. W. McCall and M. M. Lombardo, 145–149. Durham, NC: Duke University Press.

Mohr, L. B. 1982. *Explaining organizational behavior*. San Francisco: Jossey-Bass.

Moore, W. E. 1969. Occupational socialization. In *Handbook of socialization theory and research*. Edited by D. Goslin, 861–883. Chicago: Rand McNally.

Morey, N. C., and F. Luthans. 1984. An emic perspective and ethnoscience methods for organizational research. *Academy of Management Review* 9: 27–36.

Morgan, G. 1979a. Response to Mintzberg. *Administrative Science Quarterly* 24: 137–139.

———. 1979b. Cybernetics and organization theory: Epistemology or technique. Unpublished manuscript.

———. 1980. Paradigms, metaphors, and puzzle solving in organization theory. *Administrative Science Quarterly* 25: 605–622.

———., ed. 1983a. *Beyond method*. Beverly Hills, CA: Sage.

———. 1983b. More on metaphor: Why we cannot control tropes in administrative science. *Administrative Science Quarterly* 28: 601–607.

———. 1986. *Images of organizations*. Newbury Park, CA: Sage.

Morgan, G., P. J. Frost, and L. R. Pondy. 1983. Organizational symbolism. In *Organizational symbolism*. Edited by L. R. Pondy, P. J. Frost, G. Morgan, and T. C. Dandridge, 3–38. Greenwich, CT: JAI Press.

Morgan, G., and L. M. Smircich. 1980. The case for qualitative research. *Academy of Management Review* 5: 491–500.

Morrison, D. F. 1976. *Multivariate statistical methods*, 2d ed. New York: McGraw-Hill.

Moser, C. A. 1980. Statistics and public policy. *Journal of the Royal Statistical Society*, series A, 143: 1–31.

Mosteller, F. M., and R. R. Bush. 1954. Selected quantitative techniques. In *Handbook of social psychology: Vol. 1 Theory and method*. Edited by G. Lindzey, 289–334. Cambridge, MA: Addison-Wesley.

Mowday, R. T., R. M. Steers, and L. W. Porter. 1979. The measurement of organizational commitment. *Journal of Vocational Behavior* 14: 224–247.

Mulaik, S. A. 1984. Realism, pragmatism, and the implications of the new philosophy of science for psychology. *American Psychologist* 39: 919–920.

Mumby, D. K. 1988. *Communication and power in organizations: Discourse, ideology, and domination.* Norwood, NJ: Ablex.

Myers, J. L. 1979. *Fundamentals of experimental design.* 3d ed. Boston: Allyn & Bacon.

Myrdal, G. 1944. *An American dilemma.* New York: Harper.

———. 1958. *Value in social theory: A selection of essays on methodology.* London: Routledge and Kegan Paul.

Nagel, E. 1961. *The structure of science: Problems in the logic of scientific explanation.* New York: Harcourt, Brace and World.

Nagel, E., and J. R. Newman. 1960. *Gödel's proof.* New York: New York University Press.

Nelson, N., R. Rosenthal, and R. L. Rosnow. 1986. Interpretation of significance levels and effect sizes by psychological researchers. *American Psychologist* 41: 1299–1301.

Newell, A., and H. A. Simon. 1972. *Human problem solving.* Englewood Cliffs, NJ: Prentice-Hall.

Nisbet, R. A. 1962. Sociology as an art form. *Pacific Sociological Review* 5: 67–74.

———. 1969. *Social change and history.* New York: Oxford University Press.

Nunnally, J. C. 1978. *Psychometric theory.* 2d ed. New York: McGraw-Hill.

Nystrom, P. C., and W. H. Starbuck, eds. 1981. *Handbook of organizational design: Remodeling organizations and their environments.* Vol. 2. New York: Oxford University Press.

Offe, C., and H. Wiesenthal. 1980. Two logics of collective action: Theoretical notes on social class and organizational form. In *Political power and social theory.* Vol. 1. Edited by M. Zeitlin, 67–115. Greenwich, CT: JAI Press.

Olesen, V. 1994. Feminisms and models of qualitative research. In *Handbook of qualitative research.* Edited by N. K. Denzin and Y. S. Lincoln, 158–182. Thousand Oaks, CA: Sage.

Olesen, V. L., and E. W. Whittaker. 1968. *The silent dialogue: A study in the social psychology of professional socialization.* San Francisco: Jossey-Bass.

Orne, M. T. 1962. On the social psychology of the psychological experiments: With particular reference to demand characteristics and their implications. *American Psychologist* 17: 776–783.

Osigweh, C. A. B. 1983. *Improving problem-solving participation: The case of local transnational organizations.* Lanham, MD: University Press of America.

———. 1989. *Organizational science abroad: Constraints and perspectives.* New York: Plenum Press.

Owen, D. 1982. Those who can't consult. *Harpers*, November, 8–17.

Parmerlee, M., and C. Schwenk. 1979. Radical behaviorism in organizations: Misconceptions in the Locke-Gray debate. *Academy of Management Review* 4: 601–607.

Parsons, T. 1937. *The structure of social action*. New York: Free Press.

———. 1951. *The social system*. New York: Free Press.

Pateman, C. 1970. *Participation and democratic theory*. Cambridge: Cambridge University Press.

Pearson, K. 1902. On the mathematical theory of errors of judgment with special reference to the personal equation. *Phil. Trans. Royal Society of London* 198: 235–299.

Peery, N. S. 1972. General systems theory: An inquiry into its social philosophy. *Academy of Management Journal* 15: 495–510.

Peery, N. S., Jr. 1974. A structural theory of political behavior within organizations. Ph.D. diss., University of Washington.

Pei, M. 1978. *Weasel words: The art of saying what you don't mean*. New York: Harper and Row.

Perrow, C. 1981a. *Complex organizations: A critical essay*. 3d ed. New York: McGraw-Hill Publishing Company.

———. 1981b. Disintegrating social sciences. *New York University Educational Quarterly* 12(2): 2–9.

———. 1981c. Markets, hierarchies and hegemony. In *Perspectives on organization design and behavior*. Edited by A. H. Van de Ven and W. F. Joyce, 371–386. New York: Wiley.

Pfeffer, J. 1982. *Organizations and organization theory*. Boston: Pitman.

———. 1993. Barriers to the advance of organization science: Paradigm development as a dependent variable. *Academy of Management Review* 18: 599–620.

Pfeffer, J., and G. R. Salancik. 1978. *The external control of organizations: A resource dependence perspective*. New York: Harper and Row.

Pfeffer, J., G. R. Salancik, and H. Leblebici. 1976. The effect of uncertainty on the use of social influence in organizational decision making. *Administrative Science Quarterly* 21: 227–245.

Phillips, J. S., and R. G. Lord. 1986. Notes on the practical and theoretical consequences of implicit leadership theories for the future of leadership measurement. *Journal of Management* 12: 31–41.

Piaget, J. 1971. *Psychology and epistemology*. New York: Viking.

Pierce, J. L., D. G. Gardner, L. L. Cummings, and R. B. Dunham. 1989. Organization-based self-esteem: Construct definition, measurement, and validation. *Academy of Management Journal* 32: 622–648.

Pike, K. L. 1967. *Language in relation to a unified theory of the structure of human behavior*, 2d rev. ed. The Hague: Mouton.

Pinder, C. C. 1984. *Work motivation*. Glenview, IL: Scott, Foresman.

Pinder, C. C., and V. W. Bourgeois. 1982. Controlling tropes in administrative science. *Administrative Science Quarterly* 27: 641–652.

Pirsig, R. M. 1974. *Zen and the art of motorcycle maintenance*. New York: Bantam.

Platt, J. R. 1964. Strong inference. *Science* 146: 347–353.

Podolny, J. M., and J. N. Baron. 1997. Resources and relationships: Social networks and mobility in the work place. *American Sociological Review* 62: 673–693.

Polanyi, M. 1958. *Personal knowledge*. Chicago: University of Chicago Press.

———. 1961. The unaccountable element in science. *Transactions of the Bose Research Institute* 24: 175–184.

———. 1967. *The tacit dimension*. London, England: Routledge & Kegan Paul.

Pondy, L. R., and D. M. Boje. 1975. Bringing mind back in: Paradigm development as a frontier problem in organization theory. Paper presented at the meeting of the American Sociological Association, San Francisco, CA.

Pondy, L. R., and I. I. Mitroff. 1979. Open system models in organization. In *Research in organizational behavior*, 3–39. Greenwich, CN: JAI Press.

Pondy, L. R., and M. L. Olson. 1977. Theories of extreme cases. Paper presented at an American Psychological Association Symposium, San Francisco, CA.

Popper, K. R. 1959. *The logic of scientific discovery*. New York: Harper and Row.

———. 1963. *Conjectures and refutations: The growth of scientific knowledge*. New York: Harper and Row.

———. 1964. *The poverty of historicism*. New York: Harper Torchbooks.

———. 1968. *The logic of scientific discovery*. New York: Harper Torchbooks.

Preece, D. A. 1981. Distributions of final digits in data. *The Statistician* 30: 31–60.

———. 1984. In discussion of a paper by A. J. Miller. *Journal of the Royal Statistical Society* A 147: 419.

Price, J. L. 1968a. *Organization effectiveness: An inventory of propositions*. Homewood, IL: Irwin.

———. 1968b. Design and proof in organizational research. *Administrative Science Quarterly* 13: 121–134.

Pugh, D. S., and D. J. Hickson. 1976a. *Organizational structure in its context*. Vol. 1. Farnborough Hants, England: Saxon House.

———. 1976b. *Organizational structure: Extensions and replications*. Vol. 2. Farnborough Hants, England: Saxon House.

Quick, J. C., and J. D. Quick. 1984. *Organizational stress and preventive management*. New York: McGraw-Hill.

Rabinow, P. 1996. *Making PCR*. Chicago: University of Chicago Press.

Radcliffe-Brown, A. R. 1949. Functionalism: A protest. *The American Anthropologist* 51: 320–323.

Ragin, C. C. 1994. *Constructing social research*. Thousand Oaks, CA: Pine Forge Press.

Ravetz, J. R. 1971. *Scientific knowledge and its social problems*. New York: Oxford University Press.

Reed, M. 1996. Organizational theorizing: A historically contested terrain. In *Handbook of organization studies*. Edited by S. R. Clegg, C. Hardy, and W. R. Nord, 31–56. London: Sage.

Reichenbach, H. 1951. *The rise of scientific philosophy*. Berkeley: University of California Press.

Reichers, A. E. 1985. A review and reconceptualization of organizational commitment. *Academy of Management Review* 10: 465–476.

Rescher, N. 1970. *Scientific explanation*. New York: Free Press.

———. 1996. *Process metaphysics: An introduction to process philosophy*. Albany: State University of New York Press.

Reynolds, P. D. 1971. *A primer in theory construction*. Indianapolis: Bobbs-Merrill.

Rice, R. W., D. B. McFarlin, R. G. Hunt, and J. P. Near. 1985. Organizational work and the perceived quality of life: Toward a conceptual model. *Academy of Management Review* 10: 296–310.

Rickman, J., ed. 1957. *A general selection from the works of Sigmund Freud*. Garden City, NY: Doubleday Anchor.

Ricoeur, P. 1971. The model of the text: Meaningful action considered as a text. *Social Research* 38: 529–562.

Ring, K. 1967. Experimental social psychology: Some sober questions about some frivolous values. *Journal of Experimental Social Psychology* 3: 113–123.

Ritzer, G. 1975. Sociology: A multiple paradigm science. *American Sociologist* 10: 156–167.

———. 1980. *Sociology: A multiple paradigm science*. Rev. ed. Boston: Allyn and Bacon.

Roberts, K. H. 1970. On looking at an elephant: An evaluation of cross-cultural research related to organizations. *Psychological Bulletin* 74: 327–350.

Roberts, K. H., C. L. Hulin, and D. M. Rousseau. 1978. *Developing an interdisciplinary science of organizations*. San Francisco: Jossey-Bass.

Robinson, W. S. 1950. Ecological correlations and the behavior of individuals. *American Sociological Review* 15 (August): 351–357.

Roby, T. B. 1967. Computer simulation methods for organizational research. In *Methods of organizational research*. Edited by V. H. Vroom, 171–211. Pittsburgh: University of Pittsburgh Press.

Roe, A. 1961. The psychology of the scientist. *Science* 134: 456–459.

Roethlisberger, F. J., G. F. F. Lombard, H. O. Ronken, and others. 1954. *Training for human relations*. Division of Research, Graduate School of Business, Harvard University.

Rogers, C. R. 1951. *Client-centered therapy*. Boston: Houghton.

————. 1961. *On becoming a person: A therapist's view of psychotherapy*. Boston: Hougton Mifflin.

Rosen, M. 1985. Breakfirst at Spiro's: Dramaturgy and dominance. *Journal of Management* 11(2): 31–48.

Rosenthal, R. 1963. Experimenter attributes as determinants of subjects' responses. *Journal of Projective Techniques* 27: 324–331.

————. 1966. *Experimenter effects in behavioral research*. New York: Appleton.

————. 1984. *Meta-analytic procedures for social research*. Beverly Hills, CA: Sage.

————. 1987. *Judgment studies: Design, analysis, and meta-analysis*. New York: Cambridge University Press.

Rosenthal, R., G. W. Persinger, L. Vikan-Kline, and R. C. Mulry. 1963. The role of the research assistant in the mediation of experimenter bias. *Journal of Personality* 31: 313–335.

Rosenthal, R., and R. L. Rosnow. 1984. *Essentials of behavioral research: Methods and data analysis*. New York: McGraw-Hill.

————. 1985. *Contrast analysis: Focused comparisons in the analysis of variance*. Cambridge: Cambridge University Press.

Rosenthal, R., and D. B. Rubin. 1984. Multiple contrasts and ordered Bonferroni procedures. *Journal of Educational Psychology* 76: 1028–1034.

Rosnow, R. L. 1981. *Paradigms in transition: The methodology of social inquiry*. New York: Oxford University Press.

Rosnow, R. L., and R. Rosenthal. 1988. Focused tests of significance and effect size estimation in counseling psychology. *Journal of Counseling Psychology* 35: 203–208.

————. 1989. Definition and interpretation of interaction effects. *Psychological Bulletin* 105: 143–146.

Rotter, J. B. 1954. *Social learning and clinical psychology*. Englewood Cliffs, NJ: Prentice-Hall.

Rousseau, D. M. 1985. Issues of level in organizational research: Multi-level and cross-level perspectives. In *Research in organizational behavior*. Vol. 7. Edited by L .L. Cummings and B. M. Staw, 1–37. Greenwich, CT: JAI Press.

Rowan, J. 1974. Research as intervention. In *Reconstructing social psychology*. Edited by N. Armistead, 86–100. Baltimore: Penguin.

Runkel, P. J., and J. E. McGrath. 1972. *Research on human behaviour: A systematic guide to method*. New York: Holt, Rinehart and Winston.

Runkel, P. J., and M. Runkel. 1984. *A guide to usage for writers and students in the social sciences*. Totowa, NJ: Rowman and Allanheld.

Russell, B. 1945. *A history of Western philosophy*. New York: Simon and Schuster.

Ryan, A. 1974. The nature of human nature in Hobbes and Rousseau. In *The limits of human nature*. Edited by J. Benthall, 3–19. New York: Dutton.

Sahlins, M. 1974. *Stone age economics*. London: Tavistock Publications.

Salaman, G. 1981. *Class and the corporation*. Glasgow: Fontana.

Salancik, J. R. 1978. Uncertainty, secrecy, and the choice of similar others. *Social Psychology* 41: 246–255.

Sampson, E. E., and L. B. Sibley. 1965. A further examination of the confirmation or nonconfirmation of expectancies and desires. *Journal of Personality and Social Psychology* 2: 133–137.

Savas, E. S. 1970. Cybernetics in city hall. *Science* 168: 1066–1071.

Scheff, T. J. 1990. *Microsociology: Discourse, emotion, and social structure*. Chicago: University of Chicago Press.

Schein, E. H. 1985. *Organizational culture and leadership*. San Francisco: Jossey-Bass.

Schön, D. A. 1963. *The displacement of concepts*. London: Tavistock.

Schön, D. A., W. Drake, and R. Miller. 1984. Social experimentation as reflection-in-action. *Knowledge* 6(1): 5–36.

Schuler, R. S., and S. E. Jackson. 1987. Organizational strategy and organizational level as determinants of human resource management practices. *Human Resource Planning* 10(3): 125–141.

Schutz, A. 1962. *The problem of social reality*. The Hague: Martinus Nijhoff.

———. 1967. *The phenomenology of the social work*. Evanston, IL: Northwestern University Press.

———. 1971. *Collected papers*. Vol. I. The Hague: Martinus Nijhoff.

———. 1973. Concept and theory formation in the social sciences. In *Collected papers*. Vol. 1. Edited by M. Natanson, 48–66. The Hague: Martinus Nijhoff.

Schwab, D. P. 1980. Construct validity in organizational behavior. In *Research in organizational behavior*. Vol. 2. Edited by B. M. Staw and L. L. Cummings, 3–43. Greenwich, CT: JAI Press.

Schwartz, P., and J. Oglivy. 1979. *The emergent paradigm: Changing patterns of thought and belief (Analytic report 7, values and lifestyle program)*. Menlo Park, CA: SRI International.

Schwitzgebel, R. L. 1970. Behavior instrumentation and social technology. *American Psychologist* 25: 491–499.

Scott, W. R. 1965. Field methods in the study of organizations. In *Handbook of organizations*. Edited by J. G. March, 261–304. Chicago: Rand McNally.

Sears, R. R. 1977. Sources of life satisfactions of the Terman gifted men. *American Psychologist* 32(2): 119–128.

Seashore, S. E. 1964. Field experiments with formal organizations. *Human Organization* 23: 164–170.

Secord, P. F., and C. W. Backman. 1964. *Social psychology*. New York: McGraw-Hill.

Sedlmeier, P., and G. Gigerenzer. 1989. Do studies of statistical power have an impact on the power of studies? *Psychological Bulletin* 105: 309–316.

Seeley, J. 1964. Crestwood Heights: Intellectual and libidinal dimensions of research. In *Reflections on community studies*. Edited by A. Vidich, J. Bensman, and M. Stein, 157–206. New York: Wiley.

Sells, S. B. 1966. Ecology and the science of psychology. *Multivariate Behavior Research*, 1(2): 131–144.

Selltiz, C. L., S. Wrightsman, and S. W. Cook. 1976. *Research methods in social relations*. 3d ed. New York: Holt, Rinehart and Winston.

Sennett, R. 1980. *Authority*. New York: Knopf.

Shapiro, M. B. 1961. The single case in fundamental clinical psychological research. *British Journal of Medical Psychology*, 34: 255–262.

Shaw, M. E. 1977. An overview of small group behavior. In *Psychological foundations of organizational behavior*. Edited by B. M. Staw, 358–396. Santa Monica, CA: Goodyear.

Shils, E. A., and H. A. Finch. 1949. *Max Weber on the methodology of the social sciences*. Glencore, IL: Free Press.

Shontz, F. C. 1965. *Research methods in personality*. New York: Appleton-Century-Crofts.

Siehl, C., and J. Martin. 1984. The role of symbolic management: How can managers successfully transmit organizational culture? In *Leaders and managers: International perspectives on managerial behaviour and leadership*. Edited by J. G. Hunt, D. Hosking, C. Schriesheim, and R. Stewart, 227–269. Elmsford, NY: Pergamon Press.

Sievers, B. 1986. Beyond the surrogate of motivation. *Organization Studies* 7: 335–352.

Silverman, D. 1970. *The theory of organizations*. London: Heinemann.

———. 1971. *The theory of organizations: A sociological framework*. London: Heinemann.

Simon, H. A. 1957. *Models of man*. New York: Wiley.

———. 1969. *The science of the artificial*. Cambridge, MA: MIT Press.

———. 1991. *Models of my life*. New York: Basic Books.

Sims, H. P., Jr. 1979. Limitations and extensions to questionnaires in leadership research. In *Crosscurrents in leadership*. Edited by J. G. Hunt and L. L. Larson, 202–221. Carbondale: Southern Illinois University Press.

Skinner, B. F. 1953. *Science and human behavior*. New York: Macmillan.

———. 1957. *Verbal behavior*. New York: Macmillan.

———. 1971. *Beyond freedom and dignity*. New York: Knopf.

Skipper, J. K., Jr., A. L. Guenther, and G. Nass. 1967. The sacredness of .05; a note concerning the uses of significance in social sciences. *American Sociologist* 2: 16–19.

Smith, A. 1937. *Wealth of nations*. New York: Modern Library.

Smith, L. M., and P. A. Pohland. 1976. Grounded theory and educational ethnography: A methodological analysis and critique. In *Educational patterns and cultural configurations*. Edited by J. Roberts and S. Akinsanya, 264–278. New York: Mckay.

Snedecor, G. W. 1946. *Statistical methods*. Ames: Iowa State College Press.

Snedecor, G. W., and W. G. Cochran. 1967. *Statistical methods*, 6th ed. Ames: Iowa State University Press.

Sommer, R. 1968. Hawthorne dogma. *Psychological Bulletin* 70: 592–595.

———. 1969. *Personal space: The behavioral basis for design*. Englewood Cliffs, NJ: Prentice-Hall.

Stablein, R., and W. Nord. 1985. Practical and emancipatory interests in organizational symbolism: A review and evaluation. *Journal of Management* 11(2): 13–28.

Staw, B. M. 1975. Attribution of the 'causes' of performance: A new alternative interpretation of cross-sectional research in organizations. *Organizational Behavior and Human Performance* 13: 141–432.

———. 1985. Repairs on the road to relevance vigor: Some unexplored issues in publishing organizational research. In *Publishing in the organizational sciences*. Edited by L. L. Cummings and P. R. Frost, 96–107. Homewood, IL: Irwin.

Staw, B. M., S. G. Barsade, and K. W. Koput. 1997. Escalation at the credit window: A longitudinal study of bank executives' recognition and write-off of problem loans. *Journal of Applied Psychology* 82: 130–142.

Staw, B. M., and J. Ross. 1980. Commitment in an experimenting society: An experiment on the attribution of leadership from administrative scenarios. *Journal of Applied Psychology* 65: 249–260.

Steers, R. M. 1989. Organizational science in a global environment: Future directions. In *Organizational science abroad*. Edited by C. A. B. Osigweh, Yg, 293–304. New York: Plenum Press.

Steers, R. M., and L. W. Porter. 1983. *Motivation and work behavior*. New York: McGraw-Hill.

Steffy, B., and A. Grimes. 1992. Personnel/organizational psychology: A critique of the discipline. In *Critical management studies*. Edited by M. Alvesson and H. Willmott, 181–201. London: Sage.

Steinbeck, J. 1941. *The log from the Sea of Cortez*. New York: Viking.

Sterling, T. D. 1959. Publication decisions and their possible effects on inferences drawn from tests of significance—or vice versa. *Journal of the American Statistical Association* 54: 30–34.

Stern, J. P. 1963. *Lichtenberg: A doctrine of scattered occasion*. London: Thames and Hudson.

Stevenson, W. B., J. L. Pearce, and L. W. Porter. 1985. The concept of "coalition" in organization theory and research. *Academy of Management Review* 10: 256–268.

Stinchcombe, A. L. 1968. *Constructing social theories*. New York: Harcourt, Brace and World.

———. 1975. A structural analysis of sociology. *American Sociologist* 10: 57–64.

Stokes, B. 1978. *Worker participation—Productivity and the quality of work life*. Worldwatch Paper 25. Washington, DC: Worldwatch Institute.

Storey, J. 1983. *Managerial prerogative and the question of control*. London: Routledge and Kegan Paul.

Sullivan, J. J. 1986. Human nature, organizations, and managerial theory. *Academy of Management Review* 11: 534–549.

Suppe, F., ed. 1974. *The structure of scientific theories*. Urbana: University of Illinois Press.

———. 1977. *The structure of scientific theories*. 2d ed. Urbana: University of Illinois Press.

Susman, G. I., and R. Evered. 1978. An assessment of the scientific merits of action research. *Administrative Science Quarterly* 23: 582–603.

Sutherland, J. W. 1975. *Systems: Analysis, administration, and architecture*. New York: Van Nostrand.

Taggart, W., and D. Robey. 1981. Minds and managers: On the dual nature of human information processing and management. *Academy of Management Review* 6: 187–195.

Tannenbaum, R., and W. Schmidt. 1958. How to choose a leadership pattern. *Harvard Business Review* 36(2): 95–101.

Taylor, C. 1970. The explanation of purposive behavior. In *Exploration in the behavioral sciences*. Edited by R. Borger and F. Cioffi, 49–79. Cambridge: University of Cambridge Press.

Taylor, F. W. 1911. *The principles of scientific management*. New York: Harper.

Taylor, J. B. 1961. What do attitude scales measure: The problem of social desirability. *Journal of Abnormal and Social Psychology* 62: 386–390.

Taylor, S. E. 1991. Asymmetrical effects of positive and negative events: The mobilization-minimization hypothesis. *Psychological Bulletin* 110: 67–85.

Tharenou, P., S. Latimer, and D. Conroy. 1994. How do you make it to the top? An examination of influences on women's and men's managerial advancement. *Academy of Management Journal* 37: 169–194.

Thoenig, J. C. 1982. Discussion note: Research management and management research. *Organization Studies* 3: 209–275.

Thomas, D. A. 1993. The dynamics of managing racial diversity in developmental relationships. *Administrative Science Quarterly* 38: 169–194.

Thomas, K. W., and R. H. Kilmann. 1975. The social desirability variable in organizational research: An alternative explanation for reported findings. *Academy of Management Journal* 18: 741–752.

Thomas, W. I. 1951. The persistence of primary group-norms in present-day society. In *Social behavior and personality*. Edited by E. H. Volkart, 35–38. New York: SSRC.

Thompson, J. B. 1984. *Studies in the theory of ideology*. Berkeley: University of California Press.

Thompson, J. D. 1967. *Organizations in action*. New York: McGraw-Hill.

Thorngate, W. 1976. Possible limits on a science of social behavior. In *Social psychology in transition*. Edited by J. H. Strickland, F. E. Aboud, and K. J. Gerken, 121–139. New York: Plenum.

Tolman, E. C. 1932. *Purposive behavior in animals and men*. New York: Century.

Tompkins, P., and G. Cheney. 1985. Communication and unobtrusive control in contemporary organizations. In *Organizational communication: Traditional themes and new directions*. Edited by R. McPhee and P. Tompkins, 179–210. Newbury Park, CA: Sage.

Tompkins, S. S., and S. Messick, eds. 1963. *Computer simulation of personality: Frontier of psychological theory*. New York: Wiley.

Torbert, W. R. 1972. *Learning from experience*. New York: Columbia University Press.

———. 1976. *Creating a community of inquiry: Conflict, collaboration, transformation*. London: Wiley.

———. 1977. Why educational research has been so uneducational: The case for a new model of social science based on collaborative inquiry. Paper presented at the meeting of the American Psychological Association, San Francisco, CA.

Torgenson, W. 1958. *Theory and method of scaling*. New York: Wiley.

Toulmin, S. E. 1953. *The philosophy of science*. New York: Harper and Row.

Townley, B. 1993. Foucault, power/knowledge, and its relevance for human resources management. *Academy of Management Review* 18: 518–545.

Tukey, J. W. 1977. *Exploratory data analysis*. Reading, MA: Addison-Wesley.

Turner, B. A. 1971. *Exploring industrial subculture*. London: Macmillan.

Turner, R. J., and M. O. Wagenfeld. 1967. Occupational mobility and schizophrenia: An assessment of the social causation and social selection hypothesis. *American Sociological Review* 32: 104–113.

Udy, S. H., Jr. 1962. Administrative rationality, social setting, and organizational development. *American Journal of Sociology* 68: 299–308.

———. 1965. The comparative analysis of organizations. In *Handbook of organizations*. Edited by J. G. March, 678–709. Chicago: Rand McNally.

Umberson, D., M. D. Chen, J. S. House, K. Hopkins, and E. Slaten. 1996. The effect of social relationships on psychological well-being. *American Sociological Review* 61: 837–857.

Urwick, L. F. 1967. Organization and theories about the nature of man. *Academy of Management Journal* 10(1): 9–15.

Uslaner, E. M., ed. 1978. *Ecological inference.* Beverly Hills, CA: Sage.

Uzzi, B. 1996. The sources and consequences of embeddedness for the economic performance of organizations: The network effect. *American Sociological Review* 61: 674–698.

———. 1997. Social structure and competition in interfirm networks: The paradox of embeddedness. *Administrative Science Quarterly* 42: 35–67.

Vaill, Peter B. 1977. Towards a behavioral description of high-performing systems. In *Leadership: Where else can we go?* Edited by M. McCall and M. Lombardo, 103–127. Durham, NC: Duke University Press.

Vallas, S. P. 1993. *Power in the workplace: The politics of production at AT&T.* Albany, NY: State University of New York Press.

Van de Ven, A. H., and W. F. Joyce. 1981. *Perspectives on organization design and behavior.* New York: Wiley.

Van Dyne, L., J. W. Graham, and R. M. Dienesch. 1994. Organizational citizenship behavior: Construct definition, measurement, and validation. *Academy of Management Journal* 37: 765–802.

Van Maanen, J. 1979. The fact of fiction in organizational ethnography. *Administrative Science Quarterly* 24: 539–551.

Van Maanen, J., J. M. Dabbs, and R. R. Faulkner. 1982. *Varieties of qualitative research.* Beverly Hills, CA: Sage.

Venkatraman, N., and J. N. Grant. 1986. Construct measurement in organizational strategy research: A critique and proposal. *Academy of Management Review* 11: 71–78.

Vinokur, A. 1971. Review and theoretical analysis of the effects of group process upon individual and group decisions involving risk. *Psychological Bulletin* 76: 231–250.

Wagner, H. R. 1983. *Alfred Schutz: An intellectual biography.* Chicago: University of Chicago Press.

Walker, H. A., and B. P. Cohen. 1985. Scope statements: Imperative for evaluating theory. *American Sociological Review* 50: 288–301.

Wallace, W. L. 1971. *The logic of science in sociology.* Chicago: Aldine-Atherton.

Ward, J. W. 1964. The ideal of individualism and the reality of organization. In *The business establishment.* Edited by E. F. Cheit, 37–76. New York: Wiley.

Warriner, C. K. 1956. Groups are real. *American Sociological Review* 21(October): 549–554.

Warwick, D. P., and C. A. Lininger. 1975. *The sample survey: Theory and practice.* New York: McGraw-Hill.

Wason, P. C. 1960. On the failure to eliminate hypotheses in a conceptual task. *The Quarterly Journal of Experimental Psychology*: 129–139.

Webb, E. J., D. T. Campbell, R. D. Schwartz, and L. Sechrest. 1966. *Unobtrusive measures: Nonreactive research in the social sciences.* Chicago: Rand McNally.

———. 1972. *Unobtrusive measures: Nonreactive research in the social sciences*. Chicago: Rand McNally.

Webb, E. J., and P. C. Ellsworth. 1975. On nature and knowing. In *Perspectives on attitude assessment: Surveys and their alternatives*. Edited by H. W. Sinaiko and L. A. Broedling, 223–238. Washington: Smithsonian Institution.

Webb, N. M. 1980. The key to learning in groups. In *Issues in aggregation: New directions for methodology in social and behavioral science*. Vol. 6. Edited by K. H. Roberts and L. Burstein, 77–87. San Francisco: Jossey-Bass.

Webb, W. B. 1961. The choice of the problem. *American Psychologist* 16: 223–227.

Weber, Max [1904] 1958. *The Protestant ethic and the spirit of capitalism*. New York: Scribner's.

———. 1946. *From Max Weber: Essays in sociology*. Translated and edited by H. H. Gerth and C. W. Mills. New York: Oxford University Press.

———. 1949. *The methodology of the social sciences*. Glencoe, IL: Free Press.

———. 1963. Objectivity in social science and science policy. In *Philosophy of the social sciences*. Edited by M. Nathanson, 355–418. New York: Random House.

Weick, K. E. 1964. The reduction of cognitive dissonance through task enhancement and effort expenditure. *Journal of Abnormal and Social Psychology* 68: 533–539.

———. 1967. Organizations in the laboratory. In *Methods of organizational research*. Edited by V. H. Vroom, 1–56. Pittsburgh: University of Pittsburgh Press.

———. 1969. *The social psychology of organizing*. Reading MA: Addison-Wesley.

———. 1974a. Middle range theories of social systems. *Behavioral Science* 19: 657–667.

———. 1974b. Methodology and systems theory. Unpublished paper.

———. 1975. The management of stress. *MBA* 9: 37–40.

———. 1976. Educational organizations as loosely coupled systems. *Administrative Science Quarterly* 21: 1–19.

———. 1978. The spines of leaders. In *Leadership: Where else can we go?* Edited by M. W. McCall and M. M. Lombardo, 37–61. Durham, NC: Duke University Press.

———. 1979. *The social psychology of organizing*. Reading, MA: Addison-Wesley.

———. 1982. Administering education in loosely coupled schools. *Phi Delta Kappa* (June): 673–676.

———. 1983. Managerial thought in the context of action. In *The executive mind*. Edited by S. Srivastva, 221–242. San Francisco: Jossey-Bass.

———. 1985a. A stress analysis of future battlefields. In *Leadership and future battlefields*. Edited by J. G. Hunt, 32–46. Washington, DC: Pergamon-Brassey's.

———. 1985b. Cosmos vs. chaos: Sense and nonsense in electronic contexts. *Organizational Dynamics* 14: 50–64.

———. 1987a. Perspectives on action in organizations. In *Handbook of organizational behavior*. Edited by J. Lorsch, 10–28. Englewood Cliffs, New Jersey: Prentice-Hall.

———. 1987b. Theorizing about organizational communication. In *Handbook for organizational communication*. Edited by F. M. Jablin, L. L. Putnam, K. Roberts, and L. W. Porter, 97–122. Beverly Hills, CA: Sage.

———. 1989. Theory construction as disciplined imagination. *Academy of Management Review* 14: 516–531.

———. 1990a. Fatigue of the spirit in organizational development: Reconnaissance man as remedy. Paper presented at the meeting of the Academy of Management, San Francisco, CA.

———. 1990b. Technology as equivoque: Sensemaking in new technologies. In *Technology and organizations*. Edited by P. S. Goodman and L. Sproull, 1–44. San Francisco: Jossey-Bass.

———. 1991. The nontraditional quality of organizational learning. *Organization Science* 2(1): 116–124.

———. 1992. Agenda setting in organizational behavior: A theory-focused approach. *Journal of Management Inquiry* 1(3): 171–182.

———. 1993a. The collapse of sense making in organizations: The Mann Gulch disaster. *Administrative Science Quarterly* 38: 628–652.

———. 1993b. Collective conceptual options in the study of organizational learning. In *Learning in organizations*. Edited by M. M. Crossan, H. W. Lane, J. C. Rush, and R. E. White, 25–41. London, Ontario: Western Business School.

———. 1995a. *Sensemaking in organizations*. Thousand Oaks, CA: Sage.

———. 1995b. Definition of "theory." In *Blackwell encyclopedic dictionary of organizational behavior*. Edited by N. Nicholson, 563–565. Oxford: Blackwell.

Weick, K. E., and L. Berlinger. 1989. Career improvisation in self-designing organizations. In *Handbook of career theory*. Edited by M. B. Arthur, D. T. Hall, and B. J. Lawrence, 313–338. New York: Cambridge University Press.

Weick, K. E., and D. P. Gilfillan. 1971. Fate of arbitrary traditions in a laboratory microculture. *Journal of Personality and Social Psychology* 17: 179–191.

Weick, K. E., and R. E. Quinn. 1999. Organizational change and development. *Annual Review of Psychology* 50: 361–386.

Weick, K. E., and K. H. Roberts. 1993. Collective mind in organizations. Heedful interrelating on flight decks. *Administrative Science Quarterly* 38: 357–381.

Weiss, R. M., and L. E. Miller. 1987. The concept of ideology in organizational analysis: The sociology of knowledge or the social psychology of beliefs? *Academy of Management Review* 12: 104–116.

Werkmeister, W. H. 1959. Theory construction and the problem of objectivity. In *Symposium on sociological theory*. Edited by L. Gross, 483–508. New York: Harper and Row.

Wexley, K. N., and G. A. Yukl. 1984. *Organizational behavior and personnel psychology*. Homewood, IL: Irwin.

Whetten, D. A. 1989. What constitutes a theoretical contribution? *Academy of Management Review* 14: 490–495.

Whiting, J. W. M. 1968. Methods and problems in cross-cultural research. In *Handbook of social psychology*, vol. II (2d ed.). Edited by G. Lindzey and E. Aronson, 693–728. Reading, MA: Addison-Wesley.

Whitley, R. 1984. The fragmented state of management studies: Reasons and consequences. *Journal of Management Studies* 21: 331–348.

———. 1988. The management sciences and managerial skills. *Organization Studies* 9: 47–48.

Whyte, W. F. 1955. *Money and motivation*. New York: Harper and Row.

Wilden, A. 1972. *System and structure: Essays in communication and exchange*. London: Tavistock.

Willems, E. P., and H. L. Raush. 1969. Interpretation and impressions. In *Naturalistic viewpoints in psychological research*. Edited by E. P. Willems and H. L. Raush, 271–286. New York: Holt, Rinehart and Winston.

Willer, D., and J. Willer. 1973. *Systematic empiricism: Critique of a pseudo science*. Englewood Cliffs, NJ: Prentice-Hall.

Williams, T., ed. 1975. *Socialization and communication in primary groups*. Paris: Mouton.

Williamson, O. 1975. *Markets and hierarchies*. New York: Free Press.

———. 1985. *The economic institutions of capitalism*. New York: The Free Press.

Williamson, O., and W. G. Ouchi. 1981. The markets and hierarchies program of research: Origins, implications, prospects. In *Perspectives on organization design and behavior*. Edited by A. H. Van de Ven and W. F. Joyce, 347–370. New York: Wiley.

Willmott, H. 1990. Subjectivity and the dialectic of praxis: Opening up the core of labour process analysis. In *Labour process theory*. Edited by D. Knights and H. Willmott, 204–225. London: Macmillan.

———. 1993. Strength is ignorance; slavery is freedom: Managing culture in modern organizations. *Journal of Management Studies* 60(4): 515–552.

Willmott, H., and D. Knights. 1982. The problem of freedom: Fromm's contribution to a critical theory of work organization. *Praxis International* 2: 204–225.

Wils, T., and L. Dyer. 1984. Relating business strategy to human resource strategy: Some preliminary evidence. Paper presented at the meeting of the Academy of Management, Boston, MA.

Winch, P. 1958. *The idea of a social science.* London: Routledge and Kegan Paul.

Wing, K. 1994. Two cheers for the academy. *Academy of Management Review* 14: 516–531.

Wolins, L. 1962. Responsibility for raw data. *American Psychologist* 17: 657–658.

Wrong, D. 1961. The oversocialized conception of man in modern sociology. *American Sociological Review* 26: 183–193.

Wyer, R. S., and T. K. Srull. 1985. *Handbook of social cognition.* Vols. 1, 2, 3. Hillsdale, NJ: Erlbaum.

Young, R. M. 1973. The human limits of nature. In *The limits of human nature.* Edited by J. Benthall, 235–274. New York: Dutton/Plume.

Young, T. R. 1974. Transforming sociology: The graduate student. *American Sociologist* 9: 135–139.

Zabusky, S. E. 1995. *Launching Europe.* Princeton, NJ: Princeton University Press.

Zajonc, R. B. 1960. The concepts of balance, congruity, and dissonance. *Public Opinion Quarterly* 24: 280–296.

Zand, D. E., and R. E. Sorensen. 1975. Theory of change and the effective use of management science. *Administrative Science Quarterly* 20: 532–545.

Zelditch, M., and T. K. Hopkins. 1961. Laboratory experiments with organizations. In *Complex organizations: A sociological reader.* Edited by A. Etzioni, 464–478. New York: Holt, Rinehart and Winston.

Zhao, S. 1996. The beginning of the end or the end of the beginning: The theory construction movement revisited. *Sociological Forum* 11: 305–318.

Ziman, J. M. 1987. The problem of "problem choice." *Minerva* 25: 92–106.

Zucker, L. 1979. The role of institutionalization in cultural persistence. *American Sociological Review* 42: 726–743.

Zuckerman, H. 1984. Norms and deviant behavior in science. *Science, Technology and Human Values* 9: 7–13.

Credits

Chapter 1

From *Introduction to action research: Social research for social change* by Davydd J. Greenwood and Morten Levine. Copyright © 1998 by Sage Publications, Inc. Reprinted by permission of Sage Publications, Inc.

From *Surely you're joking, Mr. Feynman! Adventures of a curious character* by Richard P. Feynman as told to Ralph Leighton. Copyright © 1985 by Richard P. Feynman and Ralph Leighton. Used by permission of W. W. Norton & Company, Inc., and The Random House Group Limited.

From *The pleasure of finding things out: The best short works of Richard Feynman* by Richard P. Feynman. Copyright © 1999 by Perseus Books Group. Reproduced with permission of Persues Books Group via Copyright Clearance Center.

Chapter 3

From "Two dimensions: Four paradigms," *Sociological paradigms and organizational analysis* by Gibson Burrell and Gareth Morgan. Copyright © 1979 by Gibson Burrell and Gareth Morgan. Used by permission of Gibson Burrell.

From *Sociology: A multiple paradigm*, rev. ed., by George Ritzer. Copyright © 1975 by Allyn & Bacon, Inc. Reprinted with permission of George Ritzer.

"Bringing mind back in: Paradigm development as a frontier problem in organization theory" by Louis R. Pondy and David M. Boje. Paper presented at the annual meeting of the American Sociological Association (San Francisco, CA, 1976). Reprinted with permission of David M. Boje.

From *Organization theory and inquiry: The paradigm revolution* by Yvonna S. Lincoln. Copyright © 1985 by Sage Publications, Inc. Reprinted by permission of Sage Publications, Inc.

Chapter 4

From Stanford Research Institute, *Policy Research Report 4* (Menlo Park, CA, 1974), 22a–22d, 45–48, by permission of SRI International (formerly Stanford Research Institute).

"Intertwined paradigms, intertwined histories" by Ali H. Mir. Paper presented at the annual meeting of the Eastern Academy of Management (Crystal Springs, VA. 1996). Reprinted with permission by Ali H. Mir.

Chapter 5

"Structure of debate in organizational studies" by Ralph E. Stablein. Working paper, University of Otago (Dunedin, New Zealand, 1988). Reprinted with permission of Ralph E. Stablein.

"Alternative perspectives in the organizational sciences" by Roger D. Evered and Meryl Reis Louis. *Academy of Management Review* 6. Copyright © 1981 by Academy of Management. Reproduced with permission of the Academy of Management via Copyright Clearance Center.

"The case for qualitative research" by Gareth Morgan and Linda Smircich. *Academy of Management Review* 5. Copyright © 1980 by Academy of Management. Reproduced with permission of the Academy of Management via Copyright Clearance Center.

Reprinted by permission. "Integrating positivist and interpretative approaches to organizational research" by Allen S. Lee. *Organization Science* 2, November 1991, the Institute for Operations Research and the Management Sciences (INFORMS), 901 Elkridge Landing Road, Suite 400, Linthicum, Maryland 21090-2909 USA.

Reprinted with permission from "Administrative science as socially constructed truth" by W. Graham Astley, published in *Administrative Science Quarterly* 30: 4 (September 1985). Copyright © 1985 Johnson Graduate School of Management, Cornell University.

Chapter 6

Reprinted by permission of Sage Publications Ltd. from Mats Alvesson and Stanley A. Deetz, "Critical theory and postmodernism approaches to organizational studies." From *Handbook of organization studies*, eds. Stewart R. Clegg, Cynthia Hardy, and Walter R. Nord. Copyright © 1996 by Mats Alvesson and Stanley Deetz.

From *The cultures of work organizations* by Harrison M. Trice and Janice M. Beyer. Copyright © 1993 by Prentice-Hall, Inc. Reprinted by permission of Pearson Education, Inc., Upper Saddle River, NJ.

"Structure of debate in organizational studies" by Ralph E. Stablein. Working paper, University of Otago (Dunedin, New Zealand, 1988). Reprinted with permission of Ralph E. Stablein.

"The sociology of science" by Harriett Zuckerman. From *The handbook of sociology*, edited by Neil J. Smelser. Copyright © 1988 by Sage Publications, Inc. Reprinted by permission of Sage Publications, Inc.

From *The structure of science*, 2nd ed., by Ernest Nagel. Copyright © 1979 by Ernest Nagel. Reprinted by permission of Hackett Publishing Company, Inc. All rights reserved.

"Whose side are we on?" by Howard S. Becker. Reprinted from *Social Problems* 14, no. 3, Winter 1967, pp. 239–247, by permission. Copyright © 1966 The Society for the Study of Social Problems.

From *The conduct of inquiry* by Abraham Kaplan. San Francisco, CA: Chandler Publishing, 1964.

Chapter 7

Reprinted from *The intellectual and social organization of the sciences*, 2nd edition by Richard Whitley. Copyright © 1984, 2000 by Richard Whitley. Used by permission of Oxford University Press.

Chapter 8

"Organizational theories: Some criteria for evaluation" by Samuel B. Bacharach. *Academy of Management Review* 14. Copyright © 1989 by the Academy of Management. Reproduced with permission of the Academy of Management via Copyright Clearance Center.

Reprinted with permission from "What theory is *not*" by Robert I. Sutton and Barry M. Staw, published in *Administrative Science Quarterly* 40: 3 (September 1995). Copyright © 1995 Johnson Graduate School of Management, Cornell University.

Reprinted with permission from "What theory is *not*, theorizing *is*" by Karl E. Weick, published in *Administrative Science Quarterly* 40: 3 (September 1995). Copyright © 1995 Johnson Graduate School of Management, Cornell University.

Reprinted from "Comment on 'What theory is *not*'" by Paul J. DiMaggio, published in *Administrative Science Quarterly* 40: 3 (September 1995). Copyright © 1995 Johnson Graduate School of Management, Cornell University.

From *The conduct of inquiry* by Abraham Kaplan. San Francisco, CA: Chandler Publishing, 1964.

Chapter 9

From *The conduct of inquiry* by Abraham Kaplan. San Francisco, CA: Chandler Publishing, 1964.

From *A primer in theory construction* by Paul Davidson Reynolds. Published by Allyn and Bacon, Boston, MA. Copyright © 1971 by Pearson Education. Reprinted by permission of the publisher.

Reprinted from "A typology of explicative models," by Roger D. Evered. From *Technological Forecasting and Social Change* 9 (1976): 260–269. Copyright © 1976 American Elsevier Publishing Company, Inc. Reprinted with permission from Elsevier.

From *Explaining organizational behavior* by Lawrence B. Mohr. Copyright © 1982 by Jossey-Bass Inc., Publishers. Used by permission of Lawrence B. Mohr.

From *The social psychology of organizing*, 2nd ed., by Karl E. Weick. Copyright © 1979, 1969 by McGraw-Hill Higher Education. Reproduced with permission of The McGraw-Hill Companies.

"Empirical research strategies" from *Research methods in organizational behavior* by Eugene F. Stone. Copyright © 1978 by Scott, Foresman and Company. Used by permission of Eugene F. Stone-Romero.

"Theories of extreme cases" by Louis R. Pondy and Mary Linda Olson. Paper presented at the American Psychological Association Symposium (San Francisco, CA, 1977).

"N = 1" by William F. Dukes. From *Psychological Bulletin* 64. Copyright © 1965 by the American Psychological Association. Reprinted with permission.

"Mixing levels of analysis in organizational research" by Appa Rao Korukonda. From *Canadian Journal of Administrative Sciences* 6, no. 2, June 1989. Copyright © Administrative Sciences Association of Canada

Chapter 13

"Concept fallibility in organizational science" by Chimezie A. B. Osigweh Yg. *Academy of Management Review* 14. Copyright © 1989 by the Academy of Management. Reproduced with permission of the Academy of Management via Copyright Clearance Center.

"Field research methods" by Thomas Bouchard Jr., *Handbook of Industrial and organizational psychology*, ed. Marvin D. Dunnette,1986. Used with permission of Marvin D. Dunnette.

From *Using methods in organizational research* by Thomas W. Lee. Copyright © 1999. Reprinted by permission of Sage Publications, Inc.

"Breaking up the mono-method monopolies in organizational analysis" by Joanne Martin. From *The theory and philosophy of organizations*, edited by John Hassard and Denis Pym. First published in 1990 by Routledge. Copyright © 1990 by John Hassard and Denis Pym. Used with permission of the publisher.

"Self-reports in organizational research" by Philip M. Podsakoff and Dennis W. Organ. From *Journal of Management* 12. Copyright © 1986 by the Southern Management Association. Reprinted with permission of the Southern Management Association.

From *Experimenter effects in behavioral research* by Robert Rosenthal. Copyright © 1966 by Meredith Publishing Company. Used by permission of the author.

"Removing assumptions of bipolarity" by Philip Bobko. *Academy of Management Review* 10. Copyright © 1985 by the Academy of Management. Reproduced with permission of the Academy of management via Copyright Clearance Center.

Chapter 14

Reprinted by permission of Sage Publications Ltd. from Kenneth J. Gergen and Gün R. Semin, "Everyday understanding in science and daily life." From *Everyday understanding: Social and scientific implications*, eds. Gün R. Semin and Kenneth J. Gergen. Copyright © 1990 by Kenneth J. Gergen and Gün R. Semin.

"The initial examination of data" by C. Chatfield. From *Journal of the Royal Statistical Society* 148. Copyright © 1985 Royal Statistical Society. Used with permission of the Royal Statistical Society.

Chapter 16

Index

Italic page numbers indicate material in tables or figures.